THE BEST OF SAN FRANCISCO & NORTHERN CALIFORNIA

4th Edition

Editor-in-Chief
André Gayot

Managing Editor
Sharon Boorstin

Editor
Colin Berry

Contributing Editors
Judy Andreson, Dan Berger, Bill Citara,
Beverly Dubrin, James Gebbie, Leslie Harlib,
Sheila Himmel, Catherine Jordan, Seth Lorinczi,
Victoria Maitland-Lewis, Jamie Purviance, Marta Saunders,
Jennie Schacht, Dennis Schaefer, Kristin Spence,
Arthur von Wiesenberger, Ann Walker, Larry Walker

Publisher
Alain Gayot

GAULT MILLAU

Paris ▪ Los Angeles ▪ New York ▪ London ▪ Munich ▪ San Francisco

GAYOT PUBLICATIONS

The Best of Beverly Hills
The Best of Chicago
The Best of Florida
The Best of France
The Best of Germany
The Best of Hawaii
The Best of Hong Kong
The Best of Italy
The Best of London
The Best of Los Angeles
The Best of New England
The Best of New Orleans
The Best of New York
The Best of Paris
Paris, Ile-de-France & The Loire Valley
Paris & Provence
The Best of San Francisco
The Best of Thailand
The Best of Toronto
The Best of Washington, D.C.
The Best Wineries of North America

LA Restaurants, NYC Restaurants, SF Restaurants
The Food Paper, Tastes Newsletter
http://www.gayot.com

Published by GaultMillau, Inc.
5900 Wilshire Blvd.
Los Angeles, CA 90036
323-965-3529

Please address all comments regarding
THE BEST OF SAN FRANCISCO
& NORTHERN CALIFORNIA to:
GaultMillau, Inc.
P.O. Box 361144
Los Angeles, CA 90036
E-mail: gayots@aol.com

Advertising Sales: Debbie Eskew
Production: Walter Mladina
Page Layout and Design: Mad Macs Communications
Illustrations: Bettina Oshiro

ISSN 1520-3522

Printed in the United States of America

CONTENTS

WINE COUNTRY 237

Explore America's premier wine-producing region and its fine restaurants, hotels and health spas. Here's a list of wineries to tour and resources for surveying the countryside by horse, bicycle, boat, train and hot-air balloon.

PENINSULA 261

Travel down a coastline of unparalleled scenic splendor through redwood groves and beyond to hidden beaches. Where you should stop en route to enjoy sophisticated dining and the comforts of charming inns.

MONTEREY/CARMEL 269

From colorful Cannery Row to the legendary Seventeen-Mile Drive, discover a pair of towns rich in history and culture. Where to find the superb restaurants and the stunning resort hotels of these two popular year-round playgrounds by the sea.

PRACTICALS & INDEX 279

FREE & CHEAP THINGS TO DO 280
WHAT TO DO WITH KIDS 283
WINE SAVVY 286
COFFEE SAVVY 289
WATER SAVVY 292
INDEX 298

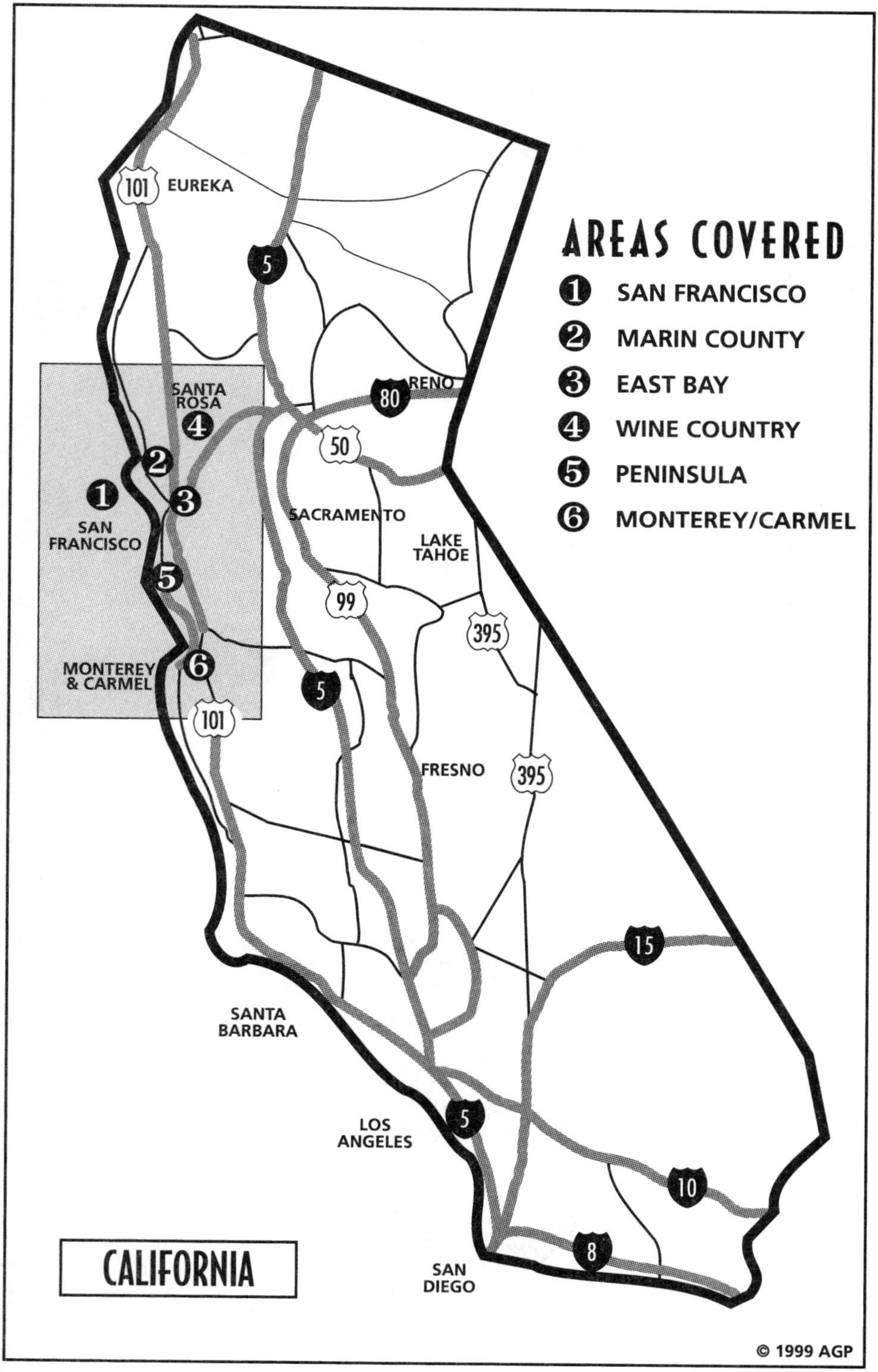
AREAS COVERED
1 SAN FRANCISCO
2 MARIN COUNTY
3 EAST BAY
4 WINE COUNTRY
5 PENINSULA
6 MONTEREY/CARMEL
101
EUREKA
5
SANTA ROSA
RENO
80
50
SAN FRANCISCO
SACRAMENTO
LAKE TAHOE
99
395
MONTEREY & CARMEL
101
FRESNO
395
15
SANTA BARBARA
LOS ANGELES
10
8
SAN DIEGO
CALIFORNIA
© 1999 AGP

EVERYONE'S FAVORITE CITY

Imagine this: you step from your sophisticated Nob Hill hotel into a balmy night and spot the moon rising over the glittering Bay Bridge. You hear the musical clang-clang as a cable car whizzes past. You take a taxi-or walk-through neighborhoods that reflect but two facets of the city's rich, multicultural personality: bustling Chinatown and energetic, celebratory North Beach. Before long, you're ensconced in a design-marvel of a restaurant, dining on cutting-edge California cuisine and award-winning California wine. After dinner, the opera starts at 8, and you're meeting friends for drinks at a hip new club later...

Now, we ask you: Is this a perfect city or what?

With its mild climate, manageable size, ethnic diversity and impeccable taste-and spectacular view after spectacular view, the City by the Bay is undoubtedly everyone's favorite. (It's a nice place to visit and you would want to live there!) San Francisco combines the urban sophistication of New York or Paris with the casual comforts of Los Angeles. Its neighborhoods are distinctive and vibrant-a walk through the Mission, Pacific Heights, or North Beach districts on a sunny Saturday will prove it. S.F. and Bay Area lifestyles reflect a combination of California's booming economy, an appreciation for arts and culture and unadulterated, fin de siècle excitement. And we can't forget that San Francisco also has the most restaurants per capita in the country-and some of the best food in the world.

We have compiled the new **The Best of San Francisco & Northern California** to direct you to the pleasures that abound here, to introduce (or re-introduce) you to this picturesque, pristine 49-square-mile grid of culinary, cultural and capitalist delights. Likewise, you'll find our guidebook essential if you're venturing outside San Francisco-into investment-heavy Silicon Valley, laid-back Marin County, the savvy East Bay cities, the dramatic coast of Monterey and Carmel or the idyllic valleys of the Wine Country.

We've enlisted the expertise of over a dozen writers, critics and experts to point out the best in dining, shopping, accommodations, sightseeing and nightlife-all waiting to be discovered. Whether you're seeking the most "in" new restaurant, the hippest nightclub, the funkiest shoe store or the classiest hotel, you have in your hands the perfect resource. With this Gayot's/GaultMillau guidebook and a decent pair of walking shoes, the city's sights, smells, sounds and tastes are yours to enjoy.

A Guide to our Restaurant Reviews

What decides the rating of a restaurant? What is on the plate is by far the most important factor. The **quality of produce** is among the most telling signs of a restaurant's culinary status. It requires a great deal of commitment and money to stock the finest grades and cuts of meat and the finest quality of fish. There is tuna, for example, and there's tuna. Ask any sushi chef. One extra-virgin olive oil is not the same, by far, as the next. Ditto for chocolates, pastas, spices and one thousand other ingredients. Quality restaurants also attune themselves to seasonal produce, whether it be local berries or truffles from Italy. **Freshness** is all-important, too, and a telling indication of quality. This means not only using fresh rather than frozen fish, for example, but also preparing everything from scratch at the last possible moment, from appetizers through desserts.

What else do we look for? **Details** are telling: if sauces are homogeneous, you know that the kitchen is taking shortcuts. The bread on the table is always a tip-off; similarly, the house wine can speak volumes about the culinary attitude and level of an establishment. Wine is food, and wine lists and offerings can be revelatory. A list doesn't have to be long or expensive to show a commitment to quality.

Finally, among the very finest restaurants, **creativity** and **innovation** are often determining factors. These qualities, however, are relatively unimportant for simply good restaurants, where the quality and consistency of what appears on the plates is the central factor. A restaurant that serves grilled chicken well is to be admired more than a restaurant that attempts some failed marriage of chicken and exotic produce, or some complicated chicken preparation that requires a larger and more talented kitchen brigade than is on hand. Don't be taken in by attempted fireworks that are really feeble sideshows.

Our rating system works as follows: restaurants are ranked in the same manner that French students are graded, on a scale of one to twenty.

The rankings reflect only our opinion of the FOOD. The decor, service, ambience and wine list are commented upon within each review.

OUR RESTAURANT RATING SYSTEM

Restaurants that are ranked 13/20 and above are distinguished with toques (chef's hats) according to the table below:

Exceptional *(4 Toques)* (ratings of 19/20)	4 toques
Excellent *(3 Toques)* (ratings of 17/20 and 18/20)	3 toques
Very good *(2 Toques)* (ratings of 15/20 and 16/20)	2 toques
Good *(1 Toque)* (ratings of 13/20 and 14/20)	1 toque

Keep in mind that we are comparing San Francisco's restaurants to the very best in the world. Also, these ranks are relative. A 13/20 (1 toque) may not be a superlative ranking for a highly reputed (and very expensive) restaurant, but it is quite complimentary for a small place without much culinary pretension. We know that diners often choose a restaurant for reasons other than the quality of the food-because of its location, type of cuisine-or just because it's a fun place to spend an evening.

The adventurous nosher can find cafés of every breed, dim sum spreads that rival those in Hong Kong, and pizzas with just about any topping a chef can dream up. And it's difficult to beat the bargains you can find at these places. So we have mixed in our favorite **Quick Bites** (where you can dine for under $15) with the more serious (and okay, sometimes expensive) restaurants. At the end of each section you'll find an **AND ALSO...** section of unrated restaurants that we wanted to mention because they're new or notable.

There are literally thousands of places in the Bay area to dine like royalty or grab a bite and save a buck. We've included only the best.

OUR RESTAURANT PRICING SYSTEM

In our reviews, we code restaurant prices using one to four dollar signs. Prices reflect the average cost of dinner for one person including appetizer, entrée, dessert, coffee, tax and tip. Not included is wine or other beverages, which vary greatly in price. Those who like to eat lightly, sharing appetizers and desserts, will spend less. Though the popularity of reasonably priced restaurants has forced many eateries to try to keep prices down, not all succeed. Forgive us if a restaurant has become more expensive by the time you visit it.

$ = under $20
$$ = under $35
$$$ = under $50
$$$$ = $50 & up

In addition, we have included noteworthy restaurants, cafés and even burger joints where you can get good food for $15 or under per person. These "Quick Bites" are noted by a ¢.

SYMBOLS

All credit cards taken .... A
Visa .... VISA
MasterCard ....
American Express ....
Diners Club ....
Discover ....
Reservations suggested ....
Valet parking ....
Ties suggested ....
Romantic setting ....
Heart-healthy dishes ....
View ....
Outdoor dining ....
Bargain Bites .... ¢

ADVICE & COMMENTS

On types of cuisine: Before Nouvelle Cuisine was introduced on the West Coast in the 1970s, followed by California Cuisine in the '80s and New American, Fusion, Pan-Asian, Mediterranean and Pacific Rim cuisines in the '90s, it was easy to classify restaurants by their cuisine-there was American, French, Italian,

Continental, Chinese, Japanese, Greek, etc. Today, however, the lines have blurred, and individual chefs create their own style of cooking, which might combine elements of some-or all-of the above.

We find it hard to slap labels on the type of cuisine that a restaurant serves, yet we must so that readers will have some hint of what they'll be served when they dine there. In most cases, we have labeled a restaurant's cuisine according to what its owners and chefs call it. But that doesn't always make things easier. For we've found that though one restaurant may describe its cuisine as Californian, another as Contemporary and another as Eclectic, their dishes may be quite similar-innovative takes on new and old themes, concocted of fresh regional ingredients and using a combination of elements from various ethnic cooking styles. But in the long run, who cares what we label restaurant's cuisine? After all, it's not the type of cuisine you're eating that's important-it's how it tastes. And we hope it tastes great.

On dressing: San Franciscans enjoy a quirky schizophrenia when it comes to dressing up, electing to think of themselves as urbane city-dwellers at one moment and casual Californians at another. In a handful of conservative restaurants, coats and ties for men are still the unspoken rule; in some of the more touristy neighborhoods, no one will feel uncomfortable in jeans and a sweater. In most of the city's eateries, however, you'll be most comfortable considering your apparel the same way the chefs treat the food they're about to serve you: with a healthy balance of respect, style, and quality.

On chefs: When you make reservations in a restaurant with a famous chef, check to be sure he or she will be there, not traveling across the country demonstrating his cooking style. Also, all chefs have good days and bad, so don't be too put off if your experience is less stellar than was ours; with luck it will be better.

On parking: If you don't already know, you'll find out soon enough-San Francisco is a nightmare for parking. Many restaurants are wisely offering valet service at a cost of $3-$8; be prepared to tip the valet an extra $2. Other restaurants have negotiated deals with nearby lots for reduced parking rates; ask when you call to make reservations. Some outlying restaurants have their own lots or plenty of street parking. But why not take a cab?

On smoking: As of January 1998, smoking is banned in all California bars and restaurants. You'll occasionally still find a bartender who looks the other way when his or her patrons light up (and a number of cigar bars are doing thriving business) but no waiter will allow it. If you must smoke, you'll need to do it outside-but look at it this way: at least you'll meet some people with whom you have something in common. We hear, however, that the non-smoking law will be repealed as of January, 1999. In the meantime, you can smoke on the patio of a restaurant.

On outdoor dining: Like available parking, outdoor dining is something of a rarity in San Francisco. For the most part, the weather-with liberal doses of fog, wind and chilly air-is the culprit. But on sunny spring or fall days, many restaurants move a few tables onto the sidewalk for impromptu al fresco dining. Too, a few have built patios with wind-blocks or installed gas heaters to attract terrace diners.

On tipping: Leaving a gratuity that reflects 15 percent of your pretax bill (including drinks) is customary. If you are with a large party, or you feel your service was above and beyond the call of duty, you may wish to leave more.

Only a small handful of restaurants handle tipping European-style, by adding 15 percent to your bill. Aside from those few, a gratuity is automatically added only for large groups (which tend to undertip). Check with your waiter or maître d'.

Top Restaurants: Food Rating

Toque Tally

Restaurants are in San Francisco unless marked otherwise:
(M) *Marin County*, (EB) *East Bay*, (WC) *Wine Country*,
(P) *Peninsula*, (MC) *Monterey/Carmel.*

18/20

Fleur de Lys
The French Laundry (WC)

17/20

La Folie
The Ritz-Carlton Dining Room

16/20

Acquerello
Aqua
Boulevard
Chez Panisse (EB)
Pacific

15/20

Absinthe
Babette's (WC)
Betelnut
Café Beaujolais (WC)
Campton Place
Catahoula (WC)
Chapeau!
Charles Nob Hill
Domaine Chandon (WC)
Farallon
Fresh Cream (MC)
Fringale
Hawthorne Lane
Jardinière
The Lark Creek Inn (M)
Palio d'Asti
Pinot Blanc (WC)
Postrio
Rivoli (EB)
The Slanted Door
Stars
Tra Vigne (WC)
Willowside Café (WC)
The Wine Spectator Greystone (WC)
Zaré
Zarzuela
Zuni

THE TOQUE, CIRCA 1700

Have you ever wondered about the origin of that towering, billowy (and slightly ridiculous) white hat worn by chefs all over the world? Chefs have played an important role in society since the fifth century B.C., but the hats didn't begin to appear in kitchens until around the eighteenth century A.D. The toque is said to be of Greek origin; many famous Greek cooks, to escape persecution, sought refuge in monasteries and continued to practice their art. The chefs donned the tall hats traditionally worn by Orthodox priests, but to distinguish themselves from their fellows, they wore white hats instead of black. The custom eventually was adopted by chefs from Paris to Peking.

OUR RATING SYSTEM

Exceptional *(4 Toques)*
(ratings of 19/20)

Excellent *(3 Toques)*
(ratings of 17/20 and 18/20)

Very good *(2 Toques)*
(ratings of 15/20 and 16/20)

Good *(1 Toque)*
(ratings of 13/20 and 14/20)

14/20

Anjou
Bay Wolf (EB)
Boonville Hotel (WC)
Brix (WC)
Buckeye Roadhouse (M)
Café Lolo (WC)
Chez Michel
Citron (EB)
Colombus Ristorante
The Covey (MC)
Cypress Club
Eos
Flea Street Café (P)
42 Degrees
Freestyle (WC)
The Girl & The Fig (WC)
Greens
Insalata's (M)
John Ash & Co. (WC)
Kincaid's Bistro (WC)
Lalime's (EB)
Left Bank (M)
Lisa Hemenway's (WC)
LuLu
Marnee Thai
The Meadowood Resort Restaurant (WC)
The Meetinghouse
Mikayla Restaurant (M)
Mustards (WC)
Oliveto (EB)
One Market
Oriental Pearl
Piazza D'Angelo (M)
Plouf
Plump Jack Café
Ristorante Milano
The Ritz-Carlton Terrace
Rose Pistola
Roti
Roy's at Pebble Beach (MC)
Rubicon
Rumpus
Spago Palo Alto (P)
Vivande
Wappo Bar (WC)
The Waterfront Restaurant & Café
Yank Sing
Zax

13/20

Ajanta (EB)
Albion River Inn (WC)
Albona Ristorante
Alegrias
Alta Plaza
Antica Trattoria
Anton & Michel (MC)
Auberge du Soleil
Avenue Grill (M)
Avenue 9
Aya Sushi
Bistro Aix
Bistro Don Giovanni (WC)
Bix
Bizou
Bolero (M)
Bruno's
Butterfield's
Byblos
Café Jacqueline
Café Kati
Café Marimba
Caffè Delle Stelle
The Caprice (M)
Carta
China Village
Crustacean
Ebisu
El Zocalo
Elan Vital
Enrico's Sidewalk Café & Restaurant
Firefly
Flying Saucer
Fog City Diner
Gira Polli
The Globe
Grand Café
The Grille (WC)
Harbor Village
Hayes Street Grill
Heritage House (WC)
Il Fornaio
Il Fornaio (M)
Indian Oven
Indigo
Jasmine House
Kenwood Restaurant & Bar (WC)
Kuleto's
Le Central
Le Charm
Lhasha Moon
Liberty Café
Lo Coco's
L'Osteria del Forno
Loongbar
MacArthur Park
Madrona Manor (WC)
Mangiafuoco
Manora's Thai Cuisine
Matterhorn
Millennium
Moa Room
Moose's
Osaka Grill
Parma Ristorante
Pacific's Edge (MC)
Pastis
PJ's Oyster Bed
Prego
Ravenous (WC)
Ristorante Ecco
Ristorante Fabrizio (M)
Ristorante Ideale
Rose's Café
Scala's Bistro
Stillwater Bar & Grill (MC)
Sushi Groove
Terra (WC)
Thanh Long
Thep Phanom
Ti Couz
Tommaso's
Trattoria Contadina
2223 Market
Universal Café
Vertigo
The Village Pub (P)
Vineria
Yabbies
Zibibbo (P)
Zinzino

No Rating

Le Colonial
Masa's

Sample Review

The following key explains the information provided in our reviews.

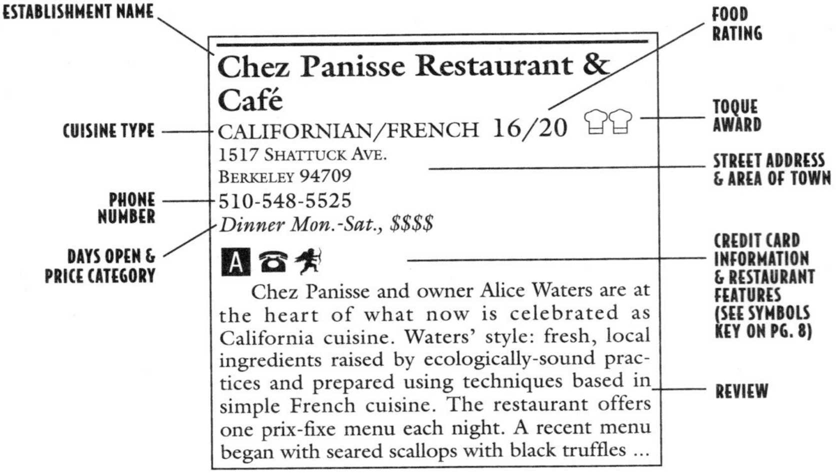
ESTABLISHMENT NAME
FOOD RATING
Chez Panisse Restaurant & Café
TOQUE AWARD
CUISINE TYPE
CALIFORNIAN/FRENCH 16/20
1517 SHATTUCK AVE.
BERKELEY 94709
STREET ADDRESS & AREA OF TOWN
PHONE NUMBER
510-548-5525
Dinner Mon.-Sat., $$$$
DAYS OPEN & PRICE CATEGORY
CREDIT CARD INFORMATION & RESTAURANT FEATURES (SEE SYMBOLS KEY ON PG. 8)
A
Chez Panisse and owner Alice Waters are at the heart of what now is celebrated as California cuisine. Waters' style: fresh, local ingredients raised by ecologically-sound practices and prepared using techniques based in simple French cuisine. The restaurant offers one prix-fixe menu each night. A recent menu began with seared scallops with black truffles ...
REVIEW

For a more comprehensive guide to dining in Northern California, see Gayot/GaultMillau's yearly updated book SF RESTAURANTS.

Gayot Publications is proud to feature restaurant, hotel and travel information from our books, newsletter and updates on many internet web sites. We suggest you start surfing with us at **http://www.gayot.com**. We welcome your questions and comments at our E-mail address: **gayots@aol.com**.

You can also find our restaurant, hotel and travel information on the following web sites:

BIGBOOK .... www.bigbook.com

DIGITAL CITY LOS ANGELES .... www.digitalcity.com

DIGITAL CITY SAN DIEGO .... www.digitalcity.com

DIGITAL CITY SAN FRANCISCO ... www.digitalcity.com

THE FOOD PAPER .... www.thefoodpaper.com

THE GRAPEVINE .... www.winery.com

LA TIMES .... www.latimes.com

PERRIER .... www.perrier.com

A Guide to our Hotel Reviews

OUR HOTEL RATING SYSTEM

To help you easily find the hotel-or inn, resort, B&B or condo- that best matches your needs and budget, we have listed establishments in sections that reflect price, service and amenities: **Top of the Line, Luxury, Moderate** and **Economy.**

Our ranking of the decor, service, comfort level, amenities, appeal and ambience of each hotel is expressed in **Golden Keys**, from one to five. The number of Golden Keys accompanying each review indicates the hotel's ranking according to the following system:

- 1 key: *Just the basics:* A clean room and private bath, and that's about it.
- 2 keys: *Comfortable:* Adequate rooms, pleasant service and some amenities.
- 3 keys: *Very comfortable:* Good rooms, amenities and service; you can't complain.
- 4 keys: *Everything you need and more:* Excellent rooms, superb amenities and service—with style.
- 5 keys: *As good as it gets; pure luxury:* Where to stay if money is no object and you demand perfection. Among the very best hotels in the world.

In the text of each hotel review, we describe and comment upon the decor, service, atmosphere, rooms, amenities, location and so on. As for the prices, there is no such thing as a fixed rate. The prices listed-given by the hotels themselves-are more an indication of their status than an unchanging room rate.

Room charges fluctuate with the season, availability and quality of view. One way to beat the high cost of lodging is to explore weekend packages at primarily business hotels, for which even some of the finest hotels slash prices to fill rooms booked by business travelers during the week. These package deals often include such amenities as champagne, dinner, brunch, and sightseeing tours. Hotels, which are favorite weekend escape spots, will often offer lower mid-week rates to those willing to make their "escape" on a Monday, Tuesday or Wednesday.

Upon check-in, we suggest that you inquire about the possibility of being upgraded to a larger room-at no extra cost, of course. If the hotel is not full-and you luck out-the management may oblige to win your loyalty. Our last tip: when phoning ahead to make reservations, don't be afraid to negotiate a lower rate, and don't take "No" for an answer until you're sure you can't negotiate any further.

SYMBOLS

- All credit cards taken
- Visa
- MasterCard
- American Express
- Diners Club
- Discover
- Health club and/or spa
- Tennis
- Golf
- Horseback Riding
- Swimming pool
- Parking
- In-room faxes
- Meeting rooms
- Business center
- Complimentary Continental breakfast

HOTEL KEY RATINGS

Hotels are in San Francisco unless indicated: M (*Marin County*), EB (*East Bay*), WC (*Wine Country*), P (*Peninsula*), MC (*Monterey/Carmel*).

Mandarin Oriental
Pan Pacific
The Ritz-Carlton

Auberge du Soleil (WC)
Campton Place Hotel
The Clift Hotel
Fairmont Hotel
Highlands Inn (MC)
The Huntington Hotel Nob Hill
The Inn at Spanish Bay (MC)
The Lodge at Pebble Beach (MC)
Meadowood Napa Valley
The Palace Hotel
Quail Lodge (MC)
The Sherman House
Stonepine Estate Resort (MC)

Albion River Inn (WC)
ANA Hotel
The Archbishop's Mansion
Casa Madrona (M)
Claremont Resort Hotel (EB)
Fairmont Hotel San Jose (P)
Grand Hyatt
Green Gables Inn (MC)
Harvest Inn (WC)
Hotel Monaco
Hyatt Regency
Hotel De Anza (P)
Hotel Griffon
Hotel Nikko San Francisco
Hotel Rex
Hotel Triton
Hyatt Regency San Francisco Airport (P)
Inn Above the Tide (M)
Inn at the Opera
The Inn at Union Square
Madrona Manor (WC)
The Majestic
The Mansions Hotel
The Mark Hopkins Inter-Continental
The Maxwell Hotel
Mill Valley Inn (M)
Mission Ranch (MC)
Monterey Plaza Hotel (MC)
Monticello Inn
Mountain Home Inn (M)
Oak Knoll Inn (WC)
Parc Fifty Five
Petite Auberge
Prescott Hotel
Radisson Miyako Hotel
Renaissance Stanford Court Hotel
San Francisco Hilton & Towers
San Francisco Airport Marriott (P)
San Francisco Marriott
Silverado Country Club & Resort (WC)
Sonoma Mission Inn & Spa (WC)
Stanford Park Hotel (P)
Villa Florence
Westin Hotel San Francisco Airport (P)
Westin St. Francis
White Swan Inn

The Abigail Hotel
Alta Mira Hotel (M)
Beresford Hotel
Best Western Tuscan Inn
Boonville Hotel (WC)
Clarion Bedford Hotel at Union Square
Doubletree Inn (MC)
The El Dorado Hotel (WC)
Embassy Suites Napa Valley (WC)

Galleria Park Hotel
Gosby House Inn (MC)
Gramma's Rose Garden Inn (EB)
Holiday Inn Fisherman's Wharf
Hotel Diva
Hotel Sofitel San Francisco Bay (P)
Hotel Union Square
Inn at the Tides (WC)
Kensington Park
La Fleur Bed & Breakfast (WC)
Manka's Inverness Lodge (M)
Mill Rose Inn (P)
Mount View Hotel (WC)
Olema Inn (M)
Panama Hotel (M)
Pelican Inn (M)
The Phoenix Hotel
The Pine Inn (MC)
Rancho Caymus Inn (WC)
San Remo Hotel
Sir Francis Drake
Stanyan Park Hotel
Vintners Inn (WC)
The Washington Square Inn
Waterfront Plaza Hotel (EB)
Whale Watch Inn (WC)

Beck's Motor Lodge
Grant Plaza Hotel
Sonoma Hotel (WC)
White Sulphur Springs Retreat & Spa (WC)

INTERNET INFO

Gayot Publications is proud to feature restaurant, hotel and travel information from our books, newsletter and updates on many internet web sites. We suggest you start surfing with us at http://www.gayot.com. We welcome your questions and comments at our E-mail address: gayots@aol.com.

You can also find our restaurant, hotel and travel information on the following web sites:

Bigbook	www.bigbook.com
Digital City Los Angeles	www.digitalcity.com
Digital City San Diego	www.digitalcity.com
Digital City San Francisco	www.digitalcity.com
France Online	www.france.com
LATimes	www.latimes.com
Perrier	www.perrier.com
Tastes	www.travelchannel.com
The Food Paper	www.thefoodpaper.com
The Grapevine	www.winery.com

THE BEST OF SAN FRANCISCO & NORTHERN CALIFORNIA

RIGHTS

Although the publishers have made every effort to ensure that the information was correct at the time of going to the press, the publishers do not assume and hereby disclaim any liability to any party for any loss or damage caused by errors, omissions, or any potential travel disruption due to labor or financial difficulty, whether such errors or omissions result from negligence, accident, or any other cause.

SPECIAL SALES

Gayot Publications are available at discounts for bulk purchases, direct sales or premiums.

- Makes a great gift that will put your name in front of important clients over and over again—and at a small cost.
- Links your firm with internationally respected publications.
- Orders over 1,000 can be customized with your logo on the cover at no extra charge.

Call our toll-free number for information and orders:

1 (800) 532-3781

OR WRITE US:

Gayot Publications
5900 Wilshire Blvd.
Los Angeles, CA 90036

E-mail: Gayots@aol.com

DISCLAIMER

Readers are advised that prices and conditions change over the course of time. The restaurants, shops and other businesses reviewed in this book have been reviewed over a period of time, and the reviews reflect the personal experiences and opinions of the reviewers. The reviewers and publishers cannot be held responsible for the experiences of the reader related to the establishments reviewed. Readers are invited to write the publisher with ideas, comments and suggestions for future editions.

San Francisco

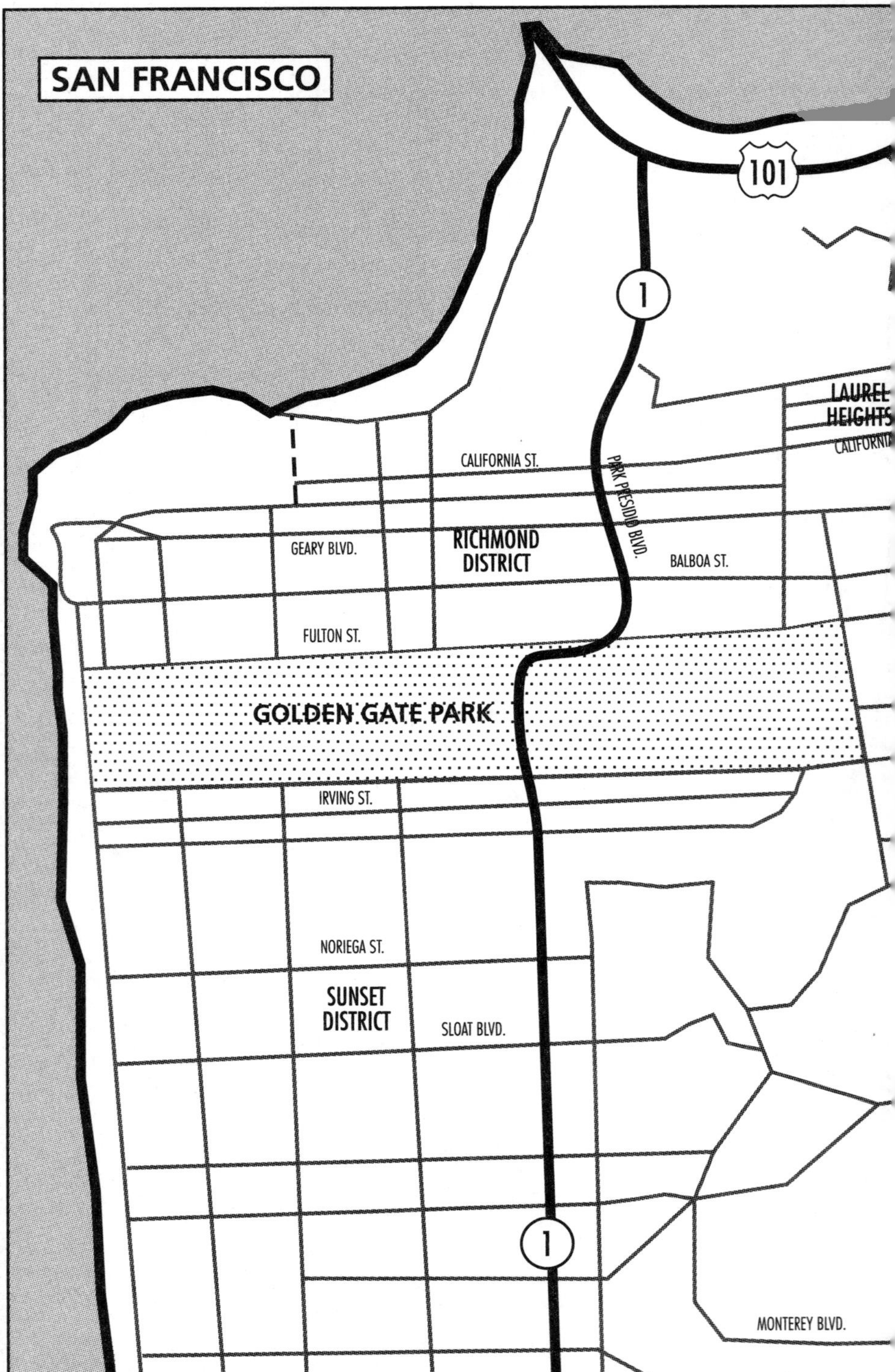
SAN FRANCISCO
101
1
LAUREL HEIGHTS
CALIFORNIA
CALIFORNIA ST.
PARK PRESIDIO BLVD.
GEARY BLVD.
RICHMOND DISTRICT
BALBOA ST.
FULTON ST.
GOLDEN GATE PARK
IRVING ST.
NORIEGA ST.
SUNSET DISTRICT
SLOAT BLVD.
1
MONTEREY BLVD.

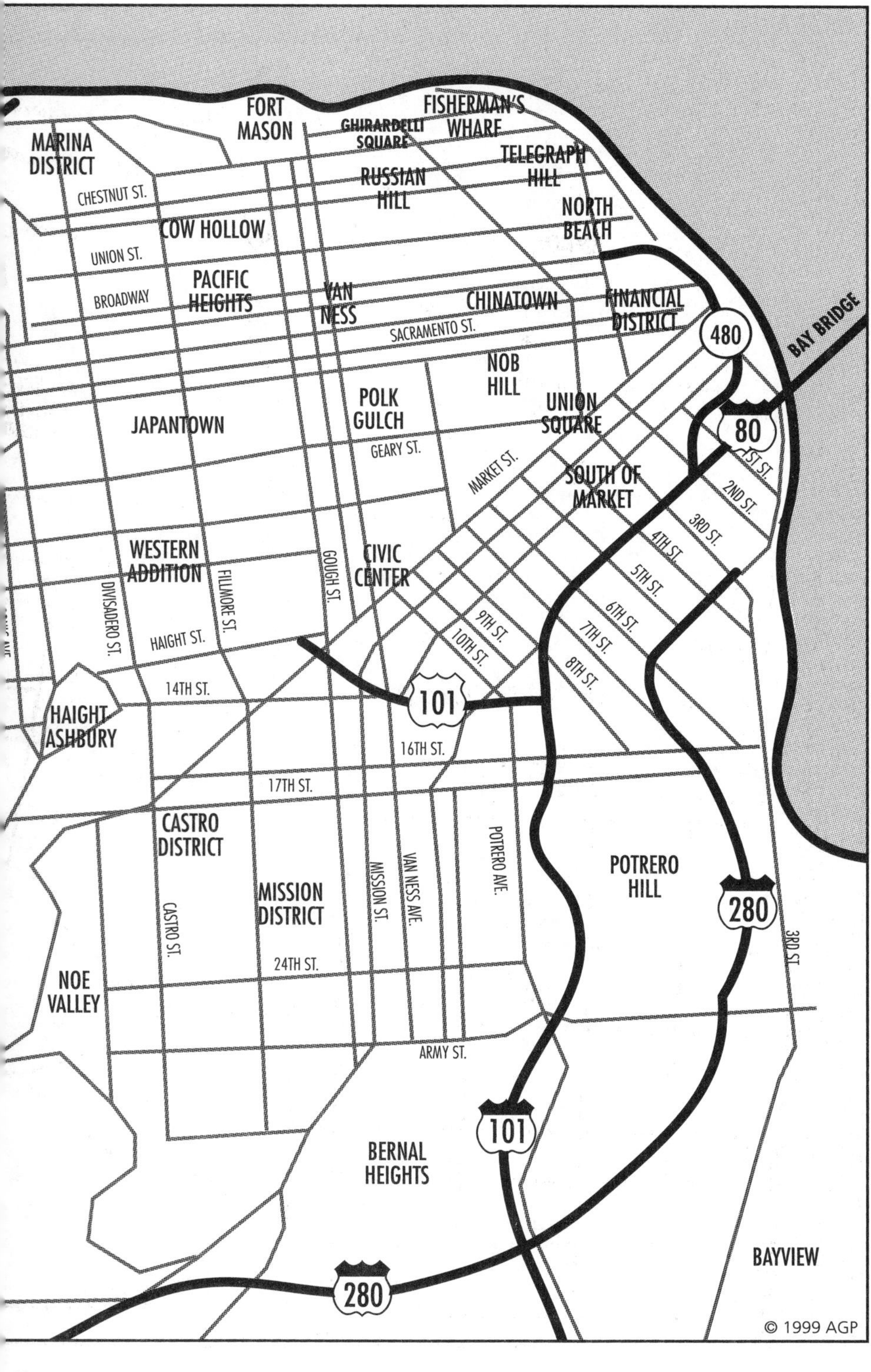
FORT MASON
FISHERMAN'S WHARF
GHIRARDELLI SQUARE
MARINA DISTRICT
TELEGRAPH HILL
RUSSIAN HILL
CHESTNUT ST.
NORTH BEACH
COW HOLLOW
UNION ST.
PACIFIC HEIGHTS
BROADWAY
VAN NESS
CHINATOWN
FINANCIAL DISTRICT
SACRAMENTO ST.
480
BAY BRIDGE
NOB HILL
POLK GULCH
UNION SQUARE
JAPANTOWN
80
GEARY ST.
1ST ST.
MARKET ST.
SOUTH OF MARKET
2ND ST.
3RD ST.
4TH ST.
WESTERN ADDITION
CIVIC CENTER
GOUGH ST.
FILLMORE ST.
5TH ST.
DIVISADERO ST.
6TH ST.
9TH ST.
HAIGHT ST.
10TH ST.
7TH ST.
8TH ST.
14TH ST.
101
HAIGHT ASHBURY
16TH ST.
17TH ST.
CASTRO DISTRICT
POTRERO AVE.
POTRERO HILL
MISSION DISTRICT
MISSION ST.
VAN NESS AVE.
280
CASTRO ST.
3RD ST.
24TH ST.
NOE VALLEY
ARMY ST.
101
BERNAL HEIGHTS
BAYVIEW
280
© 1999 AGP

DINING

From the earliest days, San Francisco has harbored the country's free spirits, from gold-addled miners and prescient Beatniks to today's rising digital stars in multimedia gulch. This cultural freedom hasn't been lost on San Francisco chefs, who routinely define the culinary trends that eventually shape the country's tastes. It doesn't hurt that its geographic location-hours from diverse farmlands, perched on the Asian Pacific gateway-marks the city as one of the world's premier sites to cook, dine, and explore the limits of culinary expression. The fruits of earth and sea are hardly confined to restaurant kitchens: nowhere else in the country are growing, cooking, and eating great food as vital a part of the lifestyle. Small wonder that many cooking schools and chefs' training programs call San Francisco home.

Faced with this educated clientele, restaurants constantly push to maintain loyal following, and big-ticket eateries must dazzle the eye as well as the palate to stay afloat. The Bay Area's chefs scour the globe in search of the freshest, newest, and most unusual ingredients. Truffles and foie gras are lavished with pre-millennial abandon on delighted diners; cardoons and house-cured salmon threaten to become commonplace. And a public that once found Chardonnay adventuresome is delving into unimagined vinicultural realms. California's once-unknown Rhone- and Alsatian-style wines are lately finding themselves the center of attention.

The following restaurants all fall within San Francisco proper. To help you get around, in each address we've included the name of the city district-**Alamo Square, Bernal Heights, Castro, Chinatown, City South, Civic Center, Cow Hollow, Financial District, Fisherman's Wharf, Fort Mason, Haight-Ashbury, Hayes Valley, Japantown, Marina, Nob Hill, Noe Valley, North Beach, Pacific Heights, Polk Gulch, Potrero Hill, Presidio Heights, Richmond, Russian Hill, SoMa (South of Market), South City, Sunset, Telegraph Hill, Tenderloin, Union Square, Upper Fillmore, Upper Market, Van Ness, Western Addition.**

Absinthe

FRENCH 15/20

398 HAYES ST.
CIVIC CENTER 94102
415-551-1590
Dinner Tues.-Sun., $$$

This new restaurant didn't wait in line but jumped right to the front of it. It's a lavish, belle époque beauty, only a few minutes walk from the opera house, and the food is superb. Executive chef Ross Browne's menu is bold and creative, based on cuisine from the south of France with a Californian accent. A bar menu runs until 1 a.m., providing a great spot for after-theater dining, and includes two classics, a solid American hamburger and a French croque monsieur as well as a superb rendition of French onion soup. On the dinner menu, the cassoulet of duck confit, pork sausage and quail with gigandes beans could match with the best of southern France; try too the risotto with roasted squab or the roasted half chicken over sage stuffing. There's a full bar, featuring a number of classic drinks, including the New Orleans favorite, Sazerac. Absinthe delivers not only on atmosphere, but food as well. Make your reservations early.

Acquerello

ITALIAN 16/20

1722 SACRAMENTO ST.
NOB HILL 94109
415-567-5432
Dinner Tues.-Sat., $$$$

A luxurious restaurant and priced accordingly, Acquerello is beautifully conceived and executed. A cool, comfortable room alive with watercolors, the restaurant feels like a comfortable home. The constantly changing menu offers antipasti, primi piatti and secondi piatti; to fully experience the artistry of the kitchen (here under the direction of co-owner Suzette Gresham), order from each category. The house-made pasta is superb, as is the filet of beef rolled with prosciutto, Parmesan and rosemary; likewise the loin of lamb with mint and Parmesan. For starters, try the veal carpaccio with lemon-egg sauce or the marinated swordfish with Sicilian baked onions and black olive parsley salad. The wine list offers an award-winning selection of Italian bottlings, as well as a number of California entries; well-trained and accommodating service staff can help you choose. A separate dolci menu offers a diverse selection of tantalizing desserts, from a warm zabaglione perfumed with orange liqueur to a house-made ice cream with a vintage balsamic vinegar sauce.

Albona Ristorante

ITALIAN 13/20

545 FRANCISCO ST.
NORTH BEACH 94133
415-441-1040
Dinner Tues.-Sat., $$

The menu in this cozy room, finished in soft colors, offers a rich and tasty blend of Italian, Slavic and Central European influences. Chef-owner Bruno Viscovi (from the hillside town of Albona, southeast of Trieste on the Italian-Yugoslavian border) has lovingly recreated the flavors he remembers from his childhood. The menu here is a veritable pan-European taste sampler. You'll find chifeleti (pan-fried potato gnocchi in a superb beef sirloin-cumin sauce) as well as capuzi garbi con luganega (mild sausage with sauerkraut, braised with onions, apples and prosciutto). The sauces, which enhance many of the dishes, are all painstakingly prepared from reductions of various stocks. A favorite is the braciole di maiale-pork loin cutlets stuffed with sauerkraut, apples, prunes and prosciutto. The wine list offers mostly Italian varietals including often-overlooked gems from the Friuli and Alto-Adige regions, as well as a few Californian wines. For dessert try a competent strudel, a chocolate-and-ricotta cream torte or a chocolate flan with Amaretto.

Alegrias

SPANISH 13/20

2018 LOMBARD ST.
MARINA 94123
415-929-8888
Dinner nightly, $$

This cheery and whimsical restaurant, decorated with hand-painted ceramics and terracotta flower boxes, gets better with every visit. Sit at the bar in the brightly colored dining room and order a few of the delicious appetizers from a list of tapas calientes and tapas frias. A plate of escalivada, grilled eggplant, peppers and onions sprinkled with extra virgin Spanish olive oil, will get your appetite in top gear. Conejo a la cazuela, stewed rabbit with vegetables and wine, is a hot tapa that could make a light lunch or starter for dinner. For a main dish, try zarzuela de mariscos-shellfish in tomato, garlic, saffron and wine sauce or (for more traditional eaters) the New York steak with Spanish blue cheese sauce. For dessert, arroz con leche, Spanish rice and milk pudding, is marvelous.

Alejandro's La Polleria

MEXICAN/PERUVIAN 12/20

2937 MISSION ST.
MISSION 94110
415-826-8260
Lunch & Early Dinner daily, $
No cards

La Polleria is an undiscovered jewel in the Mission, a 1950s-feeling roadhouse that offers well over a dozen appetizers and several main plates from Peru and Mexico. The ceviche is one of the best in San Francisco, and a rendition of octopus salad is earthy and delicious. The classic Peruvian boiled potatoes, served here with feta and ricotta cheeses, turmeric and lemon-cream sauce is smooth and velvety.

An unusual dish of pescado tipo Oriental-a filet of fish with ginger, soy sauce, green onions, sesame oil and fermented black beans-reflects the Asian influence in Peru.

Alfred Schilling

ECLECTIC 11/20
1695 MARKET ST.
CIVIC CENTER 94103
415-431-8447
Lunch Mon.-Sat., Dinner Tues.-Sat., $$

Though San Francisco has long been a confectionery capital, it took Alsatian Alfred Schilling to open a chocolate-themed eatery. Squeezed onto Market Street, the restaurant boasts a towering mural of an Egyptian goddess (presumably of chocolate?) on the side of its narrow building. A few outdoor tables make for an eminently pleasant coffee-and-pastry stop. Baked goods, ranging from pain au chocolat to futuristic opera tortes, are not to be missed. Unfortunately, the menu has veered away from chocolate-flavored savory food of late, though the results of the chef's cocoa fixation are always interesting. Tuna carpaccio comes drizzled with a balsamic-chocolate syrup, and pork chops with a red wine-chocolate sauce and beet confit. Both the kitchen and the excellent confectionery offerings display a playful sense of humor-the nightly prix-fixe is labeled the "Willy Wonka" special.

Alta Plaza

CALIFORNIAN 13/20
2301 FILLMORE ST.
PACIFIC HEIGHTS 94115
415-922-1444
Dinner nightly, Brunch Sun., $$

A

The rainbow banners that fly outside Alta Plaza's shingled exterior may mystify the folks from back home, but for locals, they indicate this restaurant's core clientele is gay. All are welcome, though, to the warmly lit and inviting spot located at the top of Fillmore Street's hopping shopping strip. The dining room is a square, airy room sitting above the bar. The menu changes daily, but expect chef Amey Shaw to prepare rib-sticking dishes such as calf's liver with applewood-smoked bacon, Jack Daniels onions and mashed potatoes and pan-roasted duck breast with a winter vegetable purée and grilled radicchio napped by a sour-cherry-Chianti sauce. Lighter salmon or scallop entrées make brief appearances among the main dishes; creative diners can also cobble together a meal with appetizers that reflect California-Asian influences. After a dessert of crème brûlée or the well-loved sour-cherry-bananas Foster, linger over a glass of port and survey the casually dressed crowd or wander out to Fillmore Street to window shop the high-end clothing and home décor boutiques. Alta Plaza is also a pleasant spot for a late-night drink after a foreign flick at the nearby Clay theater.

Angkor Borei Restaurant

PAN-ASIAN ¢
3471 MISSION ST.
MISSION 94110
415-550-8417
Lunch Mon.-Sat., Dinner nightly

The cuisine in this white-stucco room with faded pastel walls combines elements of Thai, Vietnamese, and Chinese cookery, but with a pungent and herbal flair all its own. Try a crisp Cambodian crêpe of tofu, bean sprouts, ground pork and coconut, with a lemon-garlic sauce and shredded vegetable salad. Whole fried fish topped with a sweet-hot sauce is typically Cambodian, as are rich clay pot-cooked dishes containing shrimps and vegetables. If you've gotten past your Thai and Vietnamese fixations, Angkor Borei should be next on your list.

Anjou

FRENCH 14/20
44 CAMPTON PL.
UNION SQUARE 94108
415-392-5373
Lunch & Dinner Tues.-Sat., $$

Just steps from Union Square you'll find this wonderful bistro, a favorite hideaway for Union Square shoppers and Financial District types. Chef Pierre Morin took over Janot's in 1993 and renamed it Anjou, but not much else has changed from its well-loved predecessor. Morin looks to his Loire Valley home of Anjou for inspiration, and turns out French favorites such as calf's liver with bacon and onions; warm duck confit with endive and watercress; and grilled steak with perfect French frites. Cassoulet takes a new meaning here-Morin uses lobster, monkfish and lingo beans in a crayfish sauce to lighten the traditionally heavy dish. Prices are entirely reasonable; the lunch prix-fixe is a bargain at $12 for soup or salad and an entrée. Desserts include a crème caramel and Morin's specialty, Anjou pears in a warm sabayon. The exposed brick walls, brass trim and pale yellow fabric create a casual and welcoming room, a relief from the hustle and bustle outside.

Antica Trattoria

ITALIAN 13/20

2400 POLK ST.
RUSSIAN HILL 94109
415-928-5797
Dinner Tues.-Sun., $$

Chef-owner Ruggero Gadaldi has developed a real neighborhood treasure, a casually sophisticated space with huge windows. Not only is the food amazingly good-the soft polenta with wild mushrooms alone is worth a drive from Santa Rosa-but the prices are right, with the most expensive main dish under $15. Another brilliant starter is the sliced fennel with blood oranges and red onions. Main courses change frequently, but grilled pork tenderloin with Gorgonzola and pancetta always seems to be a winner. The wine list is more than adequate, with fair prices and a good selection.

Aqua

SEAFOOD 16/20

252 CALIFORNIA ST.
FINANCIAL DISTRICT 94111
415-956-9662
Lunch Mon.-Fri., Dinner Mon.-Sat., $$$$

Chef Michael Mina, who has been at Aqua since its launch in 1991, has set a sophisticated new standard for creative preparations of the bounty from the Pacific-and other oceans of the world. The pleasures begin when you arrive at this one-time bank space, transformed into a grand but gracious arena with salmon-tinted walls and gigantic mirrors that capture the action at a curved bar the size of an ocean wave. Mina likes to send out a complimentary amuse-gueule to start your meal: it might be a few perfectly grilled scallops on an endive salad, demitasses of lobster consommé or one of several other soups. The menu changes regularly, but an Aqua standby is the fresh grilled tuna with foie gras in a Pinot Noir sauce. There is also a tasting menu-five courses of the chef's selection, a good idea if it's your first visit-and a vegetarian tasting menu. The potato-wrapped Idaho trout, served with foie gras-spiced apple stuffing and chanterelle and spinach salad is a treat. When local Dungeness crab is in season, try crab gnocchi with black truffles and a wild mushroom ragoût.

Mina brings out the full-bodied flavors of his ingredients, pairing smoked monkfish with herb-scented chanterelle mushrooms or poaching wild salmon in cabbage leaves and adding a white onion marmalade. Monterey Bay red abalone is lightly sautéed and served with basil gnocchi. Pompano and red snapper are flown in from Florida, lobster and crab from Maine. The plates are gorgeously composed, the desserts-especially the chocolate creations- intensely flavored and the wine list thoughtfully chosen and fairly priced.

Arinell Pizza

PIZZA ¢

509 VALENCIA ST.
MISSION 94110
415-255-1303
Lunch & Dinner daily
No cards

In this comfortable, noisy Mission storefront, Arinell specializes in thin-crust New York-style pizzas layered with traditional toppings and sprinkled with oregano. You can buy it by the slice or as a whole pizza. Keep the combinations to a minimum to enjoy the sharp flavors and subtle spices.

Avenue 9

CALIFORNIAN 13/20

1243 9TH AVE.
SUNSET 94122
415-664-6999
Lunch Mon., Dinner nightly, Brunch Sun., $$

Avenue 9 is part of the bumper crop of new restaurants in the Inner Sunset. Open for lunch, dinner and Sunday brunch, this busy spot has managed to satisfy the fickle tastes of its clientele. While waiting for your table, eye the dishes as they come up from the open kitchen or survey the other diners, mostly young professionals who now make this reasonably priced neighborhood their home. If dining à deux, the narrow front room is fine, but groups should escape the din and sit in the larger back room. Glance at Avenue 9's menu and you'll see the hit parade of San Francisco cuisine: seared ahi tuna, Sonoma duck confit, Niman Schell burgers, grilled salmon. Thankfully, they're well prepared, beautifully presented and reasonably priced. Other recommendations include the tasty house "pizzettas" of caramelized onion and roasted garlic, and barbecued duck with red onion, smoked gouda and cilantro. Heartier fare includes a braised lamb shank on creamy polenta and sliced Petaluma duck breast served with a mushroom flan. Servers are knowledgeable and friendly and the wine list features an interesting mix of California, Aussie and French labels; local microbrews are also available. Warm gingerbread cake with caramelized walnuts, a house specialty, still wins raves. One caveat: finding parking in the Sunset is difficult, so plan accordingly.

Aya Sushi

JAPANESE 13/20

2084 CHESTNUT ST.
MARINA 94123
415-929-1670
Lunch & Dinner Tues.-Sun., $$

With a cheerful greeting, Aya chef and owner Hiro Tanabe welcomes all to his small, unintimidating Japanese restaurant in the Marina. The stream of diners begins at 6 p.m., as regulars fall through the door eager to ditch their cell-phones and PalmPilots and join fellow diners in an ice-cold Kirin. Tanabe runs a tight ship: he mans the sushi bar; the solo waitress (literally) runs the beers and dishes to the handful of tables in the dining room; the behind-the-scenes cook turns out crisp seafood and vegetable tempuras and moist and flavorful teriyakis. For singles and couples, the sushi bar is where you want to be. One weekday visit to Aya found three women dining solo at the bar, happy to chat with their Hiro and to savor standbys such as maguro, unagi and California roll. The rich sesame dressing on the green- and purple-cabbage house salad is positively addictive; order it separately or have it as part of the sushi combination plate served with miso soup. The dining room looks onto an overgrown bamboo garden, a nice respite from ever-busy Chestnut Street out front. Reservations are not required, but expect a harried server during peak dinner hours.

Babaloo

CARIBBEAN 12/20

2030 LOMBARD ST.
MARINA 94123
415-346-5474
Dinner nightly, $$

This once dreary stretch of Lombard sports several interesting restaurants now, including Babaloo, a bright Caribbean setting that offers what chef Mark Walker calls "nuevo latino," or new Latin Caribbean cuisine. You'll find a long list of tapas, both hot and cold, including a bocadillo of pan-roasted rock shrimp cake with chipotle aïoli, an empanada of wild mushrooms and pepper jack cheese with sweet red pepper sauce and the cleverly named Amarillo, a dish of sweet plantain wedges over black beans with lime cream. Main plates include the cerdo con arroz, a plate of slow-roasted, jerk-spiced shredded pork with red beans and rice-a Caribbean classic.

Backflip

CALIFORNIAN 12/20

601 EDDY ST.
TENDERLOIN 94109
415-771-3547
Dinner Tues.-Sat., $$

The apotheosis of '90s hip makes its home at Backflip, the turquoise-toned bar and restaurant hidden in the seedy Tenderloin district. (The space, part of the Phoenix Hotel, once housed the popular Miss Pearl's Jam House.) More LA than SF, Backflip's décor is most reminiscent of a chlorinated fish bowl. And while parking and prices preoccupy some city diners, a visit to Backflip requires a consultation with your stylist; otherwise, head-to-toe Prada will suffice. The drink menu is nouveau martini bar, with colorful cocktails, a selection of 15-year-old scotch and a dozen wines by the glass. Rather than full meals, Backflip serves a tapas-style "cocktail cuisine" that roams the culinary map-hummus, sushi, prawn tamales-and is delivered via dim-sum trolley. Other dishes of grilled vegetables, house-smoked salmon and minted Moroccan lamb scooped up with endive, show imagination that almost rivals the décor. Desserts, if you dare, include cookies and truffles and a chocolate martini (chocolate-espresso mousse with a Cabernet sauce). For sheer production value, splashy Backflip is worth a lap or two.

Bahia Cabana

BRAZILIAN 12/20

1600 MARKET ST.
CIVIC CENTER 94102
415-626-3306
Dinner Tues.-Sun., $$

A

You can get the real flavor of Brazil at Bahia Cabana, not only through the food but the live music, the huge, vibrant paintings on the wall and the Carnaval atmosphere. Hot peppers, cilantro, coconut and tropical fruits are staple ingredients of this cuisine; for an authentic taste of Brazil try the feijoada completa, a rich stew of various meats, black beans and special herbs, simmered all day and served with rice, farofa (toasted manioc flour and spices sautéed in garlic and olive oil) and couve (greens sautéed the same way). Another exotic traditional dish is galinha na cerveja (chicken marinated in dark beer and baked with Brazilian spices), served with saffron rice and tutu (refried beans). If you only want a quick bite, drop in for some tapas or a dish of sopa de feijao, Brazilian black bean soup.

Baker Street Bistro

FRENCH 11/20

2953 BAKER ST.
MARINA 94123
415-931-1475
Lunch & Dinner Tues.-Sun., $$

Hearty French fare is the great strength at this tiny restaurant just off Lombard Street's motel strip, the kind of food that French truck drivers detour for kilometers and kilometers to enjoy. Service is great, too. There's a very tasty lamb stew and a superb rabbit in mustard sauce. The traditional crème brûlée for dessert is worth a trip across town.

Bangkok 16

THAI 11/20

3214 16TH ST.
MISSION 94103
415-431-5838
Dinner nightly, $

The Mission is particularly rich in Thai restaurants, and Bangkok 16 is a neighborhood favorite: spend a few moments inside this diminutive restaurant and you'll know why. The hook is the charming, home-style dining room-it feels more like a living room-and friendly, exceptionally gracious service. This isn't to denigrate the food in the least: meang-kom, for instance, is a startling and delicious appetizer. A plethora of ingredients-ginger, lemon, coconut, peanuts, onions and dried shrimps-are served with spinach leaves for rolling your own. The Bangkok 16 crêpe is similarly delicious; here, young coconut meat, dry shrimps and tofu are embedded in a light egg-and-rice-flour crêpe. All the dishes on the extensive menu are artfully presented and served, as are accompaniments of choice: Thai iced tea or Singha beer.

Barcelona

SPANISH 12/20

7 SPRING ST.
FINANCIAL DISTRICT 94104
415-989-1976
Lunch Mon.-Fri. , Dinner Mon.-Sat., $$

A

If you can find your way to tiny Spring Street, you'll find Barcelona, a stylishly fanciful restaurant hidden amongst the towers of the Financial Zone. Inside is a riot of gaudy (or is that Gaudi?) iconic Spanish images: Picasso and Miró prints battle for attention above impossibly plush booths. The menu doesn't explore new territory as far as Spanish food is concerned, but it features dishes with a level of style that sets Barcelona apart from other would-be tapas palaces. For starters, try succulent Moorish-style lamb in almond-garlic sauce, or the all-too-rare treat of scallops grilled in the shell over saffron-laced onions. Entrées, such as the classic zarzuela a la Catalonia (a rich seafood stew) and churrasco a la parilla (grilled Angus steak topped with wood-roasted piquillo peppers) receive tasteful and practiced treatment. Stop by for dinner or a leisurely cocktail hour, and as the menu invites, you'll feel "so close to a place so far away."

Beach Chalet

AMERICAN 12/20
1000 Great Hwy.
Richmond District 94121
415-386-8439
Lunch Mon.-Sat., Dinner nightly, Brunch Sun., $$

Just to be clear: it's not the Beach Chalet's food that sends diners to the far side of Golden Gate Park, and it's probably not the house-brewed beers either, although they're very good. What pulls folks to the Beach Chalet is the spectacular 180-degree view of the waves crashing on Ocean Beach. The Beach Chalet opened in 1997 after massive renovations to the vintage beachside building that now doubles as a restaurant and historic site. The dining room stretches across the second floor, while the main floor houses the history of Golden Gate Park and-more impressively-a collection of restored Depression-era murals with colorful scenes of days gone by. It's best to arrive during daylight hours to appreciate the view; when making reservations, be sure to ask for a window-side table. The food pairs nicely with the Beach Chalet's microbrews, although execution can be hit or miss: stick to basics and you won't be disappointed. The roast chicken with garlic mashed potatoes is a good choice, as is the Niman-Schell burger. Other fare includes crispy buttermilk-fried onion rings and spicy chicken wings; beer-braised dishes are also worth a try. Live music begins after the sun goes down; if you're not in the mood for dinner, join the crowd at the bar for a cold one. Thanks to the remote location, there's enough parking for everyone.

Betelnut

ASIAN/CALIFORNIAN 15/20
2026 Union St.
Cow Hollow 94123
415-929-8855
Lunch & Dinner daily, $$$

An air of drama and excitement pervades Betelnut, as if you are eating in your very own film noir. It's a noisy, comfortable place where the style-both of the clientele and the black-lacquered setting-isn't overbearing. The food here is always good, a pan-Asian fusion with a bow to European techniques. The menu reads like a wishbook if you like big, bold flavors. Start with sun-dried anchovies, wok-tossed with peanuts, chilies and garlic or chili-encrusted calamari. Move on to orange-glazed beef with Szechwan peppercorns or the tea-smoked duck. There's a whole range of those delightfully sinful drinks that could have little umbrellas stuck in them, including the classic Singapore Sling (adapted here as Singapore Sing). The wine list is chosen to match the firecracker flavors of the food, and is a classic example of what can be done with serious wines and Asian food. Could that be Peter Lorre, there at the next table with Lauren Bacall?

Big Nate's

BARBECUE ¢
1665 Folsom St.
SoMa 94103
415-861-4242
Lunch & Dinner daily

This bright yellow building, owned by basketball Hall-of-Famer Nate Thurmond, is barbecue heaven. Big Nate's serves moist and tender meats cooked slowly in a brick wood-burning oven. The sauce is tangy but not overly smoky; it comes in three degrees of hotness. Enjoy a slab of lean ribs, barbecued chicken, hot links or the house's famed Memphis pork-the best dish of all. Don't forget side dishes (baked beans, corn muffins, potato salad) or sweet potato pie. Everything here is homemade and delicious.

Bill's Place

DINER ¢
2315 Clement St.
Richmond District 94121
415-221-5262
Lunch & Dinner daily

The late Herb Caen among them, there are many stalwarts who swear this crowded diner serves the best burgers in town. Certainly this is the only place in the city with sandwiches named for Beverly Sills, Russ Riera and even Caen himself. Bill's also does well by other lunch counter staples: french fries, malts and shakes, tuna or egg salad sandwiches and a variety of green salads. The service is friendly and prompt and the atmosphere is pleasant, especially on the patio out back. Don't worry: the line at Bill's moves quickly.

Bistro Aix

FRENCH 13/20

3340 STEINER ST.

MARINA 94123

415-202-0100

Dinner nightly, $$

In a city that loves bistro fare, why not just open one and be done with it? Perhaps that's the conclusion Bistro Aix chef and owner Jonathan Beard came to when he thought up his little Marina restaurant. Starters are faves like mussels in a white-wine-shallot broth, and mesclun salad with tarragon vinaigrette and goat cheese croutons. Entrées are "cracker" crust pizzas topped with tomato, mozzarella, Fontina and Parmesan; more substantial fare includes roasted chicken with lovely crisp skin and moist meat. A pat of tarragon butter, mashed potatoes and authentic ratatouille complete the plate and make a very satisfying dinner. Beard keeps the neighborhood coming back for more by offering a prix-fixe dinner for $11.95, Sundays to Thursdays from 6 p.m. to 8 p.m. Desserts are equally delightful-tarte tatin and a caramel mousse cake with chocolate ganache. The smallish restaurant is a design hodgepodge-pretty to look at but not particularly functional: the bar takes up much of the room while café tables and chairs aren't particularly comfortable. The music is often loud, making conversation an ordeal; complain or ask to sit on the heated patio out back. The food's worth the trouble.

Bistro Clovis

FRENCH 11/20

1596 MARKET ST.

CIVIC CENTER 94102

415-864-0231

Lunch Mon.-Fri., Dinner Tues.-Sat., $$

Bistro Clovis recently underwent an extensive remodeling, but its pseudo-Parisian charm has emerged unscathed-crisp linens, brocade curtains and newly polished hardwood floors lend the dining room a homey air. Housemade pâté with onion marmalade, red snapper mousse surrounded by sliced zucchini and baked goat cheese with oyster mushroom confit are among the more intriguing of the appetizers; the trout cake with red pepper coulis also comes highly recommended. Main dishes can be hit or miss: rabbit braised in Chardonnay is paired with a creamy, bacon- and shallot-enriched sauce, but an uninspired goat cheese-stuffed chicken breast can leave you cold. Desserts are a safe bet: old standbys-poached pears, tarte tatin, and crème brûlée-find happy homes at this Parisian refugee.

Bitterroot

AMERICAN 12/20

3122 16TH ST.

MISSION 94110

415-626-5523

Lunch daily, Dinner Tues.-Sat., $

Inside this airy, Bohemian storefront overlooking the heart of the heart of the Mission, the flavors here are big and satisfying, reminding you of a roadside diner somewhere in the Midwest-only lots better. Try barbecued pork spare ribs, served with crisp roasted potatoes, spicy cole slaw and yam chips. Bitterroot also serves a great American-style breakfast.

Bix

AMERICAN 13/20

56 GOLD ST.

NORTH BEACH 94111

415-433-6300

Lunch Mon.-Fri., Dinner nightly, $$$

A

Order another martini, squint a bit and you can well believe that Scott Fitzgerald and his party are waiting for a table at the end of the bar. This 1920s-style supper club, with its dark, burnished wood and polished brass, its white-jacketed wait staff and jazz pianist, serves what might be described as "imaginative home cooking." The mezzanine dining area is quiet and intimate for romantic dinners, but lunch is more raucous. Try Bix's delicious chicken hash or the Niman-Schell hamburger with Hobb's bacon, Gorgonzola and, of course, pommes frites. Proprietor Doug Biederbeck seems to recognize everyone in town, and knows spirits the way a master sommelier knows wines. The bar here is a wonder to behold, and Biederbeck is famous for appearing at your tableside to mix his celebrated dry martinis on the spot. After dinner, ask about special Cognacs-he's got several older than your grandmother.

Bizou

MEDITERRANEAN 13/20

598 4TH ST.
SOMA 94107
415-543-2222
Lunch Mon.-Fri., Dinner Mon.-Sat., $$$

The gutsy French-California food keeps people coming back to this brisk, bright middle-class Parisian bistro. Chef Loretta Keller has a way of taking a simple dish and raising it to new levels of intensity and flavor. A wood-burning oven flickers at the heart of Bizou's menu, so try the pizzas with special toppings that change on a regular basis-if you are in luck you'll find wood-roasted onions and pancetta available. The pastas are definitely non-traditional, with bold sauces like the pappardelle in a spicy tomato broth with onions, eggplant and feta. The appetizer of batter-fried green beans with fig dipping sauce is a surprising, addictive combination. Main courses are satisfying, particularly country-style dishes such as braised beef cheeks with mashed potatoes, vegetables and fried onions, a wonderfully rich mélange of flavors. Desserts continue the bistro theme: seasonal fruit, bittersweet chocolate vacherin. Bizou's well-selected (if brief) wine list offers a number of wines by the glass at very fair prices.

Blowfish Sushi

JAPANESE 12/20

2170 BRYANT ST.
MISSION/POTRERO HILL 94110
415-285-3848
Lunch Mon.-Fri., Dinner nightly, $$

A

This stylish sushi bar brings to mind '80s L.A. Sleek lacquered-wood and traditional sake pots are set against giant video screens playing ultra-kinetic Japanese animation shorts. Add a pulsing techno soundtrack and you're blown away before you've taken your seat. The restaurant's name alludes to its dish of Northern Puffer, a cousin to the famed fugu, a potentially poisonous fish found in the Sea of Japan. As Blowfish is the only restaurant in the city serving this specialty, the fish comes at a high premium. Offerings from the kitchen are hit-or-miss, but chef Ritsuo Tsuchida's inventive sushi plates are more reliable. "Ménage à Trois" features salmon, its crispy skin and eggs wrapped in shiso, a Japanese herb related to mint, while Blowfish maki combines yellowtail, salmon, and tobiko in a fat seafood disk. All sushi is made with high-quality fish, though as a result, prices are somewhat higher than what you'll pay at other neighborhood sushi bars.

Boulevard

AMERICAN 16/20

1 MISSION ST.
FINANCIAL DISTRICT 94105
415-543-6084
Lunch Mon.-Fri., Dinner nightly, $$$

A

One of San Francisco's most beautiful restaurants is also one of its best. Manning the kitchen that overlooks a charming, turn-of-the-last-century Parisian street scene, complete with lovely tiled floors and big windows, Nancy Oakes seems to effortlessly improve as one of the nation's top chefs. Working with a basic American menu (served with a French accent, to be sure) Oakes creates flavorful dishes that linger on the palate when other meals have been forgotten. If you want to get a taste of Boulevard at a reasonable price, you could do an entire lunch just from the starters menu: open with a wood-oven pizza (a lunch all by itself) featuring white corn, roasted red pepper, applewood-smoked bacon and goat cheese, or perhaps try New England cod cakes with yellow tomato sauce, tartar sauce and baby greens. Another favorite is the crispy calamari served with a spicy Asian vinaigrette. For a main course, don't miss the honey-cured pork loin or boneless duck breast-or virtually anything from the wood-fired oven. The wine list is one of the best in San Francisco, with over two dozen varietals by the glass, including four sparkling wines and a sparkling cider from Normandy. All that wonderful food and drink in a classy belle-époque setting with views of the Bay Bridge. Let's go!

Brisas de Acapulco

MEXICAN ¢
3137 Mission St.
Mission 94110
415-826-1496
Breakfast, Lunch & Dinner daily
No cards

This friendly little place is open until midnight weeknights and until 3 a.m. on weekends, making it the perfect Mission drop-in for seafood with a Latin-American accent. Served beneath a bold mural and a lively open kitchen, most dishes on the menu are well under $10. Try their tasty seafood soups, pupusas and seafood tostadas.

Brother-in-Law's Bar-B-Que

BARBECUE ¢
705 Divisadero St.
Western Addition 94115
415-931-7427
Lunch & Dinner Tues.-Sun.

VISA MasterCard

Pilgrims from all over town line up at this brick smokehouse for some of the best 'Q going. Eugene Ponds and Demo Adams' slow-cooked pork ribs (the fat-free short ends are worth the extra charge), fork-tender beef brisket, chicken and lean beef links all carry a deep but never overpowering smoky taste. Ask for the mixed hot-and-mild sauce and don't miss the sweet baked beans and fine-grained corn muffins.

Bruno's

MEDITERRANEAN 13/20
2389 Mission St.
Mission 94110
415-550-7455
Dinner Tues.-Sat., $$

VISA MasterCard Diners Club International

A bit of Mission Street history has been recreated in Bruno's, which first opened in the 1930s. After being closed for a decade, it reopened a few years ago with chef James Ormsby serving up classic Mediterranean dishes in a supper club setting. There's music in the bar and comfortable leather booths in the dining room. The light- and sun-filled Mediterranean menu contrasts oddly with the shadowy supper-club atmosphere, but it all seems to work just fine. For starters or as a small main dish, try steamed mussels in orange-saffron broth or warm duck confit salad with Moroccan spice and a pomegranate vinaigrette, then move on to a house specialty-hearty, wine-braised oxtail with mashed potatoes. Delicious. Wonder who's playing after dinner tonight?

Buca di Beppo

ITALIAN 11/20
855 Howard St.
SoMa 94103
415-543-7673
Dinner nightly, $$

VISA MasterCard DISCOVER

Though it's loud, corny, kitsch and corporate, Buca di Beppo is a genuinely fun place to hit with a crowd. A self-styled "immigrant Italian" joint, the bright, labyrinthine restaurant is a riot of posters, photos and memorabilia. This is definitely not a place to visit with less than three or four friends; portions are mammoth, and priced to be shared family-style. The food itself is nothing new, but it is decently prepared, filling and tasty. Pizzas in particular are recommended, as are the frutti di mare pasta, which comes loaded with squid, clams and mussels in a hearty tomato sauce. The servers admirably convey the restaurant's spirit of fun, while Italian folk songs and pop vocals remind you of the childhood you never had. Frankie, we miss you.

Buca Giovanni

ITALIAN 12/20
800 Greenwich St.
North Beach 94133
415-776-7766
Dinner Tues.-Sun., $$

A

A comfortable restaurant that features a dining room below street level and scoured-brick walls decorated with scenes of Tuscany, Giovanni serves many Italian specialties not readily found elsewhere in the City. Antipasto misto has a generous serving of aromatic bresaola and sweet sun-dried tomatoes in fine olive oil. Of the excellent pastas, don't miss the panzerotti salsa di noci-al dente ravioli filled with seasoned veal and graced with a delicious, nutty sauce. Entrées range from rabbit sautéed with porcini mushrooms in a white wine sauce to ravioli stuffed with wild mushrooms and pine nuts and served in an earthy venison sauce. To finish, try the ball of chocolate gelato rolled in semi-sweet chocolate shavings. Buca Giovanni is also notable for its daily low-fat specials. The moderately priced wine list includes many good California selections and a handful of hard-to-find Italian wines, including a few affordable vintage Barolos.

Burma Super Star

BURMESE ¢
309 CLEMENT ST.
RICHMOND DISTRICT 94118
415-387-2147
Lunch & Dinner Tues.-Sun.

The audaciously titled Burma Super Star has a lot to live up to: it's one of only a handful of restaurants that claim to serve authentic Burmese cuisine. Try la pat doke, a salad of pickled green tea leaves, tomatoes, cabbage, and roasted nuts, or moo hing nga-considered Burma's national dish: a rich stew of catfish and soft noodles in spicy broth. Other winners are a chicken salad and any of the smoky Burmese-style curries. Service, though occasionally forgetful, is unfailingly friendly. Reservations are recommended.

Butterfield's

SEAFOOD 13/20
202 TOWNSEND ST.
SOMA 94107
415-281-9001
Lunch Mon.-Fri., Dinner Mon.-Sat., $$

At first glance, Butterfield's seems to be trapped in an out-of-the-way location, hidden over a bar in an old brick building at the corner of Third and Townsend. Too, it doesn't strut the way the rest of the city's restaurant gang does. Butterfield's specializes in fresh seafood, prepared in a no-fuss way for people who work in the neighborhood. Chowder two ways, crab Louis, oysters on the half shell, whole Maine lobster with drawn butter, Pacific salmon cooked on the griddle and topped with herb butter-chef and owner Stewart Butterfield Pringle serves favorites with aplomb. During Dungeness season, this is a wonderful place to indulge in some messy crab legs. If you're not a fan of the fish or seafood, you'd best avoid Butterfield's-the lone non-fish entrée is a BLT sandwich. Considering the new baseball field going in just a block away, Butterfield's may be sitting quite prettily.

Byblos Restaurant

LEBANESE 13/20
1910 LOMBARD
MARINA 94123
415-292-5672
Dinner nightly, $$

A

After you've been to Byblos once, you become part of the family at this Lebanese restaurant in the tacky heart of Lombard street. There are often local painters represented on the walls and the ambience is open and friendly. Starters at Byblos are best, little dishes called mezze in the Middle East, tapas in Spain. There are over twenty to choose from, ranging from a selection of pickled vegetables to lambs' tongues to the best dolmas in the city. Byblos makes its yogurt fresh daily; be sure and order a small pot for the table. A party of twelve or more can special-order a whole roast lamb, which comes with all the mezze you want. Entertainment has been added on the weekends-belly dancers and middle eastern music. It's amusing but can get rather loud, so go early if you want a quiet meal.

Café Claude

FRENCH 12/20
7 CLAUDE LN.
FINANCIAL DISTRICT 94111
415-392-3505
Lunch & Dinner Mon.-Sat., $$

A

If this feels like an authentic Parisian bistro, right down to its unmistakable European ambience and zinc-topped bar, that's because it is. Café Claude used to be Le Barbizon in Paris, until owner Steve Decker bought the place lock, stock and pastis pitchers, and had it shipped to San Francisco. The sandwiches, soups and salads are good enough at lunch, but we prefer the value-priced food at dinner. Cassoulet is properly robust and savory; chocolate mousse is rich and silky. Specials might include a thin filet of salmon atop sautéed greens, all crowned by aïoli and neon orange salmon roe.

Café Ethiopia

ETHIOPIAN ¢
878 VALENCIA ST.
SAN FRANCISCO 94110
415-285-2728
Lunch & Dinner daily

The plain white sign announcing Café Ethiopia doesn't promise much, but modest coffee-shop décor aside, the restaurant's identity is a welcome addition to the Mission. Eighteen dishes run the gamut from hearty kito, a buttery Ethiopian steak tartare, to delicate alecha ater, a rich purée of yellow split peas. All are served on injera (unleavened sourdough bread) and pieces are torn off to scoop up your food. Several vegetarian dishes are excellently prepared and affordable enough to share with a friend.

Café Jacqueline

FRENCH 13/20
1454 GRANT AVE.
NORTH BEACH 94133
415-981-5565
Dinner Wed.-Sun., $$

A

With only 24 seats, Café Jacqueline is a great and unexpectedly fulfilling stop on a foggy North Beach night. Aside from a daily soup and salads, the tiny North Beach landmark serves nothing but soufflés, and Jacqueline Margulis' are worth a special trip to taste. Besides more predictable egg creations, one current favorite is the black-truffle-and-lobster soufflé. For dessert, you'll find a complete lineup of sweet soufflés, from traditional selections to those infused with Grand Marnier, Bailey's, and other liqueurs.

Café Kati

CALIFORNIAN 13/20
1963 SUTTER ST.
JAPANTOWN 94116
415-775-7313
Dinner Tues.-Sun., $$

Although one of San Francisco's more innovative restaurants, softly lit Café Kati eschews the hype other hotspots encourage and concentrates on serving imaginatively prepared food to an appreciative audience. Chef and owner Kirk Webber was one of the city's first practitioners of East-West "fusion" cuisine, once raising eyebrows by using ingredients as diverse as wasabi, truffle oil and Thai curry to season his creations. Architecture plays an important role in each dish's presentation: Caesar salad towers off the plate and a napoleon of seared tuna au poivre is elaborately layered with crisp won tons, radish sprouts and seaweed. Signature appetizers are sweet potato biscuits, mango spring rolls with a tangy "diphthong" dipping sauce and crabmeat potstickers with red Thai curry. For entrées, Webber glazes salmon with miso and adds sides of avocado sushi, grilled Japanese eggplant and a seaweed salad. For more conventional fare, his lamb osso buco is served on mashed potatoes with a black-and-white chanterelle sauce and topped with a tart gremolata. (Vegetarians may need to order an assortment of appetizers to keep the faith.) Desserts are equally spectacular: Three mini-versions of crème brûlée-classic, chocolate and brown sugar-arrive under a tangle of spun sugar. Park at the Japantown lot (Café Kati will validate your parking ticket), look for Kati's storefront location on Sutter Street, enter through thick velvet curtains and make yourself comfortable at one of the city's hideaway gems.

Café Marimba

MEXICAN 13/20
2317 CHESTNUT ST.
MARINA 94123
415-776-1506
Lunch Tues.-Sun., Dinner nightly, $$

This energetic restaurant, alive with the colors and creatures of tropical Mexico, offers an upscale menu inspired by the moles and salsas from the Oaxaca region. Herbs such as epazote and hoja santa add zesty flavors to the dishes. A good introduction to Café Marimba is the Marimba Sampler, which includes a chicken enchilada with mole negro, a cuitlacoche enchilada, a spicy chorizo empanada and a mole amarillo tamale. Five different salsas and moles (using chocolate flown in from Mexico) are made fresh daily, and corn tortillas are freshly patted throughout the day. For the hearty appetite, try several meats and fish from the grill, including Zihuatanejo-style rock shrimps and Oaxacan chipotle beef.

Marimba is a long way from TexMex or CalMex border food.

Café Tiramisu

ITALIAN 12/20
28 Belden St.
Financial District 94104
415-421-7044
Lunch Mon.-Fri., Dinner Mon.-Sat., $$

Tiny Belden Street is a Californian version of a narrow side street in a hip European city: restaurants are packed like proverbial sardines into the one-block strip. A long-standing favorite is Café Tiramisu, a slightly self-conscious little trattoria next to extremely self-conscious Plouf. Trompe l'oeil murals and skylights take you to Italy, while a long, semi-open kitchen brings you right back home. Offerings are for the most part Northern Italian, meaning they're often meat-based and quite rich-though pastas tend towards sumptuous cheese and vegetable creations. While flashy preparations such as a shrimp-and-enoki Caesar with infused oils can fall flat, and rustic dishes can simply underwhelm, the majority of the food here is both well-prepared and stylishly-presented. Daily specials such as roasted eggplant and goat cheese ravioli with toasted sage and an authoritative tomato ragoût are not to be missed. The flirtatious staff are typically harried, the wine list decent and desserts highly recommended, in particular the-what else?-tiramisu.

Caffè Delle Stelle

ITALIAN 13/20
395 Hayes St.
Hayes Valley 94102
415-252-1110
Lunch Mon.-Sat., Dinner nightly, $$

Lined with wine bottles and stacks of canned tomatoes, Caffè Delle Stelle serves basic Italian fare in the heart of Hayes Valley. Location alone could keep this place busy-it's close to the opera and symphony venues and City Hall, too. But Stelle is also a warm and welcoming spot, attracting pols and cultured types as well as families, Hayes Street hipsters and folks from out of the 'hood. Lunch might mean a roasted pumpkin-and-ricotta ravioli with sage-infused butter, a timballo of grilled eggplant, roasted tomatoes, pesto and ricotta, or any of a number of reasonably priced pasta dishes. At dinner, homemade gnocchi appears on the menu, served with smoked chicken-apple sausage and Fontina; other picks include risotto studded with clams, mussels, calamari and saffron. Osso buco wins fans here, as does braised lamb served on polenta. Wines comprise a mix of Tuscan reds and California big-name favorites. After the symphony rush, Delle Stelle's is just the place to linger over dessert and watch the world go by.

Caffè Macaroni

ITALIAN 12/20
59 Columbus Ave.
North Beach 94133
415-956-9737
Lunch Mon.-Fri., Dinner Mon.-Sat., $$
No cards

This tiny space, with its charming mezzanine dining area and shoulder-to-shoulder second-floor room, offers rustic Italian fare much like you'd find on a busy side street in Rome. You'll find every imaginable size and shape of dried noodle decorating the ceiling here; between the whimsical décor and the engaging staff, any visit is bound to be pleasant. Recorded opera blasts from the kitchen, from which fresh and flavorful pasta dishes arrive in two or three paces. Pizza and hearty daily specials, all reasonably priced, are also recommended. At lunch, a grilled chicken sandwich with salad makes for a healthful, tasty meal. The owner is a wine buff, so the wine list is-like a good operatic tenor-surprisingly deep, and with an Italian accent.

Caffè Sport

ITALIAN 11/20
574 Green St.
North Beach 94133
415-981-1251
Lunch & Dinner Tues.-Sat., $$
No cards

With its mid-century pasta-joint décor and lively, clattering ambience, Caffè Sport continues to be a favorite, as the long lines waiting most evenings on Green Street will attest. However, there are some severe downsides-and we're not talking about the traffic in North Beach. It seems there is always a wait, and once you get inside, service can be abrupt and bordering on rude. While some diners

think such abuse is colorful, others have vowed to never return. The upside to dining at Caffè Sport is that the food-enormous portions of seafood or pasta spiked with loads of garlic-can be very good, particularly fist-sized prawns doused in a pungent white sauce.

Campo Santo

MEXICAN ¢
240 COLUMBUS AVE.
NORTH BEACH 94133
415-433-9623
Lunch Mon.-Fri., Dinner Tues.-Sun.

Food influenced by the Mayan region of the Yucatán Peninsula is Santo's specialty. Try quesadilla Cancun, made with nopale cactus, rock shrimps and corn or the chicken marinated in achiote and sweet chilies, grilled and topped with green tomatillo-lime sauce. Daily specials of fresh seafood are also available. You'll dine within bright blue and yellow adobe walls painted with the Día de los Muertos theme.

Campton Place

AMERICAN 15/20
CAMPTON PLACE HOTEL
340 STOCKTON ST.
UNION SQUARE 94108
415-955-5555
Breakfast, Lunch & Dinner daily, Brunch Sun., $$$$

Established years ago by Bradley Ogden (later of Lark Creek Inn and One Market fame), this comfortable dining room, one of the city's most-established, quickly earned a reputation as one of the best in San Francisco and is still considered a destination restaurant. Its décor successfully combines refinement and comfort, and its well-trained staff are friendly and helpful. Chef Todd Humphries starts with the freshest ingredients available and prepares them with imagination and style. A taste of nearly any entrée on the seasonally changing menu will make you a Campton Place fan. Pan-seared squab with butter squash gnocchi and a ragoût of salsify and truffles is an enormously appealing dish, as is roasted sea bass with caramelized endive and salsa agro dolce. Desserts are amazing, especially an apple cake with Calvados and the classic Grand Marnier crème brûlée; you can also opt for a cheese plate. Campton Place has always been renowned for its breakfasts and brunches, and the small bar off the restaurant entrance is a great place to relax with a glass of sparkling wine and a bar snack. The wine list is extensive and pricey and shows great depth in its Californian offerings.

Capital Grille

STEAKHOUSE 12/20
121 SPEAR ST.
FINANCIAL DISTRICT 94105
415-495-4109
Lunch Mon.-Fri., Dinner nightly, $$$

This new addition to San Francisco's Rincon Center appeals to bankers and brokers thanks to its dark-paneled dining room, deep booths and the oil paintings of old captains of industry. One of a chain, the Capital specializes in dry-aged beef, from 14-ounce sirloins to 20-ounce Delmonicos. Side dishes are steakhouse standbys of baked, fried or mashed spuds. Veggies are equally rich-asparagus with hollandaise, creamed spinach or bland, roasted seasonal mushrooms. Diners can opt for grilled swordfish or a salmon filet minus the buttery sauces. Desserts continue the damn-the-cardiologist theme: crème brûlée, white chocolate mousse, key lime pie. The wine list includes a sizable selection of French, South American, Italian and Californian labels. A glass of port and a fat cigar make a perfect finish to an evening at the Grille.

Capp's Corner

ITALIAN 10/20
1600 POWELL ST.
NORTH BEACH 94133
415-989-2589
Lunch Mon.-Fri., Dinner nightly, $

From the photographs of the Dimaggio brothers to the long bar that dominates one side, this restaurant is more about North Beach color than food. A tossed salad, tartly dressed and full of canned kidney beans, follows the soup. If it's on the daily special board, osso buco is one of the best dishes. Entrées are served with mixed vegetables and a plate of pasta, usually topped with a traditional "North Beach" tomato sauce. Wash it all down with an inexpensive Chianti and finish with a glass of brandy as you get to know your neighbors at the closely spaced tables. Not great food, but Capp's is fun, and its price is right.

Carta

INTERNATIONAL 13/20

1772 MARKET ST.
CIVIC CENTER 94102
415-863-3516
Lunch Tues.-Fri., Dinner Tues.-Sun., Brunch Sun., $$

Though fusion may be all the rage in San Francisco dining, Carta has an entirely different take on multiculturalism. Each month, chef Rob Zaborny's menu focuses on a specific country; diners travel via 10-odd small plates and a few entrées. Surprisingly, the results are often excellent, thanks in large part to the careful research of Zaborny and his staff. The restaurant has taken on such subjects as Eastern Europe, Scandinavia, India, and Greece, to name but a few. A well-priced and ever-changing assortment of wines is available, and the waitstaff is eager to explain the month's selections. The restaurant's Achilles heel may be its small size: there are only a dozen or so tables squeezed in between the semi-open kitchen and busy Market Street, and when the place gets busy (as it often is) service can fall far behind. Nonetheless, Carta is well worth a visit: those in the know advise a late-month meal, when the kitchen is up to speed with the month's menu. A couple of sidewalk tables beckon during warm weather, but the neighborhood panhandlers could sour this idea.

Cassis Bistro

FRENCH 12/20

2120 GREENWICH ST.
COW HOLLOW 94123
415-292-0770
Dinner Tues.-Sat., $
No cards

Unpretentious and downright inexpensive, Cassis looks to southern France for inspiration. More often than not, the small dining room echoes with both English and French speakers; a handwritten sheet of nightly specials complements the brief menu. Expect simple but classic dishes of homemade pâté, endive salad with goat cheese, and garlicky escargots in puff pastry. Entrées of savory lamb stew with tomatoes and black olives, rosemary-scented braised rabbit and simple sautéed swordfish are competently prepared, although portions can be skimpy. Fresh fruit tart on short pastry or orange sorbet served in a hollowed-out orange make for good finales. The friendly staff moves efficiently through the many-leveled space; close-set tables facilitate eavesdropping. Parking is a trial in this neighborhood (try the lot at Lombard and Fillmore) and reservations are recommended. Finally, bring cash: Cassis doesn't take credit cards.

Cha Cha Cha

CARIBBEAN 12/20

1801 HAIGHT ST.
HAIGHT-ASHBURY 94117
415-386-5758
Lunch Mon.-Fri., Dinner nightly, $$
No cards

A mainstay of the wild and crazy Haight, Cha Cha Cha's colorful setting, staff and clientele blend into a lively Caribbean concoction. Once a narrow storefront, the eatery recently moved into larger, slightly more businesslike quarters. Still brimming with the primary hues and lots of noise, it's got plenty of wacky charm. Through the throbbing music, the food remains the same omnicultural mélange it's always been: an eclectic selection of tapas-inspired dishes, ranging from mouth-tingling calamari to deep-fried new potatoes. Other tapas are Cuban-inspired, such as fried plantains with black beans and sour cream. There's a daily specials board, most always featuring fish and some form of barbecue. Don't bother calling-Cha Cha Cha rarely answers their phone.

Chapeau!

FRENCH 15/20

1408 CLEMENT ST.
RICHMOND DISTRICT 94118
415-750-9787
Dinner Tues.-Sun., $$$

Chapeau! is a bit of Paris that slipped into the avenues in 1997 and looks like it's set for a long run. Minimally decorated with white tablecloths, the bistro-style restaurant created by Philippe and Ellen Gordelle serves incredibly delicious food from chef Sean Canavan. It's a cozy little treasure and terribly romantic without trying to be. As in all good restaurants, the menu changes often; there are usually two to three prix-fixe menus, including a vegetarian offering. The current vegetarian menu offers a salad of marinated beets with roasted eggplant relish and walnut vinaigrette, followed by a ragoût of cauliflower and beluga lentils with basmati rice and curry sauce; a spiced-orange soup follows, with a tropical fruit salad and coconut sorbet with a choice of dessert. Highlights of the main menu include splendid appetizers like sautéed sweetbreads and black trumpet mushrooms with Belgian endive or a bisque of lobster with mussels. For main courses, a roasted duck breast with potato gâteau, red cabbage and quince is irresistible. Desserts at Chapeau! are similarly fabulous, and the wine list is small but very well chosen. Chapeau! is the kind of restaurant other chefs visit on their nights off-and is the next best thing to flying off to Paris for the evening.

Charles Nob Hill

FRENCH/CALIFORNIAN 15/20

1250 Jones St.
Nob Hill 94109
415-771-5400
Dinner Tues.-Sun., $$$$

For a special anniversary, birthday celebration, or elegant evening on the town, Charles Nob Hill has quietly become a San Francisco favorite. It's a true hideaway with only a subtle brass plaque to indicate its home in the Clay-Jones building. Split by a bar and decorated with sprays of flowers, the dining room is comfortable, sophisticated and quiet. Sibling to Aqua (the city's renowned seafood restaurant), Charles focuses on earthier fare-Sonoma duck, California squab, Hudson Valley foie gras-but shows the same commitment to excellence. And like Aqua, its techniques are French, but its attitude Californian. Pre-dinner teasers include a cup of richly flavored soup or a butter-poached oyster with a dab of osetra caviar. Chef Ron Siegal's tasting menu, at $65, offers seven courses that include fish, fowl and beef, followed by sorbet, dessert and cheese. A recent one opened with a circle of scallops with a roasted-onion jus, followed by sautéed Atlantic cod in lobster-infused white truffle sauce, then squab breast on black truffle risotto. The next near-perfect dishes were veal tenderloin with chestnut ravioli and sweetbreads; blood orange sorbet; and to finish, a pear financier with almond ice cream. A favorite from the regular menu is skirt steak, topped with seared bone marrow and a rich bordelaise sauce and accompanied by a short-rib ravioli. Fish and seafood also play a role here- Dungeness crab salad, Maine shrimp and day-boat scallops as appetizers; non-meat entrées include Atlantic cod, black bass and Atlantic skate wing. The only sour note we've heard at the Charles is of behavior unbecoming by amorous diners.

Chef Jia's

CHINESE ¢

925 Kearny St.
North Beach 94133
415-398-1626
Lunch & Dinner daily
No cards

Though it adheres to the Formica-and-linoleum school of decorating, Chef Jia's is no slacker when it comes to the kitchen: it serves first-rate, inexpensive, fresh Chinese food. Handwritten placards list the lunch menu, which features perennial favorites such as spicy string beans with yams, which arrive in a sweet/hot sauce brimming with garlic. The variety of mu shu (pancake-wrapped) dishes is impressive, as are the lettuce-rolls, a traditional version that wraps crunchy, nut-studded entrées in crisp lettuce leaves. Try sharing a dry-braised whole fish, the most-expensive entrée at $10.95.

Chez Michel

FRENCH 14/20

804 North Point St.
Russian Hill/Fisherman's Wharf 94109
415-775-7036
Dinner Tues.-Sun., $$$

With its subtle tones and soft lights, Chez Michel figures as one of the few elegant and romantic retreats just a stone's throw from touristy Fisherman's Wharf. Chef Daniel Schaffhauser has hit his stride here by adding a San Franciscan sensibility to his classic French training. A tamarind glaze, for example, flavors roasted quail and veal sweetbreads, while foie gras is revved up by a tart Asian pear salad and blood orange essence. Such imaginative pairings make choosing an appetizer tricky. Entrées show the same creativity-how about smoked Chilean sea bass with couscous and sweet chutney or beef tenderloin with an herb-laden blue cheese crust? The menu is meat-and-fish heavy, but Schaffhauser adds a vegetarian entrée daily. More conventional fare finishes the menu, with a selection of farm cheeses or warm Valrhona chocolate cake with honey-vanilla ice cream. The wine list provides ample opportunity to pair varietals with each course, and servers are happy to offer suggestions. This place is fairly swank, so leave Nikes and jeans at home.

China Village

CHINESE 13/20

2332 CLEMENT ST.
RICHMOND DISTRICT 94128
415-752-8833
Lunch & Dinner daily, $$

VISA MasterCard

The prawns come directly from the tanks that line the front of this chic restaurant, a bright, noisy dining room formerly known as Hong Kong Villa. Any of the fish dishes are good, but especially tasty is the whole fish steamed with ginger and green onions. Also try the whole salt-baked cod or any of the clay pot dishes. If your tastes run to dry land, the crispy chicken is also very good.

Chow

AMERICAN 10/20

215 CHURCH ST.
CASTRO 94114
415-552-2469
Lunch & Dinner nightly, $$

VISA MasterCard

This addition to the Castro's collection of mediocre restaurants seemed to wow the city's critics when it opened, but first-hand research may make one wonder what the reviewers were ordering. Granted, a dark wood interior, comfortable chairs and friendly service create a welcoming atmosphere, and prices can't be beat, but Chow's renditions of favorite ethnic dishes sometimes miss the mark. The menu ranges from pizzas and pastas to Asian-style noodles and homey roast chicken with garlic mashed potatoes. Stick to the American fare or one of Chow's daily sandwich specials, which come with soup, salad or fries. A second restaurant, Part Chow, was opening at press time at 1240 Ninth Street.

Columbus Ristorante

ITALIAN 14/20

3347 FILLMORE ST.
MARINA 94123
415-781-2939
Dinner Tues.-Sun., $$

VISA MasterCard

When May Ditano's North Beach restaurant fell victim to the neighborhood's soaring rents, she picked up her kitchen and moved it over to the Marina. A bit of a risk, true-the Marina's food scene is more about hype than the sort of well-crafted Italian food Ditano prepares. Inside an open room with a long hallway of tables (it's the former space of Cafe Adriano), Columbus is definitely worth a visit, for creative dishes like spiedini di mozzarella, an appetizer of bread and mozzeralla grilled until melted and finished with a butter-anchovy dressing. The creamy risotto del giorno might be topped with roasted vegetables or plump mussels and shrimps, and osso buco, often one of the half-dozen daily specials, is rich and tender: a must-have if it's available. Homemade gnocchi and a thick pork chop with balsamic vinegar are also winners. The restaurant avoids the kitsch that litters many Italian places; here, white tablecloths, avant-garde light fixtures and smooth service give Columbus a more modern ambience than many meatball joints in the city. As if to remind you of the hominess behind her menu, Ditano herself often patrols the dining room, checking to make sure you liked what she made for you.

Crustacean

SEAFOOD/PACIFIC RIM 13/20

1475 POLK ST.
POLK GULCH 94109
415-776-2722
Lunch Thurs.-Sat., Dinner nightly, $$

A

Crab is the name of the game in this sleek and stylish mostly Vietnamese-leaning restaurant. With neon waves and vivid murals, you could almost be underwater when you step inside. Crustacean prepares crab three basic ways: roasted, "drunken," or sweet and sour. The signature house dish is the delicious roast crab with plenty of garlic. Other items on the menu can be very tempting, but with all that wonderful Dungeness around, why bother? Their excellent wine list includes twenty by the glass.

Cypress Club

AMERICAN 14/20
500 JACKSON ST.
FINANCIAL DISTRICT 94133
415-296-8555
Dinner nightly, $$$

In lesser hands, the Cypress Club could have become one of the most elaborate and expensive practical jokes in town. Take $2 million and pour it into a voluptuous, fantasyland design that marries 1940s-style architecture with 1960s-style LSD flashback; put together an upscale menu, then try to sell the whole package to a city that prides itself on a certain resistance to flash and fashion. That Cypress Club has, in fact, survived its half-decade as one of the best restaurants in town is a tribute to the skills and creativity of proprietor John Cunin. Under new executive chef Stephan Janke, the restaurant has gone from good to better. The list of starters is filled with winners, including slow-braised veal cheeks, crispy veal sweetbreads or a simple wild mushroom salad with caramelized walnuts and shaved Parmesan. Main courses include a terrific seared monkfish, rabbit with wild mushroom ravioli or a saddle of venison with braised cabbage. All are equally good. Desserts have always been a strong point at Cypress Club, and pastry chef Patrick Coston has continued the tradition with lovely creations like Granny Smith apple frappé and a dazzling dark chocolate-hazelnut timbale; an extensive list of cheeses is also available. The fully-stocked bar is a classic, offering anything you would want in the way of spirits, including samplers of trendy new bourbons and single-malt Scotches. If you ask, the bartender will bring out the cigar humidor.

Dalla Torre

ITALIAN 12/20
1349 MONTGOMERY ST.
TELEGRAPH HILL 94133
415-296-1111
Dinner nightly, $$$

The maxim that a great view and a great meal shall never meet may be by and large true, but Dalle Torre disproves the old adage. Perched atop Telegraph Hill, the restaurant charms from inside as well as out. The cavernous main dining room is adorned with murals, a high, vaulted ceiling and large windows looking onto Montgomery Street. The upstairs room is often reserved for private parties, but should you wangle a reservation you'll be rewarded by a truly stunning view of San Francisco Bay. The menu might include Atlantic salmon cured with grappa and green peppercorns, excellent gnocchi with Parmesan cream and breadcrumbs or grilled almond-stuffed quail on black olive risotto and braised mustard greens. Attentive service and an elegant, relaxed atmosphere make this one of the city's most romantic spots to eat-on a good night, you'll be treated to a superlative dining experience.

Dame

CALIFORNIAN 12/20
1815 MARKET ST.
MISSION 94110
415-255-8818
Lunch Tues.-Fri., Dinner Tues.-Sun., Brunch Sun., $$

Opened in 1995 by caterers James and Kelly Dame, the restaurant serves uncomplicated, Italian-inspired cuisine to an eager clientele. Though dishes sometimes miss the mark, good prices, excellent service and décor-inviting, squash-orange walls and paper-covered tables-tip the balance in the restaurant's favor. The menu features such winners as a potato-encrusted filet of salmon on emerald-green spinach with spicy tomato sauce or grilled pork chops with petite roasted vegetables and addictive potato gratin. Desserts are temperamental, but an apple and sour cream cheesecake is delightful. The wine list is short and uninspired, but concentrates on value-priced bottlings. Don't miss Dame's excellent brunch offerings on Sunday.

Des Alpes

BASQUE/CALIFORNIAN 12/20
732 BROADWAY
NORTH BEACH 94133
415-391-4249
Dinner Tues.-Sun., $

Lifted straight out of a late-nineteenth-century Nevada sheepherder's hotel, one of the last North Beach family-style Basque restaurants-Spanish in this case-is a cut above most similar bistros scattered throughout the West. Des Alpes' oxtail stew is rich and intense in flavor and the roast chicken is crispy and perfectly cooked. There's always a huge bowl of soup to get started. After dinner in the funky front bar, as you enjoy a sol y sombra made of brandy and anise, you can sometimes hear four languages spoken at the same time-Basque, English, French and Spanish.

Doidge's

AMERICAN 12/20
2217 UNION ST.
PACIFIC HEIGHTS 94123
415-921-2149
Breakfast & Brunch daily, $

Arguably one the city's most elegant nooks, Doidge's serves breakfast and brunch to those wise enough to make reservations beforehand. From the outside, Doidge's looks charming, with a welcoming bench and café curtains dressing the windows. Once inside, guests pass by the long, diner-style counter to enter the bright, New Englandy dining room, with tasteful artwork, white tablecloths and fresh flowers to start their day Servers rush about with coffee pots and pewter creamers, while diners enjoy Doidge's selections-buttermilk pancakes with fresh strawberries, rich eggs Benedict with hollandaise, home-fried potatoes. Omelets with avocado, artichoke hearts and chicken-apple sausage also entice, as do french toast, hot oatmeal and fresh fruit.

E & O Trading Company

PACIFIC RIM 12/20
314 SUTTER ST.
FINANCIAL DISTRICT 94108
415-693-0303
Lunch & Dinner Mon.-Sat., $$

A

This bustling newcomer has received rave reviews, and its crowded dining room would suggest the public feels the same. Done up in theatrical fabric and faux woven bamboo, E & O's spacious dining room evokes the colonial spirit that drives its food. The food culls inspirations from India, Indonesia, Thailand and Japan, and dishes are split, tapas-like, into small and large plates. The results are satisfying, if somewhat uninspirational. Salty, Indian-style naan breads are quite good, and fried items like the crisp squid and greens with a subtle pommelo vinaigrette are expertly prepared. Main dishes fuse some delicious elements together: one of the kitchen's signature entrées is seared sushi-grade ahi with a dome of green-onion-spiked rice, baby bok choy and shiitake mushrooms. House-made beers and sodas are quite good. Live music entertains on most nights.

Ebisu

JAPANESE/SUSHI 13/20
1283 9TH AVE.
SUNSET 94122
415-566-1770
Lunch & Dinner daily, $$

Some naysayers may claim that other sushi restaurants serve fresher fish, or that others are more attractive, but for creative, excellent-quality sushi, wonderfully idiosyncratic service, and sheer fun, Ebisu can't be beat. Behind the long sushi bar stand four master sushi chefs. Each makes suggestions, and occasionally dispenses amuses bouches of fishy treats. If it's available, get toro-fatty tuna belly-at all costs; the succulent meat seems to melt in your mouth. Yellowtail, sea urchin, and sweet shrimps are reliably excellent (the latter served with its tempura-fried head) and oysters, served with lemon and ginger, are unbelievably good. Kitchen dishes are well prepared, but don't distract yourself from the sushi. Ebisu is no secret, and their no-reservations policy means that you can spend an hour and a half waiting in the little anteroom.

El Balazo

MEXICAN/CENTRAL AMERICAN ¢
1654 HAIGHT ST.
HAIGHT-ASHBURY 94117
415-864-8608
Lunch & Dinner daily
No cards

Painted in vibrant, swirling murals and featuring "Jerry's" and "Bob's" (both of the Grateful Dead) specialty burritos, Balazo makes no secret of its commercial aspirations. That's the bad news. The good news is that the food is quite good, and certainly a bargain. Fillings such as Mexican goat cheese, tender nopales cactus, and sautéed rock shrimps bring the offerings up a notch or two from the cheap-meat burrito circuit. Add to this an excellent salsa and condiment bar, an extensive soda, agua fresca, and Central American beer selection, and set it all in a clean, attractive and pleasant duo of dining rooms, and you've got one great burrito joint.

El Castellito

TAQUERIA ¢
2092 MISSION ST.
MISSION 94110
415-621-6971
Lunch & Dinner daily
No cards

Though at first glance you might suspect that El Castellito stands out only for the unsavoriness of its surrounding neighborhood, determined diners will be rewarded by excellent, simple and nourishing Mexican fare: burritos, tacos, and a few special platters. Marinated, roasted and chopped pork al pastor is superb. House-made aguas frescas are excellent, and an extensive selection of Latin- and Central American sodas and beers rounds out the meal.

El Farolito

MEXICAN ¢
4817 MISSION ST.
MISSION 94110
415-337-5500
Lunch & Dinner daily
No cards

The prospect of a first-rate taco or burrito after a night of bar-hopping or sight-seeing makes the trip to El Farolito an entirely worthwhile adventure. Lest you doubt the origin of the savory meat fillings-the grilled steak is fantastic-all preparation is done behind the long counter in front of you. If watching your quesadilla cook on the griddle doesn't spark your appetite, nothing will. You'll be well fed and content for under $5.

El Nuevo Fruitlandia

CARIBBEAN ¢
3077 24TH ST.
MISSION 94110
415-648-2958
Lunch & Dinner Tues.-Sun., Brunch Sun.

Fruitlandia was on the scene long before the Caribbean food trend surfaced. In the heart of the 24th Street strip, it's a hopping place, particularly on weekends, when there is sometimes live music with no cover. The food is delicious and plentiful, with hefty portions of Cuban- and Puerto Rican-inspired fare. Main courses emphasize beef, pork or seafood; most dishes come with black beans and rice. The house specialty is ropa vieja, shredded flank steak cooked in Creole sauce with onions, tomatoes, bell peppers and wine. There's even a decent Spanish wine list.

El Zocalo

MEXICAN/SALVADORAN 13/20
3230 MISSION ST.
MISSION DISTRICT 94110
415-282-2572
Lunch & Dinner daily, $

A

With its fake leather booths crammed into a narrow, deep room, this is undoubtedly one of the few restaurants in the Bay Area (or the world) where you can get a decent, whole steamed or fried red snapper at 2 a.m. If you aren't in a fishy mood, go for the Bonanza, a top sirloin served with Salvadoran sausage, beans, rice and salad. On the Salvadoran side of the menu, pupusas comprise patties of fresh corn meal batter, filled with your choice of stuffing-chicken, beef, cheese, pork, beans-and grilled. They are utterly delicious.

Elan Vital

MEDITERRANEAN 13/20
1556 HYDE ST.
RUSSIAN HILL 94109
415-929-7309
Dinner nightly, $$

Roughly translated, Elan Vital means "spirit of life," an appropriate moniker for this intimate, softly lit restaurant perched atop Russian Hill. Chef/owners Will Dodson and Ruth Schimmelpfennig also run acclaimed Frascati across the street, but Elan Vital is the cozier-and more romantic-of the two. The menu jumps around the globe quite a bit, but centers somewhere in the Mediterranean. Depending on the season, selections might include Sonoma foie gras with a vibrant kumquat gastrique, marvelously rich pan-seared spinach gnocchi or excellent-quality salmon tartare with tobiko, avocados and a carrot-lime vinaigrette. A tiny bar in the front serves a nice selection of wines and after-dinner treats, while dinner itself is served in a comfortable room that looks out onto Hyde Street. Don't forget to make reservations: tiny Elan Vital fills up quickly.

Elephant Bleu

VIETNAMESE ¢
3232 16TH ST.
MISSION 94110
415-553-6062
Lunch & Dinner Tues.-Sun.
No cards

One of the Mission's rare Vietnamese restaurants, Elephant Bleu serves food with a hearty, home-cooked feeling and that accompanies perfectly the lively setting. There's a wide selection of filling vermicelli dishes and first rate barbecued pork. The eatery is open until midnight on Friday and Saturday, which makes it a good after-theater stop.

Eliza's

CHINESE 12/20
1457 18TH ST.
POTRERO HILL 94107
415-648-9999
Lunch & Dinner daily, $

A neighborhood favorite on the 18th Street restaurant row, Eliza's updates Hunan and Mandarin cooking without sacrificing an iota of the cuisine's hot, sweet, salty and pungent appeal. In fact, the great food and low prices seem out of place in this airy, arty eating space. Beautiful potted plants, colorful paintings, and whimsical sculpture vie for your attention, while the food itself arrives on attractive, hand-painted dishes. The menu includes many war-horses-kung pao chicken, mu shu pork, vegetarian Buddah's delight-but they receive fresh treatment in the form of light sauces and fresh, crisp vegetables. For specials, you'll find beef paired with mango (a surprisingly satisfying combination) or Eliza's spicy eggplant with shrimps, chicken, basil and chili. Occasionally surly service comes as something of a shock in such a pleasant environment, but it may be due more to a lack of fluency than bad attitude. In all, Eliza's delivers the goods admirably, and, in case one should wonder, without benefit of MSG.

Ella's

AMERICAN 12/20
500 PRESIDIO AVE.
PRESIDIO HEIGHTS 94115
415-441-5669
Breakfast & Lunch daily, Dinner Mon.-Fri., Brunch Sun., $

Ella's is a classy little place decked out in spiffy navy-blue awnings and weathered shingles. It promises neoclassical American cooking, delivered in well-prepared basics like grilled pork loin, meatloaf with gravy and chicken pot pie. Ella's serves breakfast, lunch and dinner to regulars from the nearby Presidio Heights and Laurel Heights neighborhoods, but the big deal here is weekend brunch. On Sunday mornings, diners sit cheek to jowl, vying for Ella's open-face omelets topped with sausage, Asiago, grilled eggplant and roasted red peppers. In addition, fresh fruit, buttermilk pancakes, homemade sticky buns and coffee cake get washed down with bottomless cups of coffee; service is calm and organized despite the weekend pandemonium. Bring the Sunday *Chronicle* to read while you wait outside for your table.

Elroys

CALIFORNIAN 12/20

300 BEALE ST.
FINANCIAL DISTRICT 94105
415-882-7989
Lunch Mon.-Fri., Dinner nightly, $$

Elroys's space-age décor appeals to the young MBAs from the nearby Financial District, who commandeer this warehouse-sized restaurant and bar as a fun after-work watering hole. The finger food is pub-grub-wings, spare ribs, fried calamari, barbecued oysters-and the drink list includes thirteen martinis, nine margaritas and eleven draft beers, as well as some pretty decent wines. Throw in a huge heated patio, a view of the bay, and a second level for pool tables and you've got a hot new spot. Dinner entrées offer more sturdy California fare, including a chili-cured pork chop and wood-fired mahi mahi. Menu prices are marked in teeny-tiny type.

Elysium Café

CALIFORNIAN 11/20

2434 MISSION ST.
MISSION 94110
415-282-2447
Dinner Tues.-Sun., $

It's difficult to tell if Elysium Café is a restaurant attached to a bar or the other way around. Dark, moody and a little off-kilter, the restaurant serves decent bistro fare to the late-night bar-hopping crowd. There aren't culinary epiphanies here, but it's a welcome alternative to the burrito circuit. Past appetizers have included an antipasto plate with grilled portobello mushrooms, mozzarella and garlic toast, while pan-roasted half chicken was served with satisfying jack cheese polenta, blue lake beans and wild mushrooms. The short wine list concentrates on bargains, though a '95 Ravenswood Merlot lent a little elegance. Physically, Elysium manages to be both hip and disarming: a table sited over an aquarium is a highlight.

Enrico's Sidewalk Café & Restaurant

MEDITERRANEAN 13/20

504 BROADWAY
NORTH BEACH 94133
415-982-6223
Lunch & Dinner daily, $$

When partners Rick Hackett, Meredith Melville and Mark McLeod sought to revitalize the former Enrico Banducci's historic café on Broadway, the area was at the time a wasteland of strip joints and barkers cajoling tourists to chat with a "live nude girl." The area is up-and-coming again, with no small thanks due to this restaurant-a big, noisy room with full windows and haphazard table placement. For starters, try a bowl of clams in a spicy broth or rings of perfectly-fried calamari with ginger-garlic black bean mayonnaise; pizzas come with a variety of toppings (try the wild mushroom-pancetta model); a hamburger with house-made condiments and crusty polenta "fries" is great. A recent and welcome addition is a list of almost two dozen California-inspired tapas, including seared tuna with Asian greens and a sesame vinaigrette or squab with hoisin sauce and eggplant. Live jazz goes on nightly, and large gas heaters on the sidewalk patio make it warmer-and more conducive to people-watching-than ever.

Eos

PACIFIC RIM 14/20

901 COLE ST.
HAIGHT-ASHBURY 94117
415-566-3063
Dinner nightly, $$$

A cool, gray space that looks like a movie set, Eos is a delightful neighborhood restaurant and wine bar with an eclectic menu centered on Asian-Californian dishes. Inside the minimal, squared room set in white linens and colorful flowers, the food reflects chef Arnold Wong's background: Trained as a French-chef, Wong has worked for many years in his family's grocery and wine shop. His menu changes often, but some favorites include Caesar salad laced with ginger, green-papaya spring rolls and grilled marinated steak accompanied by bok choy. Other standouts are tea-smoked duck with mashed sweet potatoes and tamarind-marinated rack of lamb with cherry chutney. It's often easier to get seated at Wong's wine bar, which offers the same menu. Sommelier Debbie Zachareas has assembled a thoughtful collection of wines by the bottle and glass that are a treat on their own.

Esperpento

SPANISH 12/20

3295 22ND ST.
MISSION 94110
415-282-8867
Lunch & Dinner Mon.-Sat., $

No cards

From the Spanish for a ridiculous person or situation, Esperpento (which looks vaguely like a college caféteria) serves a menu largely comprised of tapas-tasty tidbits of everything from mushrooms to seafood to sausage to olives that are among the glories of Spanish cuisine. You can hardly go wrong with any of them, but our favorites include plump mussels in a tangy red pepper vinaigrette, chicken livers in a rich red wine sauce and the thick and filling torta de patata-a classic Spanish tapa of potatoes, eggs and olive oil prepared like a hard omelet. Main course specials and paellas are also available; house-made flan is the dessert of choice. To accompany your meal, try the house sangría or one of several good Spanish wines. The best seats are on the second floor balcony.

Farallon

AMERICAN 15/20

450 POST ST.
UNION SQUARE 94108
415-956-6969
Lunch, Mon.-Sat., Dinner nightly, $$$$

Famed Bay Area restaurant designer Pat Kuleto teamed up with chef Mark Franz to open this spectacular restaurant in 1997. The décor, a watery theme fitting the restaurant's namesake (the Farralons are a small group of Pacific islands west of San Francisco) seems just one step ahead of the food. Farallon's rich menu features signature dishes like truffled mashed potatoes with crab and sea urchin sauce and a fish stew with mussels, clam and shrimps in a tomato-fennel-leek broth. Check out the prawn, sea scallop and lobster pyramid, suspended in a shellfish gelée with leeks and saffron essence. If land-based cuisine is more to your liking, try the simple but delicious grilled chicken breast with warm spinach salad, fingerling potatoes and red pepper purée. Menu changes occur on a daily basis, depending on what the sea has to offer. Bring a pocketful of cash or a high-limit credit card: Farallon has the reputation as the most expensive restaurant in town.

Faz

MEDITERRANEAN 12/20

161 SUTTER ST.
FINANCIAL DISTRICT 94104
415-362-0404
Lunch Mon.-Fri., $$

Owner Fazol (Faz) Poursohi has built a tempting menu around pizza, pastas, basmati rice and special grilled dishes, including prawns and lamb shanks. The pizza in this pleasant, well-lit space is practically perfect, especially a version with grilled eggplant, garlic, tomato, basil and mozzarella. Faz is definitely a cut above most Financial District lunch stops.

Fina Estampa

PERUVIAN 12/20

2374 MISSION ST.
MISSION 94110
415-824-4437
Lunch & Dinner Tues.-Sun., $

One of the great things about eating out in San Francisco is the range of ethnic food available. A half-dozen Peruvian restaurants are open at any given time, yet this storefront space with glass-topped tables remains one of the best. The menu reflects a full range of foods from the Peruvian geography: wonderful seafood soups or a whole fried fish with hot green salsa from the Pacific; a range of potatoes, beef heart and various beef and chicken dishes from the mountains. All are perfectly cooked. A grilled chicken dish, aji panca, rubbed with a spicy red paste, is superb. Fina Estampa's spirit selection includes beer from Peru and red wines from Chile and Spain.

Firecracker

CHINESE 12/20
1007 VALENCIA ST.
MISSION 94110
415-642-3470
Lunch Tues.-Sat., Dinner Tues.-Sun., $
No cards

This newcomer to the rapidly gentrifying Valencia strip has already won a devoted following, which unfortunately makes it harder than ever to get a table. A soothing, pastel vision of late Imperial China, Firecracker's artful iron chairs and fanciful under-lit stools beckon to the clusters of hungry diners outside, while elegant woodwork anchors the swaths of crimson decorating the interior. Food-wise, Firecracker seems to have listened to Westerners' complaints about cheap Chinese food: its version is spicier, more herbal and noticeably less greasy than the competition's. The menu includes old standbys but veers toward the unexpected: a favorite alternative to egg rolls is Fujien rolls, a light dough wrapper surrounding lettuce, crunchy sprouts and chewy tofu skin. Similarly, pinenut chicken pairs curry-flavored diced meat with fresh spinach. Service is warm and professional, and a nice wine selection rounds out the meal.

Firefly

ECLECTIC 13/20
4288 24TH ST.
NOE VALLEY 94114
415-821-7652
Dinner nightly, $$

VISA MasterCard

This neighborhood favorite has garnered excellent press in the past few years, and for good reason: Chef Brad Levy creates home cooking without borders, bringing life to hearty, balanced foods. Though there's plenty of protein to be found here, some of the kitchen's best work is found in its vegetarian selections: a smoky kale-and-beluga lentil stew is paired with griddled pesto-laced grits, and portobello mushrooms replace beef in an eminently satisfying Wellington. Shrimp and scallop potstickers are a textural delight, as are carefully composed salads employing top-notch produce. All meats come from the Niman Schell ranch, and the menu touts their "happy drug-free animals with an ocean view." The two little dining rooms are funky and modern, with a flair for the absurd as well as the quaint. The wine list leans towards excellent value-priced bottles, and artful desserts are highly recommended.

Fleur de Lys

FRENCH 18/20
777 SUTTER ST.
UNION SQUARE 94108
415-673-7779
Dinner Mon.-Sat., $$$$

A

When chef Hubert Keller is paying attention, his food tastes effortless, as if all lobsters swim in coconut milk, enhanced in broth and braced by lemon grass and ginger; as though baby lamb is born with chops crowned by an ethereal herb mousseline; as if sea bass are pulled from the ocean wearing thin scales of crispy potato and a tangy rhubarb purée. Where other chefs strive to be creative, Keller simply creates. Keller came to San Francisco from the south of France in the 1980s to open Sutter 500, where his cooking showed flashes of brilliance. That venture led to Keller's teaming with restaurateur Maurice Rouas at Fleur de Lys. The chef's already enviable reputation continues to grow with every exquisite meal he prepares here. Hundreds of yards of red-hued, hand-painted fabric drape the ceiling to give the restaurant an intimate, vaguely Moorish feel; this is an ideal spot for a romantic assignation. The 10,000-bottle wine cellar offers fine vintages from France and California, including many California Chardonnays. The menu changes often, but highlights from the current version include roasted sea scallops with wild mushrooms on a cream of artichokes; crispy veal sweetbreads dressed with truffle vinaigrette; and pan-seared foie gras with grapes, served on julienned cabbage with a port wine-and-aged sherry vinegar reduction. Turning to the main course, an "untraditional" lobster bouillabaisse features Maine lobster tail on garlic toast with rouille and saffron potatoes; boneless quail are stuffed with ris de veau, morels and spinach; sautéed veal loin medallions pair with leek compote, black chanterelles and truffle sauce. As you would hope, Keller's desserts match the quality of his main courses.

The Fly Trap

AMERICAN 12/20
606 FOLSOM ST.
SOMA 94107
415-243-0580
Lunch Mon.-Fri., Dinner nightly, $$

The nether regions of Folsom Street might not be the first place you think of finding dinner, but if you're craving solid, old-time food in a clean, well-lit environment, Fly Trap is the place for you. The walls in this bright little dining room are decorated with antique maps and botanical prints in homage to the original "Fly Trap," Louie's Restaurant on Market Street, while the rest of the eatery is done up in pleasant natural wood. A full bar, well stocked with various wines, dominates the room around quitting time, but hearty eaters will be more interested in the food. The restaurant concentrates on simple, old-style favorites. Sweetbreads with pancetta, sautéed calf's liver with bacon and onions and a hangtown fry are featured here, although lighter offerings, including San Francisco favorite Celery Victor, leaven the menu somewhat. Desserts are not to be missed.

Flying Saucer

CALIFORNIAN 13/20
1000 GUERRERO ST.
MISSION 94110
415-641-9955
Dinner Tues.-Sat., $$$

A visual combination of kitsch curio and post-industrial cool, Flying Saucer seems to exist in a parallel universe; many have speculated that chef/owner Albert Cordjman is not of this earth. However eccentric his peculiarities-such as ejecting food critics of any stripe-his restaurant turns out consistently stunning food, from border-hopping appetizers to massive, baroque entrées and satisfying, intensely architectural desserts. Part of the fun is trying to anticipate what your plate will bring: though the menu might describe dry-aged New York steak with horseradish pommes dauphinoise and roasted garlic thyme jus, it's a guarantee that these are only a few of the delicious, visually inventive items that will appear with your order. Cordjman practices a sure hand in several cuisines at once: an appetizer of raw ahi with a clam-and-shiso potato cake might appear next to Sonoma foie gras with a cranberry, pear and lime chutney and lemon verbena oil. Desserts infuse traditional foods-vanilla ice cream, apple pie, sorbets-with flavors as intense and satisfying as the entrées. All retain the kitchen's playful visual style, though some are so outrageously styled it seems a crime to actually eat them. Service is professionally hip, if occasionally, how-shall-we-say spacey, and the wine list is as adventurous as it is balanced. The room itself (dominated by a painting of a relaxed Greek deity wearing chef Cordjman's trademark horn-rimmed glasses) is a delight to behold.

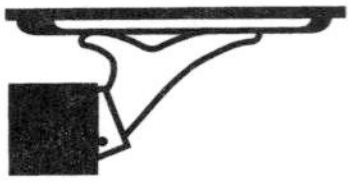

Fog City Diner

CALIFORNIAN 13/20
1300 BATTERY ST.
EMBARCADERO 94111
415-982-2000
Lunch & Dinner daily, $$

Though not the hot spot it once was, Fog City Diner remains a quintessential San Francisco restaurant. Situated on the now-appealing Embarcadero and not far from Telegraph Hill, the Diner is decorated with wooden booths and a long bar; the chrome exterior with neon trim gives it a distinctive 1950s look; inside, its long room and cozy tables have the feel of a swanky dining car which, along with goodies like scallop ceviche, ahi tuna carpaccio and mu-shu pork burritos as appetizers, means nobody will mistake this place for a greasy spoon. Among the tapas-style small plates, creamy crabcakes with sherry-cayenne mayo remain a top pick. A pork chop with apple gravy, a grilled hanger steak with fries and the diner's own cioppino (with Dungeness crab, prawns and fish) are part of the large plates selections, with mashed potatoes, fries and other side dishes ordered separately. To finish, warm banana-chocolate bread pudding with rum caramel sauce is a favorite. Tourists and visitors can order a T-shirt or baseball cap from the menu.

42 Degrees

AMERICAN 14/20
235 16TH ST.
SOMA 94107
415-777-5558
Lunch Mon.-Fri., Dinner Wed.-Sat., $$$

The creation of chef-owner Jim Moffat, who also owns the Slow Club, this clean, sleek, post-industrial supper club is located in a showplace design space with high ceilings and a curving iron staircase leading to a mezzanine looking over the Bay. The menu changes weekly and dances to a Spanish-Mediterranean beat with dishes like Iberian blood sausage with candied tomatoes or bacalao, warm salt cod baked with garlic, potatoes and cream. For main dishes, grilled cider-cured pork loin with baby turnips, braised greens and a rhubarb demi-glace is super. One recent menu featured both cassoulet and a coq au vin, both of which were superb. Portions are huge-two could share a main course-and the well-paired wine list is excellent, with a number of little-known bottlings. Desserts affect a wide range, from traditional to adventurous; you'll probably be enjoying yours when the music starts. The bar also stocks over a dozen single malt Scotches and an extensive selection of brandies.

Fringale

FRENCH 15/20
570 4TH ST.
SOMA 94107
415-543-0573
Lunch Mon.-Fri., Dinner Mon.-Sat., $$$

Serving homey, deceptively simple bistro-style fare inspired by his native Basque country in Southwest France, chef Gerald Hirigoyen has for nearly a decade fashioned a menu of unusual and appealing dishes. Soups such as the potato-garlic are balanced and flavorful. In addition, try shredded duck confit, topped with bits of toasted walnuts and sandwiched in a mound of mashed potatoes, or Roquefort ravioli with basil and pine nuts. Fresh fish, too, is always a treat here: should monkfish be on the menu, don't miss it. We've also enjoyed tuna steak with onion marmalade and roast rack of lamb. The wine list is short but focused on wines that match the food, including rare bottlings from Basque wineries. They're superb. With only 50 seats and continued popularity, Fringale requires that you book well ahead for reservations. Should you have to wait, however, you'll find a little room at the handsome curved bar that stands near the entrance.

Gira Polli

ITALIAN 13/20
659 UNION ST.
NORTH BEACH 94133
415-434-4472
Dinner nightly, $$

This North Beach gem takes the humble chicken, roasts it rotisserie-style and serves it for take-out or eating in. It's delicious, and it is also one of the few reasons to risk the stress of finding parking near Washington Square. Seasoned with a squirt of lemon, there's no better bird in town. The meat is juicy and tender, the vegetables are flavorful and seasoned by a light broth, and the crusty Italian rolls catch the runaway juices. Meals can be also made of appetizers alone: prosciutto wrapped around fresh melon; a tomato-and-mozzarella salad with basil, olives and olive oil; an antipasto of fresh artichokes, roasted red peppers, basil, Gorgonzola and olives. Counter help is friendly, and the service is both smooth and casual. Gira Polli also has outlets in Mill Valley and Walnut Creek.

The Globe

AMERICAN 13/20
290 PACIFIC AVE.
FINANCIAL DISTRICT 94111
415-391-4132
Lunch Mon.-Fri., Dinner Mon.-Sat., $$$

A

Mary Kingbell and Joseph Manzare have taken a former brick livery stables and turned it into a comfortable, warming restaurant that serves until 1 a.m.-the kind of place in which chefs from some of the city's top spots go after they close their own kitchens. Besides daily pizza specials, the changing lunch menu includes items like grilled salmon on parsnip purée with salsa verde and house-made spaghetti with roasted new potatoes and basil pesto. For dinner you might start with baked mussels, bay scallops and rock shrimps with basil and garlic butter, then continue with a tasty braised veal shank on lemon risotto or pork chop on sweet and spicy cherry pepper ragoût with green olive tapenade.

Gold Spike

ITALIAN ¢

527 COLUMBUS AVE.
NORTH BEACH 94108
415-421-4591
Dinner Thurs.-Tues.

Plain and unadorned, the Spike steadfastly retains the spirit of a neighborhood hangout, despite being a tourist mecca. The family-style Italian menu offers the predictably standard soup, salad, pasta, main course and dessert, but there's plenty of it, it's cheap and it tastes pretty good, too. The bar is always lively.

Golden Gate Park Brewery

ECLECTIC/BREWPUB 12/20

1326 9TH AVE.
SUNSET DISTRICT 94122
415-665-5800
Lunch & Dinner daily, $$

A new addition to the Sunset dining scene, Golden Gate Park Brewery is a splashy bistro serving pub fare several cuts above the norm. From a graceful, curved balcony that mirrors the polished wood and zinc-plated bar below, you'll enjoy standard burgers and hearty sandwiches, but also unusual (and unusually good) dishes such as Manila clams in sake-soy broth, maple-cured smoked pork chops and seared ahi with red miso dressing and sprout salad. Not everything shines here, but the restaurant is still young. Seven house-made beers are by and large very good, the standouts being refreshing cream and sweet, nut-brown ales. The physical plant is striking as well-over the balcony and bar, one can spy the polished vats from which come the brewery's lifeblood.

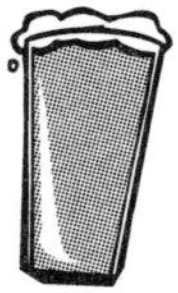

Golden Turtle

VIETNAMESE 12/20

2211 VAN NESS AVE.
NOB HILL 94109
415-441-4419
Dinner Tues.-Sun., $

This attractive split-level dining room (it's quiet even on a busy night) is one of the top Vietnamese restaurants in the city. Chef/owner Kim Quy Tran's distinguished Vietnamese cuisine employs simple, fresh flavors enhanced by sweet and savory sauces. Try charboiled prawns, catfish in a clay pot or a whole sea bass steamed and topped with ginger. Dig into house specialties such as five-spice chicken, Saigon pork chops and shrimp-and-pork salad roll with a zesty cilantro tang. In fact, there is nothing on the menu that isn't a treat. An extensive vegetarian selection, including the exotic lotus blossom salad, is available; likewise an excellent wine list, chosen to match the exotic flavors of Golden Turtle's succulent food.

Grand Café

FRENCH 13/20

501 GEARY ST.
UNION SQUARE 94109
415-292-0101
Breakfast, Lunch & Dinner daily, $$

Grand Café captures the turn-of-the-nineteenth-century feel of a Parisian brasserie. The dining room, once a hotel ballroom, has the whimsical yet impressive look of the belle époque, and the food, under the direction of Enis Soriano, matches the restaurant's soaring look. Standouts from the lunch menu include a pan-seared duck leg confit with Napa cabbage and walnut dressing or a polenta soufflé with wild mushroom ragoût and Cambozola fondue as starters. For main course selections, choose pheasant ravioli with sautéed wild mushrooms and duck consommé. At dinner, braised beef cheeks with white beans and red wine sauce is a sure winner, as is sweetbread fricassée with mixed vegetables and truffle sauce. A daily vegetable plat du jour is available for vegetarians. Day or night, the Grand's banana cream pie is a standout dessert.

Gordon Biersch

MICROBREWERY/
CALIFORNIAN 12/20
2 HARRISON ST.
SOMA/FINANCIAL DISTRICT 94105
415-243-8246
Lunch Mon.-Fri., Dinner nightly, $$$

Following the success of its original Palo Alto location, this Bay-side yupeteria opened in 1992 and became known for the young, corporate crowd that jams the downstairs bar after work. The hearty and spicy fare is designed to stand up to Biersch's four German-style lagers, and it isn't bad-mostly finger food of satays, pizzas and sandwiches, plus a selection of pastas and stir-fried dishes. Larger appetites will want to try the roasted King salmon on focaccia with sun-dried tomato rémoulade. A number of microbreweries have bubbled up in the city recently, but Gordon Biersch takes care of the basics and people keep coming back for more.

Great Eastern

CHINESE ¢
649 JACKSON ST.
CHINATOWN 94133
415-986-2500
Lunch & Dinner daily

With fish tanks lining its walls, Great Eastern more closely resembles an aquarium than a typical Chinese restaurant. No matter: make your selection from the chalkboard specials, nod politely when the waiter presents your choice for inspection, and wait a few minutes for one of the best-priced, freshest plates of seafood in town. Rock cod is a house specialty, either as soup or stir-fried with seasonal vegetables.

Greens

VEGETARIAN/
CALIFORNIAN 14/20
FORT MASON, BUILDING A
MARINA 94123
415-771-6222
Lunch Tues.-Sat., Dinner Mon.-Sat., Brunch Sun., $$$

For vegetarians in the know, Greens represents the ultimate destination in organic gourmet dining. The daily menu displays the pick of the crop from Greens' produce purveyors, including the Zen Center's renowned Green Gulch Farm in Marin. Chef Annie Somerville transforms the veggies into appetizers even a carnivore can love, like mesquite-grilled asparagus with watercress, radicchio, shaved Parmesan and niçoise olives with a Meyer lemon vinaigrette. Another toothsome starter is golden griddlecakes made of potato and grilled fennel and topped with crème fraîche and an apple-cherry confit. Entrées might include a "Mediterranean sampler" of apricot-, currant- and rice-stuffed dolmas, tabouli, grilled Japanese eggplant, hummus and pita; or spinach, goat cheese, roasted garlic, Fontina, provolone and thyme pizza. For dessert, a warm apple-rhubarb cobbler with Calvados ice cream or a chocolate pot de crème with praline cookies may tempt you. The wine list is peerless and the service attentive. Somerville and Greens' founder Deborah Madison have spun out a number of cookbooks, some of which can be purchased at the restaurant; there's also a take-out counter in case you'd like to dine al fresco. Greens can't be beat for location: housed in Fort Mason and imbued with a bit of 1970s polished-wood décor, the restaurant is blessed with an unmatched view of the Golden Gate Bridge and the Marin Headlands. After dinner, stroll along Marina Green and savor San Francisco at its most beautiful.

Hama-Ko

JAPANESE/SUSHI 12/20
108B CARL ST.
HAIGHT-ASHBURY 94117
415-753-6808
Dinner Tues.-Sun., $$

Hama-Ko is a Japanese version of the Mom-and-Pop diner: Guests are greeted warmly by the Kashiyamas before sitting at one of the overturned barrels that serve as tables. The décor is sparse, but the little dining room is comfortable in the way that only a family-owned restaurant can be. Fish and shellfish are of excellent quality, and the chef is open to special requests. If ordered in advance, he'll prepare a special menu of hot and cold specialties for your party. On the downside, orders can take quite a while once the tiny restaurant fills up. Mrs. Kashiyama only asks your patience and understanding, and in return you'll have an unrushed and satisfying meal at this unusual little eatery.

Harbor Village

CHINESE 13/20

4 EMBARCADERO CENTER, SECOND LEVEL
FINANCIAL DISTRICT 94111
415-781-8833
Lunch & Dinner daily, $$

Harbor Village offers a sumptuous array of dim sum delicacies in a vast, well-appointed dining room in the Embarcadero Center. It's a favorite lunch spot for Hong Kong émigrés and businesspeople who savor the hundreds of dim sum goodies, from translucent shrimp balls to chili-spiked octopus and crunchy pork dumplings with peanuts, dried shrimps and celery. By night, the waiters park the trolleys, dim the lights and serve elaborate Chinese fare, often starring a selection of seafood fished from the nearby tanks. Duck is also a treat at Harbor Village, especially the crackling Peking duck served tableside. Service can be hit or miss; inquire about banquet menus that can be shared by groups of ten or more.

Hard Rock Café

AMERICAN ¢

1699 VAN NESS AVE.
VAN NESS 94109
415-885-1699
Lunch & Dinner daily

There's one in every major city in the world these days, yet tourists and non-locals flock to the Hard Rock seeking an experience all their own. Centrally located and always packed, the place is famous for rock memorabilia, great hamburgers...and the smugness of knowing for certain that no one who lives in SF will see you walking in the door.

Harris'

STEAKHOUSE 12/20

2100 VAN NESS AVE.
RUSSIAN HILL 94109
415-673-1888
Dinner nightly, $$$

Owner Ann Harris hangs sides of beef in the window to age, a sure way to frighten off any vegetarian who strays near the revered Van Ness institution. The décor is classic masculine-dark wood, heavy curtains, vast leather booths. Harris' has mastered the favorites, including the martini, so it's best so throw caution to the wind and indulge. Oysters on the half shell, Caesar salad and escargots lead the openers, but steak is the main event, from a 16-ounce "Harris Steak" (a bone-in New York steak) to the 25-ounce T-bone. Party-poopers can opt for grilled Atlantic salmon or breast of chicken. Service is excellent; prices are beefy-pack your plastic or have out-of-town relatives pick up the tab. Harris' bottles its own Cabernet Sauvignon.

Hawthorne Lane

AMERICAN 15/20

22 HAWTHORNE ST.
SOMA 94103
415-777-9779
Lunch Mon.-Fri., Dinner nightly, $$$

A dramatic space near the new San Francisco Museum of Modern Art, Hawthorne Lane was opened in 1995 by David and Anne Gingrass, who pulled out of Postrio to try their own restaurant. The warehouse space is exciting, with an oval bar and great artwork on display; clientele has included President Clinton and members of U2; several coveted booths overlook Hawthorne Street. The cooking is American fused with an Asian touch. Menus change on almost a daily basis, but you'll always find an extensive hors d'oeuvre list, featuring several pizzas, Chinese-style duck on steamed buns with blood orange sauce or braised lamb short ribs with peppered five-spice sauce. From the lunch menu, favorites include lemon and artichoke ravioli, house-made ham and radicchio pizza or spicy gingered seafood stew. The dinner menu includes pan-roasted sturgeon with crispy potato-apple cakes or roast rack of veal with caramelized onion sauce. Desserts from pastry chef Nicole Plue are worth every calorie: warm strawberry shortcake with Tahitian vanilla bean ice cream rates a bus ride across town. The wine list is predictably superb.

Hayes Street Grill

SEAFOOD/AMERICAN 13/20
320 HAYES ST.
HAYES VALLEY 94102
415-863-5545
Lunch Mon.-Fri., Dinner nightly, $$$

Owned in part by San Francisco restaurant critic Patricia Unterman, the doyen of Hayes Valley, HSG caters to civic center pols at lunchtime and theatergoers in the early evening. Cream-colored walls and wood trim give the place a continental feel, and the service (once the mad dash to the show is over) is delightful. Fish is the Hayes' main attraction, its menu changing to reflect the day's catch. Preparations are refreshing and unfussy; from Hawaiian yellow fin tuna to Puget Sound salmon, filets are mesquite-grilled and served with a choice of sauces. Appetizers are basic but tasty-standbys include a Caesar salad for two and a warm goat cheese salad with toasted pecans. For dessert, you might find an apple dried-cherry crisp or the crème brûlée, a version with few peers in a city seemingly obsessed with the dessert.

Hazahez

INDIAN ¢
3083 16TH ST.
MISSION 94110
415-621-4189
Lunch & Dinner daily

A great late night stop for Indian food lovers, phone-booth-sized Hazahaz is open until 3 a.m. on the weekends and offers a full menu. Most dishes are fairly standard, with good vegetarian items and wonderful falafel balls. Plan to take out-there are about three seats in the place.

The Helmand

AFGHAN 12/20
430 BROADWAY
NORTH BEACH 94133
415-362-0641
Dinner nightly, $$

In the heart of North Beach lies an elegant setting in which to enjoy a unique menu of Afghan specialties. Served in a narrow, brick dining room, accented with Afghani goodies, the Helmand's food is reminiscent of Indian, Asian and Middle Eastern cuisines, but has its own highly aromatic character. Start your meal with skorwa, a piquant broth brewed with lamb and vegetables. Main courses run to beef, chicken and lamb, marinated in fragrant spice and accompanied by stewed vegetables. A fresh fish special and vegetarian dishes are offered daily. Service is polished and professional and the wine list well chosen. Turkish coffee is prepared tableside-an elegant finish to any meal in this sophisticated spot.

House of Nanking

CHINESE ¢
919 KEARNY ST.
CHINATOWN 94133
415-421-1429
Lunch Mon.-Sat., Dinner nightly
No cards

While its cooking is tailored to the Caucasian palate, there's no denying that Nanking is fresh, inventive and delicious. Try the famous spring onion cakes, or the spicy, dry-cooked string beans. Shrimps cooked in Tsing Tao beer are heavenly, and thick, chewy noodles are not to be missed. If it's ambience you crave, you're out of luck: the bare-bones restaurant is always frantically busy, the service notoriously curt. Get there early to beat the crowds.

Hung Yen

VIETNAMESE ¢
3100 18TH ST.
MISSION 94110
415-621-8531
Lunch & Dinner Mon.-Sat.
No cards

Hung Yen's menu proclaims "Lunch & Dinner at popular prices," and it's no exaggeration: you'd be hard-pressed to find livelier, more satisfying Vietnamese cuisine at twice the price. Though décor is sparse, the dining room has a pleasant, bungalow-like feel. Selections run from simple pork, shrimp or tofu roll appetizers (each hearty enough for a main course) to a delightfully pungent sweet-and-sour fish soup, which features an entire fried flatfish. Wash it all down with a characteristically grassy Hue beer or bittersweet Vietnamese iced coffee-more a dessert than a beverage.

Il Fornaio

ITALIAN 13/20

1265 BATTERY ST.
FINANCIAL DISTRICT 94111
415-986-0100
Breakfast, Lunch & Dinner daily, Brunch Sun., $$

Il Fornaio has mastered breakfast, lunch and dinner and all the goodies in between, making it one of the city's favorite eateries. Like its corporate partners, the restaurant is warm and comfortable, with views of the open kitchen. The patio overlooking the fountain in Levi's Plaza is a perfect place to enjoy a pizza margherita at lunch, while the sleek interior welcomes at night, when diners can be seen tucking into a tender veal chop with roasted potatoes or rotisserie cooked chicken. With nearly a dozen pastas on the menu, good picks include paglia e fieno con gamberetti-homemade spinach and egg linguine, with rock shrimps, chopped tomatoes and chili flakes-and linguine mare chiaro-seafood in a tomato-wine sauce. In addition to the long menu of antipasti, salads, pastas and grilled meats, the eatery offers a bit of culinary education. Each month, Il Fornaio's chef introduces diners to a new regional Italian cuisine, with a menu of the area's best-loved food and wine.

Indian Oven

INDIAN 13/20

233 FILLMORE ST.
HAIGHT-ASHBURY 94117
415-626-1628
Dinner nightly, $

Owner Partap Singh and chef Mohammed Aslam serve some of the city's best North Indian food, so it's not surprising that Indian Oven is busy every night. Unlike many South Asian places, some effort has been put into the décor: café curtains and climbing plants along with the requisite Indian art hint this isn't your run-of-the-mill curry shack. Sizzling non-vegetarian dishes come from the deep tandoor oven in the open kitchen, where chicken, lamb, prawns and fish are cooked at high heat in the traditional North Indian style. Savory potato and pea samosas are encased in a light pastry; favorites like chana masala (stewed chickpeas) and saag paneer (a mild farmer's cheese in creamed spinach) are also reliable. Vegetarians will appreciate thali, a collection of small pots of stewed and curried vegetables that are scooped up with warm naan bread or chapatis. The Lower Haight crowd, from hempy locals to graying couples, offers an added element of entertainment to the evening.

Indigo

CALIFORNIAN 13/20

687 MCALLISTER ST.
CIVIC CENTER 94102
415-673-9353
Dinner Tues.-Sun., $$

Indigo joined the pre-theater dinner crowd in 1997 and hits all the right notes, with an unpretentious, airy, blue-toned dining room and a pre-theater fixed-price menu of $22.95. Chef John Gilbert favors Californian cuisine with lots of seasonal local produce and grilled and roasted fish and seafood. For starters, try lobster-fennel soup or oak-smoked salmon with a crisp potato pancake. Entrées include barbecued Gulf prawns with roasted polenta, fresh asparagus in a tart lemon vinaigrette, and roasted trout with a wild rice and dried cranberry stuffing. Side dishes (mashed potatoes, cannelini bean cassoulet) are ordered separately; one worthy pick is the herb-scented bread pudding. Desserts are rich and fruity, from bananas Foster and apple-cranberry crisp to poached pears with sorbet. Wine selections reveal a love of California.

Jackson Fillmore

ITALIAN 12/20

2506 FILLMORE ST.
PACIFIC HEIGHTS 94115
415-346-5288
Dinner nightly, $$

This Italian trattoria, found at the intersection of its namesake streets, remains busy most every night. Jackson Fillmore takes reservations for only three or more, so couples can wait for a table or opt to sit at the long counter and watch as antipasti are assembled. It's an entirely casual operation, best for a bright, noisy night out with friends or as an easy meal when you can't face the kitchen.

Antipasti include bruschetta, carciofi ripieni (artichoke stuffed with breadcrumbs and prosciutto), and eggplant al forno (eggplant baked with garlic until it's black and smoky-tasting). Basic Italian piattis make up the entrées here, such as linguine with prawns and scallops in a spicy tomato sauce and creamy mushroom risotto; veal is also a good bet. A long list of medium-priced Italian reds and half as many whites add to a robust trattoria ambience.

Jakarta

INDONESIAN 12/20

615 BALBOA ST.
RICHMOND DISTRICT 94118
415-387-5225
Dinner Tues.-Sun., $

A charming restaurant with an extensive menu of Indonesian dishes is a surprise find on a quiet Richmond district street. The restaurant comprises a series of small rooms, each with a center of interest, such as a wall of masks or shadow puppets. The space invites one to relax and enjoy the parade of dishes that cross the table. Shrimp cakes, dotted with corn and hot peppers, are a good start; also try deep-fried squid, grilled rockfish, braised beef served with various vegetables and a spicy, very hot fried chicken in chili sauce. Jakarta offers an extensive vegetarian selection, including an excellent gado gado-a heaping platter of vegetables served with classic Indonesian peanut sauce.

Jardinière

FRENCH/CALIFORNIAN 15/20

300 GROVE ST.
CIVIC CENTER 94102
415-861-5555
Dinner nightly, $$$$

Restaurant designer Pat Kuleto's latest stellar creation is a joy to see. Jardinière's theme is celebration, from the inverted Champagne glass above the bar to the oval dome that sparkles like rising bubbles; a balcony-level dining area offers the best view of the party scene below. The menu, created by Traci des Jardins (the chef who developed Rubicon's opening menu) includes such innovative dishes as house-cured salmon with German potato salad,house-made duck terrine with foie gras and Perigord black truffles and calamari and Peruvian white bean salad with oven-dried tomatoes and olives. For main courses, try crispy sweetbreads with glazed cipollini onions or red-wine-braised short ribs with roasted root vegetable-and-parsley coulis. Save room for the fanciful desserts and keep in mind that Jardinière is one of the few restaurants in the U.S. with a special cheese cellar to keep its superb collection of cheeses at the right temperature. An outstanding addition to the San Francisco restaurant repertoire, Jardinière is much more than just another pretty face.

Jasmine House

VIETNAMESE 13/20

2301 CLEMENT ST.
RICHMOND DISTRICT 94121
415-668-3382
Lunch Wed.-Sun., Dinner nightly, $$

Warm and tasteful, Jasmine House is on a busy stretch of Clement Street; its delicious Vietnamese food drawing families from the neighborhood to sample chef Nhan Nguyen's clean flavors and fresh ingredients. Good bets are the curried eggplant, which is grilled beforehand to give it a smoky flavor and added to a rich coconut-curry sauce with onions and red peppers. Fried imperial rolls are served with wrappers of lettuce, cucumber and mint and a sweet-and-sour dipping sauce. Through crab season (November-April), this is a popular place to dig into fresh local Dungeness-cracked, roasted and served with butter and spices. Service is friendly and helpful, and dessert is a plate of sweet orange sections.

Julie's Supper Club

CALIFORNIAN 12/20

1123 FOLSOM ST.
SOMA 94103
415-861-0707
Lunch Thurs.-Fri., Dinner nightly, $$

Standby Julie's is kitschy, vibrant and fun, with a menu to match. At lunchtime, you're likely to be seated next to a table of Webheads who work in the warehouse offices nearby;

dinner hosts a better-dressed crowd who find the eatery a not-too-intimidating entrée to the SoMa scene. The appetizers don't take themselves too seriously: "Jewelees," for example, are fried won tons stuffed with cheese, jalapeño and coriander and dipped in a zingy salsa. Grilled Atlantic salmon with saffron-Sambuca aïoli on saffron fettuccine (!) arrives moist and flavorful, yet pasta dishes can be uncharacteristically insipid. Veggies are sold separately, and it's best to load up on appetizers. Tables in the front room provide a ringside seat to the busy bar; the back room offers a more intimate atmosphere.

Julius' Castle

ITALIAN/CONTINENTAL 11/20
1541 MONTGOMERY ST.
TELEGRAPH HILL 94133
415-392-2222
Dinner nightly, $$$$

Perched on the city's most charming hill and commanding a majestic view of the Bay Bridge, Alcatraz and Treasure Island, Julius' Castle is the place to go when you want to pop the question or impress out-of-town guests. It's a real castle, built in 1922 on Telegraph Hill by dreamer/restaurateur Julius Roz. While locals shun such tourist-pleasers, Jeffery Pollock, the current owner, is slowly winning over the town. In 1995, the castle underwent $1 million worth of renovations, adding new marble and hardwood flourishes and an exhibition kitchen. Two Victorian-style dining rooms offer glittering chandeliers, ornate moldings and comfy chairs, plus a turret room that seats ten. The menu features fancy Italian/Continental dishes, with imperial prices. Starters include beluga caviar on blinis, Dungeness crab gnocchi and seared Atlantic scallops on endive. Main courses are rack of lamb, poached Maine lobster, and roast Muscovy duck breast. The wine list earns accolades and the service is old-world and solicitous. After dinner, it's a short walk up to Coit Tower to smooch or survey the kingdom.

Just For You Café

AMERICAN ¢
1453 18TH ST.
POTRERO HILL 94107
415-647-3033
Breakfast & Lunch daily, Brunch Sat.-Sun.
No cards

In a simple, straightforward style often associated with small-town diners, Just For You serves up hearty breakfasts and lunches to those lucky enough to get in. No reservations are accepted; the miniscule restaurant boasts only a couple of tables and a very skinny counter for eat-in service. Lucky customers enjoy grits, huevos rancheros and excellent hot cakes. Décor is kept to a minimum, but the café exudes a cheery, laid-back charm.

Kate's Kitchen

SOUL FOOD 12/20
471 HAIGHT ST.
HAIGHT-ASHBURY 94117
415-626-3984
Breakfast & Lunch daily, $
No cards

This unpretentious little restaurant, with hand-painted walls and geographical artifacts, attracts bleary-eyed students, slumming artistes and local kooks hungry for Kate's famous ginger and peach pancakes. Hush puppies are surprisingly good, and soul food such as greens, beans and rice are made with a practiced hand. Don't mind the downscale digs-no reservations, no credit cards, a long wait and a walk through the kitchen to the bathroom are part of the bargain. Just remember to arrive early, and remind yourself how good the simple things in life can be.

Kowloon Vegetarian Restaurant

CHINESE ¢
909 GRANT AVE.
CHINATOWN 94108
415-362-9888
Lunch & Dinner daily

Dining here is informal at best, though an attractive and incense-laden Buddha watches over the utilitarian gloom. "Vegetarian M & M" refers to mushrooms cooked with sea moss, a tiny seaweed-like vegetable that raises the dish from the ordinary. Vegetarian eel contains crispy pieces of "eel" (mushrooms) tossed with bean sprouts, a surprisingly hearty and satisfying meal. What the restaurant has over the competition is a baked goods counter, which makes it an ideal place to pop in for a snack. The ice creams-ginger, green tea, and lychee-are excellent.

Kuleto's

ITALIAN 13/20

221 POWELL ST.
UNION SQUARE 94102
415-397-7720
Breakfast, Lunch & Dinner daily, $$$

Pat Kuleto is a restaurateur-phenomenon about town. He began as a designer (of Fog City Diner, Lascaux and Postrio) and went on to become a partner in such places as McCormick & Kuleto's and Boulevard. His eponymous eatery in the Villa Florence Hotel is quintessential Kuleto, with rich marble and burnished wood; focal points are a Florentine ceiling and a magnificent mahogany bar from the old Palace Hotel. Beneath a forest of hanging salamis and garlic garlands, the bar is a great place to relax, sip wine and nibble antipasto. The kitchen's best starter is grilled radicchio wrapped in pancetta and served with a basil vinaigrette. A favorite meal here consists of house-made focaccia, a bulb of roasted garlic and an order of fried calamari served with tangy aïoli; likewise the torta rustica, a thick-crust pizza with cheese, pancetta and pine nuts. The wine list, mostly Italian and Californian, is modestly priced.

La Folie

FRENCH 17/20

2316 POLK ST.
RUSSIAN HILL 94109
415-776-5577
Dinner Mon.-Sat., $$$$

This chic yet unpretentious storefront French restaurant is run by chef Roland Passot and his wife, Jamie, with the help of brother Georges who handles the wine. Overhead in the intimate, whimsically decorated dining room, the painted blue sky is always filled with billowing clouds. But the pale azul and wispy billows are no match for the drama of Passot's plate presentation, which belie a keen mind and great sense of humor. Dishes arrive at your table looking like works of art. Sculpted edibles often rise vertically from the plate; vegetables lie in colorful swirls, appetizers in architectural arcs; entrées are designed in artful collages. La Folie is a proverbial feast for the eyes. Yet the food tastes even better than it looks. The smallish menu changes regularly and tends to focus on seasonal ingredients. The best deals are the three- and five-course prix-fixe dinners; the former is offered Monday through Thursday. Starters establish the high level of creativity at work here: We recently enjoyed parsley and garlic soup with a ragoût of snails and shiitake mushrooms before launching into a roti of quail and squab, stuffed with wild mushrooms wrapped in crispy potato strings and served in natural jus with truffles. A roasted venison loin on a leek fondue with a gâteau of root vegetables and sauce poivrade proved another palate-charmer. La Folie's ever-changing desserts-meal-sized plates containing curls of color in extraordinary shapes and textures-fairly fill your mouth with happiness. Even usually heavy strudel becomes ethereal in Passot's hands, not to mention his fabulous lemon mousse tucked into crêpe "purses." La Folie is nothing if not delicious fun. It is a restaurant of the highest distinction and Passot an artist who deserves to be counted among the city's super chefs. The wine list is one of the most imaginative in San Francisco, with a tasty selection of undiscovered regional French varietals.

La Villa Poppi

ITALIAN 11/20

3234 22ND ST.
MISSION 94110
415-642-5044
Dinner Tues.-Sun., $$

This charming little eatery makes you feel instantly at home, though it would be hard not to feel the warmth in a restaurant the size of your living room. A tiny open kitchen in the corner surveys a handful of artfully decorated tables. The weekly menu matches the restaurant size-wise-typically, a soup, a pizza and a salad join two pastas and two entrées. Simple, bold flavors tend to work best: hearty main courses such as pan-roasted monkfish with marinated vegetables, or pastas with tomato or sage butter sauces are guaranteed winners. The diminutive wine list centers on inexpensive Italian bottlings, perfect accompaniments to the rustic food. Given Poppi's size, reservations are a good idea.

La Paz Restaurant and Pupuseria

MEXICAN/SALVADORAN ¢
1028 POTRERO AVE.
MISSION 94110
415-550-8313
Breakfast, Lunch & Dinner daily

VISA MasterCard

Pupusas, a kind of Salvadoran tamale, are always tasty, stuffed with seafood or vegetables and served with traditional Salvadoran cabbage salsa. Other special treats include beef tongue in a sauce of tomatoes, onion and wine and a special chicken dish prepared in a zingy red sauce. You can eat very well here for very little money.

La Rondalla

MEXICAN ¢
901 VALENCIA ST.
MISSION 94110
415-647-7474
Lunch & Dinner Tues.-Sun.

No cards

It's always navidad at this crazy-quilt restaurant, one amply decorated with Christmas tree lights, balloons, stuffed birds, fake Tiffany lamps and other kitsch. From its long counter, La Rondalla's open kitchen serves fine Cal-Mex food, including a rare-grilled steak smothered with fresh onions, potatoes and tomatoes, an equally tasty adobada (marinated pork similarly topped) and the best guacamole north of the border. Threadbare mariachis and nonplused waitresses in red ruffled blouses add to the fun.

La Santaneca

SALVADORAN/MEXICAN ¢
3781 MISSION
OUTER MISSION 94110
415-648-1034
Lunch & Dinner daily

VISA MasterCard

A delicious combination of Mexican and Salvadoran foods: pupusas are the highlight, especially a savory cheese version. If you are really hungry, go for chorizo soup or a huge Salvadoran-style steak with a delicious green pepper- and-tomato sauce. Chile rellenos are also outstanding.

La Taqueria

MEXICAN ¢
2889 MISSION ST.
MISSION 94110
415-285-7117
Lunch & dinner daily.

No cards.

With its distinctive whitewashed facade, street-side seating and gleaming tiles, La Tacqueria is perhaps the most visually appealing bargain in the Mission. Yet no one comes for the décor: rather, they line up for perfectly composed burritos and corn tortilla tacos and the most authentic fruit drinks, perhaps, in the Bay Area. Carnitas cooked in lard are meltingly tender; chorizo sausage is spicy and lean; and carne asada may be the best in the neighborhood.

Laghi

ITALIAN 11/20
1801 CLEMENT ST.
RICHMOND DISTRICT 94118
415-386-6266
Dinner Tues.-Sun., $$

VISA MasterCard Diners Club International American Express

Eating at Laghi is very much like stepping into a neighborhood trattoria in Italy. Run by the Laghi family, the restaurant offers a complete Italian dining experience. Ingredients are fresh; focus on the food is sure and unfuzzy. The menu changes constantly, but look for lamb and rabbit or risotto with red wine and black truffles. The wine list is very good with many Italian bargains, most of which are available by the glass.

Le Central

FRENCH 13/20
453 BUSH ST.
UNION SQUARE 94108
415-391-2233
Lunch & Dinner Mon.-Sat., $$

A

A San Francisco institution and the favorite of several mayors including Willie Brown, eating at Le Central comes close to the experience of dining in a Paris bistro. In a setting of functional, no-frills décor and menu scrawled on blackboards, traditional dishes arrive to warm the soul and please the stomach. An individual onion tart is tasty-if sometimes a little soggy-while the celery root rémoulade is rich and satisfying. A steak served with pommes frites is chewy but flavorful, while charcuterie garnie is lusty comfort food. Close with tarte tatin or crème brûlée. The wine list would benefit greatly from more fruity Alsatian wines and fewer standard-issue California bottlings. Stop by for lunch and you might score a table next to Da Mayor.

Le Charm

FRENCH 13/20

315 Fifth St.
SoMa 94107
415-546-6128
Lunch Mon.-Fri., Dinner Tues.-Sat., $

Like its SoMa compatriots Fringale, Bizou and South Park Café, Le Charm offers classic French fare-but often at half the price of the others. The bright, airy room fills regularly for lunch and dinner, creating a din as diners and an open kitchen compete for airspace. Still, if you're craving classics such as frisée aux lardons, steamed mussels or salade niçoise, you've come to the right place. Lunch-either in the dining room or on the back patio-offers an expert croque monsieur or a grilled lamb chop with fries. At night, Le Charm features a $20 fixed-price menu with lots of choices: perhaps fish soup Provençal followed by steak frites, then tarte tatin and coffee, or maybe house-cured gravlax with cucumber salad, followed by duck confit and orange crème brûlée...it's difficult to decide. Fresh flowers, capable service and an interesting crowd make Le Charm a worthwhile trip down this somewhat shabby stretch of 5th Street.

Le Colonial

FRENCH/VIETNAMESE No Rating

20 Cosmo Pl.
Union Square 94108
415-931-3600
Lunch Mon.-Fri., Dinner Mon.-Sat. $$$

As we went to press, the latest in this chic French-Colonial Vietnamese family restaurant opened in the old Trader Vic's location. The gorgeous setting is right out of 1920's French-Colonial Vietnam: Antique oriental carpets, tall shuttered windows, palm fronds, and twirling fans on the stamped tin ceiling. The action takes place in the upstairs lounge, a sumptuous recreation of a decadently elegant French Colonial club. Expect light and subtly tasty French-Vietnamese cuisine.

Lhasha Moon

TIBETAN 13/20

2420 Lombard St.
Marina 94123
415-674-9898
Lunch Thurs.-Fri., Dinner daily, $$

This charming little restaurant is an exciting find on outer Lombard. Maps and pictures on the wall offer a Himalayan ambience. Try steamed momo buns, a kind of dumpling stuffed with meats or vegetables and flavored with basil, mint and chives. Vegetable momos were laid on to appease California diners, while the beef and chicken are more authentic. You'll find a large selection of vegetarian dishes, including bean thread strings, potatoes and celery, sautéed with ginger and emma, a kind of Tibetan peppercorn. Try several different breads, including bhaley, a dry fried flat bread and loko momo, a steamed bread. Meat dishes include kongpo shaptak, a hot, spicy, cheese-flavored beef-and-chili pepper dish and gutse rithuk, a hearty pasta dish made of hand-rolled noodles cooked in a lamb stew with daikon radish and spinach. A glass of Tibetan-style rice wine makes a perfect apéritif.

Liberty Café

AMERICAN 13/20

410 Cortland Ave.
Bernal Heights 94110
415-695-8777
Lunch Tues.-Fri., Dinner Tues.-Sun., $$

Bernal Heights residents generally don't trek down to Cortland Street for dinner, at least not until the Liberty opened. With two small, modestly decorated rooms, Cathie Guntli's little café won fans from across the city for its homemade bread, fresh local produce and brief menus. At lunch you'll find homey chicken pot pie and a sandwich of deep-fried littleneck clams on crusty French bread. Dinner might include warm chicken livers on pan-fried focaccia or risotto with Meyer lemons, rock shrimps and clams. Game lovers will appreciate aromatic braised rabbit with cabbage and tomato and served with green-garlic mashed potatoes; another pick is a salmon filet with tarragon, anchovy and caper butter. Locals especially love weekend brunch at the Liberty, with warm apple turnovers and sticky buns on the menu, as well as eggs Benedict and challah french toast. The Café might be the perfect launching point to explore this up-and-coming neighborhood full of friendly bookstores, sleepy cafés and almost-affordable houses.

Little City Antipasti Bar

ITALIAN 11/20
673 UNION ST.
NORTH BEACH 94133
415-434-2900
Lunch Mon.-Fri., Dinner nightly, Brunch Sat.-Sun., $$

A great place to sit at the window, Little City was one of the first places in San Francisco to pioneer the concept of making an entire meal from antipasti. Sip a glass of sparkling wine or share an appetizer at the gleaming brass bar, gazing out at North Beach while you wait for a table. Once seated, try small plates such as grilled asparagus with pistachio tahine sauce, Szechuan lamb sausages with spicy pickled vegetables and grilled prawns borrachos, marinated in tequila, lime and chilies, and served with tomatilla salsa. A perennial favorite is baked Brie with a whole roasted garlic bulb. A changing wine list features a brief selection of Californian and Italian wines by the glass.

Little Italy

ITALIAN 11/20
4109 24TH ST.
NOE VALLEY 94114
415-821-1515
Dinner nightly, $$

Little Italy is perhaps the most popular restaurant in Noe Valley, packed nightly with hungry diners appeasing their appetites in a sea of hearty Italian comfort food. Start with the house specialty, spiedini la Romana-a fat block of bread and mozzarella that's battered, deep-fried and served with bracing anchovy-parsley-wine sauce. Linguine with clam sauce is a garlicky treat, and fans of sweetbreads will delight in their preparation with tomatoes, olives and capers. For dessert, zabaglione is as ridiculously rich and ethereal. An Italian-tilted wine list is quite good, and waitstaff are up-to-speed on its vintages. Little Italy is about as close as San Francisco gets to a Brooklyn-style Italian café.

Lo Coco's

ITALIAN 13/20
510 UNION ST.
NORTH BEACH 94133
415-296-9151
Dinner Fri.-Sun., $$

As we go to press Lo Coco's is planning to re-open for lunch and additional nights for dinner, with a new menu reflecting the owner's Sicilian heritage. But whatever is on the menu, go for the pizza, one of the best in the city. Also good is an Arab-influenced pasta con sarde, a spaghetti with saffron, sardines, anchovies, fennel, pine nuts, currants and bread crumbs.

Los Jarritos

MEXICAN ¢
961 SOUTH VAN NESS AVE.
MISSION DISTRICT 94110
415-648-8383
Lunch & Dinner nightly

Los Jarritos, named for the tiny clay jars strung around the walls, is a colorful place. People come from all over San Francisco for birria, the warming and restorative goat stew served here on weekends in huge bowls with house-made corn tortillas. Jarritos is also a good lunch spot, serving tacos and burritos with fresh ingredients. Service is friendly.

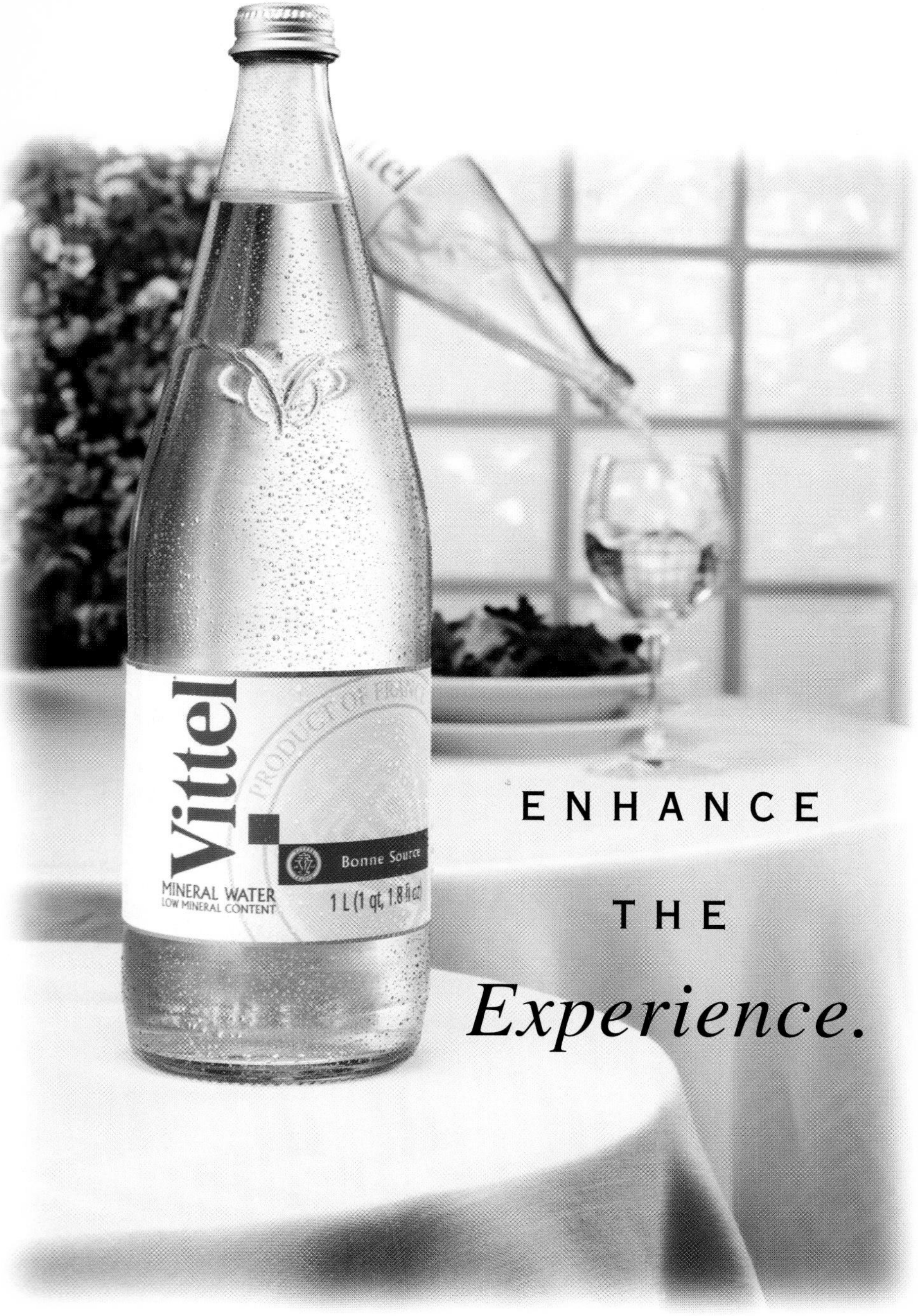

ENHANCE

THE

Experience.

Vittel®
YOUR SOURCE *of* VITALITY.

L'Osteria del Forno

ITALIAN 13/20

519 COLUMBUS AVE.
NORTH BEACH 94133
415-982-1124
Lunch & Dinner, Wed.-Mon., $$
No cards

Some of the tastiest food in North Beach can be had in a space the size of a large walk-in closet. You will almost always experience a wait for a table (they don't take reservations) but it's worth it. L'Osteria hardly has a real kitchen-the cooking is all done in one oven-but this hasn't stopped the owners from presenting an imaginative, ever-changing menu. L'Osteria is famous for its focaccia bread and for milk-braised pork roast, a Tuscan favorite. The anchovy pizza is delicious, and a short but good selection of Italian wines is available by the glass.

Loongbar

PAN ASIAN 13/20

900 NORTH POINT ST.
GHIRADELLI SQUARE 94109
415-771-6800
Dinner daily, $$$

Mark Miller's impressive new restaurant is named for the Chinese word for dragon, and the fiery beasts compose his decorating motif. An eclectic menu, executed by chef Jeffrey Inahara, features bold flavors from Japan, China, Indonesia and South Asia. Appetizers include tea-smoked quail nested on Szechuan eggplant salad and a bamboo steamer basket of five-treasure buns, each holding a different filling; main courses range from a rice-paper-wrapped roast salmon with coconut curry sauce to a pork chop with smoked clams. A number of large seafood platters can be shared family style. In a wine-friendly touch, varietals by the glass are suggested with each starter and main course. The dessert menu focuses on ice creams and sorbets.

Lucky Creation

CHINESE/VEGETARIAN ¢

854 WASHINGTON ST.
CHINATOWN 94108
415-989-0818
Lunch & Dinner Thurs.-Tues.
No cards

Don't judge Lucky Creation by its euphemistic-sounding name. There's little left to chance at this little hole-in-the-wall, though carnivores may disagree: the restaurant serves only vegetarian cuisine. Deep fried taro rolls are winners: in this incarnation, the purple tuber is surrounded by a crispy and delightfully flaky crust. Lucky Creation's forte, however, is its clay pot dishes. Essentially Chinese versions of hearty stews, all are excellent, though braised eggplant with bean sauce is a standout.

LuLu

MEDITERRANEAN 14/20

816 FOLSOM ST.
SOMA 94107
415-495-5775
Lunch & Dinner daily, $$$

This SoMa mainstay has had its ups and downs, the most serious after the departure of star chef Reed Hearon, but it remains one of the most popular restaurants in the city. A striking, double-vaulted dining room is flanked by a long bar and imposing brick ovens, from which issue forth LuLu's notable wood-roasted meats and forceful vegetable preparations. LuLu's food is nothing if not full-flavored, and it's served family style: sand dabs cooked a la plancha receive chilies, garlic, olives and preserved lemons, while rotisserie items-in particular the popular rosemary-scented chicken-are knockouts. Whole petrale sole and rock snapper arrive on rustic hand-painted oblong platters, as do spit-roasted slabs of pork loin nestled in a mound of olive-oil-mashed potatoes. Add to this a superb raw bar and an adventurous wine list: though primarily Californian, the restaurant makes its vinicultural selections from all over the world. LuLu is a consistent crowd-pleaser, and justifiably so. On the downside, noise levels are high, and the bar is often so crowded as to preclude comfortable interaction. Such is the price of popularity. Don't forget to make a reservation.

MacArthur Park

AMERICAN 13/20
607 FRONT ST.
FINANCIAL DISTRICT 94111
415-398-5700
Lunch Mon.-Fri., Dinner nightly, $$

This cavernous restaurant in the Financial District employs a simple recipe for success: prepare good quality American food like ribs, steaks, burgers and grilled fish; throw in a selection of microbrews on tap; and add fast friendly service. Décor is warm polished wood, high ceilings and exposed brick walls with lots of tables that can be pushed together to accommodate groups. On the tables are crayons and white butcher paper for kids and doodlers; for grown-ups there's a sizable wine list featuring a number of smaller California wineries. The most desirable seats are near the front door looking out onto leafy Jackson Square. Every Tuesday evening, the bar features a different West Coast microbrew, plus high-end appetizers like grilled pasilla peppers stuffed with three cheeses and popcorn shrimps. There's take-out too, in case you're craving ribs to go.

Magnolia

AMERICAN/BREWPUB 12/20
1398 HAIGHT ST.
HAIGHT-ASHBURY 94117
415-864-7468
Lunch & Dinner daily, $$

Magnolia brings solid, unpretentious food back to Haight-Ashbury. Attractive and comfortable though it is, the restaurant's pastel tiled and mirrored décor might start to remind you of your own bathroom. The food is down-to-earth: sandwiches are well-executed and filling, and more adventurous dishes such as grilled sesame-soy eggplant with Fontina-stuffed risotto cakes and spicy tomato jam are exciting, if a little short on presentation. House-made "Cole Porter" brew is first-rate, and an inexpensive, thoughtful wine list rounds out your choices. Perhaps the best comes last: desserts are homey, generous, and excellent. Be sure to try the warm blood-orange upside-down cake, if it's offered, and wash it down with a glass of "Willie Brown" ale.

Mandalay

BURMESE 12/20
4248 CALIFORNIA ST.
RICHMOND DISTRICT 94121
415-386-3895
Lunch & Dinner daily, $

Mandalay is an undiscovered joy of San Francisco dining. Fishnets, a large aquarium and paper lanterns on the walls lend a cheerful dowdiness to the place; the pungent food, however, is cheerful and fascinating, packed with the fragrant flavors of Burmese spices. Favorite dishes here include the Mandalay prawns and the chicken in garlic sauce. Salads are particularly tasty: try a lap path thok, a Burmese tea-leaf salad with artfully arranged portions of peanuts, split beans, fried garlic, fried coconut, roasted sesame seeds, dried shrimps and special tea leaves. There are those who insist on beer with this food, as Mandalay's wine list is minimal; bring your own and you won't be charged corkage.

Mangiafuoco

ITALIAN 13/20
1001 GUERRERO ST.
MISSION 94110
415-206-9881
Dinner nightly, $$

The past few years have transformed the corner of 22nd and Guerrero streets into a veritable gourmet ghetto; Flying Saucer, Moa Room, and Mangiafuoco all call it home. The latter (whose name means "fire eater" in Italian) serves credible Italian specialties at surprisingly low prices. A wood-fired oven makes its presence known not only by the aroma of burning kindling but by hearty, comforting meat dishes-Sonoma lamb chops with a mustard and huckleberry sauce is a standout. Pastas are uniformly superb: the filled varieties might contain gingered sea bass, or squash with crumbled amaretti cookies. Daily risottos and gnocchi are highly recommended as well. The décor is charmingly hip, with bright miniature lamps hanging over diners' heads, and a pair of Italian scooters mounted over the kitchen. A mostly Italian wine list covers the bases.

Manora's Thai Cuisine

THAI 13/20

1600 FOLSOM ST.
SOMA 94103
415-861-6224
Lunch Mon.-Fri., Dinner nightly, $

Though the name might suggest an unfortunate Kosher fusion experiment, Manora's in fact serves innovative, affordable and intense Thai food. Classics including the ubiquitous phad Thai, galanga and tom yan gung soups receive simple and artful treatment. Other dishes such as pong pang, a seemingly bottomless clay pot of squid, shrimps, scallops, mussels and fish cloaked in an authentically hot chili sauce, or the deceptively simple som-tum-a salad of unripe papaya and tomato-only raise the stakes. Service is blindingly efficient, and the warmly paneled room is a delight. Reservations are only accepted for parties of four or more, so you may have to cool your heels a few minutes. Be patient. There are few restaurants offer that perfect mix of heat, sweetness, spice and vibrant herbal flavors that make a great Thai meal, but Manora's does it every time.

Marina Central

AMERICAN 12/20

2001 CHESTNUT ST.
MARINA 94123
415-673-2222
Dinner nightly, Brunch Sat.-Sun., $$

A

This noisy Marina restaurant is just what the neighborhood needs-a non-chain eatery with a brasserie ambience. It's a great place for a casual dinner and a decent glass of wine, especially when the chain eateries down the street have an hour's wait. The high-ceilinged room with butter-colored walls and banquettes all add to a come-in-from-the-cold feeling; service, once slow, has improved greatly. Food-wise, roast chicken from the open kitchen is a good bet, as is the Bradley Ranch burger and the grilled portobello mushroom, served with spaghetti squash and Parmesan. Fish specials can be tasteless, so quiz your server before deciding. A Sunday brunch menu finds a decent eggs Benedict, huevos rancheros and Maine crab cakes. The bar area is a great place to catch the game or sip a glass of wine after a day spent in the Marina.

Mario's Bohemian Cigar Store

ITALIAN ¢

556 COLUMBUS AVE.
NORTH BEACH 94133
415-362-0536
Lunch & Dinner daily

Don't believe it when cynics proclaim the death of North Beach: as long as Mario's is around, the neighborhood's spirit is alive. Wonderful cappuccini, delicious focaccia sandwiches and a lemony ricotta cheesecake are served at the bar or one of the small tables. Try Mario's "campari," which tastes even better than the real stuff. The recently opened Polk Street Mario's (2209 Polk St., 415-776-8226) has a slightly more extensive menu, but it ain't the quintessential North Beach coffeehouse, babe. You dig?

Marnee Thai

THAI 14/20

2225 IRVING ST.
SUNSET 94122
415-665-9500
Lunch & Dinner Wed.-Mon., $

As crowded with Thai tastes as San Francisco is, Marnee stands out as a beautifully appointed temple to fresh, vibrant flavors. Woven mats and hanging plants transport you to another world, where chef/owner Chaiwatt Siriyan is a master of his craft, combining the building blocks of Thai flavor-heat, acidity, sweetness and salt-with a practiced hand. Try any of the vivid salads, the perfectly fried appetizers (corn fritters are a standout) or the rich, pungent soups, and you'll know you've found a winner. Green and red curries are authentically ardent, yellow versions mellower. The indecisive often defer to hostess May Siriyan, who seems to know just what you want. Unfortunately, you're not the only one to stumble across this lonely outpost, and the unreserved will wait long for their place in the Thai sun.

Masa's

FRENCH/
CALIFORNIAN No Rating
648 BUSH ST.
UNION SQUARE 94108
415-989-7154
Dinner Tues.-Sat., $$$$

As we were about to go to press, we learned that celebrated Chef Julian Serrano was about to leave. Thus, we cannot give Masa's the high rating (18/20) it earned before. Serrano's sous chef, Chad Callahan, is taking over and expects to produce the same high-quality French/California cuisine as his predecessor. Stay tuned. Meanwhile, expect an elegant, understated setting and one of the best wine lists in town.

Matterhorn

SWISS 13/20
2323 VAN NESS AVE.
NOB HILL 94109
415-885-6116
Dinner Tues.-Sun., $$$

A cozy wood-paneled interior of knotty pine, Matterhorn is fondue central: nine different kinds are available, served in traditional style with a bubbling pot of oil and broth and accompanied with side dishes and condiments. After a fondue starter, try the grilled veal sausage or traditional Wiener schnitzel. For dessert, go for (what did you expect?) chocolate fondue. Yodel-ay-he-ho! Reservations are required on the weekend.

Maye's Original Oyster House

ITALIAN 11/20
1233 POLK ST.
POLK GULCH 94109
415-474-7674
Lunch Mon.-Fri., Dinner Mon.-Sat., $$

Opened in 1867, Mayes' is San Francisco's second-oldest restaurant, and its clientele at various times have included the city's political and cultural elite. These days, Maye's serves rather predictable old-style Old Country dishes: veal Parmigiana, lobster thermidor and shrimp Newburg feature prominently. But there's an undeniable charm to this old warhorse. Genial, barrel-chested waiters seat you in a dark, cozy room filled with photos of old San Francisco, where you can get comfortable with oysters Rockefeller or the signature pan-fried sand dabs. The regal bar is a good place to find yourself at happy hour, when you can enjoy cocktails, munch hot hors d'oeuvres and gaze at glossies of long-departed celebrities.

Mecca

MEDITERRANEAN 12/20
2029 MARKET ST.
UPPER MARKET 94114
415-621-7000
Dinner nightly, $$$

A recent addition to the rather barren Market Street restaurant scene, Mecca comprises a large, curtained room and impressive curved bar, with tables for dining or drinking around the perimeter. The space is huge, the setting noisy and the crowd occasionally on the pretentious side, but in general the concept seems to work. From the dinner menu, try the wine-steamed mussels, or pick a pizza from the changing selection offered daily. Also delicious are the perfectly crisp calamari-a true test of any San Francisco restaurant. In addition to a large regular menu, Mecca features a good selection of bar snacks served until midnight.

The Meetinghouse

AMERICAN 14/20
1701 OCTAVIA ST.
WESTERN ADDITION 94109
415-922-6733
Dinner Tues.-Sat., $$$

As austere and solid as any Shaker design, the Meetinghouse reminds us of what restaurants were like before the marketing gang got hold of them. Wood gleams, lights glow softly and fresh flowers add a note of indulgence to the otherwise-unadorned room. American cuisine here seems to be a calling, not a niche; from the appetizers' distinct flavors to the simple but satisfying entrées, good food is clearly this restaurant's labor of love. The brief menu changes daily, but could include warm goat cheese-and-leek tart with arugula, fingerling potatoes with a citrus vinaigrette or a warm parsnip soup with curried apples and garlic chives. A favorite entrée is roasted duck breast with red onion marmalade, rosemary polenta crisps and steamed greens-the oniony marmalade acts as a wonderful foil to the duck's richness. Fish is also first rate: pan-seared salmon with lentils, winter vegetables, red wine jus, applewood-smoked bacon and crispy leeks sounds like a lot of commotion, but works well. The wine list takes the best of Northern California vineyards, and prices are reasonable. Desserts require advance planning-a "freeform" praline napoleon with caramel cream, roasted bananas and caramel sauce, and pippin apple and raisin turnover with cinnamon ice cream take effort to finish but are worth the attempt. With the exception of parking (use the valet), the Meetinghouse makes running a good restaurant look effortless.

Millennium

VEGETARIAN/
CALIFORNIAN 13/20
246 MCALLISTER ST.
CIVIC CENTER 94102
415-487-9800
Dinner nightly, $$

If vegetarianism brings forth unpleasant memories of marching eggplant Parmesans, perhaps you need a visit to Millennium, an elegant, softly lit room that aims to make vegetarian food exciting by using organic produce and creative, low-fat cooking. Chef Eric Tucker uses an unusual collection of ingredients including plantain, kumquats and jicama, and protein-rich seitan, tempeh and soy; a single menu draws on Italy, the Caribbean, the American South, Japan and California for inspiration. Appetizers might include Caesar salad; grilled vegetables with focaccia and aïoli; or an empanada stuffed with tempeh chili, olives and raisins and garnished with an avocado-jicama salsa. Entrées are equally intriguing: the "winter harvest purse" is a light pastry stuffed with roasted veggies and wild mushrooms; the Asian-style napoleon has layers of crisp sesame filo, oyster mushrooms, Japanese eggplant, asparagus and smoked tofu. One caveat: Stick to vegetables you can readily identify, unlike the Millennium steak, which is seitan or soy (your choice) masquerading as beef. Service is professional and the wine list works well with the non-traditional menu. Millennium hosts holiday dinners if you're seeking alternate plans for Thanksgiving or Christmas.

Moa Room

ECLECTIC 13/20
1007 GUERRERO ST.
MISSION 94110
415-282-1007
Dinner Wed.-Mon., Brunch Sun., $$

This relative newcomer to the Mission fine-dining scene has made quite a name for itself in its brief tenure in the Guerrero Street gourmet ghetto. Chef Jan Gardner's "borderless cuisine" is only one facet of a thoroughly pleasing, well-integrated project. A cleanly elegant white dining room is set off by vivid orange and lime-green curtains and banquettes, while tight clusters of tables are tended by a gracious staff. The menu rotates regularly, following the seasons via the owner's organic farm in Calistoga. Quality produce and meats are the restaurant's hallmark, and the chef's creations hail from Asia, the Americas, Europe and her native New Zealand. Try corn cakes and prawns with a richly hot chipotle butter, a jambalaya filled with massive, blood-red crawdads or any of the simple, fresh salads. A short, well-chosen wine list pairs nicely with the food, and desserts are inventive and satisfying.

Mom Is Cooking

MEXICAN ¢
1166 GENEVA AVE.
SOUTH CITY 94112
415-586-7000
Lunch & Dinner daily
No cards

This quirky, family-run restaurant is located in a working-class neighborhood not likely on most visitors' itineraries. Home-cooked Mexican food is served in humble, wood-paneled surroundings. "Mom" is diminutive Abigail Murillo, who turns all the food out herself, from a soul-warming hominy soup to crab enchiladas and shrimps in a potent red chili sauce that's sure to singe its way into your memory.

Moose's

CALIFORNIAN 13/20
1652 STOCKTON ST.
NORTH BEACH 94133
415-989-7800
Lunch Mon.-Sat. Dinner nightly, Brunch Sun., $$$

For over two decades, Ed and Mary Etta Moose have reigned as the San Francisco equivalent of the First Family of Washington Square. With Moose's, their eponymous eatery across the green from their longtime digs at the Washington Square Bar & Grill, the City's most convivial hosts have created for themselves a grander setting. The bustling open kitchen turns out something for every taste and budget, from lightly battered-and-fried calamari and a perfect Caesar salad to a pizza strewn with smoked chicken and leeks and an imposingly thick "Mooseburger" of tasty Niman-Schell beef. Whether a magnificent veal chop, a fresh pasta or a grilled fish, the food you eat will never disappoint at Moose's. The wine list is well chosen and reasonably priced, with many good selections available by the glass. The bar-an all-important element of any Ed Moose establishment-is a cozy mahogany beauty, a great place for a quiet drink. The restaurant features a live jazz pianist or trio several nights a week.

Nippon (No Name) Sushi

JAPANESE/SUSHI ¢
314 CHURCH ST.
MISSION 94114
NO PHONE
Lunch & Dinner Tues.-Sun.

No cards

This very homey little box just off Market Street is almost always crowded with voracious diners. Plain tuna, salmon and in particular unagi (roasted eel with sweet/salty ponzu sauce) are quite good. Vegetarian selections are available, from simple sliced cucumber to sour umeboshi plum- and natto-fermented soybeans. Arrive early or stand in line outside; once seated, if you prefer alcohol to the excellent toasted rice/green tea, brown-bag it from nearby stores.

Oberon

CALIFORNIAN/
MEDITERRANEAN 12/20
1450 LOMBARD ST.
COW HOLLOW 94123
415-885-6555
Dinner nightly, $$

If lamb is a favorite of yours, this is a good stop: you'll find rack of lamb and lamb shank on the main menu, or an appetizer of skewered ground lamb with mint and garlic. Lamb moussaka is a classic, as is lamb shank braised on a bed of white beans with Swiss chard and tomatoes. Other dishes available include roast half chicken with couscous and steamed clams. Big flavors reside here in a charming, three-room dining area hidden behind the facade of a dreary-looking motel.

One Market

AMERICAN 14/20
1 MARKET ST.
FINANCIAL DISTRICT 94111
415-777-5577
Lunch Mon.-Fri., Dinner Mon.-Sat., $$$

One Market serves wholesome American classics both new and old in a chic setting. Don't arrive expecting the pace of chef Barry Ogden's Lark Creek Inn in Marin County: the feeling here is bustling, even slightly rushed, in a huge dining room with an open kitchen at the back. Lunch starters include a number of salads, as well as oysters served with a Champagne mignonette and Danish black bread-a bit like the wonderful black loaves found in the oyster bars of Paris. Fish and chips and juicy three-cheese lasagne with tomato fondue and pesto round out the lunch main courses. The dinner menu is much more extensive, although starters are still heavy on salads; split pea soup with smoked ham hock and tortellini is a treat. For a main course, cioppino or house-made fettuccine with truffle butter are hard to beat. Ogden's near-legendary pot roast was sadly missing from a recent menu, a result of extensive changes when George Morrone took over the kitchen. The new roster reflects Morrone's love of seafood while retaining some of Ogden's American comfort foods. To accompany your meal, a daily wine list offers a number of nice selections by the glass, as well as an "Expanded List and Cellar Selections" that spans an astoundingly broad range (and several decades) of exceptional all-American winemaking. Desserts? Outstanding-find any excuse to try One Market's house-made vanilla ice cream.

Oriental Pearl

CHINESE 14/20

778 CLAY ST.
CHINATOWN 94108
415-433-1817
Lunch & Dinner daily, $$

A

Don't go to Oriental Pearl expecting the usual Chinatown dining experience: the bill here will be a little higher, the service more attentive, the food arriving in courses rather than in one massive wave, and the quality exceptional. Start with the peppery tofu soup or a chicken meatball (which sounds pedestrian but is a heavenly bite). All the main course dishes are a step up from ordinary Chinatown fare. What's more, the waiters are familiar with wine and the list is reasonable.

Osaka Grill

JAPANESE 13/20

1217 SUTTER ST.
NOB HILL 94109
415-440-8838
Lunch Mon.-Fri., Dinner nightly, $$

Inside this attractive, minimal space, matched by the look and taste of the food, meals are prepared on hibachis while the customer watches. Chef-owner Noel Mok has created a light and tasty style of cuisine that keeps people coming back for more. Highlights include the shrimp appetizer, sea bass with ginger sauce and a terrific steak in garlic sauce. Grilled scallops are on the menu most nights, always perfectly cooked and deliciously fresh.

Pacific

PACIFIC RIM/
CALIFORNIAN 16/20

500 POST ST.
UNION SQUARE 94102
415-929-2087
Lunch Mon.-Fri., Dinner nightly, Brunch Sun., $$$

A

Hidden away on the third floor of the Pan Pacific Hotel is a comfortable, quiet and corporate-looking restaurant that serves some of the city's best fusion cuisine. Monochromatic, sound-absorbing décor and well-spaced tables allow for quiet conversation, a sane alternative to the many deafening restaurants in the neighborhood. Chef Michael Otsuka joined the team in late 1997 and quickly won enthusiastic reviews for his ability to work within a number of culinary traditions-French, Mediterranean, Japanese and Vietnamese. One trademark appetizer is pan-roasted foie gras with Granny Smith apples served three ways: caramelized, sliced and brushed with parsley oil, and as a tart sorbet. Entrées might include grilled ahi tuna served rare with spinach, roasted garlic and a wild rice and mushroom miso or a decadent Asian duck salad with hoisin sauce served in a crisp fried lumpia wrapper basket. Flavors are clean and precise, and the presentation is fantastic. Desserts are slightly more conventional-warm brioche bread pudding, tarte tatin and crème brûlée.

Palio d'Asti

ITALIAN 15/20

640 SACRAMENTO ST.
FINANCIAL DISTRICT 94111
415-395-9800
Lunch Mon.-Fri., Dinner Mon.-Sat., $$$

A

As we went to press, owner Gianni Fassio couldn't say what would comprise the new dinner menu at his outstanding Italian restaurant, but standouts among his lunch menu, developed by chef Keld Laustsen, include a risotto of the day, butternut squash gnocchi with brown sage butter and oven-roasted portobello mushroom sandwich on toasted Pugliese olive bread. For dessert, a piece of Sicilian Meyer lemon-ricotta cheese cake is hard to resist. The good news is that Fassio has just opened Enoteca della Douja, a wine bar next door that serves a selection of small plates. Of these, standouts include a tender and delicious grilled cuttlefish, grilled sardines with marinated fennel and onion salad, pappardelle with rabbit ragoût, lamb shank braised in aromatic vegetables with polenta and sautéed quail with roast artichokes. A selection of pizzas arrives from the wood oven. To accompany all this, sommelier Pamela Busch has put together an exciting wine list offering a number of little-known Italian wines as well as a good mix of recognized favorites.

Pancho Villa Taqueria

MEXICAN ¢
3071 16TH ST.
MISSION 94110
415-864-8840
Lunch & Dinner daily
No cards

Don't be deterred by the line out the front door. It moves fast, as Mission locals and out-of-the-neighborhood fans flock to this taqueria for some of the best Mexican food in town. Burritos and soft tacos are the main draws; house special is the carne asada burrito, a huge flour tortilla filled with rice, red or black beans, grilled chopped steak, guacamole and fresh salsa. There are also chicken, pork, red snapper and vegetarian varieties.

Pane e Vino

ITALIAN 12/20
3011 STEINER ST.
PACIFIC HEIGHTS 94123
415-346-2111
Lunch Mon.-Sat., Dinner daily, $$

Look under the awning on Steiner and follow the scent of garlic. This lively trattoria is a pleasant surprise, considering it's so close to the homogenous Union Street strip. As the name will tell you, Pane e Vino serves rustic, simple fare, although the spare, tasteful decor is several notches above your neighborhood pasta place. Diners waiting for tables idle near the open kitchen, sipping a glass of house wine and eyeing the plates as servers whisk them away. Pastas are basic and sometimes hit-or-miss-stick to grilled entrées and wonderful cold appetizers like a timballo di melanzane of eggplant stuffed with salmon mousse, goat cheese and tomato sauce. Rack of lamb in a red wine sauce and a thick veal chop with rosemary butter make excellent secondi, as does the whole grilled fish. Desserts include a good rendition of tiramisu, but don't miss the affogato al caffè-white chocolate ice cream, espresso and cocoa. Pane e Vino's two adjoining rooms are often full of exuberant diners enjoying the restaurant's warm and casual atmosphere.

Parma Ristorante

ITALIAN 13/20
3314 STEINER ST.
MARINA 94123
415-567-0500
Dinner Mon.-Sat., $

Parma's robust pastas and hearty Italian red wines keep this Marina favorite hopping late into the night. The waitstaff are a lively bunch whom you half expect to break into a chorus of "That's Amore" as they dash from table to table in the narrow room. Crusty, thick-cut Italian bread arrives with a dish of herbs and olive oil for dipping; linguine alla vongole is heaped with clams and mussels in a garlicky white wine sauce; the daily risotto, however, can be lackluster. Once the place fills up, no one seems to notice the noise, engrossed as they are in their own conversations. Reservations aren't necessary; just put your name on the clipboard and settle on the park bench out front. Tables turn quickly.

Pasta Pomodoro

ITALIAN ¢
655 UNION ST.
NORTH BEACH 94108
415-399-0300
Lunch & Dinner daily
No cards

This hot local chain specializes in pasta, pasta and a little more pasta. Servings are large and cheap and consistently tasty, the staff is friendly and the wine is plentiful. What more can you ask? Best bets are dried pastas like penne putanesca or spaghetti frutti di mare; good salads are available in half servings; sandwiches, polenta and a popular tiramisu for dessert are also available. The chain intends to open ten local branches by 2000.

Pastis

FRENCH/CALIFORNIAN 13/20
1015 BATTERY ST.
SOMA 94111
415-391-2555
Lunch Mon.-Fri., Dinner Mon.-Sat., $$$

Gerald Hirigoyen of Fringale has created a much different feeling here than at his original restaurant. Though Pastis feels industrial, its customers soon warm to chef Isabella Alexandre's dishes—hearty and homey plates from Languedoc, southeastern France and Toulouse, from which Alexandre hails. Like Fringale's, Pastis' menu reflects some of Hirigoyen's Basque influence, but Alexandre has opened it up to include dishes like the oxtail rouelle or the steamed mussels au Pastis. A three-course prix-fixe lunch menu, which changes daily, costs $15; a daily dessert list includes a "skinny" apple tart and a popular triple chocolate mousse with espresso sauce.

Patio Español

SPANISH 12/20
2850 ALEMANY BLVD.
MISSION 94112
415-587-5117
Lunch & Dinner Wed.-Sun., $$

A

Even native San Franciscans rarely venture into this outlying reach of the city, but it's worth a visit. Patio Español is in the Spanish Cultural Center, a big rambling white building that looks like a roadside hotel in central Spain. It features a large bar with small tables (perfect for tapas) or a big dining room for full lunches and dinners. New chef Jose Pérez Garcia has made some interesting changes with the main menu: family-style meals-such as baked lamb shank roasted with vegetables-change daily. But go to Patio Español for the tapas: prawns grilled in garlic sauce, squid poached in its own ink, grilled sausages, slices of ham, dried in the Spanish style...the list includes more than two dozen hot and cold tapas. Patio Español offers an extensive and reasonably priced list of Spanish wines.

Pazzia

ITALIAN 12/20
337 THIRD ST.
SOMA 94107
415-512-1693
Lunch Mon.-Fri., Dinner Mon.-Sat., $$

This sunny little trattoria isn't big on furnishings: the airy, tiled dining room might be described as "stylishly barren." What Pazzia does excel in are thin, crisp-crusted pizzas-some say they're the city's best-and delicious, rustic pastas and panini. Around lunchtime, the café is filled with hungry office-workers; on sunny days, a lucky few get to enjoy the sidewalk tables. Dinner is a little less harried. Peruse the excellent Italianate wine list; entrées as good as their rosemary-grilled lamb chops deserve an apt bottle. The restaurant draws an interesting clientele from the nearby SFMOMA and surrounding art schools.

Piaf's

FRENCH 11/20
1686 MARKET ST.
CIVIC CENTER 94102
415-864-3700
Lunch Tues.-Fri., Dinner Tues.-Sat., $$

There's something about Market Street that seems to attract French-style bistros. Newcomer Piaf's joins Bistro Clovis and Alfred Schilling as the resident purveyors of Francophilia, but Piaf's plush, elegant décor, attentive service and rich cuisine set it apart from its cousins. The restaurant is devoted to vocalist Edith Piaf; her recordings grace the dining room when a live singer isn't performing. The dishes are evocative of the singer's era; you'll find escargots in Champagne, vol-au-vent of duxelles with Gruyère, and grilled entrecôte. The wine list includes some nice value-priced Southern French bottles, but nothing extraordinary. Piaf's is a lovely choice for a special occasion.

PJ's Oyster Bed

CAJUN/CREOLE 13/20
737 IRVING ST.
SUNSET 94122
415-566-7775
Lunch & Dinner daily, $$

A

PJ's has been serving heaping portions of Southern-style seafood for almost 20 years, and shows no signs of slowing down. The emphasis is on heat, but chef Pachi Calvo y Perez also turns out some excellent paellas that won't singe the roof of your mouth. It's hard to choose a favorite here: the iron-skilleted Avery island shellfish roast, blackened catfish and spicy jambalaya are all superb, as are the oyster bar selections. Unfortunately, space is at a premium and the unreserved will have to wait upwards of an hour (many wait across the street at Yancy's) for one of the cramped tables. If you can finagle a seat at the counter, you can watch the chefs at work. Be forewarned: the fruits of the sea don't come cheap, but you'll leave generously stuffed-and probably sweating.

Plouf

SEAFOOD 14/20
40 BELDEN PLACE
UNION SQUARE 94109
415-986-6491
Lunch Mon.-Fri., Dinner Mon.-Sat., $$$

French onomatopoeia for the sound a stone makes falling into water, Plouf bills itself as a seafood bistro. Whatever you call it, the food is exceptional. The menu changes daily, reflecting what's available in the market. Steamed mussels and clams are a house specialty and come in many different styles, ranging from marinière (garlic, white wine and parsley) to poulette (cream, shallots, white wine and parsley.) The fish side of the menu starts with fish and chips with aïoli and includes a traditional bourride, a fish stew from southern France. The restaurant also features delightful outdoor dining on sunny days, making it popular with both the Union Square and the Financial District dining crowds.

Plump Jack Café

CALIFORNIAN 14/20
3127 FILLMORE ST.
COW HOLLOW 94123
415-563-4755
Lunch Mon.-Fri., Dinner Mon.-Sat., $$$

Plump Jack attracts publicity like a Getty attracts money-just pick up a paper or a food magazine and you'll see that the Cow Hollow restaurant and its famed owners are in the news again. The most recent publicity centers on one of Plump Jack's owners, Gavin Newsom, a young businessman who took office as a city Supervisor in 1997. Despite the ballyhoo, Plump Jack chef Maria Helm manages to hold her own with hearty Californian cuisine. Starters include a bruschetta of roasted eggplant, peppers, feta cheese, olives and chives, and smoked salmon with two caviars served on a potato "waffle" and topped with a lemon-chive crème fraîche. Delicious! Helm's crisp-skinned duck confit and roasted duck breast is also a favorite in town: It's served with a golden potato rösti and thyme-roasted apples. Plump Jack's gray-toned décor and luxurious leather banquettes create a soothing ambience; mesh-like curtains filter the incoming light from Fillmore Street. Wine aficionados will go gaga over the house list, brimming with varietals they always wanted to taste; better yet, the list's prices are near-retail. Landing a reservation in the somewhat cramped, deep-hued room sometimes requires a large dose of patience. Getty bucks lie behind the operation, and the empire is growing: the remarkable Plump Jack wine store is down the street, a Plump Jack restaurant lies at the foot of Squaw Valley in Lake Tahoe, and a Plump Jack vineyard was recently christened in Napa Valley. Too, the owners have bought and renovated the historic Balboa Café half a block to the north.

Postrio

CALIFORNIAN 15/20
545 POST ST.
UNION SQUARE 94102
415-776-7825
Breakfast & Lunch Mon.-Fri., Dinner nightly, Brunch Sun., $$$$

Since it opened in 1989, Postrio has been one of the city's premiere restaurants, partly because it has the imprimatur of L.A. überchef Wolfgang Puck. Designed by Pat Kuleto (Fog City Diner, Farallon, Jardinière, et al), Postrio's three levels still impress; people love to watch who's coming down the stairs. One night it might be the mayor and a big-name Democrat, the next a Hollywood star who's shooting her film in town. Since chefs David and Annie Gringrass left Postrio in 1995 to open Hawthorne Lane, brothers Mitchell and Steven Rosenthal have taken the helm. Things were rocky at first, but the pair seems to have found their way. Their culinary influences are

San Francisco favorites: Californian, American, Italian, French and Asian. Dinner entrées range from Chinese-style duck with braised endive and a green peppercorn-citrus sauce to grilled Sonoma lamb chops with a roasted garlic-port sauce and pan-seared tuna with roasted shiitakes and a port-five-spice sauce. Pastry chef Janet Rikala continues to win accolades for homey faves like Granny Smith apple pie with ice cream and an elegant tangerine sorbet on pomegranate granita. Postrio is open for breakfast and lunch, as well as weekend brunch; guests at the adjacent Prescott Hotel get first dibs on tables.

Powell's Place

SOUTHERN/SOUL 11/20
511 Hayes St.
Hayes Valley 94102
415-863-1404
Breakfast, Lunch & Dinner daily, $

A

For more than 20 years, Powell's has served soulful Southern food to locals and diners who want a break from the city's trend-setting restaurant scene. Occasionally, owner and gospel singer Emmit Powell is on hand to welcome you to his comfortable, frill-free Hayes Street restaurant, now surrounded by fashionable boutiques and chi-chi shops. If your foodie spirit cries out for crisp and tender fried chicken, black-eyed peas with sausage, corn muffins, red beans or mashed potatoes and greens, Powell's offers redemption. Sweet potato pie with subtle spices and a good flaky pastry make a rousing finish; blues and R & B play on the jukebox. What could be more satisfying?

Pozole

MEXICAN ¢
2337 Market St.
Upper Market 94114
415-626-2666
Lunch Fri.-Sun., Dinner nightly
No cards

Chef Jesus Acevedo, who hails from Mexico's Michoacan province, turns out some of the kickiest Mexican food in the City. In these striking quarters while cheery Latin pop blares, candle wax sculptures play against electric blue walls. On the overhead menu, you'll find cactus, rock shrimps and roasted garlic, folded into a quesadilla Cancun and accented with vibrant salsas. Cinnamon-and-chocolate chicken mole is superb, as are airy corn masa tamales.

Prego

ITALIAN 13/20
2000 Union St.
Cow Hollow 94123
415-563-3305
Lunch & Dinner daily, $$

This local favorite serves sophisticated Italian cuisine in chic Cow Hollow. Airy and open, Prego consists of several dining areas with a stately bar in its center. The slightly raised room in the back is a favorite: on sunny days the skylight opens to give a patio-like feel. The menu ranges from familiar pizzas, calzones, antipasti and sandwiches to more adventurous dishes such as polilpi alla luciana-octopus braised in tomato sauce, chili peppers, garlic and oregano. A selection of house-made pastas includes the enticing agnolotti d'aragosta: pasta half-moons filled with lobster, prosciutto and ricotta and served with a lemon-lobster cream sauce. Open all day, Prego is also a nice spot to catch a soda or a selection from the nicely rounded Italian/American wine list.

R & G Lounge

CHINESE 12/20
631 Kearny St.
Chinatown 94108
415-982-7877
Lunch & Dinner daily, $

A

Here's a two-story dining experience: downstairs is a family-style Chinese restaurant with astonishingly low prices and daily Cantonese lunch specials, including a tasty five-spice oxtail soup. Upstairs is a serene, rather elegant dining room where you can order fish pulled right from the tank. In this upper altitude, start with the salt and pepper shrimps-they're crisp, salty and delicious, much like eating popcorn. Eat the heads and shells along with the bodies. The vegetables are always fresh and perfectly cooked. Only downside? R & G's selection of wine isn't much-it's best to bring your own bottle.

Raw Experience

CALIFORNIAN/HEALTH/
VEGETARIAN 12/20
1224 NINTH AVE.
SUNSET DISTRICT 94122
415-665-6519
Lunch & Dinner Tues.-Sun., $

Located in the sleepy Sunset is an unusual restaurant in a town full of them: Raw Living Foods is not only 100% vegan-meaning no dairy products are used-but serves only uncooked food, save that which is baked by the sun. Sound terrible? Guess again: Raw's New Agey treats are surprisingly satisfying, such as novel cold soups like "fat mushroom" (a "bio-dynamic herb" concoction featuring yellow tomatoes and portobello mushrooms). Pizzas are built on a sun-dried buckwheat crust that resembles crusty cornbread in consistency; toppings include sea palm, house-made kraut and marinated eggplant. Complement your meal with the hot shots of puréed pepper juice. The restaurant itself is a perfect slice of California, overgrown with lush plants, framed photos of reclining goddesses and a soothing techno soundtrack. Against your preconceptions, you may well find the food as innovative, soothing, and artfully prepared as do many San Franciscans. Groovy.

Ristorante Ecco

ITALIAN 13/20
101 SOUTH PARK
SOMA 94103
415-495-3291
Lunch Mon.-Fri., Dinner Mon.-Sat., $$

This is a warm, relaxing space, tucked away on the east side of South Park across the greenery from Ristorante Ecco's sibling South Park Café. Staff is young and friendly, if sometimes a trifle undertrained; ambience is easy and the food is equally satisfying. This is a pleasant place to spend a leisurely evening. You might begin with a dish of arancine, deep-fried risotto balls stuffed with Fontina and mozzarella or a sharable Antipasto all'Ecco, a large plate of prosciutto and coppa with roasted peppers, marinated vegetables, olives and grissini. Try a starter of carpaccio di salmone, a plate of fresh salmon drizzled with olive oil, topped with red caviar and served with crostini and fluffy, horseradish-scented Mascarpone. Of the half-dozen pastas and as many grilled meats and fish, the Linguine dell'Ecco-a flavorful combination of pears, pecans, Gorgonzola, mint and Reggiano-is particularly pleasing. Osso buco alla Milanese is one of the best in town, and the filetto di maiale-pancetta-wrapped pork tenderloin with roasted pears, braised cabbage and garlic-mashed potatoes-is a delight. The lunch menu includes a short list of pizzas. Dessert highlights include house-made fruit ices and a seasonal fruit tart. The Californian and Italian wine list is good and reasonably priced.

Ristorante Ideale

ITALIAN 13/20
1309 GRANT AVE.
NORTH BEACH 94108
415-391-4129
Lunch & Dinner Tues.-Sun., $$

With its red-tiled floors and walls covered in paintings, bustling Ideale has rapidly become one of the most popular Italian restaurants in San Francisco, and for good reason. The menu in this double-storefront eatery changes daily, and pastas are first-rate. Try house-made fettuccine in fresh tomato sauce with porcini, seasonal mushrooms, garlic and red pepper, or gnocchi in a lamb ragu. Main course highlights include a baked boneless pork chop stuffed with fresh mozzarella and sage or fresh mussels and cannelini beans sautéed in white wine, garlic and thyme. The wine list is short but more than adequate.

Ristorante Milano

ITALIAN 14/20
1448 PACIFIC AVE.
RUSSIAN HILL 94109
415-673-2961
Dinner Tues.-Sun., $$

A small and very romantic space, Milano is jammed until late in the evening. Pasta here, especially the puttanesca, is always a treat; skewered chicken livers and smoked bacon served with grilled endive are a must. Main courses are fairly simple-try a grilled veal chop with rosemary and sage or a chicken breast with prosciutto, mozzarella, Marsala and sage. For sweets, the tiramisu is one of the best in town. Because of the charming staff and the good food, you won't notice (as you're gazing deeply into the eyes of your significant other) that the diner at the next table has his elbow nearly in your bread plate.

The Ritz-Carlton Dining Room

CALIFORNIAN 17/20

RITZ-CARLTON HOTEL, 600 STOCKTON ST.
NOB HILL 94108
415-773-6198
Dinner Mon.-Sat., $$$$

On any given night, The Ritz-Carlton Dining Room may be the best restaurant in San Francisco. Its exquisite décor, top-of-the-line wine list, professional service and live dinner music combine to create a showcase for Chef Sylvain Portay's magnificent cuisine. Detailed, flavorful food artfully presented is at the heart of the great dining experience you'll have here. If you prefer, you may devise your own prix-fixe meals of three, four or five courses, or you may choose to leave yourself in Portay's hands with a special dining menu-six courses for $69, plus $43 for wine with each course. If you decide to construct your own, open with braised sweetbreads or a rabbit ballentine, then move to a roasted Maine lobster or sautéed monkfish with onion confit, red bell pepper and zucchini cake. Main courses might include a roasted duck breast with rosemary-niçoise-olive sauce and polenta gratin or a tenderloin of beef braised in white wine with a potato-vegetable gratin. Gregory Gourreau's dessert selections include a festival of delights, highlighted by a chocolate bombe crème brûlée and a selection of fruit desserts and sorbets. Master Sommelier Emmanuel Kemiji can choose the perfect wine for any occasion, including just the right glass to go with The Ritz-Carlton's superlative cheese course. The bar outside the dining room offers an amazing line of desserts for before- and after-theater nibbling and 90 single-malt Scotches from which to choose. Indulge in the city's best.

The Ritz-Carlton Terrace

AMERICAN 14/20

RITZ-CARLTON HOTEL, 600 STOCKTON ST.
NOB HILL 94108
415-773-6198
Breakfast, Lunch & Dinner daily, Brunch Sun., $$$

Chef Paul Murphy has created an eclectic menu which can work as a quick lunch for business travelers or a destination for locals. A pan-seared Dungeness crabcake with avocado and tomato salsa will be enough lunch for many diners. Another good starter, also a generous portion, is lobster risotto with tarragon, Mascarpone and truffles. For those with simpler tastes, a smoked turkey breast sandwich or grilled ahi tuna niçoise salad make excellent choices. Grilled filet mignon with sweet potato purée makes for a hearty lunch. In addition to its fine food, the Terrace boasts one of the largest and most attractive outdoor dining areas in the Bay Area, a superlative Sunday brunch (buffet or table service) and excellent live jazz-at brunch as well as most evenings. In keeping with the Ritz-Carlton tradition, service here never falters, and an excellent wine list features a wide selection of California vintages.

Rose Pistola

ITALIAN 14/20

532 COLUMBUS AVE.
NORTH BEACH 94133
415-399-0499
Lunch & Dinner daily, $$$

Named for a legendary North Beach woman who once owned the Washington Square Bar & Grill, Rose Pistola features an open kitchen, a large bar and a simple cuisine that has won chef-owner Reed Hearon good reviews from opening day. Highlights include Ligurian seafood salad, cured swordfish with green peppercorns and a roasted, fresh-market filet of fish with fennel. Oven-roasted rabbit with white runner beans is also a favorite, as is anything that comes from the wood-burning oven. Rose Pistola also has the dubious distinction of being one of the loudest restaurants in San Francisco: go early if you want to have a conversation with your dinner companions. At lunch, try for a sidewalk table, where you're only competing with traffic noise on Columbus Avenue. A late-night menu is available until midnight.

Rose's Café

ITALIAN 13/20

2298 UNION ST.
PACIFIC HEIGHTS 94123
415-775-2200
Breakfast, Lunch & Dinner daily, $

This recent Union Street addition marks another successful project by Reed Hearon. Rose's offers a casual Italian take on breakfast, lunch and dinner in a high-end cafeteria setting. Homemade Italian breads are a real success here, especially strawberry or black currant focaccias. For breakfast, don't miss the "breakfast pizza," a thin blistered-crust torte topped with ham, Cheddar and eggs and baked in the oven. At lunch, several sandwiches entice-grilled chicken with roasted tomatoes and aïoli or steak with blue cheese, radicchio and roasted onion. The fresh salads are also good; try the goat cheese with arugula and tapenade bruschetta. Table service begins at dinner, when the specials get posted beside the front door. From the menu, you'll discover bistro-style fare such as a wonderful grilled chicken with mashed potatoes and tender lamb chops with white beans and a sage aïoli. The tables inside fill up quickly; during peak hours you can sit outside on a heated and covered sidewalk patio. This is a busy place and a perfect spot to watch the Pacific Heights nobles as they emerge from double-parked Range Rovers to pick up dinner chez Rose.

Roosevelt Tamale Parlor

MEXICAN ¢

2817 24TH ST.
MISSION 94110
415-550-9213
Lunch & Dinner Tues.-Sun.

No cards

This 24th Street institution has been in business since 1922. Order huge servings of pork or chicken tamales à la carte or on a dinner plate, along with a wide range of other Mexican specialties. Several tasty moles are house-made daily.

Roti

AMERICAN 14/20

155 STEUART ST.
FINANCIAL DISTRICT 94105
415-495-6500
Lunch Mon.-Fri., Dinner daily, $$

Roti stretches from Steuart Street to the Embarcadero, allowing it multiple personalities. On the Steuart Street side, it's a busy sidewalk café; further in, it's a warm brasserie with deep banquettes; on the Embarcadero side, Roti encloses a semi-private dining room with a beautifully framed view of the Bay Bridge. Roasted and grilled meats from the rotisserie are its main attraction, but the longish menu includes wonderful alternatives that show fresh ingredients and bold flavors. A summer appetizer included savory gazpacho garnished with grilled gulf prawns and coriander. Other starters include oysters on the half shell with a tomatillo cocktail sauce and fat, grilled scallops with avocado-lime salsa and cumin aïoli. From the grill, fire-roasted gulf prawns puttanesca, served bubbling in a skillet with artichokes and potatoes, are wonderful-be sure to have bread handy to sop up the tomato and caper broth. Spit-roasted chicken is so-so, but the mashed potatoes go beautifully with the rich pan gravy. Desserts are formidable; one winner is the Kentucky Derby, a warm chocolate cake with a truffle center, caramel bourbon sauce and mint ice cream; warm apricot and cherry brioche bread pudding comes a close second. Service is near-perfect.

Rubicon

CALIFORNIAN 14/20

558 SACRAMENTO ST.
FINANCIAL DISTRICT 94111
415-434-4100
Lunch Mon.-Fri., Dinner Mon.-Sat., $$$

When star chef Traci Des Jardins left Rubicon in 1997 to open Jardinière, many wondered who could fill her toque. Happily, Scott Newman, Des Jardins' former chef de cuisine, has taken his promotion and run with it. The Sacramento Street restaurant has a cachet that only money can buy-restaurateur Drew Nieporent owns the place; backers include Francis Ford Coppola, Robert De

Niro and Robin Williams; the sommelier is Larry Stone, the grand kahuna of American wine specialists. Despite the high-powered talent, some people still grumble that Rubicon should be more consistent, especially for the money you're spending. At lunch, dealmakers gather for the two-course fixed-price lunch for $19.98 (a good choice for bargain-hunters, too). At dinner, the chef's tasting menu is the best way to take measure of the place ($59; $79 with wine). Everyone at your table must take part, but it's a great opportunity to learn what Stone will match with each course (and don't be surprised if Coppola's own Rubicon label is among the varietal picks). Newman's menu might include a delicate salmon carpaccio with cucumbers and mint vinaigrette; a crisp crabcake with fennel-and-apple salad; perfect duck confit alongside apple-smoked bacon hash, and roasted lamb accompanied by artichokes, tomato confit and niçoise olives.

À la carte prices are among the city's most expensive, so you might as well splurge: try house-cured salmon with warm fennel and onion tart to start, or herb gnocchi with lobster and basil. Entrées include grilled quail with cabbage and bacon and seared tuna with a ragoût of root vegetables and gremolata. Desserts are worth the wait-the tempting "Cardinal Sin" layers chocolate genoise, peanut butter mousse and peanut pralines. Profiteroles, "liquid center" chocolate cake, and almond crème brûlée will also have you repenting at the gym.

Rumpus

AMERICAN 14/20

1 TILLMAN PLACE
UNION SQUARE 94108
415-421-2300
Lunch Mon.-Sat., Dinner daily, $$

An upscale hideaway tucked into a small Union Square alley, Rumpus is a favorite among those who like full-flavored foods and hard-to-find wines. A lively feeling pervades the space, perhaps due to the long bar, which is ideal for an afternoon of hanging out while sampling a few wines by the glass. The menu features unusual items: a starter of Hudson Valley foie gras with caramelized mango, ginger and polenta or a New Zealand venison carpaccio with red onions and capers. Main dishes include grilled calf's liver with sweet potato mash and applewood-smoked bacon. More standard fare features a splendid risotto with assorted wild mushrooms or a delicious moussaka with béchamel. Desserts range from rice pudding to crème brûlée and include a nightly sorbet. Every summer Rumpus hosts a rosé wine festival with special dishes paired to serve with dry rosés from around the world.

Sam's Grill

SEAFOOD/AMERICAN 12/20

374 BUSH ST.
FINANCIAL DISTRICT 94104
415-421-0594
Lunch Mon.-Fri., Dinner nightly, $

With a history that starts in 1867, Sam's is old-time San Francisco. From the brick exterior to the neon sign to the vintage cash register on the bar, the eatery is imbued with a sort of crusty charm that only a sentimentalist could love. The food is seconded by the décor-the wooden booths make Sam's a good pick if you actually want to hear what your companions are saying-and the monosyllabic waiters will remind you of Walter Matthau. And despite the history seeping from Sam's creaky frame, it's the scotch-drinking lunch crowd from the financial district who keeps this place afloat, not the tourists. Fish is the main item here; stick to grilled or sautéed basics and you won't be disappointed.

Scala's Bistro

ITALIAN 13/20

432 POWELL ST.
UNION SQUARE 94102
415-395-8555
Lunch & Dinner daily, $$

Warm and welcoming, clubby and comfortable-countless exemplary adjectives describe Scala's, a perfect Union Square refuge. At lunch, the place fills with suits, shoppers and tourists who want a break from the hustle and bustle outside. And who couldn't relax in this brasserie-style restaurant, with its sepia- toned décor, glowing brass and polished wood? At dinner, the theater crowd and office dwellers meet at the bar for drinks and a view of the cable cars rumbling down Powell Street. Located beside the Sir Francis Drake Hotel, Scala's feels like a San Francisco institution even though it opened in 1994. The all-day Italian menu addresses most appetites with a choice of antipasti, salads, pizzas, pastas and meaty secondi. House favorites are the grilled pear salad with cabbage and topped with Maytag blue cheese, caramelized walnuts and bacon; for entrées, it's a perfectly seared salmon filet with buttermilk mashed potatoes. Pastas include ricotta and pesto ravioli with a lemon-cream sauce and linguine and clams with an oven-roasted tomato and white wine sauce. Scala's signature dessert, Bostini cream pie, combines vanilla custard and chocolate-glazed orange chiffon cake-definitely worth a try if you have room. Scala's is also a good place for parents who want a decent meal but must accommodate picky eaters-the Niman-Schell burger suits teens and kids. Lineups are frequent at peak hours, so be sure to make reservations. With full meals offered until midnight, the place never really slows down.

Shalimar

INDIAN ¢
532 JONES ST.
TENDERLOIN 94102
415-928-0333
Lunch & Dinner daily
No cards

Though it's located on one of the trashiest blocks in the city, Shalimar works daily miracles by turning out excellent, affordable Northern Indian and Pakistani dishes in a barren dining room. Try murg boti tandoori (marinated roast chicken) or tandoori lamb chops. Vegetarian selections and stuffed breads are both excellent and inexpensive. Bring your own beverages, and don't be alarmed by the clientele-they too know a great deal when they see one.

The Slanted Door

VIETNAMESE 15/20
584 VALENCIA ST.
MISSION 94110
415-861-8032
Lunch & Dinner Tues.-Sun., $$

Plan ahead for a visit to The Slanted Door, which remains one of the hottest restaurants in town. Décor is sleek and upscale; food is superb. Chef Charles Phan has attracted national attention by elevating Vietnamese street food to new heights, and his house specialties include clay-pot catfish, lamb chops with tamarind, chicken sautéed in caramel sauce and ginger, grilled lemon grass rack of lamb or a steamed filet of sea bass with shiitake mushrooms and fresh ginger. At another visit, try spicy squid with tofu, bamboo shoots and basil, curry vegetables, eggplant with green onions in spicy coconut sauce-one could return again and again. Choose from an outstanding dessert list that includes warm chocolate-caramel bread pudding with fresh cream and a zingy toasted hazelnut-pear tart topped with vanilla ice cream. The wines are thoughtfully chosen to pair well with the dishes; there is also a list of teas.

The Slow Club

MEDITERRANEAN/
ECLECTIC 12/20
2501 MARIPOSA ST.
POTRERO HILL 94103
415-241-9390
Lunch Mon.-Fri., Dinner Tues.-Sat., $$

This post-industrial clubhouse is a local favorite. A changing Mediterranean-based menu works the basics and throws in some surprises: a recent dinner featured excellent seared albacore tuna over a bed of lentils, leeks and mushrooms. Tuesday nights are devoted to tapas, though favorites can be found through the week on the antipasto plate, which might include minted chiogga beets, brusque feta or gorgeous balsamic-glazed onions. The small bar is attractive and chic; its thoughtful selections include locally made Old Potrero rye. Unfortunately, the restaurant's own intimacy works against it: tables are hard to come by, and the noise level in the paneled room is intense.

South Park Café

CALIFORNIA/FRENCH 12/20
108 SOUTH PARK AVE.
SOMA 94107
415-495-7275
Breakfast & Lunch Mon.-Fri., Dinner Mon.-Sat., $$

South Park Café can be claustrophobic at lunchtime, but if you can get a table, it's worth the crush. Cuisine here tempers the rich flavors of lusty country French cookery with the light touch of California. At lunch start with pistou, a classic Provençal vegetable-and-white bean soup; or try a frisée salad-chicory with chicken livers and a bacon vinaigrette. The lunch menu also offers a croque monsieur or a grilled chicken sandwich with roasted tomatoes, cabbage and curry mayonnaise. In addition, mussels steamed with white wine and cream are superb, as is boudin noir with sautéed apples and potato purée. At dinner, start with a lovely mussel soup with leeks and saffron or a cured duck salad with carrot, celery root and shallot confit. Move on to roast duck breast with green peppercorn sauce and cabbage braised with bacon or a classic roast leg of lamb with rosemary sauce and garlic potato purée; superb. The lemon tarte is a perfect finish to either lunch or dinner. An excellent wine list is augmented with chalkboard additions of wines by the glass. This is a great place to linger in the afternoon over a glass of fino sherry and watch the action in South Park.

Stars

CALIFORNIAN 15/20

555 GOLDEN GATE ST.
CIVIC CENTER 94102
415-861-7827
Lunch Mon.-Fri., Dinner nightly, $$$$

Until recently, Stars was resting on its laurels, not seeming to care that it was being eclipsed by other sexy young starlets. (In fact, the opulent Stars in Palo Alto fell off the marquee altogether and is now home to Wolfgang Puck's newest Spago.) But in 1997, with a new chef and renewed vigor, Stars began to shine again. With its fresh flowers, creamy walls and soft lighting, the dining room remains the archetypal San Francisco restaurant, and most nights the place is jammed. Chef Jeremiah Tower still has a hand in the menu, although he's often jetting about developing the next JT production. Signature appetizers include "Jeremiah's oyster cocktail shooters" (oysters with a cilantro gremolata) and crab cakes with cilantro salad and chipotle-avocado salsa. More substantial appetizers include roasted duck broth and Sonoma foie gras, and smoked sea bass with prawn rémoulade, lentils and jerusalem artichokes. Entrées are a seafood-rich bouillabaisse-clams, mussels, lobster, scallops and prawns with aïoli croutons-and mesquite-grilled Colorado rack of lamb with a chanterelle mushroom sauce, horseradish potato gratin and grilled green pearl onions. Tempting desserts include a Meyer lemon tart with a raspberry sorbet and a Valrhona chocolate soufflé with an espresso crème anglaise. Entrée prices nudge $30; bring your plastic. Located across the back of the lush, well-appointed dining room, Stars' legendary bar remains the crossroads of the city's elite, where city hall dealmakers rub shoulders with Silicon Valley CEOs, wealthy Democrats and fans of opera.

Storyville

CAJUN/CREOLE 11/20

1751 FULTON ST.
HAIGHT-ASHBURY 94117
415-441-1751
Dinner Tues.-Sun., $$

Though San Francisco nourishes a proud history of jazz appreciation, there's a scarcity of venues in which to see first-class acts and eat more than a burger and fries. Storyville fills the void in baroque-, crimson- and black-swathed style. Guests lounge before a roaring electric fireplace to enjoy the music and chef "Gator" Thompson's fiery New Orleans cuisine. Nouveau classics such as blackened catfish with fried corn and peppers receive admirable treatment, and the chef doesn't skimp on his namesake: you can sample alligator prepared several ways-in jambalaya, for instance, over bayou-style rice. Be forewarned: The food is somewhat rich and heartily spiced with cayenne. But what else would you eat when listening to sizzling jazz? There's a cover charge for shows in the capacious back room, and a two-drink minimum for the cozier front room.

Suppenkuche

GERMAN 12/20

525 LAGUNA ST.
HAYES VALLEY 94102
415-252-9289
Dinner nightly, Brunch Sat.-Sun., $$

Suppenkuche, offers light nouveau German cuisine and more than a dozen

German beers. The spare décor-pine tables, benches and communal seating-makes sense once you realize Suppenkuche means "soup kitchen"; the food, however, is a several notches above charitable handouts. Breads are chewy and flavorful in good German tradition; potato soup is warm and rich; and appetizers include many vegetarian selections. Golden potato pancakes with homemade applesauce and house-cured gravlax in a mustard and dill sauce make unusual starters. Entrées include venison medallions in a sweet-tart red wine-plum sauce and served with spätzle, a tender noodle dumpling. German traditionalists will appreciate the wiener schnitzel and grilled bratwurst with a grainy hot mustard and homemade sauerkraut. With all the beers on tap, it's no surprise that Suppenkuche doubles as a noisy bar, but good service keeps everything running smoothly.

Sushi Groove

JAPANESE/SUSHI 13/20

1916 HYDE ST.
RUSSIAN HILL 94109
415-440-1905
Dinner daily, $$

Don't be put off by the Western-sounding name: this newcomer on the Hyde Street strip serves the real deal. Quality fish is paired with a level of artistry not often found at mid-price sushi joints. Place it all in a smartly designed, diminutive dining room beset with Japanese artifacts, and you've got quite a happening little eatery. As it is, the restaurant is often full to capacity, and navigating between the tiny tables will take a great deal of poise. Fortunately for the proprietors, the crowd tends toward the sleek Russian/Nob Hill set, so grace and good grooming are a given. Dig into any of the nightly specials, which might include a refreshing octopus, bonito and cucumber salad or tofu skin-wrapped salmon and scallions. Nigiri (finger-shaped single pieces of fish) are superb: ask for the prized toro (tuna belly) if it's available. A thoughtful selection of sakés and Japanese beers whets your wasabi-scorched palate. Sushi Groove isn't exactly a bargain, but if you're looking for superb, beautifully presented fish away from the Japantown crush, you can't go wrong here.

Swan Oyster Depot

SEAFOOD 12/20

1517 POLK ST.
POLK GULCH 94109
415-673-1101
Lunch & Dinner Mon.-Sat., $$
No cards

The Swan Oyster Depot is a true San Francisco landmark; it's been selling and serving fresh, frill-free seafood since 1912. Behind the well-worn marble counter, convivial employees shuck impeccably fresh oysters to order. Steamed crab, shrimps, and lobster are also offered, but not much in the way of prepared foods. A couple of draft beers including San Francisco's own Anchor Steam complete the dining experience. You may have to wait for one of the few precarious wooden stools, but the place is so nondescript from the outside most tourists seem to miss it entirely. It's difficult to imagine a nicer way to while away the afternoon than at Swan, a cold beer in one hand, and an oyster fork in the other.

Tadich Grill

SEAFOOD/AMERICAN 12/20

240 CALIFORNIA ST.
FINANCIAL DISTRICT 94111
415-391-1849
Lunch & Dinner Mon.-Sat., $

Behind the huge plate window is a warmly lit room full of the clatter and bang of an old-time fish house. Tadich doesn't take reservations, so you'll probably end up at the long polished bar while you wait for a table. No matter; watching the white-jacketed bartender pour martinis and scotches will be as entertaining as whatever you've got planned for the rest of the evening. At lunch, Financial District folks dine here, while dinner is a hodgepodge of tourists and regulars. The menu is locked in a time warp; prawn cocktail and shrimp Louie are devoid of irony and often garnished with iceberg lettuce. Fish cooked most any way is delicious: try to avoid anything too creative. Petrale sole, snapper or salmon won't disappoint, although the basic potatoes and tartar sauce lack zing. Tadich has been around since 1849 and some of the waiters look, the old joke goes, as if....

Taiwan

CHINESE ¢
445 CLEMENT ST.
RICHMOND 94118
415-387-1789
Lunch & Dinner daily

This small space is always crowded, and for good reason. Their dumplings, pot stickers and noodles are super, soups are delicious-try the pork tripe-and the stir fries are worth coming for every day. For a full meal, try crispy chicken in a rich brown sauce with a side of dry-fried long beans.

Taqueria Cancun

MEXICAN/CENTRAL AMERICAN ¢
2288 MISSION ST.
MISSION 94110
415-252-9560
Lunch & Dinner daily
No cards

The little shop, festooned with colorful banners and blasting mariachi music, is often crowded, but one bite of any of their benchmark comidas will explain why. Carne asada is a standout, as is pork marinated al pastor. For the more adventurous, beef tongue, head and brains are available as fillings; most will be satisfied by spicy chorizo or grilled chicken. The vegetarian burrito is also consistent: slabs of creamy avocado play off fresh tomato salsa to create a winner. Horchata, a cinnamon-laced rice beverage, is the perfect antidote to an overdose of jalapeños.

Taqueria San Jose

MEXICAN ¢
2830 MISSION ST.
MISSION 94110
415-282-0203
Lunch & Dinner daily
No cards

Fill up on some of the heftiest burritos in captivity, fashioned around grilled beef, chicken, greasy and indulgent barbecued pork al pastor, carnitas and the more exotic lengua (tongue) and cabeza (brain). The high-ceilinged space has no ambience: you might want to tote your foil-wrapped meal elsewhere.

Thanh Long

VIETNAMESE 13/20
4101 JUDAH ST.
THE AVENUES 94122
415-665-1146, *$$*

The predecessor of the venerable Crustacean, and still going strong after 27 years, San Francisco's first Vietnamese restaurant in the Avenues was remodeled recently in a welcoming bamboo-garden style. The whole roasted Dungeness crab and garlic noodles, from the An family's "secret" (literally) kitchen, are alone worth a visit.

Thanya & Salee

THAI 12/20
1469 18TH ST.
POTRERO HILL 94107
415-647-6469
Lunch Mon.-Fri., Dinner nightly, $$

While waiting for a table at this tiny, plant-filled neighborhood eatery, have a drink at the adjoining Li-Lo Lounge, a dimly lit tiki bar. Once seated, you'll find a sheet of specials to consider: salmon larb-grilled salmon with roasted Thai chilies, lime leaves and cilantro-or roast duck with mint, lime, cilantro, green onions and chilies served in a pineapple "boat." Soups are particularly flavorful; tom kha gai or hot and sour coconut has countless flavors melded together-chicken, galangal, lemongrass, lime and chilies. Spring rolls are crispy and stuffed with shrimps, pork and rice and served with a cool cucumber salad. Thanya and Salee also offers the ultimate luxury: street parking that doesn't require hours of circling.

Thep Phanom

THAI 13/20
400 WALLER ST.
HAIGHT-ASHBURY 94117
415-431-2526
Dinner nightly, $$

It's rare to find a Thai restaurant with Thep Phanom's low-key elegance and genuine charm; perhaps this lessens the surprise that this cozy little dining room serves some of the nation's best Thai food. The delicacy of the treatments-from the crisp and light tod mun plah (fried fish cakes) to startlingly complex sam kasatr (beef, chicken and pork with bamboo shoots, basil and lemon leaves)-are more evocative of French than Thai cuisine, though dishes can smolder with authentic heat. Naree gun-saeng earns its moniker "the crying lady": in this incarnation, crisp-fried prawns are cloaked in "Chef's new spicy sauce" and fresh basil. Though the menu is extensive, be sure to check the specials boards for more enticing dishes. Another of the restaurant's surprises is an extensive wine list, heavy on older French bottlings. Though Cabernet with phad Thai might seem odd, at least you have the option of enjoying first-class wines with your dinner. Thep Phanom is no secret: make reservations, or be prepared to wait a very long time for a table.

Thirsty Bear

SPANISH 12/20

661 HOWARD ST.
SOMA 94103
415-974-0905
Lunch Mon.-Sat., Dinner nightly, $$

This zesty brewpub with a Spanish accent has proved a huge success, opening recently in the restaurant-lean region near SFMOMA. The crowd is young, excited and noisy. Like the two floors that comprise its dining room, Thirsty Bear's food has its ups and downs, with the paella mostly down but some of the house specials (grilled fennel with sausage or grilled shrimps sautéed with garlic and chili flakes) proving quite tasty. Fish cheeks came highly recommended, and proved a delicious accompaniment to two different house-brewed beers. Service is cheerful and prompt; pool tables are upstairs and tapas are served all day long.

Ti Couz

FRENCH 13/20

3108 16TH ST.
MISSION 94110
415-252-7373
Lunch & Dinner daily

Its name means "old house" in Gaelic, and Ti Couz, a stuccoed storefront with rows of tightly-spaced tables in one room, and a long bar with seating in the other, serves one thing-traditional, earthy buckwheat crêpes ("krampouz") of Brittany. Choosing from a menu that meanders between Gaelic and French in its description of the sweet and savory dishes, patrons order crêpes individually so that they arrive hot and fresh at the table. Uncomplicated fillings such as tomato and basil or cheese and slivered almonds result in wonderful dishes. The best crêpes here are the simplest, like one spread only with butter and sprinkled with sugar. Onion soup makes a good starter; a mighty seafood salad is a bargain, easily split between two diners. Dessert crêpes are exceptional: the "Sylvette" is filled with apple slices sautéed in Calvados and served with vanilla ice cream. Wines include reasonably priced French classics as well as a low-alcohol French cider, served in terra-cotta bowls, that perfectly complements Ti Couz's food. Perhaps it's the care that chef-owner Sylvie Le Mer takes with each order or the good spirits of the quick and dependable wait staff that make this place feel like a favorite from the first visit.

Timo's

SPANISH 12/20

842 VALENCIA ST.
MISSION 94110
415-647-0558
Dinner nightly, $$

Carlos Corredor has a solid background in Spanish and Latin American cooking, having worked one of the Bay Area's pioneer Spanish restaurants, El Greco in Marin County. At Timo's Corredor's skills stand out on dishes like Catalán-style rabbit in red wine and herbs, duck confit cassoulet and gambas a la plancha-whole prawns grilled in the shell with a picada of garlic and parsley. His spicy pork tenderloin with romesco sauce is delicious, and marinated calamari, served at room temperature, are a real treat. The décor isn't fabulous, but don't let the restaurant's outdated Beat-era artwork keep you from sampling the tortilla española, a potato-onion frittata that remains Spain's best known tapa.

Tommaso's

ITALIAN 13/20
1042 Kearny St.
North Beach 94133
415-398-9696
Dinner Tues.-Sun., $$

Stepping into Tommaso's is like entering the set of a vintage Francis Ford Coppola movie: Everything about this North Beach pizza haven makes time stand still. To start, ask for marinated roasted peppers, glistening string beans, or whatever vegetables are in season-never have vegetables tasted brighter. Order a bowl of vinegar-accented steamed coo-coo clams for the table. Then get serious: chewy, thin-crust pizzas and rich calzones from the wood-fired oven are what Tommaso's is all about, perfectly sauced and anointed with fennel-flecked sausage and other impeccable toppings. A light house red wine is served in ceramic pitchers and seems to go with everything. This popular place doesn't take reservations.

Tommy Toy's Haute Cuisine Chinoise

CHINESE 12/20
655 Montgomery St.
North Beach 94111
415-397-4888
Lunch Mon.-Fri., Dinner nightly, $$$$

Tommy Toy's models itself after the city's top-end French restaurants, offering a prix-fixe menu of elaborately-prepared dishes served in a dining room full of Chinese antiques and lacquered furniture. The prix-fixe menu at $49.50 assembles seven dishes, seemingly dreamed up by a French chef trapped in a Chinese restaurant kitchen. It starts with classic minced squab and follows with a seafood bisque served in a fresh coconut and topped with a puffed-pastry hat. Shelled Maine lobster, sautéed with pine nuts, mushrooms and a peppercorn sauce, precedes the Peking duck; then on to medallions of beef in a garlic, wine and rosemary sauce. Dessert is a peach mousse in a strawberry compote. Seafood and fish star on the à la carte menu, and appetizers include such favorites as pot stickers and barbecued baby-back ribs with a sweet passion fruit sauce. Altogether, Tommy Toy's is a fun place that should make you feel like Mandarin royalty at least once in your life.

Tommy's

MEXICAN ¢
5929 Geary Blvd.
Richmond District 94121
415-387 4747
Lunch & Dinner daily

Tommy's family is from the Yucatán, a part of Mexico known for delightful regional foods. While there's nothing wrong with this restaurant's basic menu-the usual selections of beans and rice, tacos and burritos-ask for Yucatán specials. In addition, be sure to order a margarita: for the price, theirs is the best in San Francisco.

Ton Kiang

CHINESE 12/20
3148 Geary Blvd.
Richmond District 94118
415-752-4440
Lunch & Dinner daily, $

Ton Kiang is one the city's top practitioners of Hakka, or "guest" cuisine, a conglomeration of Chinese regional styles accrued by gypsy clans fleeing the Mongol invasions some 1500 years ago. The result is a complex, pungent, and earthy style. Though the gaudy gold wallpaper and formally attired staff may hearken back to an earlier decade, the cooking is fresh, lively, and reliably delicious. The emphasis is on fresh seafood prepared to order: local species of rock cod and steelhead trout (some of them alive just moments earlier in the tanks at the back of the room) can be prepared in a number of styles, though paired with scallion and ginger is a favorite; house chicken is superb. Vegetables receive admirable treatment here too: dry-fried string beans, asparagus and sugar pea tips are strongly recommended. A second branch is located is at 5821 Geary.

Trattoria Contadina

ITALIAN 13/20
1800 Mason St.
North Beach 94133
415-982-5728
Dinner nightly, $$

Chef Salvatore Parra makes his home at this Italian family eatery, infusing both the tried-and-true and more-adventurous offerings with a practiced, elegant touch. The restaurant itself is a comfortable wood-paneled refuge from the madness of Columbus Avenue below; genuinely gracious service and large portions will further soothe the ruffled traveler. On the "must-try" list is fettuccine alla Salvatore: imported noodles, smoked chicken, Mascarpone, peas and sun-dried tomatoes swim in a rosemary and garlic-spiked chicken broth. Vitello Correnti pairs scaloppine of veal with a seductively rich porcini and cream sauce. Desserts can stray from typical Italian bittersweet models to outright richness.The restaurant delivers solid North Beach Italian cuisine without crowding or attitude.

Truly Mediterranean

MIDDLE EASTERN ¢
3109 16TH ST.
MISSION 94103
415-252-7482
Lunch & Dinner daily

No cards

It's hard to go wrong in this bargain-priced falafel joint. Falafel sandwiches-with or without pungent feta, fried eggplant or potatoes-are cheap, quick, and hot, while the rotating cone of roasting shwarma has been known to convert more than a few vegetarians. The carrot juice is renowned, though the salty garlic/mint/yogurt drink makes an unusual and refreshing substitute. Service is unfailingly friendly and quick.

Tu Lan

VIETNAMESE ¢
8 SIXTH ST.
SOMA 94103
415-626-0927
Lunch & Dinner Mon.- Sat.

No cards

Consistently fresh, inspired and delicious, Tu Lan's food-seemingly bottomless bowls of beefy noodle soup, richly herbal stir-fries and braises and sparkling salads and spring rolls-are the essence of culinary economy. $8.95 buys asparagus and crab soup, shrimp salad, fried fish with ginger sauce and prawns with bamboo shoots and mushrooms. Don't forget Vietnamese iced coffee for dessert-a perfect pick-me-up after a sublime meal.

2223 Market

CALIFORNIAN 13/20
2223 MARKET ST.
CASTRO 94114
415-431-0692
Dinner nightly, Brunch Sat. -Sun., $$

VISA MasterCard

Among the Castro's ever-changing array of mediocre, trend-loving restaurants-please, no more yuppie taquerias, wheat-grass joints or noodle houses-you'll find relief at 2223 Market. The food is just one of the attractions here. Others include the daily happy hour(s) at the bar and the light and airy décor that lets diners to see and be seen. Chef Wesley Saunders replaced chef Melinda Randolph in late '97; Saunders' résumé includes stints at LuLu Bis and the now-defunct Miss Pearl's Jam House. Open for dinner and weekend brunch, 2223 Market shows off American bistro faves such as crisp-skinned roast chicken with garlic mashed potatoes and onion rings and a thick, smoked pork chop with a root vegetable purée. For more West Coast flavors, diners can make a meal of the well-priced appetizers of Dungeness crab tempura or house-smoked salmon with red and gold caviar and potato chive pancakes, followed by one of the pizzas. While waiting for your table, join the fashionable throng at the bar to sip one of 2223's inventive house cocktails.

Universal Café

AMERICAN 13/20
2814 19TH ST.
MISSION 94110
415-821-4608
Breakfast, Lunch & Dinner Tues.-Sun., Brunch Sat.-Sun., $$

VISA MasterCard

Lunch or Dinner at the tiny Universal is like eating in a hip and attractive art gallery with an industrial accent. It's a fun and joyful place to eat, but regulars would go for the food even if it were served in a garage. At lunch the restaurant features a changing daily list of chalkboard specials, in addition to a regular menu of pizzas and focaccia sandwiches. Chef Julia McClaskey stretches a bit more at dinner, offering an eclectic selection including, on one visit, a fresh egg fettuccine entrée with asparagus, roasted garlic, Meyer lemon, black olives and Reggiano cheese. Her oven-roasted pork chops with polenta are outstanding, as is a warm duck confit. A morning latte taken al fresco on the Universal's sunny sidewalk patio tastes doubly good.

Val 21

AMERICAN 12/20
995 VALENCIA ST.
MISSION 94110
415-821-6622
Dinner nightly, Brunch Sat.-Sun., $$

Located in the Mission District at the corner of Valencia and 21st streets, Val 21 remains one of the best cafés in the neighborhood. To start, try the uncommonly good butternut-squash-and-sage tamales with a chipotle salad or hangtown oysters served with a green bean horseradish and a bloody mary vinaigrette. Main courses might include grilled salmon on a coconut-red curry sauce and grilled pork chop with mashed potatoes. The braised lamb shank with saffron lima beans also is outstanding. The Sunday brunch is a standout, the house specialty being Mission scramble-eggs scrambled with green onions, blue corn tortilla bits and melted jack cheese, all topped with sour cream.

Valentine's Café

VEGETARIAN 12/20
1793 CHURCH ST.
NOE VALLEY 94131
415-285-2257
Dinner Wed.-Mon., Brunch Sat.-Sun., $$

Though this is San Francisco, good vegetarian restaurants aren't all that easy to find. Valentine's does a fairly good job of it, though what it lacks in subtlety it makes up for in warmth and earnestness. The little restaurant doesn't accept reservations; once inside, be charmed by the softly lit and homey dining room. The menu features a number of vegan (dairy-less) options, and their overall use of fresh, seasonal produce is innovative and satisfying. Try scaloppini of portobello with a lemon "butter" (actually a canola oil roux), or mushroom korma with dahl, basmati rice and a Bengal tomato-fruit chutney. A list of inexpensive wines pairs nicely with the menu, bringing a little elegance to the world of meatless cuisine.

Veecha Thai Cuisine

THAI ¢
500 HAIGHT ST.
HAIGHT-ASHBURY 94117
415-861-2550
Dinner nightly

Almost half the menu at this plain-Jane Thai house is devoted to vegetarian selections. An excellent tour kact-a melange of string beans, roasted coconut, cashews and fried onion in a spicy, lemony sauce-relies on inventive interpretations of fresh vegetables. But try Veecha's version of pla muk crob-crisp fried squid in a spicy chili sauce with fried basil leaves, or the classic roast duck in red curry, which receives a delicious accompaniment of spinach, basil and pineapple. Wholesome food; bargain prices.

Vertigo

CALIFORNIAN 13/20
600 MONTGOMERY ST.
FINANCIAL DISTRICT 94111
415-433-7250
Lunch Mon.-Fri., Dinner Mon.-Sat., $$$

Vertigo is nestled at the bottom of the Transamerica Pyramid, a landmark as distinctive to the city as Coit Tower. Looking up from the dining room through the skylights might make you dizzy, but Vertigo's menu is grounded in California conventions: seasonal produce, international influences and several flavors on each plate. Chef Derek Burns took over the kitchen in 1997 after chef Jeff Inahara moved on to new projects; Burns pared down Inahara's Asian and French influenced creations and added a new emphasis on San Francisco's favorite dishes, a move that's sure to please the suits who frequent the place. Appetizers include a moist duck confit salad with winter greens and a citrus vinaigrette, and veal sweetbreads, cooked until crisp and served with a puff pastry filled with a wild mushroom ragoût. Enticing main courses range between osso buco on brown butter and sage polenta and seared day boat scallops with a gingery parsnip sauce. Vertigo has a distinctly corporate feel that isn't leavened by its vast size and multiple dining levels. For business folks doing deals, this place impresses, but if you want intimacy, seek it elsewhere.

Vicolo Pizzeria

PIZZA ¢
201 Ivy St.
Civic Center 94102
415-863-2382
Lunch Mon.-Sat., Dinner nightly

The fresh ingredients and crisp cornmeal crusts served at this high, square, industrial-styled alleyway eatery add up to one of San Francisco's best pizzas. Available whole or in slices, a typical pie comes topped with zucchini, red onion, sun-dried tomatoes and basil. A Greek model might include olives, feta, peppers and rosemary. More traditional standards are available, as are great salads. Counter service is informal and friendly.

Vietnam 2

VIETNAMESE 12/20
701 Larkin St.
Tenderloin 94109
415-885-1274
Lunch & Dinner daily, $
No cards

A huge sprawling restaurant that may intimidate the fastidious, Vietnam 2 specializes in seafood. Spicy squid and shrimp dishes, whole, roasted fish, various clever uses for clams-it just keeps coming from the (comparatively) spotless kitchen. Pack your own wine, put yourself in the hands of the waiter, tell him anything you positively don't like, and relax. Once you taste Vietnam 2's cooking, your worries will melt away.

Vineria

ITALIAN 13/20
3228 16th St.
Mission 94110
415-552-3889
Dinner Wed.-Sun., $$

This sleek trattoria has made quite a splash since its opening in 1997; its success is due in large part to dishes taken from its parent restaurant, L'Osteria del Forno. Both serve simple, refined pan-Italian fare, but Vineria updates (and enlarges) the tiny North Beach eatery's home-style digs. Almost everything is excellent, from antipasti and salads, to delicious, elegant pastas and crisp pizzas; portions, in the Italian style, can be somewhat underwhelming. Be sure to try insalata rustica, a heady salad of tuna, white beans, celery and oregano that begs to be mopped off the plate with crusty slices of focaccia. Grilled whole sea bass surrounded by a bed of fresh herbs is sure to arouse your neighbors' envy, and skewered lamb (marinated in ginger, rosemary and garlic) is as delicious as it is simple. The Italianate wine list is brief but purposeful, with many selections available by the glass. Unfortunately, a place this good is no secret; the ochre-hued room is usually full and quite noisy. Residents have little to complain about now that a first-class neighborhood Italian restaurant can call the Mission its home.

Vinga

CATALAN 12/20
320 3RD ST.
SoMa 94107
415-546-3131
Lunch Mon.-Fri., Dinner Mon.-Sat., $$

Chef Antonio Buendia is from a small town near Barcelona, where he learned the basic skills of Catalan cooking. Locally he was chef de cuisine at Café Tango in San Rafael and managed the kitchen at Stars restaurant. Vinga, which means "come here" in Catalán, offers a daily prix-fixe lunch menu that features fresh garlic soup and a potato omelet. For main courses, try the vegetarian noodle paella or grilled sausage with white beans. The dinner menu offers four paellas as well as grilled rabbit with aïoli and a filet of salt cod with garlic and tomato sauce. A "pica pica" menu offers what would be called tapas in Spain. While its food is terrific, Vinga isn't perfect: the wine list is short and could do with more traditional Spanish wines, and little has been done to make the restaurant's interior attractive. Dim lighting and pedestrian ambience lend Vinga the air of a Midwest hotel diner that has seen better days.

Vivande

ITALIAN 14/20
670 Golden Gate Avenue
Civic Center 94122
415-673-9245
Lunch & Dinner daily, $$

Carlo Middione's little Vivande Porta Via on Fillmore is still humming along, but his recently opened Opera Plaza restaurant is a magnificent space, a large, open-kitchened room that's elegant for a pre-theater or opera dinner (and a great place to get a late supper until midnight). One of the best dishes is panino del oro-focaccia with grilled radicchio, eggplant and fennel, served with wood-oven roasted cherry tomatoes and blue lake green beans. Try the cannelloni ripieni di pesce, pasta rolled around chunky pieces of poached rock fish. You can't go wrong with any of the pastas. Vivande's wine list is rather special, filled as it is with rare Italian wines, many of which available by the glass.

Washington Square Bar & Grill

AMERICAN 12/20
1707 POWELL ST.
NORTH BEACH 94133
415-982-8123
Lunch & Dinner daily, Brunch Sat.-Sun., $$

People sometimes forget this legendary hangout (a big, curtained room with stodgy, early-twentieth-century décor) also has pretty good food, especially if you stick with simpler selections like a barbecue-glazed meatloaf sandwich with fries or the braised tri tip with roasted yellow finn potatoes. Pastas are reliable, and the osso buco is first-rate. Chef Timothy Au also does a spectacular job with a banana bread ice cream sundae. The Washbag, as it is called, was the original restaurant opened by the legendary Rose Pistola and has for decades been an unofficial North Beach office for visiting media and politicians. Bigwigs now split their time between The Washbag and Moose's across Washington Square.

The Waterfront Restaurant & Café

ASIAN FUSION 14/20
PIER 7 ON THE EMBARCADERO
FINANCIAL DISTRICT 94111
415-391-2696
Lunch Mon.-Fri., Dinner nightly, $$$$

Yes, it really exists: a view restaurant with great food. The Waterfront affords views of San Francisco Bay and the Bay Bridge, and its décor is contemporary, with accents of Asian antiques and culinary-themed artwork. Bruce Hill, one of the originators of fusion fare at Oritalia, has created a pan-Asian menu that offers bold and vivid flavors, with highlights including pumpkin seed-seared ahi tuna, lotus-braised monkfish with daikon, grilled filet of beef with taro gnocchi, smoked sturgeon and roasted beet terrine in a tomato gelée with osetra caviar. Try a honey-soy cured steelhead trout salad frisée with fennel and caviar. The spectacular dessert menu sparkles with a number of standout offerings, like tangerine-cheesecake tart or a chocolate midnight cake with crème chantilly. The Waterfront hosts a full bar and a good selection of wines.

Yabbies

SEAFOOD/CALIFORNIAN 13/20
2237 POLK ST
RUSSIAN HILL 94109
415-474-4088
Dinner nightly, $$$

Yabbies are crayfish in Australian argot, and you'll find lots of them at this sleek Polk Street restaurant. Chef Mark Lusardi often adds subtle Asian flavors such as ginger, chili, Thai basil and curry to fish and seafood from both coasts. The best appetizers come from the ice bar, including six kinds of shucked oysters, peel-and-eat shrimps and cracked Dungeness crab. Less work (but less fun) are the Rhode Island chowder and Maine crab-cakes. The handful of entrées might feature shrimps and scallops with ginger, chilies and Thai basil or a moist, grilled ahi tuna seasoned with Szechuan pepper and accompanied by spicy sesame-shiitake soba noodles. Yabbies' menu suggests wines to go with each entrée, either by the bottle or the glass-perhaps an Edna Valley Pinot Noir with the wild salmon or a Cambria Viognier with the ahi. It's a wonderful way to try new labels and enhance the flavors on the palate. Desserts include a homey apple, quince and cranberry crisp with Tahitian vanilla ice cream and a roast banana-and-pecan tart with rum-raisin ice cream and hot fudge sauce. Yabbies can be noisy, so do your talking before or after dinner.

Yamo

THAI ¢

3406 18TH ST.
MISSION 94110
415-553-8911
Lunch Mon.-Sat., Dinner nightly

No cards

What Yamo lacks in adornment, it makes up for with simple, fresh versions of Thai classics such as tom yum (sweet and sour shrimp soup) and phad Thai. Meat and poultry are given forceful treatment: try gai himaparn, sliced chicken with cashews, onion, and a smoky underpinning of crisp-fried chili. Vegetarian dishes range from subtle praram pak (steamed vegetables and tofu with peanut dressing) to fiery prig khing tofu-crisp chunks of bean curd with string beans in chili paste.

Yank Sing

CHINESE/DIM SUM 15/20

427 BATTERY ST.
FINANCIAL DISTRICT 94111
415-362-1640
Lunch Mon.-Fri., Dinner Mon.-Sat., $$

VISA MasterCard

Sure, there are dim sum palaces in the Richmond District and Chinatown that pack them in all weekend, but from Monday to Friday, Yank Sing rules-and it's not even in Chinatown. Diners are seated quickly and before they can catch their breath, the dim sum trolley rolls by. Yang Sing wins fans with the more than 80 items in its repertoire, from pristine shrimp dumplings to savory barbecued pork buns to crunchy braised chicken feet. Moist slices of golden Peking duck are served from one trolley: sandwich the meat between steamed buns and use the scallion brushes to dab on some hoisin sauce. Office workers from the surrounding Financial District keep this place busy, so avoid peak lunch hours if you're lacking a reservation. Tea is the drink of choice, but a cold Tsingtao does nicely. The restaurant itself, a seemingly endless maze of rooms, is a notch above much of the Chinatown competition thanks to white tablecloths and helpful service. Don't bother phoning unless you plan to leave your reservation on their machine.

Yuet Lee

CHINESE 12/20

1300 STOCKTON ST.
CHINATOWN 94133
415-982-6020
Lunch Wed.-Mon., Dinner Wed.-Sun., $

No cards

The fluorescent surroundings are decidedly unglamorous, but looks have no bearing on the famous pepper-and-salt roast squid, steamed fresh crab or deep-fried oysters that emerge from Yuet Lee's kitchen. The crowds keep coming until 3 a.m. for some of the cleanest tasting Hong Kong-style seafood to be found. Maine lobster and Dungeness crab, two of Yuet Lee's best dishes, are netted from a tank and quickly stir-fried with black beans and chilies or with ginger. Vegetable dishes, particularly a water spinach called "long green" cooked with a dry shrimp sauce, are good bets, too. Try decent, sweetish Peking spareribs. No beer or wine is served, though both can be brought in. At the newer branch in Noe Valley (3601 26th St., 415-550-8998), closing time is at 10 or 11, but the food is even better.

Zaré

MEDITERRANEAN 15/20

568 SACRAMENTO ST.
FINANCIAL DISTRICT 94123
415-291-9145
Lunch Mon.-Fri., Dinner nightly, $$

VISA MasterCard Diners Club International

Chef-owner Hoss Zaré's Mediterranean cuisine has won raves since he opened his eponymous restaurant in the Financial District in 1997. At lunch and dinner, the warm, cave-like room fills with suits and other folks who love Zaré's satisfying dishes-braised rabbit with mushrooms and artichokes in tarragon cream sauce or grilled lamb sirloin with rosemary and red-wine-truffle oil sauce. Zaré uses bold flavors in unusual combinations: a foie gras appetizer is wrapped in salmon and matched with a port wine reduction; a napoleon of artichokes and Dungeness crab meat is melded with a spicy chive-infused oil. Half the fun is watching Zaré and his crew work at the open kitchen. Desserts include Zaré's signature dish of Champagne zabaglione and the popular chocolate soufflé with Mascarpone. The copper ceiling, stone floor and charming accented waiters add to the continental feel of this place, but with none of the stuffiness found in some Euro-style spots. Wines are mostly Californian, although a few varietals from France and Italy fill out the list.

Zarzuela

SPANISH 15/20
2000 HYDE ST.
RUSSIAN HILL 94109
415-346-0800
Dinner Tues.-Sat., $$

Zarzuela is the best of many tapas bars that have sprung up in San Francisco in the past few years, a crowded corner space overflowing with prints and travel posters. Owner-chef Lucas Casco has created what could be taken for a bustling bar in the heart of Madrid's Old Quarter, yet even there, you wouldn't find tapas much better than those at Zarzuela. Almost anything on the menu is good, but croquettes (either chicken or ham), cold grilled marinated vegetables, duck leg, poached octopus or the classic tortilla Español are favorites. The restaurant takes its name from a seafood stew that is always available. The wine list includes a number of good Spanish bottlings and a good sherry selection.

Zax

AMERICAN 14/20
2330 TAYLOR ST.
NORTH BEACH 94133
415-563-6266
Dinner Tues.-Sat., $$

In this out-of-the-way corner of North Beach, Barbara Mulas and Mark Drazek have created a very special California-Mediterranean style restaurant, one named for the character in a Dr. Seuss book. Zax's room evokes a provincial French restaurant, serene and charming; the food is frequently stunning. Special dishes include roast rabbit with artichokes and mushroom ragoût, a Niman-Schell flatiron steak with spicy onion rings and sautéed greens or a fresh fish of the day with seasonal vegetables. The wine list is inexpensive and well-suited to the food.

Zinzino

ITALIAN/PIZZA 13/20
2355 CHESTNUT ST.
MARINA 94123
415-346-6623
Dinner nightly, $

For those of us raised on cardboard pizzas, Zinzino is a revelation. The restaurant's crusts are thin and cooked at a roaring heat until they blister, giving them a satisfying crunch. A mushroom pizza is thick with wild funghi and sprinkled with ricotta and white truffle oil. Another with roasted eggplant, herbed breadcrumbs and mozzarella shows simplicity that can never be matched at home. The pizza oven turns out wonderful roast chicken and baked dishes. A few basic pastas lack appeal, especially when compared to the scintillating pizzas. Décor-wise, the deep, shadowy room features a waterfall on one end and Italian posters on the other. Service is wonderful; the open kitchen is the entertainment; and the heated back patio is one of Chestnut Street's best-kept secrets.

Zuni

MEDITERRANEAN 15/20
1658 MARKET ST.
HAYES VALLEY 94102
415-552-2522
Lunch & Dinner Tues.-Sat., $$$

Sexy, urban and oh-so-San Francisco, Zuni wears its age well. The open-air bar still attracts a well-dressed crowd of hip professionals both straight and gay, and the menu still satisfies every appetite at every hour. Chef Judy Rodgers continues to preside over the Mediterranean cuisine, preparing delectable dishes such as house-cured anchovies with celery and Parmesan. Rodgers' signature dish, chicken roasted in the brick oven until golden and served on a bread salad with currants and pine nuts, first won her recognition and it still works, as does her fragrant Caesar salad. The two levels and many rooms make this a fun place to see and be seen, so dress accordingly—you're likely to run into someone you know (or want to get to know). Attitude, both good and slightly haughty, is in the air at Zuni, from both the staff and the other diners; be ready to play along.

HOTELS

CONTENTS

IF YOU GO TO SAN FRANCISCO...

The hippie song about the "Summer of Love" crooned, "If you go to San Francisco, be sure to wear some flowers in your hair...." You might want to do the floral-tonsorial thing, but it's probably more practical to wear a cap-and a warm sweater. Every summer, tourists arrive in shorts and tank tops only to find themselves freezing in a swirl of icy fog. As Mark Twain put it: "The coldest winter I ever spent was a summer in San Francisco."

When it comes to places to stay in the City by the Bay, you're not going to find many swimming pools. What you will find, however, in San Francisco hotels is style and grace and wonderful, friendly staff. In certain Nob Hill palaces, even your toothbrush seems to be gilded, and the room in which you're staying only costs a grand a night. Elsewhere, the city is also studded with oodles of boutique hotels that ooze charm and fashion, these for more reasonable prices. We've even included some real bargains here, such as the Grant Plaza, just inside the Chinatown gate, where you can rest your head without taking out a second mortgage. The most efficient way to secure a room in the City by the Bay is to call the official booking agent approved by the San Francisco Convention & Visitors Bureau: San Francisco Reservations (888-782-9673 or 415-227-1500; fax 415-227-1520). They can also be found on-line at www.hotelres.com. Ask about special rates.

The following hotels all fall within San Francisco proper. To help you get around, in each address we've included the name of the city district—**Alamo Square, Bernal Heights, Castro, Chinatown, City South, Civic Center, Cow Hollow, Financial District, Fisherman's Wharf, Fort Mason, Haight-Ashbury, Hayes Valley, Japantown, Marina, Nob Hill, Noe Valley, North Beach, Pacific Heights, Polk Gulch, Potrero Hill, Presidio Heights, Richmond, Russian Hill, SoMa (South of Market), Sunset, Telegraph Hill, Tenderloin, Union Square, Upper Fillmore, Van Ness, Western Addition.**

TOP OF THE LINE

Campton Place Hotel

340 STOCKTON ST.
UNION SQUARE 94108
415-781-5555, 800-235-4300,
FAX 415-955-5536
Singles & Doubles $240-$360, Suites $470-$1,050

VISA MasterCard Diners Club International P

Campton Place was a hit from the beginning, as much for its acclaimed restaurant as for its supremely elegant rooms. Opened in 1983 after an $18-million renovation, Campton Place doesn't have the old San Francisco aura of some of the city's other great hotels, but the location-just off Union Square-is great, and the ambience is refined and discreet. With just 117 rooms, Campton Place is never overrun with large tour groups. The lobby, lounges, snug guest rooms and large suites are exceptionally attractive and comfortable, with a skillful mix of rich colors, antique and contemporary furnishings, plush carpets and fresh flowers. Service is emphasized: you'll enjoy intelligent concierges, prompt room service, a brigade of business and secretarial services (on request) and valet parking ($25 a day). The restaurant, also named **Campton Place** (see Dining), is as good as the hotel's formidable reputation.

The Clift Hotel

495 GEARY ST.
UNION SQUARE 94102
415-775-4700, 800-65-CLIFT,
FAX 415-441-4621
Singles & Doubles $255-$305, Suites $360-$1,260

P

Unquestionably one of the finest of San Francisco's grand old hotels, the Clift is perhaps best known for its atmospheric **Redwood Room** piano bar, magnificently appointed with polished redwood paneling and beautiful art deco light fixtures. The adjoining restaurant, **The French Room**, is an old-fashioned delight, dressed up in gleaming chandeliers and painted woodwork and serving good food. The lobby makes an appropriately dramatic statement to this venerable establishment, and most of the long-term staff serves from the heart (guests sometimes complain about the bell people). Its bathrooms feature black tiles, marble furnishings and lots of amenities. The Clift continues to woo the business traveler tired of the sterility and impersonality of the glass-tower hotels: here they'll find a full-service business center, as well as conference rooms, computer modems and fax machines. At press time, new manager, ultra-hip hotelier Ian Schrager is expected to soon update this old favorite in order to compete with today's hot hotels.

Fairmont Hotel

950 MASON ST.
NOB HILL 94108
415-772-5000, 800-527-4727,
FAX 415-772-5013
Singles & Doubles $229-$319, Suites $500-$830

A P

San Francisco socialites love the Fairmont. So do visitors. This Nob Hill legend gained even more fame after a several-year run as the St. Gregory on the TV series *Hotel*. The lobby is everything you'd expect of a grand hotel: gigantic columns and a dramatically ornate, seemingly built-for-Cinderella marble staircase. The hotel houses four restaurants, including the exotic **Tonga Room**, where you experience a tropical rainfall and a band floating across a pool (see Bars). Rooms in the old section are particularly spacious; the views from the tower wing are spectacular. The service is excellent, the old San Francisco ambience unbeatable.

Grand Hyatt

345 STOCKTON ST.
UNION SQUARE 94108
415-398-1234, 800-233-1234, FAX 415-391-1780
Singles & Doubles $260-$300, Club level $295-$335, Suites $450-$1,300

A P

The 36-story Hyatt, smack in the heart of Union Square, is Grand indeed. Each of the 693 large, smartly decorated rooms features great views, minibars, two phones with voice-mail, hair dryers and TVs in the bedroom and bathroom. Regency Club rooms on the upper floors provide additional niceties: a concierge, robes, special amenities and a lounge, which serves complimentary Continental breakfast each morning and hors d'oeuvres each afternoon. Nearly $1.5 million was spent on each of the six penthouses. The top-floor **Grandviews** restaurant and lounge (see Nightlife) appeals to several senses: panoramic vistas of downtown for the eyes and live jazz music for the ears. Hotel facilities include an award-winning concierge, health club, business center and town car service to the Financial District on weekday mornings. Valet parking costs $24 per day. Nonsmoking floors available.

The Huntington Hotel Nob Hill

1075 CALIFORNIA ST.
NOB HILL 94108
415-474-5400, 800-652-1539, FAX 415-474-6227
Singles & Doubles $210-$345, Suites $400-$935

A P

This low-key gem re-creates the experience of a stay in one of Europe's fine old hotels.

The Huntington's quiet refinement makes it one of our Nob Hill favorites, and its regulars have included such celebrities as Placido Domingo, Luciano Pavarotti and Paloma Picasso, all of whom care more about discretion and the quality of their rooms than about passing through a dramatic lobby. The Huntington's small entrance features cream-colored walls, earth-tone furnishings and burgundy accents. Designed by Charles Gruwell, the décor throughout is classic yet contemporary. Each of the 140 rooms is furnished opulently with antiques, objets d'art and original paintings; each flaunts a marble bath; each of the 38 suites has been individually designed. There's a complete range of business services as well as an excellent concierge. Personal service is emphasized here: the pleasant staff is happy and shows it. The dark, wood-paneled **Big Four Restaurant**, a handsome tribute to San Francisco's Victorian-era railroad magnates, changes menus three times a year. Parking is a very-reasonable $19.50 a day.

Hyatt Regency

5 EMBARCADERO CENTER
FINANCIAL DISTRICT 94111
415-788-1234, 800-233-1234,
FAX 415-398-2567
Singles $225-$290, Doubles $250-$315, Suites $395-$525

This waterfront giant sits at one end of the sprawling Embarcadero Center, also the easternmost terminus of the California Street cable car line. Such a location makes it popular with both visiting businesspeople and tourists. The Hyatt Regency has more than 800 rooms, plus large meeting facilities: expect to see a lot of people milling around the atrium-style lobby, the city's largest entryway which soars 17 stories overhead. The hotel has undergone a recent multimillion-dollar remodeling of all suites and rooms on the Regency Club and Business Plan floors, which focus on the needs of traveling executives. Standard rooms are spacious and tastefully furnished in a masculine, corporate fashion, with blue or burgundy color schemes and cherry-wood furnishings. Each includes a working desk, in-room coffee service and phones with data ports and voicemail. Upper rooms can have fine vistas of the North Bay. Drinking and dining establishments include the lobby-level **Eclipse Café** and **13 Views Bar**, which overlooks Justin Herman Plaza and the waterfront. Visit the newly renovated, revolving rooftop restaurant **Equinox** for a dizzying panorama on a fogless day. The daily tab for on-site parking is $25.

Mandarin Oriental

222 SANSOME ST.
FINANCIAL DISTRICT 94104
415-885-0999, 800-622-0404,
FAX 415-433-0289
Singles & Doubles $325-$520, Suites $475-$1,650

Part of the hotel group of Bangkok and Hong Kong fame, the Mandarin landed in this city with a bang in 1987. In what may be one of the oddest configurations in town, the property occupies the top 11 floors of a commercial building-the third tallest in San Francisco-smack in the heart of the Financial District. Those floors, numbered 38 through 48, place guests above most of the surrounding high-rises. The 158 lavish rooms and suites feature unobstructed views of the city and portions of San Francisco Bay (even plate-glass views from your bathtub in the Mandarin king rooms). Take the skybridge from one tower to another-it's like walking on air. A $1.8-million renovation in all rooms recently changed the Mandarin's hues to sage, crimson, gold and cream, as well as adding new artworks, fabrics and silk-covered headboards. You'll pay steep prices for the privilege of being surrounded by furnishings worthy of a Park Avenue penthouse, but for quality, service and business convenience, these accommodations are hard to beat. A fitness center is also new. Business services and the excellent **Silks** restaurant are located off the lobby. Valet parking is $25 a day.

The Palace Hotel

2 NEW MONTGOMERY ST.
FINANCIAL DISTRICT 94105
415-546-5005, 800-325-3535,
FAX 415-543-0671
Singles and Doubles $215-$285, Suites $475-$2,000

Palace truly describes this grand old dowager, which underwent a massive, three-year, $150-million renovation that was completed in 1991. Kings and presidents have slept here;

a feeling of old world luxury surrounds it. The 550 rooms (17 of which are two-bedroom suites) feature original or reproduction mahogany antiques, as well as elegant appointments in hues of cream, butter and white. Don't miss the **Pied Piper Bar/Maxfield's Restaurant** (the clubby, wood-paneled grill and bar with a wonderful, original Maxfield Parrish mural) and the Garden Court (a breathtaking room of marble columns, crystal chandeliers and rich carpeting, all beneath a remarkable leaded-glass dome). Once the hotel's carriage entrance, this latter restaurant remains a choice spot for tea, Sunday brunch or Friday night dinner-and-dancing. **Kyo-Ya** is the hotel's superb Japanese eatery. Other amenities include a health spa, sky-lit swimming pool and conference and business centers. Valet parking: $22 a day. The only complaints from guests are that service and food quality have slipped a bit in recent years.

Pan Pacific Hotel

500 POST ST.
UNION SQUARE 94102
415-771-8600, 800-327-8585, FAX 415-398-0267
Singles & Doubles $280-$370, Suites $410-$1,700

This exquisite, 21-story, 330-room property was built in 1987 by architect-developer John Portman. It is managed by Pan Pacific, the Pacific Rim hotel group whose Asian philosophy of hospitality translates into such services as assigning one valet for each room and suite. Despite its size, the Pan Pacific has an intimate atmosphere. Once you get past the first three floors of public spaces, smallish rooms echo some of the contempo-classical architectural details of the exterior, designed with lots of arches, recesses and expanses of marble. The entire property was redone in the fall of 1997, to fine effect: elegantly decorated with custom-designed furniture, the rooms have built-in storage cabinets and spacious desks. The bathrooms are nearly as large, with all-marble surfaces and a separate tub-shower arrangement. The business center is full service, and guests who must travel to meetings or the airport can hop into a BMW or Rolls-Royce. Valet parking is $20 a day. **The Pacific** restaurant (see Dining) features contemporary Californian cuisine. A fitness center is also new.

Renaissance Stanford Court Hotel

905 CALIFORNIA ST.
NOB HILL 94108
415-989-3500, 800-HOTELS-1,
FAX 415-391-0513
Singles & Doubles $240-$300, Suites $675-$875

On the Powell Street cable car line, the 400-room Stanford Court projects an image of refined luxury. The "Court" in its name refers to the courtyard automobile entrance, which flaunts a large, stained-glass dome over a fountain. The almost-hidden covered entrance is as discreet as they come, leading into an intimate marble lobby that is uncluttered yet inviting. Rooms are large and comfortable: you may feel like you're staying in a fine, old Virginia country house. A recent $6-million refurbishment added cushy but more modern furnishings to the rooms, with Asian accessories and calming color schemes in cool blue or leaf green. Bathrooms have towel warmers and a small TV; suites are dressed with original antiques; complimentary coffee and newspaper arrive on your doorstep every morning. Make sure to request a room with a view-not all have one. Public facilities include a beautiful ballroom, a lovely bar and **Fournou's Ovens** restaurant. Valet parking is $25 a day, with in-and-out privileges.

The Ritz-Carlton

600 STOCKTON ST.
NOB HILL 94108-2305
415-296-7465, 800-241-3333,
FAX 415-986-1268
Singles & Doubles $350-$550, Club floor $395-$600, Suites $550-$3,000

It's terribly chic to meet for tea at the **Lobby Lounge** of the Ritz-Carlton, a fashionable Nob Hill establishment that takes up a full square block. The hotel's motto? "Ladies and gentlemen serving ladies and gentlemen." The columned, neoclassical building, built in 1909, reopened as a 336-room luxury hotel in 1991. Museum-quality artworks decorate the hotel's public areas. Rooms are on the smallish side, but the hotel just underwent a $4-million renovation and most are elegantly appointed. Guests look out on views of the city: San Francisco Bay or the hotel's landscaped courtyard; a two-floor club level with 52 rooms and 15 suites has a dedicated concierge and is accessible with a separate elevator key. Rooms feature marble bathrooms with double sinks and telephones; most have separate water closets. Other amenities include remote-control color TVs; private voicemail; luxurious terry-cloth robes; safes and honor bar/refrigerators that offer just about everything. The 44 suites also come with VCRs. Guest services include a 24-hour concierge and room service, valet parking ($29 a day) and a fitness center with an indoor pool. For dining and entertainment, the Ritz has the highly rated **Dining Room** and the alfresco **Terrace** (see Dining), the **Ritz-Carlton Bar** and the **Lobby Lounge**. What more could you ask for?

The Sherman House

2160 Green St.
Pacific Heights 94123
415-563-3600, 800-424-5777,
Fax 415-563-1882
Singles & Doubles $310-$395, Suites $625-$775

A P

Northern California is full of enterprising people who are converting charming old houses into homey inns, but none have created one as luxurious and opulent as the Sherman House. Built in 1876 by Leander Sherman, founder of the Sherman Clay Music Company and a devoted opera buff, the house boasts a three-story recital hall. In 1980, Manou Mobedshahi and his wife, Vesta, bought the old mansion and spent nearly three years (and a considerable fortune) restoring the buildings and extensive gardens. The main house has 11 rooms and suites; the carriage house has three suites. Every room is large and furnished with exceptionally fine antiques and rugs, and most have canopied beds, down comforters, marble fireplaces, modernized black granite bathrooms, whirlpool tubs, color TVs, stereo systems and in-room laptop computers. Some have such extras as a private garden or rooftop deck; a few rooms and the restaurant (open only to guests) offer Bay views. The Sherman's personal service is exemplary: butlers will unpack your luggage; the skilled chef will prepare a refined snack or full-blown feast any time of the day or night. Sited near the Union Street and Cow Hollow shopping districts, The Sherman is located far from downtown, a factor that does not recommend it to the dining-and-dancing set. Valet parking is $16 a day.

LUXURY

ANA Hotel

50 3rd St.
SoMa 94103-3198
415-974-6400, 800-ANA-HOTELS,
Fax 415-543-8268
Singles & Doubles $165-$225, Executive level $190-$250,
Suites $265-$1,500

A P

This 667-room, wedge-shaped property operated by the Japanese ANA airline/hotel company. The ANA and the Marriott are the nearest major hotels at Yerba Buena Gardens, the site of Moscone Convention Center and the SFMOMA. Guests enter an art deco lobby, a graceful expanse of marble and mahogany with masses of fresh flowers. The ground floor houses a reception area, concierge desk, lounge and **Café 53**, a sort of Alice-in-Wonderland restaurant serving Californian cuisine with accents from France, Italy and Japan. Rooms come in varying shapes (nothing square or rectangular) with floor-to-ceiling windows. Décor is contemporary-slightly Japanese, simple but elegant. Each room has three phones with voicemail and data ports, safes, minibars and air conditioning. There are four executive-level floors. Hotel amenities include an in-house fitness center, above-average business center, valet parking for $25 per night and same-day laundry and room services.

Hotel Diva

440 Geary St.
Union Square 94102
415-885-0200, 800-553-1900,
Fax 415-346-6613
Singles $169, Doubles $179, Suites $179-$450

A P

The Hotel Diva, a moderately sized, moderately priced Union Square hotel, has undergone a complete facelift. The entrance greets you with a new-millennium look of stainless steel and glass, polished black granite tiles and cobalt-blue carpeting. The postage stamp-sized lobby still centers around four large TV monitors tuned to a vintage movie. But the small rooms are as well-equipped and cleverly designed as can be, featuring high-tech TVs with VCRs (videos available), minibars, comfortable beds with down comforters and sculptural steel headboards that sail to the ceiling. Furniture looks like office file cabinets warmed up with wooden surfaces. Views, mostly of neighboring brick walls, actually help ensure quiet in a noisy Theater District neighborhood. The amenity package includes an amusing modern touch: a single condom locked in the room safe; bathroom reading changes weekly. Other features: a bamboo wishing well, a 24-hour business hub and fitness center with Nautilus equipment. The next-door **California Pizza Kitchen** serves pizzas, salads and sandwiches and doubles for Diva room service; complimentary breakfast includes yogurt and granola. The hotel provides slick conference and meeting rooms and an accommodating staff. If you can't abide the neighborhood noise, request a room on an upper floor.

Hotel Griffon

155 STEUART ST.
EMBARCADERO 94105
415-495-2100, 800-321-2201, FAX 415-495-3522
Singles & Doubles $215-$260 Suites $315

Hard by the Embarcadero, the 62-room Hotel Griffon stretches only five stories, but is high enough to afford some views of San Francisco Bay and downtown skyline. The hotel has small rooms and suites, the latter with petite redwood balconies. Lofty ceilings and whitewashed brick walls reveal the structure's origin (and renaissance) as a waterfront hotel-it was built just after the 1906 earthquake. Mahogany headboards sport images of the legendary taloned griffon (or "griffin"); the same wood is used generously for desks and occasional tables. Rooms are simple and handsome, with window seats, good-looking, Italian alabaster light fixtures, marble vanities and subdued color schemes such as cream and blue. Roman shades are new. It's a great location for doing business in the nearby Financial District or taking a stroll to waterfront attractions, such as Pier 39 or the art-movie house Embarcadero Center Cinema. Amenities include room service, honor bars and a complimentary Continental breakfast. A nearby fitness center with a swimming pool is available; parking is $15 a night. Downstairs, **Roti** (see Dining) is popular for its rotisserie fare.

Hotel Monaco

501 GEARY ST.
THEATER DISTRICT 94102
415-292-0100, 800-214-4220,
FAX 415-292-0111
Singles & Doubles $199-$269, Suites $369-$429

In 1995, Bill Kimpton took the sow's ear of the once fashionable Bellevue Hotel, built in 1910, and created a proverbial silk purse. The Monaco sits across the street from the venerable Clift Hotel, but here you'll feel like you've boarded the Orient Express. Designer Cheryl Rowley has an audacious way of mixing shades of gold and yellow with vertical stripes and Chinese red to create a rich, warm environment. It's a 1990s version of the 1930s-but with high energy and fresh style. The lobby sports lots of marble, fresh-cut flowers, two fireplaces and a reception desk that looks like a giant, leather steamer trunk, complete with brass studs and trim. The lobby ceiling features a trompe l'oeil travel motif with biplanes and hot-air balloons. The hotel has 201 rooms and 35 suites, all of which are bravely decorated with green-and-yellow or charcoal-and-ivory stripes; eclectic desks and other odd but tasteful furnishings accompany the rooms. Amenities include irons and boards, robes, complimentary coffee and in-room faxes. The Monaco has a fitness center/mini-spa and business center. Valet parking costs $24. When dining at the Monaco, you'll probably smell the wood-burning ovens of the **Grand Café**, once the Bellevue ballroom, which serves light Californian-French fare. The restaurant features a 30-foot-high ceiling, massive columns and French art nouveau posters painted on the walls, all with a warm, amber glow. The adjoining **Petit Café** offers pizza and burgers, and is decorated with whimsical bronze statues of rabbits and chimpanzees.

Hotel Nikko San Francisco

222 Mason St.
Union Square 94102
415-394-1111, 800-NIKKO-US,
Fax 415-394-1106
Singles $280-$320, Doubles $310-$350, Suites $375-$625

The Hotel Nikko used to count on foreign trade for the bulk of its business, but the domestic market now counts for 70%. The lower levels of this 25-story white tower are devoted to restaurants, public rooms and an executive assistance center, complete with televisions, VCRs and a multilingual staff. The open lobby is warmed up with potted trees and jewel tones of emerald, topaz and ruby. But the Nikko's best amenity is the health club, with its workout room, sauna, deep Japanese baths and full-size, heated, indoor swimming pool beneath an arched roof of glass. Rooms and suites are simple yet elegant with an Asian touch; the sleek, contemporary furnishings and understated color schemes (beige and silver) may seem severe by Western standards. The Nikko is a good bet for business travelers keen on Japanese high-tech savvy; ask about procuring one of their superb Japanese suites. On Sundays, enjoy brunch at **Café 222** while local KKSF radio deejays play smooth jazz. Employees are all smiles; valet parking is $25 a day.

Hotel Triton

342 Grant Ave.
Chinatown 94108
415-394-0500, 800-433-6611,
Fax 415-394-0555
Singles & Doubles $164-$194, Suites $279-$305

When Bill Kimpton built the Triton just outside the entrance to Chinatown, he decided to do it differently from his other small, successful accommodations. The result is a 140-room showcase hotel, both sophisticated and whimsical, that features the works of Bay Area artisans on the cutting edge of design. Entering the lobby is like walking into a huge mural with mythological Greek images. Artworks include two columns in gold, teal and purple, dervish chairs with undulating backs and other curved and padded furniture. Even the bellmen's uniforms were designed to impress-depending on the season, they may sport edgy Mao jackets or Hawaiian-print shirts. The rooms, not overly large, are furnished with armoires, framed watercolors, honor bars, phones and cable-equipped televisions. The postmodern angularity of light fixtures and furniture, custom-made of stained mahogany, can almost make you seasick. The Triton offers three celebrity-inspired rooms, such as the Jerry Garcia Room, and 24 "EcoRooms" that incorporate environmentally savvy products and energy-saving features. Neighboring **Café de la Presse** (see Newsstands) serves up good espresso drinks, light café fare and international periodicals. Pets cost a flat $50 flat; valet parking is $24.

The Mark Hopkins Inter-Continental

999 California St.
Nob Hill 94108
415-392-3434, 800-327-0200,
Fax 415-421-3302
Singles & Doubles $220-$300, Concierge level $340,
Suites $425-$1,500

The Mark Hopkins is a longtime San Francisco favorite that, while it shares the crest of Nob Hill with the Fairmont, doesn't compare to that more famous neighbor. What draws travelers and tourists here is the **Top of the Mark** (see Bars), a romantic rooftop lounge that overlooks the city and has been a high-altitude meeting place for generations. Upgraded in 1996, the bar is a must-visit, especially on a clear night. Back on the ground, the hotel lobby, renowned for its marble floors, mirrored walls and magnificent crystal chandeliers, has been modernized and flooded with light. Upstairs, rooms and suites are large and feature alternating color schemes of either silver and blue or khaki and gold, thick carpeting, minibars and Regency-style writing desks. The Club floor, with a separate lounge, has 21 rooms. There's first-come, first-served limo shuttle for all guests; hotel service is bright and friendly. In addition, the Mark offers room service until 1 a.m., a fitness center and a "video checkout"-guests can preview their bill from the room's own television screen.

Prescott Hotel

545 Post St.
Union Square 94102
415-563-0303, 800-283-7322,
Fax 415-563-6831
Singles & Doubles $245, Club level $295, Suites $285-$1,200.

The Prescott, which opened in 1989 in conjunction with Wolfgang Puck's **Postrio** restaurant (see Dining), is one of the best projects of omnipresent hotelier Bill Kimpton. Cherry-wood furnishings, a Ralph Lauren paisley look and a color scheme of burgundy, teal and navy with camel outlines suit the masculine architecture of the hotel, a blend of neoclassical and Empire. There's a member's-only feeling to the 164 suites and smallish rooms, 82 rooms of which comprise the Club Level. All are outfitted with armoires and marble-clad baths. The clubby theme is underscored in the living room-style lobby, complete with a wood-burning fireplace and overstuffed furniture. Altogether, the Prescott's extremely handsome interior design, first-rate location and fine service (not to mention a leg up on reservations at Postrio) make the Prescott a top Union Square choice.

Radisson Miyako Hotel

1625 Post St.
Japantown 94115
415-922-3200, 800-333-3333,
Fax 415-921-0417
Singles $169, Doubles $189, Club level $189-$209,
Japanese-style Singles & Doubles $209, Suites $299

With 218 rooms, the Miyako is one of the smallest of San Francisco's large and modern hotels, and certainly one of the most pleasant, offering as it does the flair of a luxury accommodation. We prefer the simple, handsome, Japanese-style rooms (tatami mats, futon-style beds and deep soaking tubs) over the Western-style rooms, though the latter still include Japanese touches such as shoji screens and wood-block prints. Stressed executives should request one of the eight suites, some with private redwood saunas. There is a club floor with 14 rooms (one with a private steam room). From the marble lobby, enjoy the view out upon a Japanese garden with a pond full of koi; likewise, the mezzanine lounge is a peaceful spot to wait for seating at the **Yoyo Bistro**, a restaurant specializing in Californian-Asian dishes. Service is perfect; parking is $15 a night.

Renaissance Parc 55 Hotel

55 Cyril Magnin St.
Union Square 94102
415-392-8000, Fax 415-403-6602
Singles & Doubles from $189, Executive Club level $265, Suites $249-$300

This high-rise hotel offers 1,008 rooms and suites. The hotel completed a major renovation in early 1997, and its rooms are modern in a soft, corporate way. Each has fresh-air vents, hair dryers and ironing boards. Amenities include room service, overnight laundry (including one-hour pressing), a business center and a health club. The Executive Club, with stepped-up service, occupies the 31st floor. The staff is courteous. For dining, try **The Veranda** (a casual breakfast for lunch and dinner), **Rikyu** (for Japanese favorites) or the atrium-style **Piazza Lounge**, a pleasant place to listen to piano music and enjoy a light meal, or hang at the new **Barley 'N Hops Bar & Grill**. Parking will set you back $25 a day. If you stay at the Parc 55, you'll be a ten-minute walk to Union Square and only a minute to the San Francisco Centre, home to Nordstrom and other upscale stores (see Shopping). Take a flight of steps from the hotel down to Hallidie Plaza, a local transportation nexus where you can catch the Powell Street cable car, BART or a Muni bus.

San Francisco Hilton & Towers

333 O'Farrell St.
Union Square 94102
415-771-1400, 800-445-8667,
Fax 415-771-6807
Singles $185-$240, Doubles $205-$260, Suites $400-$2,900

Business is booming at the full-service Hilton. The current room count is an impressive 1,896-making this the largest hotel on the West Coast. The size (a whole square block) can be exciting, and provides enough distractions and services to satisfy every one of its thousands of customers. There are other points to recommend it: tower rooms are large, quiet and comfortable; the location is convenient to Union Square shopping and downtown office buildings; views can be wonderful; two ATMs in the lobby provide security and convenience when you need cash. In 1996, 400 rooms were upgraded at a cost of $8 million. Finally, there's a heated, rooftop swimming pool-one of few in town. Expect to encounter ranks of conventioneers and plan on getting lost now and then. On-site parking costs $27 per day.

San Francisco Marriott

55 4TH ST.
SOMA 94103
415-896-1600, 800-228-9290,
FAX 415-777-2799
Singles & Doubles $249, Suites $299-$2,100

Everyone loves the Marriott-particularly its guests. Because of its scalloped shape, San Franciscans affectionately (or not) call this Marriott the "Jukebox." It opened on October 17, 1989-the day the city experienced its second-most-famous earthquake. The 1,500-room hotel provides one of the anchor corners to Yerba Buena Gardens, which puts it near both the San Francisco Museum of Modern Art and Moscone Convention Center. The five-story atrium lobby and other public areas are handsome, adorned with lots of marble, splashing fountains and brass trim. Rooms, large and well decorated in shades of pink and green, all have air conditioning, TVs and phones with voicemail. Restaurants are plentiful in this hotel, and the **View Lounge** affords spectacular vistas through a three-story-high arched window. Not surprisingly, this convention-friendly hotel offers all the basic services, including video checkout and valet parking for $25 a day. A new Sony multi-screen cineplex is scheduled to open sometime in the new century across Mission Street from the property.

Westin St. Francis

335 POWELL ST.
UNION SQUARE 94102
415-397-7000, 800-WESTIN-1,
FAX 415-774-0124
Main building: Singles & Doubles $229-$405, Suites $395-$475. Tower: Singles $330-$375, Doubles $360-$405, Suites $575-$1,850

We do love visiting the St. Francis, one of San Francisco's most famous grand old hotels, just to see the exceptional rosewood-paneled lobby and enjoy a drink in the evocative **Compass Rose** lobby bar (see Bars). Queen Elizabeth hung her hat here in 1983, as have all U.S. presidents since Taft. A modern tower was added to the property in the 1970s, which brought the room total up to 1,189 (and filled the place with tourists). Facing Union Square, its location is probably the nicest in the city, although for some, it's a little too close to the action; lower-level rooms can be noisy. Westin is currently spending $55 million to renovate the St. Francis: the sandstone facade has been cleaned, and all rooms now shine with new furnishings and in-room safes, hair dryers and ironing boards with irons. Take one of the outside elevators for a thrilling, city-view ride. Valet parking is $26 a day.

White Swan Inn

845 BUSH ST.
UNION SQUARE 94108
415-775-1755, 800-999-9570,
FAX 415-775-5717
Singles & Doubles $150-$165, Suites $195

Without a doubt our favorite B & B-style San Francisco inn. The White Swan, sister to the Petite Auberge, makes large and modern hotels seem as if they belong to a science fiction world of the future. Though officially a bed-and-breakfast, the White Swan exhibits none of the problems that keep some travelers away from B & Bs. Each of its 26 rooms is spacious and boasts a fireplace, refrigerator, phone, color TV and decent-sized (if a bit dated) bathroom. In addition, the inn offers such amenities as valet parking and a small meeting room for business. The English-country look has been treated with remarkable skill; every nook and cranny is attractive and inviting. The lower level houses a large breakfast room, whose doors open onto a small garden, as well as a lounge and a cozy library-and all three have fireplaces. The full buffet breakfast is more than generous, as are the afternoon hors d'oeuvres, tea and wine. Each room has a stuffed bear that guests can "take care of." Add $19 a day for parking.

MODERATE

The Archbishop's Mansion

1000 FULTON ST.
ALAMO SQUARE 94117
415-563-7872, 800-543-5820, FAX 415-885-3193
Singles & Doubles $139-$419, Suites $229-$419

Despite the name, these are no parson's quarters. Built in 1904, this out-of-the-way bed-and-breakfast is a resplendent example of old San Francisco wealth. Built not for some captain of industry, but for the city's one-time archbishop, the three-story mansion faces historic Alamo Square, and has been lovingly restored to its original beauty: rich, polished woodwork; thick carpets, vaulted ceilings, crystal chandeliers and a lovely, stained-glass dome over the staircase. Ten large rooms and five suites feature queen-size beds, nineteenth-century French antiques, fine linens and silks and private baths; several have fireplaces or Jacuzzis. Amenities include an extended Continental breakfast served in your room and complimentary cheese and wine in the evening. The staff can arrange limousine service to the Opera House or nearby Symphony Hall. Another plus: free off-site parking on a first-come, first-served basis...anywhere in this residential neighborhood.

Beresford Hotel

635 SUTTER ST.
UNION SQUARE 94102
415-673-9900, 800-533-6533,
FAX 415-474-0449
Singles $109, Doubles $119

A

At the Beresford you'll feel as if you've arrived in jolly old England. The 114-room, seven-story, family-owned hotel has not been over-designed by a professional decorator-rather, the place feels comfortable and homey, if a touch dated. Two blocks from Union Square, the location couldn't be any better (safe neighborhood, almost no panhandlers), nor finer suited for theater, shopping and transportation options. The lobby, with chandeliers and English-style furniture, is comfortable, as are the clean rooms, which come with honor bars, satellite TVs and fridges. Complimentary are Continental breakfast and a morning newspaper. The on-site **White Horse Restaurant & Pub** is an authentic replica of an Old English tavern. In addition, the Beresford has safety-deposit boxes and accepts small pets. Nearby parking is $15 a day. One tip: Interior rooms are quieter.

Best Western Tuscan Inn

425 NORTHPOINT ST.
FISHERMAN'S WHARF 94133
415-561-1100, 800-648-4626,
FAX 415-561-1199
Singles & Doubles $138-$188, Suites $188-$238

A P

In 1990, Bill Kimpton took an ordinary Days Inn and waved his magic wand to create the Tuscan, a luxury inn on Fisherman's Wharf. From the Italianate lobby with a fireplace to the excellent **Café Pescatore**-the classic trattoria just off the lobby-this 220-room establishment is much more than a motel. Rooms, in typical Kimpton fashion, are smallish in size, so this is not the place for families. The Tuscan is, however, rich in the necessities: floral spreads and upholstery, stocked honor bars, writing desks and phones with data ports. Complimentary features include weekday limousine service to the Financial District, morning coffee and tea and evening wine by the fireside. The hotel offers a concierge and meeting facilities; Café Pescatore provides room service. On-site parking is $17 a day.

Galleria Park Hotel

191 SUTTER ST.
UNION SQUARE 94104
415-781-3060, 800-792-9639,
FAX 415-433-4409
Singles & Doubles $125-$199, Suites $199-$470

A P

The predecessor to this smart little hostelry was the Sutter Hotel, which opened its doors in 1911. In 1984, after extensive restoration, the property reopened as the Galleria Park-a 177 rooms-and-suite creation of developer Bill Kimpton and interior designer Nan Rosenblatt. The lobby, with warm burgundy colors and wrought-iron touches, is an art nouveau vision with crystal skylight, etched glass and a sculpted fireplace. In 1996, all rooms underwent complete renovation, and service was upgraded to include a doorman and concierge. Rooms are small but exceptionally attractive, with yellow-striped wall coverings and floral spreads and drapes. Suites are well-designed in soothing colors, with Jacuzzis, fireplaces, stereos and large TVs. Amenities include a short, outdoor jogging track, well-appointed conference rooms and two restaurants: **Brasserie Chambord** and **Perry's Downtown**. A wine reception is held nightly for guests. Parking is $23 a day.

Holiday Inn Fisherman's Wharf

1300 COLUMBUS AVE.
FISHERMAN'S WHARF 94133
415-771-9000, 800-942-7348, FAX 415-771-7006
Singles & Doubles $149-$224, Executive Level $184-$239, Suites $300-$500

For families, this above-average Holiday Inn is the best bet in the touristy Wharf area, where attractions are within walking distance. The 585-room facility was renovated in 1998. Clean rooms in shades of wine and beige are done in the usual Holiday Inn fashion. Amenities include phones with data ports, cable TV, safes, irons and ironing boards. The kids will love the heated outdoor pool; cribs, pull-out sofa beds and baby-sitting all can be arranged. A fitness center is new, as well as the **Bristol Bar & Grill**, serving American/ Californian cuisine. An Executive Level offers 74 rooms, each with two phones, hair dryers, robes and bottled water. Business travelers can also take the free limo to the Financial District. Overseas visitors appreciate the hotel's 24-hour currency exchange. Inside courtyard rooms are quieter.

Hotel Rex

562 SUTTER ST.
UNION SQUARE 94102-1102
415-433-4434, 800-433-4434,
FAX 415-433-3695
Singles & Doubles $135-$195, Suites $575

Literati, please take note. Modeled after New York's Algonquin Hotel in the 1930s, the salon-style Rex (formerly the Orchard) showcases well-known Bay Area authors, such as Jack London and Ambrose Bierce. In the extensive lobby library, their works line the mahogany bookshelves, and their portraits brighten the beige walls. In keeping with the bookish theme, the hotel holds poetry readings once a month in the lobby. The hotel, opened by the Joie de Vivre group in 1997, sits hard by Union Square on relatively quiet Sutter Street, surrounded by art galleries. The Rex's 94 compact rooms are homey, light and airy, with (appropriately) writing desks, updated bathrooms, remote-control TVs, minibars, ironing boards and phones with data ports, private voicemail and call waiting. The Rex also has a bar and complimentary evening wine service. Extras include a concierge, salon/meeting room and adjoining antiquarian bookshop. Valet parking is $25 a day.

Hotel Union Square

114 POWELL ST.
UNION SQUARE 94102
415-397-3000, 800-553-1900,
FAX 415-399-1874
Singles & Doubles $99-$135, Suites $149-$179

Completely renovated in 1998 and tremendously popular-no doubt because of its good location and low prices-the Union Square won't wow you with its service; nor is it as sophisticated as its sister hotels, Hotel Diva and Kensington Park. But most doubles cost just $125 (parking adds $17 per day), so one needn't be too fussy. There's complimentary Continental breakfast on each floor in the morning; coffee and tea every afternoon in the lobby. Avoid the rooms facing the street, unless you don't mind the sounds of the Powell Street cable cars grinding and clanging. Non-smokers have their choice among three floors.

Inn at the Opera

333 Fulton St.
Civic Center 94102
415-863-8400, 800-325-2708, Fax 415-861-0821
Singles $146-$190, Doubles $165-$215, Suites $215-$290

A P

This marvelous, five-story, 47-room inn has many unique qualities: history (it was built in 1927 to house opera stars), location (a few steps from the Opera House and Symphony Hall), décor (shades of peach, tasteful artwork and objets d'art) and ambience (luxuriously low-key). Rooms' size are their only drawback, well-equipped as they are with wet bars, mini-refrigerators and microwaves; all have queen-size beds. Guests can get terry robes on request, a nightly shoeshine and reliable advice from a concierge. Rates include a continental breakfast. **Ovation at the Opera**, which provides room service here, features a pianist most evenings and serves after-performance desserts. Valet parking adds $19 a day.

The Inn at Union Square

440 Post St.
Union Square 94102
415-397-3510, 800-288-4346,
Fax 415-989-0529
Singles & Doubles $165-$205, Suites $215-$360

A P

Entering the Inn at Union Square is like walking into the library of a genteel country manor. With its small parlors on each floor and its reasonably priced Continental breakfast and afternoon tea served fireside, this small, European-styled hotel could almost be considered a bed-and-breakfast. Yet the place offers a level of service most B & Bs do not, including a 24-hour concierge and complimentary newspapers. The 30 rooms are inviting, if a bit fussy; half come with florals, canopies and Georgian furniture, while the rest have been recently redone in an airy contemporary mode. Most are furnished with king-or queen-size beds, down pillows and phones with voicemail and data ports. The penthouse suite pampers guests with a powder room, fireplace, bar, sauna and whirlpool tub. The suites, which face Post Street, can be noisy. No smoking is allowed-nor is tipping! Parking is $22 a night.

Kensington Park

450 Post St.
Union Square 94102
415-788-6400, 800-553-1900, Fax 415-399-9484
Singles & Doubles $139-$170, Suites $550

A P

A handsome but eccentric little hotel minutes from Union Square, 86-room Kensington Park carries on the British-style hotel tradition, and its staff makes an effort to make each guest feel welcome. The small, attractive lobby (shared with neighbor Theater on the Square) is on the ground floor, but the hotel's rooms don't start until the fifth. Newly renovated chambers are good-sized, with mahogany furnishings and soft goods in shades of blackberry and muted greens. Small baths are done in marble and brass. Complimentary coffee, tea and croissants are served each morning on every floor; in the late afternoon, guests gather around the lobby piano for tea and sherry. There's a new fitness center on the fifth floor, and Pat Kuleto's latest restaurant **Farallon** (see Dining) adjoins the hotel on the ground level. Valet parking is $20 a day; nonsmoking on three floors.

The Majestic

1500 Sutter St.
Cathedral Hill 94109
415-441-1100, 800-869-8966,
Fax 415-673-7331
Singles & Doubles $135-$150, Deluxe rooms $165-$185, Suites $325

A P

One visitor said this five-story, Edwardian hotel reminded her of her grandmother's house. Tasseled pillows, lace curtains, antiques and four-poster beds announce the Majestic's turn-of-the-century heritage. In 1997, the hotel fixed up each of its 60 rooms-spending some $14,000 on each. All are color-coordinated with almost-matching fabrics, rugs and patterned wallpaper. The lobby exudes an old-manor feel appropriate to the residential neighborhood. The restaurant, **Café Majestic**, serves Californian cuisine with Asian undertones. The restaurant's tiny bar came from a Paris bistro (1821) and features an old and rare butterfly collection. New are in-room velour robes, a concierge and 24-hour room service.

The Mansions Hotel

2220 SACRAMENTO ST.
PACIFIC HEIGHTS 94115
415-929-9444, 800-826-9398,
FAX 415-567-9391
Singles $129-$159, Doubles $149-$179, Suites $225-$350

The Mansions is located on a quiet street in fashionable Pacific Heights. An upscale bed-and-breakfast exhibiting old-world charm: today, because of its famous magic shows, neighbors call it the Haunted House. (In fact, some guests have reported ghost encounters.) The 1887 Queen Anne houses have 21 guest rooms and suites. The rooms, all with private bath, are furnished with Victorian antiques, TVs, phones and fresh flowers. For those who opt to spend a bit more, a few rooms are furnished with canopied beds, marble fireplaces or private terraces. A full breakfast is served. Every evening The Mansions puts on an hour-long magic show that climaxes with a "snowstorm." The hotel's full-service restaurant serves a four-course dinner (Californian and Continental cuisine) at a prix-fixe tab of $47 on weeknights and $57 on weekends, and includes the cost of the performance. The hotel houses several museum collections, including original signed documents from past presidents and the ultimate master of escape—Houdini; as well as a complete collection of pigs. Parking is available nearby for $10 a day. Barbra Streisand, who stayed here once, said it offered "marvelous hospitality."

The Maxwell Hotel

386 GEARY ST.
UNION SQUARE 94102
415-986-2000, 888-734-6299,
FAX 415-397-2447
Singles & Doubles $135-$195, Suites $450-$670

Known a few year ago as The Raphael, this smart little property in the heart of the Theater District was taken over by Joie de Vivre in late 1996. It is ideal for visitors who want see the downtown sights and take in a play or two. The smallish rooms, outfitted with a sort of art deco Victoriana (mahogany furniture, red brocades with moss-green accents), are surprisingly quiet. Each is provided with AM/FM radio; remote control, cable TV, two phones with voicemail, hair dryers, ironing boards and air-conditioning. Your kids can rent videos or Nintendo games. On your way out in the morning, pour yourself a cup of complimentary coffee or tea, drop off your laundry and ask the valet for your car and the tour desk to arrange an itinerary for you. There's also room service as well as a nearby health club. Guests can sign for meals at the full-service, 1940s-style Gracie's restaurant, dishing up "American brasserie" cuisine. Non-smoking rooms are available. Parking costs $17 a day.

Monticello Inn

127 ELLIS ST.
UNION SQUARE 94102
415-392-8800, 800-669-7777,
FAX 415-398-2650
Singles & Doubles $120-$175, Suites $160-$230

Thomas Jefferson might have liked the Monticello Inn, a decent, diminutive Kimpton hotel with a Southern colonial theme. The 63-room, 28-suite property is just around the corner from the Powell Street cable car turnaround and, consequently, close to everything downtown. The renovated 1906 building features a lobby with Federal-period décor, a library, a grandfather clock and a wood-burning fireplace. Rooms are outfitted with writing desks, cable TVs (VCRs on demand), stocked honor bars, refrigerators and phones with voicemail and data ports; king and queen rooms sport canopied beds. Suites add coffeemakers, robes and ironing equipment. Complimentary are the Kimpton's Continental breakfast, coffee throughout the day and evening wine, all served in the library. Non-smoking rooms are available, as is valet parking ($18 a day).

Petite Auberge

863 BUSH ST.
UNION SQUARE 94108
415-928-6000, 800-365-3004,
FAX 415-775-5717
Singles & Doubles $110-$160, Suites $225

Perhaps the only inn in all of San Francisco that is as cozy as this one is the neighboring

White Swan-which happens to be owned by the same good people (see above). A romanticized interpretation of the French country look has been skillfully assembled here: earth-colored tile floors, delicately flowered wallpaper, country furnishings and French windows and doors. The basement level comprises a breakfast room with French doors opening onto a small garden, and a lounge/bar area, where good California wines and tea are served in the afternoon. The upper floors comprise 26 small and adorable rooms, all with private bathrooms and queen-size beds, and many with fireplaces. The suite has a private entrance, and its own patio and a Jacuzzi. It's a short walk to Union Square, yet comfortably distanced from the tourist throngs. Valet parking is $19 a day.

The Phoenix Hotel

601 Eddy St.
Civic Center 94109
415-776-1380, 800-CITY-INN,
Fax 415-885-3109
Singles & Doubles $109, Suites $149

Balanced precariously on the edge of the Tenderloin, the Phoenix was once a 1950s cinder-block motel, known for its Magic Fingers beds. In 1987, Joie de Vivre Hotels bought the dilapidated property and reincarnated it into a funky, 44-room inn. The lemon-and-turquoise-painted motel attracts various trendsetters-artists and actors, filmmakers and movie stars, bands, hip musicians. Among the celebrity overnighters: Brenda Lee, Keith Haring, k. d. Lang, Dan Rather and Sinead O'Connor. Colorful room décor runs to bamboo furniture, tropical plants and original pop art. Outside in the art garden, a heated swimming pool with a famous underwater mural lies between the motel and **Backflip** (see Dining), the next-door lounge that glows with a kitsch underwater theme. Continental breakfast and parking are free; services include massage, concierge, same-day laundry and access to a nearby health club. The Phoenix's quintessential blunder? Accidentally booking John F. Kennedy, Jr. and Deborah Harry of Blondie in the same room.

Sir Francis Drake

450 Powell St.
Union Square 94102
415-392-7755, 800-227-5480,
Fax 415-391-8719
Singles & Doubles $205-$250, Suites $350

Though hardly luxurious, the Sir Francis Drake is one of the better-known San Francisco's landmark hotels. Its clientele love the doormen (who dress up as London Beefeaters), the front-door cable car stop and the ornate (some would say tired) lobby and lounges. The rooms are ordinary-each seems to cry, "Fix me up!"-but the nearby bars and restaurants help save the Drake. Streetside, you'll find **Scala's Bistro** (see Dining), serving good country French-Italian cuisine and **Caffè Espresso**, offering wine and light fare all day. On the rooftop, **Harry Denton's Starlight Room** (see Nightlife) attracts young stockbrokers and Perry Como couples to drink and dance to live music nightly. The staff at the Drake is friendly, its location a Union Square bull's-eye and its prices palatable. Parking costs $24 a day.

Villa Florence

225 Powell St.
Union Square 94102
415-397-7700, 800-553-4411,
Fax 415-397-1006
Singles & Doubles $125-$185 Suites $165-$185

Villa Florence is another old hotel that has been skillfully spruced up for clients reluctant to spend more than $135 for a Union Square location. This particular site on the Powell Street cable car line is a little tawdry outside-don't mind the panhandlers-but is well-situated for a downtown shopping spree. The Italianate lobby is moderately attractive, with a fireplace, plush seating and a fresco depicting Florence. To one side is the long-established Italian restaurant, **Kuleto's** (see Dining). The 180 rooms, fixed up in 1997, combine modern dressers and armoires (which hide TVs) with mustard-green-and-crimson-colored bedspreads, drapes and overstuffed chairs. New is **Caffè Kuleto's**, serving sandwiches and light fare streetside; valet parking is $23 a day. A good home-away-from-home for the price.

The Washington Square Inn

1660 STOCKTON ST.
NORTH BEACH 94133
415-981-4220, 800-388-0220,
FAX 415-397-7242
Singles & Doubles $120-$200

A P

Those enamored with the old-world charm of North Beach and Washington Square will be pleased to find this friendly, pleasant hideaway. Fifteen of the Washington Square Inn's rooms face the park, and two have bay windows overlooking the square. The English-style rooms, updated in 1997, are cozy and often small, and are as quiet as can be from the public park location. All have private baths, and some have king-size beds. Prices include breakfast, afternoon tea, wine and hors d'oeuvres. The personable staff acts as the concierge; ask to see their restaurant menu file. You'll be lucky to find parking in North Beach, so be prepared to pay $20 a day to stash your car. The area excels in great restaurants.

ECONOMY

The Abigail Hotel

246 MCALLISTER ST.
CIVIC CENTER 94102
415-861-9728, 800-243-6510,
FAX 415-861-5848
Singles & Doubles $94, Suite $149

A

Bargain hunters who don't mind being away from downtown-or who want to be near Civic Center and the Opera House-immediately call up The Abigail, a Joie de Vivre property and the quieter relative of the funky Phoenix. You can't beat the charm, friendliness and comfort for the price. "Faux California" best describes the décor at this otherwise-European-style hotel: the small lobby displays black-and-white tile floors, faux marble walls and faux copper lacquer furnishings. The small rooms are not immune to street noise, but they are comfortable. Each is equipped with handsome antiques, a down comforter in bright colors, a cable TV, a phone and a private bath that is clean and large, if not especially modern. A sunken-level restaurant, **Millennium**, open only for dinner, serves superb meatless meals (see Dining). Parking around the corner costs $12.50 a day.

Beck's Motor Lodge

2222 MARKET ST.
CASTRO DISTRICT 94114
415-621-8212, 800-227-4360,
FAX 415-241-0435
Singles & Doubles $75-$115, Deluxe rooms $105-$115

A P

A huge rainbow flag proudly waves at the corner of Market and Castro streets, flying over the heart of San Francisco's gay and lesbian mecca. An old-fashioned motel only two blocks away, Beck's Motor Lodge offers typical motel-style accommodation straight out of the 1950s. The cream-colored facility, with wood-and-sandstone facade and dark-blue trim offers 57 rooms, including two deluxe rooms with fireplace. The clientele is 80% gay and lesbian, although many families and relatives of gays stay here too. Rooms are functional, some small; all are tastefully decorated in shades of blue with touches of green or rose. Furnishings include phone, cable TV, small fridge, coffee pot (for a self-brewed cup) and oak- or walnut-veneer furniture. The low-rise Beck's offers a sundeck and a coin-operated washer/dryer on site. There's a good selection of nearby restaurants (Mexican, Thai, Indian, Italian) that front handsome, palm-lined, noisy Market Street. The staff is friendly. It's clean if not fancy; and Beck's is a short stroll to all the hot bars, trendy shops and gay scene of the Castro District. Parking is free.

Clarion Bedford Hotel at Union Square

761 POST ST.
UNION SQUARE 94109
415-673-6040, 800-227-5642,
FAX 415-563-6739
Singles & Doubles $89-$169, Suites $155-$195

A P

The European-style Bedford, a member of the Kimpton chain, offers one of the best deals in the downtown area: most singles and doubles are just $119. The old hotel was renovated skillfully and tastefully, and though not opulent, is elegant enough for the price. The cheerful lobby opens onto **Crushed Tomato's Café & Bar**, serving Californian- and Italian-style fare. Its 144 rooms are clean and comfortable, with mini-refrigerators, cable TVs, in-room coffeemakers, phones with data ports, pastel walls and floral fabrics; bathrooms are old-fashioned but certainly not feeble. Seven one-bedroom suites are located on the upper floors. The small staff is friendly. Three blocks west of Union Square, the Bedford offers convenience but is located just far enough removed to be out of earshot of the clanging cable cars. Valet parking is $18 a night; don't miss their evening wine reception.

Grant Plaza Hotel

465 GRANT AVE.
CHINATOWN 94108
415-434-3883, 800-472-6899,
FAX 415-434-3886
Singles $52-$62, Doubles $62-$85, Suite $109

There are few amenities-no concierge, no restaurant, no room service-but this slightly-out-of-fashion little hotel is a great find for the frugal. The chandeliers and pink leather sofa in the lobby don't quite match the fake flowers and French provincial chairs. Who cares? The location is swell, one block up from the Bush Street (Dragon Gate) entrance to Chinatown. Clean and comfortable, the Grant Plaza has 71 small, Holiday Inn-like rooms on six floors; all are equipped with phones with voicemail, TVs, showers and wall-mounted hair dryers. Décor is on the mauve side with floral spreads and light-colored wooden furnishings (and nice plantation shutters on the top floor). Don't miss the beautiful stained-glass dome and windows in the hallway of the sixth floor, once a nightclub and Chinese tea garden. Last year, the hotel changed the locks to electronic key cards. Request a corner room: it's larger, but at no extra cost, and lets you look out at St. Mary's Square and the Financial high-rises. The area abounds in Chinese restaurants and other dining spots.

San Remo Hotel

2237 MASON ST.
FISHERMAN'S WHARF 94133
415-776-8688, 800-352-7366,
FAX 415-776-2811
Singles $50-$60, Doubles $60-$70, Triples $80, Penthouse double $125

The San Remo is a charming, restored Victorian hotel built by A. P. Giannini (founder of Bank of America) to house maritime workers displaced by the earthquake of 1906. The three-story, 62-room Italianate inn is located far from the expensive Union Square accommodations, but it offers very reasonably-priced rooms near Fisherman's Wharf, North Beach and the Powell-Mason cable car line. All rooms except the penthouse share bathrooms. Authentic furnishings give the San Remo the air of a lovely old home, down to the claw-footed tubs, brass fixtures, redwood wainscoting and pull-chain toilets. Rooms are decorated with antiques, including brass and iron beds, oak, maple and pine armoires, pedestal sinks and wicker furniture. A bar serves snacks. The penthouse is often booked-but good luck trying.

Stanyan Park Hotel

750 STANYAN ST.
GOLDEN GATE PARK 94117
415-751-1000, FAX 415-668-5454
Singles & Doubles $99-$145, Suites $185-$225

Built in 1904 and renovated in 1997, the Stanyan Park is on the National Register of Historic Places. Just across the street from Golden Gate Park and around the corner from the hip Haight-Ashbury, this small three-story hotel offers both comfort and Victorian-era ambience. Bathrooms have been reasonably modernized; reproduction antique furnishings are simple and homey; each room has cable TV and phones with data ports. For a larger group or an extended stay, consider one of the one- or two-bedroom suites, which sleep up to six and include four-poster beds, kitchens and living and dining rooms. The room rate includes a decent expanded Continental breakfast and evening tea and cookies. Weekend visitors should be prepared for daytime noise from the surrounding neighborhood; parking can be a headache.

NIGHTLIFE

CONTENTS

SLEEP IS OVERRATED

Since the days of the Barbary Coast, San Francisco has always been a town known for lively nightlife. Whether you're seeking live music, cabaret or dancing, or you just want to meet friends-straight or gay-at the neighborhood saloon to hoist a few, the city caters willingly to your needs. In **North Beach**, friendly Beat-poet ghosts haunt the cafés and late-night bookstores. In the **Mission** and **SoMa**, dozens of clubs and pubs reflect a healthy new Bohemian economy. In the **Castro**, streets and bars are alive with buffed bodies and stylish clothes. And on **Nob Hill**, several establishments offer dizzying bird's-eye vistas of the dazzling city, one where everyone, it seems, is on the move.

San Franciscans' nightlife preferences are changing: currently, martini bars and dance clubs compete with many live music venues-the city marks the birthplace of several musical trends, after all-and the neighborhood pubs. Establishments that serve food and liquor and also provide live music are experiencing an upswing. Included at the chapter's end are a list of these supper clubs, where you can enjoy a full evening's entertainment without giving up your seat (or looking for more parking). A word to the smoker: at press time, it is illegal to smoke in all bars.

We could easily publish an entire guidebook on the city's after-dark activities, but we present the best of them here. For the most up-to-date nightlife listings, do as the locals do: pick up either the ***Datebook*** ("Pink Section") of the Sunday *San Francisco Chronicle* and *Examiner*, or any of the free weekly papers that come out on Wednesday-the ***SF Weekly*** or ***San Francisco Bay Guardian*** remain your best bet, and the ***Bay Area Reporter*** delivers the inside scoop on the gay and lesbian scene.

CASUAL BARS & BREWPUBS

The Albion

3130 16TH ST.
MISSION 94110
415-552-8558
Open daily 2 p.m.-2 a.m.
No cards

With a new sign and a recent paint job, you'd think The Albion might be revamping its image as the quintessential Mission hideaway. But-thank heaven-it's still the same, a friendly dive with a pool table, a cave-like back room, and a general ambience of comfort and familiarity. It's got some competition of late from Dalva, down the street, but The Albion is here to stay. No live music anymore, but lots of interesting souls to talk to.

The Balboa Café

3199 FILLMORE ST.
COW HOLLOW 94123
415-921-3944
Open daily 11 a.m.-2 a.m.

A

Making up one-third of the infamous "triangle" (the Pierce Street Annex and Golden Gate Grill form the triumvirate)," Cow Hollow's original fern bar remains a monument to the young pick-up scene. Long in a state of unkempt shabbiness, the establishment was recently bought by the owners of Plump Jack, up the street, and refurbished to its original grandeur. A singles exchange at night, The Balboa boasts the best burger in town by day. Sunday brunches (and their killer Bloody Marys) remain popular.

Brain Wash

1122 FOLSOM ST.
SOMA 94103
415-861-3663
Open daily 7 a.m.-11 p.m.

Where else can you order an espresso, chat up a foreigner from the international hostel across the street, get a bite to eat and catch an act from a young and up-and-coming band-all between the wash and spin cycles of your laundry? This funky pub-cum-Laundromat also offers avant-garde theater upstairs, with an eclectic roster that includes plays, various performing artists and poetry readings.

Buddha Lounge

901 GRANT AVE.
CHINATOWN 94108
415-362-1792
Open daily 10:30 a.m.-2 a.m.
No cards

Quietly stowed away in the middle of one of the busiest parts of Chinatown, the Buddha has grown more popular lately, filling at lunch and overflowing after 5 p.m. It's still, however, very comfortable. The smell of incense wafting through the air and Cantonese-style red vinyl booths set the mood of this unique neighborhood meeting place, where curious Caucasians sip drinks alongside the local businesspeople, all beneath the five-foot-tall altar to Buddha behind the bar.

Buena Vista

2765 HYDE ST.
NORTH BEACH 94133
415-474-5044
Open Mon.-Fri. 9 a.m.-2 a.m., Sat.-Sun. 8 a.m.-2 a.m.
No cards.

Legend has it that this ever-crowded hangout introduced Irish coffee to San Francisco in 1953. Now, it reputedly serves a couple thousand of the drinks a day to the locals and (mostly) tourists who jam the round oak tables and the old mahogany bar. To enjoy its vista overlooking the Bay, Ghirardelli Square, the Cannery and Fisherman's Wharf, expect to queue up for seat.

Eagle Café

PIER 39, #201
FISHERMAN'S WHARF 94133
415-433-3689
Open daily 7:30 a.m.-11 a.m.

A refuge from the tourist trap bars of the Fisherman's Wharf area, The Eagle Café lies in the heart of Pier 39. Originally located across the street in a more humble structure, this friendly bar/café serves the local fishing and sailing community, who come in to relax after a long day of life on the water. Folk music performances on weekend nights. In the evening, you can sit outdoors to catch a miraculous view of the fog rolling into the bay.

Edinburgh Castle

950 GEARY BLVD.
UNION SQUARE 94109
415-885-4074
Open Mon.-Fri. 5 p.m.-2 a.m.

The Edinburgh's countryside pub atmosphere is accented by heavy wooden tables, beamed ceilings, dartboards and intimate balconies, and the bagpipe music will soothe the homesick Scot. Bartenders pull rich drafts of Bass, Watney's, John Courage, Guinness and the local favorite, half-and-half (ale and stout). Like many of the city's Celtic bars, however, the Edinburgh suffers from lack of upkeep. It's a bit of a dump-albeit a friendly, bustling dump-lately.

El Rio

1358-A MISSION ST.
MISSION 94110
415-282-3325
Open Mon. 3 p.m.-midnight, Tues.-Sun. 3 p.m.-2 a.m. Cover $5-$7 with live bands.

No cards

One of the nicest places in the City to sit outside in the Mission and have a margarita is on the deck behind El Rio. As culturally diverse as its neighborhood, a friendly, mixed-orientation crowd patronizes this establishment, taking in a game of bar-size shuffleboard or billiards. At the end of the week, regulars flock there for happy hour to shoot free oysters until the last mollusk is shucked. The upbeat Rio is popular with those who love to dance to everything from world beat and Latin salsa to live music. A great spot to hear live salsa on a sunny Sunday afternoon.

Elbo Room

647 VALENCIA ST.
MISSION 94110
415-552-7788
Open nightly 5 p.m.-2 a.m. Cover varies.

The two-floor Elbo Room is best known as the showcase for San Francisco's Acid Jazz movement. The club still books many local favorites-the Broun Fellinis have a permanent gig there-and fills in other nights with talented deejays. Decent happy hours and generally accommodating staff complement a noisy, barn-like ambience downstairs; upstairs, the stage is tucked at the back end of a long, narrow room. Customers seem to come from other districts (mainly the Marina) and, unfortunately, seem more interested in cruising for the opposite sex than enjoying the great music.

Gordon Biersch

2 HARRISON ST.
FINANCIAL DISTRICT 94105
415-243-8246
Open Sun.-Tues. 11:30 a.m.-11 p.m., Wed.-Sat. 11 a.m.-1 a.m.

A

When this popular Palo Alto-based microbrewery/restaurant opened its doors in 1992, it solely revitalized the heterosexual, fraternity-like Financial District singles scene. Immortalized in *The New York Times*, it packed such a mob that you couldn't squeeze your way through the front door, and brewmaster Dan Gordon couldn't brew enough beer to meet the demand. The dust has settled quite a bit since then, but guys and dolls continue to flock to this watering hole (see Dining).

Hotel Utah Saloon Bistro

500 4TH ST.
SOMA 94103
415-421-8308
Open Mon.-Fri. 11:30 a.m.-2 a.m., Sat.-Sun. 5 p.m.-2 a.m. Cover varies.

A legend among SoMa establishments, this long narrow bar fills up with cool folks who want to hear live music in close quarters or play a game of pinball. Some ten different kinds of draft are poured by the pint, and a wide selection of export beers are available. The Utah has great bar food, too. Pick a spot in the upper-floor balcony for the best view of the bands.

Johnny Love's

1500 BROADWAY, VAN NESS 94109
415-931-6053
Open nightly 5 p.m.-2 a.m. Cover $5 Mon.-Thurs., $10 Fri.-Sat.

Sexy and successful bartender Johnny "Love" Metheny is the host of this popular bar, restaurant and nightclub. The primped and coiffed upwardly-mobiles stand four-deep at the bar, shouting for drinks and looking to get coupled. If you can't score at the Balboa, Johnny Love's is just the spot for you.

Kezar Bar & Restaurant

900 COLE ST.
SAN FRANCISCO, CA 94117
415-681-7678
Open Mon.-Fri. 5 p.m.-2 a.m., Sat.-Sun. 4 p.m.-2 a.m.

Though it's also a restaurant with a decent casual menu, the Kezar is best known as the neighborhood pub for Cole Valley yuppies, students, and those wishing to escape the panhandlers in the nearby Haight. The bar is dark and cordial, with TVs showing ESPN or old movies. It's staffed by capable waitresses and bartenders, and feels like exactly what it is: a local hangout that's been there forever.

Mad Dog in the Fog

530 HAIGHT ST.
HAIGHT-ASHBURY 94117
415-626-7279
Open Mon.-Fri. 11:30 a.m.-2 a.m., Sat.-Sun. 10 a.m.-2 a.m.
No cards

This hugely popular Haight Street bar takes its inspiration from a basic English pub complete with darts, draft beers, greasy fare, and bartenders with honest-to-goodness cockney accents. It's a good counterpart to the funkier bars across the street-Noc Noc and Toronado-and will make the international traveler feel quite at home.

Noc Noc

557 HAIGHT ST.
HAIGHT-ASHBURY 94117
415-861-5811
Open nightly 5 p.m.-2 a.m.

A friend best described Noc Noc as "a 747 that crashed into the Flintstones house." Exactly. Looking more like something out of a Werner Fassbinder movie than a bar, this self-consciously cool establishment offers cavernous fabricated granite-like booths, numerous static-screened TV sets, and a full selection of wine, beer, and saké. One of the Lower Haight's most established hangouts, it's a favorite among hip night crawlers, European wannabes and locals alike.

Pat O'Shea's Mad Hatter

3754 GEARY BLVD.
RICHMOND DISTRICT 94121
415-752-3148
Open daily 11 a.m.-2 a.m.

With three satellite dishes, nine 25-inch televisions and sporting memorabilia galore, Pat O'Shea's is one of San Francisco's premier sports bars, impossibly crowded when the 49ers are on the tube. But football jocks aren't the only patrons. In the evening, University of San Francisco students make this a regular hangout. Local blues and rock bands play on Friday and Saturday nights for dancing. The bar pours more than 25 beers on tap, including a healthy sampling of microbrews and imports.

Pier 23 Café

PIER 23
FISHERMAN'S WHARF 94133
415-362-5125
Open Mon.-Thurs. 11:30 a.m.-12:30 a.m., Fri.-Sat. 11:30 a.m.-2 a.m., Sun. 11 a.m.-9 p.m.

Down the wharf from the ringing registers of the tourist boutiques, you'll find this lively place tucked away on Pier 23. During the daytime, the place is warmed by the sun, beaming down on the bright patio, but at night the heat is generated from the Latin beat and cooled with the sweat of salsa dancing. Sunday afternoons are particularly eventful, especially on a sunny day.

The Plough and Stars

116 CLEMENT ST.
RICHMOND DISTRICT 94121
415-751-1122
Open daily 2 p.m.-2 a.m. Cover $3 with live bands.

No Irish pub crawl would be complete without a stop at this no-frills, no-nonsense, music-oriented bar. The crowd is an unpretentious mix of Irish nationalists, serious drinkers from the old country and blue-jeaned young folk from the neighborhood. The biggest attraction is the evocative live and recorded Irish songs-the best airs, reels and jigs in the City, for listening or dancing.

The Rite Spot

2099 FOLSOM ST.
MISSION 94110
415-552-6066
Open Mon.-Thurs. 4 p.m.-2 a.m., Sat.-Sun. 2 p.m.-2 a.m.
No cards

As the neighborhood surrounding the Rite Spot changes from blue to white collar (this part of the Mission marks ground zero for many new Internet and media businesses), it will be interesting to see how the bohemian haunt holds up. Most nights, you'll find the bar lined with reporters and editors from the Bay Guardian; the weeknight crowd includes folks dispersing from the nearby clubs and theaters. On weekends, suburbanoids who've discovered this art bar come by to absorb some of its flavor. The Rite Spot's great virtue is its deliberate lack of hipness. Can it survive?

The Saloon

1232 Grant Ave.
North Beach 94133
415-989-7666
Open daily noon-2 a.m.
No cards

Sometimes called the 1232, this venerable North Beach institution has become a haven for hippie holdovers. Here, musicians from the golden era of San Francisco rock bands (Quicksilver Messenger Service, Country Joe and the Fish, Big Brother and the Holding Company) can play for fans who knew them when. The musical mainstay is raw, gritty blues. The bar itself is even more of a survivor than the clientele, having been around since 1861.

San Francisco Brewing Co.

155 Columbus Ave.
North Beach 94133
415-434-3344
Open daily noon-midnight

If you're a brew enthusiast and you find yourself in North Beach, eschew that second glass of Chianti and head for the San Francisco Brewing Company. This microbrew pub pours over 20 types of domestic beers plus four made on the premises. The dark mahogany bar with brass trim dates back to 1907.

Skylark

3089 16th St.
Mission 94110
415-621-9294
Open daily 6 p.m.-2 a.m.

The classiest bar in the heart of New Bohemia, the recently opened Skylark attracts a different crowd on different nights. During the week, it's a casual hangout for Mission locals, who commandeer the pub's booths and back room during happy hour. But come the weekend, the place turns well-heeled, catering to the martini-tipping swing dance crowd dressed in tight shirts and poodle skirts, flashing their tattoos on their way to (or from) the Deluxe, Bimbo's or another jitterbug party.

Specs' Twelve Adler Museum Café

12 Adler St.
North Beach 94133
415-421-4112
Open Mon.-Fri. 4:30 p.m.-2 a.m. Sat.-Sun. 5 p.m.-2 a.m.
No cards

Brick walls in this haunt, located in an alley off Columbus Avenue, are practically hidden beneath signs and memorabilia from Barbary Coast days, and old black-and-white photographs capture the images of the neighborhood's heyday. While a few stalwarts have attempted to re-create the golden age of jazz in North Beach, Specs' has been the real thing all along, filling nightly with local regulars in search of a strong drink or good music.

Tosca Café

242 Columbus Ave.
North Beach 94133
415-986-9651
Open nightly 5 p.m.-2 a.m.
No cards

The opera discs on the jukebox add one more element of old-world charm to this classic North Beach hangout. High ceilings, old photos and a feel of unchanged history are additional draws. Slide into one of the old leather booths and order a legendary "house cappuccino," made with chocolate, steamed milk and brandy. Weeknights are quieter and therefore better for a casual drop-in; on weekends, throbbing beats from the Palladium club downstairs dominate the conversation.

Trad'r Sam's

6150 Geary Blvd.
Richmond District
415-221-0773
Open daily 10 a.m.-2 a.m.
No cards

You know the drill: tropical drinks, concocted mostly of rum and fruit juices, with names like Polynesian Punch and Hawaiian Honeypot. Sam's isn't even remotely as classy as the late Trader Vic's nor the overpriced Tonga Room, but the place fills nonetheless, with undergraduates and the occasional local looking for a rummy romance. Easy parking, and a logical stop on your way back from Ocean Beach.

Vesuvio Café

255 COLUMBUS AVE.
NORTH BEACH 94133
415-362-3370
Open daily 6 a.m.-2 a.m.
No cards

Although North Beach boasts precious few reminders of the Beat era when Kerouac, Ginsberg, Corso and others scrawled or read their poetry in the bookstores and cafés, Vesuvio has hardly changed since it opened in 1949. Located across Kerouac Alley from City Lights bookstore, this delightfully casual bar is dark and cozy, with a balcony for people-watchers. Poets and chess players are always in evidence.

SOPHISTICATED BARS

Café du Nord

2170 MARKET ST.
CASTRO 94114
415-861-5016
Open Sun.-Tues. 6 p.m.-2 a.m., Wed.-Sat. 4 p.m.-2 a.m.

It's hard not to like Café du Nord, once a 1930s speakeasy that now houses a long bar, tangerine-covered pool table and intimate back room with a curtained stage. On certain nights it's a dance club, with local deejays spinning a mixture of tunes; on others it sways to the sound of live jazz and salsa bands; lately, it's trying its hand at booking comedy shows. It's dark, funky and usually packed with locals in sharp clothes, chatting, dancing and generally kicking back. Admission on certain weekend nights is still a bargain-usually $3.

Club Deluxe

1511 HAIGHT ST.
HAIGHT-ASHBURY 94117
415-552-6949
Open 8 p.m.-2 a.m. Cover varies.
No cards

The wear and tear of recent rediscovery by a younger crowd hasn't hurt this Haight Street hangout one bit. A warm wood bar is framed by swank booths, a checkerboard floor, and a touch of the underworld, and the joint's charismatic bartenders can mix a highball as well as pull a pint of your favorite hefeweizen. The clientele seems a little lost, since the recent passage of anti-smoking measures, at their smoke-free status, but they still pack the place, jostling for space between the chrome stools.

Compass Rose

WESTIN ST. FRANCIS HOTEL
335 POWELL ST.
UNION SQUARE 94102
415-774-0167
Open daily 11 a.m.-11 p.m.

A

This lush, clubby bar next to the Westin St. Francis lobby is a fitting respite from shopping in Union Square. For a terribly romantic date, indulge in a glass of Champagne and dip into the extensive selection of caviar served by the ounce. Jazz trios and lounge singers round out the evening's entertainment. Legend has it that Ernest Hemingway won over Ingrid Bergman in this bar, where she reportedly agreed to star in *For Whom the Bell Tolls.*

Elysium

2434 MISSION ST.
MISSION 94110
415-282-2447
Open nightly 5 p.m.-2 a.m.

Another winner in a series of fine retro bars, Elysium occupies the main floor of the Andora Hotel, attracting a posh young crowd to the Mission and the warm blue glow of its fish tank. A corner jukebox dispenses tunes from bygone decades, but the place never turns cheesy; rather, it feels like something distinctly out of time, an adventurous setting from a piece of bygone cinema.

Harry Denton's Starlight Room

SIR FRANCIS DRAKE HOTEL
450 POWELL ST.
UNION SQUARE 94102
415-395-8595
Open Tues.-Sat. 4:30 p.m.-2 a.m., Sun.-Mon. 4:30 p.m.-midnight

VISA MasterCard Diners Club International

With the second-best view in town, Harry Denton's is the young, single set's answer to the Top of the Mark. Additional characteristics include a high door charge, cheaper drinks, a loud band playing covers and a wall-to-wall, hormone-soaked clientele on the make. If you can handle all that, the Starlight Room makes for a pleasurable evening. Don't say we didn't warn you.

London Wine Bar

415 SANSOME ST.
FINANCIAL DISTRICT 94111
415-788-4811
Open Mon.-Fri. 11:30 a.m.-9 p.m.

A

With a wide selection of premier California and imported wines by the glass, this cozy, English-style bar located in the Financial District fills up with businesspeople of both sexes looking to blow off steam at the end of the day. The knowledgeable bartenders will help you find your way around the daily menu.

Orbit Room

1900 MARKET ST.
CASTRO 94102
415-252-9525
Open Sun.-Thurs. 7 a.m.-1 a.m., Fri.-Sat. 7 a.m.-2 a.m.

No cards

Look skyward as you enter this classy neighborhood lounge, one frequented by scooter-riders and sharp-dressed couples: the faux tin ceiling is just one of several elegant touches that make Orbit a hit. Tall, spindle-shaped tables surround a tiny bar, and window tables fill first; snag a seat near the jukebox fortified with great jazz and classical discs. Plan to arrive early, and don't be surprised to find yourself poured out the door at closing time.

Persian Aub Zam Zam

1633 HAIGHT ST.
HAIGHT-ASHBURY 94117
415-861-2545
Open Mon., Wed. & Fri.-Sat. 4 p.m.-2 a.m. (closing time varies.)

No cards

Don't tell Bruno you heard about his place from a guidebook-he probably won't serve you. Do, however, appreciate the Persian Aub Zam Zam for what it is: one of the most perfect bars in San Francisco. Bruno's father opened the place more than 40 years ago, as he will tell you in his curmudgeonly commentaries, and his specialty is the martini-order one with Finlandia and you've really befriended this guy. The dim decor is punctuated with the sweet, swinging music of the big-band era.

Rasselas

2801 CALIFORNIA ST.
PACIFIC HEIGHTS 94115
415-567-5010
Open Sun.-Thurs. 5 p.m.-12:30 a.m., Fri. & Sat. 5 p.m.-1:30 a.m.

A

Named after the hero of the Samuel Johnson story, this restaurant and nightclub is a local institution, offering tasty Ethiopian food and toe-tapping jazz nightly. Stylish patrons of mixed ethnicity lines up three-deep at the bar for a good vantage point from which to watch the band. Joe Handy plays here regularly, as well as the upper echelon of the local jazz acts. A pleasant find in an otherwise barren lower Pacific Heights neighborhood.

Red Room

827 SUTTER ST.
UNION SQUARE 94109
415-346-7666
Open nightly 5 p.m.-2 a.m.

VISA MasterCard

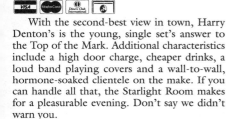

Nearly as hip as Backflip, its azul counterpart in the Phoenix, the Hotel Commodore's hot new Red Room suffers slightly from cooler-than-thou-itis. Curvy bartenders in leather pants swirl your $5 martini almost as efficiently as the dose of attitude it's served with. Part of Red Room's snobbery is legit-the place is undeniably attractive-but we hope the place will become genuinely friendly soon. Get there early and claim a seat beneath the curved wall of red liquid-filled bottles, or, if you're persistent, a thick-padded stool at the bar itself. A great place to people-watch.

Redwood Room

FOUR SEASONS CLIFT HOTEL
495 GEARY ST.
UNION SQUARE 94102
415-775-4700
Open Sun.-Thurs. 10 a.m.-12 a.m., Fri.-Sat. 10 a.m.-2 a.m.

A

Located in the grand old Clift Hotel, this elegantly appointed room is a San Francisco classic. High ceilings, gorgeous dark wood, art deco lighting fixtures and furnishings, majestic paintings, brass railings and beveled glass create an aura of impeccable good taste. Unbelievably, this entire room was paneled by one redwood tree. Businesspeople, tourists and lovers soak in the grand style while the piano player serenades them with snappy jazz.

Tonga Room

FAIRMONT HOTEL
950 MASON ST.
NOB HILL 94108
415-772-5278
Open Sun.-Thurs. 5 p.m.-midnight, Fri.-Sat. 5 p.m.-2 a.m.

A

The reputation of the Tonga Room precedes it. This Fantasy Island-style bar serves palatable Polynesian food and oversized, overpriced tropical drinks. But it's really the famed "tropical thunderstorms," (with real water that pours down around the pool), which hit every half hour after 5 p.m., that bring in the tourists. Great for an after-work party or an augmented evening of dancing and drinking.

Top of the Mark

MARK HOPKINS INTER-CONTINENTAL HOTEL
1 NOB HILL
NOB HILL
415-392-3434
Open Mon.-Sat. 4 p.m.-12:30 a.m., Sun. 10 a.m.-12:30 a.m.

A

Is it worth the troublesome parking, the long elevator ride, the sky-high drink prices? Absolutely. The Top of the Mark Hopkins Hotel is the city's most popular view for a reason-it's stunning. Whether a sunset, a foggy Saturday afternoon or a crystal-clear night, the vista afforded to patrons is phenomenal, and everyone-from starry-eyed honeymooners to jaded locals setting out on a weeknight-deserves that pleasure of sipping a drink here. Here's a parking tip: call a cab!

GAY BARS

Esta Noche

3079 16TH ST.
MISSION 94110
415-861-5757
Open daily 2 p.m.-2 a.m. Cover varies.
No cards

For a truly special San Francisco experience, check out Esta Noche, San Francisco's first and foremost Latin drag-queen bar. Unpretentious as it is authentic, this is the place where the guys and "girls" go to disco dance with reckless abandon to the sounds of a salsa beat. The club hosts a draggy striptease night on Fridays.

Lion Pub

2062 DIVISADERO
PACIFIC HEIGHTS 94117
415-567-6565
Open daily 3 p.m.-2 a.m.
No cards

Smack in the middle of conservative Pacific Heights sits the city's classiest gay bar, a Victorian housefront with a cozy, clubby, cruise-y interior. The bartenders are legendarily good-looking, and the music vacillates between smoky jazz and the incessant, throbbing *uhn-sss-uhn-sss* of Castro Street bar disco. From boy toys to ascot-wearing senior queens, the Lion roars with them all.

Martuni's

4 VALENCIA ST.
HAYES VALLEY 94103
415-241-0205
Open daily 4 p.m.-2 a.m.

VISA MasterCard

Duck inside the triangular porch at the corner of Valencia and Market: the flamboyant singing at the piano should dispel any misconceptions the minute you walk in that Martuni's isn't a gay bar- but everyone can feel comfortable here. Friendly waitresses, generous drinks, and a good-looking crowd comprised mostly of couples and young businessmen are among the many attractive qualities of this comfortable neighborhood addition. Don't worry about getting home: the restored F Muni line out front runs deep into the night.

Midnight Sun

467 18TH ST.
CASTRO 94114
415-861-4186
Open daily noon-2 a.m.
No cards

One of the oldest of the Castro bars, the Midnight Sun was already an institution in the Village People-loving '70s. Though the faces behind the bar have changed, this is still a popular spot for watching soap operas by day and good-looking men by night. Investigate their drink specials, and don't choose the Sun if you're claustrophobic-it's a popular place.

Rawhide

280 7TH ST.
SOMA 94103
415-621-1197
Open Mon.-Thurs. 4 p.m.-2 a.m., Fri.-Sun. noon-2 a.m.

San Francisco's best-known country-western bar is usually commandeered by gay men, coiffed cowboys who fill the dance floor with the clomping of boots and waves of bobbing ten-gallon hats. But if it's two-step, swing, waltz and line dancing you're seeking, this is the place to do it. Rawhide offers lessons most nights, and the crowd varies from experienced rug-cutters to the most novice. Yeee-haww!

CABARET & COMEDY

Club Fugazi

678 GREEN ST.
NORTH BEACH 94133
415-421-4222
Shows Wed.-Thurs. 8 p.m., Fri.-Sat. 7 p.m. & 10 p.m., Sun. 3 p.m. & 7 p.m. Tickets $20-$50.

The Fugazi, an old North Beach Italian music hall, has retained its cozy charm amid the frenetic antics of the late Steven Silvers' larger-than-life *Beach Blanket Babylon.* In its third decade and its umpteenth incarnation, the production (a spoof on a lovelorn Snow White and her adventures in topographically-challenging SF) still draws tourists and locals who can't get enough of the high-camp song-and-dance routines, outrageous costumes and outlandish hats. Sunday's matinee is the only show open to those under 21 of age.

Cobb's Comedy Club

THE CANNERY, 2801 LEAVENWORTH ST.
FISHERMAN'S WHARF 94133
415-928-4320
Shows and covers vary.

The Monday night showcase at this unadorned, 200-seat club is one of the best places to catch San Francisco's aspiring comics. For only five bucks and a two-drink minimum, you hear fourteen comedians in a grab bag of styles. National headliners are featured the rest of week, with strong opening and supporting acts; look in the weekly papers for discount coupons. If you're hungry, you can always grab a bite to eat at the adjoining Belle Roux before or after the show.

Finocchio's

506 BROADWAY
NORTH BEACH 94133
415-982-9388
Shows Fri.-Sat. 8:30 p.m., 10 p.m. & 11:30 p.m. Cover $14.50.
No cards

Long before gay pride provided San Francisco's gays and lesbians freedom to express themselves, the female impersonators at Finocchio's were all the rage. The novelty of cross-dressing has undoubtedly worn off some, and campy stage drag by today's standards seems tame, but Finocchio's-donning heels and feather boas since 1936-is still a prime nightlife attraction, especially for busloads of giddy tourists. There's no drink minimum; three different shows are performed nightly.

Josie's Cabaret & Juice Joint

3583 16TH ST.
CASTRO 94111
415-861-7933
Shows and covers vary.
No cards

Josie's tiny Cabaret and Juice Joint is the resurrection of Valencia Rose, a gay and lesbian theater forum popular in the mid-eighties. Primarily a venue for live comedy and one-person shows, Josie's has offered its stage to such national and up-and-coming gay talent as Lypsinka, Marga Gomez, local politician Tom Ammiano and actor Scott Capurro, as well as more serious introspective pieces on gay life. Mondays are open mike. Get here early for popular shows-they sell out quickly.

Mock Café

1070 VALENCIA ST.
MISSION 94110
415-641-0235
Admission varies.
No cards

A spin-off from the successful Marsh performance space, the Mock is a relatively new venue with irregularly scheduled spoken word performances. Poetry, commentary, soliloquy-there's something different every Saturday night.

Punch Line

444 BATTERY ST.
FINANCIAL DISTRICT 94111
415-397-7573
Shows vary. Cover $8-$12.

As local comics climb the ladder of success, they pass through the Punch Line, San Francisco's most professional comedy club. Part of the late Bill Graham's nightlife empire, the comfortable, brick-walled club presents some of San Francisco's most polished performers and national headliners, along with regularly scheduled amateur showcases. It is also one of the regular sites for the annual comedy competition. Italian food, pizza, deli sandwiches and snacks are available, and there's a two-drink minimum. Reservations recommended.

COFFEE HOUSES

Café Abir

1300 FULTON ST.
WESTERN ADDITION 94115
415-567-7654
Open daily 5:30 a.m.-12:30 a.m.

Commanding a larger and larger piece of real estate at Divisadero and Fulton, Abir's current empire includes a café, international newsstand and organic market. All are excellent, but the coffee house started it all: an airy, incense-scented room with Middle Eastern paintings, superb music (played at levels that allow conversation) and quick, accommodating staff. Arrive on the weekend anticipating a line for service, but once served, you'll always find a chair inside or out.

Café Flore

2298 MARKET ST.
CASTRO 94114
415-621-8579
Open daily 7 a.m.-11:30 p.m.
No cards

Flore stands as one of the Castro's great institutions: a funky, open-air café that's packed with people (mostly gay men and lesbians) every hour, every day they're open. Peruse the baked goods while you're in line, or choose from the overhead menu of sandwiches, soups and salads. You'll be given your drink and a number to take to your table; they'll deliver food for you, giving you plenty of time to strike up a pleasant conversation with the hunk at the next table.

Caffè Trieste
601 VALLEJO ST.
NORTH BEACH 94133
415-392-6739
Open Sun.-Thurs. 6:30 a.m.-11 p.m., Fri.-Sat. 6:30 a.m.-midnight.
No cards

Its name means "sad," but there's nothing weepy about this North Beach favorite, one of the city's oldest coffee houses. Tiled tables stretch along the walls, where Bohemians and Beat aficionados read, converse or play backgammon. Food is standard café fare: baked goods and simple sandwiches. Kerouac and Ginsberg loved the place, and you will, too.

Peets Coffee and Tea
2156 CHESTNUT ST.
MARINA 94123
415-931-8302
Open Mon.-Thurs. 6 a.m.-8 p.m., Sat.-Sun. 7 a.m.-8 p.m.

With a growing preponderance of Seattle-based Starbucks branches, San Francisco has legitimate cause for concern that some local roasters-namely Peets and other independent stores-stand to be usurped by Big Green. But this Marina district café feels healthy and strong, catering to a broad cross-section of healthful young clients. Order your latte at the back of the store, then peruse the comestibles and brewing paraphernalia while it's steaming. You can enjoy it at the small tables in the front or the long wooden bench outside, though many opt to carry theirs to go while they study the shops. **Other locations.**

DANCE CLUBS-STRAIGHT & GAY

Bahia Tropical
1600 MARKET ST.
CIVIC CENTER 94102
415-626-3306
Open daily 5 p.m.-2 a.m. Live music Sun.-Thurs. 9 p.m.-1 a.m.
Fri.-Sat. 9:30 p.m.-1:30 a.m. Cover varies; 2-drink minimum.

Blaring Brazilian beats will lure you off the street and into this tropical dance club featuring live Latin music nightly. Sultry samba dancers take the floor on Friday and Saturday nights after 11:30 p.m. A footloose, tropicalismic crowd packs the dance floor, despite the steep cover charges and the two-drink-minimum rule. Dance classes are offered Friday and Saturday nights.

Big Heart City
836 MISSION ST.
SOMA 94103
415-777-0666
Open daily 8 p.m.-2 a.m. Cover $10.

Big Heart City suffers from club schizophrenia lately, unable to decide if it's a hip hop club, modern dance Mecca, house palace or performance art space. No matter-you'll probably have a great time anyway, with a two-story dance floor and a young, mixed clientele. Goth rockers take over the club for Death Guild on Monday, and New Wave City, an '80s lovefest, happens on occasion.

The Café
2367 MARKET ST.
CASTRO 94114
415-861-3846
Open daily 12:30 a.m.-2 a.m.
No cards

In its umpteenth incarnation, the cheesy Café San Marcos is hot again, this time with the hottest lesbian dance venue in the Castro. Two floors of pulsating bodies, a patio, pool, pinball and a tiny outdoor deck for observing the passers-by-the Café is the epicenter for the gay weekend dance music scene. Don't miss this piece of San Francisco history.

Club 181
181 EDDY ST.
TENDERLOIN 94102
415-673-8181
Open Fri.-Sun. 9 p.m.-2 a.m. Cover $10.

In the heart of one of the city's roughest neighborhoods, the 181's opening reflected a remarkable gamble: would bar-hoppers forego dicey parking, long lines, dress codes and high cover charges to hang in the stylish S-shaped bar? Sure they would: 181 still fills on the weekends, a crowd of magnificently mixed colors, orientations and musical tastes, dancing and sweating for hours to a variety of deejays. Catch a cab to and from the 181, bring a purseful of cash and leave your hang-ups at home.

DNA Lounge

375 11TH ST.
SOMA 94103
415-626-1409
Open Fri.-Sun. 9 p.m.-2 a.m. Cover varies.
No cards

Years ago, the DNA was the happening SoMa nightspot, with live music and deejay dancing every night of the week. Lately, the club has all but atrophied, failing to compete with the more-adventurous v/SF, Endup and Covered Wagon clubs. But it's still a safe bet, particularly after hours when the bridge-and-tunnelers have lurched toward home. Leather and lycra (as well as tattoos and piercings) are de rigueur.

Endup

995 HARRISON ST.
SOMA 94103
415-357-0827
Open Wed.-Sun. 9 p.m. Closing time varies. Cover $5-$10.
No cards

Crammed under the freeway, this run-down-looking club hosts the most interesting crowds and the city's most colorful dance parties, complete with go-go dancers, an artificial outdoor waterfall and a pool room. Every night the venue hosts a different club, each with its own name and theme. Fag Fridays are followed by Saturday nights' G-Spot, a women-only dance party. But the club's Sunday Tea Dance, an all-day, everyone-welcome event that begins at 5 a.m., remains one of the city's longest, sweatiest and most-loved dance marathons.

Minna Street Gallery

111 MINNA ST.
SOMA 94105
415-974-1719
Open 7 p.m.-2 a.m. Wed.-Sun.

VISA MasterCard

Edgy art gallery by day, trendy dance club by night, postage-stamp-sized Minna is worth the trip. The city's best deejays weave a mix of auralia that goes hand-in-hand with the surrounding visuals. Occasionally, live artists take the stage, which occupies the far corner of the dance floor. Beer and wine flow freely, and the crowd is the most diverse and pleasant you'll find in the city; the Wednesday-after-work "electronicool" lounge is excellent. Check Minna out-during the day, and again after the sun goes down.

Nickie's

460 HAIGHT ST.
HAIGHT-ASHBURY 94117
415-621-6508
Open daily 9 p.m.-2 a.m. Cover $3-$5.
No cards

You haven't been dancing in San Francisco if you haven't been to Nickie's, the restaurant-turned-nightspot whose funky vibe and friendly clients are legendary. Check your local paper for listings: some nights are hip hop, others soul, still others 1970s disco, but any night you're there you'll revel in the sweaty, intimate thrill of its tiny dance floor.

Sound Factory

525 HARRISON ST.
SOMA 94105
415-979-8686
Open Sat. 9:30 p.m.-4:50 a.m. Cover $15.

VISA MasterCard

If you've outgrown the Palladium but are still in the mood for a mind-numbing suburban dance setting, check out the Sound Factory, a mouse-maze of a club with eight rooms and three floors for rugcutting. Like the Palladium, however, this isn't where the locals go.

Stud

399 9TH ST.
SOMA 94103
415-252-7883
Open daily 5 p.m.-2 a.m. or later. Cover $2-$5.

VISA MasterCard

And then there's the Stud, the funky, dark gay club that hosts dance nights including the ever-popular Trannyshack-a loud, fun drag show held every Tuesday night. Bet you never knew those red pumps came in a 13DDD and that bustier came in XXXL!

1015 Folsom

1015 FOLSOM ST.
SOMA 94103
415-431-1200
Open Tues.-Sun. 9 p.m.-2 a.m. or later. Cover $5-$10.

VISA MasterCard

Second only to Townsend for massive dance clubs, 1015 features three floors and six rooms of different scenes-from house and techno to drum-n-bass and trippy hip hop. Plan to stand in line for your entrance, but once inside, feel free to explore 1015's cavernous floorplan. It's hard not to have a good time here-check the *Bay Guardian* or the *SF Weekly* to investigate the week's listings.

Townsend

177 TOWNSEND
SOMA 94103
415-974-6020
Open Fri.-Sun. 10 p.m.-6 a.m. Cover $7-$10.

No cards

Big and ungainly as only a city club can be, Townsend features different themes on different nights. Saturday night's Universe is most popular, a line-out-the-door event featuring a broad mix of locals and hopefuls. Other nights of the week feature varying themes and hosts.

LIVE MUSIC CLUBS

Bimbo's 365 Club

1025 COLUMBUS AVE.
NORTH BEACH 94133
415-474-0365
Hours & covers vary according to bookings.

No cards

The lush, crimson-curtained walls of this nightclub exude the retro feel of a bygone era in which fedoras and fenders were in bloom, supper clubs reigned and the Mob ruled North Beach. Nowadays, however, it hosts a grab-bag of entertainment. Rock, jazz, lounge, surf-the music coming out of Bimbo's is always adventurous. Keep an eye out for the swing dance nights, when the club and its patrons are decked out in impeccable '40s style.

Boom Boom Room

1601 FILLMORE ST.
JAPANTOWN 94115
415-673-8000
Hours 2 p.m.-2 a.m. daily; cover varies.

No cards

When blues legend John Lee Hooker recently bought Jacks, the long-standing tavern opposite the Fillmore theater on Geary, no one had any doubt the place would be a success. Gracefully redecorated and imbued with a dollop of class, the club presents live blues and boogie seven nights a week, from pickup and jam bands to legends of the genre. And yes, John Lee himself occasionally joins the groups onstage to defend his status as one of the history's greatest bluesmen.

Bottom of the Hill

1233 17TH ST.
POTRERO HILL 94107
415-626-4455
Open Mon.-Fri. 3 p.m.-2 a.m., Sat. 8:30 p.m.-2 a.m., Sun. 3 p.m.-9 p.m. Cover for live shows $4-$8.

VISA MasterCard

Located at the foot of Potrero Hill, this neighborhood restaurant and bar has a sterling reputation for booking excellent local and medium-name artists. The stage has been widened, the patio cleared and a full array of draft beers stocked. Inside, check out the pool tables and the impromptu gallery of rock poster art. For alternative live music junkies, the Bottom of the Hill should be at the top of your list.

Grandviews Bar

GRAND HYATT HOTEL, 345 STOCKTON ST.
UNION SQUARE 94108
415-885-2800
Open daily 2 p.m.-2 a.m. No cover.

A

The best live jazz venue with a view, the Grandviews only recently began promoting its live music schedule, which ranges from piano combos to Middle Eastern drummers, vocalists and solo players. It's a gorgeous room overlooking the city's northern neighborhoods, and for a sky-high, its drink prices are well grounded. As always, you'll find the local crowds there during the week, and plenty of out-of-towners on the weekend. A newly rediscovered gem.

Great American Music Hall

859 O'FARRELL ST.
TENDERLOIN 94109
415-885-0750
Open 1 hour before early show (usu. 8:30 p.m.); closing times varies-end of show. Cover $5-20.

San Francisco's most eclectic live club is a beautifully-maintained turn-of-the-century music hall, complete with Corinthian pillars, ornate red-and-gold rococo trim and a U-shaped balcony overlooking the stage and main floor. Although it has the standard small round tables and cane-back chairs (usually jammed together), the Great American remains the most comfortable spot in town to see a great variety of music. Popular Bay Area dance bands hold forth when out-of-town headliners aren't booked. The promoters aren't afraid to take a risk when they know the music is of a high artistic quality.

Last Day Saloon

406 CLEMENT ST.
RICHMOND DISTRICT 94121
415-387-6343
Open daily 2 p.m.-2 a.m. Showtimes & cover vary.

No cards

One of the least pretentious rock clubs in the City, the Last Day is an old standby. Pop styles may come and go, but as long as there are audiences for earnest rock, blues and reggae, this solid nightspot will be packing them in. The dance floor is small, surrounded by tables, with a walk-up bar and a rear room for overflow seating. In addition to local favorites who churn out a multitude of boogie grooves, often for no cover, the Last Day books great blues, rock and rhythm-and-blues artists from around the country.

Lou's Pier 47

300 JEFFERSON ST.
FISHERMAN'S WHARF 94133
415-771-0377
Open daily 10 a.m.-1 a.m. Showtimes vary. Cover free-$10.

A

Right in the heart of the tourist mecca, Lou's retains a bit of Barbary Coast flavor largely through the gritty sounds of the live music booked nightly. The blues-and-roots music revival of recent years has been buoyed by bars such as this.

Maritime Hall

450 HARRISON ST.
SOMA 94105
415-974-0634
Shows & covers vary.

No cards

One of the city's newest venues, the Maritime is like a gymnasium converted into a music hall-with appropriate acoustics to boot. Several different stages are available, though shows are generally limited to two boxy rooms. Bands reflect a wide mix, from great rappers and reggae artists to local blues, punk and some oldie bands.

Noe Valley Ministry

1021 SANCHEZ ST.
NOE VALLEY 94114
415-282-2317
Shows Fri.-Sat. 8 p.m. Ticket prices vary.

No cards

Borrowing the sanctum of an actual Sanctuary Movement church, the Noe Valley Ministry presents an eclectic mix of folk, jazz, new-age and experimental music. Nearly every weekend some nationally known troubadour or adventurous music group takes the small stage and makes good use of the room's intimate seating and fine acoustics. The volunteer staff sells homemade refreshments.

Paradise Lounge

1501 FOLSOM ST.
SOMA 94103
415-861-6906
Open daily 6 p.m.-2 a.m. Cover $5 Fri.-Sat.

No cards

The crowd that supports the neighborhood's burgeoning new music scene starts their evening at the Paradise, a labyrinthine venue which boasts three stages and offers as many as five shows a night. The free entertainment Sunday through Thursday night includes jazz, pop cabaret and poetry. Serious pool playing and spoken-word performance occur upstairs. The club has expanded recently into the Transmission Theater next door on 11th Street. A tip: the bands alternate stages so score your seat for the next band while the current one is playing.

Pearl's
256 COLUMBUS AVE.
NORTH BEACH 94133
415-291-8255
Open Tues.-Sun. 9 p.m.-1 p.m. No cover.

Pearl's remains the mainstay for North Beach jazz, a nondescript, crowded room with a great house band and a variety of singers and soloists. It's great on a warm night, with the windows open to the parade of passers-by; a two-drink minimum is strictly enforced, and a limited menu is available if you're hungry.

Slim's
333 11TH ST.
SOMA 94103
415-255-0333
Open 1 hour before early show. Cover $3-$20. Showtimes vary.

Though not solely a blues club, Slim's has established itself as one of the City's most dependable stage for roots music with exceptionally good sound. Slim's has also become a stop for modern rockers who want to play to more intimate crowds. Earlybird patrons secure the limited table seating, but it's standing room only for the rest of the crowd. Wear layers you don't mind peeling: Slims can become sweltering on hot summer nights.

SUPPER CLUBS

(see reviews in Dining)

Backflip
601 EDDY ST.
TENDERLOIN 94109
415-771-3547
Dinner Tues.-Sat., $$

Page 24

Bix
56 GOLD ST.
NORTH BEACH, 94111
415-433-6300
Lunch Mon.-Fri., Dinner nightly, $$$

A

Page 27

Bruno's
2389 MISSION ST.
MISSION 94110
415-550-7455
Dinner Tues.-Sat., $$

Page 29

Enrico's Sidewalk Café & Restaurant
504 BROADWAY
NORTH BEACH 94133
415-982-6223
Lunch & Dinner daily, $$

A

Page 41

42 Degrees
235 16TH ST.
SOMA 94107
415-777-5558
Lunch Mon.-Fri., Dinner Wed.-Sat., $$$

Page 45

Piaf's
1686 MARKET STREET
CIVIC CENTER 94102
415-864-3700
Lunch Tues.-Fri., Dinner Tues.-Sat., $$

Page 65

Rose Pistola
532 COLUMBUS AVE.
NORTH BEACH 94133
415-399-0499
Lunch & Dinner daily, $$$

Page 69

Storyville
1751 FULTON ST.
HAIGHT-ASHBURY 94117
415-441-1751
Dinner Tues.-Sun., $$

A

Page 73

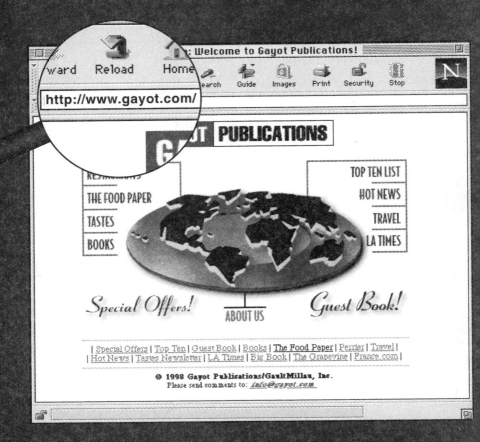

SHOPPING

CONTENTS

A SHOPPER'S HAVEN

Since its founding a century and a half ago, San Francisco has been an eccentric town, a strange collaboration between conservative and crazy. It's this mix that gives San Francisco's shopping scene its character. No matter what you're seeking, from the classic to the bizarre, you'll find a shop that sells it.

Shopping in San Francisco is defined by neighborhoods, each with an individual charm and character. In recent years, big-name chain stores have been popping up in every shopping mall and regional shopping center. San Francisco has not been spared this trend, and has its share of **Gap**, **Disney**, **Limited**, **Sanrio** and the like. For those who need their **Old Navy** and **Victoria's Secret** fix, we've included what we consider the best of these stores (or at least the branch we consider the most interesting); you may even see some regional differences in the merchandise they carry.

San Francisco does have its share of shopping centers, but they're malls with a difference. **The San Francisco Shopping Centre**, with its prestigious **Nordstrom** on the top five floors, is also rumored to have Bloomingdales moving in next door. **Crocker Galleria** is a European-style arcade in the heart of the Financial District. Also in the Financial District, the **Embarcadero Center** has a cinema that features independent first-run films, as well as four bi- and tri-level blocks of tony shops. Tourist-mobbed **Ghirardelli Square** and **Pier 39** offer great shopping and spectacular views of the San Francisco Bay. Outlying **Stonestown Galleria** is the closest you'll find to a suburban mall, with **Macy's** and **Nordstrom** as its anchors.

But where San Franciscans head for the most rewarding shopping is into the neighborhoods, to quirky, one-of-a-kind boutiques that give each neighborhood a slightly different character. For this reason, we've attempted to include only the best of the chain stores, and focused primarily on shops that you'll only find in San Francisco.

Here are our favorite neighborhoods where you'll find the best shopping:

UNION SQUARE

The most famous of San Francisco's shopping districts, this downtown region centers on a one-block spot of greenery of the same name. Aside from the **department stores**, **art galleries** and big-money **retail stores** adjacent to Union Square, make sure to wander Sutter and Post streets, Grant Avenue and Maiden Lane. Head down Stockton or Powell Street to the San Francisco Shopping Centre on Market Street. So many of the big-name **designer boutiques** have set up shop on the block of Post Street between Stockton and Grant Avenues that we've named it "Designer Row." (Note that some of the addresses listed here as Union Square may actually be a few blocks away-within easy walking distance for inclusion in a shopping trip. The **Financial District** and **Chinatown** are likewise close by.)

CASTRO

This area caters to the neighborhood's trendy, urban fashion-conscious residents, and most of the shopping is centered around the intersection of Castro and 18th streets. The area is growing, though, with more and more shops springing up along Market Street. For a cutting-edge **urban fashion** scene, the Castro-though it caters mostly to gay men-is as close as it's going to get in San Francisco. You'll also find great shops selling **housewares**, **sunglasses**, and **books**.

UNION STREET & THE MARINA

Union Street remains a favorite of the young and the upscale for its **boutiques**, **jewelry shops** and **antique stores** as well as its **cafés** and **bars**. Start at Van Ness Avenue, head west and you'll pass through a shopper's paradise. A few blocks south, Chestnut Street marks the heart of the Marina, a favorite residential area for the interesting mix of young professionals and retirees. Walking along Chestnut between Fillmore and Divisadero Streets, you'll get a sense of what it's like to live in San Francisco: you'll find all the necessities of life-**dry cleaners**, **delicatessens**, **produce markets**, stores with **home furnishings**, **juice bars** and lots of **restaurants** and **coffee bars**. After dark, the bar scene in both neighborhoods becomes quite lively.

FISHERMAN'S WHARF

Every visitor to San Francisco makes at least one trip to Fisherman's Wharf. We consider the most interesting shopping spots to be **Pier 39**, a Cape Cod-like complex of stores overlooking a colony of sea lions, and **Ghirardelli Square**, a former mill and factory. Both are almost always crowded with tourists, as is Jefferson Street, the most direct walking route between the two.

UPPER FILLMORE/JAPANTOWN

Fillmore Street, from Post to Pacific Streets is a bustling shopping route in a residential neighborhood packed with trendy **boutiques**, unique **home furnishing shops** and some of the city's best **thrift shops**. At Post, the Upper Fillmore gives way to Japantown, San Francisco's center of Japanese cultural and social life. In the heart of Japantown is the **Japan Center**, an indoor complex which includes **shops**, **restaurants**, the **Miyako Hotel**, a **spa** and a **multiplex cinema**.

THE UPPER HAIGHT

For a look at how the times have been a-changing, head over to Haight Street in the Haight-Ashbury from Masonic to Stanyan Streets, the locus of flower power in the 1960s. Smartly dressed baby boomers mix in with street people and diehard hippies. The best **vintage clothing** and **CD and record stores** are here.

HAYES VALLEY

A mere three blocks of Hayes Street between Laguna Street and the Civic Center, Hayes Valley marks the most up-and-coming shopping area at the moment. Each store radiates a different ambience: trendy **shoe shops**, funky **boutiques**, quirky **jewelry** shops and eclectic **art galleries**-all worthy of perusal. Once a month, Hayes Valley shops stay open late, and bar patrons spill out onto the streets. The neighborhood is rapidly expanding, with a number of interesting **antique shops** that have opened on Market and Gough Streets, a few blocks south.

MISSION

You'll find **bookshops** in every neighborhood, but the highest concentration of both new and second-hand tomes is on Valencia Street in the Mission district. Stores here reflect the ethnic diversity of the neighborhood, with **markets** selling Mexican and South and Central American **produce**. The Mission is also a great source for affordable items for the home; **lamps**, **candles**, **bedspreads**, **picture frames** and much more.

NOE VALLEY

This quiet residential neighborhood has a small-town feel. When the sun shines, dogs, children and parents line the sidewalk along 24th Street, the one main shopping corridor between Douglas and Church. The neighborhood remains low-key and friendly, perhaps because this area doesn't get a lot of through traffic. Shopping in Noe Valley-for kids' clothes, shoes, books, and records and CDs-is a relaxing experience.

NORTH BEACH

North Beach is San Francisco's most "European" neighborhood. We love to wander up and down Grant and Columbus Avenues, north of Broadway, past the busy coffee houses, restaurants and shops where Italian is more often the language of choice. For more than a century, offbeat North Beach has represented the Little Italy of the West, attracting Beatniks in the 1950s and topless dancers in the 1960s. It continues to be free-spirited. Yet North Beach is also home to many high-style shops specializing in European imports, as well as clothes and household goods.

SACRAMENTO STREET & PRESIDIO HEIGHTS

Farther west in prosperous Presidio Heights, the several-block-long stretch of Sacramento Street is lined with fashionable shops for clothing and home furnishings. We like the calm, civilized character of this neighborhood.

SOUTH OF MARKET

Also known as SoMa, this is where you'll find the outlets and discount stores for a growing number of San Francisco clothing manufacturers. The most interesting outlets are clustered in the area bounded by Brannan, Fourth and Townsend streets. A number of edgy art galleries have taken root as well. When you get tired of shopping, stop off at the South Park Café (on South Park, off Third Street) for refreshments.

ANTIQUES & COLLECTIBLES

Artiques

2167 UNION ST.
UNION STREET 94123
415-929-6969
Open daily

Billing itself as "affordable art," Artiques is a major dealer in Louis Icart and Maxfield Parrish lithographs. The gallery also sells a varied assemblage of seventeenth-century to early twentieth-century etchings, lithographs and oils. If you poke around a bit, you're sure to find something you not only love but can afford.

Butterfield and Butterfield

220 SAN BRUNO AVE.
POTRERO HILL 94103
415-861-7500
Open Mon.-Fri.

A San Francisco institution since 1865, Butterfield's appraises all collectibles, but is better known for its year-round auctions of furniture, art, antiques, silver, rugs, jewelry and wine.

Designers Center

UPPER LEVEL, TANFORAN PARK
SAN BRUNO 94066
650-871-4462; 888-410-GIFT,
FAX 650-827-7312
Open Daily

An incredible selection of gift items, collectibles and limited-edition art awaits your visit—so complete that it is the largest gift and collectible store in Northern California (by the SFO airport.) Some of the prestigious lines here include Swarovski Crystal, Walt Disney Classics Collection, Lladro, Armani, Thomas Kinkade paintings, Walt Disney Animation cells, Lena Lui and more. Designers Center often hosts exclusive collector events that are done with style and panache. Ask the friendly and knowledgeable staff about perks such as free gift wrapping, free shipping on any purchase over $100 and more.

Don's Antiques

560 & 572 Valencia St.
Mission 94110
415-586-3022
Open Sat.-Sun.

If you're in the neighborhood on the weekend, stop in and check out the 9,000 square feet of distinctive lamps, avant-garde home furnishings, kitchenware, and much, much more. Don't be put off by the disarray, Don's is the kind of place to find that trinket you were always looking for—or vintage furniture for your entire house.

Edward Davidson

2014 Broadway
Union Street 94123
415-563-2404
Call for hours.

Some of the most arresting items in this collection of silver and antiques are the pieces of antique jewelry. The rest is comprised of primarily vintage English, American and San Francisco silver-a set of silver napkin rings makes an unusual gift. Davidson also has antique paintings in his collection.

Halcyon Antiques

2263 Union St.
Union Street 94123
415-586-3022
Open Sat.-Wed.

Halcyon's eclectic collection includes eighteenth-century American Chippendale pieces, carved Chinese wooden screens, silver, jewelry, books and the obligatory English furniture. Owner Don Fried buys entire estates, displays the best pieces in this Union Street shop and puts the remainders in his Don's Antiques on Valencia Street (see entry above) in the Mission. Great prices; terrific selection.

Kimberly Bragg Design

3640 Sacramento St.
Presidio Heights 94118
415-563-8122
Open Mon.-Sat.

Kimberly Bragg specializes in French and English antiques, but keeps an eye out for other interesting household eccentricities. You'll find quality items in a good range of prices. The shop also offers interior design services, including chair upholstering and curtainmaking.

Paris 1925

1954 Union St.
Union Street 94123
415-567-1925
Open Tues.-Sun.

This store sells an ever-changing collection of vintage and pre-owned watches, all of which come with a one-year warranty. Some of the more valuable include signed Vacheron and Constantin pieces that date to the 1940s and Patek Philippes from the 1950s. Paris 1925 is also an authorized dealer for new watches by Jaeger LeCoultre, Porsche by IWC, Fortis and many other fine makers. Should you be in the market for the Fortis Limited Edition Platinum Alarm chronograph alarm watch, you can purchase one here. If you are looking for something special, be sure to ask; the shop offers much more than the mainly new pieces on display in the showcases.

Serge Matt Antiques

1878 Union St.
Union Street 94123
415-921-7656
Open Mon.-Sat.

Eighteenth- and nineteenth-century antique furniture and accessories are sold here at reasonable prices. The basement contains English and French country furniture and some prints.

Telegraph Hill Antiques

580 Union St.
North Beach 94133
415-982-7055
Open Mon.-Sat.

You'll find countless treasures at this tiny store: you may come across an original Lalique or Verlys piece.

Therien and Co.

411 Vermont St.
SoMa 94107
415-956-8850
Open Mon.-Fri.

A serene, civilized establishment standing in the shadow of the 101 Freeway, Therien's shop features old Sheffield plates and antique porcelain, much of which is beautifully displayed on seventeenth- and eighteenth-centu ry furniture. You'll also find some especially lovely silver pieces, including a few contemporary tea services and serving utensils.

BEAUTY & HEALTH

COSMETICS & BEAUTY PRODUCTS

BeneFit Cosmetics

2219 Chestnut St.
Marina 94123
415-567-1173
Open daily

Makeup is fun at a BeneFit salon, where you are invited to "play with" anything you desire from their cosmetics line. Who can resist the promise of kissable lips from "Smoo...ch," getting rid of frown lines with "Bo-ing!" or firming up thighs with "Thigh Hopes"? Two local girls, twin sisters Jane and Jean Ford, are the brains behind BeneFit. **Other locations.**

Body Time

1932 Fillmore St.
Upper Fillmore 94115
415-771-2431
Open daily

More than twenty years ago in Berkeley, Body Time (then known as The Body Shop) made its mark in the toiletries world by opening a small shop selling quality handmade soaps in traditional and exotic fragrances that were cut, wrapped and labeled on the premises. It also was a pioneer of recycling containers and customizing scents. The Body Time line includes bath oils, bubble baths, lotions, soaps, shampoos, masks, creams, cleansers and intoxicating oils, all offered in a range of scents from Canton rose to muguet (lily of the valley). **Other locations.**

MAC on Union

1833 Union St.
Union Street 94123
415-771-6113
Open daily

Previously available only in department stores, the vamp-look cosmetics sold in this huge, well-lit shop have been popularized lately by entertainer and drag queen RuPaul. Make an appointment with their professional make-up artists. Their outrageous lipstick colors include Fetish, Viva Glam, and Twig.

HAIR SALONS

Architects and Heroes

580 Bush St.
Union Square 94108
415-391-8833
Open Tues.-Sat.

2239 Fillmore St.
Upper Fillmore 94117
415-921-8383
Open Tues.-Sun.

You feel like you've entered into an art gallery rather than a hair salon, but if you want a hair experience, book in advance for a cut with one of A & H's professionals. The pre-cut shampoo is more like a luxurious head massage (and will probably lull you to sleep); cuts or coloring here are top-notch.

Di Pietro Todd Salon

177 Post St.
Financial District 94108
415-397-0177
Open Tues.-Sat.

Enjoy lunch at the in-salon café while you observe the latest hairstyles being created. A full crew of stylists, colorists, manicurists and a few "aestheticians" wander around this attractive, airy space, working magic on their chic clientele. Di Pietro Todd is the place to try out that new super-short haircut you've always wanted or to change your hair from blond to raven black. Prices range from $50 to $115.

Mister Lee

834 Jones St.
Union Square 94109
415-474-6002
Open Mon.-Sat.

The eve of the opera or symphony's opening night is booked up months in advance by the local social set, but Mister Lee or one of his associates can probably fit you in with San Francisco's finest at any other time. Haircut prices range from $35 to $65. The salon's full range of European-style spa services includes body massage, manicure, hair extension and reflexology.

77 Maiden Ln.

77 MAIDEN LN.
UNION SQUARE 94108
415-391-7777
Open daily

With an eye on ecology, Sherlee Rhines' 77 Maiden Lane salon make use of natural cosmetics and doesn't use aerosols. The full-service salon charges between $50 and $70 for a haircut. Makeup lessons, a specialty of the house, range from $45 to $125; ask about using 77 Maiden Lane's own line of makeup. For a day of pampering, we recommend one of their spa packages for men or women (see "Spas" in Sports & Leisure).

Yosh

173 MAIDEN LN.
UNION SQUARE 94108
415-989-7704
Open Tues.-Sat.

Specializing only in hair and constantly written up in *Elle*, *Vogue*, and *Marie Claire*, this internationally renowned salon is tucked away behind Union Square on the second floor of a peaceful cul-de-sac. Prices range from $45 to $125 for a haircut.

HERBALISTS

An-Da-Jiang

2272 MISSION ST.
MISSION 94110
514-861-3959
Open Mon.-Sat.

Chinese herbalism is one of today's hottest trends in alternative medicine, and this shop caters to the city's ills. Inspect the splendid array of roots and ancient remedies to cure what ails you. Other services include acupuncture and acupressure.

Vinh Khang Herbs and Gensengs

512 CLEMENT ST.
RICHMOND 94118
415-752-8336
Open daily

Tell them your condition, however trivial you think it is, and let Vinh Khang's herbal specialists mix up a customized concoction of herbs that you can take in pill form or in tea. They may not smell good, but they're reputed to do the trick.

Great China Wok Co. and Herbs

857 WASHINGTON ST.
CHINATOWN 94108
415-982-2195
Open daily

If you don't speak Chinese, you may have trouble communicating with the specialists here. But use a bit of sign language to describe your symptoms, and chances are good the herbalist will dip into his neatly organized drawers and concoct a mixture that might make you feel better. If Ginseng is your thing, here you'll have your choice of it-in every imaginable form.

BOOKS & NEWSSTANDS

BOOKS

A Clean Well-Lighted Place for Books

OPERA PLAZA
601 VAN NESS AVE.
HAYES VALLEY 94102
415-441-6670
Open daily

The name of this bookseller, taken from an Ernest Hemingway short story, is apt; it also boasts a nicely chosen poetry and contemporary fiction section, a well-stocked mystery section and titillating shelves of biographies and travel books. The shop frequently hosts book signings and popular authors' readings.

A Different Light

489 CASTRO ST.
CASTRO 94114
415-431-0891
Open daily

A Different Light stocks a thorough selection of books by and about the gay community. Come here for gay, lesbian, and transgender-oriented literature, videos, magazines and novelty items. This specialty bookstore carries many works by local authors.

Anderson Harrison Books

552 HAYES ST.
HAYES VALLEY 94102
415-554-0435
Open Wed- Sun.

If you're looking for a hard-to-find or out-of-print title or want to establish a personal collection or library, look no further: Anderson

Harrison specializes in literature arts and fine bindings. Amid a setting of warm yellow walls, green leather chairs and fresh-cut flowers, the store's owners will help you find any volume you're seeking. Also open by appointment.

Argonaut Book Shop

786 SUTTER ST.
UNION SQUARE 94109
415-474-9067
Open Mon.-Sat.

This peaceful, uncluttered shop is stocked with rare and out-of-print books, prints, maps and manuscripts. Owner Robert Haines has an especially fine collection of books and maps from early California, including the Gold Rush days, along with lovely prints of old San Francisco. A must for the California history buff.

Barnes & Noble

2552 TAYLOR ST.
FISHERMAN'S WHARF 94133
415-292-6762
Open daily

San Francisco prides itself on the city's wealth of independent book merchants, yet this big B&B-the only one within the city proper-remains a destination for those seeking discounted bestsellers, international magazines, and most pop culture publications under the sun. With a newly added multimedia aisle and a large selection of computer books, Barnes & Noble appeals to out-of-town businesspeople, browsing tourists, and locals looking to save time with one-stop shopping. Other locations in Oakland, Berkeley, San Jose, and several on the Peninsula.

Books Inc.

2275 MARKET ST.
CASTRO 94114
415-864-6777
Open daily

These large well-stocked book stores have something for everyone, plus good personal service and late evening hours. **Also in the Marina (2251 Chestnut St., 415-931-3633) and Laurel Village (3515 California St., 415-221-3666).**

The Booksmith

1644 HAIGHT ST.
HAIGHT-ASHBURY 94117
415-863-8688
Open daily

A good, all-purpose bookstore in the Haight, with a commendable mix of new and second-hand books and magazines, the Booksmith is known for its helpful staff. It's a bit of an oddball shop, highly recommended for the dedicated browser, with an admirable collection of contemporary fiction.

Borders Books and Music

400 POST ST.
UNION SQUARE 94108
415-399-1633
Open daily

Occupying four floors of prime real estate overlooking Union Square, Borders' vast space enables it to have in-depth selections of books on almost every imaginable topic. In the children's area you'll find a place to sit, read and play. We were impressed with the extensive computer and cookbook sections, as well as the selection of newspapers and magazines from around the world. The top two floors are dedicated to recorded music, audio books, videos and new media, including laser discs, DVDs and CD-ROMs. Most hardcover books are discounted. The daily schedule of events features author appearances, movie screenings, live music and book discussion groups; an in-store café overlooks Union Square and serves light meals and snacks.

The Brick Row Book Shop

49 GEARY ST.
UNION SQUARE 94108
415-398-0414
Open Mon.-Sat.

Brick Row's shelves are sculpted to look like those of a medieval castle's, and on them sit rare and antiquarian books of every genre. Emphasis is on first-edition eighteenth- and nineteenth-century English and American literature. Book lovers and collectors must make a detour to visit this curious shop, located on the second floor of a downtown office building. Single books or entire libraries are purchased from private collections.

Browser Books

2195 FILLMORE ST.
UPPER FILLMORE 94115
415-567-8027
Open daily

Browser offers a cozy, bookwormish atmosphere, with its volumes attractively arranged on wooden shelves. Their selection continues to be strong in contemporary and classic fiction as well as unusual travel books. Help yourself to a cup of coffee and plop down for a lengthy appraisal of your selection before committing to a purchase.

Builders Booksource

GHIRARDELLI SQUARE, 900 NORTH POINT
FISHERMAN'S WHARF 94109
415-440-5773
Open daily

Every respectable source of information on building or remodeling-even on building code specifications-is available at Builders Booksource. Their selection covers architecture, interior design, landscaping, gardening, construction and engineering. A visit here is a must before undertaking any do-it-yourself home project.

City Lights Books

261 COLUMBUS AVE.
NORTH BEACH 94133
415-362-8193
Open daily

A literary meeting place since 1953, City Lights is synonymous with the city's literary life. Through its door have passed the movers and shakers in every branch of the arts from the Beat era to the present. It was here that Allen Ginsburg first read *Howl* (it was published by City Lights owner and poet Lawrence Ferlinghetti). Still going strong, the North Beach bookstore has a room devoted entirely to poetry and boasts a decent selection of periodicals and unusual books. While away an hour or two as you check out City Lights' latest small-press publications; then buy the latest novel by some twentysomething literary prodigy and read it over an espresso down the street.

European Book Store

925 LARKIN ST.
TENDERLOIN 94109
415-474-0626
Open Mon.-Sat.

A must for European emigrés and European wannabes, this shop stocks foreign-language textbooks and dictionaries, plus wide selections of fine literature, children's literature and magazines, mostly in French, Spanish and German.

Great Expectations

1512 HAIGHT ST.
HAIGHT-ASHBURY 94117
415-863-5515
Open daily

Here's where to find hip reading material, underground comics, rock-star biographies and cult classics such as Charles Bukowski's Love is a Dog from Hell. Great Expectations stocks as many T-shirts as they do books.

National Park Store

PIER 39
FISHERMAN'S WHARF 94133
415-433-7221
Open daily

This store features literature of the American West: Native Americans, cowboy culture, the Southwest, California history, backpacking, hiking and more. It also features a comprehensive selection of San Francisco guides, history books and videos of every National Park in the West. A portion of each sale goes to National Park Services.

Richard Hilkert Bookseller

333 HAYES ST.
HAYES VALLEY 94102
415-863-3339
Open Mon.-Sat. & by appt.

We stop in to say hello to Richard Hilkert whenever we are in the area, which gives us a chance to browse his eclectic selection of new and used books. A visit here is like going to a private library: we've found children's books, cookbooks and even novels never seen in other bookstores. Hilkert supplies libraries and schools throughout the country with their interior-design texts-a specialty of the shop. Drop in later in the afternoon and Hilkert just might pour you a drink.

Rizzoli

117 POST ST.
UNION SQUARE 94108
415-984-0225
Open daily

How refreshing to escape the megastore atmosphere and do your book shopping at Rizzoli! Packed floor-to-ceiling shelves remind you of a university library or European bookstore. You'll like the calm and quiet of the store, as well as its eclectic selection.

Stacy's

581 MARKET ST.
FINANCIAL DISTRICT 94111
415-421-4687
Open daily

The best place for reference books, including those about computers and computer software, is gargantuan Stacy's, where you'll find an up-to-date selection of technical and business volumes as well as current fiction, nonfiction and periodicals. The shop has a lively list of in-person authors' readings.

Thomas Bros. Maps

550 JACKSON ST.
FINANCIAL 94133
415-981-7520
Open Mon.-Fri.

Ground zero for map fanatics and travelers, this store carries domestic and world guidebooks, maps of all kinds, as well as the entire collection of Thomas Brothers' California county maps--don't drive without one.

Used Books Company

4190 24TH ST.
NOE VALLEY 94114
415-648-8733
Open Tues.-Sun.

You're sure to walk out with a couple of finds after visiting this well-organized shop, one whose shelves boast an intriguing collection of used hardcover and paperback books. Prices are very fair, and friendly owners will be happy to fill any special requests for hard-to-find titles.

William K. Stout Architectural Books

804 MONTGOMERY ST.
FINANCIAL DISTRICT 94111
415-391-6757
Open Mon.-Sat.

Woman- and man-made structures are featured here-an outstanding collection of both new and rare architectural books for scholars and novices alike.

Writers Bookstore

2848 WEBSTER ST.
UNION STREET 94123
415-921-2620
Open daily

This small, friendly store discounts new titles on all topics by 20%-80%. Its constantly changing stock includes cookbooks, tomes on interior design and architecture, best-sellers, paperbacks, used books and review copies. Neighborhood regulars drop in to chat about what they've been reading and invariably leave with an armload of new books.

NEWSSTANDS

Café de la Presse

352 GRANT AVE.
UNION SQUARE 94108
415-398-2680
Open daily

The international news hound will find a truly superlative collection of foreign-language books, newspapers and magazines at this tiny store, as well as a smattering of overseas travel guides and maps. All this, coupled with a French-style café, makes Café de la Presse both a destination and hangout for those who enjoy all things European.

Eastern Newsstand

1 EMBARCADERO CENTER
FINANCIAL DISTRICT 94111
415-433-4007
Open daily

When you're looking for the current issue of *New York Magazine* or regional magazines for other cities, you can find them here, as well as a selection of foreign periodicals.

Harold's International Newsstand

524 GEARY ST.
UNION SQUARE 94108
415-441-2665
Open daily

Whatever newspaper or magazine you want, it's likely that Harold's will have it. In addition to sporting, literary or photographic titles, this is the best place in town to find out-of-town newspapers.

Kinokuniya Bookstore

JAPAN CENTER, KINOKUNIYA BUILDING
1581 WEBSTER ST.
JAPANTOWN 94115
415-567-7625
Open daily

Japanese magazines, books, videos and recorded music fill this enormous bookstore. Whether the Japanese edition of Newsweek or

Seventeen or translation of *Diana, Princess of Wales*, chances are good they are here. A large "Asia in English" department features English-language books on all aspects of Japanese history and culture. We know of no other place to find a larger selection of instructional books on origami, in both Japanese and English. Those interested in learning Japanese can purchase audio and video tapes, CDs and other learning aids.

CIGARS & TOBACCONISTS

Dunhill

250 Post St.
Union Square 94108
415-781-3368
Open daily

Proper San Franciscans come to the venerable Dunhill for their tobacco and their pipe and cigar accessories, including lighters. Cigars are kept at the correct temperature in the humidor at the back of the store. The full line of Dunhill menswear, leather goods and accessories are also available here.

Grant's Tobacconists

562 Market St.
Union Square 94108
415-981-1000
Open Mon.-Sat.

Beginning cigar smokers and longtime aficionados stop to talk cigars with Grant's staff members, who make a point of trying out all the cigars-and there are many-they carry. Those who enjoy smoking (or who need the ideal gift for the smoker) will find what they're looking for in this well-rounded selection of pipes, cigars, tobaccos, humidors and smoking accessories.

Jim Mate Pipe and Tobacco Shop

575 Geary St.
Union Square 94102
415-775-6634
Open Mon.-Sat.

A well-known tobacconist, Jim Mate sells fine pipes from the likes of Sasieni, Dunhill and GBD, along with the world's finest cigars and tobaccos. Mate's house blend is exceptional; also quite respectable are his house-brand cigars.

Sherlock's Haven

275 Battery St.
Financial District 94111
415-362-1405
Open daily

In addition to the requisite large selection of cigars, the shop offers a range of cigarettes, from dizzying French Gitanes to smooth Virginia Plains, fine South American cigars and the standard French and English brands of pipes. Sherlock's Haven is the only authorized Davidoff merchant in the city.

CLOTHES, SHOES & ACCESSORIES

CHILDREN'S CLOTHES

Dottie Doolittle

3680 Sacramento St.
Presidio Heights 94118
415-563-3244
Open daily

A pleasant, spacious shop that's supply central for Daddy's little princesses aged 4-14 (and considering their prices, let's hope Daddy claims royalty of some sort), Dottie Doolittle sells stylish sportswear as well as a multitude of classic pretty dresses. Fetching, beautifully made infant wear is displayed in pink and blue sections at the rear of the store, where you'll also find exquisite silk and linen christening gowns.

Kids Only

1608 HAIGHT ST.
HAIGHT-ASHBURY 94117
415-552-5445
Open daily

If you can't abide clutter, stay out of this shop, but if you're looking for attractive, practical, fairly priced clothing for infants and children, you'll have come to the right place. No $150 designer playsuits here, just fun clothes that wear well. Accessorize each outfit with one of their brightly printed hats in a variety of styles. A must-visit for clothing historians and dedicated hippies, Kids Only also stocks tiny tie-dyed T-shirts in psychedelic colors.

Kinder Sport

3566 SACRAMENTO ST.
PRESIDIO HEIGHTS 94118
415-563-7778
Open daily

Apparently, it's never too early to take sports seriously, judging by the success of this ski-clothing shop for children from 8 to18. Eschewing animal prints, French skiwear manufacturers such as Killy and Boy have miniaturized their chic, streamlined adult lines for the small-but-earnest skier.

Mudpie

1694 UNION ST.
UNION STREET 94123
415-771-9262
Open daily

Every time we turn around, Mudpie has opened another branch. This is the main store, where you'll find everything from lunch boxes to layettes, stuffed animals, Madame Alexander dolls, dance costumes, books, toys and, of course, oodles of clothes-some imported from France, some from local designers. The Mudpie Homeworks shop a block away carries cribs, tables, chairs, all for kids, and beds and furniture for their parents too. **Other locations.**

Peek-A-Boutique

1306 CASTRO ST.
NOE VALLEY 94114
415-641-6192
Open daily

Peek-A-Boutique is the place to find second-hand children's clothing for as much as 50%-75% off its original price. This utterly charming shop for clothes and toys is full of unique, hand-made gifts for privileged tots.

Small Fry's

4066 24TH ST.
NOE VALLEY 94114
415-648-3954
Open daily

Small Fry's specializes in comfortable and affordable play clothes, sleepwear and dresses. They carry newborn-7 sizes for boys, newborn-10 for girls. Look no further for babies' tie-dyes, Oshkosh overalls and Converse trainers for tots, as well as fake leopard furs for toddlers. Pop star Madonna's child, Lourdes, has an account here.

Thursday's Child

1980 UNION ST.
UNION STREET 94123
415-346-1666
Open daily

As at so many children's clothing shops, this packed basement shop is filled with merry pandemonium. If you have the patience to sort through their towering stacks on the tables and shelves, you'll find great bargains on all kinds of kids' clothes.

Young Man's Fancy

3527 CALIFORNIA ST.
LAUREL HEIGHTS 94118
415-221-4230
Open Mon.-Sat.

Boys and young men are outfitted in the traditional prep-school look at this San Francisco institution. They sell button-down oxford cloth shirts, Shetland sweaters and tweed jackets galore by such labels as Boston Trader and Polo University. A wide selection includes tennis, golf and ski attire, and Young Man's Fancy's own well-made, well-priced labels. The store attracts such a loyal following that many formerly youthful clients continue to outfit themselves here.

Yountville

2416 FILLMORE ST.
UPPER FILLMORE 94115
415-922-5050
Open Mon.-Sat.

Doting grandmothers love the well-rounded selection of upscale clothes and accessories for newborns through preteens at this bright little shop, which represents many trendy top European outfitters.

EYEWEAR

Eyewear is a fashion statement these days, but if you leave your favorites at home, **Sunglass Hut** and **Sun Shade Optique** carry both cheap and stylish frames and seem to have branches on every other street corner. Consult your telephone directory for locations.

Eyedare

3199 16TH ST.
MISSION 94103
415-241-0240
Open Mon.-Sat.

Sometimes shopping for frames can be traumatic-too many to choose from and too many people telling you how they look. The staff at Eyedare are in sync with your needs and will give you their honest opinion on how you look in the latest designs by Magli, Gaultier, Ferrè and Oliver Peoples.

Eyes in Disguise

2189 UNION ST.
UNION STREET 94123
415-474-5321
Open Mon.-Sat.

As everyone knows, sunglasses are the necessary accessory for the terminally hip, the budding *vedette* or the incurable nightowl. At Eyes in Disguise, you'll find every look and make of sunglasses that anyone could possibly want, including Gucci, Alain Mikli and Isaac Mizrahi. We were intrigued by the Beausoleil sun version of Granny glasses. The store fills prescription sunglass orders, too.

HATS

Krazy Kaps

PIER 39
FISHERMAN'S WHARF 94133
415-296-8930
Open daily

Go hat crazy here with the straw hats, Aussie hats, nautical hats, propeller beanies, Afro hats with dreadlocks and velvet jester hats. Krazy Kaps will even embroider your name (or whatever you wish) on the baseball cap of your choice. The challenge is making a choice from the vast selection. Who can resist one of their "Bad Hair Day" caps?

CASUAL CLOTHES FOR MEN & WOMEN

(For straight-up sportswear, see also the "SHOPPING-SPORTING GOODS.")

A/X Armani Exchange

2090 UNION ST.
UNION STREET 94123
415-749-0891
Open daily

If the Gap just doesn't do it for you, give A/X a try for the Giorgio Armani slant on Gap-like clothes. Choose among jeans, T-shirts, sweaters for men and women and, of course, a little slip dress or two.

Bolla

1764 HAIGHT ST.
HAIGHT-ASHBURY 94117
415-386-3290
Open daily

Bolla sells contemporary, eclectic sportswear for young-in-spirit men and women from such makers as Marithé et Francois Girbaud, Paris Blues and Renaissance. Great rayon separates, cotton trousers, chic skirts, clompy shoes and funky sunglasses and watches make up their fashionable look. The selection is small but reasonably priced.

Button Down

3640 SACRAMENTO ST.
PRESIDIO HEIGHTS 94118
415-563-1311
Open Mon.-Sat.

Button Down carries primarily its own handsome line of traditional, outdoorsy clothing for men and women. No rugged camping gear, just great swashbuckling raincoats, thick hand-knit sweaters, formidable bathrobes and practical separates for career women. This cozy shop usually has a friendly dog greeting customers at the door.

Diesel

101 POST ST.
UNION SQUARE 94108
415-982-7077
Open daily

Diesel picks up where the Gap leaves off with its line of jeans, sweats, T-shirts, backpacks, shorts, sunglasses and lots and lots of denim attire, all sporting the Diesel logo. The younger crowd can't get enough of Diesel's clothes, and will appreciate the loud music that assaults you throughout the store. Affordable? That depends on how you look at it-we were hooked on a pair of leather jeans that cost barely over $100.

Johnson's Leather Co.

1833 POLK ST.
POLK GULCH 94109
415-775-7393
Open daily

With motorcycle jackets all the rage, renewed interest has been taken in this vendor and manufacturer of leather clothing for men and women. For a reasonable fee, you can have a jacket made to order from the finest cowhide, with as many laces, studs, buckles and snaps as you wish. A lovely lambskin blazer, tailored in your choice of colors, can be imported from England or Australia. Johnson's sells wholesale to other stores and retails some labels, such as Greenwich, Mid Way, Mirage and Casablanca. Their stock of jackets, pants, skirts and vests is sizable; you can also have leather garments repaired, cleaned and altered here.

Na Na

2276 MARKET ST.
CASTRO 94114
415-861-6262
Open daily

With chains in Los Angeles and New York, Na Na offers up-to-the-minute cheap shoes, outrageous fashions and obnoxious accessories for urban-dwelling Gen X-ers. The clubbers do their shopping here, whether for a flamboyant Hawaiian polyester shirt or a dependable black dress.

Rolo

450 CASTRO ST.
CASTRO 94114
415-626-7171
Open daily

Each Rolo store caters to a slightly different crowd: The Market Street store has stylish casual menswear, including brands such as Mossimo, Stucy, and Lucky Brand jeans, as well as trendy Nose sneakers and Airwalks. The downtown store has more upscale designers for both men and women, such as Dolce e Gabbana, and Katherine Hamnett. Rolo Garage, South of Market, sells regular items from others stores at substantial discounts. **Other locations.**

Uko

2070 UNION ST.
UNION STREET 94123
415-563-0330
Open daily

This small, select array of Japanese contemporary clothing features tailored white cotton shirts for men and women and natural-fiber trousers, skirts, jackets and dresses, most of them by Japanese designer Emico. Women on the lookout for an unusual raincoat will delight in the array of colors and styles. The minimalist elegance of these garments will make you feel like royalty, with prices more moderate than you'd expect from Japanese designer clothing.

Versace Jeans Couture

CROCKER GALLERIA
50 POST ST.
FINANCIAL DISTRICT 94111
415-616-0600
Open Mon.-Sat.

Versace's chic "casual" line-with jeans for women costing $175 and men's sports jackets in the $500 range-will boost your image and not impact your wallet as much as the Versace couture clothes. We love the vivid colors used in much of the sportswear.

DISCOUNT CLOTHES

Esprit Factory Outlet

499 ILLINOIS ST.
POTRERO HILL 94110
415-957-2550
Open daily

The Esprit outlet carries young hip women's clothes at substantial savings: 30%-70% department-store prices, often at a further 20% markdown. Serious shoppers grab one of the supermarket-style shopping carts and load up on Esprit's lively, youthful sportswear and dresses and hip, young-professional separates. It's worth driving that little bit further for a "Green Eggs and Ham" T-shirt: Esprit is the only store in the U.S. that carries Dr. Seuss clothing.

Gunne Sax

35 Stanford St.
SoMa 94103
415-495-3326
Open daily

This Gunne Sax outlet is not just for the high-school prom crowd or the bridesmaid, though you'll see plenty of young women flocking here for the romantic, feminine dress designs of yesteryear. The store also carries all lines made by this company, including Jessica McClintock and Scott McClintock, as well as an entire floor of fabulous fabric and trim (the bolts of lace are to die for). Everyone from infants to career women are assured of many choices, all at discounts of as much as 80%.

Isda and Company Outlet

29 South Park
SoMa 94103
415-247-0930, ext. 110
Open Mon.-Sat.

Isda's target market is a woman who likes an intelligent, well-designed look: if that describes you, you'll find fabulous gabardine skirts and jackets, pleated slacks and shorts, and the occasional smashing yet simple evening dress. This outlet sells past-season styles at close to wholesale prices. The company is launching a men's line in the fall of 1998.

Jeremys, New West Inc.

2 South Park
SoMa 94107
415-882-4929
Open daily

If you can't afford Armani, but you like the look, this designer's sale house is the place to stop. It's in beautiful South Park, within walking distance of other outlets. Prepare to riffle and you'll likely come up with a big-name second: 50%-60% off Mikaki, Yamamoto, Moschino, Donna Karan, Jill Sander, TSE Cashmere, Versace Jeans and Prada Bags. Sizes might resemble items found in Kate Moss's wardrobe, but keep digging. Jeremy's also stocks Neal's Yard cosmetics: sandlewood and coriander soaps, honey and orange scrubs, jasmine body creams, and lots of massage and skin-conditioning oils.

Loehmann's

222 Sutter St.
Financial District 94108
415-982-3215
Open daily

This designer discount department store in the heart of the Financial District caters to the New York business woman who never pays full price for her power suit.

Simply Cotton

610 3rd St.
SoMa 94103
415-543-2058
Open daily

Simply Cotton's factory outlet specializes in 100% all-American cotton clothing. Each garment is hand-dyed and pre-shrunk; teens or the young at heart can put together outfits of matching or contrasting separates from the array of colorful, comfortable casual wear. Jackets, tights, bike shorts, crop tops, long tops, short skirts, long skirts and more are all considerably discounted from retail prices.

Six-Sixty Center

660 Third St.
SoMa 94103
415-788-3144
Open daily

The Six-Sixty Center is an indoor mini-mall with two floors of discount outlets. Among our favorite stops are **Designer Man/Woman**, **Dress Market**, **Kidswear Outlet**, **Nomadic Traders** and **Carole's Shoe Heaven**. The Six Sixty's Center Court Deli is one of the few lunch places for SoMa area shoppers.

Yerba Buena Square

899 Howard St.
SoMa 94103
Open daily
No phone

You'll find some twenty discount outlets here, offering great deals on women's and men's fashions, sportswear and home furnishings. A worthy stop for the bargain hunter.

MENSWEAR

Brooks Brothers

201 POST ST.
UNION SQUARE 94108
415-397-4500
Open daily

Designed for the man who dresses in nothing but the most classic fashions, Brooks Brothers' clothes are extremely well made, of mostly natural fabrics, with cuts that are impervious to fads or passing fancies. The venerable clothier's suits, ties and shoes stick closely to tradition and have become almost a uniform for Financial District businesspeople. Their cotton button-down shirts, popularized in this country by Brooks several decades back, remain very good buys. Some of Brooks' current sportswear shows a hint of fashion flair.

Bryan Lee

1840 UNION ST.
UNION STREET 94123
415-923-9923
Open daily

We never thought a short-sleeved polyester shirt with a front zipper would come back, much less be considered hip, but that's what men who shop at Bryan Lee consider as an essential addition to their wardrobes. Avant-garde women find clothing to their liking here too.

Bullock and Jones

340 POST ST.
UNION SQUARE 94108
415-392-4243
Open Mon.-Sat.

Since 1853, Bullock and Jones has been a favorite of conservatively dressed businessmen. Inside the handsome three-story building you'll find Hickey-Freeman and Brioni suits, Pringle cashmere sweaters and Bullock and Jones' own shirts, ties, pajamas, sportswear and undergarments. Cole-Haan, Ferragamo, Edward Green and Bally are represented in the shoe department. The third floor features Aquascutum of London rainwear and clothing, for women as well as men. There is even an in-house barber shop.

Burberrys Limited

225 POST ST.
UNION SQUARE 94108
415-392-2200
Open daily

The famous Burberry trenchcoat is offered for men and women in a variety of colors. Accessorize it with a plaid umbrella and a Burberry scarf, and you'll be stylishly set for the most blustery of days. Tailored men's clothing includes topcoats, suits, sport coat jackets, sweaters, slacks, belts, shirts and ties.

Cable Car Clothiers, Robert Kirk, Ltd.

441 SUTTER ST.
UNION SQUARE 94108
415-397-4740
Open Mon.-Sat.

For close to 60 years, Cable Car Clothiers has been San Francisco's most complete store for British goods for men. You'll find several lines of English toiletries and such names in clothing at Daks and Southwick.

Emporio Armani

1 GRANT AVE.
UNION SQUARE 94108
415-677-9400
Open daily

If there is such a thing as "low-end" Giorgio Armani, that's what is featured at this fabulous boutique, which caters to a younger, designer-wearing crowd. You'll find everything from T-shirts and formalwear to gorgeous coats and shoes. The majestic building at the foot of Grant Avenue, once home to a bank, still has reminders of its past-pale marble walls and stately Corinthian columns. Today, the center of the first floor is a café and bar. Branching off from a first-floor central café and bar area are intimate, room-sized mini-boutiques, each featuring a different collection from the Emporio Armani line.

Giorgio Armani

278 POST ST.
UNION SQUARE 94108
415-434-2500
Open Mon.-Sat.

Seasoned Armani wearers head to this uptown boutique for the couture Black Label line. Finely tailored suits for men and women remain classics.

The Hound

140 SUTTER ST.
FINANCIAL DISTRICT 94104
415-989-0429
Open Mon.-Sat.

As its name implies, The Hound effects the atmosphere of an English haberdashery, and although it does carry some English goods-such as Alan Paine sweaters-it's best-known for its custom-made shirts, available at a reasonable price. Suits feature a natural shoulder, by designers such as Hickey Freeman, Southwick, Ralph Lauren and Freeburg of Boston. **Also at 275 Battery St., 415-982-1578.**

J. Crew

SAN FRANCISCO SHOPPING CENTRE,
865 MARKET ST.
UNION SQUARE 94103
415-546-6262
Open daily

Though the store offers a fraction of the selection you'll find in this popular clothier's catalog, J. Crew is fast-becoming a favorite for well dressed young men and women in search of high-quality suits, dress shirts, casual clothes, shoes and accessories with a classic urban look and feel.

M.A.C.

5 CLAUDE LN.
UNION SQUARE 94108
415-837-0615
Open daily

M.A.C. stands for "Modern Appealing Clothing," and the friendly shop lives up to its acronym. It was at M.A.C. that the avant-garde duds by Texan Todd Oldham were introduced to San Francisco a few years ago; currently, you can continue to count on the shop for the newest in East Coast and European chic.

Macy's Men's Store

120 STOCKTON ST.
UNION SQUARE 94108
415-397-3333
Open daily

Across the street east from the main Macy's store, most of this five-story edifice is devoted to men's clothing and accessories. Virtually every menswear designer is represented, from Ralph Lauren and Giorgio Armani to Issey Miyake. Macy's merchandise is well-organized, its price range fairly wide, its selection staggering and-should you become overwhelmed-its restaurant located in the basement.

Nicole Miller

CROCKER GALLERIA, 50 POST ST.
FINANCIAL DISTRICT 94104
415-398-3111
Open Mon.-Sat.

If the waiter at a restaurant where you recently dined was wearing a printed tie, chances are good it was a Nicole Miller, whose signature clothing is made from whimsical, limited-edition printed silks. With themes including "Killer," "Oz," "Weight" and "Israel 50," the prints don't stop at ties: the store also retails printed shirts, jackets, boxer shorts, cummerbunds, bow ties, socks, vests and jackets, as well as hundreds of scarves. Prices are steep: a distinctive Nicole Miller neckwrap costs about $60.

Polo/Ralph Lauren

90 POST ST.
FINANCIAL DISTRICT 94104
415-567-7656
Open daily

Ralph Lauren's clothing strikes a perfect balance between high fashion and conservative good taste. His dress and casual lines are infinitely appealing, and they'll look equally at home on Wall Street or a world-class yacht. Suits, sport coats and shirts have an American cut, while sportswear has an Yankee sense of color and preppiness with a touch of European sophistication.

Saks Men's Store

220 POST ST.
UNION SQUARE 94108
415-986-4300
Open daily

Saks Fifth Avenue recently moved its high-style menswear department to its own shop, located a block and a half from the main Saks store. Here men (and the women who shop for them) can browse in a shop of their own. Should hunger call you from your shopping, Saks Men's Store has its own café.

St. Croix

651 MARKET ST.
FINANCIAL DISTRICT 94105
415-538-8700
Open Mon.-Sat.

Fans of St. Croix's multicolored sweaters will think they've died and gone to heaven when they discover the full array of clothing that this store carries. Splurge on a bomber jacket, and add a pair of slacks and shirt to complete the outfit.

Think Tank

349 9TH ST.
SOMA 94103
415-255-9313
Open Mon.-Sat.

A combination gallery and boutique, Lat Naylor's shop-designed down to its hangers-features the menswear he designs, small art exhibitions and theme installations that change seasonally. If the art doesn't always appeal, Naylor's clothing certainly does: a basic jacket, trousers, overcoat and several styles of white shirts are cunningly cut and beautifully made in muted tones.

Wilkes Bashford

375 SUTTER ST.
UNION SQUARE 94108
415-986-4380
Open Mon.-Sat.

A veritable supermarket of clothing for the fashionable man, Wilkes Bashford accrues six floors of suits, sport coats, tuxedos, shoes, shirts, overcoats and accessories-cutting-edge fashion for men who want more than a basic button-down. Valentino, Brioni, Matsuda, Armani, plus many European brands that we've not see elsewhere: it's all here. Womenswear and home accessories are also sold.

DISCOUNT MENSWEAR

Men's Wearhouse

601 MARKET ST.
DOWNTOWN 94105
415-896-0871
Open daily

If you find yourself in San Francisco without a suit and need something in a hurry for cheap, you'll find it here. Men's Wearhouse also does quick alterations and offers free pressing. They claim to have known-label makers construct their suits. **Other locations.**

MEN'S LARGE & SMALL SIZES

Rochester

700 MISSION ST.
SOMA 94103
415-982-6455
Open daily

Rochester is a lifesaver for the fashion-conscious large man. The well-established store has an especially good selection of business wear: suits, sport coats and trousers from the likes of Chaps, Hickey-Freeman, Lanvin and Hart, Schaffner and Marx. Also featured are sportswear from a variety of makers and Cole-Haan and Bally shoes up to size 16.

The Short Shop

49 KEARNY ST.
UNION SQUARE 94108
415-296-9744
Open Mon.-Sat.

The short (and shorter and portlier) man will find the answer to all his clothing needs at The Short Shop. Shirts are available in 30 to 32 sleeve lengths. You'll also find a full line of business and casual wear.

SHOES

Arthur Beren Shoes

222 STOCKTON ST.
UNION SQUARE 94108
415-397-8900
Open daily

Foreign visitors rush to this upscale shop to stock up on French Arche, Robert Clergerie and Mephisto styles priced lower than they are overseas. Arthur Beren always stocks a wide selection of the latest Ferragamo styles.

Bally of Switzerland

238 STOCKTON ST.
UNION SQUARE 94108
415-398-7463
Open daily

The name is legendary in the *chaussure* trade: supple leathers and skilled craftsmanship combine to make Bally's shoes solid and sensible. Loafers (many featuring little gold fetishes on the vamp) are plentiful, and prices are high.

Bulo

437A HAYES ST.
HAYES VALLEY 94102
415-864-3244
Open daily

Selling some of the most interesting shoes in the city, Bulo imports Italian footwear in the latest styles for both for men and women. Makes such as Gatsby's, Debu and XS line the walls. Renowned in Italy, shoes here are one-of-a-kind...and pricey; you'll also find a good sale rack, however.

Insolent Shoes

1418 GRANT AVE.
NORTH BEACH 94133
415-788-3334
Open daily

If you are in the market for an expensive pair of European shoes, this is the place to find them-at the kind of store one finds in New York's upper East Side.

Gimme Shoes

416 HAYES ST.
HAYES VALLEY 94102
415-864-0691
Open daily

2358 FILLMORE ST.
UPPER FILLMORE 94115
415-441-3040
Open daily

If you're a shoeaholic, enter Gimme Shoes with caution: you'll find European designer footwear for men and women, such as Dirk Bikkenbergs, Freemance, Costume Nationale, and Patrick Cox. The store also stocks hard-to-find trainers by Adidas and other exclusive manufacturers. So many gorgeous shoes to choose from!

Joan and David

172 GEARY ST.
UNION SQUARE 94108
415-397-1958
Open daily

Joan and David shoes are all beautifully made and manage successfully to combine sensible form and imaginative style. Be sure to check the sale section on the lower level, which offers a decent assortment of bargain-priced shoes.

Kenneth Cole

2078 UNION ST.
UNION STREET 94123
415-346-2161
Open daily

Kenneth Cole has carved out an enviable niche in the footwear trade. Like his witty print ads, his shoes are well-designed and original; they're also well-made and economically feasible. For men, styles are just hip enough; his man-tailored women's shoes are quite sexy. Don't overlook Kenneth Cole for women's dress shoes-his formal line, especially for weddings, is sensational. Also in the San Francisco Shopping Centre (865 Market St., Union Square, 415-227-4536).

Laku

1069 VALENCIA ST.
MISSION 94110
415-695-1462
Open daily

This unique boutique sells beautifully handmade velvet shoes for children and adults-charming, one-of-a-kind footwear that can be worn as slippers and have a fairytale quality. Their wares are made to order, starting at $25 for children and $58 for adults.

Macy's

170 O'FARRELL ST.
UNION SQUARE 94102
415-397-3333
Open daily

Every shoe imaginable can be found in Macy's multi-level, intelligently organized shoe department-from Sperry Topsiders to Pfister pumps, Keds tennis shoes to Ralph Lauren loafers. Highlights include Macy's own Charter Club line of stylish, reasonably-priced women's shoes in wide, narrow and large sizes. Cole-Haan, Anne Klein, Bruno Magli, Reebok, Van Eli, Joan and David, Timberland, Amalfi...you name it, it's here.

Nordstrom

SAN FRANCISCO CENTRE
865 MARKET ST.
UNION SQUARE 94103
415-243-8500
Open daily

Nordstrom started as a Seattle shoe store, and continues to pay tribute to its roots with every brand of shoe you can imagine. Footwear for men, women, and children, trendy and conservative, expensive and moderate-they are all here. Young women will find Doc Martens, as well as for colorful strappy dress sandals, at Brass Plum; the store's Salon shoes have more appeal to the society crowd. Nordstrom's knowledgeable salespeople make this a place parents bring their children for a first pair of shoes.

Shaw

2001 UNION ST.
UNION STREET 94123
415-922-5676
Open daily

Shoppers with a serious shoe fetish have their own map of the city, and Shaw is a star on it. The boot selection is ample, and the women's shoes range from trendy platforms in animal prints to sophisticated Lagerfeld and Charles Jourdan numbers and sensible Mephistos.

VINTAGE & RECYCLED CLOTHING

Aaardvark's Odd Ark

1501 HAIGHT ST.
HAIGHT-ASHBURY 94117
415-621-3141
Open daily

Original Hawaiian shirts are here in abundance, each with a marvelous flair lacking in today's common copies. Other goodies include lacy lingerie, feather boas and vintage leather jackets, shorts and shirts.

American Rag

1305 VAN NESS AVE.
POLK GULCH 94109
415-474-5214
Open daily

If you're planning on going swing dancing, this store has racks of stylish pants, jackets, coats and shoes to choose from, including a mixture of designer labels and vintage clothing in excellent condition and taste. American Rag specializes in denim: Calvin Klein, BCBG, Diesel (and for $200 you could buy the limited edition Levi reproductions). Arguably the best place in the city for shoes and accessories, they're also good source for vintage costume jewelry and gowns.

Goodbyes

3464 SACRAMENTO ST.
PRESIDIO HEIGHTS 94118
415-345-6380
Open daily

This new and used-clothing consignment store has an huge selection of top-designer fashions. Both the women's store and the men's across the street are exceptionally well-stocked and -organized: finding the right color and size is easy-and the result will be a fraction of its original price. The selection is top-notch: no grunge, funk, retro '70s or power '80s.

La Rosa

1711 HAIGHT ST.
HAIGHT-ASHBURY 94117
415-668-3744
Open daily

This unusual store rents new tuxedos and vintage evening gowns and sells used clothing. They offer an excellent selection of near-perfect used overcoats, sport coats, leather jackets and vintage tuxedos and dinner jackets.

Next To New Shop

2226 FILLMORE ST.
UPPER FILLMORE 94115
415-567-1627
Open Mon.-Sat.

San Francisco's finest-including its flamboyant mayor-donate their slightly worn designer togs to this shop, the Junior League of San Francisco's thrift and consignment store. Society wannabes and budget-conscious shoppers alike make Next To New a regular stop; the local newspaper has even been known to publicize when a shipment of the mayor's suits will be on its racks.

Old Vogue

1412 GRANT AVE.
NORTH BEACH 94133
415-392-1522
Open daily

The previously worn leather jackets, tuxedos, shirts, khaki trousers, Hawaiian shirts, party dresses and many denim pieces in this cheerful shop are clean, moderately priced and in good condition.

WOMENSWEAR

Ambience

1458 HAIGHT ST.
HAIGHT-ASHBURY 94117
415-552-5095
Open daily

One of our favorite boutiques in town, this split-level shop houses an array of young-in-spirit dresses, costume jewelry and accessories-some trendy, some discreet, most falling somewhere in between. We love Ambience's own cotton knit separates and felt hats, their '40s-style Rayon items and delicate, embroidered cotton underwear.

Ann Taylor

240 POST ST.
UNION SQUARE 94108
415-543-2487
Open daily

The selection at this multi-story boutique on "Designer Row" seems to be more interesting, elegant and complete than at the city's other branches. As the years have passed, more of the clothing has become Ann Taylor's own-even the shoes now bear the store label. Worthy as ever are the tailored shift dresses, pleated trousers, seasonal linens and wools, and smart, elegant shoes. A safe bet for the young urban professional. **Other locations.**

Avant Premiere

372 SUTTER ST.
UNION SQUARE 94108
415-788-5588
Open Mon.-Sat.

1942 FILLMORE ST.
UPPER FILLMORE 94115
415-673-8875
Open daily

Business women seeking to jazz up their conservative image flock to Avant Premiere for the Parisian look in tailored jackets, slacks and skirts. An assortment of tops by other designers (many also from France) complement the outfits.

Bébé

2095 UNION ST.
UNION STREET 94115
415-563-2323
Open daily

Bébé caters to the European taste in a formulaic sort of way-their boutiques keep popping up in shopping centers. But, when it comes to leather jackets, business suits for thirtysomethings and drapey blouses or smashing slacks to wear under them, this store hits the spot. **Other locations.**

Bella Donna

539 HAYES ST.
HAYES VALLEY 94102
415-861-7182
Open daily

Bella Donna sells contemporary, handmade clothing that looks like you've stepped back in time to Edwardian England. Straw hats by Laurel Fenenga complement linen garden party dresses; you'll also find hand-dyed cotton stockings, antique buttons, hand-knit women's sweaters, printed scarves and plush velvet slippers. If the clothing weren't enough, they also sell hand-dipped chocolates and sweet-smelling bath salts. Their bridal salon is open by appointment.

Betsey Johnson
2031 Fillmore St.
Upper Fillmore 94115
415-567-2726
Open daily

160 Geary St.
Union Square 94108
415-398-2516
Open daily

If you've never abandoned your '60s free-spiritedness, yet insist on being fashionably up-to-date, you'll be in your element here. Betsey Johnson's wacky, sexy line of clothing is definitely night-on-the-town stuff. It also helps if you have the figure to wear skimpy slip dresses and skirts cut up to...there!

Bryan Lee
1840 Union St.
Union Street 94123
415-923-9923
Open daily

Who'd have thought that a slip dress could be successfully paired with a leather jacket and a funky little handbag? Somehow, this retro look works when Bryan Lee puts it together. Hip men will find clothing to their liking here, too.

Burberrys Limited
225 Post St.
Union Square 94108
415-392-2200
Open daily

Burberry's tailored women's clothing includes suits, overcoats, jackets, sweaters, skirts, blouses and jumpers in a distinctive plaid.

CP Shades
1861 Union St.
Union Street 94123
415-292-3588
Open daily

CP Shades' cotton jersey T-shirts, cardigans, sweaters and elastic-waist skirts, pants and shorts for women are comfortable, ultra-casual and great for traveling or simply lounging around. Identical basic pieces are arranged in sections by color. Each season brings a new set of hues and slight changes in styles.

Donna
1427 Grant Ave.
North Beach 94133
415-397-4447
Open daily

Donna's look is loose, unconstructed and natural and features linens, cottons and knits in attractive earth tones. They also sell sensual washable silks, designs by European and New York designers and European shoes.

Dosa
2063 Union St.
Union Street 94123
415-931-9939
Open daily

This tiny boutique looks more like a thrift shop than a designer salon. Surprisingly, it features marvelous filmy dresses and blouses with the Dosa label, sweaters from Ireland and shoes by Materia Prima and Sigerson Morrison to complete the outfit.

Dreamweaver
171 Maiden Ln.
Union Square 94108
415-981-2040
Open daily

Dreamweaver's hand-knit fashions (sweaters in particular) come from around the world; many are elegant enough to wear to opening night at the Opera. The quality and styling make them worth their price.

Earthly Goods
1981 Union St.
Union Street 94123
415-922-0606
Open daily

The racks and racks of natural-fiber clothing in this popular shop occasionally become smothered in veritable traffic jams of shoppers. At earthly prices, the shop offers a staggering choice of reasonably priced, mostly cotton items. Racks of sale clothing can be found in the back room. A few lines of moderately priced shoes are sold here, too.

Eddie Bauer
250 Post St.
Union Square 94108
415-986-7600
Open daily

Eddie Bauer is adding to its image as a supplier of rugged outdoor wear-which it still is-with its new A/K/A line of tailored and dressy clothes for women. These outfits can carry the professional woman through the workday and out for an evening on the town.

Emporio Armani

1 GRANT AVE.
UNION SQUARE 94108
415-677-9400
Open daily

If there is such a thing as "low-end" Giorgio Armani, that's what is featured at this fabulous boutique, which caters to a younger, designer-wearing crowd. You'll find everything from T-shirts and formalwear to gorgeous coats and shoes. The majestic building at the foot of Grant Avenue, once home to a bank, still has reminders of its past-pale marble walls and stately Corinthian columns. Today, the center of the first floor is a café and bar. Branching off from a first floor central café and bar area are intimate, room-sized mini-boutiques, each featuring a different collection from the Emporio Armani line.

Gianni Versace

60 POST ST.
FINANCIAL DISTRICT 94111
415-616-0604
Open Mon.-Sat.

Gianni Versace's family is continuing his legacy with attractive, dramatic Italian haute couture for women who like to make a statement . Be prepared to pay close to $3,000 for a woman's suit and $375 for the tiniest of hot pants. For younger, more casual styles, visit Versace's Jeans Couture (just down the walkway in the Crocker Galleria) where the clothing is more modestly priced.

Giorgio Armani

278 POST ST.
UNION SQUARE 94108
415-434-2500
Open Mon.-Sat.

Seasoned Armani wearers head to this uptown boutique for the couture Black Label line. Finely tailored suits for men and women remain classics.

Girlfriends

1824 UNION ST.
UNION STREET 94123
415-673-9544
Open daily

Shopping here is almost like going through your closet at home with a girlfriend. You'll find a little bit of everything in this cozy store-Margaret O'Leary sweaters, Lily Pulitzer sun dresses, David Dart separates. The Girlfriends logo wear is hard to pass up, especially T-shirts for kids and pajamas for grownups.

Gladrags

3985 24TH ST.
NOE VALLEY 94114
415-647-7144
Open daily

Dress yourself from the inside out at Gladrags, with delicate silk lingerie, beautiful printed pants with matching tops, velvety chenille sweaters, and endless scarves, hats, bags, and jewelry. They also have an excellent selection of sleepwear. Ask to look at their sales rack for excellent Eileen Fisher markdowns.

Grand

1435 GRANT AVE.
NORTH BEACH 94133
415-951-0131
Open daily

Grand is the place for upscale, "with-it" women's clothing. We can easily imagine Madonna or Gloria Estefan shopping here.

J. Crew

SAN FRANCISCO SHOPPING CENTRE
865 MARKET ST.
UNION SQUARE 94103
415-546-6262
Open daily

Long known for its tailored classic sportswear, J. Crew now also has a more sophisticated line of moderately priced clothing (separates under $200), including simple, elegant dresses, fabulous white shirts and silk pants.

Knitz and Leather

1429 GRANT AVE.
NORTH BEACH 94133
415-391-3480
Open daily

A minuscule, one-of-a-kind shop that's a must for any woman who loves knitwear,

Knitz and Leather is a partnership of two women-one who designs and knits stylish sweaters, scarves and skirts, and one who designs and fabricates leather jackets and other leather clothing. Both create unique, elegant fashions for women. Don't miss the jewelry they've selected to accent their creations: not only does it complement the store's selection, it may also brighten up an outfit you already own.

Jim Elle

2237 FILLMORE ST.
UPPER FILLMORE 94115
415-567-9500
Open daily

"Clothes for the Fashion Confident" is Jim Elle's motto, and if you're confident enough to shell out several hundred bucks for a Romeo Gigli outfit, you'll fall in love with the place. It's all crisply modern and tasteful, and not everything is expensive.

Joshua Simon

3915 24TH ST.
NOE VALLEY 94114
415-821-1068
Open daily

Loose-fitting women's clothing in natural fibers is available at Joshua Simon, from flowing pants to unusual woven vests and romantic-looking dresses. Many block-printed cottons and linens in muted colors from New Mexico and Indonesia. For comfy, flowy and natural clothes, look no further.

Jessica McClintock

180 GEARY ST., 4TH FL.
UNION SQUARE 94108
415-398-9008
Open daily

Many brides-especially those over 30-find Jessica McClintock's romantic silk and lace dresses to have just the right level of sophistication. This salon is all bridal, with a good selection of feminine bridesmaid and flower girl dresses as well.

Kalf

1971 SUTTER ST.
UPPER FILLMORE 94115
415-563-6788
Open Mon.-Sat

These exquisite clothes-pants, jackets, shorts and skirts-are all designed by Japanese couturier Fumio Tanuma. Everything is done in neutral hues, and exudes elegance.

Laura Ashley

253 POST ST.
UNION SQUARE 94108
415-788-0190
Open daily

Now a virtual emporium for the English country look, Laura Ashley provides you the opportunity to dress yourself, and your daughter of almost any age, in romantic-looking flowered prints from head to toe. The shop also custom-designs upholstery, pillows, linens, curtains and more in its own English country-style fabrics, displayed here in enormous bolts.

M.A.C.

1543 GRANT AVE.
NORTH BEACH 94133
415-837-1604
Open daily

M.A.C. stands for "Modern Appealing Clothing," and that's what this store is all about. You can count on it for the newest in East Coast and European chic. We enjoy wide selection of Vivienne Westwood pieces and always find an intriguing accessory or two. We've been told that when Madonna is in town, this is one of her clothing stops.

Metier

355 SUTTER ST.
UNION SQUARE 94108
415-989-5395
Open Mon.-Sat.

There is a sleek sophistication to the clothes at Metier: Italian silk dresses and suits, leather coats and jackets, sweaters from Scotland. The shop's unique pieces mean you won't meet yourself walking down the street-that is, see another wearing the same thing-when you outfit yourself at Metier.

Nicole Miller

CROCKER GALLERIA
50 POST ST.
FINANCIAL DISTRICT 94104
415-398-3111
Open Mon.-Sat.

If the waiter at a restaurant where you recently dined was wearing a printed tie, chances are good it was a Nicole Miller, whose signature clothing is made from whimsical, limited-edition printed silks. With themes including "Killer," "Oz," "Weight" and "Israel 50," the prints don't stop at ties: for women there are printed shirts, jackets, dresses, shoes, purses, scarves and even lingerie. At Nicole Miller, the basic little black dress can be found in a slew of solid colors and (of course) in prints.

Martha Egan

1127 FOLSOM ST.
SOMA 94103
415-252-1072
Open Mon.-Sat.

This up-and-coming designer has her own studio and shop among the clubs in SoMa. Women's blouses, dresses and jackets, with vintage styling in contemporary cuts, are all decorated with unique, sometimes handcut buttons. Prices are moderate.

Ovation

2124 CHESTNUT ST.
MARINA 94123
415-931-5445
Open daily

Ovation can be counted on for its selection of under-$100 dresses in the newest of styles. They always have the latest Kenar designs as well as clothes from the French Connection and many local designers. Young career women make this a regular shopping stop.

Talbots

128 POST ST.
UNION SQUARE 94108
415-398-8881
Open daily

2 EMBARCADERO CENTER
EMBARCADERO 94111
415-781-2128
Open daily

Talbots' new flagship store here on "Designer Row" is a delight to the suit-wearing women who rely on its classic styles the same way some men we know only buy their suits at Brooks Brothers. Rely on Talbots for well-made clothing that is moderate to expensive in price; a complete line of petite sizes is included.

Three Bags Full

2181 UNION ST.
UNION STREET 94123
415-567-5753
Open daily

Known for its high-quality wool sweaters, many of which are hand-knit, this store has items for women, men and children. Three Bags Full also stocks special soaps for wool and an astounding variety of socks. Going one step beyond wearable art, the store has a lovely assortment of another kind of art-the colorful English pottery of Mary Rose Young. **Other locations.**

Trendy Inc.

404 SUTTER ST.
UNION SQUARE 94108
415-399-9867
Open daily

Most of the clothes here are by local designer Joanie Char, whose knits and tailored clothing are staples in many a professional woman's wardrobe. Although this is a retail outlet for Char's clothing, you'll always find many sale racks loaded with great bargains.

TSE Cashmere

171 POST ST.
UNION SQUARE 94108
415-391-1112
Open Mon.-Sat.

Seasoned travelers swear by TSE Cashmere's sweaters and slacks for their travel wardrobe. They are warm and comfy, especially on an overnight flight, and, when you arrive, look fresh and unwrinkled. TSE takes the classic hand-knit cashmere sweater to new heights in up-to-date styles of cashmere T-shirts, skirts, dresses and jackets.

Yanagi

2271 UNION ST.
UNION STREET 94123
415-922-2218
Open daily

Japanese designer Evan Yanagi's finely tailored two-piece suits and ensembles are meant to take chic women through their busy days-from the office to cocktails-without a change of clothes. This hard-to-find tiny shop is worth searching for.

Zoe
2400 Fillmore St.
Upper Fillmore 94115
415-929-0441
Open daily

If you are looking for something different in a slip dress or a classic pair of gabardine slacks, chances are you'll find it at Zoe. Bianca Nero, Helen Wang, and Think Tank are among the brands carried.

WOMEN'S LARGE & SMALL SIZES

In addition to these shops that specialize exclusively in large or small sizes, we suggest that you visit **Macy's** and **Nordstrom**, both of whom have well-stocked departments for petite and plus-sized clothing.

Forgotten Woman
550 Sutter St.
Union Square 94102
415-788-1452
Open daily

You'll know you're in for a special shopping excursion as you head up the flower-filled path toward the white facade of The Forgotten Woman. Once inside, you'll be dazzled by the selection of larger-size clothing. Styles cover everything from sportswear to formal wear. Once you've selected your outfits, you can complete them with carefully chosen accessories and jewelry.

Elizabeth
4 Embarcadero Center
Financial District 94111
415-397-1831
Open daily

Liz Claiborne's special plus-sized line of clothing, Elizabeth, fills this store with larger versions of our favorite Liz styles. The plus-sized petite is in luck, too; she'll find a wide variety of clothes in her size.

Liz Claiborne Petites
San Francisco Shopping Centre,
865 Market St.
Union Square 94103
415-495-8982
Open daily

Our shorter women friends rely on Liz Claiborne Petites for both their work and weekend wear. You'll find the full petite line here.

LINGERIE

Aricie
Crocker Galleria
50 Post St.
Financial District 94104
415-989-0261
Open Mon.-Sat.

Such European makers as Lejaby, Aubade and Lise Charmel are well represented here, as are American favorites. There are tons of frilly bras, panties, camisoles and the like, as well as drop-dead lounge wear, including some hand-painted silk gowns. A few well-heeled gentlemen shop here, buying expensive, tasteful and seriously sexy gifts for their wives and girlfriends.

Carol Doda's Champagne and Lace Lingerie
1850 Union St. #1
Union Street 94123
415-776-6900
Open daily

Hidden away in a courtyard at the end of an alley, you'll know you are in the right place when you spot the outdoor display of frilly things. Yes, this shop is owned by the Carol Doda who made San Francisco a topless mecca in the '60s. The comprehensive collection of wispy undergarments assembled here includes full-figured sizes for women and intimate wear for men.

Toujours
2484 Sacramento St.
Presidio Heights 94118
415-346-3988
Open daily

Everywhere you look in this tiny lavender-scented shop your eye is greeted by pastel silks, fragile lace and fine cottons. The shop is run by Beverly Weinkauf, who has collected the prettiest natural-fiber lingerie made by various European and Bay Area designers.

Victoria's Secret

WESTIN ST. FRANCIS HOTEL
335 POWELL ST.
UNION SQUARE 94102
Open daily

Although it seems like there is a Victoria's Secret in every shopping center in the United States, we never tire of this shop that brought sexy lingerie to mainstream America. In addition to the push-up bras in a rainbow of colors and the silky nightgowns that catalog shoppers covet, there are cotton items, menswear-styled underthings, such as silk boxers and cotton T-shirts (available for men, too), cuddly chenille robes and a whole line of fragrance, bath and body products. **Other locations.**

MATERNITY

Japanese Weekend

500 SUTTER ST.
UNION SQUARE 94102
415-989-6667
Open Mon.-Sat.

Not your traditional maternity wear by any means, this line was created by a choreographer who has some very precise ideas about how maternity clothing should look and feel. Japanese Weekend is known for the invention of the Obi-Katsurogi (O.K.) waistband, which allows garments to rest comfortably on the hips. The pants, tunics, skirts and nursing tops, all of cotton interlock, are stylish and contemporary. Japanese Weekend clothing is carried in maternity shops around the country, but only at this, the company store, is the full line available.

A Pea in the Pod

290 SUTTER ST.
UNION SQUARE 94104
415-391-1400
Open daily

Pregnant women call shop for their entire maternity wardrobe at A Pea in the Pod. Everything from swim suits to cocktail dresses are here in this cheerful boutique.

DEPARTMENT STORES

Macy's

STOCKTON & O'FARRELL STS.
UNION SQUARE 94108
415-397-3333
Open daily

At first glance it looks like Macy's is the only department store on Union Square. Its buildings occupy most of the Stockton Street block between Geary and O'Farrell and extend west almost an entire city block. It's a jangling, chaotic, big-city department store, with everything from discount racks to haute couture, along with a continual crush of tourists, locals and suburban shoppers. Come here for menswear, children's clothing, electronics and all sorts of women's clothing and accessories. A walk through the enormous, ever-bustling cosmetics department is worth a special trip. The women's shoe department is spectacular. For the gourmand, **Macy's Cellar** houses a marketplace of delicious foods to eat on the premises or take out, as well as the largest assortment of cookware and housewares in town. There's a also Macy's at the Stonestown Galleria.

Neiman-Marcus

150 STOCKTON ST.
UNION SQUARE 94108
415-362-3900
Open daily

Neiman's Texas roots are disguised under San Francisco's old City of Paris dome, but the merchandise selection still displays a certain flash and flair that suggests its heritage. You'll find some wonderfully luxurious departments, especially the lingerie, gourmet foods, couture and cosmetics wards. One of our very favorite downtown lunch spots is the Rotunda restaurant on the top floor under the beautiful dome. For a quick meal, we highly recommend the **Fresh Market**, a comfortable café on the third floor.

Nordstrom

SAN FRANCISCO SHOPPING CENTRE,
865 MARKET ST.
UNION SQUARE 94103
415-243-8500
Open daily

The grandest Nordstrom anywhere, this one occupies five floors atop the San Francisco Shopping Centre. Included in the spread are four restaurants and a spa, all accessed by a huge, circular central escalator. When you enter the store by the optional elevator, You'll come upon the concierge, who will provide you with a map of the store and details about restaurant reservations (the Champagne Exchange is our favorite, and some of our men friends like to duck into The Pub to get game scores and some refreshment). Nordstrom is unbeatable for its shoes, purses, menswear and women's designer clothing. Live music from a grand piano player will serenade you as you make your way through the store. There's a less-splendid-though still very satisfying-branch at the **Stonestown Galleria**.

Saks Fifth Avenue

384 POST ST.
UNION SQUARE 94108
415-986-4300
Open daily

This lovely West Coast version of the classic New York society department store has a well-rounded selection of upscale merchandise for women. Some of the designer mini-boutiques have more merchandise here than in their full-store counterparts in other parts of town. If Jeanne-Marc clothing (made and designed in San Francisco) is a staple in your wardrobe, Saks is your place to find the latest additions to the line. We like the Dolce e Gabbana salon, too. Saks' own moderately priced lines, Real Clothes and The Works, offer good quality and design. **Café SFA** on the top floor is exceptional for a relaxing meal and a spectacular view of Union Square. **Saks menswear is sold in the new Saks men's store at 220 Post St.**

ELECTRONICS

PHOTOGRAPHY

Adolph Gasser

181 2ND ST.
SOMA 94103
415-495-3852
Open Mon.-Sat.

With a complete range of cameras, including all of the world's finest, Adolph Gasser caters to a professional clientele, who can also buy and rent video and movie equipment. **Also in the Richmond District (5733 Geary Blvd., 415-751-0145.)**

Brooks Cameras

125 KEARNY ST.
UNION SQUARE 94108
415-362-4708
Open Mon.-Sat.

Professionals and amateurs alike shop at Brooks, a large, all-purpose photography store that sells cameras, accessories, film and darkroom supplies. It also rents and repairs cameras and has a good-quality overnight developing service.

Film Processing

There are hundreds of one-hour photo shops that count on you to part with big bucks for instant developing; the best bargains are at the Walgreens drugstore and Fox Photo chains, which offer one-hour and over-night processing at low rates. You can choose large or small and single or double prints. Make the daily deadline (around 1pm) to guarantee next-day service. Check the telephone directory for branches.

RECORDS, TAPES CDS, DVDS

Amoeba Music

1885 HAIGHT ST.
HAIGHT-ASHBURY 94117
415-831-1200
Open daily

What used to be the old Rock and Bowl bowling alley is now one of the largest independent new and used record store in the Bay Area, with over 30,000 used CDs and 100,000 used LPs. Amazing. Trade in your used CDs and LPs for cash or credit.

102 Music

513 GREEN ST.
NORTH BEACH 94133
415-392-6368
Open daily

If you're a used record collector, jampacked 102 Music is not to be missed. The sheet music mural on the store's facade, painted by artist Ellen Byrnes, is worth seeing.

Star Classics
1401 Haight St.
Haight-Ashbury 94117
415-552-1110
Open daily

The most reliable source for classical music in the city and a noted San Franciscan institution for opera, jazz and Broadway musicals, Star Classics also offers free concerts in their recital hall at noon every Friday.

Streetlight Records
3979 24th St.
Noe Valley 94114
415-282-3550
Open daily

Along with a complete range of records and CDs in every category, Streetlight sells new, used, vintage, rare and out-of-print discs. **Also in the Castro (2350 Market St., 415-282-8000).**

Tower Records
2280 Market St.
Castro District 94114
415-621-0588
Open daily

There are no actual records at this Tower Records, just CDs, tapes, DVDs and laser discs. They stock a decent selection of new rock, pop, country, soul, jazz, blues and classical releases. There's also a great collection of old rock and pop singles, classic rock and rhythm-and-blues. Hot new selections are usually discounted; check out their book and magazine selection in the back. You might still find a few records at the North Beach location, and the Bay Street Tower Classics sells only classical discs. **Other locations.**

Virgin Megastore
2 Stockton St.
Union Square 94108
415-397-4525
Open daily

If more is better, then Virgin Megastore wins hands down. Walk into the store and you'll be bombarded with sound, video and an unfathomable selection of recorded music and video. Yes, they even have classical music, lots of it, occupying close to 20% of the store on the second floor. Virgin brand clothing and souvenirs and a small selection of books and computer software round out the merchandise. If the checkout lines are too long on the street level, take your purchases to one of the upper floors where cashiers are more readily accessible.

MUSICAL INSTRUMENTS

Haight-Ashbury Music Center
1540 Haight St.
Haight-Ashbury 94117
415-863-7327
Open daily

A stop-off point for musicians of all sorts, but a particular favorite with local and out-of-town rock-and-rollers, the Music Center sells new and second-hand instruments, sheet music and amps; they also posts notice about bands looking for new members. A Haight Street institution.

STEREO & VIDEO

Circuit City (1200 Van Ness) and **Good Guys** (1400 Van Ness) are the supermarkets of home electronics, well worth a look to compare prices. They carry all the name brands and may well provide the best deal in town; the salespeople can be sharks, though. For more individualized service, we recommend the following:

Audio Excellence
101 Henry Adams St.
SoMa 94111
415-255-7066
Open Mon.-Sat.

1336 Van Ness Ave.
Civic Center 94109
415-440-9197
Open Mon.-Sat.

When we are visiting designer showrooms with our decorators we often stop at Audio Excellence to check on the latest in state-of-the art sound and video equipment.

Bang and Olufsen

345 Powell St.
Union Square 94108
415-274-3320
Open Mon.-Sat.

For decades, this Danish line has offered state-of-the-art stereo and audio equipment.

Harmony Audio Video

333 W. Portal Ave.
West Portal 94127
415-661-2525
Open daily

It's not just the demonstration surround-sound and the home theater systems that draw customers to Harmony Audio Video: it's knowledgeable and personal service, along with prices that compare favorably with those at the big chains. Owner Frank Mari truly cares what you purchase and wants to insure that you will continue to be happy with your sound or video system. Some of the brands he carries are Yamaha, Denon, Rotel and Panasonic as well as the sought-after Vidikron Front Projection Systems. Harmony services all its products and includes extended warranties with most purchases at no extra charge.

FLOWERS

Bed of Roses

2274 Union St.
Union Street 94123
415-922-5150
Open Mon.-Sat.

The smell of damp earth and cut greens will lure you into this lovely little shop. In addition to a healthy array of cut flowers, the store boasts walls lined with interesting old (or just old-looking) baskets and vases, along with wonderful reproductions of antique garden ornaments. Bring in your favorite vase and the agreeable staff will creatively fill it.

Bloomers

2975 Washington St.
Pacific Heights 94115
415-563-3266
Open Mon.-Sat.

Stacked on towering shelves against Bloomers' formidable white walls are vases, baskets and ribbons of every conceivable sort to complement your armful of lovely cut flowers. The best idea, however, is to let the Bloomers' pros design a bouquet for you. It's well-known locally that they create some of the most creative and soulful arrangements anywhere. The potted plants and specially planted herb pots are also tempting.

Fleurtations

1880 Fillmore St.
Upper Fillmore 94115
415-923-1070
Open Tues.-Sun.

The choice selection of fresh flowers here includes some you rarely see at other florists. Silk and dried flowers, along with baskets and other containers, become the makings of magnificent permanent floral displays. The flower theme is further reflected in a fanciful array of printed napkins and tablecloths.

Ixia

2331 Market St.
Castro 94114
415-431-3134
Open Mon.- Sat.

You should at least window-shop at this Castro florist, the likes of whose living plant and flower sculptures have never been seen. This tiny shop magically builds bouquets into floral masterpieces. While the flowers are sure to dazzle the recipient, they may also stun your wallet. Their window displays are changed weekly.

Podesta Baldocchi

508 4th St.
SOMA 94107
415-346-1300
Open Mon.-Sat.

This long-established San Francisco megaflorist does it all: tiny bouquets, huge parties, balloon bouquets, potted plants, plant rentals, plant maintenance, fruit baskets-you name it. The self-service selection of fresh, cut flowers and indoor plants is complete, and Podesta's own designs can be stunning.

FOOD & WINE

BAGELS

Noah's
1887 UNION ST.
UNION STREET 94123
415-346-4095
Open daily

Responsible for popularizing bagels in the Bay Area, Noah's New York memorabilia-filled bakeries can be found in almost every neighborhood, offering every imaginable choice of bagel-from pumpernickel and sesame to exotic flavors such as chocolate chip and cranberry-orange. Try a shmear to go with yours-light, regular and flavored spreads in sun-dried tomato or with lox. **Numerous other branches.**

BAKERIES

Boudin Sourdough Bakery and Café
156 JEFFERSON ST.
FISHERMAN'S WHARF 94133
415-928-1849
Open daily

The San Francisco sourdough here is made purely with sourdough starter-no yeast, no preservatives. In addition to standard loaves, Boudin makes special decorative breads in the shape of dinosaurs, Easter bunnies and such; watch the whole process through a window that looks into the baking room. Tourists love to use Boudin's mail-order service to ship loaves to out-of-state friends; for more immediate needs, the café serves sandwiches, salads, soup and pastries. **Other locations.**

Casa Sanchez
2778 24TH ST.
MISSION 94110
415-282-2400
Open Mon.-Sat.

This Mexican bakery specializes in fresh corn and flour tortillas, made here all morning long. From miniature, Mexico-City-style rounds to giant flour 14-inchers, Casa Sanchez offers every variety of tortilla just waiting to be stuffed or rolled into a jumbo burrito.

Danilo
516 GREEN ST.
NORTH BEACH 94133
415-989-1806
Open daily

The display of baked goods in this venerable North Beach bakery changes throughout the day, as fresh batches of Italian bread-from big, country-style loaves to grissini, or hand-rolled breadsticks-emerge from the oven. Danilo also bakes cialde (lacy anise-flavored cookies) and Genovese-style panettone.

Dianda Italian American Pastry
2883 MISSION ST.
MISSION 94110
415-647-5469
Open daily

565 GREEN ST.
NORTH BEACH 94133
415-989-7745
Open daily

Elio Dianda, once the pastry chef at Salza in Lucca, Italy, developed all the recipes for the Italian pastries at Dianda; his three sons now carry on the tradition. They bake moist amaretti, delicate allumettes and other cookies, along with a classic torta de mandorle and a bevy of other sweets. The zabaglione tha goes into the torta de zabaglione e rum and the zuppa inglese is still whisked by hand in a big, copper bowl. The Diandas's chewy, subtly spiced panforte is dense with nuts and covered with a delicate wafer, and their tall panettone is a classic.

Dominguez Bakery: Flor de Jalisco

2951 24TH ST.
MISSION DISTRICT 94110
415-821-1717
Open daily

These panes (Hispanic breads) are good and always fresh, baked several times a day. You'll find egg bread, sweet crescent rolls and large, leaf-shaped hojaldre, turnovers, jelly rolls, custard fills and miniature Central American pastries, as well as panes dulces in dozens of fanciful shapes and various flavorings-anise, vanilla, lemon and pineapple.

Eplers

LAUREL VILLAGE
3465 CALIFORNIA ST.
LAUREL HEIGHTS 94118
415-752-0825
Open Mon.-Sat.

Bought from Ernest Weil who started Fantasia, Eplers has carried on the same tradition: If you want napoleons, petits fours, Black Forest cake or Sachertorte, you've come to the right place. At Christmas, in addition to all sorts of German holiday cookies, they make Baumkuchen, a cake of Gypsy origin cooked over an open fire. The batter is poured onto a rotating spit and cooked layer by layer to resemble the rings of a tree; the whole cake is then glazed with sugar or chocolate.

Just Desserts

3 EMBARCADERO CENTER
FINANCIAL DISTRICT 94111
415-421-1609
Open daily

Founded in 1974, Just Desserts is a wholesale bakery that also operates half a dozen retail stores and cafés throughout the city. All are comfy, low-key spots where people go to chat cozily over a slice of banana-walnut cake or apple-crumb pie and a good cup of coffee. Everything is baked from scratch, from the New York-style cheesecake that launched the business to the black-bottom cupcakes, blueberry muffins and danishes. You can even enjoy a '70s relic-carrot cake with cream-cheese frosting. **Other locations.**

La Nouvelle Pâtisserie

2184 UNION ST.
UNION STREET 94123
415-931-7655
Open daily

Jean-Yves Duperret fills the shelves of this Union Street shop with beautifully crafted French pastries: feather-light palmiers, slender allumettes and buttery croissants. His shimmering fruit tarts, on display in the window, stop passersby in their tracks. He also serves light luncheon fare, making La Nouvelle Pâtisserie as close as you can get to a Parisian salon de thé. The San Francisco Shopping Centre location is popular with shoppers and downtown business people who pick up dessert on their way home. **Other locations.**

La Palma Mexicatessan

2884 24TH ST.
MISSION 94110
415-647-1500
Open daily

A fine source for fresh tortillas, La Palma bakes both the corn and flour varieties on large iron griddles in the back of the shop. You can also stock up on bundles of dried chiles, beans, searing hot sauce and corn husks for making tamales.

La Victoria

2937 24TH ST.
MISSION 94110
415-550-9292
Open daily

La Victoria's windows are filled with dozens of kinds of Mexican cookies and panes dulces glazed with sugar and baked in fantasy shapes. Go in, grab a tray and tongs and help yourself to a heap of these sweet treats. Great (and inexpensive) party fare.

Liguria Bakery

1700 STOCKTON ST.
NORTH BEACH 94133
415-421-3786
Open daily

This venerable North Beach bakery is known for its delicious focaccia. The mainstay of countless Italian delis and cafés (including Mario's, across the park), the Ligurian pizza bread is sold here over the counter in sheets. Baked night to morning in an old brick oven, it comes plain, seasoned with olive oil and salt or topped with scallions, tomato sauce or raisins.

Stella Pastry and Café

446 COLUMBUS AVE.
NORTH BEACH 94133
415-986-2914
Open daily

Stella is known for its Sacripantina, an incredible cake made of thin layers of sponge cake filled with a tasty rum, Marsala and sherry flavored zabaglione. On a sunny day, enjoy the North Beach scene with a pastry at one of Stella's sidewalk tables.

Tassajara Bread Bakery

1000 COLE ST.
HAIGHT-ASHBURY 94117
415-664-8947
Open daily

Mostly students at the Zen Center, the Tassajara bakers bake bread-at least a half dozen kinds every day-with tender care. Try their stone-ground whole wheat, tender challah, sourdough corn rye and excellent potato bread (made moist with grated russet). Recently merged with Just Deserts, Tassajara also sells tempting walnut-cranberry scones and hefty morning pastries, along with oversized brownies and macaroons; the bakery is a nice place to take a book and sit. Tassajara bread is also sold at many locations throughout the Bay Area. There's another bakery shop inside **Greens** in Fort Mason (see Dining).

Victoria Pastry

1362 STOCKTON ST.
NORTH BEACH 94133
415-781-2015
Open daily

The famous cake at Victoria is the St. Honoré, an incredible concoction decorated with cream puffs. While we cannot justify Victoria's St. Honoré or frozen Zuccotto as everyday fare, we never pass this bakery without buying their loaf-style cornmeal cake-a terrific breakfast or dessert cake, especially with fresh fruit or sorbet.

CANDIES & CONFECTIONS

Alfred Schilling

1695 MARKET ST.
MISSION 94103
415-255-1666
Open Mon.-Sat.

Mouth-watering, handmade European truffles-filled with champagne, Grand Marnier and espresso in dark, milk, and white chocolate-are Schilling's signature (see also Dining).

Chocolates from Chocolates

218 CHURCH ST.
MISSION 94110
415-431-3640
Open Mon.-Sat.

The heady scent of chocolate fills this bandbox of a shop that produces competent truffles in a dozen or so flavors. Many items that are already tasty alone become richer after taking a dip in the shop's own melted chocolate. Chocolate-coated items run from graham crackers to Oreo cookies to pretzels.

Confetti le Chocolatier

4 EMBARCADERO CENTER
FINANCIAL DISTRICT 94111
415-362-1706
Open daily

One of the city's prettiest chocolate stores, Confetti sells Chocolatier Le Manon chocolates, imported fresh directly from Brussels, and local master Chocolatier Joseph Schmidt's truffles and chocolates. Equally wonderful is their awesome selection of packaged confections; health-conscious chocoholics will find a tempting array of sugar-free chocolates. Some of these sweets are very expensive, but you can always afford just a piece or two as a special treat. Linger here in their café, enjoying a cup of coffee or hot chocolate. Other locations.

Ghirardelli Chocolate Manufactory and Soda Fountain

GHIRARDELLI SQUARE, 900 NORTH POINT
FISHERMAN'S WHARF 94133
415-771-4903
Open daily

The Ghirardelli Chocolate Company has been making premium chocolate in San

Francisco since 1852, and has maintained its Ghirardelli Square location since 1895. Take a souvenir menu on your way in and choose from such temptations as the World Famous Hot Fudge Sundae, the Golden Gate Banana Split, or the $19.06 Earthquake Sundae, which serves four or more and is made with eight flavors of ice cream and eight different toppings. The retail shop sells the entire line of packaged Ghirardelli chocolate products. At Ghirardelli Too!, a second store at the other end of the Square, individual pieces of chocolate candies are sold by the pound from self-service bins.

Joseph Schmidt Confections

3489 16TH ST.
MISSION 94110
415-861-8682
Open Mon.-Sat.

Swiss-trained Joseph Schmidt is a master chocolatier, sufficiently confident of his craft to step outside tradition and create such wonderful, goofy innovations as a chocolate spiny cactus or a dark- and white-chocolate saddle shoe. He also makes miniature chocolate tennis balls, baseballs and golf balls with nougat fillings, not to mention white-chocolate swan boats and free-form chocolate bowls swirled with color. This is the most enchanting chocolate shop in the city, especially at Easter, when it practically bursts with chocolate bunnies, huge speckled white-chocolate eggs and demure little baskets filled with realistic eggs and maybe a woodsy chocolate mushroom or two. Prices are the lowest in town.

Teuscher Chocolates of Switzerland

255 GRANT AVE.
UNION SQUARE 94108
415-398-2700
Open daily

This Swiss firm, which has been at its craft since the 1950s, is best known to chocolate fanciers for its seductive Champagne truffle. Try a small sampling of flavors, about a dozen in all, made with the same care and craftsmanship and flown in once a week from Zurich. We are equally intrigued by the packaging for the chocolates-boxes topped with fanciful characters and colorful flowers.

Yamada Seika Confectionery

1955 SUTTER ST.
JAPANTOWN 94115
415-922-3848
Open Tues.-Sun.

For more than 35 years this tiny shop has been making traditional Japanese pastries such as manju (a sweet bean pastry) and yokan (candies jelled with agar-agar, a seaweed derivative). These may be something of an acquired taste; the helpful shopkeeper will guide you in your selections. We prefer manju made from red beans. The shop also sells lovely packaged crackers, cookies and sweets.

CHEESE

Country Cheese

415 DIVISADERO ST.
WESTERN ADDITION 94115
415-621-8130
Open Mon.-Sat.

This nondescript storefront is a great place to buy such cheeses as Gruyère and Cheddar. You'll find intelligent staff and good prices on both imported and domestic cheeses sold by weight. Watch for specials on Reggiano and other pricey cheeses used in cooking. The store stocks Ferrante Cheese Company's locally made mozzarella, too. While you're here, stock up on flour, grains and nuts in bulk.

Creighton's Cheese and Fine Foods

673 PORTOLA DR.
TWIN PEAKS 94127
415-753-0750
Open daily

It's hard to come up with a cheese that Creighton's does not stock. They also sell meat, salads, frittatas, desserts and pastries. If you're in need of a box lunch for an outdoor concert at Stern Grove, Creighton's will put together a spread that will make you the envy of the rest of your table.

Say Cheese

856 COLE ST.
HAIGHT-ASHBURY 94117
415-665-5020
Open daily

Much of San Francisco received an education in cheese after Bob Wiskotzil and George

Kovatch opened this store in 1976. These days, new owners stock 150 to 200 cheeses, depending on the season. Buy Swiss Raclette, and they'll rent you the machine and all the fixings to broil it. The shop often has unusual cheeses-perhaps sheep's milk Manchego from Spain or Montosio from the Veneto.

COFFEE & TEA

With the exception of the downtown location (22 Battery), **Peet's** shops are found mostly in the neighborhoods. Omnipresent **Starbucks** have blanketed the downtown area and are all over the city. **Spinelli** and **Pasqua** are home-grown favorites with a faithful local following. Pasqua is best known for its walkup coffee bars in the Financial District and has a few cafés that serve tasty sandwiches, salads, and pastries; they are also at San Francisco Airport.

Coffee, Tea & Spice

1630 HAIGHT ST.
HAIGHT-ASHBURY 94117
415-861-3958
Open daily

This no-nonsense coffee store roasts its own beans, and also sells spices and teas in bulk, as well as every gadget you need for making a steaming cup of your favorite. Some candies and gourmet food items are also available.

Freed, Teller and Freed

1326 POLK ST.
POLK GULCH 94109
415-673-0922
Open Mon.-Fri.

Since 1899, Freed, Teller and Freed has been quietly selling its own roasted coffees and imported teas to discriminating customers. Prices are very low, and the company really knows its business. The Darjeeling tea is exceptional: ask the staff how to make the perfect brew. Also for sale are herbs and spices in bulk and well-chosen tea- and coffee-making implements.

Graffeo Coffee Roasting Co.

735 COLUMBUS AVE.
NORTH BEACH 94133
415-986-2420
Open daily

The seductive smell of roasting coffee will lure you to the door of this North Beach coffee roaster. A fixture in the neighborhood for over 50 years, Graffeo has been tops in San Francisco for Italian-style (read: espresso) coffee through three generations of the Repetto family. The Rube Goldberg-like roaster and rough burlap bags from Costa Rica, New Guinea, Java and Colombia take up most of the floor space. Just as in Italy, they keep it simple with just one Graffeo blend, roasted light or dark, and a single, water-processed, 100% Colombian decaf.

Tea and Company

2207 FILLMORE ST.
UPPER FILLMORE 94115
415-929-8327
Open daily

If tea is your beverage of choice, you must visit Tea and Company's World Tea House. Here you will be dazzled by over 40 tea blends and an impressive number of pure tea varieties. Enjoy a cup here with a pastry and/or buy the loose tea to brew at home. With your cup of tea to go, be sure to investigate Tea and Company's specially designed Tea Loft lid and Tea Pouch bag, which keeps loose tea out of the cup after it is brewed.

FOOD DELIVERY

Dine One One

415-908-3463
Open daily

This up-market restaurant delivery service brings dishes from more than 80 restaurants to your doorstep. Call them for a current menu selection.

Waiters on Wheels

415-252-1470
Open daily

In business for 10 years, this service delivers from over 110 restaurants to your home. Call WOW for a current menu selection or look online at www.waitersonwheels.com.

ICE CREAM

Ben & Jerry's

543 COLUMBUS AVE.
NORTH BEACH 94133
415-249-4684
Open daily

What better place to enjoy Cherry Garcia than here in the home of the Beatniks? Customers are welcomed by life-sized, stuffed tourists, who smile at them through the window. **Other locations.**

Mitchels's Ice Cream

688 SAN JOSE AVE.
MISSION 94110
415-648-2300
Open daily

This outlying ice cream shop specializes in imported tropical fruit and gourmet flavors. We love the mango!

Rory's Twisted Scoop Ice Cream

2015 FILLMORE ST.
UPPER FILLMORE 94115
415-346-3692
Open daily

Choose the candies, nuts or other confections that you want with your ice cream, select your ice cream flavor and voila!-Rory's special "twist-in" process will mix them for you. Many San Francisco's restaurants feature Rory's ice cream pies on their menus. **Also in Noe Valley (1300 Castro St., 415-648-2837).**

St. Francis Fountain and Candy Store

2801 24TH ST.
MISSION 94110
415-826-4200
Open daily

A throwback to the days when Americans headed for the soda fountain after school or a movie, the St. Francis is an old-fashioned ice cream counter. Perch on a swivel stool and dig into a sundae made of rich homemade ice cream, chocolate syrup and gooey marshmallow. Purchase some handmade chocolates for a snack later in the evening.

MARKETS

Ethnic Markets

Bombay Bazaar

INDIAN
548 VALENCIA ST.
MISSION 94110
415-621-1717
Open Tues.-Sun.

It's hard to walk into this enticing Indian grocery and not load up on enough supplies to cook Indian food for the next couple of years. It features unusual dhals, special flours for making Indian bread and Indian spices that are hard to find elsewhere. You'll even find tikka spice paste for grilled meats and poultry and an arsenal of pickles, chutneys and chili condiments-plus edible gold and silver leaf and Indian cooking implements.

Casa Lucas Market

LATIN AMERICAN & CARIBBEAN
2934 24TH ST.
MISSION 94110
415-826-4334
Open daily

This is the place to get the ingredients you'll need to cook Caribbean, Central American and Latin American dishes. Hundreds of specialty items are stocked on the crowded shelves-everything from Brazilian palm oil and dried hominy to salt cod, dried potatoes and tins of chorizo imported from Spain. The produce department displays fresh tamarind, coconuts in the husk, mangoes, papayas and cherimoyas.

Hans Speckman

GERMAN
1550 CHURCH ST.
MISSION 94110
415-282-6850
Open daily

A splendid array of wurst awaits at this German deli-everything from Bratwurst and Liverwurst to paprika sausage and Westphalian ham, along with Swiss Bündnerfleisch (air-dried beef) and the house Leberkäse (a pork and veal meatloaf). You can buy German-style horseradish, plus pumpernickel and rye breads collected from local Eastern-European bakeries. You'll also find more than twenty German beers.

K. Sakai

JAPANESE
1656 POST ST.
JAPANTOWN 94115
415-921-0514
Open daily

Dozens of different types of sake, soy sauce, rice, miso, kim chee and other staples of Japanese cuisine are featured at this old-line, family-run Japanese-American market. Don't miss the produce and fresh fish departments.

Lucca Delicatessen

ITALIAN
2120 CHESTNUT ST.
MARINA 94123
415-921-7873
Open daily

The folks at Lucca Delicatessen have been roasting chickens, making salads and baking zucchini frittatas for more than 60 years. This Italian deli is a necessity for cooks in search of salt-packed anchovies, well-aged Parmesan, pancetta and polenta flour. Early morning twice a week, they make their own ravioli by hand, stuffed with finely chopped meat, Swiss chard and cheese for a truly delicious take-home meal. If you buy a small quantity of everything on display in the window, you will have the makings of the perfect antipasto. **Also in the Mission (1100 Valencia St., 415-647-5581).**

Metro Food Co.

CHINESE
641 BROADWAY
CHINATOWN 94108
415-982-1874
Open daily

An emporium of Shanghai foodstuffs, Metro Food proffers a grand selection of ingredients for Chinese cooking: several grades of jellyfish in big crocks, dried Chinese mushrooms and other fungi, packaged spices, Szechuan vegetables and more. The refrigerator cases harbor fresh egg noodles and rice noodles, fish cakes and rice cakes, dumplings, fresh bean-curd skin and fermented rice pudding. Metro is also a favorite for all kinds of canned or preserved goods.

Molinari Delicatessen

ITALIAN
373 COLUMBUS AVE.
NORTH BEACH 94133
415-421-2337
Open Mon.-Sat.

Heroic Italian sandwiches, typical Italian-American salads, a respectable array of cold cuts and cheeses and a mixed bag of Italian wines are the basic fare at this North Beach deli. Italian cooks also can find baccalà (salt cod) and fish for making stock, musky porcini mushrooms, semolina, arborio rice and other hard-to-find imported goodies. Tuscan olive oils, widely considered among the world's best, are priced accordingly.

Sunny Food Mart and Packaged Goods

CHINESE
1210 STOCKTON ST.
CHINATOWN 94108
415-989-2350
Open daily

Sunny Food Mart is one of the best places in Chinatown for Chinese produce: fresh water chestnuts, baby bok choy, Chinese mustard and broccoli, handsome cabbage and watercress. Get your packaged goods and seasonings here too.

Super Koyama

JAPANESE
1790 Sutter St.
JAPANTOWN 94115
415-921-6529
Open daily

The fishmonger at this upscale Japanese supermarket cuts to order, and you can pick up all the fixings for a Japanese meal, including fish cakes, snack crackers, and pickles. A fresh produce and a large in-depth grocery section fill out the store.

Gourmet Markets

Tsar Nicoulai Caviar/ California Sunshine Fine Foods

144 KING ST.
SOMA 94107
415-543-3007, 800-95-CAVIAR
Open Mon.-Fri.

Walk-in and phone-in customers are welcome at this wholesale caviar purveyor to such tony restaurants as Aqua and Postrio. In addition to fresh malossol Tsar Nicoulai caviar (from $18 to $65 an ounce), you'll find such other gourmet goodies as smoked sturgeon and smoked Norwegian salmon.

Epicure at Neiman-Marcus

150 STOCKTON ST.
UNION SQUARE 94108
415-362-3900
Open daily

The best thing about Neiman-Marcus's gourmet department is the Petrossian boutique, tucked discreetly into a corner and painted the same blue as the caviar purveyor's famous store in Paris. If you want to splurge, this is the place to buy sevruga and beluga caviar, smoked eel, smoked salmon and cod roe. Epicure's other strong points include their selection pastries from the best bakeries in San Francisco and the Neiman-Marcus Red River brand of packaged foods-especially the Texas chili.

Macy's Cellar

120 STOCKTON ST.
UNION SQUARE 94108
415-397-3333
Open daily

Its hard to know where to start in the Cellar, the most complete of downtown's gourmet markets. There are chocolates, imported or domestic, by the pound or by the package; a selection of Fortnum and Mason preserves, biscuits and teas is unsurpassed; there's an excellent wine department. If you feel like a bite to eat, try the Boudin Café, or you can choose among the counters that sell salads, sandwiches, Wolfgang Puck pizzas, Tom's cookies and frozen yogurt. Whether you need a gift for your dinner host or the makings for a picnic, this is your downtown stop.

Health Food Markets

San Francisco Health Food Store

333 SUTTER ST.
UNION SQUARE 94108
415-392-8477
Open Mon.-Sat.

Long before juice bars and vitamin stores were trendy, the San Francisco Health Food Store was serving freshly-made carrot salad and vegetable juices and offering a full line of vitamin and mineral supplements. Their lunch counter is one of our favorite places for a quick bite to eat-salads and soups are tasty and nutritious-and we can't pass up a scoop of ginseng ice cream for dessert. Check the back of the store for nuts and dried fruits sold in bulk.

Whole Foods

1765 CALIFORNIA ST.
PACIFIC HEIGHTS 94109
415-674-0500
Open daily

This is the newest gourmet shop to hit San Francisco, and it's already quite a scene. Yuppie shoppers exploit a bakery, a deli, a meat market, a cheese market, and a fish market. Whole Foods' in-house salad bar is to die for. Cater a dinner party and do no work: buy everything already prepared and serve a gourmet meal. Whole Foods even has brown rice sushi.

Outdoor Markets

We've listed two of the city's most popular outdoor markets. For information on about 16 more outdoor markets, most in areas outside of the city, call the **Pacific Coast Farmers' Market Organization (800-949-3276).**

Civic Center Farmer's Market

UNITED NATIONS PLAZA
MARKET & 7TH STS.
415-558-9455
Open Wed. & Sun. only, year-round

This busy market is the place to buy the freshest locally grown produce, as well as olive oil, honey and dried fruit.

Ferry Plaza Farmer's Market

EMBARCADERO & GREEN STS.
415-981-3004
Open Sat.only year-round & Sun. April through Nov.

A popular farmer's market. Buy your fresh produce, sit down on the wall along the promenade and watch the rollerbladers and ships go by.

Supermarkets

The trend in supermarket shopping is towards healthful food, much of which is organic, locally grown and prepared without any preservatives. These are some of the city's best:

Rainbow Grocery

1745 FOLSOM ST.
MISSION 94110
415-863-0621
Open daily

A trip to Rainbow Grocery is like traveling back to the '60s but with a '90s healthful twist-fresh, natural food in an earthy, unpretentious setting. Besides enjoying Rainbow's superb selection of organic produce and vegan comestibles, we have a hard time keeping away from their enormous selection of dried spices, bulk foods, olive oil from the barrel, maple syrup and molasses from vats, nut butters and salsa from plastic tubs and bulk hair- and skin-care products. Shoppers are encouraged to bring their own shopping bags and to bag their own purchases; sales receipts contain political messages.

Real Food Co.

1023 STANYAN ST.
HAIGHT-ASHBURY 94117
415-564-2800
Open daily

Real Food sells both organic and nonorganic produce, with everything clearly marked and handsomely displayed. The range of products is quite a bit broader than you'll find at other organic produce stores. While you're here you can stock up on organic flours, polenta, whole grains, imported olive oils, raw milk cheeses, gourmet ice creams and more. There's good bread and fresh fish for sale, too. **Other locations.**

Trader Joe's

555 9TH ST.
SOMA 94103
415-863-1292
Open daily

You'll find delicious organic goods, healthy fast food, and the least-expensive (but best selection of) wine and beer in the city at Trader Joe's, fast-becoming one of the city's favorite food stops. Their cheese prices are the lowest you'll find anywhere in town. Out-of-towners have been known to load up their luggage with their wild rice, peanut butter pretzels and ginger cookies. **Also in the Western Addition (3 Masonic Ave., 415-346-9964).**

MEAT, POULTRY & GAME

Bryans

3473 CALIFORNIA ST.
LAUREL HEIGHTS 94118
415-752-3430
Open Mon.-Sat.

The meat at Bryans is beautifully displayed in modest quantities, which means they cut it just as they need it. Steaks are labeled "prime" and "choice." Roasts are good-looking, and you'll see such old-fashioned cuts as flat-iron pot roast and cross-rib roast, plus handsome corned beef briskets, pale veal and corn-fed Eastern pork.

Cheung Hing Chinese Deli & Meat Inc.

1151 STOCKTON ST.
CHINATOWN 94108
415-951-8628
Open daily

One of the many good Chinatown butcher shops, Cheung Hing is the place for fresh meat and poultry as well as prepared foods, breads and pastries.

Janmae Guey

1222 STOCKTON ST.
CHINATOWN 94108
415-433-3981
Open daily

Janmae Guey is an informal Chinese restaurant with Formica tables and a small deli where you can buy what may be the best roast pig in Chinatown. The roast duck and barbecued pork are also excellent. While you wait for your take-out order, sit down for a bowl of congee (Chinese rice porridge).

Little City Meats

1400 STOCKTON ST.,
NORTH BEACH 94133
415-986-2601
Open Mon.-Sat.

This longtime North Beach butcher shop specializes in locally-raised veal weighing in at just 60 to 70 pounds. Look for thick-cut veal chops, scaloppine, veal shoulder for stews and meaty veal shanks for osso buco. The store always has breast of veal ready to stuff, and sometimes sells veal filet. Don't worry if you don't have a recipe-they're plastered all over the walls.

Roberts Corned Meats
1030 BRYANT ST.
SOMA 94103
415-621-2624
Open Mon.-Fri.

In business since 1910, Roberts is renowned for corned beef cured from the inside out by directly injecting the beef with spice-laden brine rather than soaking it. In addition to a unique curing method, owner Jim Dixon claims the San Francisco climate has something to do with the quality of his corned beef. Roberts is also a good source for New York pastrami, hams, smoked or pickled tongue, pork hocks and bacon.

Vivande Porta Via
2125 FILLMORE ST.
UPPER FILLMORE 94115
415-346-4430
Open daily

Vivande celebrates Carlo Middione's love affair with Italian cooking. The author of several books on the subject, Middione stocks his Fillmore Street salumeria with the best possible ingredients, and cooks antipasti and other dishes perfect for take-home dinners, picnic outings or simply for eating at Vivande's in-house café. Assembled goodies include prosciutto, pâtés, terrines, galantines, Italian cheeses, fresh sausages flavored with fennel and pepper, a profusion of fried sausages, various antipasti and salads and homemade pastries and biscotti. Shop here for distinguished Italian wines, Tuscan olive oils, arborio rice, dried porcini mushrooms and all manner of special Italian ingredients.

PASTA

New Hong Kong
874 PACIFIC AVE.
CHINATOWN 94108
415-982-2715
Open daily

Twenty-five sizes and types of Chinese noodles are produced by this Chinatown noodle company, including Shanghai-style noodles, very thick Hong Kong-style noodles and wide noodles. You'll also find several types of skins for wontons, potstickers and other dumplings. Prices are only slightly above wholesale.

Pasta Gina
741 DIAMOND ST.
NOE VALLEY 94117
415-282-0738
Open daily

Pasta Gina sells fresh pasta in many widths, shapes and flavors, as well as fresh-made sauces and other essentials for preparing a pasta-based meal- olive oil, imported plum tomatoes, salad fixings, wine and great bread. Expect to find a half dozen different pastas, flavored with roasted peppers, fresh garlic, red chile, beets or lemon. To top them, pick from several sauces, including tomato-basil, sweet red pepper and, for garlic-lovers, cream sauce with roasted garlic and porcini mushrooms.

SEAFOOD

Antonelli and Sons
CAL MART SUPER
3585 CALIFORNIA ST.
LAUREL HEIGHTS 94118
415-752-7413
Open daily

The Antonelli family has decades of experience with local seafood, buying their catches at the wharf in the early morning and cleaning, scaling and cutting it back at the store. You'll find thick, freshly-cut fish steaks-halibut, swordfish and salmon-plus lots of whole fish, fresh filets and some shellfish. Live lobsters are available by request.

Luen Sing Fish Market
1207 STOCKTON ST.
CHINATOWN 94108
415-399-8788
Open daily

Crabs scurry around in a box, shrimp crowd shallow ponds and fresh-water fish swim back and forth in tanks. Could you buy any fresher fish than that at Luen Sing? We doubt it, and, judging by the crowds who shop here just before dinner time, we think much of the Chinese community is of the same opinion.

Swan Oyster Depot
1517 Polk St.
Polk Gulch 94109
415-673-1101
Open Mon.-Sat.

The friendly staff at this decades-old café and fish market will sell you whatever oysters they're shucking for customers that day, plus any fresh fish they're serving-steelhead salmon, swordfish, ling cod or red snapper (see Dining).

WINE & SPIRITS

Ashbury Market
205 Frederick St.
Haight-Ashbury 94117
415-566-3134
Open daily

A family business, Ashbury Market has served the neighborhood for close to 40 years. Owner Wilfred Wong's wine shop is small, but well-stocked with personal selections that fill the floor-to-ceiling shelves.

California Wine Merchant
3237 Pierce St.
Marina 94123
415-567-0646
Open daily

The California Wine Merchant is true to its title: a tidy shop with one of the widest selections of California wines in the city. Their stock includes a fine stash of older vintages.

Coit Liquors
585 Columbus Ave.
North Beach 94133
415-986-4036
Open daily

Tony Giovanzana has managed to fit a remarkable selection of Italian, French and California wines into his corner liquor store in North Beach, along with cases good Champagne at some of the best prices in town. Customers buy steadily all day long, yet the shelves are always fully stocked. How does he do it? He has a huge cellar beneath the store. Coit is particularly known for its selection of hard-to-find Italian wines; its grappa selection is similarly unsurpassed.

Connoisseur Wine Imports
462 Bryant St.
SoMa 94103
415-433-0825
Open Tues.-Sat.

Its warehouse space a maze of stacked wine crates, Connoisseur is the place to bone up on German wines and their intricate classification system. It also has great old Bordeaux, a splendid collection of Sauternes, fine Burgundies and respectable vintage ports, plus a well-edited selection of California wines, many from wineries with limited production.

Cost Plus World Market
2552 Taylor St.
Fisherman's Wharf 94133
415-928-6200
Open daily

Savvy wine shoppers come to Cost Plus for the best prices on wines, particularly California vintages. This vast wine supermarket is well-organized, with write-ups and recommendations posted next to the wines. There is a decent selection of imports, too. While you are here, check out the rest of the store for its terrific assortment of bargain-priced, packaged gourmet foods and home furnishings. Validated parking is in the lot underneath the store.

D and M
2200 Fillmore St.
Upper Fillmore 94115
415-346-1325
Open daily

This unassuming little Mom-'n'-Pop liquor store on the corner sells an intelligent collection of wines, scotches, grappas, Armagnacs and Cognacs. D and M's Champagne assortment includes many splits of world-class sparklers that are rarely found elsewhere. Many prices are discounted. If you're headed to a celebration of any kind and need a speedy but special gift for the hosts, you can be sure to find a vintage spirit or memorable bottle here.

Hennessey's Wines & Spirits
3600 16th St.
Castro 94114
415-864-6677
Open daily

Wine lover Les Hennessey scours the world for special wines and spirits in all price ranges. Whether a tasty Chardonnay from a tiny winery in California's Anderson Valley or a prize-winning Cabernet from Australia or Rioja from Spain, we are always pleased with Les's finds. He's usually there to share his insights and, as way of introduction to the wines, hosts a tasting bar. An ever-changing assortment of cheeses, gourmet snacks and cigars is also available for purchase. **Also in Soma (199 Brannan, 415-777-9403.)**

John Walker and Co.

175 SUTTER ST.
UNION SQUARE 94104
415-986-2707
Open Mon-.Sat.

If you have a taste for legendary Bordeaux vintages or fine old Burgundies, you can find more than enough to keep you happy at John Walker, whose namesake has kept some of these wines maturing in his warehouse for years. Surprisingly, even in this high-rent district, prices are a touch lower than you might pay elsewhere. A selection of Jameson Irish whiskies is awesome.

The Jug Shop

1567 PACIFIC AVE.
POLK GULCH 94115
415-885-2922
Open Mon.-Sun.

Perhaps because it was once a humble liquor store, this wine shop tends to cater to the I-need-a-bottle-for-dinner-tonight crowd. If you need a fail-safe choice for a party or are interested in exploring California Cabernets and Chardonnays, The Jug Shop has your desires well-covered. The strength here is in California wines (all of them discounted), but look into their a decent array of German, Italian and French wines. If you're in the area, stop by for their wine tastings.

Plump Jack's

3201 FILLMORE ST.
UNION STREET 94123
415-346-9870
Open daily

This beautiful store, with its abundant gleaming woods and fresh flower arrangements, is the most exclusive-looking wine store in the city. The younger generation of the J. Paul Getty clan and a San Francisco Supervisor own the shop and restaurant (see Dining), and they have amassed a comprehensive collection of big American names, especially Californians, and a smaller French selection. When in doubt, you won't go wrong with the Plump Jack label Chardonnay or Cabernet, both from the Napa Valley. Ask about the tastings and seminars held frequently in the back room of the store.

The Wine Club

953 HARRISON ST.
SOMA 94107
415-512-9086
Open daily

People come here with serious intent: to hunt down great wines at great prices. And they always succeed, often leaving with armloads of new finds as well as old favorites. A discount wine warehouse, the Wine Club stocks a constantly-changing roster of interesting California wines, as well as French, Italian, German, Australian and Chilean varietals. Load up on any wines the buyers have procured for a stupendous deal that month; a varied selection is usually open at the tasting counter. If you discover a sensational wine, though, hurry back and buy a case-some varietals and vintages are one-time purchases and may not be carried again.

The Wine House

535 BRYANT ST.
SOMA 94103
415-495-8486
Open Mon.-Sat.

John Carpenter is an importer who specializes in the wines of Bordeaux and Burgundy, although he has digressed into other, lesser-known French wine areas. Since his customers enjoy drinking vintage wines as much as investing in new ones, a good portion of his business is in older bottles. Look here for rare California vintages, noble Italian wines and vintage ports, Sauternes and Champagnes.

GIFTS

ARTS & CRAFTS

The African Outlet
524 OCTAVIA ST.
HAYES VALLEY 94102
415-864-3576
Open daily

Step inside this delightful shop and you'll feel as if you've been transported to Africa. Everything in the store is authentic, and you'll find hundreds of treasures: brilliantly colored fabrics, beautiful jewelry, intricate carvings, painted masks, musical instruments and clothes for men, women, and children.

Atys
2149-B UNION ST.
UNION STREET 94123
415-441-9220
Open Wed.-Sat.

Atys was a Roman god who had an interest in design; this shop pays tribute to him with an assortment of contemporary living accessories that remind us of those at the Museum of Modern Art's gift shop, yet even more interesting. You'll find curved Danish silver letter openers, light-as-a-feather Japanese business card cases, sinuous wooden chairs and a classic Beachcruiser bicycle.

Australia Fair
700 SUTTER ST.
UNION SQUARE 94109
415-441-5319
Open Mon.-Sat.

A cheery spot for rarely seen products from down under, this is the place to buy a boomerang or didgeridoo as well as the instruction books on how to use them. Children and other animal lovers will enjoy lifelike koala stuffed animals; for outdoors types, ranch coats and bush hats; for skiers, wool underblankets and lambskin rugs to decorate the cabin; and, for homesick Aussies, tins of vegemite. Call for Sunday hours.

Babushka Russka Dolls
PIER 39
FISHERMAN'S WHARF 94133
415-788-7043
Open daily

We are always fascinated by the Babushka Dolls that stack one into another. The ones here are the real thing-as is everything in the store, filled with goods imported from Russia. Many items can be considered collectibles.

The Balloon Lady
1263 HOWARD ST.
SOMA 94103
415-864-3737
Open daily

The Balloon Lady creates amazingly creative balloon bouquets and structures out of 100% biodegradable latex. Balloons can be delivered for any occasion; prices range from $34.95 and up, with delivery by a tuxedo-clad man singing a song: Watch for the arrival of the pink van.

Dandelion
55 POTRERO AVE.
SOMA 94103
415-436-9500
Open Tues.-Sat.

Everything here is a little different: a delightful assortment of imported soaps, cards, wrapping papers, candles, children's playthings, coffee-table books and fine fountain pens. Among the housewares is a great selection of tablecloths in varied designs and fabrics, and you can even indulge your sweet tooth at the old-fashioned candy counter.

De Vera
580 SUTTER ST.
UNION SQUARE 94102
415-861-8480
Open Mon.-Sat.

Federico de Vera sells the most beautiful collectibles from the most beautiful places in the world. Each store is different: Sutter Street houses objects including Japanese lacquer from the Edo period; Hayes Street houses a gallery of blown Italian and Scandinavian glass art; and Maiden Lane houses Victorian jewelry, including a collection of Indian jewelry. **Other locations.**

The Disney Store

400 Post St.
Union Square 94108
415-391-6866
Open daily

As over-exposed as we are to Disney fare, we are still amazed by this store, which is usually so crowded you may have to wait in line just to get close to the merchandise. Everything is Disney-stuffed toys, watches, mugs and pencils to swimsuits and athletic wear; clothing is not just for kids. Be sure to visit the portion of the shop dedicated to Disney art and fine gifts, including limited-edition glass vases and plates, fine china, dessert sets and prints. Other locations.

EC Studio Store

347 Hayes St.
Hayes Valley 94102
415-621-1355
Open Tues.-Sat.

EC sells imported fabric portfolios that wrap packets of fine stationery, and is also turned into unusually shaped sachets and elegant napkins. Silk flowers are fabricated into napkin rings, hair combs and decorative pins. The fabric items are all unique designs of this store; most are priced under $30 and are real treasures. Lovers of paper products will delight in EC's assortment of notebooks and writing papers.

Folk Art International Gallery/Boretti Amber

Ghirardelli Square, 900 North Point
Fisherman's Wharf 94133
415-928-3340
Open daily

This showroom for the Folk Art International group, which includes the Xanadu Gallery next door, offers an intriguing selection of folk arts and crafts from around the world: masks from Mexico, South America and the Philippines; hand-woven baskets from Africa; paintings from China, Ecuador and France; sculptures and artworks from as close as the Appalachians and as far as Sri Lanka; and antique bronzes, porcelains and ivory carvings from Asia. You'll also find winsome toys, unusual furniture, Berber jewelry from Morocco's Atlas Mountains, tribal art and amber jewelry.

Fumiki Fine Asian Arts

2001 Union St.
Union Street 94123
415-922-0573
Open daily

An eclectic array of antique and contemporary art objects and fine jewelry from Japan, China and Korea, includes elegant silk obi (sashes for kimonos) and a noteworthy group of ivory and wooden netsuke-intricately carved toggles used to fasten small containers.

Gump's

135 Post St.
Union Square 94108
415-982-1616
Open daily

No trip to San Francisco can end without a visit to Gump's, the fabulous china/stationery/jewelry/gift store that opened its first downtown doors in 1862. Gump's own designs in jade jewelry tempt shoppers. The china and crystal departments are unequaled: there are more than 400 patterns from every fine maker in the world, including Waterford, Baccarat, Steuben, Limoges, Fitz and Floyd and Spode. Curiously, there is now a bed and bath department and a section devoted to gardening accessories-both supposedly a reflection of Gump's clientele's current-day interests. An immense, wooden Lama Buddha greets you as you enter.

Left Hand World

Pier 39
Fisherman's Wharf 94133
415-433-3547
Open daily

"Where the customer is not always right" is the motto of this store dedicated to making life easier for left-handed people. You'll find left-handed measuring cups, calligraphy pens, spatulas, watches, scissors, Swiss Army knives and even special decks of playing cards designed for the southpaw.

Mashiko Folk Craft

Japan Center, Kinokuniya Building
1581 Webster St. #216
Japantown 94115
415-346-0748
Open Wed.-Mon.

This tiny shop features hand-crafted oven-proof pottery from the village of Mashiko, where pottery has been made for over 2000 years. Many of the tea cups, some selling for hundreds of dollars, have been made by Living National Treasures, a title awarded to a few very special traditional craftsmen. Don't be put off by the aloof shopkeeper: treasures in all price ranges can be found here.

The Poster Source

PIER 39
FISHERMAN'S WHARF 94133
415-433-1995
Open daily

What better souvenir of San Francisco than a poster of the Golden Gate Bridge or a row of Victorian houses? If *The Scream* by Edward Munch is more your cup of tea, you'll find it-and many other art prints and museum graphics-as well. Most posters are in the $3 to $35 category and the Poster Source offers same-day mounting and framing.

The San Francisco Music Box Company

PIER 39
FISHERMAN'S WHARF 94133
415-433-3696
Open daily

Customers are encouraged to try out every music box in the store. Once you select the style, you can customize your box with your choice of a tune. Some of the more popular boxes are those depicting Disney characters and popular shows such as *Phantom of the Opera* and *Les Misérables.* In recognition of the sea lions who have taken up residence at the pier, there is a barking *California Sea Lions* at *Pier 39* music box. **Also in the San Francisco Shopping Centre (865 Market St., 415-546-6343).**

The Sharper Image

532 MARKET ST.
FINANCIAL DISTRICT 94111
415-398-6472
Open daily

The famous and innovative catalog comes to life here with state-of-the-art items you may never have seen before, such as massage recliners, electronic organizers, laser golf trainers, neon license plate frames and even a few pedestrian shirts, ties and casual jackets. Other locations.

Smile

500 SUTTER ST.
UNION SQUARE 94108
415-362-3436
Open Mon.-Sat.

We smile even when we think about Smile, which describes itself as "a gallery with tongue in chic." A mix of playful ceramic pieces, decorative sculptures, jewelry, natural fiber clothing and lots of cheerful tchotchkes are sure to brighten your life.

Sonoma Country Store

3575 SACRAMENTO ST.
PRESIDIO HEIGHTS 94122
415-923-1600
Open daily

If you haven't got time to make it up to Sonoma, then why not have Sonoma come to you? Everything here is beautifully intricate: lace Victorian night shirts, rabbit candlesticks, dried flowers, and porcelain tea pots. This is the kind of store where you go to buy a gift for someone else and can't resist one for yourself. They are also one of the only stores that stock Eileen West clothing at discounted prices.

Panetti's

3927 24TH ST.
NOE VALLEY 94114
415-648-2414
Open daily

Panetti's describes itself perfectly: "A charming place to find witty and wonderful gifts in San Francisco's sunny Noe Valley."

Tibet Shop

1807 POLK ST.
POLK GULCH 94109
415-982-0326
Open daily

Run by a disciple of the Dalai Lama, this shop sells bells, incense, singing bowls, carved skulls and prayer beads, as well as lapis lazuli, turquoise, silver and coral necklaces. You'll also find clothing, crafts, artifacts, and paintings from Tibet, including everything you need for the practice of Tibetan Buddhism.

TT Globe Trotter USA

418 SUTTER ST.
UNION SQUARE 94108
415-434-1120
Open daily

Tintin's origins go back to before World War II, when his Belgian creator, Hergé, began writing and drawing cartoons about this boy's adventures. With this cheerful boutique, American children can join their European counterparts in following Tintin and his loyal dog Snowy in the books that chronicle his good deeds and travels. Adults and kids alike will delight in the Tintin porcelain dishes and figurines, watches, neckties and T-shirts.

Twig

2162 UNION ST.
UNION STREET 94123
415-928-8944
Open daily

Sharing an entryway with Union Street Papery, Twig is a gallery of American crafts. The pottery pieces, jewelry and picture frames are such perfect gifts that you might want to buy two and keep one for yourself. The woven rugs are lovely functional art.

Virginia Breier

3091 SACRAMENTO ST.
LAUREL HEIGHTS 94118
415-929-7173
Open Mon.-Sat.

Dealing in crafts for over 20 years, this contemporary folk art gallery specializes in the works of local artists. A good place for one-of-a-kind gifts, such as jewelry, ceramics, glass, furniture outdoor sculpture, and housewares, Breier's is an eclectic mix of folk and ethnic artwork in bright colors.

Wings America

262 SUTTER ST.
UNION SQUARE 94108
415-989-9464
Open daily

This fabulous store for those who love aircraft and flying specializes in hand-painted mahogany sculptures. You'll also find a nice selection of Leather Flight Jackets and other flight-oriented clothing and accessories, including famous brands and styles made especially for Wings America. Their main store is in Carmel.

Worldware

336 HAYES ST.
HAYES VALLEY 94102
415-487- 9030
Open daily

It feels like a warm spring morning when you enter this Hayes Valley store, with cotton sheets blowing in the wind. Worldware sells all-natural, eco-friendly clothing, bedding, cosmetics and baby clothes-even clothing made from hemp. The cuts are very simple, stylish and wearable.

MODERN/FUNKY/FAR OUT

Botanica Yoruba

998 VALENCIA ST.
MISSION 94110
415-826-4967
Open daily

Candles, potions, powders, oils, herbs, statues of saints-Yoruba sells everything you need for the practice of Santeria, the African-Cuban religion practiced in some Latin countries. From the opposite side of the world, this shop is also an oasis of Eastern-inspired spiritual products to heal the mind, body, and soul.

Haight-Ashbury T-shirts

1500 HAIGHT ST.
HAIGHT-ASHBURY 94117
415-863-4639
Open daily

Even if you're not looking for a T-shirt, once you step inside you'll marvel at the display: the whole shop is covered from floor to in tie-dyes, Jerry Garcia collectibles, and Beatles mania.

Harley Davidson Motor Cycles

66 PAGE ST.
CIVIC CENTER 94102
415-703-9494
Open Mon.-Sat.

Part of Dudley Perkins, the original Harley Davidson dealership has been in San Francisco since 1914. The shop sells everything you could imagine in Harley-Davidson paraphernalia-including new bikes. For more apparel and collectibles stop by the other location at **Fisherman's Wharf (2595 Taylor St., 415-776-7779).**

Lyle Tuttle Tattooing

841 COLUMBUS AVE.
NORTH BEACH 94133
415-775-4991
Open daily

Tattooist Lyle Tuttle opened his studio in North Beach close to 50 years ago, and quickly established a reputation for providing the best and safest tattoo artistry in San Francisco. His tradition continues, and today Tuttle's is still the place of choice for body art from abound the world. Not up to a design for yourself? Tuttle's gallery of tattoo art is worthy of a visit.

Neverland

241 COLUMBUS AVE.
NORTH BEACH 94133
415-788-7883
Open daily

This store is pure fantasy: who can pass up the magic wands from Brazil, fanciful masks, and lavish jester hats? Owner Bob Hemphill also runs the Gallery of Ethnic Art (245 Columbus Ave.) next door, and its Dreaming Room, a magical room filled with large-scale, sometimes rare, works of ethnic art. The Dreaming Room can be rented at reasonable rates for private parties, dinners, photo and movie shoots.

Pipe Dreams

1736 HAIGHT ST.
HAIGHT-ASHBURY 94117
415-431-3553
Open daily

This Haight shop will take you back in time to when the neighborhood was known as the 'Hashbury'. The shop offers a full selection of smoking paraphernalia, T-shirts and psychedelic sundries.

Quantity Postcards

1441 GRANT AVE.
NORTH BEACH 94133
415-986-8866
Open daily

Quantity Postcards sell thousands of strange, outlandish and hilarious postcards. You'll find all of its wacky cards here, along with boxes of vintage postcards and some produced by other publishers. Bring your sense of humor and plenty of stamps.

SF Rock Posters and Collectibles

1851 POWELL ST.
NORTH BEACH 94133
415-956-6749
Open Mon.-Sat.

Handbills, tickets, original art and posters galore fill this store, a vault of the art from San Francisco's early rock and roll history.

Uncle Mame

2241 MARKET ST.
CASTRO 94114
415-626-1953
Open daily

Mame is the quintessential establishment for procuring American memorabilia. Customers take a trip down memory lane as they seek out Oscar Weiner whistles, Mr. Peanut salt-and-pepper shakers, Charlie's Angel's rubber stamps, and much, much more.

Winterland Products

100 HARRISON ST.
SOMA 94105
415-597-9700
Open Wed.-Sat.

If you've missed the rock show, you can still get the T-shirts: Iron Maiden, the Doors, Pink Floyd.

PETS

Cool Doggy O's

468 GREEN ST.
NORTH BEACH 94133
415-788-2665
Open Mon.-Fri.

If 1950s-era Beatniks were to set up a shop for pets, it would look a lot like Cool Doggy O's: look for the colorful sign with Cool Doggy-O pointing the way from his perch on a window sill. The store itself features an array of "parafurnalia" for pets and their people, including cookies, snacks, frozen entrées, hand-painted pet food bowls from Guatemala, cards, pet art, cat condos (check out the Southwest pueblo model), and such basics as nutritious pet food, kitty litter, and pet shampoo. If your pooch is in need of a new coif or a flea dip, Doggy O's does grooming, too.

George
2411 California St.
Upper Fillmore 94115
415-441-0564
Open daily

Pampered dogs and cats thrill to the thought of receiving a terry cloth towel, food bowl, or edible treat from George; their owners enjoy the selection of books about pets and picture frames. All purchases are wrapped in a George's bone bag, and many items bear the George label logo.

Ken Grooms
3429 Sacramento St.
Presidio Heights 94118
415-673-7708
Open Mon.-Sat.

In addition to handsomely-decorated water and food bowls and a selection of healthful dog and cat treats, Ken Grooms sells French leather collars with matching leashes, which must be seen to be fully appreciated.

HOME

BED & BATH

Scheurer Linens
340 Sutter St.
Union Square 94108
415-392-2813
Open Mon-Sat.

If Scheurer's 330-count Egyptian cotton sheets are too rich for your budget, check out the more attractively priced Italian sheets, finely woven with a 210-count that feels like a 300-count sheet. Other temptations include Cashgora blankets, hotel robes and towels, white goose-down pillows and hypo-allergenic synthetic down pillows. We can't resist the Vogue print hand towels, despite their extravagant $22 price.

Sue Fisher King
3067 Sacramento St.
Presidio Heights 94118
415-922-7276
Open Mon.-Sat.

You can realize any domestic fantasy in this elegant, densely packed shop. The walls are lined with fine Italian, French and Portuguese linens, shower curtains, woolen blankets, pretty placemats and silver picture frames-items for the upscale hope chest. Sue Fisher King Home is also located inside **Wilkes Bashford (375 Sutter St.)**

CHILDREN'S FURNITURE

Jonathan-Kaye
3548 Sacramento St.
Presidio Heights 94118
415-563-0773
Open daily

Jonathan-Kaye sells unfinished pine furniture for children, so much of it that it's nearly spilling out the door and onto the sidewalk. You'll find well-made bunk beds, dressers, chairs and desks, all reasonably priced and awaiting the stroke of a paintbrush or a natural finish. Jammed in among the furniture are some high-quality toys by Brio and Gund, a respectable assortment of Paddington bears and a good selection of books.

COOKWARE

HomeChef Kitchen Store & Cooking School
3525 California St.
Laurel Village 94118
415-668-3191
Open daily

This kitchen store is always bustling, and sells everything you could ever need for cooking: great cookware and tools, elegant dishes, stylish glassware, specialty foods—even chefs' apparel. The Cooking School offers its signature "Essential Cooking Series," which covers everything from stocks to soufflés, as well as a range of single classes from cake decorating to Thai cuisine.

Sur La Table
77 Maiden Ln.
Union Square 94108
415-732-7900
Open daily

Dozens of whisks, wooden spoons in every length and width, cookie cutters, coffee makers, mixers, salt cellars-you name the kitchen utensil and Sur La Table probably has several to choose from. Add to this an almost-daily schedule of cooking classes and demonstrations and you have the ultimate store for those who love to cook. **Also in Berkeley (Fourth Street District, 1806 Fourth Street).**

Williams-Sonoma

150 Post St.
Union Square 94108
415-362-6904
Open daily

Thousands of customers have made the Williams-Sonoma catalog immensely successful: now residents of many American cities have a Williams-Sonoma of their very own. There are several in the Bay Area, but this branch-the company's headquarters-is the best of the bunch, with spacious rooms on two levels, filled with the best kitchen products available. Dishes range from white classics to Italian charmers, cookware from copper to Calphalon and appliances from cappuccino machines to food processors. We especially like the cotton table linens, colorful dish rags, copper cookware, cookbooks and gadgets. Heavy wooden chairs and tables and handsome outdoor furniture are displayed on the second level. Other locations.

FABRIC

Britex Fabrics

146 Geary St.
Union Square 94108
415-392-2910
Open Mon-Sat.

Traveling tailors and seamstresses head straight for Britex when they get into town. They know that few places in the world have such an extensive collection of fine fabrics, leathers, trims, buttons and notions. From sea-island cotton to cashmere, couture knits to crêpe de chine, Britex satisfies almost any kind of sewing need imaginable.

Laura Ashley

253 Post St.
Union Square 94108
415-788-0190
Open daily

Beyond the racks of flouncy dresses, corduroy jumpers and cuter-than-cute little-girl clothes are shelves filled with Laura Ashley's English country fabrics, the majority of which are heavy, upholstery-weight high-quality cotton weaves in the company's traditional flowered designs.

Mix

309 Sutter St.
Union Square 94108
415-392-1742
Open Mon.-Sat.

Once at the vanguard of modern Scandinavian fabric design in this country, Marimekko has brightened many a household with these bold, colorful fabrics and linens from Finland. Mix also features Marimekko clothing and apparel from other European lines.

Pierre Deux

134 Maiden Ln.
Union Square 94108
415-296-9940
Open Mon.-Sat.

This handsome French country store is filled with purses, cosmetic cases, pillows and notebooks covered with Pierre Deux's trademark provençal cotton prints. These same fabrics are sold by the yard if specially ordered.

FURNITURE & FURNISHINGS

Bay Commercial Lighting Center

1140 Folsom St.
SoMA 94103
415-552-4110
Open Mon.-Sat.

Bay Lighting sells high-style and Euro-style lighting fixtures, floor lamps, wall sconces, table lamps, hanging fixtures from European and American designers. The selection of cutting-edge contemporary fixtures is exceptional. It's also a good place for well-made track lighting and recessed lighting.

Centrium Furnishings

2166 Market St.
Castro 94114
415-863-4195
Open Tues.- Sun.

Centrium sells furniture, lighting and decorative arts from the 1930s to the 1970s.

Echo

3775 24TH ST.
NOE VALLEY 94114
415-282-3330
Open daily

Looking to furnish your contemporary lifestyle? Echo offers everything you need for the home and garden: upholstered furniture, bed and bath accessories, kitchen and tabletop accessories, gifts and rugs.

Fillamento

2185 FILLMORE ST.
UPPER FILLMORE 94115
415-931-2224
Open daily

Whenever we are looking for the unusual in tabletop items or furniture, we always come to Fillamento first. Young, modern and somewhat Euro-styled, this is a good place for attractive rugs, glassware, terra-cotta dishes, designer stainless flatware, dining room tables, bar stools and bathroom accessories. The complimentary gift wrap is special.

Jeffrey Davies, Inc.

575 SUTTER ST.
UNION SQUARE 94108
415-392-1722
Open Mon.-Sat.

Silk and dried flowers-many of them handmade and handcolored in Europe-dominate this exclusive shop that also sells antiques. Custom arrangements can be made to your order, or you might just be pleased with an already-potted Iceland Poppy or Lily of the Valley. You'll appreciate the attentive professional service.

Galisteo

590 10TH ST.
SOMA 94103
415-861-5900
Open daily

San Francisco's best of the Southwest, Galisteo comprises an entire building devoted to furniture, both antique and contemporary, memorabilia, cowboy relics, rugs, jewelry and art of the American West.

Limn

290 TOWNSEND ST.
SOMA 94103
415-543-5466
Open Mon.-Sat.

Limn stocks "intriguing currents and lasting influences in contemporary design," and carries extraordinary tables, desks, chairs and couches. The artist- and architect-designed furniture, some of it created by owner Lee Friedlander, ranges from subtle to extreme. Radical and expensive lighting fixtures are sometimes in stock, and there's usually an exhibition of painting or sculpture. Limn's art gallery is located next door at 292 Townsend.

Pottery Barn

2100 CHESTNUT ST.
MARINA 94123
415-441-1787
Open daily

Casual California living is personified in Pottery Barn's moderately priced vases, lamps, glassware, coffee tables, rugs, mirrors, beds and just about everything else needed to furnish a yuppie household. We like the young contemporary look of it all. Other locations.

Ralph Lauren Home Collection

CROCKER GALLERIA, 90 POST ST.
FINANCIAL DISTRICT 94111
415-788-7656
Open daily

Adjacent to the Polo/Ralph Lauren store, the Home Collection provides the rest of the preppy look that we love in Ralph Lauren clothing. You'll find luggage, sheets, towels, items for the tabletop and even furniture here-truly a Ralph Lauren heaven.

Swing Song

PIER 39
FISHERMAN'S WHARF 94133
415-399-9504
Open daily

Hop into one of their indoor/outdoor hammock chairs and chances are good you'll be so comfortable that you'll take one home. Likewise, it's hard to resist the rainbow-colored traditional hammocks ready to hang between two trees-especially after the staff shows you how to add a few pillows for even more comfort. A wide selection of wind chimes and bells is also featured.

Z Gallerie

2071 UNION ST.
UNION STREET 94123
415-346-9000
Open daily

High in design and moderate in price, Z Gallerie exhibits a strong predilection for modern decorative items and furnishings for home and office. The "gallerie" moniker is justified by the large stock of framed posters. **Other locations.**

HOUSEWARES & TABLETOPS

Biondi Art Imports

412 COLUMBUS AVE.
NORTH BEACH 94133
415-392-8096
Open Mon.-Sat.

The remarkable hand-painted dinnerware, vases, platters and objets d'art, made by the best of Italian Majolica artists, are Biondi's main draw, both in the store and through its large mail-order business. But there's more: espresso and cappuccino machines, authentic Italian cookware, pasta rollers and ornate Capodimonte china.

Crate and Barrel

125 GRANT AVE.
UNION SQUARE 94108
415-986-4000
Open daily

Crate and Barrel is a marvel of merchandise, with three floors of great-looking household basics. It's difficult to leave this place without a carful of goods, from reasonably priced Adirondack chairs and storage systems to terra-cotta dishes and champagne flutes.

E.M. Hundley Hardware Co.

617 BRYANT ST.
SOMA 94107
415-777-5050
Open Mon.-Sat.

Hundley Hardware is a favorite shopping place for designers, contractors and builders because of its wide selection of home building and home decorating items. If you have the urge to change the knobs and pulls on your kitchen cabinets, you're sure to find something to your liking from the selection that covers one entire side of the store.

Forrest Jones, Inc.

3274 SACRAMENTO ST.
PRESIDIO HEIGHTS 94118
415-567-2483
Open daily

Once you get past the baskets and leather shopping bags festooning this doorway, you can lose yourself in the maze of shelves filled with glasses, candles, napkins, napkin rings, travel accessories, cooking utensils and hand-painted Italian and French dishes.

Fredericksen Hardware

3029 FILLMORE ST.
UNION STREET 94123
415-292-2950
Open daily

Since 1896 Fredericken's has been the place to shop for all manner of hardware and housewares. Whether it be a Le Creuset pot, a colander in a special size, cookie cutters, straw baskets, a coffee grinder or a packet of flower seeds, you'll find them all in this jam-packed hardware store. If you need a tool for a one-time use, you can rent it here. We especially appreciate the personalized service, no matter how small or big our purchase.

Whole Earth Access

401 BAYSHORE BLVD.
SOUTH CITY 94124
415-285-5244
Open daily

The offshoot of the popular Marin and Berkeley stores, Whole Earth's retail business grew out of the Whole Earth Access catalog, the bible of the socially-conscious '70s consumer. Today, Whole Earth is an appealing warehouse full of high-quality PCs, televisions, appliances large and small, cookware, dishes, kitchen tools and some furniture-all at excellent prices.

GARDENING & YARD

Lumbini

156 SOUTH PARK
SOMA 94107
415-896-2666
Open Mon.-Fri.

A design studio and gardening store in one! Lumbini describes itself somewhat-pretentiously as "A Store: The celebration of physical expressions; A Spirit: The symbol of transformation; A Garden: the sight of transformation; A Place: The birthplace of Buddha." Lumbina has seeds for the garden, books on gardening, decorations, stationary, recycled maps and candles beautifully displayed. This special store is sure to lift your spirits.

Smith and Hawken

2040 FILLMORE ST.
UPPER FILLMORE 94115
415-776-3424
Open daily

Smith and Hawken is best known for its catalogs of gardening equipment, supplies and clothing and outdoor furniture. What a treat to visit one of its only-in-California stores! We love their colorful Jolly brand gardening clogs from Germany which keep our feet dry and free of mud. Don't miss the live plants, exotic flower and vegetable seeds and wooden benches for sale at this upscale shop.

JEWELRY & WATCHES

Cartier

231 POST ST.
UNION SQUARE 94108
415-397-3180
Open Mon.-Sat.

This large branch of the venerable Parisian jeweler and watchmaker is as opulent an establishment as the name would suggest. Glass cases glow with displays of watches and extravagant jewels. The staff is content to let you browse; don't neglect the fabulous array of silver.

Edmund R. Weber

210 POST ST., STE. 308-309
UNION SQUARE 94108
415-781-0218
Open Mon.-Fri.

One of the few jewelers in the Bay Area to work in platinum, Ed Weber and his son Alberto specialize in custom-made fine jewelry, and their selection of precious stones includes diamonds, jade, emeralds and sapphires. The Webers are also appraisers, and will gladly educate first-time diamond buyers in the intricacies of evaluating the quality of a stone. We appreciate their personal service and design expertise. Describe your lifestyle and taste and they will create a competitively priced ring, bracelet, necklace, or brooch to complement it. Appointments recommended.

Gump's

135 POST ST.
UNION SQUARE 94108
415-982-1616
Open daily

The choicest pearls and jade and the finest gold and silver are crafted into exquisitely simple pieces in this quintessential San Franciscan store. Equally attractive are the necklaces, earrings, brooches and rings made of such stones as tourmaline and lapis lazuli. Because Gump's combs the world for the finest raw materials and then designs and manufactures these pieces, you can be assured of their quality.

Harry Mason Design Studio

PIER 39
FISHERMAN'S WHARF 94133
415-296-7009
Open daily

Imagination has no limit when it comes to the earrings, earcuffs and earpins for pierced and non-pierced ears that Harry Mason and his stable of artists and designers create. We love the trademarked Earspirals, attention-grabbing gold wire spirals. Those without pierced ears can achieve the pierced look with trademarked Earwraps; many wear three or four of them on one ear.

Imposters

295 GEARY ST.
UNION SQUARE 94108
415-391-9491
Open daily

"Inspired by" is the way Imposters describes its knockoffs of jewelry by Cartier, Tiffany, Bulgari, Gucci and just about every other premier jeweler you can imagine. You will feel like a million dollars, while rarely spending even a hundred, when you don their classic faux jewelry. **Also in the San Francisco Shopping Centre (865 Market St., 415-541-4922).**

The Jerusalem Shop

313 Noe St.
Castro 94114
415-626-7906
Open daily

This little women's clothing and jewelry shop-which recently relocated to a new, expanded location-has been lauded as the best in town for hand-crafted jewelry. Knowledgeable and personable help will assist you with their wide-ranging selection, with an emphasis on silver and semi-precious stones.

Jest Jewels

2049 Union St.
Union Street 94123
415-563-8839
Open daily

A pricier, adult version of the five-and-dime, you could walk out of Jest Jewels with a collection to rival the late Dutchess of Windsor's in style, though not in cost. The store's selection runs the gamut from faux baroque pearls to bits of anodized engine parts; an assortment of watches range from cheap tickers to handsome quartz knockoffs of serious timepieces. **Also in the Embarcadero Center (415-986-4494).**

The Magical Trinket

524 Hayes St.
Hayes Valley 94102
415-626-0764
Open daily

A sea of beads and baubles for jewelry making awaits you. The Trinket's staff are very helpful in offering suggestions and even offer bead-making workshops; call for a schedule. Take plenty of time to enjoy the riches found in this store, overflowing with plastic buckets containing every imaginable color of beads.

Peter Macchiarini

1529 Grant Ave.
North Beach 94133
415-982-2229
Open Mon.-Sat.

If we were to single out one special shop in North Beach, it would be the studio of Peter Macchiarini, who has been making avant garde jewelry for more than 60 years. With 50 years at this location, Mr. Macchiarini is still at work here just about every day; his daughter and son now work with him. Each piece of his jewelry is made to the customer's specifications. You can select your ring, pendant, brooch, or earrings from a portfolio of his designs or work with him to design something entirely new.

Shreve and Co.

200 Post St.
Union Square 94108
415-421-2600
Open daily

An established San Francisco jeweler in an historic building that has survived many an earthquake, Shreve and Co. is a bastion of conservative good taste. The window displays are always a treat, and the silver pieces are especially lovely. They also sell a full range of crystal, stationery and fine gifts.

St. Eligius

1748 Union St.
Union Street 94123
415-771-2282
Open Tues.-Sat.

Reminiscent in spirit of the work of Tiffany's famous designer Jean Schlumberger, the gold jewelry made here includes clever accents of precious stones: a pheasant's eye is a tiny ruby; diamonds comprise the dewdrops on a leaf; a marked art deco influence is expressed in many of the pieces. The special child in your life will cherish their necklaces on which dangle a golden bear balancing on a freshwater pearl ball. As well as providing gem appraisal and brokerage, St. Eligius is linked to a computer network that can locate that flawless, marquise-cut stone you've been searching for.

Swatch Store

Pier 39
Fisherman's Wharf 94133
415-788-4543
Open daily

Swatch wearers know there is always room for another timepiece in one's wardrobe-see the newest as well as vintage watches here. We like the new Swatch "Skin" watch for dressier wear. Macy's is the only other place in town that sells a large selection of Swatches.

Tiffany and Co.

350 Post St.
Union Square 94108
415-781-7000
Open Mon.-Sat.

Even the least materialistic among us delights in receiving one of Tiffany's famous little pale blue boxes, for inside will surely be something wonderful. We especially like Gene Moore's "Fantasy" children's party china, the Atlas watches that are inspired by the 1853 clock on Tiffany's facade and the company's timeless silver gift items-from teething rings and money clips to picture frames and keyfobs.

Tom Wing and Sons

208 Grant Ave.
Union Square 94108
415-391-2500
Open Mon.-Sat.

Gump's isn't the only place in town for jade: Wing's small, elegant shop features an unusual collection made of striking lavender, apple-green and emerald-green stone.

Zeitgeist

437B Hayes St.
Hayes Valley 94102
415-864-0185
Open Tues.-Sat.

One of the most highly-regarded watch repair shops in the city, Zeitgeist also sells an extensive array of second-hand clocks and watches, including timepieces by Patek Philippe and Rolex. While there, take note of the fascinating map on the wall illustrating the inside workings of a clock, as well as vintage watch ads from old magazines.

LEATHER GOODS & LUGGAGE

Bottega Veneta

108 Geary St.
Union Square 94108
415-981-1700
Open Mon.-Sat.

A marvelous array of Italian leather goods is displayed In this celebrated shop. The luggage, briefcases, purses, belts and wallets are supple, handsome and unspoiled by logos or initials.

Brava Strada

3247 Sacramento St.
Presidio Heights 94118
415-567-5757
Open Mon.-Sat.

Against a postmodern backdrop of rough-textured concrete and smooth marble, Brava Strada displays an eclectic sampling of Italian leather handbags, art jewelry and various accessories.

The Coach Store

190 Post St.
Union Square 94108
415-392-1772
Open daily

Many a woman still carries the Coach bag she bought five (or ten) years ago-a bit scuffed, perhaps, but still going strong. Since the leather is crafted to last, the bags, belts, wallets and accessories are styled so they won't look foolishly dated in the years to come. That's not to say Coach merchandise is stodgy: many of these bags-especially the briefcases and drawstring purses-are beautiful. The new Coach for Men store, just down the block, carries shoes, briefcases, telephone cases, neckties and other masculine goodies. **Also at 170 Post St., 415-391-7770.**

Edwards

3 Embarcadero Center
Financial District 94111
415-981-7047
Open daily

The array of leather goods, luggage and gift items at Edwards will make you feel like a child on Christmas morning. The name-brand luggage is available in leather as well as in space-age materials; small leather items include wallets, purses and attaché cases. They also sell fountain pens, travel accessories, luggage tags, desk accessories and umbrellas; novelty gifts will amuse the busy executive or the bored child. Edwards is a family-run business, and their services include complimentary monogramming and gift wrapping. Other locations.

Louis Vuitton
230 Post St.
Union Square 94108
415-391-6200
Open daily

Many consider Louis Vuitton's pieces major status symbols. The coated canvas bags and luggage covered with "LVs" still exist, but the line has been given some new life with purses, wallets and portfolios in vivid solid colors: yellow, green, red and blue.

SERVICES

AUDIO/VISUAL

Star Audio/Visual
2061 Willow Way
San Bruno 94066
650-588-4666
Open Mon.-Fri.

Star supplies audio and visual equipment to most of San Francisco's hotels and restaurants. Though their offices are in San Brunó, they're happy to deliver the projector, screen, sound system or podium and mike directly to the site of your event-and pick it up the next day, with efficient, reliable service.

COSTUMES

Costumes on Haight
735 Haight St.
Haight-Ashbury 94117
415-621-1356
Open daily

This shop provides rentals and sales of vintage, and contemporary clothing-and if you fall in love with your costume, you can also buy it.

DRY CLEANERS

Locust Cleaners
3585 Sacramento St.
Presidio Heights 94118
415-346-9271
Open Mon.-Sat.

Locust may not be as convenient (or as cheap) as the downtown one-day cleaning operations, but if you want quality alterations, bring your garments here. Staff that work at many of the Pacific Heights' mansions say they wouldn't send clothes anywhere else.

Walnut Cleaner
2266 Chestnut St.
Marina 94123
415-921-0495
Open daily

Shops that sell sweaters direct their customers to Walnut Cleaners to assure that, when they are cleaned, the clothes are blocked back into their original shape.

SHOE REPAIR

Anthony's Shoe Service
30 Geary St.
Union Square 94108
415-781-1338
Open Mon.-Sat.

You name it, they mend it. We highly recommended this cobbler, who can make your favorite bag or pair of shoes look like new again. You'll need to leave your item for repair overnight. Also at 135 Post St., 415-984-9439.

Galletti Shoe Repair
22 Battery St.
Financial District 94111
415-398-5474
Open Mon.-Fri.

427 Columbus Ave.
North Beach 94133
415-982-2897
Open Mon.-Sat.

You've just set out for a day of shopping and the heel of your shoe falls off. Hobble over to Galletti Brothers and in minutes you will be on your way, good as new. We hate the slippery plastic heels that even the most expensive shoes seem to come with these days, so we go to Galletti's straight from the shoe store for replacements with something more practical.

TAILOR

Macchione

564 Market St.
Financial District 94104
415-956-3597
Open Mon.-Sat.

The downtown business crowd, both men and women, have relied on Macchione for custom suits for years. Choose your fabric and style and the garment of your choice will be made to your measure. Bring your alterations here, too.

SPORTING GOODS

Avenue Cyclery

756 Stanyan St.
Haight-Ashbury 94117
415-387-3155
Open daily

Just across the street from Golden Gate Park, Avenue Cyclery sells impressive machines for the serious cyclist. They also provide an in-house repair shop that is well-stocked with parts.

City Cycle

3001 Steiner St.
Union Street 94123
415-346-2242
Open daily

For serious pedalers, the bicycles sold here are all hand-built and custom-made, using high-quality frames by the best makers in the world. The staff are all experienced cyclists who will custom-build and -tailor your bike and keep it in perfect repair. Brands carried include Merlin Titanium, Kestrel, Salsa, Serotta and, for women only, Georgia Terry. You'll also find a good selection of Pearl Izumi clothes, helmets, books, shoes and auto racks.

Don Sherwood's Sport Shop

320 Grant Ave.
Union Square 94108
415-989-5000
Open daily

A bustling two-story emporium with a full inventory of golf and tennis equipment and fashions, Sherwood's has a large, professional staff that will put you on the right track-whether you need a tune-up on your swing, court shoes or covers for your clubs or racquet.

Eddie Bauer

250 Post St.
Union Square 94108
415-986-7600
Open daily

Eddie Bauer caters to rugged outdoor types, as well as those who like to limit their activity to sitting in front of a roaring fire in a handsome flannel shirt. Most of the cotton and wool clothing for hiking, running, cycling and skiing carries the Eddie Bauer label, which ensures durability and fair prices; the same goes for the camping, fishing and other sports equipment sold here. Down jackets are especially good values. We like the selection of well-made shoes for walking, hiking and running. Catalog shoppers can place orders here, too.

Kite Flite

Pier 39
Fisherman's Wharf 94133
415-956-3181
Open daily

Kite Flite sells stunt kites, sport kites, or traditional kites in your favorite colors. If you've never flown a kite before, the staff will gladly give you advice and send you to practice them in nearby Aquatic Park. You'll also find a selection of decorative wind socks, sure to brighten up any balcony or backyard.

McCafferys Golf Shop

80 Sutter St.
Financial District 94104
415-989-4653
Open daily

A golfer's dream, this full-service golf shop in the heart of the Financial District sells balls, shoes or clothes, in a variety of familiar brands and at a good price. Should you have special needs, PGA professional Doug Talley is on hand to assist.

Niketown

278 Post St.
Union Square 94108
415-392-6453
Open daily

As would be expected, the theme of Niketown is sports and athletic performance. The ride up the elevator is a noisy, visual one-much the same as an airline terminal, with flashing lights and messages. The profiles, pictures and displays of Nike sporting equipment and well-known athletes will make sports fans think they've died and gone to heaven. Of course, this is the first place to come looking for Michael Jordan's newest shoe, Tiger Woods' golf jacket or Mary Pierce's tennis dress.

The North Face

180 Post St.
Union Square 94108
415-433-3223
Open daily

The outdoors type looks to North Face tents, packs, sleeping bags and outerwear for reliability and high quality; the fashion-conscious looks to it for a modern statement of couture. Whatever your needs, you'll find no better source for it than this Union Square location. Travelers and outdoor enthusiasts will enjoy the books, maps and accessories for outdoor adventures.

Patagonia

770 North Point
Fisherman's Wharf 94133
415-771-2050
Open daily

Whether your outdoor sporting takes you on the water, up a mountain, or to an equestrian event, you'll find all the necessary attire at Patagonia. If sports are not your thing, but you just want to look good outdoors while keeping warm and dry, Patagonia's cheerfully colored clothing is for you. From underwear to outerwear, you'll find attire for men, women and children.

Skates on Haight

1818 Haight St.
Haight-Ashbury 94117
415-752-8375
Open daily

Skates on Haight has been providing quality rental skates to the Golden Gate Park crowd for close to two decades. To assure a safe return, rentals include wrist guards and knee pads. If you want to buy a new pair of in-lines or more traditional quads, you cannot find a better selection anywhere.

Valencia Cyclery

1077 Valencia St.
Mission 94110
415-550-6600
Open daily

Locals say Valencia is the best place in the city for new bikes, biking accessories, and repairs. Starting at $219, the Mission district cyclery sells mountain, hybrid, and racing bikes.

STATIONERY

The Brown Bag

2000 Fillmore St.
Upper Fillmore 94115
415-922-0390
Open daily

Witty, ever-changing display windows will lure you inside this neighborhood favorite, a stationery/office supply store with much, much more. Brown Bag sells hip greeting cards, fanciful magnets, rubber stamps, art supplies, paper party goods and great toys. Perhaps you've always desired "Last Supper" paint-by-the-numbers or velvet painting kit-you'll find them here.

Desk Set

3252 Sacramento St.
Presidio Heights 94118
415-921-9575
Open Mon.-Sat.

One of life's pleasures is to own good stationery and desk accessories. Desk Set understands, and stocks elegant stationery and cards that can be imprinted on their premises. Tempting knickknacks include picture frames, blank books bound in leather and cloth, letter openers, metal seals with sealing wax, stacks of agendas and smart address books, French Elysée fountain pens and even personalized computer paper.

Flax

1699 Market St.
Mission 94110
415-552-2355
Open Mon.-Sat.

Considered by San Franciscans the premiere place for art supplies, Flax offers everything your heart desires in the way of stationary, pens, paper, inks, paint, brushes, gift wrap, and handmade specialty papers. A slightly snobby staff will begrudgingly explain the craft of papermaking, faux finishing, and bookbinding. Don't forget to ask for a list of current workshops being offered. Feed your fetish-it's worth those few extra pennies.

Union Street Papery

2162 Union St.
Union Street 94123
415-563-0200
Open daily

High-quality announcements, invitations and personal stationery are the specialty here, with a selection that will occupy you for hours. Their large assortment of one-of-a-kind handmade greeting cards is bound to improve even the most lugubrious epistle.

TOYS & GAMES

FAO Schwarz

48 Stockton St.
Union Square 94108
415-394-8700
Open daily

San Franciscans are proud to have this acclaimed toy store in their downtown area. Kids are encouraged to play with most of the merchandise, and play they do when faced with captivating train sets, Steiff and Trupa stuffed animals and extravagant, child-size race cars. As it's always been, FAO Schwarz is for those parents who don't mind splurging on special-and expensive-toys.

Game Gallery

1 Embarcadero Center
Financial District 94111
415-433-4263
Open daily

Monopoly, Scrabble and Chess are stacked side by side with such newer parlor games as Pictionary and Risk at Game Gallery. They sell fine jigsaw puzzles and old standbys such as dice, jacks and darts. If you're lacking a chess partner, take a look at their computerized chess games.

The Game Keeper

San Francisco Shopping Centre, 865 Market St.
Union Square 94103
415-543-8540
Open daily

Games for older children and adults are a specialty of this store-particularly chess games, imported from around the world. Twelve Caesars, a card game set in Rome, and Listen Up!, a game where you say what you see and draw what you hear, are two of many games sold here exclusively. You'll also find such game basics as backgammon, dominoes, cribbage, jigsaw puzzles and family board favorites.

Imaginarium

3535 California St.
Laurel Village 94118
415-387-9885
Open daily

The slogan of this delightful playground of a shop is "A Store Kids Can Handle": In addition to the usual educational playthings by Playskool, Ambi and Brio, kids can try out Slinkys, wind-up dinosaurs and elaborate hand puppets by Gund. Equally enchanting are Imaginarium's dolls: Madame Alexander's Storybook Dolls; Carolle dolls from France (which are geared to the age of the child and behave accordingly); dolls by Pauline, with porcelain-colored flesh and realistic hair; and kids' perennial favorites Raggedy Ann and Andy. There's also a wide assortment of books and cassettes, and a few interesting mineral collections for the budding geologist.

Jeffrey's

7 3RD ST.
FINANCIAL DISTRICT 94103
415-243-8697
Open daily

An all-purpose, independent toy store with a representative collection of contemporary kids' toys, Jeffrey's carries everything from Ninja Turtles to educational toys. Dolls range from Madame Alexander to Barbie. Be sure to take advantage of their free gift wrapping when you buy.

The Littlest Mouse

700 SEVENTH ST.
SOMA 94107
415-864-5814
Open Tues.-Sat. and by appointment.

Can't afford the down payment on that Victorian dream house? Then have the skilled and accommodating staff here build a dollhouse replica of it for you or your child. Models are beautifully furnished, down to the last detail, with Chippendale dining sets, chintz curtains and electrically-wired chandeliers. The craftspeople here will copy any house, or build one for you from their selection of kits; you can also buy a kit and build your own. Once it's done, you can fill it with furniture made to order or with their selection of miniature accouterments. Ask to see the hooked rugs, painstakingly rendered in needlepoint.

Star Magic Space Age Gifts

4026 24TH ST.
NOE VALLEY 94114
415-641-8626
Open daily

Star Magic sells toys for grownups as well as children-New Age and Space Age toys, books, music, jewelry, and gift items, each with scientific and/or spiritual meaning.

ARTS & CULTURE

CONTENTS

AUCTION HOUSES

Butterfield & Butterfield
220 SAN BRUNO AVE.
SOMA 94103
415-861-7500
Call for viewing & auction times.

Established in 1865, the West's most venerable auction house brings the hammer down on paintings, photographs, prints, furniture and decorative arts, antiques and collectibles, silver, rugs, jewelry and wine. Previews take place on weekends before the sales, which occur throughout the year and are open to the public.

Christie's
400 MONTGOMERY ST. , STE. 920
UNION SQUARE 94104
415-982-0982
Call for viewing & auction times.

The venerable New York auctioneers maintain a West Coast office, coordinating the California command center for sales of art, jewelry, furniture and assorted heirlooms. Telephone Christie's main number for a schedule of upcoming auctions.

ART GALLERIES

One of the world's great artistic cities, San Francisco supports a lively and varied gallery scene. Painting, sculpture, conceptual, multimedia, installation-the arts found in the city's galleries is as dynamic as its regional weather. Look for big-name galleries clustered near **Union Square** and the **San Francisco Museum of Modern Art (SFMOMA)**, but feel free to explore other areas in order to expand your artistic boundaries: some of the city's most innovative work can be found in outlying neighborhoods. The listings below reflect our preferences for the best of the locals, with emphasis on contemporary American and Bay Area artists' works.

Art Exchange
77 GEARY ST., 2ND FL.
UNION SQUARE 94108
415-956-5750
Open Tues.-Sat.

Specializing in the resale of art from museums and private collections, including paintings, sculpture and fine art prints, Art Exchange chooses regularly from among a strong roster of Bay Area artisans.

Bomani Gallery
251 POST ST., 6TH FL.
UNION SQUARE 94108
415-296-8677
Open Tues.-Sat.

Owned by Asake Bomani and her husband Danny Glover, this well-established gallery specializes in contemporary African-American art.

Braunstein/Quay Gallery

250 SUTTER ST., 3RD FL.
UNION SQUARE 94108
415-392-5532
Open Tues.-Sat.

A gallery with a keen sense of humor, Braunstein/Quay showcases contemporary sculpture and paintings, as well as works on paper, in a broad range of styles and subjects.

Capp Street Project

525 2ND ST.
SOUTH PARK 94107
415-495-7107
Open Mon.-Fri.

Known for stunning installations and witty, edge-plumbing exhibitions, Capp Street remains one of the Bay Area's best alternative galleries. Recent works by Glen Seator and Ilya Kabakov have proved stellar.

Gallery 16

1616 16TH ST.
MISSION 94103
415-626-7495
Open Mon.-Fri.

This walk-up Mission gallery pumps new blood into the local art scene, showcasing a wide range of works, artists and media. Off the beaten track and definitely worth the trip.

John Berggreun

228 GRANT AVE.
UNION SQUARE 94108
415-781-4629
Open Mon.-Sat.

This three-floor gallery stands at the heart of the art-dealing district and features works by Matisse, Steinberg and Giacometti, in addition to established artists from the Bay Area.

New Langton Arts

1246 FOLSOM ST.
SOMA 94103
415-626-5416
Open Wed-Sat. noon-5 p.m., Tues. by appointment. Free.

An experimental performance space as well as a nonprofit gallery, New Langton regularly presents visual arts exhibitions, literary events, experimental music, media arts, and interdisciplinary projects. Truly marginal art can be found here, including group shows incorporating a variety of media, innovative video projects and installations that transform the second floor space into drastic new spaces. Lousy parking, great art.

Refusalon

20 HAWTHORNE ST.
SOMA 94105
415-546-0158
Open Tues.-Sat.

A locally known artist himself, Refusalon curator Charles Linder maintains this austere basement gallery that remains the epicenter for progressive, po-mo conceptual art in San Francisco. Like most art spaces, exhibits change monthly.

Rena Bransten Gallery

77 GEARY ST.
UNION SQUARE 94108
415-982-3292
Open Tues.-Sat.

A fascinating mix of contemporary painting, sculpture, video and photography. Rena Bransten maintains an emphasis on local artists.

San Francisco Art Commission Galleries

401 VAN NESS AVE.
CIVIC CENTER 94102
415-554-6080
Open Tues.-Sat. 11 a.m.-5:30 p.m. Admission free.

The SFAC maintains two good public galleries in this neighborhood: on the first floor and second- and third-floor hallways of the Memorial Opera House and in a public lot and storefront at 155 Grove Street. Themes range from environmental and social to historical and whimsical, and change frequently. For additional public art, watch for SFAC's "Art In Transit" works, exhibited at bus shelters and train stations throughout the city.

PHOTOGRAPHY GALLERIES

Ansel Adams Center

250 4TH ST.
SOMA 94103
415-495-7000
Open Tues.-Sun. 11 a.m.-5 p.m. (until 8 p.m. the first Thurs. of every month). Adults $5, students $3, seniors & children 13-17 $2, children under 13 free.

In the vanguard of Yerba Buena arts institutions is this museum, operated by the Friends of Photography and dedicated to one of its founding members, the great California photographer Ansel Adams. Its five galleries reflect the diversity of historical and modern photography. Events range from individual shows to group presentations under an abiding theme. The building also houses a bookstore and library.

Forty-Nine Geary

49 GEARY ST.
UNION SQUARE 94108
No phone
Open Tues.-Sat.

This building houses some of the best photo galleries in the city:

The **Fraenkel Gallery** (4th floor, 415-981-2662) exhibits nineteenth- and twentieth-century fine art photography, including works by the likes of Diane Arbus and Edward Weston. The Fraenkel remains one of the primary showcases for photography in San Francisco.

The **Robert Koch Gallery** (5th floor, 415-421-0122) tends to showcase provocative photographic works. A recent exhibit by Jock Sturges raised a predictable outcry controversy, and another by Czech photographer Josef Koudelka sounded an environmental theme.

The **Stephen Wirtz Gallery** (3rd floor, 415-433-6879) shows mostly contemporary painters, but also is the primary U.S. gallery for outstanding British art photographer Michael Kenna, who is possibly the best-selling photographer in the world.

MUSEUMS

Asian Art Museum

8TH AVE. & JOHN F. KENNEDY DR.
GOLDEN GATE PARK 94118
415-668-8921
Open Wed.-Sun. 9:30 a.m.-5 p.m. (first Wed. of the month 10 a.m.-8:45 p.m.). Adults $7, seniors $5, children under 12 free. Admission free 1st Wed. of the month.

When Avery Brundage donated his collection of more than 10,000 pieces to San Francisco in 1966, the City cleared out the west wing of the De Young Museum to make room. Only a portion of the paintings, ceramics, sculptures, jades, bronzes and textiles can be exhibited at one time. Don't miss the stunning blue-and-white porcelains or the Jade Room, where some objects date back more than 3,000 years. The Asian will be moving into the Civic Center space once occupied by the old Main Library sometime around 2000.

California Palace of the Legion of Honor

LINCOLN PARK, CLEMENT ST. & 34TH AVE.
RICHMOND DISTRICT 94121
415-750-3600
Open Tues.-Sun. 9:30 a.m.-5 p.m.; Adults $7, seniors $5, youth ages 12-17 $4; children under 12 free. Admission free 1st Thurs. of the month.

This spectacular museum recently reopened with some splendid improvements. Built in 1924, the palace was a gift of the Spreckels family and was designed by George Applegarth after the Palace of the Légion d'Honneur in Paris. Its permanent collection includes a Rodin sculpture garden, decorative arts and tapestries and eighteenth- and nineteenth-century French paintings including Impressionist works by Monet, Renoir and Dégas. Downstairs, the expanded garden level features the Achenbach Foundation for Graphic Arts, which houses more than 100,000 works of art on paper-the largest collection of its kind in the West.

Cartoon Art Museum

814 MISSION ST., 2ND FL.
SOMA 94107
415-227-8666
Open Wed.-Fri. 11 a.m.-5 p.m., Sat. 10 a.m.-5 p.m., Sun 1 p.m.-5 p.m. Adults $5, seniors & students $3, children 6-12 $2, under 6 free. Admission optional 1st Wed. of the month.

A one-of-a-kind gallery of art from the strips, books and pages of history, the Cartoon Art exhibits everyone from Bill "Zippy the Pinhead" Griffith, Robert Crumb and MAD magazine artists to a history of Hanna-Barbera characters and everything (really!) in between. Anime, graphic novels, New Yorker cartoons-it's all here. Additionally, the CAM's CD-ROM gallery and killer bookstore make this a unique favorite among 'toon junkies.

Exploratorium

PALACE OF FINE ARTS, 3601 LYON ST.
MARINA 94123
415-561-0360
Open Tues.-Sun. 10 a.m.-5 p.m. Wed. until 9:30 p.m. Adults $9, seniors & students $7, children 3-17 $5, children under 3 $2.50. Admission free 1st Wed. of the month.

This hands-on learning center, designed by scientist and educator Frank Oppenheimer, opened in 1969. Even if you or the kids in your life never cared much for experimentation, this museum of science, art and human perception will change your mind. Its innovative exhibits are designed to be manipulated in all kinds of ways. Scientific principles are not demonstrated for you-you make them happen by pushing, pulling, talking and listening. It's more fun to learn about physics, biology and meteorology than you've ever imagined possible. A separate exhibit, the Tactile Dome, is so popular that it requires reservations and separate admission.

Mexican Museum

FORT MASON CENTER, BLDG. D
MARINA 94123
415-441-0404
Open Wed.-Fri. noon-5 p.m. (until 7 p.m. first Wed. of the month) & Sat.-Sun. 11 a.m.-5 p.m. Adults $3, seniors & students $2, members & children under 10 free. Admission free first Wed. of the month.

This museum honors California's Mexican heritage, displaying Mexican and Mexican-American art in five thematic settings-Hispanic, colonial, folk, Mexican fine arts and Mexican-American fine arts.

M.H. De Young Memorial Museum

8TH AVE. & KENNEDY DR.
GOLDEN GATE PARK 94118
415-750-3600
Open Wed.-Sun. 9:30 a.m.-5 p.m.. Adults $7, seniors $5, youth 12-17 $4, children under 12 free. Admission free Sat. morning & 1st Wed. of the month.

The De Young Museum houses the most eclectic permanent collection in San Francisco. Although its genesis was the 1894 California Midwinter International Exposition, the building expanded dramatically after 1917, when newspaper baron Michael De Young sparked new construction. The permanent collection includes works from ancient Egypt, Greece and Rome from the Renaissance to the present: Rubens, seventeenth- and eighteenth-century Italian paintings and an extensive American collection that includes donations from John D. Rockefeller III. Another gallery contains traditional arts of Africa and the Americas. Currently, the De Young's future remains uncertain, as seismic concerns have compromised its future in Golden Gate Park.

San Francisco Art Institute

800 CHESTNUT ST.
RUSSIAN HILL 94133
415-771-7020
Open Tues.-Sat. 10 a.m.-5 p.m. Admission free.

Founded in 1871, this art school is the oldest in the western U.S. and continues to be an important institution in the Northern California art world. A short walk up from Columbus Avenue in North Beach, the Institute's three galleries-the Diego Rivera, Walter/McBean and Project Space-exhibit the work of both students and professionals. A tiny café just past the Diego (open daily 9 a.m.-9 p.m.) is open during school hours and sells decent sandwiches and soups.

San Francisco Craft and Folk Art Museum

FORT MASON CENTER, BLDG. A
MARINA 94123
415-775-0990
Open Tues.-Sun. 11 a.m.-5 p.m. Adults $3, seniors, students & children 12-17 $1, children under 12 free. Free 1st Wed. of the month & Sat. 10 a.m.-noon.

Witty and elegant exhibitions of contemporary craft, American folk art and worldwide tribal art are featured here, with displays that run the gamut from traditional to contemporary. The visitor can also enjoy lectures and demonstrations of their chosen crafts.

San Francisco Museum of Modern Art

151 3RD ST.
SOMA 94103
415-357-4000
Open Fri.-Tues. 11 a.m.-6 p.m. Thurs. until 9 p.m. Adults $8, seniors $5, students $4, children under 12 free. Half price admission Thurs. 6 p.m.-9 p.m. Free 1st Tues. of the month.

The 225,000-square-foot SFMOMA, designed by Swiss architect Mario Botta and opened in 1995, remains the jewel in the crown of the city's arts community. Located just a short walk from the Moscone Convention Center, the museum houses a decent selection in its permanent collection: you'll find Matisse, Picasso, Klee and Kandinsky, along with a good roster of post-modern and contemporary living artists. The excellent permanent collection of photographs, strong on 20th-century American and European photographers, rotates with traveling photography exhibits, such as a Paul Strand show. For an architectural and vertiginous thrill, take the elevators to the top floor and stroll across the catwalk. The gift shop is superb, and **Caffè Museo**, the ground-level restaurant, offers a fresh (though pricey) selection of homemade soups, focaccia sandwiches, and scrumptious pastries. Eat al fresco to watch the hip crowds as they enter and leave the museum.

San Francisco State University Art Department Gallery

ART AND DESIGN BUILDING
1600 HOLLOWAY AVE.
RICHMOND DISTRICT 94132
415-338-6535
Open Mon.-Sat. noon-4 p.m.

Housed in the imposing new Art and Design building at State, the SFSU gallery features a rotating lineup of shows and artists. Some exhibitions are devoted to Bay Area movements; others to student or faculty work; occasional appearances by the works of international sculptors and painters are less frequent. It's worth the trip if you're exploring the southwest section of the city, but if you're hungry, you're out of luck: State's on-campus food is unequivocally lousy.

Yerba Buena Center for the Arts

701 MISSION ST.
SOMA 94103
415-978-2787
Open Tues.-Sun. 11 a.m.-6 p.m., until 8 p.m. 1st Thurs. of the month. Adults $5, students & seniors $3. Admission free 1st Thurs. of the month.

Every city should have a YBCFA: This complex for the visual and performing arts opened its doors in late 1993, and has since maintained the leading edge of cultural creativity. Five galleries are available for one entrance price; the state-of-the-art theater and screening rooms are intimate and acoustically superior. The grounds are magnificent-a five-acre verdant spread of walks, fountains, picnic spots and countless pieces of public art. Located just west of the San Francisco Modern Art Museum, YB is the perfect destination, whether after museum-hopping, as a summer outdoor concert venue, or as an art-packed end itself. Indulge in the city's best.

PERFORMING ARTS

American Conservatory Theater (A.C.T.)

415 Geary St.
Union Square 94108
415-749-2228
Box office open Sun.- Mon. noon-6 p.m., Tues.-Sat. noon-8 p.m.

The ACT is one of the nation's leading resident professional theaters and the recipient of a Tony Award for outstanding theater performance and training. With Artistic Director Carey Perloff at the helm, this company continues to challenge the artistic sensibilities of San Francisco's theatergoing public, with performances of classic and world-premiere dramatic works. The gorgeous Geary theater, a 1,000-seat venue recently reopened in the theater district, is a national historic landmark. For more information, look on-line at www.act-sfbay.org.

Curran Theatre

445 Geary St.
Financial District 94108
415-551-2000
Box office open Mon. 10 a.m.-6 p.m., Tues.-Sat 10 a.m.-8:30 p.m., Sun. noon-4 p.m.

The "other" theater in the block with the Geary has, since 1993, been under the spell of Andrew Lloyd Webber's *Phantom of the Opera*. Tickets are pricey, but try calling 415-433-7827 for half-price admissions the day of the show.

Fillmore

1805 Geary Blvd.
Fillmore 94117
415-346-0600
Box office opens 2 hours before performances.

A classic dance hall that remains forever a 1960s institution, the Fillmore was the favorite of the late, legendary rock producer Bill Graham. It's a great place to see a rock and roll show, whether that of a local band that's hit the big time, or a nationally touring act. Book tickets through BASS (510-762-BASS) and expect to pay a hefty service charge.

Herbst Theater

401 Van Ness Ave.
Civic Center 94102
415-621-6600
Box office open 90 minutes before performances.

Chamber music, classical and modern dance performances, recitals, readings and lectures are among the year-round presentations offered by internationally renowned cultural figures. Its scale makes it most suitable for small theatrical pieces, dance groups and recitals, and it is home to the San Francisco Chamber Symphony. The City Arts and Lectures series brings writers, politicians, pundits and pop culture icons to this small hall.

The Marsh

1062 Valencia St.
Mission 94110
415-641-0235
Call for box office hours.

Self-described as "a breeding ground for new performance," this small theater showcases almost exclusively local emerging talent. The venue's focus is on solo performance; they offer admission prices on a sliding scale.

San Francisco Ballet

War Memorial Opera House
301 Van Ness Ave.
Civic Center 94102
415-865-2000
Box office hours Mon.-Sat. noon-6 p.m.

Led by artistic director Helgi Tomasson, the San Francisco Ballet is the oldest professional ballet company in the country. The ballet is most cherished by locals and tourists alike during the Christmas season, when they bring new life to the ubiquitous *Nutcracker*. The regular season runs from February to May and features varied classical and contemporary ballets. Note that although both perform in the Opera House, the Ballet and the Opera have separate box offices.

San Francisco Opera

War Memorial Opera House
301 Van Ness Ave.
Civic Center 94102
415-864-3330
Box office hours Mon.-Sat. 10 a.m.-6 p.m.

With more than three-quarters of a century of performance behind it, the San Francisco

Opera has returned recently to a delightfully renovated War Memorial Opera House. The hall's improvements-$85.7 million worth-gave director Lotfi Mansouri the venue his talented company so richly deserves. World premieres by André Previn and Phillip Littell, Wagner's *Der Ring des Nibelungen*, a full menu of Puccini, Strauss, and Verdi, as well as the more approachable "Femme Fatale" and Opera In the Park series-all these and a dazzling marquee of singers more make the San Francisco Opera the city's favorite production. The SFO also maintains a decent web site at www.sfopera.com.

San Francisco Symphony

LOUISE M. DAVIES SYMPHONY HALL
210 VAN NESS AVE.
CIVIC CENTER 94102
415-552-8000, TICKETS 415-864-6000
Box office open Mon.-Fri. 10 a.m.-6 p.m., Sat. noon-6 p.m.

The big news in recent years for the SF Symphony was the arrival of Michael Tilson Thomas, the Wünderkind superconductor who successfully rescued the group from their doldrums and resuscitated their desire for passionate music. Acoustic improvements made to Davies Hall (built in 1980) didn't hurt, either, particularly for MTT's preferred repertoire of more-contemporary American and European composers. If your tastes are highbrow but your budget is low, attend an open rehearsal; otherwise, check the Symphony box office for last-minute and discounted ticket availability. Like the Opera, the Symphony has a good Website: www.sfsymphony.org

Theatre Rhinoceros

2926 16TH ST.
CASTRO 94103
415-861-5079
Call for box office hours.

For over 20 years San Francisco has been home to the nation's oldest and largest gay and lesbian theater company, presenting innovative works to a variety of audiences. The theater, founded by Allan Estes in 1977, takes its name from the animal that is "mild and peace-loving unless provoked."

Warfield

982 MARKET ST.
TENDERLOIN 94102
415-775-7722
Call for box office hours.

The slightly smaller "big rock club" is perfect for lesser-known bands. Its acoustics are a little better than the Fillmore, and its setting a bit more intimate. Tickets available through Bass (510-762-BASS) or the box office.

CITY LORE

A LAND IN TRANSITION

Originally formed by the receding glaciers from the most recent Ice Age, the topography and geology of San Francisco Bay and its surrounding region are also defined by the swelling waters of the Sacramento River delta and by the tectonic jostling of the Pacific plate, a continental shelf in constant motion. The most unsettling and famous geological forces in the Bay Area are earthquakes, which reflect shifts along the major fault lines that criss-cross the region. The longest and most famous fault, the San Andreas, runs 650 miles (1,046 km) up the California coast, slipping into the sea just south of San Francisco and joining the mainland to the north at Point Reyes. The most famous quakes, in 1906 and 1989, are the largest on record, but they are not the last. As any San Francisco resident can attest, the ground beneath the Bay Area is always in motion.

DANCING ON THE BRINK OF THE WORLD

The Bay's original inhabitants were the Costanoan Indians, a community of neighboring Native American tribes who lived peaceably with each other and the land. Locally, the Ohlone and Miwok people exploited the bounty of flora and fauna that surrounded and filled the not-yet-named San Francisco Bay. From the sandy peninsulas they took shellfish and small game; from the hilly terrain further inland they found freshwater fish, elk, deer, and larger animals, in addition to a host of native vegetation. A spiritual people known for diplomacy and peaceful ways, relying only on land and sea for their livelihoods, these hunter-gatherers thrived in the region for thousands of years.

Because the Costanoans considered it bad luck to maintain oral or written histories of their traditions, much of the Ohlone culture remains unknown in modern times. Little has survived, save the record of their initial hospitality to the Spanish explorers that began to arrive in the region in the late 1500s. After their conquest of Mexico in 1521, the Spanish began scouting the region, giving it the name "El Dorado." It was an English admiral and explorer, Francis Drake, who claimed California for Queen Elizabeth in 1579; he sailed into a bay further north, near what is now Point Reyes.

THE COMING OF THE FRONTIER

In the fall of 1775, Captain John Bautista de Anza set out with 250 soldiers and colonialists from Sonora, Mexico, to establish Spanish settlements on the Bay of San Francisco, named six years earlier. In 1776, two important landmarks were founded in the area: a Spanish military garrison (which later became the Presidio) and the Mission San Francisco de Assis next to La Laguna de lost Dolores (the lake of sorrows), later called Mission Dolores. The establishment of Mission Dolores, run by Father Junipero Serra, proved the downfall of the Ohlone tribes. Xenophilic and friendly, the outgoing natives soon found themselves in servitude to the new strangers, who offered slavery, smallpox and a healthy dose of Christian religion in return for their kindness. Within 200 years of Spanish arrival, the native Ohlone were all but extinguished.

Various explorers and admirals-among them Capt. George Vancouver, Nikolai Petrovich Rezanov, Fr. Ramon Abella and Gabriel Moraga-investigated the surrounding land and coastline, while trappers, hunters and frontiersmen like Capt. Jedediah Smith and John Bidwell navigated the land. By the early 1830s, the small harbor of Yerba Buena began to be known as a natural anchorage for trading ships in the Bay. In his book *Two Years Before the Mast*, writer Richard Dana called the climate "as near perfect as any in the world, Immigrants heeded the word and cut south from the Oregon trail. The first attempts at accommodating a community in the area occurred in 1835, a pueblo founded with the first building by William Richardson. The original site is near Grant Avenue and Filbert Street, in the township Richardson dubbed Yerba Buena. The same year, the Territorial Deputation granted the provision of lots on which to build the first homes.

Thirteen years later, as a result of the Mexican-American War, the Treaty of Guadalupe Hidalgo granted the Union all the land from the Rio Grande to Oregon and, after an unsuccessful revolt staged by the Bear Flag Republic in 1846, the village began to take shape, renamed San Francisco in 1847. The first newspaper, *The California Star*, published its first issues that year; the first bank, public school, and post office in 1848. The frontier and its apologists like Kit Carson, began to emerge as the future for the quickly growing union. European civilization had moved in to stay.

EUREKA!

When James Marshall discovered gold in 1849 at the Coloma mill of Swiss homesteader John Sutter, the last thing the prospectors wanted was publicity. But news of riches brought the first wave of fortune seekers to California, and from around the world they came, abandoning some 600 of their ships at the city's new coastline and racing into the Sierra hills. For its part, San Francisco was too young to brace itself for the onslaught: As the welcome mat to the Forty-Niners' climb to the heights of (perceived) riches, she was not a destination herself, but rather means to a mean end.

The city at the time of the Gold Rush was a brutal one: It comes as no surprise to learn that the San Francisco police force was borne in 1849, and the first jail shortly thereafter. Hooliganism, theft, burglary, prostitution, gambling, rape, robbery-all the predictable livelihoods of a disorganized and restless citizenry came to light. The truth, of course, was that there was far less gold in the hills than the hopeful naively suspected, and most dreams were vanquished in a few short months of reality. The city's merchants at the time felt free to cheat prospectors on their way to Sacramento and gouge them again when they returned a year later, penniless.

The news records of this era in the city's history are marked by countless tragedies and squabbles: stories of fires, bank runs, strikes, executions, gang activities, assassinations and racial intolerance filled the papers. San Francisco's population grew from 800 to more than 20,000, and with it arrived the trappings of modern humanity: brothels, churches, fire departments and restaurants. Journalists Mark Twain and Bret Harte sought to capture the era in writings at the time, and remain, 150 years hence, some of the township's best early chronologists. Newspapers were published in French, Chinese and German; specialty publications shipped their premiere issues.

The city's first mayor, George W. Geary, began his tenure in San Francisco as the city's first postmaster, in a building at Washington and Montgomery streets. As mayor, he gave police broader powers and established the town's first city council. On Geary's watch, streets were gaslit; hospitals built; the Academy of Sciences organized; brothels routinely raided; a cemetery was dedicated; a water works was created. A few years after the gold rush began, it appeared that San Francisco might begin to enjoy the first of a few city services.

BARBAROUS COAST

But history repeated itself ten years later, when the Comstock Silver Lode was discovered in Western Nevada, and the Silver Boom brought more optimistic men to the region. This time, however, individual prospectors were stymied at the hands of large ore mining companies, the heads of whom settled in the city's first elite neighborhood: Nob Hill. Here the silver barons built mansions of unparalleled wealth overlooking the largely blue-collar city, with commanding views and opulent fixtures. Simultaneously, drunken sailors and innocent newcomers to the Barbary Coast were inadvertently finding themselves "shanghaied"-plied with alcohol or drugs until they passed out, then awakening to find themselves "volunteered" for servitude aboard ships. Women had it worse: many entered a life of prostitution or slavery, eking out an existence just down the hill from California's richest citizens.

Other events drew more inhabitants to California and to San Francisco: The Civil War jolted many young Americans into examining prospects on the other side of the continent; blooming business ventures (the Pacific Stock Exchange opened in 1862) and strengthening unions offered workers of all creeds the promise of a future upon arrival. The creation of the Central Pacific Railway, whose "Big Four" investors' names-Charles Crocker, Mark Hopkins, Leland Stanford and Collis Huntington-still appear on the city's best hotels, drew workers and homesteaders alike. Similarly, the construction of the Transcontinental Railway lured European and Asian immigrant laborers, many of whom stayed on after work was done, raising families and establishing new roots in the young city.

Such an influx of citizenry had an unexpected effect on San Francisco, one which remains a century and a half later. Each brought with him the regional food and drink of their homeland, and before long, the city was home to fine French bread, Irish beer and Swiss chocolate, as well as Cantonese, Italian, German and many other cuisines. It's a history for which the city is known today.

THE SAN FRANCISCO TREAT

A ride up one of the city's steep hills on a cable car may be a quaint attraction for tourists, but it was born of that age-old combination of necessity and ingenuity. By the mid-1870s, city public transportation was dominated by a half-dozen companies operating horse-drawn streetcars, hauling produce, lumber, masonry, and animals up the imposing inclines of Nob, Russian and Telegraph Hills. But in 1869, a horrible accident occurred when a team of horses with a heavy load broke down trying to negotiate a slippery slope. One of the witnesses was an immigrant from London named Andrew Hallidie, who had been manufacturing wire rope for the quartz mines of the Mother Lode. Hallidie dreamed and schemed for three years and came up with a wild plan for an endless underground steel cable-to which the streetcars would latch themselves through a slot-that would tow the cars up the hills. The cable was to be kept in motion by giant flywheels driven by steam engines and enclosed in large barns. The first cable car went into operation in 1873. Today, the cable cars are the only mobile National Historical Monument.

QUAKES!

San Francisco residents had long been familiar with tremors and temblors, but nothing prepared them for the rocking and rolling that hit at 5:13 a.m. on April 18, 1906. The San Andreas fault gave way with a two-minute shift that has been estimated as measuring 8.3 on the Richter scale (devised later). Some 120 aftershocks continued to wrack the already rattled citizens. In three days, nearly a third of the city's buildings were destroyed in the ensuing firestorm. Losses were valued at $400 million; in addition, 250,000 people were left homeless (out of a population of 400,000) and there were more than 500 deaths.

On October 17, 1989, at 5:04 p.m., the second game of the "Bay Bridge" World Series between the Oakland Athletics and the San Francisco Giants began. The lights went out, fans cheered, and Candlestick began to tremble as the Bay Area was hit with the largest earthquake since 1906. within 15.24 seconds, more than 60 people were killed, most by falling concrete on the Nimitz freeway. Over 3,700 people were injured; the Marina and SoMa neighborhoods (both built on landfill) were hardest hit. Freeways through the city also suffered major damage. Damages from the quake have been estimated at $10 billion. The Loma Prieta Earthquake, as it was later dubbed, was centered in the Santa Cruz mountains and registered 7.1 on the Richter scale.

DIFFERENT DRUMMERS

San Francisco has always been a magnet for fringe cultures, starting with the Forty-Niners who eschewed a mid-nineteenth-century life of relative safety and serenity for one of adventure, risk and potential riches. Since then, the city has continued to attract those outsiders, to offer a place of comfort alongside those around them who feel similarly disenfranchised. The Beat Generation, so named by novelist Jack Kerouac, was another group of misfits, seeking to escape the rampant consumerism and ultra-conformity of the 1950s. Kerouac and his compatriots Neal Cassidy and Allen Ginsberg sought to achieve in fiction and poetry what the bebop musicians were in jazz music. As Kerouac's *On The Road* demonstrates so well, the Beats rejected established forms and, commandeering the cafés in the city's North Beach Neighborhood, were determined to make their mark on literary history.

Ground zero for the Beats-who took their name from the musical beatitude, being beatific, and feeling beat (tired)-was Lawrence Ferlinghetti's City Lights Bookstore. A poet who vowed to open his own bookshop after discovering the wonders of literature as a G.I., Ferlinghetti created the mecca to which fans of the rebellious writing still flock. Today, the establishment remains the neighborhood's best bookseller, with late hours and two floors of elaborately stacked books.

Similarly, the hippies and flower children who flocked to the Haight-Ashbury district in 1968 to celebrate the "Summer of Love" were expressing their repulsion at current attitudes and morals. Though couched in flowery clothes and fogged with the haze of marijuana smoke, their 'flower power'-ful ideas (germinated years earlier during the Free Speech Movement, sparked at U.C. Berkeley, and the House Committee Hearings on Un-American Activities, held in San Francisco's City Hall in 1960) rejected the establishment and sought to inspire action and political activism. Such events as Ken Kesey's Acid Test in 1966 and 1967's Human Be-In drew an estimated 8,000 hippies to the city; by 1968, the spread of LSD and heroin had tarnished the hippie movement.

Ironically, by the time the "Summer of Love" was in full swing, many of the crucial players were already established. Three years earlier, a concert featured Jefferson Airplane, the Great Society, and the Charlatans. Impresario Bill Graham, having previously hosted a fundraising party for the San Francisco Mime Troupe, leased the Fillmore Auditorium and triggered a whole new wave of musical and cultural events he would eventually parlay into a multimillion-dollar entertainment empire. At the time, though, no one was aware that long hair, psychedelic music, Eastern spiritualism and a diet of hallucinogenic drugs would set the course for an entire generation.

Such thinking (and the subsequent empowerment that comes from surrounding oneself with co-conspirators) is still a part of the San Franciscan mindset: Political causes, musical genres, artistic movements, philosophical and religious innovations, sea changes in accepted thinking-many frequently find sympathy with local citizenry, who are well-accustomed to living on the fringes. Whether pagans or punks, Acid Jazz instrumentalists or Information-Age cyber-rebels, the city remains home to those who prefer their ideologies as they do their geography: on the edge.

BRIDGE AND TUNNEL CROWDING

The Golden Gate Bridge is a suspension bridge 6,450 feet in length, 90 feet wide, and 746 feet in height above San Francisco Bay. It incorporates 80,000 miles of pencil-thick cable, some 27,572 strands that weigh 22,000 tons. During its building, which took just over four years, the bridge required 25 million man-hours and claimed eleven lives. Currently, it handles over 112,000 vehicles a day, each car slowing to pay the $3 toll at the south end. The painting of "international orange" never ceases.

The San Francisco-Oakland Bay Bridge, a suspension and cantilevered span, is 43,500 feet long, its main structure comprising some 4.5 miles over water. Like the Golden Gate, the Bay Bridge is designed to sway some 28 feet during high winds. A portion of the upper deck collapsed during the 1989 earthquake but was later repaired. Plans are underway to rebuild the span, though at press time the new design was undermined. Currently, it costs $2 to cross.

Completed as they were in 1937 and 1936, the Golden Gate and Bay Bridge were never designed to handle the automobile traffic required of them daily. Their congestion reflects the state of the entire Bay Area traffic system, more clogged with automobiles every year.

WE'RE QUEER, WE'RE HERE

Since the Gold Rush days when men outnumbered women by fifty to one, San Francisco's gayness, however underreported, has always been a part of its heritage. (Alice B. Toklas, Gertrude Stein's lover, was born here in 1877.) But the city's international reputation as an epicenter for gay life seems to have its roots in the number of discharged soldiers-lesbian women and gay men-arriving on its docks during World War II. Coupled with the 1950s bohemian literary scene, 1960s counter-cultural events and the rebellion at the Stonewall Inn in New York in June of 1969, the crystallizing of attitudes on the Left Coast solidified the city's reputation as a gay mecca.

Following a mixed record for pro-gay legislation in the city, much of San Francisco's modern homosexual history is entwined with one man, Harvey Milk, a business owner elected to the city's governing Board of Supervisors in 1977. Milk was the first publicly gay elected official to win office (though not the first to run), and his subsequent assassination in 1978 by former SFPD officer Dan White catalyzed the gay movement. In a city already leading the nation in gay film festivals, helplines, professional organizations and civil rights laws, Milk's unintentional martyrdom set in motion an irreversible political spin.

Sadly, the salad days of 1970s San Francisco gay life were undermined almost immediately by the diagnosis of "gay cancer" in the early 1980s, which subsequently took the form of AIDS and HIV-related illnesses. Nearly twenty thousand San Franciscans have died from AIDS to date, and although HIV-related mortality in the city has declined, the continued lack of a cure means undue suffering in the city. Financial catastrophe threatens many San Franciscans living with HIV; cost of protease inhibitors and other promising treatments are skyrocketing; hospices and other support organizations continue to be impacted.

But such somber statistics fly directly in the face of the levity many gays and lesbians find from living in San Francisco. A walk through the Castro district on a spring evening is the best indication of what it's like to be gay and live here: exceptional. The community has never looked better, enjoyed a higher standard of living nor felt better supported by itself and the surrounding city. The Gay and Lesbian Center in the new Main Library stands as the first research hub devoted specifically to the documentation of gay and lesbian history and culture. The Lesbian and Gay Freedom Parade and Celebration, held the last Sunday in June, has become the single most widely attended event in the city, metamorphosing Market Street into a sunny, hospitable, all-day street party. This is a great city for anyone-especially if you're gay.

SLICK WILLIE

If you're here for more than a day, you're sure to hear about him: Mayor Willie Brown, the well-haberdashed, fedora-wearing top city official, as controversial now as when he ruled as Speaker of the California State Assembly. Thwarting former Police Chief Frank Jordan in his bid for incumbency, Brown came to mayoral office in 1995 and looks for all the world likely to win re-election in 1999. Like him or not, Mayor Brown stands to usher San Francisco across the threshold of the 21st century.

A seasoned palm-presser who can wheel and deal when he needs to, Brown (nicknamed "Da Mayor") seems able to inspire local coalitions to get things done. He has bullied MUNI into relative reliability and made inroads to address the city's homeless problem. He's a loud-mouthed advocate for students, workers, and gays. He's pulling for San Francisco to host the Summer Olympic Games in 2008. As the city's first African American mayor, Brown has given minorities a strong voice in local government, and counts on black voters to support his ideas. True, his methods smack of old-school machine politics based on influence and favoritism; he's audacious, obnoxious and irritating; he's lost some of the support that rolled him into office, yet he remains highly popular.

On his watch, Brown lobbied for the building of two new sports stadiums. The 42,000-seat Pacific Bell Baseball Park is scheduled to open in April 2000 in the city's China Basin district. The other, a behemoth $525-million rebuild of the aging 3Com (formerly Candlestick) Park includes plans for a mall, restaurant, shopping and sports complex dedicated to the city's beloved San Francisco 49ers football team. The measure passed voters by a razor-thin margin in 1997, but is, at press time, still mired in controversy. Accusations of elections fraud and influence peddling, paired with recent shifty business dealings by 49ers owner Eddie DeBartolo, may mean lengthy delays for the groundbreaking of Da Mayor's pet project.

ETHNIC SF

ASIAN TASTES

Fleeing domestic wars and seeking work on the transcontinental railroad, San Francisco's Cantonese population began to arrive in the late 1840s. By century's end, Chinatown became the second-largest Asian community in the world-a neighborhood subsequently destroyed by the 1906 earthquake and fire. Just inside the **Chinatown Gateway** at Bush and Grant streets, today's Chinatown is probably even more crowded, bursting with tourists and locals lured by the scent of Chinese food markets and hundreds of restaurants offering regional cuisine. Here you can watch (and smell) cookies being made at the **Golden Gate Fortune Cookie Factory**, and explore the **Ten Ren Tea Shop**, the largest in San Francisco. Stockton Street is lined with Chinese fish markets, supermarkets, grocery stores, dim sum restaurants and windows displaying roast ducks and pigs, as well as a host of produce markets offering seasonal fruits and vegetables.

NOODLES AND PINS

Japanese immigrants who settled in the city's original Japantown were forced to move after the bombing of Pearl Harbor. In 1968 San Francisco's urban planners, in a vague spirit of reparation, created the Japan Center, a huge shopping, dining and entertainment complex, which takes up six city blocks between Post Street and Geary Boulevard and between Laguna and Webster Streets. Indulge in a relaxing massage from **Kabuki Hot Spring**, a traditional Japanese bathhouse, or sit in the **Peace Plaza** garden, overlooked by the five-tiered concrete Peace Pagoda. Superb noodle and sushi restaurants abound in this neighborhood as does five-star cuisine in the Miyako Hotel. After dinner, enjoy a movie at the **Kabuki 8 Cinema** complex or a few frames at the city's only bowling alley, **Japantown Bowl**. If you're feeling vocal, any of a dozen karaoke bars lie within walking distance.

THE MISSION'S RICH HISTORY

The city's oldest neighborhood has seen the influx of Latin, European and, most recently, Asian populations. 200-year-old **Mission Dolores** was the region's first building; don't miss its ancient graveyard, where Hitchcock's Vertigo was filmed. In the business districts, countless bars, cafés, clubs. For the best food, try the many tacquerias on or near Valencia street (**El Toro** and **Pancho Villa** are the best), or the paneterias selling fresh baked goods on 24th Street. The **Casa Lucas La Hacienda** produce store at Valencia Street, with its fresh Latin groceries, is also worth exploration. Other restaurants include those serving Spanish tapas, French crêpes, and fine Italian delis - 21st and Valencia marks the center of a thriving restaurant ghetto. As you walk, you can't help but notice the many remarkable historical murals; for a guided tour, telephone the **Precita Eyes Mural Arts Center** (415-285-2287).

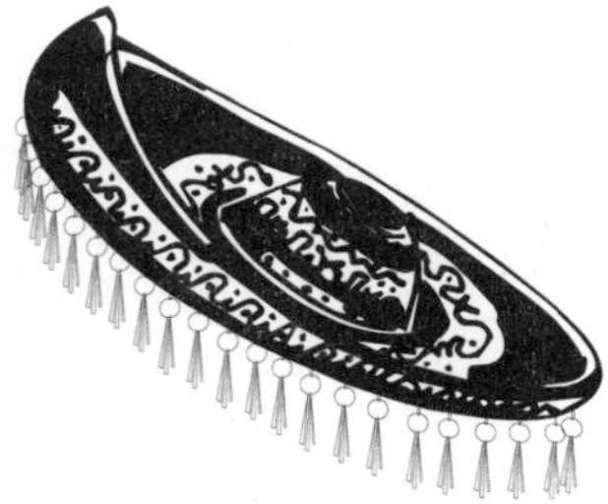

BOCCE BALL AND FOCACCIA

Few urban neighborhoods have retained their sense of ethnic history better than North Beach. Despite being a popular tourist attraction as much for its Beat heritage as for its thriving Italian bars and cafés, North Beach retains a sense of authenticity. **Columbus Avenue** defines the central artery, as close to a West Coast "little Italy" as you'll find: Italian pottery, bakeries, delicatessens, and numerous restaurants line both sides. For true flavors of the old country, spend an hour in **Washington Square Park** beneath the spires of **Sts. Peter and Paul** (Joe DiMaggio and Marilyn Monroe had their wedding photos taken here); **Columbus Tower**-the curious green building on the corner of Columbus and Kearny-marks the office for filmmaker Francis Ford Coppola. For a flavor of the Beats, you deserve a trip to the City Lights Bookstore, just alongside **Jack Kerouac Alley** at Broadway and Columbus.

LITTLE RUSSIA

Not on Russian Hill as its name might suggest, a relatively-undiscovered Russian ethnic epicenter lies in the Richmond district, on Geary Boulevard between 19th and 25th Avenues. In the shadow of the minarets on the **Holy Virgin Cathedral Church** can be found a mother lode of Russian culture in a city better-known for Asian, Italian, and Latin heritage. Russian bakeries, restaurants, tea rooms, bookstores, churches, travel agents and other businesses that cater to the city's Eastern European immigrant populations fill the neighborhood. Not surprisingly, the nearby section of **Golden Gate Park** is another favorite Russian hangout, with couples walking their dogs, having picnics or sailing model boats on (and sitting playing dominoes around) **Spreckels Lake**.

THE PRESS ACCLAIMS

Gayot Publications

"Their spicy reviews are fun."– Associated Press

"For picking restaurants, you can't do better than GaultMillau."– Travel & Leisure

"Entertaining... you will enjoy their prose."– US News & World Report

"GaultMillau is the toque of the town."– San Francisco Examiner

"The best money you'll spend: get a copy of GaultMillau."– The Star

"Great fun- An "A" for the authors."– Daily Herald

"GaultMillau is the authority on the subject."– South China Morning Post

"Witty, breezy, opinionated."– New York Times

"GaultMillau is provocative and frank."– Los Angeles Times

"Honest and specific. Booksellers are high on GaultMillau."– The Chicago Tribune

"They are the top choice."– Glamour

SIGHTSEEING

CONTENTS

ATTRACTIONS

Alcatraz Island

DEPART VIA BLUE & GOLD FLEET FROM PIER 41, POWELL ST.
FISHERMAN'S WHARF 94133
INFORMATION 415-773-1188;
415-705-5555 FOR TICKETS.
Open daily 8 a.m.-5 p.m. Ferries depart every thirty minutes from 9:30 a.m.-4:15 p.m. (9:45 a.m.-2:45 p.m. during late fall & winter months). Adults $11, seniors $9.25, children 5-11 $5.75, under 5 free. Admission includes audio tour. Also available in the summer are evening tours at 6:15 p.m. & 7 p.m.; Adult admission $18.

Hospitable only to the pelicans for which it was named, La Isla de Alcatraces-Alcatraz Island-is one of the most famous detention facilities of all time. The once-notorious federal penitentiary closed in 1963, but due to the fame of the criminals who were housed there, and those who attempted escape, the legend of The Rock lives on. **Blue and Gold Fleet** offers a variety of tours of the city's most popular attraction, including guided walks given by Parks Service rangers to pre-recorded tours you listen to on a Walkman. Bring a jacket, plan on a two-and-a-half-hour trip and buy your tickets in advance. The **Red & White Fleet** (415-447-0591) offers a "Round the Rock" boat-only tour if you're not in the mood to walk.

Cable Car Museum

WASHINGTON & MASON STS.
NOB HILL 94109
415-474-1887
Open daily 10 a.m.-6 p.m. Admission free.

If you've ever wondered how this wonderfully anachronistic form of transportation works, visit this refurbished cable car barn, built in 1887 and rebuilt after the 1906 earthquake. Here you can peruse old photos and memorabilia and watch the giant gears, pulleys and loops of steel cable that power the cars. Cable cars are synonymous with San Francisco, but only three lines remain: the **Powell-Hyde**, **Powell-Mason** and **California**.

California Academy of Sciences

MUSIC CONCOURSE
GOLDEN GATE PARK 94122
415-750-7145
Open daily 10 a.m.-5 p.m. (9 a.m.-6 p.m. Memorial Day-Labor Day) Adults $8.50, seniors & children 12-17 $5.50, children 3-11 $2, children under 3 free. Admission free first Wed. of the month. Separate admission for Planetarium and Laserium shows; call 415-750-7138 for Laserium schedule.

Dinosaurs, lasers and water creatures of all creeds and colors reside together in this wonderful science complex, a collection of the **Museum of Natural History**, **Steinhart Aquarium** and **Morrison Planetarium** under one roof. Among the exhibits are the lifelike dioramas of African and North American animal and plant life, daily star shows, stunning laser light performances and more than 14,000 species of fish. As you walk up the spiral ramp inside the aquarium's **Fish Roundabout**, sharks, tuna, yellowtail, rays and other large ocean dwellers swim around you in an endless current. The fish are fed at 2 p.m., dolphins and seals every two hours starting at 10:30 a.m. and penguins at 11:30 a.m. and 4 p.m.

Chinese Historical Society of America

644 BROADWAY, SUITE 401
NORTH BEACH 94133
415-391-1188
Open Tues.-Fri. 10 a.m.-4 p.m. Admission free.

Arriving en masse to work on the Transcontinental Railway in the nineteenth century, Chinese and other Asian immigrants have played a crucial part in shaping San Francisco history. This museum-it moved into new digs in 1998-celebrates the importance of Chinese-American history and traditions with photographs, documents and artifacts.

Exploratorium

PALACE OF FINE ARTS
3601 LYON ST.
MARINA DISTRICT 94123
415-561-0360
Open Tues.-Sun. 10 a.m.-5 p.m., Wed. 10 a.m.-9:30 p.m. Adults $9, seniors $7, youth 6-17 $5, children 3-5 $2.50, under 6 free. Admission free first Wed. of the month. Tactile Dome $12 (415-561-0362 for reservations).

This hands-on learning center designed by scientist and educator Frank Oppenheimer opened in 1969. Even the kids in your life never cared much for experimentation, this museum of science, art and human perception will change their mind. Its innovative exhibits are designed to be manipulated in all kinds of ways. Scientific principles are not demonstrated for you-you make them happen by pushing, pulling, talking and listening. It's more fun to learn about physics, biology and meteorology than you've ever imagined possible. A separate exhibit, the **Tactile Dome**, is so popular that it requires reservations and separate admission.

Fisherman's Wharf

ALONG THE WATERFRONT BETWEEN JEFFERSON & HYDE STS.

Tourist, know thyself. If you wouldn't be caught dead in schlock central, don't go there. If, in your heart, you know you might have fun making snide remarks to your companions and marveling at the variety of souvenir items shaped like or covered with cable cars, you might just join the hordes and check it out. Among the attractions are the **Wax Museum**, **Ripley's Believe or Not Museum** and the **Guinness Book of World Records Museum**. The Wharf was once the City's center of commercial fishing and still harbors fishing vessels, whose crews can be seen around the docks-though they are far outnumbered by tourists toting loaves of sourdough bread. If hungry, try the street food, especially the bread-bowl clam chowder or the walkaway cocktails of shrimp or Dungeness crab from the open-air fish markets.

Ghirardelli Square & The Cannery

NORTH POINT & LEAVENWORTH STS.
FISHERMAN'S WHARF 94109
415-775-5500

Just west of Fisherman's Wharf, these two renovated factory complexes house scores of shops, galleries and restaurants. Ghirardelli Square, originally a woolen mill in the mid-1800s and later the Ghirardelli chocolate factory, was converted to its present commercial state in the early 1960s. It boasts a lively outdoor scene, including street vendors and sidewalk performers, a lovely central plaza and some fine upscale chain shops. The Cannery, so called because it was the home of Del Monte's peach-canning operation, was remodeled in 1968 and is another early example of San Francisco's clever commercial redevelopment of old buildings. The mix of shops is less interesting than at Ghirardelli, but both centers are usually packed shoulder-to-shoulder with tourists. The **Museum of the City of San Francisco** is located in the Cannery's third floor.

National Maritime Museum and Historical Park

HYDE ST. PIER AT THE WATERFRONT
FISHERMAN'S WHARF 94109
415-556-3002
Museum open daily 10 a.m.-5 p.m.; admission free. Ships open 9:30 a.m.-5 p.m.; admission: Adults $4, children 12-17 $1, seniors & children under 12 free. Family rates available.

When commuting across the Bay to San Francisco was a more romantic venture, the Hyde Street Pier was the docking point for the Golden Gate ferries. Docked here today are five antique ships (three of which you can board), including the **Eureka**, the last of the side-wheel ferries to run in the United States. The most recent addition to the collection is the **Balclutha**, a century-old sailing ship with three masts reaching skyward and classic square rigging. Built in Scotland in 1883, the Balclutha has been a cargo ship, a lumber ship, a salmon cannery, a carnival ship and a Hollywood prop.

Pier 39

NORTHERN WATERFRONT NEAR BEACH & POWELL STS.
FISHERMAN'S WHARF 94133
415-981-7437

Where once stood a cargo pier now stands this two-level shopping arcade, one of the most popular tourist spots in the country. It's a Disney-like version of turn-of-the-century San Francisco, housing tourist-oriented specialty shops, fast-food joints and a **merry-go-round** for the kids. An unexpected attraction is the colony of **sea lions** who have made the pier their seasonal home.

San Francisco Zoo

SLOAT BLVD. & 45TH AVE.
SOUTH CITY 94132
415-753-7080
Open daily 10 a.m.-5 p.m. Adults $9, children 12-17, seniors $6, children 3-11 $3, under 3 free. SF residents receive a discount. Free the first Wed. of the month.

This 70-acre park is popular for such features as **Monkey Island**, **Gorilla World**, the **Seal Pool**, **Wolf Woods** and other natural environments for the more than a thousand animals. There's also a popular **children's zoo** and a delightfully creepy insect "petting" zoo.

LANDMARKS

Balmy Alley

BETWEEN 24TH, 25TH, TREAT & HARRISON STS.
MISSION 94110
415-285-2287

In a city known for spectacular street art, Balmy Alley stands as one of the most historic public galleries in the city. Here you'll find dozens of murals depicting chapters in immigration history. A rotating exhibition (though some of the works are more than ten years old), the works here are by artists who hail from El Salvador, Mexico, Guatemala, Vietnam and elsewhere and bring to Balmy's fences and garage doors colorful biographies of their homelands. A San Francisco institution.

Civic Center

POLK ST. TO FRANKLIN ST.
GROVE ST. TO MCALLISTER ST.
CIVIC CENTER 94102

In 1905, architect Daniel Burnham envisioned the Civic Center complex as part of a total city redesign which, like that of Paris, would include boulevards extending outward from the Beaux Arts campus. Ultimately, the Civic Center was the only portion of Burnham's plan to be built. The first building was completed in 1913, with original construction continuing into the 1930s. Several buildings are worth particular note: the beautifully domed and detailed **City Hall**, designed by Bakewell and Brown is scheduled to reopen (after a major seismic upgrade) on New Year's Day 2000; the **War Memorial Opera House**, sporting its recent $85.7 million renovation includes a foyer with a stunning gilt ceiling, new curtains and seats and a twinkling new chandelier; finally, the new 375,000-foot **Main Library**, a state-of-the-art learning and technology center designed by James Ingo Freed and Cathy Simon boasts soaring interior atriums and exceptional resources. There are many other beauties, including the **Civic Auditorium**, the **State Office Building** and the **Federal Office Building**. The presence of many homeless San Franciscans in the Civic Center area juxtaposes the Beaux ideals of civic planning and civic pride with the complex contemporary urban realities of American cities.

Cliff House

1090 POINT LOBOS AVE.
RICHMOND DISTRICT 94121
415-386-3330
Restaurant: Lunch & Dinner Mon.-Sat. Bar open daily. Musée: daily 11 a.m.-7 p.m. Admission free.

Today's Cliff House can't match the grandeur of the earlier structures on this sight, especially Adolph Sutro's 1896 castle, but the setting near Point Lobos, the westernmost tip of San Francisco, remains as spectacular as ever. The building houses a bar and restaurant, popular more for location than food, as well as the Musée Méchanique (415-386-1170), one of the world's largest collections of coin-operated automatic musical instruments. A camera obscura (admission $1) looks out over the Seal Rocks, where sea lions and an occasional harbor seal spend their time.

Coit Tower

TELEGRAPH HILL ST.
TELEGRAPH HILL 94133
415-362-0808
Open daily 10 a.m.-6 p.m.; Adults $3, seniors (65+) and children 13-17 $2, children 6-12 $1, under 6 free.

Perhaps you've heard that Coit Tower was built to look like the nozzle of a fire hose? It's a good story-just not quite true. As a girl, Lillie Hitchcock Coit had much admired her local fire department. In 1929, she left money to the city for beautification. Arthur Brown designed the cylindrical tower which was completed in 1934. It stands as a monument to both the San Francisco Volunteer Fire Department and Lillie Coit's husband. An elevator takes you to the top, where you can enjoy a 360-degree view of the Bay and lands beyond. Inside the tower lobby is a series of powerful and once controversial murals, including several by Diego Rivera, painted during the Great Depression as a WPA project and depicting working class life in California.

Ferry Building

EMBARCADERO & MARKET ST.
FINANCIAL DISTRICT 94111

Built in 1896, the Ferry Building with its galleries and arcades was modeled after the cathedral tower in Seville, Spain. Before the bridges were built, it served as the gateway to the city, towering high at the end of Market Street, receiving millions of ferry passengers. After the 1989 earthquake, the Embarcadero freeway was torn down, revealing the full grandeur of this clock tower at the end of Market Street. In addition, the removal of the freeway has resulted in the renovation of the Embarcadero as a pristine promenade, with benches, sculptures and historical markers. Enjoy it during the day or night for magnificent views of the city, East Bay, and the Bay Bridge. On Saturday mornings, just opposite Justin Herman Plaza, a farmer's market takes place.

Fort Mason

MARINA BLVD. & BUCHANAN ST.
MARINA 94123
415-441-5705

Under the auspices of the Golden Gate National Recreation Area, the pier-situated buildings of this former nineteenth-century army post have been transformed into a fine array of workshops, galleries, museums, theaters and restaurants. **Greens**, located in Building B, is a nationally acclaimed vegetarian restaurant (see Dining). Life on the Water presents progressive theater and music in Building B, and the new, acoustically marvelous Cowell Theater is used for various types of performance (most notably KQED's West Coast Weekend radio show on Saturday mornings). Two warehouse buildings house annual crafts fairs, and the Great Meadow is home to the rousing San Francisco Blues Festival each September. Just to the west, extending to the yacht harbor, is the Marina Green, a vast bayside lawn typically dotted with kite-flyers, joggers and sunbathers.

Golden Gate Bridge

101 FWY. BETWEEN SAN FRANCISCO & MARIN COUNTY
415-923-2331
Toll $3 in the southbound direction.

San Francisco's most popular and most photographed symbol does not disappoint when seen in real life. One of the longest suspension bridges in the world (with a 4,200-foot span), this photogenic masterpiece, completed in 1937 by Joseph Strauss, is also one of the most beautiful. Its orange paint flashes brilliantly against the blue of the sky and water, and its grand scale is rendered human and graceful through fine modern styling. It is possible to walk or bicycle across the bridge but be sure to dress warmly if you do. Walking is permitted on the east side of the bridge, bicycling on the west.

Grace Cathedral

1100 CALIFORNIA ST.
NOB HILL 94109
415-749-6310

This poured-in-place Gothic Episcopal cathedral was begun in 1914 but not completed until 1965. It's as grand as most European cathedrals, with twin towers rising some 170 feet high (the North Tower is stocked with 44 working bells). After inspecting the doors cast from a mold of the famous doors on the Baptistery of Florence, walk inside for a look at the impressive marble and stained glass and the mammoth pipe organ.

Mission Dolores

DOLORES AVE. NEAR 16TH ST.
MISSION DISTRICT 94110
415-621-8203
Open daily 9 a.m.-4 p.m. Adults $2, children $1.

Having survived four major earthquakes, this simple Mexican church, built of sun-dried adobe by Native Americans between 1782 and 1791 as one of the string of Junipero Serra's California missions, is San Francisco's oldest building. Originally built of brush, the Mission's walls are four feet thick. Its three original bells are still in place but are rung only during Holy Week. The first burial in the cemetery to the south took place on December 21, 1776.

Palace of Fine Arts

3601 LYON ST.
MARINA 94123
415-563-6504

The Panama-Pacific International Exhibition of 1915 marked the city's dramatic rise from the ashes of the 1906 earthquake and fire. This building, originally constructed of plaster and later replaced by concrete, is the only building that remains from the fair, but it's a beauty: a curved colonnade whose Grecian friezes and statues supports a neoclassical domed rotunda. Reflecting pools, fountains and weeping trees complement the Palace and make it a favorite strolling spot. Inside, the **Exploratorium** is a unique, hands-on science museum, and the 800-seat auditorium provides one of the best theater settings in the city.

San Francisco-Oakland Bay Bridge

I-80 FWY. BETWEEN SAN FRANCISCO & OAKLAND, ENTRANCES FROM SOMA AND FINANCIAL DISTRICT
Toll $2 in westbound direction.

The San Francisco-Oakland Bay Bridge is more than just a bridge. In fact, it's two-a two-level, double-suspension bridge on the San Francisco side and a cantilever bridge on the Oakland side connected by a tunnel through Yerba Buena Island. The two-level span was engineered by Charles H. Purcell and completed in 1936. It was damaged by the 1989 earthquake, which sent a piece of the top level down onto the lower level, but reopened one month later completely repaired and resurfaced. The longest steel high-level bridge in the world, the entire structure is more than 8 miles long, on-ramps included, and spans 4.5 miles of water. Closed to pedestrians, the views of San Francisco, the Bay, the port of Oakland, the Oakland Hills and beyond are limited when driving east on the lower level, but beautiful on the westward trip by day and by night. Avoid rush hour at all costs.

St. Mary's Cathedral

1111 GOUGH ST. AT GEARY BLVD.
CIVIC CENTER 94109
415-567-2020

Cathedral does not, by definition, mean Gothic, as this ultra-modern 1971 structure makes clear. Its 190-foot roof (many have compared it to the inside of a large washing machine) is formed by four deeply sloping concave sides that meet in a cross at the top. Inside is an altar canopy composed of fourteen tiers of shining aluminum rods. Roman Catholic mass is celebrated Sundays at 7:30 a.m., 9 a.m., 11 a.m. and at 1 p.m. in Spanish.

Transamerica Pyramid

600 MONTGOMERY ST. AT COLUMBUS AVE.
FINANCIAL DISTRICT 94133

This narrow white pyramid was designed by William Pereira & Associates of Los Angeles and drew much criticism when it was completed in 1972. Decades later, it remains the city's most famous-and, at 853 feet, the tallest-skyscraper and serves, like the Golden Gate Bridge and the Cable Car, as an icon representing San Francisco itself. Art exhibits in the lobby change monthly; no public access to upper floors.

NEIGHBORHOODS

CASTRO & NOE VALLEY

Filled with upscale shops, bars, cafés and restaurants, the Castro was once a center for the Catholic community and the working-class Irish. It's now the center of gay life in the city, a hubbub of activity at all hours of the day and night. Highlights include the remarkably restored **Castro Theater**, where before each movie you'll be entertained on the mighty Wurtlitzer organ before each movie; the **Café Flore**, where you can get an espresso, enjoy a bite of lunch and meet your next date all in one stop. The neighborhood is also the epicenter for Gay Pride, as well, and includes a commemorative plaque outside Harvey Milk's original camera store, and headquarters the Names Project, originators of the AIDS Memorial Quilt. Just over the Castro Street hill, Noe Valley is a mellow neighborhood filled with young parents and a fine variety of health food and unique clothing shops.

CHINATOWN

Rising from the ashes of the 1906 earthquake and fire, Chinatown is perhaps the most authentic neighborhood in the city-still feeling very much as it must have a century ago. Two good sources, the **Chinese Cultural Center** and the **Chinese Historical Society Museum**, trace the demographics of the borough. The historical center of Chinatown once was Portsmouth Square, and the comestible center was Wentworth Alley, where fresh and dried fish, brine-preserved eggs and produce were bought and sold. Now, most of the Epicurean commerce centers on Stockton and Grant Avenues, where kitchenware stores, grocers and restaurants fill the air with enticing smells. Herbalists, too, are easily found in Chinatown, mostly on Jackson and Clay Streets: **Li Po** is the best-known, but many more can satisfy your holistic health needs.

HAIGHT-ASHBURY

Teetering on the edge of Golden Gate Park, the Haight-Ashbury is one of the most commercially active in the city, despite its reputation as the nucleus of the Summer of Love. It's a neighborhood filled with local color-mohawked punks, homeless vets, fashion plates, fashion disasters-and thrumming with activity. Though there are more clothing shops and smoking paraphernalia sellers than eateries here, you'll find a good mix of ethnic restaurants, including Ethiopian, Middle Eastern, Italian, and Mexican. The Haight's early history as a weekend resort in the later 1800s lives on in a series of funky, comfortable hotels and B&Bs, namely the **Red Victorian** and **Stanyan Park Hotel**. The echoes of Janis Joplin, the Grateful Dead, and Jefferson Airplane can still be heard in some of the shops, though most of the record stores have updated their merchandise. **The Booksmith** is the Haight's favorite source for newspapers, magazines and books of all kinds; and any of a number of bars cater to any of a number of customers. While safe in general, the Haight gets dicey after dark: be alert.

MISSION

The Mission is conducive to a book all its own, rich as it is with history and culture. What was first one of the city's Irish communities gave way in the '60s to the Spanish-speaking immigrant populations, primarily Mexican and other Latin Americans. As a result, the best ethnic food in the city can be found here at the many taquerías and cafeterías that line its streets. Take your food to go and enjoy it in the delightful **Dolores Park** or on **Bernal Hill**, both lovely and quite different. Other characteristics of the Mission are changing: the eastern perimeter is gentrifying with the arrival of multimedia companies, upscale restaurants and edgy art galleries. The bookshops so well-known to **Valencia Street** are struggling for survival with larger chain stores threatening their business. Likewise, several live music venues have either shut down or cut their hours. But don't worry: the Mission, like the original **Mission Dolores** on 16th Street, will survive as a lifeblood for the city's bohemian nature. The cafés and bars are always packed, the markets busy; the sun is almost always warm. As always, public art thrives in the region (especially near Balmy Alley on 24th Street), and there's scarcely a wall that isn't brightly decorated. Some things about the Mission never change-like the very fact it's changing constantly.

NORTH BEACH

A walk through North Beach, which fills the valley between Russian and Telegraph Hills reminds you of the city's long-standing hospitality to bohemian culture. It was here that the Beat writers of the mid-1950s took to the cafés and bookstores to "Howl," as Allen Ginsberg did in his poem of the same name, about the materialism and values they perceived from the Eisenhower era. North Beach retains the same flavor of cool rebellion today, filling on weekends with out-of-towners who troll the topless clubs, the tattoo parlors or the jazz bars, bustling on weekdays with Italians of new- and old-world origin. The late Herb Caen, the longtime columnist for the *San Francisco Chronicle*, loved this 'hood more than any, bending elbows in the **Washington Square Bar and Grill**, digging the jazz at **Enrico's** and **Pearl's** and **Moose's**. Despite the traffic, it's retained a feel of timelessness. Don't believe us? Enjoy dinner at any of the superb trattorias, then make your way to **Tosca** for an after-dinner drink. As the arias play on the jukebox and the well-dressed crowd moves slowly in and out, you'll swear nothing has changed since Ginsburg, Kerouac, and Ferlinghetti held court as kings of the Beat Generation.

RICHMOND & SUNSET

It seems cruel to combine two neighborhoods of such different character under one heading, but the Richmond District and Sunset have much in common. Besides three great beaches—**Ocean Beach** in the Sunset and **China Beach** and **Baker Beach** in the Richmond-Both have a mainstay of Asian and Pacific Islander populations, as well as an influx of white residents looking to escape the crowdedness of the inner neighborhoods. Investigate the Sunset's new restaurant ghetto: around the corner of Ninth and Irving, nearly a dozen quality establishments have taken root. In the Richmond, the quintessential destination seems to be **Mountain Lake Park**, where parents, children, nannies and grandparents stroll, walk dogs or play friendly games of checkers. The two neighborhoods are flat in topography but diverse in qualities; spend some time getting to know them.

BEACHES, HILLS & PARKS

BEACHES

Baker Beach

GIBSON RD. OFF BOWLEY ST.
PRESIDIO
415-556-0560

A part of the Golden Gate National Recreation Area, this mile-long stretch of clean, sandy beach attracts fishermen, family picnickers and sunbathers. Nude bathers head to the north end of the beach, nearest the Golden Gate Bridge; elsewhere, sunbathers are a mix of pale and picturesque, flocking to the beach on sunny afternoons and eschewing it when the fog rolls in. Overnight camping is prohibited, but picnic and barbecue facilities, restrooms and drinking water are all provided by the park service. Although the water at Baker is often warmer than other local beaches, its waves are hazardous and swimming is discouraged.

Ocean Beach

GREAT HWY., SOUTH OF CLIFF HOUSE
RICHMOND DISTRICT
415-556-0560

Where Golden Gate Park ends its long stretch toward the sea, San Francisco's most accessible beach begins. When most city dwellers want surf and sand, this is where they come-to a long strip of beach, just south of the **Cliff House**, often heavily populated with joggers, Frisbee throwers, sunbathers and beachcombers. Surfers can be seen catching waves off the shore, but because of the rough tides and dangerous undertow, wading and swimming are frequently unsafe.

Phelan ("China") Beach

SEACLIFF AVE. OFF EL CAMINO
RICHMOND DISTRICT
415-556-0560

At last a beach where you can swim! Nestled in a small cove, Phelan is a tiny stretch of beach sufficiently protected from the tides and undertows so that swimming is feasible during the warmest months. Lifeguards are on duty from April to October, but call ahead to check on the conditions. On sunny afternoons in the spring and fall the beach is packed.

HILLS

Bernal Hill

This bald, rocky hill, accessible from Folsom at Ripley Sts., is actually quite a friendly place, a promontory where dog-watchers and view-admirers meet above the city for a little meditative escape. It affords fine views of the East Bay, downtown, the Mission and (on a clear day) Peninsula cities; it's similarly appealing at night. For those interested, the hill is atop a well-established lesbian neighborhood.

Lombard Street

LOMBARD STREET BETWEEN HYDE & LEAVENWORTH, RUSSIAN HILL

It's hard to determine why the act of waiting in a long line of cars to take your turn descending a 27% grade, nine-hairpin-turn is a thrill, but many, many tourists do it every hour of every day of the year. More notable than the slow flow of automobiles is Lombard's fine brick paving and attractive landscaping (all recently renovated) that make the city's crookedest street visually pretty. Step lively or you'll find yourself in someone else's photograph.

Nob, Russian & Telegraph Hills

Each of the city's best-known hills are famous for a different reason. Nob Hill, at the top of California Street, owes its glittery character to the wealth created by the railroads, which finally spanned the nation in 1869. The "Big Four" Sacramento merchants who financed the Central Pacific Railway built their mansions on Nob Hill in the 1870s-spending up to $3 million of nineteenth-century money-and created a hill of nabobs, or "nobs." Except for the Flood, at 1000 California, these mansions perished in the fire that swept the city after the 1906 earthquake.

Moviemakers love Russian Hill with its bohemian neighborhoods and famous San Francisco views-the perfect spot for car chases. Contemporary poetry lovers can walk up the steps at Greenwich and Hyde to the secluded George Sterling Glade. Sterling, San Francisco's King of Bohemia, was known for his macabre writing and friendship with Jack London. For those whose hearts and calf muscles are strong, the walk down the breathtakingly steep east slope of Telegraph Hill is memorable. From Coit Tower, follow the easternmost stairway (Filbert Street) until it turns into a neatly landscaped walkway. As the path snakes down the hillside, you can look from side to side at the rich array of architectural styles and out across the Bay.

Twin Peaks

TWIN PEAKS BLVD. SOUTH OF CLARENDON AVE.

Ohlone legend states that the two hills that comprise Twin Peaks were once twin daughters of an Indian chief, frozen forever by the Great Spirit. Choose a clear day to drive to the top of the southernmost, where you'll enjoy one of the city's best views. Market Street unfurls before you, and your vista from Berkeley to the Golden Gate Bridge will be unobstructed. Don't miss this photo opportunity.

PARKS

Angel Island

DEPART VIA BLUE AND GOLD FLEET FROM PIER 41, POWELL ST.
FISHERMAN'S WHARF
INFORMATION 415-773-1188;
TICKETS 415-705-5555

Open daily 8 a.m.-5 p.m. Ferries depart at 10 a.m. Wed.-Fri., 9:30 a.m., 11:45 a.m. & 2 p.m. Sat., Sun. & holidays (9:45 a.m.-2:45 p.m. during late fall & winter months); last ferry returns 3:20 p.m. (Wed.-Fri.) & 4:40 p.m. (Sat., Sun., holidays). Adults $10, children 12-18 $9, children 5-11 $5.50, children under 5 free.

Once called the Ellis Island of the West, Angel Island's history is just as long and notorious as Alcatraz. Angel once was a military outpost, and has restored and upkept the garrisons and compounds that once dotted the island. It's now a California State Park and a wildlife preserve, with miles of biking and hiking trails, picnic grounds, beaches, forests and flowery meadows. Bike space is limited on ferries, but bicycling around Angel Island is one of San Francisco's best-kept pleasurable secrets.

Aquatic Park

NEXT TO GHIRARDELLI SQUARE
FISHERMAN'S WHARF
415-556-3002

On a clear day, this terraced park by the Bay is filled with sunbathers, picnickers and joggers. The view is splendid, out to Alcatraz and across the Golden Gate Bridge to Sausalito and Angel Island. There is a large lawn and a small beach for wading. Watch for the homeless artists who create rock sculptures when the tide is out; on weekends, a group of drummers gathers for a spontaneous, afternoon-long jam session.

Dolores Park

DOLORES & 18TH STS.
MISSION
415-831-2700

Just two blocks away from Mission Dolores, this small oasis of greenery in the densely populated Mission district is a frequent rallying point for political demonstrations and marches. On most days its quiet setting affords a view of San Francisco, from downtown to the southern waterfront. When the sun is out, it turns into a sunbathing destination. At night, visiting this park is inadvisable.

Golden Gate Park

BOUNDED BY FULTON & STANYAN STS., GREAT HWY. & LINCOLN BLVD.
415-831-2700
Maps and information available at the McLaren Lodge, at the corner of Stanyan & Fell Sts.

Golden Gate Park is a masterwork of creative urban transformation. More than a pocket of city greenery, this wonder of urban landscaping is a world unto itself. Inspired by Frederick Law Olmsted's pioneering work with Central Park in New York City, Engineer William Hammond Hall, the park's first superintendent, along with John McLaren, the tireless landscape gardener who took over as superintendent in 1876 and served for the next 55 years, designed, planted, nurtured and tended the 1,000 acres until they flourished with lush, green foliage and more than one million trees.

The narrow **Panhandle**, the jogger-filled peninsula between Fell and Oak streets on the park's east side, leads into a dazzling maze of wooded drives. The spectacular **Strybing Arboretum**, the **Dutch windmill**, the **Rhododendron Dell**, the **California Academy of Sciences**, the **M. H. De Young** and **Asian Art Museums**, are all worth investigating, as are the **Children's Playground**, the peaceful **Japanese Tea Garden**, several lakes (including Stow and Spreckels), a buffalo paddock, a nine-hole golf course, tennis courts, baseball diamonds, handball courts and designated roller-skating areas, all brilliantly tucked into their own green havens within the park.

The pristine Conservatory of Flowers is closed until 2002 because of damage from severe winter storms, and the future of the DeYoung museum (compromised by the earthquake of 1989) remains uncertain. Voters will decide whether to construct a parking structure beneath the park to ease its traffic woes. But all these changes are indicative of Golden Gate Park's importance to every San Franciscan. The entire realm is a supreme example of man tempering a harsh urban landscape with natural wonders. The park headquarters are in **McLaren Lodge**, the Romanesque house at Fell and Stanyan streets that served as John McLaren's home during his tenure.

Presidio

VISITOR'S CENTER, 102 MONTGOMERY ST.
PRESIDIO 94129
415-561-4323
Entrances on Park Presidio (Hwy 1), Arguello Blvd., Presidio Blvd., Lombard St. & Marina Blvd.

Originally a Spanish garrison, The two-and-a-quarter-century-year-old Presidio was a Mexican outpost and, later, a U.S. military post until 1994, when it officially transferred to the jurisdiction of the Golden Gate National Recreation Area. It contains 11 miles of hiking trails, including an ecology trail and portions of the **Bay Area Ridge Trail** and the **Anza National Historic Trail**. Cyclists can explore its 14 miles of paved roads; a world-class sailboarding area borders **Crissy Field** on the Bay side; fishing and crabbing opportunities abound at the nearby rocks and pier. **Fort Point**, one of the few Civil War-era forts west of the Mississippi, offers several tours beneath the south tower of the **Golden Gate Bridge**. The park also contains 510 historic buildings, a cemetery, airfield, forests, beaches and bluffs, as well as a golf course, bowling alley, tennis courts and athletic fields. Group camping facilities are available. A calendar of events are available at the visitors center; you can also look online at www.nps.gov/prsf.

Sigmund Stern Memorial Grove

19TH AVE. & SLOAT BLVD.
SUNSET
415-252-6252
Open during daylight hours.

Given to San Francisco in 1931 by Rosalie M. Stern in memory of her husband, 63-acre

Stern Grove hosts a summer festival of afternoon concerts in its natural tree-lined amphitheater. Classical, popular and jazz artists perform in a sylvan setting of redwoods, eucalyptus and fir trees. The Grove is also a lovely spot for a picnic or barbecue.

TOURS

BY BOAT

Blue & Gold Fleet

PIER 39 & 41
FISHERMAN'S WHARF 94133
415-773-1188; 415-705-5555 FOR TICKETS.
Open daily 8 a.m.-5 p.m. Fall & winter hours limited. Adults $16, seniors & children 12-18 $12, children 5-11 $8, under 5 free. Call for departure times.

Blue & Gold's just-under-an-hour Bay cruise covers the waterfront, passes under the Golden Gate and Bay Bridges and loops around Alcatraz Island. You won't find any locals on this trip, but sometimes it's fun to be the tourist you are. If the day is clear, the views are memorable. Blue and Gold also provides tours of Muir Woods, Alcatraz and Wine Country, and offers ferry service to Sausalito, Tiburon, Marine World Africa USA in Vallejo and Angel Island.

Hornblower Dining Yachts

PIER 33
FISHERMAN'S WHARF 94133
415-394-8900
Admission $25-$75. Holiday cruises & special events available. Reservations essential.

It's not the Queen Mary, but the City of San Francisco, the Hornblower fleet's flagship yacht, is the most luxurious way to cruise the San Francisco Bay. Dinner-dance cruises are offered every evening, lunch cruises every Friday and champagne brunch cruises every weekend. Special events are scheduled throughout the year, including full-moon cruises, holiday luncheons and galas, Big Game (Cal-Stanford football) cruises and a New Year's Eve dinner-dance.

Red & White Fleet

PIER 43 1/2
FISHERMAN'S WHARF 94133
415-447-0591
Golden Gate Bay Cruise departs ten times daily between 10:50 a.m. & 5:05 p.m. Price includes a headset for a recorded audio tour in English, German, Japanese or Mandarin. Adults $15; seniors, military & children 12-18 $12; children 5-11 $8; under 5 free. Hours & prices of other trips vary.

The Red & White Fleet offers two tours: an hour-long Golden Gate Bay Cruise, a headset-narrated tour available in six languages that takes tourists past the Golden Gate Bridge, waterfront, and Alcatraz island, and the 45-minute "Round the Rock" tour of Alcatraz (you'll never leave the boat). Red and White also provides commuter service to Point Richmond in the East Bay.

BY BUS

Gray Line Tours

350 8TH ST.
SOUTH OF MARKET 94103
415-558-9400
City tours depart daily 9 a.m., 10 a.m., 11 a.m., 1:30 p.m. & 2:30 p.m. Adults $28, seniors (65+) $26, children 5-11 $14, under 5 free. Times & prices of other tours vary. Day tours depart from Transbay Terminal, 1st & Mission Sts., evening tours from Union Square, Powell & Geary Sts.

Pre-packaged travel does not appeal to many, precluding as it does the joys of serendipity. For those who don't mind the lack of adventure, Gray Line bus tours do run often and hit all the best-known attractions. The three-hour deluxe city tour includes the Civic Center, the Mission District, Golden Gate Park, the Cliff House, Presidio, Fisherman's Wharf and a drive across the Golden Gate Bridge, with stops along the way. It can be supplemented with a Bay cruise package or an Alcatraz walking tour. A different "San Francisco by Night" tour is also available, as well as tours to Muir Woods, Sausalito and the Wine Country. Finally, Gray Line is also the source for double-decker bus, motorized cable car and helicopter tours of the city.

ON FOOT

City Guides

FRIENDS OF THE LIBRARY, MAIN LIBRARY
LARKIN & GROVE STS.
CIVIC CENTER 94102
415-557-4266
Call for schedule and meeting places. Tours free.

If you've hungered to know more about historic Market Street, the Civic Center and City Hall, Japantown, Haight-Ashbury or the Gold Rush history of San Francisco, the well-informed representatives at City Guides will walk with you, talk with you, and share all they know. Other tours include Chinatown, North Beach, Yerba Buena Gardens, Coit Tower, Mission Murals, Pacific Heights Mansions, Alamo Square, Palace of Fine Arts, Victorians, Japantown, Sutro Park, Presidio, Golden Gate Bridge, art deco, hotels and more. Whew! The roster of tours changes often, with the greatest number offered during summer months. Access their schedule on the Web at www.hooked.net/users/jhum.

Cruisin' the Castro

375 LEXINGTON ST.
CASTRO DISTRICT 94110
415-550-8110
Tours Tues.-Sat. 10 a.m.-2 p.m. $35 per person including brunch. Reservations required.

Join Trevor Hailey and cruise the Castro, San Francisco's lively gay neighborhood, from a historical perspective. Trevor shares her knowledge of the history of San Francisco's gay and lesbian communities, from the Gold Rush through the present, and visits such sights as the Castro Theater and the Names Project (birthplace of the AIDS Memorial Quilt).

Dashiell Hammett Tour

STARTS FROM SAN FRANCISCO MAIN LIBRARY,
LARKIN & GROVE STS.
CIVIC CENTER 94102
510-287-9540
Tours Saturdays at noon, $10.

For more than two decades, trenchcoated tourguide Don Herron has led a Saturday walking excursion that explores the place names and characters of his hero, Dashiell Hammett. The author of The Maltese Falcon and other classics still lives in San Francisco, and this is the best way to trace the gumshoe progress of his main character, Sam Spade. You'll see where Brigid Shaughnesy was "murdered" and visit Spade's apartment on Post Street. The tour wraps up at Hammett's favorite restaurant, John's Grill, at 63 Ellis Street, where you can enjoy lunch at additional cost.

Precita Eyes Mural Arts Center

348 PRECITA AVE.
MISSION DISTRICT 94110
415-285-2287
Tours vary; call for information. Cost free-$5.

Founded in 1977, Precita Eyes serves as a community cultural center, offering mural workshops and classes. An eight-block walking tour of the Mission District murals begins with a slide presentation in the center highlighting mural history and the San Francisco mural movement. The tour covers 60 murals and is a bargain at $3. Ask about additional tours-some on bikes, BART, or the Mexican Bus-that vary by theme, time and price.

Victorian Home Walk

STARTS FROM THE WESTIN ST. FRANCIS HOTEL LOBBY
225 POWELL ST
UNION SQUARE 94102
415-252-9485, FAX 415-863-7577
Tours 11 a.m. daily, $20 per person, reservations necessary.

Jay Gifford meets interested folks by the big clock in the lobby of the St. Francis Hotel. For the next two-and-a-half hours, he leads them-by public transportation and by foot-past (and in some cases into) some of the city's best remaining examples of Victorian houses. Along the way, Gifford entertains one and all with his rendition of San Francisco history (particularly the periods just before and after the great earthquake and fire of 1906). It's an enjoyable way to see what you'll never see from a tour bus (tour buses are forbidden on most of the streets Gifford explores).

Wok Wiz Chinatown Tours

654 COMMERCIAL ST.
CHINATOWN 94111
415-981-8989
Tours daily
$37 including dim-sum lunch, $25 for tour only. Reservations required.

Chef and cookbook author Shirley Fong-Torres offers daily tours of San Francisco's Chinatown, sharing her knowledge and experience of the neighborhood's history, food and folklore. Reservations required. Ask about other excursions, including the "I Ate My Way Through Chinatown" and various historical tours. Fong-Torres also offers cooking classes.

OTHER TOURS

Many other tours of San Francisco are available. If you're a bicyclist, the Department of Parking and Traffic has organized a series of bicycle routes that traverse the city. Call the **Bicycle Information Hotline** (415-585-2453) and check the current Pacific Bell Yellow Pages for a map. For automobile drivers, the city pre-mapped 49-mile-long scenic drive in and around the city: look for the signs with the seagull on them. For a map, contact the **San Francisco Visitor Information Center** (415-391-2000). You can also request a map from their Website: www.sfvisitor.org.

San Francisco Helicopter Tours

EXECUTIVE TERMINAL, SF AIRPORT
P.O. BOX 280776
SAN FRANCISCO 94128
800-400-2404, 650-635-4500
Cost $79-$250. Reservations required.

If you think the Bay is beautiful from the top of Telegraph Hill, imagine how it will look from a low-flying helicopter. Bay tours range from 15 to 30 minutes in length; also available are a half-day tour to the wine country, including lunch and wine tasting and sunset city tours-with or without dinner after the flight. Complimentary shuttle service is available from downtown and Fisherman's Wharf hotels to this company's heliport at the executive terminal of San Francisco International Airport.

Spas, Sports & Leisure

CONTENTS

HEALTH & FITNESS CLUBS

Club One

2 EMBARCADERO CENTER
EMBARCADERO 94111
415-788-1010
Open daily
Cost $15 daily, $40 weekly.

The most exclusive of the city's fitness chain, Club One offers state-of-the-art equipment, hundreds of group exercise classes, sauna, steam rooms, whirlpools and a full array of personal workout programs. Five other locations.

Gold's Gym

1001 BRANNAN ST.
SOMA 94103
415-552-4653
Open daily
Cost $10 daily, $30 weekly.

The newest of the weight-training epicenters, Gold's is a huge space located between the Mission and Financial districts. For hard-bodies, it's the place to pump iron.

Koret Health and Recreation Center

PARKER & TURK STS.
WESTERN ADDITION 94117
415-422-6820
Open daily
Cost $8 daily.

The University of San Francisco's health center, located at the northwest edge of campus, is a good alternative spot for swimming, weight training and aerobic machines. Arrive in the middle of the day for the best chance of missing the undergraduate crowds.

Pacific Heights Health Club

2356 PINE ST.
PACIFIC HEIGHTS 94115
415-563-6694 (MEN),
415-563-5341 (WOMEN)
Open daily
Cost $10 daily.

This small club, tucked a block off the Fillmore shopping district, offers a rarity-separate workout facilities for men and women. It's not a big club, but conducive to a good, scene-free workout.

Pinnacle Fitness

345 SPEAR ST.
EMBARCADERO 94105
415-495-1939
Open daily
Cost $15 daily, $75 for 10-day pass.

As the middle-range club, Pinnacle is trying hard to gain members from Club One and 24 Hour Fitness. Each of their facilities (four currently in the city) offer a full range of programs and equipment. Other locations.

24 Hour Fitness

1200 Van Ness Ave.
Civic Center 94109
415-776-2200
Cost $15 daily, weekly discounts offered.

The former 24 Hour Nautilus centers are sprouting up everywhere. With huge aerobic studios, cardio areas, tons of free weights and swimming pools and steam rooms in selected clubs, they're becoming the most popular-and most crowded-fitness chain in the city. Other locations.

YMCA

1530 Buchanan St.
Japantown 94115
415-931-9622
Open daily
Cost $7.50 daily.

The Y remains a good, unglamorous standby in a city filled with glittery clubs. Seven other locations including Stonestown and Chinatown.

SPAS

Claremont Resort and Spa

41 Tunnel Rd.
Berkeley 94705
510-549-8566
Open daily

Just across the Bay Bridge from San Francisco, the Claremont is a long-kept secret for area pleasure-seekers. With over 100 services, choose among massages, body treatments, baths, facials and other pampering treats. Herbal and body wraps start at $55; a 50-minute Swedish massage is $92. Day packages include use of facilities (steam room, whirlpool, sauna), lockers, slippers and robe and range from $99-$325. Claremont also features a full-service salon and restaurant.

Harbin Hot Springs

P.O. Box 782
Middletown 95461
800-622-2477
Open daily

Harbin Hot Springs is a 1160-acre nonprofit retreat located an hour north of San Francisco. Guests soak in natural spring pools, bask on clothing-optional sun decks, receive massages from certified staff, attend workshops, hike or otherwise relax. Reservations are not required for day use of the spa, but are for use of dormitories or cabins. Adult fees range from $20 daily to $145 weekly; children from $15-$115. A one-time membership fee costs $5 for a one-day trial ($20 for one year). Accommodations range from $30 dormitories to $185 cabins.

Kabuki Hot Spring

Japan Center
1750 Geary Blvd.
Japantown 94115
415-922-6002
Open daily

While we only recommend a Shiatsu massage for the hearty, if you can take it, afterwards you will feel incredibly invigorated. Other services at this Japanese Spa include communal or private hot baths, sauna, steam room and backscrub. Get the "works" with one of the ten packages offered; the Shogun plan at $69 includes a 55-minute massage; the Kabuki plan at $45 includes a 25-minute massage.

Novella Salon

2238 Union St.
Union Street 94123
415-673-1929
Open daily

From the moment you walk into the door, you are engulfed in the relaxing fragrances of the Aveda beauty products that Novella uses. Come in for a half-hour mini facial ($35) or spend the whole day here having a massage, facial, body polish, body wrap, manicure, pedicure, shampoo and blow dry ($300). Either way, you will feel like a pampered princess or prince.

Spa Nordstrom

San Francisco Centre
865 Market St.
Union Square 94103
415-978-5102
Open daily

For $275, you'll enjoy at least five hours of healthy self-indulgence with the "Day Spa" package which includes thalassotherapy, full-body massage, body wrap with scalp treatment, therapeutic facial, sports manicure and pedicure and a delicious spa cuisine meal. Add aromatherapy services to this package for an additional $25. A complete menu of individual services is offered in addition to full-day packages. These include a choice of seven varieties of massage, French manicure, facials and hair removal.

WINE COUNTRY SPAS

The best-known and most luxurious of Sonoma and Napa county spas are located at the **Sonoma Mission Inn** (18140 Sonoma Highway, Boyes Hot Springs; 707-938-9000) and the **Meadowood Resort** (900 Meadowood Ln., St. Helena; 707-963-3646). **Calistoga** has a dozen spas with mud baths, mineral baths and volcanic ash treatments; **Indian Springs Resort and Spa** (1712 Lincoln Ave., Calistoga; 707-942-4913) is perhaps the oldest. **Roman International Spa** (1300 Washington St., Calistoga; 707-942-4441) offers an large range of spa treatments. **Dr. Wilkinson's Hot Springs** (1507 Lincoln Ave., Calistoga; 707-942-4102) is also well-equipped to pamper you.

SPORTS TO DO

BICYCLING

Although downtown's fast and furious bicycle messengers are legendary, we don't recommend imitating their dangerous weaving through autos and pedestrians. The Department of Parking and Traffic has created a series of east-west and north-south bike routes through the city whose signs point you toward the safest and least topographically challenging routes; check the map found in the Yellow Pages or call 415-585-2453.

Golden Gate Park Bike & Skate

3038 FULTON ST.
RICHMOND DISTRICT 94118
415-668-1117
Open 10 a.m.-6 p.m. daily.

Start To Finish Bicycles

672 STANYAN ST.
HAIGHT-ASHBURY 94117
415-750-4760
Open 10 a.m.-6 p.m. daily.

BOATING & SAILING

If you're by yourself and feel contemplative, or with a loved one and feel romantic, you might consider boating in Golden Gate Park's largest lake. The boathouse is located in Stow Lake's northwest corner. Its rowboats, pedal boats and electric motorboats rent from $10 to $16 per hour. For the sailor, the San Francisco Bay enjoys a challenging reputation worldwide.

Stow Lake Boathouse

LAKE DR. OFF JOHN F. KENNEDY DR.
GOLDEN GATE PARK
415-752-0347
Open daily 9 a.m.-4 p.m.

Sailing Education Adventures

FORT MASON 94123
415-775-8779
Call for hours & location.

FISHING

Along with the charter fishing boats that depart from Fisherman's Wharf in search of deep-sea denizens, San Francisco has its own large freshwater fishing hole. Explore this long, narrow lake in a rented rowboat, electric motorboat, canoe, or pedal boat. In addition to its boathouse, Lake Merced, a backup reservoir just south of the San Francisco Zoo, has a bar, restaurant and plenty of picnic areas.

Lake Merced Boating & Fishing

HARDING PARK, SKYLINE BLVD. & HARDING RD.
SOUTH CITY 94132
415-753-1101
Open daily 6 a.m.-7:30 p.m. Rowboats $7 per hour, 3 to 5 hours $16 & $21 for the full day.

GOLF

Tough, hilly nine-hole Gleneagle's makes up for the frustrations it imparts with the southern Bay view it allows from the clubhouse. The course is privately operated. At Golden Gate Park, the short, tight fairways, tricky turns, ample hills and surrounding trees mix well with the wisps of fog that blow in from the nearby Pacific.

Gleneagle's Golf Course

MCLAREN PARK
2100 SUNNYDALE
PORTOLA 94134
415-587-2425
Open daily 7 a.m.-5 p.m. (last tee time) Greens fees weekdays $11 for 9 holes, $17 for 18 holes, weekends & holidays $14 and $24.

Golden Gate Park Golf Course

47TH AVE. AT JOHN F. KENNEDY DR.,
GOLDEN GATE PARK
415-751-8987
Open daily 6 a.m.-7 p.m. (last tee time) Greens fees weekdays $10, weekdays and holidays $13.

HORSEBACK RIDING

You can't gallop off by yourself across the park, but you can take an hour-long guided walking trail ride or an English riding lesson by yourself or with friends.

Golden Gate Park Stables

JOHN F. KENNEDY DR. & 34TH AVE.
GOLDEN GATE PARK
415-668-7360
Open 8 a.m.-6 p.m. daily. 1-hour group lessons $24 per person, semi-private $30 for two people. Reservations required.

ROLLER SKATING & ROLLERBLADING

The rollerblading trend has brought new life to skating and skinned knees to skaters. During daylight hours on Sundays, a large stretch of John F. Kennedy Drive in Golden Gate Park is closed off for skating and cycling.

Bikes & Blades in Golden Gate Park

50 STOW LAKE DR.
GOLDEN GATE PARK
Open daily.

Skates on Haight

1818 HAIGHT ST., HAIGHT-ASHBURY 94117
415-752-8375
Open daily.

RUNNING

The city is well-known for its annual San Francisco Marathon and wacky Bay-to-Breakers footraces. If you're interested in running these or other races with the locals (and helping worthy causes) look for a magazine called The Schedule in specialty sporting goods stores. This monthly publication lists runs throughout the Bay Area, from 5K races to marathons, many of which raise money for local charities. If you can't find the publication call 415-472-RACE.

Our favorite routes are Lake Merced in Harding Park, with five flat miles of asphalt and dirt; the Marina Green, a popular one-mile stretch of grass with spectacular views of the Golden Gate Bridge, Alcatraz and the Bay; the Polo Field, just off Middle Drive in the center of Golden Gate Park, with pleasant tracks and trails; and Stow Lake, a short, scenic course around the water with the option of more difficult dirt trails on Strawberry Hill. Finally, The climb up Bernal Hill is a heart-stopper, but the resulting view is superb.

SWIMMING

The Parks and Recreation Department maintains several municipal pools, each of which have their own operating hours; it's best to call in advance to ascertain rates and times. They include Garfield (26th Ave. & Harrison St., 415-695-5001), Hamilton (Geary Blvd. at Steiner St., 415-292-2001) and North Beach (Lombard & Mason Sts., 415-274-0200). Several fitness clubs have swimming pools as well.

TENNIS

One call to the Parks Department (415-753-7100) will give you the location of more than 100 city courts, most of which are free to use. The most popular courts, located on the east end of Golden Gate Park, do require a fee. To reserve those courts call 415-753-7101.

San Francisco Recreation & Parks Department

McLaren Lodge, Fell & Stanyan Sts.
Golden Gate Park
415-753-7001
Open daily 9 a.m.-5 p.m. Mon.-Fri.: Adults $4, seniors 65+ $2, children under 18 free. Sat.-Sun. (reservations required): adults $6, children $2. Walk-ons $5 for 90 minutes of play.

SPORTS TO WATCH

In addition to its many amateur recreational sporting activities the Bay Area is also home to professional athletic teams and their devoted fans. Until the new baseball park is completed early in the new century, 3Com (Candlestick) Park, home to the San Francisco Giants and the San Francisco 49ers, remains the only major sporting venue. 3Com is eight miles south of the City and accessible by car or the MUNI Ballpark Express bus service. In the East Bay, catch the Oakland Athletics and Oakland Raiders at the Oakland-Alameda County Coliseum Complex, aka the Oakland Coliseum, accessible by BART. Call (510) 762-BASS to charge tickets for any professional sporting events in the Bay Area.

For tickets to major college football and basketball games, call UC Berkeley (800-462-3277) or Stanford (650-723-1021) athletic ticket offices.

AUTO RACING

Sears Point Raceway

State Highways 37 & 121
Sonoma 95476
707-938-8448
Admission $5-$55.

BASEBALL

Oakland Athletics

Oakland Coliseum
510-638-4627
Tickets $4-$20

San Francisco Giants

3Com Park
415-467-8000
Tickets $5.50-$20

BASKETBALL

Golden State Warriors

Oakland Coliseum
888-479-4667
Tickets $13.75-$220

FOOTBALL

Oakland Raiders

Oakland Coliseum
510-949-2626
Tickets $35-$200

San Francisco 49ers

3Com Park
415-656-4900
Tickets $40-$250

HOCKEY

San Jose Sharks

San Jose Arena
800-888-2736
Tickets $15-$78

Horse Racing

Bay Meadows Racecourse
2600 Delaware St.
San Mateo 94403
650-574-7225
Admission $3-$15

Golden Gate Fields

1100 Eastshore Hwy.
Albany 94710
Tickets $3-$17.50

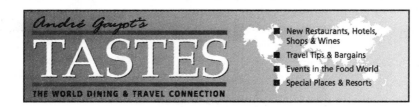

BASICS

CONTENTS

TRANSPORTATION

BY AIR

San Francisco International Airport (SFO)

Located 15 miles south of San Francisco on U.S. 101. This distance can take up to 50 minutes to travel during rush hour or any time when traffic is heavy. In light traffic it's a short 25 minutes from downtown. A Nationwide Transportation Hotline (800-SFO-2008) can help with all airport transportation questions. (General information, 650-761-0800; parking information 650-877-0227.) SFO has three terminals and serves more than 50 carriers: the **South Terminal** serves small carriers including Southwest, US Air, Alaska, Air Canada, Delta and others; the **International Terminal** serves all international flights; the **North Terminal** serves United, United Express, American, American Eagle, Canadian, Reno Air and others. CitySpan maintains a good plan of SFO on line at http://www.ci.sf.ca.us/sfo/.

Arriving flights are met on the airport's lower level. Hotel and car rental shuttles serve the upper level only. For departures, use the upper level. Among the numerous shuttle services providing transportation to and from SFO (for around $10 per person to downtown) are **SFO Airporter** (415-495-8404), **SuperShuttle** (415-558-8500) and **Yellow Airport Express** (415-282-7433). Cab fare from the airport into the City averages $40 (see "Taxi! Taxi!" in this chapter). For information on lodging located near the airport, see the "Hotels" sections of the Peninsula chapter.

Free bus connections between the airport and the Millbrae Caltrain station are available on average three times per hour.

Oakland International Airport

Located just south of Oakland, off U.S. Hwy. 880, at the Hegenberger exit. Fewer carriers fly into this airport, which can be to the benefit of travelers looking for a slightly less frenetic travel experience. United, Alaska, American West, American, Delta, City Bird, Corsair and Martinair fly from Terminal 1; Southwest commands Terminal 2. Shuttles and taxis from here to downtown San Francisco are very costly; **BART** offers a more economical, if more circuitous, option. For Oakland airport information, call 510-577-4000, or go to http://www.flyoakland.com/ on the Web.

Other Airports

San Jose on the Peninsula, and Santa Rosa in Sonoma County also have small airports. **San Jose International Airport** (408-277-4759), off the Guadalupe exit, is an easy one-hour shot down U.S. 101. When traveling on American, Southwest, or Reno Air go to Terminal A; all other major airlines are in Terminal C; find on line information at http://www.sjc.org/. To reach the **Sonoma County Airport** (707-524-7240), drive through Santa Rosa on U.S. 101 and take the Airport Blvd. exit heading west. This airport has only limited service provided by regional carriers.

BY LAND

Car Rental

An average weekday rate for car rental in Northern California is around $40, and an average weekly rate is around $250 with unlimited mileage. There is usually an additional charge for dropping off a rental car in a location different from the one where you rented it. Many national rental companies offer special rates, so call around to compare prices. Drivers must all be licensed and at least 25 years old and must pay using a credit card. Among the bigger companies with large fleets in the region are **Avis** (800-331-1212), **Dollar** (800-800-4000), **Enterprise** (800-325-8007), **Hertz** (800-654-3131), **National** (800-227-7368) and **Thrifty** (800-367-2277).

Limousine service to and from the airport as well as around town is provided by a variety of agencies including **The Finishing Touch** (415-921-5000) and **Squire Limousine** (650-761-3000).

Getting Into San Francisco

From Marin County and points north: travel south along scenic Pacific Coast Highway (also known as Highway 1) to U.S. 101, which takes you across the Golden Gate Bridge ($3 toll). Upon entering San Francisco, stay left to reach the Marina or straight, following the signs to Lombard Street, to get downtown.

From the Peninsula and points south, take U.S. 101 heading north or Interstate 280 north, a much prettier route. From the East Bay and points east, Interstate 80 west takes you across the upper deck of the San Francisco-Oakland Bay Bridge (the toll is $2 westbound). Always allow for plenty of time to travel by car when navigating into or out of San Francisco; traffic frequently gets snarled during rush hour or at other times of the day. For updated traffic info, tune to KCBS (740 AM).

Driving Tips & Rules

Generally speaking, California highway numbers ending in 1 and other odd numbers run north-south, while freeways ending in 0 and other even numbers run east/west. The speed limit on highways in California is 65 m.p.h. or lower, as posted. In metropolitan areas where no speed limit is posted, assume it to be 25 m.p.h.

Drivers' licenses from all Western nations allow visitors to drive in California for up to one year. International Driver's Licenses are also valid in California. The Department of Motor Vehicles (1377 Fell St., Western Addition, 415-557-1191) issues drivers' licenses and car registrations. Lines are always long, so call ahead to make an appointment.

Navigating the City

San Francisco is designed in a simple grid pattern, and is bisected from north to south by Van Ness Avenue, east and west by Geary Boulevard and diagonally from northeast to southwest by Market Street. If you are able to determine your location relative to these streets, you will seldom be lost. The Embarcadero Freeway (Interstate 480) has been torn down where it parallels the waterfront, and the junction of I-80 and I-40 has been demolished, both in the aftermath of the 1989 earthquake. The rebuilding of the Central Freeway is scheduled to begin sometime early in the 21st century.

Finding Parking

Street parking in San Francisco can be truly vexatious. There are far fewer spots on the street than there are cars in most business neighborhoods. But towaway zones (such as bus stops and fire hydrants) are watched assiduously by the police, and fines can be as much as $250-in addition to the $100 towing fee and storage charges. Street signs and colored curbs should be observed at all times: red curbs indicate no parking, white curbs are for five minutes, green curbs for ten, blue curbs are reserved for disabled persons and yellow curbs are for commercial vehicles. Metered parking is everywhere; all meters require quarters. The fine for expired meters is $25. For parking in residential zones for more than two hours, temporary or yearly permits are available at the Department of Parking and Traffic, 370 Grove St.

When parking on the streets and especially on a hill, always curb your wheels. This will not only protect against the possibility of a runaway car, but also against the imposition of a $40 fine.

Parking garages offer a sometimes pricey alternative to street parking. There are several around town that have reasonable hourly rates: the Sutter-Stockton Garage near Union Square, the Portsmouth Square Garage in Chinatown, the Fifth and Mission Street Garage near the San Francisco Shopping Center, and the North Point Shopping Garage at Fisherman's Wharf all charge around $18 for all-day parking, about $2 for one-hour parking, and at least $6 for evening parking.

The Muni Lines

The San Francisco Municipal Railway (Muni) encompasses the diesel and electric buses, underground metro cars and cable cars that crisscross the city in over 70 public transit lines, some of which run 24 hours. Bus and underground Muni fares are $1 (35 cents for children under 18), regardless of distance traveled. Free bus transfers allow for two changes of vehicle within 90 minutes of issuance.

A Muni Passport provides unlimited bus travel for $6 per day, $10 for three days or $15 for seven days. A monthly Fast Pass is priced at $35. The best places to purchase Muni Passports are at the Powell/Market cable car turnaround, the Hyde/Beach cable car terminal, and the City Hall Information Booth. Fast Passes are available during the first week of each month at all Safeway grocery stores, numerous small shops, and corner groceries. One-time tickets can be purchased upon boarding, with exact change (you can use $1 bills).

Cable car fares are $2 per ride for adults and children, with no transfers allowed. Tickets can be purchased at self-service machines at all major cable car stops. Cable cars and electric buses are not wheelchair accessible.

For more detailed Muni information, call 415-673-MUNI or consult the large Muni maps in most bus shelters. Official Muni route maps can be found at most bookstores and newsstands for $1.50, or in the San Francisco Yellow Pages.

BARTing It

Bay Area Rapid Transit (415-788- BART) affectionately known as BART, is the 71-mile, high-speed rail network that runs under Market Street, connecting the City with the East Bay and Daly City. BART makes six San Francisco stops (25th Street, 16th Street, Civic Center, Powell, Montgomery, Embarcadero) on four separate lines: Richmond/Fremont, Concord/Daly City, Fremont/Daly City, and Richmond/Daly City. The system is entirely automated: machines dispense magnetic-strip tickets valued at anywhere from 80 cents to $40, and these tickets are read by computers at the turnstiles when you enter and exit a BART station. A computer calculates your fare and automatically subtracts the amount from your ticket.

BART trains run approximately every 15 or 20 minutes Monday through Friday 4 a.m. to midnight, Saturday 6 a.m to midnight, and Sunday 8 a.m. to midnight. Fares range from 80 cents for a one-stop jump to $3.25 from Daly City to Fremont; discount tickets are available for senior citizens and children 5 to 12. Children under 5 ride free. BART is wheelchair accessible.

Taxi! Taxi!

Order a cab by phone whenever possible (hotel and restaurant staffs will usually call for you), or make your way to Van Ness Avenue, Broadway, Market or California streets, where you may have the good fortune to find one. Taxi meters start at $1.70; add 30 cents for each additional sixth of a mile. Drivers should be tipped about 15 percent. The fare from Market Street to Fisherman's Wharf is about $9. Yellow Cab (415-626-2345), Veteran's Cab (415-552-1300) and Luxor Cab Co. (415-282-4141) are equally reliable, which isn't saying much in this cab-hungry city. Fares for cab trips fifteen miles or more-that is, to or from SFO-are half again higher.

Traveling Out of the City

CalTrain (800-660-4287) provides rail service from the City to the Peninsula and San Jose. Trains depart from the CalTrain station at 4th and Townsend streets at 20-minute intervals during peak hours, otherwise at 1-hour intervals. A one-way fare, San Francisco to San Jose, is $4.50.

Greyhound Bus Lines (415-495-1575 or 800-231-2222) has buses running from the Transbay Terminal (1st & Mission streets) to many cities around the country. Value-priced fares have, in recent years, once made this a viable means of transportation.

If you're Peninsula-bound, **SamTrans** (800-660-4287 or 650-508-6200) municipal buses numbered 7B and 7F serve San Mateo County, including the San Francisco Airport

(3B) and Palo Alto. Buses depart San Francisco from the Transbay Terminal at First and Mission streets, and run from the airport to the Daly City BART station every 30 minutes.

In Marin county, **Golden Gate Transit** (415-923-2000) buses connect San Francisco to Marin County and Sonoma by way of the Golden Gate Bridge. Buses stop in the City on Lombard Street, Van Ness Avenue and Geary Street, in the Financial District, and at the Transbay Terminal. The one-way fare between San Francisco and San Rafael is $2.50, to Sonoma is $4.50.

BY SEA

The **Alameda-Oakland Ferry** (510-522-3300) provides daily commuter and excursion service between Alameda, Oakland and San Francisco with departures from **Pier 39** and the **S.F. Ferry Building** at the foot of Market Street. **Golden Gate Ferries** (415-923-2000) leave daily for Sausalito and Larkspur from the Ferry Building. The **Blue and Gold Fleet** (415-773-1188) offers ferry service to Sausalito, Tiburon, Vallejo, Alcatraz and Angel Island; the **Red & White Fleet** (415-447-0591) provides commuter service to Point Richmond in the East Bay. For a listing of pleasure cruises and tourists' boat tours, see the "Sightseeing" chapter.

VITAL NEEDS

VISITORS INFORMATION

The **San Francisco Visitor Information Center**, (900 Market St., lower level of Hallidie Plaza at Powell and Market Sts.) has multi-lingual assistants that can answer virtually any question. **The San Francisco Convention and Visitors Bureau** hotline (415-391-2000) provides recorded information about events in the city. The SFCVB can also be accessed online at http://www.sfvisitor.org; it offers fax-back service at 800-220-5747.

LATE NIGHT

Automotive Assistance

Golden Gate Towing Co. (355 Barneveld St., 415-826-8866) provides towing services 24 hours.

Currency Exchange

Thomas Cook Currency Services (International Terminal, Departure Level, San Francisco International Airport, 800-287-7362), is open from 7 a.m. to 11 p.m.

Film Processing

Photo Motion, with three locations at 514 Frederick St., 415-682-3982; 350 Bay St., 415-398-6088; and 1850 Fillmore St., 415-346-1850, offers excellent same-day service and a 24-hour drop box.

Pharmacy

Walgreen Drugstore (Divisadero & Lombard Sts., 415-931-6417; 498 Castro St., 415-826-8533) fills prescriptions 24 hours.

Photocopy/Fax

Kinko's Copies is open 24 hours, 7 days per week, at both 1967 Market St., 415-252-0864 and 25 Stanyan St., 415-750-1193.

Pickup & Delivery

It's not a universally known fact, but most cab drivers will act as errand runners for you after normal courier services (see below) have closed for the day. You'll pay what's on the meter plus a flat service fee, negotiated with the cabby.

Phoning in S.F.

All telephone numbers in San Francisco and Marin counties are preceded by the 415 area code. The area code for Alameda and Contra Costa counties is 510; for outlying part of East Bay, dial 925. For Peninsula phone numbers, the area code is now 650. The Wine Country (Napa, Sonoma and Mendocino counties) area code is 707; in Silicon Valley it's 408. For telephone information within your area code, dial 411, and for information in another area code, dial 1-area code-555-1212. A local pay phone call of any duration is a minimum of 35 cents.

EMERGENCY NUMBERS

Police/Ambulance/Fire-911
Poison Control Center-800-876-4766
Emergency Road Service-415-565-2012
Dental Referral-415-421-1435
Doctor Referral-415-776-7364
Suicide Prevention-415-781-0500
Alcoholics Anonymous-415-621-1326
Narcotics Anonymous-415-621-8600
AIDS-HIV Hotline-800-367-2437

Other Useful Numbers

Courier Services:
Emery Worldwide-800-443-6379
Federal Express-800-463-3339

Credit Cards, Lost or Stolen:
American Express-800-528-2121
Carte Blanche-800-234-6377
Diners Club-800-234-6377
Discover Card-800-347-2683
MasterCard-800-826-2181
Visa-800-336-8472

Travelers Checks, Lost or Stolen:
American Express-800-221-7282
Citicorp-800-645-6556
Visa-800-227-6811

Foreign Currency Exchange:
Bank of America-415-622-2451
Thomas Cook-800-287-7362

International Currency Transfers:
Thomas Cook-800-287-7362
Western Union-800-325-4176

Automatic Teller Information:
Cirrus Network-800-424-7787
Diners Club-800-248-4286
Plus System-800-843-7587

MISCELLANEOUS:

Better Business Bureau-415-243-9999
Chamber of Commerce-415-392-4511
City Hall-415-554-4000
Convention & Visitors Bureau-415-391-2000
District Attorney Consumer Protection Unit-415-553-1814
Golden Gate National Recreation Area 415-556-0560
Highway Conditions-415-557-3755
Office of the Mayor, S.F-415-554-6141
Passport Information-415-538-2700
Postal Information-800-276-9850
S.F. Bar Association Lawyer Referral-415-989-1616
S.F. Dept. of Parks and Recreation-415-831-2700
Senior Citizens-415-626-1033
Time of Day-415-767-8900
Weather-510-562-8573
Western Union-800-325-6000

MEDIA

NEWSPAPERS

Both of the City's daily papers, the ***San Francisco Chronicle*** (morning, 50 cents) and the ***San Francisco Examiner*** (afternoon, 25 cents) are available from newsstands and boxes all over town. Locals tend to be partisans of one or the other. The papers are combined in a single, large Sunday edition that includes news, features and **Datebook**, (referred to as the **Pink Section**) which outlines cultural, theatrical and culinary events for the week.

The ***San Francisco Bay Guardian*** and ***SF Weekly*** are distributed free on Wednesdays at shops, cafés and in street boxes all over the City. Both are undeniably liberal, providing useful commentary on city politics and culture as well as information about Bay Area happenings.

In the East Bay, the is widely available, and many smaller communities have their own local papers. On the Peninsula, The Times in San Mateo and the ***Mercury News*** in San Jose are large-circulation dailies. In Marin, locals look to the ***Independent Journal*** for regional news.

MAGAZINES

There are myriad weekly, monthly, and quarterly publications that cover life in the Bay Area. Many serve individual ethnic groups and special interest groups. For general coverage of what there is to do and see in San Francisco, try ***San Francisco Focus***.

LIBRARIES

The **San Francisco Public Library**'s recently opened main branch (415-557-4400) is located on Larkin and Grove Sts. in the Civic Center area. It houses 1.2 million volumes, a number of special and rare collections, and the San Francisco Historic Room. There are 26 neighborhood branches throughout the city; see the phone book for a complete listing. The **UC Berkeley Library** (510-643-9999) is one of the best in the western U.S. The general public is welcome to visit, but the stacks are closed.

TV & RADIO

The main San Francisco national TV network affiliates are channel 2 **KTVU** (FOX), channel 4 **KRON** (NBC), channel 5 **KPIX** (CBS), channel 7 **KGO** (ABC), and channel 9 **KQED** (PBS). Cable television is widely available in homes and hotels. Here's a smattering of Bay Area radio:

88.5 FM KQED—News and information/NPR
91.7 FM KALW—News and information/NPR
94.9 FM KYLD—Urban Top 40
98.5 FM KOME—Alternative rock
100.9 FM KKHI—Classical
104.5 FM KFOG—Soft rock
105.3 FM KITS—Alternative
106.1 FM KMEL—Hip hop, dance music.
610 AM KFRC—Sports and oldies
740 AM KCBS—News, sports, weather

WEB SITES

Check out our Gayot/GaultMillau information on www.perrier.com, www.digitalcity.com, www.gayot.com and www.thefoodpaper.com

CHURCHES & SYNAGOGUES

These are some of the city's better-known places of worship; all of them welcome visitors.

Calvary Presbyterian, 2515 Fillmore St., Pacific Heights, 415-346-3832

Congregation Emanuel (Jewish, Reform Movement), 2 Lake St., Presidio Heights, 415-751-2535

First Congregational Church, 432 Mason St., Downtown, 415-392-7461

Glide Memorial Church (Methodist), 330 Ellis St., Downtown, 415-771-6300

Grace Cathedral (Episcopal), 1051 Taylor St., Nob Hill, 415-749-6310

Old Saint Mary's Church (Roman Catholic), 660 California St., Chinatown, 415-288-3800

Saint Mary's Cathedral (Roman Catholic), 1111 Gough St., Western Addition, 415-567-2020

St. Paulus Lutheran Church, 950 Gough St., Western Addition, 415-673-8088

Vineyard Christian Fellowship (Charismatic), 1098 Harrison St., South of Market, 415-558-9900

Zen Center (Buddhist), 300 Page St., Western Addition, 415-863-3136

CALENDAR OF EVENTS

For up-to-date information on these and other events, call the **San Francisco Visitors' Information Bureau** at 415-391-2000.

JANUARY

- **Martin Luther King, Jr. Celebrations**, various venues, 415-771-6300.
- **Tet Festival**, Vietnamese New Year in the Tenderloin, 415-885-2743.
- **San Francisco Ballet performances** (through mid-May), War Memorial Opera House, 301 Van Ness Ave., Civic Center, 415-865-2000.
- **San Francisco Symphony** (runs year-round), Davies Symphony Hall, Grove St. and Van Ness Ave., Civic Center, 415-552-8000.

FEBRUARY

- **Chinese New Year Celebration and Parade**, Chinatown, 415-982-3000. Colorful, firecracker-punctuated parade through Chinatown's streets.
- **San Francisco Tribal, Folk and Textile Art Show**, Fort Mason, 310-455-2886. Over 100 dealers sell North American pottery, baskets, textiles and jewelry.
- **Pacific Orchid Exposition**, Fort Mason Center, 415-546-9608. The festival is nearly 50 years old.

MARCH

- **St. Patrick's Day Celebration**, 415-661-2700. A festive parade, ceremonies and parties are held on the Sunday closest to St. Patrick's Day (Mar. 17).
- **The Bay Area Music Awards** (BAMmies) are held at the Civic Auditorium, 99 Grove St., Civic Center, 415-970-4000, in recognition of the wealth of musical talent in the Bay Area.
- **Tulipmania**, Pier 39, 415-981-7437, is a free tour of the City's largest tulip beds.
- **Mostly Mozart Festival** (last weekend of March), Davies Symphony Hall, Civic Center and Herbst Theater, Civic Center, 415-552-8000.

APRIL

- **Cherry Blossom Festival**, Japantown, 415-563-2313. Parades, martial arts performances and tea ceremonies.
- **Baseball season opens**. San Francisco Giants, 3Com Park, 415-467-8000; Oakland Athletics, Oakland Coliseum, 510-430-8020.
- **Britain Meets the Bay**, various locations, 415-274-0373. Sporting events, symposia mark U.S.-Britain relations.
- **San Francisco International Film Festival**, held in various venues, 415-931-FILM.
- **Yachting Season** opens with the Annual Boat Parade, first day of daylight saving time, San Francisco Bay, 415-771-9500.

MAY

- **Mural Awareness Month**. Learn more about the city's favorite public art medium. 415-285-2287.
- **Black & White Ball**, Civic Center, 415-864-6000. This gala ball, held every odd-numbered year, benefits the San Francisco Symphony. Tickets $150.
- **Cinco de Mayo Celebration**, Mission District, 415-826-1401. Held the first weekend in May.
- **Bay to Breakers Race**, 415-808-5000, ext. 2222. The famous 7.5-mile foot race draws more than 100,000 runners to the city's streets.

JUNE

- **Lesbian and Gay Pride Month**: SF International Lesbian and Gay Film Festival, Castro Theater and other venues, 415-703-8650; Lesbian-Gay Parade, from Market St. to the Civic Center, 415-864-3733.
- **Ethnic Dance Festival**, Palace of Fine Arts Theater, 415-474-3914. Dancers from around the world perform.
- **Carnaval**, Mission & 24th Sts., Mission District, 415-826-1401. Mardi-Gras-style festival with dancing and parades.
- **Stern Grove Midsummer Music Festival**, Sigmund Stern Memorial Grove, 19th Ave. and Sloat Blvd., 415-252-6252. This long-running music celebration showcases classical artists and also features jazz and pop. Through August.
- **San Francisco Symphony Beethoven Festival**, Davies Symphony Hall, 201 Van Ness Ave., Civic Center and Herbst Theater, 401 Van Ness Ave., Civic Center; 415-552-8000.

JULY

- **Midsummer Mozart Festival**, Davies Symphony Hall, Civic Center and Herbst Theater, Civic Center; 415-552-8000.
- **Jewish Film Festival**, U.C. Berkeley Theater, Castro, and other Bay Area theaters, 510-548-0556. The largest Jewish film festival in the world.
- **Blues and Art on the Bay**, Embarcadero between Folsom and Beale, 415-346-4446. A three-day celebration of live blues music.
- **Fourth of July Celebration** (July 4), Crissy Field, Presidio waterfront. Festivities go on all day; fireworks start at 9 p.m.
- **San Francisco Marathon**, San Francisco, 800-722-3466. Thousands complete a 26-mile route around the city.
- **San Francisco Symphony Pops** season, Davies Symphony Hall, 415-552-8000.

AUGUST

- **Shakespeare in the Park**, Liberty Meadow, Golden Gate Park, 415-422-6041. This reputable company performs one play, through September, for free.
- **Nihonmachi Street Fair**, Japantown, 415-771-9861. Merchants and food vendors line Japantown's streets.
- **San Francisco 49ers** season opens, 3Com Park, 415-468-2249.
- **American Crafts Council Fair**, Fort Mason, 415-896-5060. Largest juried craft fair on the west coast.
- **Absolut à la Carte**, à la Park, Golden Gate Park, 415-458-1988. An al fresco delight featuring more than 50 restaurants, 40 wineries, plus guest chefs and live entertainment.

SEPTEMBER

- **San Francisco Opera** season (through mid-Dec.), War Memorial Opera House, Civic Center, 415-864-3330.
- **Renaissance Pleasure Faire** (through September), Blackpoint Forest, Novato, 909-880-6211. Food, crafts, entertainment, clothing, and whimsy of the fifteenth and sixteenth centuries.

- **Festival de las Americas**, Mission District, 826-1401. Latin American food festival serves up plenty of dancing and live entertainment as well.
- **San Francisco Blues Festival**, Justin Herman Plaza and Fort Mason, 415-979-5588. A weekend festival that showcases the best blues talent in the country.
- **Folsom Street Fair**, Folsom between 8th and 11th Sts., 415-861-3247. Thousands, clad mostly in leather, attend this unique event.

OCTOBER

- **Fleet Week**, Pier 32-45, Fisherman's Wharf, 415-705-5500. The U.S. Navy flexes its air and sea muscle, and the Blue Angels fly overhead.
- **Columbus Day Celebration**, North Beach and Aquatic Park. The City's Italian heritage is celebrated with a parade, bocce ball and more.
- **International Street Performers Festival**, Pier 39, Fisherman's Wharf, 415-705-5500.
- **San Francisco Jazz Festival**, various venues, 800-627-5277. Features international and local artists.
- **Halloween Night** (Oct. 31), Castro, Civic Center, and Embarcadero. The gay community-and plenty of straight friends-parade in wild costumes.

NOVEMBER

- **Dia de los Muertos** (Nov. 1), Mission District, 415-826-8009. Traditional celebration of the Mexican Day of the Dead.
- **San Francisco International Auto Show**, Moscone Center, 3rd & Howard Sts., South of Market, 415-673-2016. Car makers show off new models and future prototypes.
- **Run to the Far Side**, Golden Gate Park, 415-564-0532. 10K and 5K footraces begin and end at the California Academy of Sciences.

DECEMBER

- **A Night in Old Vienna**, Davies Hall, Civic Center, 415-552-8000. A New Year's Eve gala presented by the San Francisco Symphony.
- **New Pickle Circus**, Cowell Theater, Fort Mason, 415-441-3687. A small, local circus with panache.
- **The Nutcracker**, San Francisco Ballet, War Memorial Opera House, 301 Van Ness Ave., Civic Center, 415-865-2000. The Christmas ballet classic.
- **A Christmas Carol**, American Conservatory Theatre (A.C.T.), Geary Theater, 415 Geary St., Union Square, 415-864-3200. A.C.T.'s acclaimed adaptation of Dickens' beloved holiday tale.
- **New Year's Eve Extravaganza**, Cow Palace, Geneva Ave., and Santos St., South City, 415-469-6000. Pop musicians rock in the new year.

Marin County

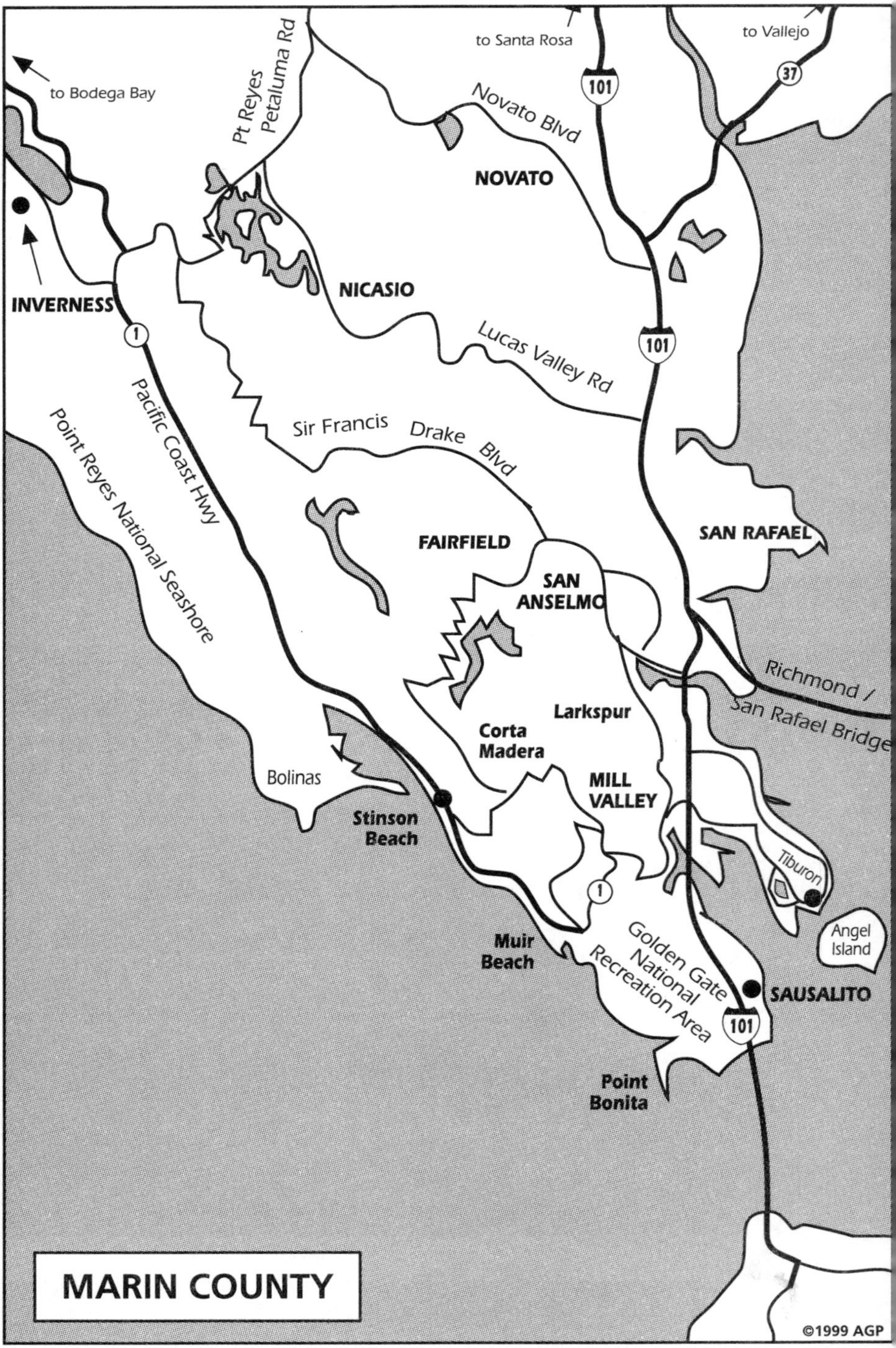

to Bodega Bay
Pt Reyes Petaluma Rd
to Santa Rosa
to Vallejo
101
37
Novato Blvd
NOVATO
INVERNESS
NICASIO
1
101
Lucas Valley Rd
Sir Francis Drake Blvd
Pacific Coast Hwy
Point Reyes National Seashore
FAIRFIELD
SAN RAFAEL
SAN ANSELMO
Richmond / San Rafael Bridge
Larkspur
Corta Madera
Bolinas
MILL VALLEY
Stinson Beach
Tiburon
1
Angel Island
Muir Beach
Golden Gate National Recreation Area
SAUSALITO
101
Point Bonita
MARIN COUNTY
©1999 AGP

RAINBOWS, REDWOODS & ARUGULA

For years, Marin County had a reputation as a haven for over-the-hill hippies and sun-tanned yuppies weaned on designer lettuce. And though it's true that you'll find more Birkenstocks and Volvos here than anywhere in the country, you'll also find real beauty and substance. Marin is home to some of the most charming communities, gorgeous scenery in Northern California-many would say in all of the state-and to their credit, most Marin towns have shown a deep commitment to preserving and protecting nature's bounty from the ravages of progress. **The Golden Gate National Recreation Area** controls thousands and thousands of acres here; almost every neighborhood in every township has designated open space and striated with hiking trails; vistas from Sausalito to Novato are uniformly striking.

For all its rusticity, however, Marin offers a tremendous amount of style. Here you'll find unusual, **independent shops** of all kinds: **bookstores, art and craft galleries, furniture, clothing** and **antique boutiques**-and, of course, a multitude of amazing **restaurants**. In addition to upscale dining rooms such as **The Lark Creek Inn**, **The Left Bank**, and **Buckeye Roadhouse**, the county boasts a wealth of good eating, at small, inexpensive ethnic restaurants. And since the filmmaking community has discovered Marin as well, you might run into Star Wars director George Lucas or actors such as Robin Wright or Sean Penn in any of Marin's unpretentious eateries.

DINING

A. G. Ferrari Foods

DELI ¢
107 CORTE MADERA TOWN CENTER
CORTE MADERA 94925
415-927-4347
Lunch & Dinner daily

This kitschy, refreshing deli is the Marin link in a mini-chain of gourmet food shops. A central kitchen makes seasonal salads, pastas, sauces, frittati soups, tortes and sandwiches on fresh baked foccacia. Try a deep-fried eggplant sandwich (two slices of the veggie holding prosciutto and mozzarella), panini sandwiches, and house-made tiramisu.

Avenue Grill

AMERICAN 13/20
44 E. BLITHEDALE AVE.
MILL VALLEY 94941
415-388-6003
Dinner nightly

Avenue Grill is one of the new breed of restaurants that tries to put the fun back into fundamental American food. When its cooks are on, they can turn out anything from delicious meatloaf with garlic mashed potatoes to coconut-crusted, deep-fried shrimp. The restaurant isn't always consistent, however, mainly when it tries too hard to be wackily inventive, but eclecticism is part of its charm. Nightly specials range from Spanish paella to Caribbean cuisine to Jewish comfort food. There's also a good selection of wines by the glass.

Azteca

MEXICAN 12/20

555 E. FRANCISCO BLVD. #20
SAN RAFAEL 94901
415-485-5682
Breakfast Sat.-Sun., Lunch & Dinner daily, $

The fiery salsa at this starkly furnished storefront in a shopping center in San Rafael's heavily Hispanic Canal District could take the paint off your car, but it's so good you can't stop eating it. Also terrific is queso fundido (with big chunks of oily chorizo), savory goat stew and a stellar chicken with a mole sauce-one of the few we've run across that doesn't taste smothered in canned chocolate.

Bolero

SPANISH 13/20

125 E. SIR FRANCIS DRAKE BLVD.
LARKSPUR 94939
415-925-9392
Lunch & Dinner daily, $$

Formerly a brick factory and an upscale French restaurant, this Spanish eatery is a place to take a hot date when you want to impress and don't want to spend a lot of money. Dishes sing with garlic and fresh herbs; tapas are scrumptious, including shrimp in garlic sauce, stuffed red peppers in a seafood sauce, grilled chicken and beef skewers and garlic soup. Paella for two is rife with seafood and meats in fragrant saffron rice and dotted with peas and red peppers. Desserts are uninspired but tasty; live Spanish music and flamenco dancing happens on weekend nights.

Bubba's Diner

AMERICAN 12/20

566 SAN ANSELMO AVE.
SAN ANSELMO 94960
415-459-6862
Breakfast & Lunch Wed.-Mon., Dinner nightly, $$

Chef/owner Steve Simmons has created one of the hippest little restaurants in the Bay Area. Classic, '50s-style dishes like chicken pot pie, meat loaf, fried catfish and barbecued ribs are made from scratch-even the pickles are house-made. Portions are huge. Great desserts, including butterscotch banana cream pie or hot fudge sundaes, and extraordinary corned beef hash at breakfast.

Buckeye Roadhouse

AMERICAN 14/20

15 SHORELINE HWY.
MILL VALLEY 94941
415-331-2600
Lunch & Dinner daily, Brunch Sun., $$

When it opened its doors nearly ten years ago, this place instantly became one of the most popular in Marin, its clubby bar and dining room jammed at all hours with assorted folks who love chef/owner Cindy Pawlcyn's brand of sophisticated yet down-home American cooking. We've visited repeatedly and have yet to have a bad dish here: among our favorites are some of the world's greatest onion strings and french fries. Other irresistibles include oysters Bingo (a playful take on oysters Rockefeller), savory barbecued baby back ribs, and liver and onions so good even your kids will eat it. What else could you have for dessert here except strawberry shortcake or s'more pie?

Cactus Café

CALIFORNIAN/MEXICAN 11/20

393 MILLER AVE.
MILL VALLEY 94941
415-388-8226
Lunch & Dinner daily, $

This funky little Mill Valley eatery next door to the Marin Theatre Company blends

California freshness with Mexican flavors and a little local vegetarianism for good measure. Flour tortillas are filled with goat and ricotta cheeses, spinach and caramelized onion, topped with guacamole, salsa and mesclun; black bean tostadas are stuffed with sautéed wild mushrooms and a wealth of baby greens. Carnivores will find fresh Cal-Mex seafood tacos.

The Caprice

CALIFORNIAN 13/20
2000 PARADISE DR.
TIBURON 94921
415-435-3400
Dinner nightly, $$$$

For years, The Caprice was the Mercedes Benz of Marin restaurants-prestigious, upscale and rather stern. The restaurant's old-fashioned menu, stiffly formal service and bayside location made it a favorite of conservative diners and the romantically inclined, who could take in the terrific view of the waterfront while their waiter flambéed cherries jubilee beside the table. But the restaurant changed ownership in January 1996 and became more of a Porsche. Still a special-occasion destination, the Caprice's decor has been refurbished. The room is much lighter and brighter, and the menu now changes regularly, featuring fresh fish dishes such as seared sea scallops, shellfish paella, or a seafood sampler in a bamboo steamer basket. Caprice also serves a wide range of meats-duck breast, rabbit, filet mignon, rack of lamb, prepared in various ways.

Chai of Larkspur

TEA HOUSE ¢
25 WARD ST.
LARKSPUR 94939
415-945-7161
Morning & Afternoon Tea daily, Evening dessert & wine, Fri.-Sat.

Marin's only true British-style tea house sports an exquisite interior of deep green and flower-cushioned wicker chairs, lined with antique tea pots. Several different 'set' teas with sweet and savory dainties are served on three-tiered plates. Entertainment includes a concert harpist on Sundays, blues and jazz the fourth Saturday evening of every month, adult storytelling, teas for kids, lectures and more. Chai's backyard patio is an extremely pleasant place in nice weather.

Comforts

CALIFORNIAN ¢
335 SAN ANSELMO AVE.
SAN ANSELMO 94960
415-454-9840
Breakfast & Lunch daily, To-go until 7:30 p.m.

Comforts' stylish, sponge-painted walls offer contemporary style: look through sliding glass doors onto the outdoor patio, or through big, open windows onto downtown San Anselmo. The breakfast and lunch menu changes every Tuesday; take-out selections vary all the time. You might find such dishes as chicken satay, composed salads notable for their size and freshness; and a wide range of pastas. There's also a good selection of reasonably priced wines and local beers.

Frantoio Ristorante

ITALIAN 12/20
152 SHORELINE HWY
MILL VALLEY 94941
415-289-5777
Lunch Mon.-Sat., Dinner nightly, $$

One of Marin's busier Italian eateries, Frantoio is a dramatic, theatrical space with a working olive press visible behind a tall glass window. (The restaurant makes and serves its own olive oil.) Two heated patios make for pleasant if austere outdoor dining from a large, seasonal menu. Toothsome fried calamari come with potato tartar and spicy tomato sauces; pizzas offer crackling-crisp crusts with toppings such as portobello mushrooms or baby artichokes and free-range chicken. Something for everyone.

Gira Polli

ROAST CHICKEN ¢
590 E. BLITHEDALE AVE.
MILL VALLEY 94941
415-383-6040
Dinner nightly

This smart-looking Mill Valley restaurant specializes in roasted chicken. Fresh Petaluma birds are stuffed with lemons and oranges, sprinkled with herbs, cooked over an almond-wood fire on an Italian-made rotisserie and served with potatoes, veggies and soup or salad. There are also tasty pastas and excellent spit-roasted lamb.

Guaymas

MEXICAN 12/20
5 MAIN ST.
TIBURON 94920
415-435-6300
Lunch & Dinner daily, $$

This restaurant's sleek decor, thriving bar scene and drop-dead waterfront location are as much a part of its appeal as the food. As at most suburban Mexican eateries, seasonings here are applied with a timid hand. The salsas, however, deliver real flavor-you'll want to apply them liberally to goose some life into many of the dishes. Among our favorite menu items are sopas and chalupas. Top entrées include roasted duck with pumpkin seed sauce, fat prawns cooked on rock salt and served with a piquant sauce of lime juice, jalapeños and cilantro, and rich, lush carnitas (chunks of fork-tender pork). Try a terrific coconut flan-one of the best of its type-for dessert.

Il Fornaio

ITALIAN 13/20
223 CORTE MADERA TOWN CENTER
CORTE MADERA 94925
415-927-4400
Lunch & Dinner daily, $$

Thanks to a recent remodel, this popular Italian trattoria now offers two fireplaces-one to amuse diners on the outdoor patio, and one inside. But the real heat comes from the creative menu. Two weeks out of every month they do regional specials, featuring an area of Italy. Crisp, juicy rotisserie chicken from the wood-burning oven is always good; tagliata (sirloin steak grilled, sliced, and served with balsamic vinegar sauce); spaghettini bolognese; capellini al pomodoro; pizzas, house Caesar salad-all work favorably upon your stomach. The kitchen will provide a roasted vegetable platter with triangles of grilled polenta upon request. Pastries and coffee are served for breakfast daily.

India Village

INDIAN 12/20
555 FRANCISCO BLVD.
SAN RAFAEL 94901
415-456-2411
Lunch Mon.-Sat., Dinner nightly, $

Expertly prepared tandoori dishes include chicken tikka masala, tandoori mixed grill (lamb, prawns and white and dark meat chicken), special vegetarian thali, and minced lamb. Even prawns emerge juicy and properly cooked. Samosas are first-rate, too, as are most vegetarian dishes; seasonings haven't been blanded down to avoid offending Western palates. Service can be slow and a bit brusque.

Insalata's Restaurant

MEDITERRANEAN 14/20
120 SIR FRANCIS DRAKE BLVD.
SAN ANSELMO 94960
415-457-7700
Lunch Mon.-Sat, Dinner nightly, Brunch Sun., $$

Chef Heidi Insalata Krahling has become one of Marin's favorite culinary personalities, especially since she opened this restaurant a couple of years ago. The menu offers some of the county's most delicious dishes: Fattoush salad is a Syrian concoction of hearts of romaine, crunchy pita triangles, feta cheese, Del Cabo tomatoes and Kalamata olives in a cilantro-lemon-mint vinaigrette; pan-roasted salmon appears with Venetian pinenut relish, fennel, spinach, all piled atop a crispy saffron risotto cake. Chive fettucine with Gulf prawns, asparagus, sherry and almonds is a winner, too. The décor is modern yet down-to-earth, and with desserts like "Pigs in Mud" (a pig-shaped shortbread cookie plunked in a bowl of chocolate pudding), it's a great place for kids.

Jennie Low's

CHINESE 11/20
38 MILLER AVE.
MILL VALLEY 94941
415-388-8868
Lunch Mon.-Sat., Dinner nightly, $

Cooking instructor, cookbook author and restaurateur Jennie Low has built two wildly successful Chinese restaurants with coolly modern interiors (done in purple, Low's lucky color), exhibition kitchens, a prohibition on MSG, a staff that speaks perfect English and very reasonable prices. You won't find any Chinese culinary exotica here, only dishes that have become Chinese standards everywhere, prepared with skill and top-quality ingredients. **Also in Novato (120 Vintage Way, 415-892-8838).**

Jhan Thong

THAI ¢
5835 NORTHGATE MALL
SAN RAFAEL 94901
415-499-3501
Lunch & Dinner daily, $

Amid the burgers, hot dogs and ersatz Mexican food served up at the local shopping mall, Jhan Thong turns out pretty good food. Best bets are the grilled and deep-fried dishes, all of which are cooked to order. Excellent roast duck, phad Thai (noodles), and spicy eggplant can be good, as can salads and stews.

Joe's Taco Lounge & Salsaria

MEXICAN ¢
382 MILLER AVE.
MILL VALLEY 94941
415-383-8164
Lunch & Dinner daily

Painted in vibrant colors and decorated with ceramic Madonnas, Joe's offers good, cheap Mexican peasant food with a California accent. Enjoy tacos, burritos, enchiladas, salads and even a burger. Dishes come conservatively seasoned and require plenty of Joe's salsas to give them some zip.

The Lark Creek Inn

AMERICAN/
CALIFORNIAN 15/20
234 MAGNOLIA AVE.
LARKSPUR 94939
415-924-7766
Lunch Mon.-Fri., Dinner nightly, Brunch Sun., $$$

Bradley Ogden's country-elegant Larkspur restaurant serves the kind of hearty food Mom might serve-if Mom were a trained chef whose talent and palate were matched by her growing national celebrity. The yellow-and-white wood-framed building is tucked away in a grove of redwood trees; inside furnishings are plain and simple. A lushly landscaped patio makes one of the most romantic outdoor dining spots in Marin. Much of the food served here comes off the oak-fired grill/oven-whether pork chops, flavorful Niman-Schell steaks, or exquisitely fresh fish, you can count on its being perfectly cooked and imaginatively presented. The kitchen also does a terrific job with slow-cooked dishes such as braised oxtails, pot roast and lamb or veal shanks. We've enjoyed crisply-fried softshell crabs, lush and savory risotti and the best hamburger north of the Golden Gate Bridge. Brunch is special, too. Egg dishes, french toast, homemade maple-scented jam-filled beignets and savory hash are served in ample portions and complemented nicely by a housemade Ramos gin fizz or mimosa. Though pricey, the wine list here is exclusively American and very well chosen.

Left Bank

COUNTRY FRENCH 14/20
507 MAGNOLIA AVE.
LARKSPUR 94939
415-927-3331
Lunch & Dinner daily, Brunch Sun., $$

Chef Roland Passot, who owns elegant La Folie in San Francisco, opened this family-style bistro in Larkspur that is one of Marin's most delightful places to eat. From the thick beef burger with Parisian-style fries to the mussels in wine and garlic or bouillabaisse, this restaurant is a winner. The large menu, with wide range of appetizers, entrées, and daily specials, is hard to choose from. Light eaters can opt for a daily-changing salad with warm entrée, or a great lamb sandwich with tapenade and roasted red peppers. A superb kids menu, too.

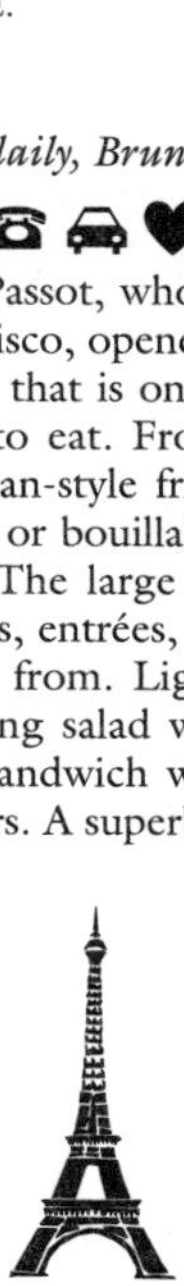

Mikayla Restaurant at Casa Madrona

CALIFORNIA CUISINE 14/20
801 BRIDGEWAY BLVD.
SAUSALITO 94965
415-331-5888
Dinner nightly, Brunch Sun., $$$

As we write this, chef David Button has taken over what has become one of the most popular-and elegant-kitchens in Marin. Button's new menu will emphasize strong, clear flavors, natural reductions of sauces, herbal essences, and seasonal local produce. Even without details, we can rave about Mikayla for its spectacular views, and casually dramatic atmosphere, a space designed by Laurel Burch (of jewelry and handbag fame). Sunday brunch in this room is one of the most romantic around.

Piazza D'Angelo

ITALIAN 14/20
22 MILLER AVE.
MILL VALLEY 94941
415-388-2000
Lunch & Dinner daily, $$

Paolo and Dominic Petrone spent nearly $1 million remodeling their downtown Mill Valley restaurant, transforming it into a beautiful, airy Cal-Ital trattoria that's one of Mill Valley's hottest hangouts. The food is mostly terrific: stick with familiar Italian dishes-vitello tonnato, calamari fritti, veal saltimbocca and the like. Don't miss a superb roasted half chicken, grilled portobello mushroom appetizer, risotto or outstanding crème brûlée for dessert.

The Rice Table

INDONESIAN 12/20
1617 4TH ST.
SAN RAFAEL 94901
415-456-1808
Dinner Wed.-Sun.

The specialty at this small, evocative Indonesian restaurant is rijstaffel (rice table), a dozen or so small dishes that constitute an exotic form of grazing. The sambals, or sauces-creamy peanut, tart cilantro, spicy chile-are very good, as are Indonesian-style egg rolls and prawns cooked in tangy butter-tamarind sauce. Salads here are fresh and clean-tasting; long-simmered curries are savory and flavorful.

Ristorante Fabrizio

ITALIAN 13/20
455 MAGNOLIA AVE.
LARKSPUR 94939
415-924-3332
Lunch Mon.-Fri., Dinner nightly, $$

A few years ago, Fabrizio Martinelli remodeled what used to be claustrophobic, unappealing dining room (albeit a popular one) into an airy Cal-Ital trattoria. The menu has been updated too, but there's been no change in the quality of the food: Fabrizio's still serves some of the county's best Italian cuisine. Try the crisply fried calamari or the simple, perfect carpaccio appetizers. Pasta and seafood, alone or in combination, are among the best bets here. The house's linguine tutto mare is stellar.

Royal Thai

THAI 12/20
610 THIRD ST.
SAN RAFAEL 94901
415-485-1074
Lunch Mon.-Fri., Dinner nightly, $

Royal Thai has earned a reputation as one of the North Bay's best Thai restaurants, a distinction that neither time nor competition has mitigated. Their superb hot and sour prawn soup has marvelous restorative powers; Thai crêpe is among the best we've eaten; a sneakily incendiary beef salad is indeed-as the menu promises-curiously refreshing. A caveat: dishes labeled 'hot' can set your tongue afire.

Station House Café

CALIFORNIA 12/20
11180 STATE ROUTE 1
PT. REYES 94956
415-663-1515
Breakfast, Lunch & Dinner daily, $$

No trip to Point Reyes would be complete without a stop at this charming restaurant to slurp fresh oysters and steamed Manila clams and lift a couple of beers before returning to civilization. Oysters come from the nearby Johnson's Oyster Farm and are as plump and briny as you could desire: they're as good breaded and deep fried or barbecued and slathered with pesto as they are raw on the half-shell. Fresh fish, steaks, a basket of puffy popovers-all are well executed. Don't miss butterscotch pudding, one of the best ever, topped with organic whipped cream from the Straus Family organic dairy.

Stinson Beach Grill

CALIFORNIA CUISINE 10/20
3465 STATE ROUTE 1 (SHORELINE HWY.)
STINSON BEACH 94970
415-868-2002
Lunch & Dinner daily, Brunch Sat.-Sun., $

If there's a better way to dine at the beach than to sit out on the Grill's wood-planked patio, watching the sunset while sipping a glass of Chardonnay, we have yet to discover it. There's a heated deck, full bar, tons of oysters both raw and cooked on a menu that features everything from pastas and sandwiches to grilled steaks and a variety of fresh fish. If the Almighty were to create an archetypal beachfront restaurant, it would probably be identical to this laid-back, unpretentious spot.

HOTELS

TOP OF THE LINE

Inn Above the Tide

30 EL PORTAL
SAUSALITO 94965
415-332-9535, 800-893-8433,
FAX 415-332-6714
Doubles $195-$425

Built on pilings that hang over San Francisco Bay, brand-new Inn Above the Tide is arguably one of Marin's most romantic hotels. The 30 rooms, decorated in whites and seafoam green, range from great to spectacular, with floor-to-ceiling windows offering panoramic views. Most have decks and fireplaces; grand deluxes ($265) also feature Jacuzzis in the tubs. The $425 Vista suite seduces with a king-sized canopy bed, wraparound deck, hot tub, and giant TV with VCR. Continental breakfast is included for all guests-you can opt to have it delivered right to the room. Several good **downtown Sausalito** restaurants are within walking distance.

LUXURY

Pelican Inn

HWY. 1
MUIR BEACH 94965
415-383-6000, FAX 415-383-3424
Doubles $174-198

The Pelican Inn's rough-hewn Tudor facade might not be to everyone's taste, but it's a perfect fit for its sylvan site, just a few minutes' walk from both **Muir Beach** and **Muir Woods**. Seven cozy guest rooms comprise this converted old farmhouse that looks like the setting for a Thomas Hardy novel: all have private baths and are furnished with English antiques, canopied beds and Oriental rugs over hardwood floors. Windows open onto expansive lawns and flowering gardens. The friendly ground-floor pub is complete with roaring fireplace and a lovely brick-floored patio for outdoor dining. Hotel guests get a full English breakfast which includes bangers, eggs, tomato and toast. The **dining room** is open for lunch, dinner and Sunday brunch.

MODERATE

Casa Madrona

805 BRIDGEWAY
SAUSALITO 94965
415-332-0502, 800-567-9524,
FAX 415-332-2537
Singles & Doubles $138-225, Suites $245-260

Some of the 39 rooms here are small, some are more stylish than others, but most have gorgeous views of Sausalito harbor, San Francisco Bay and the city skyline. Casa Madrona offers the size and amenities of a small hotel, with all the warmth and comforting ambience of a bed-and-breakfast. Room décor ranges from romantic Victorian in the main house to a mix of contemporary styles in the newer rooms and suites that cascade down the hillside. There's a **hot tub** on the property and an elegant restaurant, **Mikayla**, with some of the best food and views in Marin County.

Manka's Inverness Lodge

CALLENDAR WAY AT ARGYLE
INVERNESS 94937
415-669-1034, 800-539-1872,
FAX 415-669-1598
Singles & Doubles $135-$365

VISA MasterCard P

A rustic former hunting lodge in the hills above quaint Inverness, Manka's is an idyllic spot for urban refugees. The lodge consists of four rooms in the main building, four in a nearby annex and four private cottages. Some rooms are decorated in contemporary style; others are done in hunting lodge decor; all have private baths. The **dining room** here is such a charming, homey room that you'll want to take at least one meal here. A full lodge breakfast (not included with your room rate) is available à la carte; at dinner, game is a menu staple.

Mill Valley Inn

165 THROCKMORTON AVE.
MILL VALLEY 94941
415-389-6608, 800-595-2100, FAX, 415-389-5051
Doubles $139-$199

A

Within walking distance of Mill Valley's **town center**, this dramatic new inn offers the twin bonus of a great redwood getaway with a hip town attached. Twenty-five rooms, each different in design, feature king or queen beds, large soaking tubs and separate showers and cable TV. Complimentary Continental breakfast is served to all guests. Great **restaurants**, **coffee houses**, **bookstores** and **shops** are literally yards away, yet you'll fall asleep to the sound of a **gurgling creek**.

Mountain Home Inn

810 PANORAMIC HWY.
MILL VALLEY 94941
415-381-9000, FAX 415-381-3615
Singles & Doubles $139-$259

VISA MasterCard P

All ten rooms of this stunning redwood and glass inn-seemingly flung off the side of a winding hill on the road to Mt. Tamalpais-offer views so spectacular as to make mere panoramas pale by comparison. The entry-level lobby is split by slim redwood trunk pillars, which rise through the floor to the sky above. A small bar and dining deck both offer commanding views; a more formal restaurant downstairs serves a complimentary full breakfast here. This inn is a romantic's dream come true, particularly if you get a room with a private Jacuzzi, deck and/or fireplace.

ECONOMY

Alta Mira Hotel

125 BULKLEY AVE.
SAUSALITO 94965
415-332-1350, FAX 415-331-3862
Singles & Doubles $80-$190

VISA MasterCard Diners Club International

If you desire a room with a view, check into this 63-year-old mansion-cum-hotel perched high atop Sausalito. Twenty-two rooms offer spectacular **views of San Francisco and the Bay** (a few have private terraces); lower-end rooms offer views of hotel grounds and gardens. Rooms are done in Victorian period style, and the hotel itself has a quality of old, slightly faded luxe that suggests the romanticized decadence of a foreign film. A restaurant of middling quality serves breakfast, lunch, dinner, and Sunday brunch.

Olema Inn

10,000 SIR FRANCIS DRAKE BLVD.
OLEMA 94950
415-663-9559, FAX 415-663-8783
Singles & Doubles $95-$115

VISA MasterCard DISCOVER

Originally built as a hotel and stagecoach stopover, the Olema Inn gained notoriety early in the century as a house of ill repute and during WWII was used to house Gen. Dwight Eisenhower, John Steinbeck and Jack London. Only portions of the original structure still stand, but its six Victorian-style, antique-filled rooms are charming reminders of an earlier, less stressful era. All rooms have private baths and/or showers. Only a stone's throw from **Point Reyes National Seashore**, the inn contains a very good restaurant which serves lunch and dinner seven days a week.

Panama Hotel

4 Bayview
San Rafael 94901
415-457-3993, Fax 415-457-6240
Singles & Doubles, $55-$129

This rambling, fifteen-room Inn offers true character in a suburban city hotel, filled as it is with funky antiques, found objects and just plain junk. It may not be right for your Boston relatives, but if you don't mind giving up a little luxury, you'll be quite comfortable here. Many of the rooms face a lovely outdoor garden and patio, where lunch and dinner are served by an adept kitchen staff.

SHOPPING

SOUTHERN MARIN

Sausalito is a shopper's paradise, boasting a huge range of antique stores, clothing boutiques and craft and gift shops all along **Bridgeway and Caledonia Streets. Tiburon** is famous for its **Main Street** and Victorian-flavored **Ark Row**, both streets filled with eclectic antique, clothing, and curio shops and little restaurants. **Mill Valley**, the largest town in Southern Marin, is renowned for its shopping on **Miller and Throckmorton avenues**, where you'll find some state-of-the-art furniture stores, art galleries, gift shops and clothing boutiques. Here are some of our favorites:

Armchair Sailor Bookstore

42 Caledonia St.,
Sausalito 94965
415-332-7505
Open Mon.-Sat.

There's a lot more than books for sale here: reproductions of vintage ship's fittings, brass lamps, ship's bells, Bosun's whistles, reproduction sailing ships, watercolor nautical scenes and ship-oriented puzzles are all part of the charm.

Kachina

771 Bridgeway
Sausalito 94965
415-332-0663
Open daily

Everything here is Native American-oriented, from scads of jewelry and a huge Sioux feather war bonnet, to bows and arrows and dozens of beautiful Hopi and Zuni kachina dolls.

Parsley's Hats and Garnishes

84 Main St.
Tiburon 94920
415-435-6380
Open daily

Marin's best hat shop sells chapeaux for men, women and children and lovely padded cloth-covered hat boxes in which to keep them.

Susan Cummins Gallery

12 Miller Ave.
Mill Valley 94941
415-383-1512
Open Mon.-Sat.

One of Marin's most popular galleries showcases contemporary painting, mixed media sculpture and contemporary art jewelry in shows that rotate every month.

MID MARIN

The towns of **Larkspur** and **Corte Madera** are called the "Twin Cities" because they are so close to each other. **Corte Madera** offers two of the best shopping centers in Marin—**Town Center** and **The Village**—containing stores such as Nordstrom, Macy's, Bridgestone, Williams Sonoma, Victoria's Secret, and two excellent food courts. **Magnolia Avenue** in Larkspur is also a wonderful place to stroll for gift and card shops, clothing and hanging out in **Emporio Rulli**, one of the best coffee houses in the Bay Area.

Emporio Rulli

64 Magnolia Ave.
Larkspur 94939
415-924-7478
Open daily

From one small storefront, expert patissier Gary Rulli has expanded his bakery/coffee house into a huge operation with excellent sandwiches, extraordinary cakes, cookies, homemade candies and gelato, imported coffee beans and other delicacies from Europe, wines and more. Spending time here is like taking an instant trip to Venice-but without the canals.

NORTHERN MARIN

San Rafael, the capital of Marin County, is a small municipality with all the energy, seediness and variety of shops that you'd find in bigger city. Everything from Tibetan and Haitian artifacts to vintage bookstores to gamestores, billiards emporiums, coffee houses and a multitude of restaurants make Fourth Street and its immediate side blocks (between Lincoln and E Streets) one of the county's premier stroll-and-shop experiences. Just west and over the hill from San Rafael are the towns of **San Anselmo** and **Fairfax**, where antique shops, more bookstores, and a distinctly artistic feeling characterize many of the buildings and stores. Marin's northernmost township, **Novato**, is known for **Grant Avenue**, also called "Old Town," where unusual boutiques, coffee houses, restaurants and all sorts of independent stores provide a great place to cruise.

Gunning's Hobbies

550 San Anselmo Ave.
San Anselmo 94960
415-454-3087
Open daily

Beaver Cleaver and his dad would have shopped here. They've got everything from trains, cars, trucks, airplanes, model-making and other marvels of male toy technology. Great miniature vintage cars.

French Toast

808 Grant Ave.
Novato 94945
415-898-4101
Open daily

Opulent and dazzling, French Toast reflects the way Auntie Mame might decorate if she were alive today, with brocade and tapestry pillows, throws of all types, candles by the score, clocks, picture frames, hatboxes, mirrors, albums, and everything seemingly printed with fruits, vegetables, flowers or other patterns.

Open Secret

923 C St.,
San Rafael 94901
415-457-4191
Open daily

Open Secret sells New Age paraphernalia, including mystical and philosophical trinkets and remarkable collection of Eastern religious artifacts. How about a statue of the Buddha no bigger than your thumbnail or a complete six-foot gilded-metal shrine for $5,000? It's all available here, along with jewelry, books, music, prayer drums, meditation materials, herbs and videos.

SIGHTSEEING

Angel Island State Park

San Francisco Bay
415-435-1915
Open daily 8 a.m.-sunset. From Tiburon: Angel Island State Ferry, 415-435-2131. From San Francisco: Blue and Gold Fleet, 415-773-1188.

Accessible by ferry from downtown Tiburon or from Pier 39, this 750-acre State Park is devoted entirely to hiking, biking, boating, barbecuing, camping and fishing. Once an army outpost in the 1800s, the island's many buildings offer glimpses of architecture ranging from the Civil War through World War II; historically oriented special events held on the Island from time to time. A small deli and café sell food if you don't wish to pack in your own

Bay Area Discovery Museum

557 E. Fort Baker
Sausalito 94965
415-487-4398
Open Tues.-Thurs., 9 a.m.-4 p.m., Fri.-Sun., 10 a.m.,-5 p.m., closed Mon.
Admission: Children ages 1-18 $6; adults $7.

Housed in several old Fort Baker buildings in the eastern section of the Marin Headlands, this hands-on children's museum offers not only art, science and history activities aimed at kids ages 1 to 10, but opportunities for crawling and climbing indoors and outdoors as well. There's a nifty café and store on site.

The Bay Model

2100 BRIDGEWAY
SAUSALITO 94965
415-332-3870
Open Tues.-Sat. 9 a.m.- 4 p.m. Free admission.

The Army Corps of Engineers was thinking small when they made this highly detailed copy of the San Francisco Bay and its tributaries. The model is filled with water only when a project is actually under study, but even when empty, it is most impressive. Groups of 10 or more can arrange for a ranger-led tour; otherwise, it's a self-guided experience.

Marin County Civic Center

3501 CIVIC CENTER DR.
SAN RAFAEL 94901
415-499-6646
Open daily, 9 a.m.-5 p.m.

Frank Lloyd Wright designed this striking, gold-spired complex, commissioned in 1959 and visible from Highway 101. It houses county offices and the county courthouse in addition to a circular public library, a large, multi-use theater (the Marin Veteran's Memorial Auditorium) and a smaller showcase theater. Both the on-site gift shop and cafeteria are open to the public.

The Marin Headlands

415-561-3000

The craggy cliffs on your left as you cross the Golden Gate Bridge heading out of San Francisco are part of the Golden Gate National Recreation Area, which encompasses much of the Bay Area's coastline. A Visitor's Center provides maps and other literature.

Marin Museum of the American Indian

2200 NOVATO BLVD.
NOVATO 94947
415-897-4064
Open summer Wed.-Fri. 10 a.m.- 3 p.m., Sat.-Sun. noon-4 p.m. Call for non-summer hours. Free admission.

This small museum emphasizes aboriginal Northern California Miwok culture and has a garden of indigenous plants. Artifacts from other locally native tribes are displayed as well. The museum is tucked away in a park filled with live oak trees and a lovely stream that roars away during the winter season.

Marine Mammal Center

MARIN HEADLANDS, GOLDEN GATE NATIONAL RECREATION AREA,
SAUSALITO 94965
415-289-7325
Open daily 10 a.m.- 4 p.m. Free admission.

Ill and wounded pinnipeds (walruses, seals, sea lions) from all around Northern California are brought here to rest and recuperate in saltwater tanks. Friendly volunteers will gladly take you around to view the patients and can speak informatively about the work being done at the Center. An on-site gift shop features pinniped-related toys, objects and more.

Muir Woods National Monument

MILL VALLEY 94941
415-388-2595
Open sunrise to sunset.
Admission: Adults $2, kids under 17 free.
Parking free.

This old-growth redwood forest of around 560 acres is one of the Bay Area's most popular attractions. Established in 1908, it offers hiking trails through grove upon grove of extraordinary ancient redwoods, with the tallest trees approximately 260 feet in height. It's wonderfully peaceful place-if you get there before the tourist buses.

Mt. Tamalpais State Park

MILL VALLEY 94965
415-388-2070

Hiking interest you? There's nothing like this 900-acre park, which offers a remarkable range of environments and trails. Grasslands, chaparral and laurel groves, steep peaks, waterfalls, woods and lakes are all within half an hour's drive of San Francisco.

East Bay

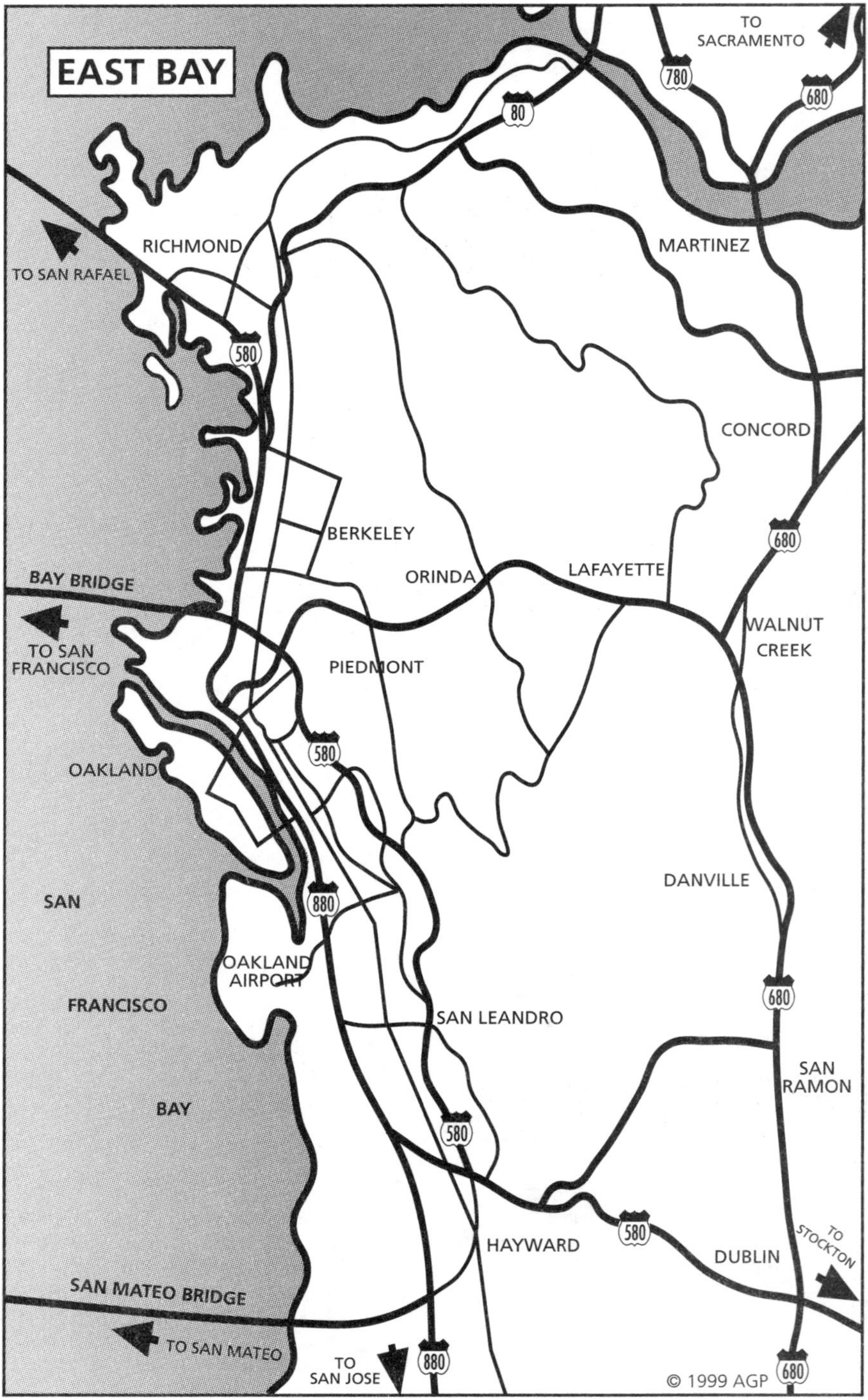
EAST BAY
TO SACRAMENTO
780
680
80
RICHMOND
MARTINEZ
TO SAN RAFAEL
580
CONCORD
BERKELEY
680
BAY BRIDGE
ORINDA
LAFAYETTE
TO SAN FRANCISCO
WALNUT CREEK
PIEDMONT
580
OAKLAND
DANVILLE
SAN
880
OAKLAND AIRPORT
FRANCISCO
680
SAN LEANDRO
SAN RAMON
BAY
580
580
HAYWARD
DUBLIN
TO STOCKTON
SAN MATEO BRIDGE
TO SAN MATEO
TO SAN JOSE
880
680
© 1999 AGP

To The East

Only a short ride over the Bay Bridge from San Francisco, the East Bay offers better weather most of the year, less congestion, and a lower cost of living. **Oakland** and **Berkeley** are two of the region's most prominent cities, but the population continues to migrate beyond to the cities and suburbs of **Alameda** and **Contra Costa Counties**.

Oakland first was settled in the early nineteenth century, when soldier Luis Peralta claimed 48,000 some-odd acres to graze his cattle. In 1852, Horace Carpentier secured a town site and named it Oakland for its live oaks. The transcontinental railroad was completed in 1869 with Oakland its western terminus, contributing to business growth and a thriving logging industry. Many San Franciscans moved east following the 1906 earthquake; the opening of the Bay Bridge in 1936 made for an easy commute.

Originally a tiny hamlet called Ocean View, Berkeley was renamed in 1866 for Irish clergyman George Berkeley, who came to convert the natives to Christianity. **The University of California at Berkeley**—called "Cal"—has helped transform this town into a thriving intellectual and cultural center.

DINING

Ajanta

INDIAN 13/20

1888 Solano Ave.
Berkeley 94706
510-526-4373
Lunch & Dinner daily, $

Chef/owner Lachu Moorjani offers an Indian dining experience a cut above most others, with attentive and cordial service and a changing selection of lesser-known regional Indian specialties. Large reproduction murals depicting paintings from the Ajanta caves for which the establishment is named warm the restaurant's walls. Dinner entrées are spiced to your heat tolerance, and come with papadam, appetizer, naan, rice, vegetable, chutney and pickles. Moorjani's beverage list includes carefully-selected wines and beers that bring out the best in his food.

Bay Wolf

MEDITERRANEAN 14/20

3853 Piedmont Ave.
Oakland 94611
510-655-6004
Lunch Mon.-Fri., Dinner nightly, $$$

If Chez Panisse is the hallowed cathedral of California cuisine, Bay Wolf is the friendly parish church, offering fresh ingredients in creative combinations in a converted craftsman-style house. Owners Michael Wild and Larry Goldman offer a tour of the Mediterranean, with menu selections inspired by the diverse culinary styles of France and Italy. A recent menu celebrating the cuisine of Lyon proffered duck liver flan with green peppercorns and Marsala; potato and Fontina ravioli with butternut squash and white truffle oil; and Liberty Ranch duck with lavender, prunes, and duck fat-fried potatoes. The wine list includes attractive selections from France, Italy and California.

Breads of India

INDIAN ¢
2448 SACRAMENTO
BERKELEY 94702
510-848-7684
Lunch & Dinner daily
No cards

If it's Indian food you're after, try this new bakery, serving a daily-changing selection of curries and tandooris paired with house-baked Indian breads.

Cactus Taqueria

MEXICAN ¢
5525 COLLEGE AVE.
OAKLAND 94618
510-547-1305
Open daily.
No cards

The East Bay offers bargain dining spots too numerous to detail. For a delightful Mexican must, try the Cactus, with its changing selection of fresh salsas. A second restaurant is located in **Albany (1881 Solano Ave., 510-528-1881).**

Cheese Board Pizza

PIZZA ¢
1512 SHATTUCK AVE.
BERKELEY 94709
510-549-3055
Lunch & Dinner daily
No cards

Craving an inspired slice of pizza? Stop by this tiny storefront pizzeria, serving up daily changing specials by the slice, half-pie, or pie, using cheeses from the Cheese Board a few doors down.

Chez Panisse Restaurant & Café

CALIFORNIAN/FRENCH 16/20
1517 SHATTUCK AVE.
BERKELEY 94709
510-548-5525
Dinner Mon.-Sat., $$$$

Chez Panisse and owner Alice Waters are at the heart of what now is celebrated as California cuisine. Waters' style: fresh, local ingredients raised by ecologically-sound practices and prepared using techniques based in simple French cuisine. The restaurant offers one prix-fixe menu each night. A recent menu began with seared scallops with black truffles and pancetta, followed by tortelli filled with wild mustard greens, fresh ricotta, and pine nuts. The main course offered a mixed grill of lamb, garlic sausages and sweetbreads with cardoons and artichokes; dessert brought Marsala-baked pears with Mascarpone. A less expensive prix-fixe menu is available on Monday.

The casual **Chez Panisse Café** upstairs (510-548-5049) serves daily-changing lunch and dinner menus that feature salads, pizzas and pastas alongside more substantial entrées. The wine list features interesting offerings by the glass and bottle.

Citron

MEDITERRANEAN 14/20
5484 COLLEGE AVE.
OAKLAND 94618
510-653-5484
Dinner nightly, $$$

Citron draws diners from the East Bay and beyond to enjoy inventive, Mediterranean-inspired cuisine in a cozy bistro setting. Chef/Owner Chris Rossi's weekly-changing menu may feature the likes of grilled angus New York steak on a bed of Swiss chard with caramelized onions, pommes frites and green peppercorn sauce or a tagine of opah fish and mussels, paired with large pearl couscous, peppers and grilled olive bread. Don't miss desserts like a red wine-poached pear served with lavender mousse. Additional niceties may include an amuse bouche of puff pastry filled with a dab of lemon crème fraîche and a snip of smoked salmon, or tiny complimentary butter cookies with your coffee. The short wine list includes selections from California, Washington, and France.

Lalime's

MEDITERRANEAN 14/20

1329 GILMAN ST.
BERKELEY 94706
510-527-9838
Dinner nightly, $$

Lalime's serves California-inspired Mediterranean fare to a loyal following in a warm, bi-level dining room. Owners Haig Krikorian and Cindy Lalime's robust fare borrows from France, Italy, Spain and the Middle East. A newsletter gives regulars the jump on daily-changing, fixed-price menus, which might include celeriac, onion and cider soup with Stilton croutons; sliced smoked pork filet with goat cheese-apple strudel in Calvados sauce; and pear frangipane tart with crème anglaise. An à la carte menu also is offered. Wines by the bottle or glass are paired expertly with each night's selections.

Le Cheval

VIETNAMESE ¢

1007 CLAY ST.
OAKLAND 94607
510-763-8495
Lunch Mon.-Sat., Dinner nightly

No cards

Le Cheval offers generous portions of authentic curries, noodles, and other dishes in a massive setting that manages to maintain its upscale feel.

Nan Yang Rockridge

THAI ¢

6048 COLLEGE AVE.
OAKLAND 94618
510-655-3298
Lunch & Dinner daily

No cards

For something completely different, try the green papaya salad and Burmese garlic noodles with curried spinach and tomatoes at this superb little spot.

Oliveto

ITALIAN 14/20

5655 COLLEGE AVE.
OAKLAND 94618
510-547-5356 (Restaurant);
510-547-4382 (Café)
Lunch Mon.-Fri., Dinner nightly, $$$

Chef Paul Bertolli is on a mission to teach Bay Area diners to appreciate Italian cuisine the way it's served back home. His is inspired by a love for the simple and traditional, coupled with a reverence for fresh, local ingredients. Bertolli may offer a salad composed of duck, pears, curly endive and treviso, followed by house-made pastas and soups redolent of the Italian countryside. Try anything from the grill, perhaps spit-roasted pigeon or rabbit. The wine list features Italian and California vintages, several by the glass. A casual café downstairs, complete with wood-burning oven, offers table service during mealtimes and counter service between.

Rivoli Restaurant

MEDITERRANEAN 15/20

1539 SOLANO AVE.
BERKELEY 94707
510-526-2542
Dinner nightly, $$

Recently remodeled to cover the cinder block walls and soften the restaurant's feel, this little treasure has gone from wonderful to better. With talented chef Wendy Brucker in the back and husband Roscoe Skipper out front, Rivoli offers a friendly, enticing dining experience. The best place to sit is facing the glass wall looking into the garden, where you feel as if you're dining outdoors in the country. Regularly changing menus feature the likes of portobello mushroom fritters with lemon aïoli, delicately poached salmon with chervil butter and a spring-like mix of carrots and asparagus as well as a world-class hot fudge sundae for dessert.

Uzen

JAPANESE ¢

5415 COLLEGE AVE.
OAKLAND 94618
510-654-7753
Lunch & Dinner Tues.-Sun.

No cards

For impeccably fresh sushi and other Japanese items, Uzen offers beautifully presented cuisine at reasonable prices in a pretty little postage-stamp of a restaurant. Try the udon, a huge bowl of intensely-flavorful, steamy broth with toothsome noodles and a choice of tempura or other toppings.

AND ALSO..

Autumn Moon

INTERNATIONAL
3909 GRAND AVE.
OAKLAND 94610
510-595-3200
Breakfast, Lunch & Dinner daily, $$

Near Lake Merritt, Wendy Levy and Kerry Heffernan's always-packed restaurant serves modern International specialties like house-made blintzes, a Parisian-style falafel sandwich, and grilled teriyaki salmon with snap peas and sticky rice in a casual, lively atmosphere.

Garibaldi on College

MEDITERRANEAN
5356 COLLEGE AVE.
OAKLAND 94618
510-595-4000
Lunch Mon.-Fri., Dinner Mon.-Sat., $$

An outpost of the San Francisco Garibaldi, this new spot offers sophisticated Mediterranean cuisine in the most swank, cosmopolitan atmosphere you'll find this side of the Bay. Don't miss desserts by pastry chef Jennifer Millar, formerly of Square One.

Nava

CALIFORNIAN
5478 COLLEGE AVE.
OAKLAND 94618
510-655-4770
Dinner nightly, $$

Pierre Charbel's welcoming neighborhood venue offers friendly service and southwest-inspired Californian cuisine.

HOTELS

TOP OF THE LINE

Claremont Resort Hotel

41 TUNNEL RD.
OAKLAND 94705
510-843-3000, FAX 510-848-6208
Singles $204-$300, Doubles $229-$289, Suites $295-$875

The Claremont is the ultimate luxury spot in the East Bay. Completed in 1915 and lucky to survive a major nearby fire in 1991, this landmark is surrounded by beautifully landscaped gardens, and remains a favorite for conferences and romantic getaways. The hotel's full service European-style spa offers health, fitness and beauty programs, along with two Olympic-size pools, lighted tennis courts, a lounge with live music and the recently renovated Jordan's restaurant. Guest rooms are individually decorated and offer hillside garden or Bay views.

LUXURY

Waterfront Plaza Hotel

10 WASHINGTON ST.
JACK LONDON SQUARE
OAKLAND 94607
510-836-3800, FAX 510-832-5695
Singles & Doubles $165- $185

The Waterfront Plaza is the only hotel in the area with front-door ferry service to San Francisco and private docking facilities. The hotel offers 144 guest rooms and suites, and is walking distance from Oakland's historical district, Chinatown and the convention center. A favorite with business travelers, the Waterfront offers a range of services, a pool and a small fitness facility. Jack's Bistro serves breakfast, lunch and dinner daily.

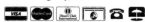

MODERATE

Gramma's Rose Garden Inn

2740 TELEGRAPH AVE.
BERKELEY 94705
510-549-2145, FAX 510-549-1085
Singles & Doubles $99-$175

Gramma's offers 40 rooms in two belle époque, Tudor-style mansions with period comforts like rose-patterned wallpaper and handmade quilts, stained- glass windows, intricate woodwork and elaborate, nineteenth-century furnishings. Three newer buildings with fireplaces and other period amenities seem oddly out of place. All share a central courtyard with fountains, picnic tables and lots of roses. Rates include a full breakfast, wine, hors d'oeuvres, coffee and homemade cookies.

NIGHTLIFE

East Bay venues offer smaller crowds, lower cost, and easier parking than in the city. **Kimball's East** (5800 Shellmound, Emeryville; 510-658-2555) books live music Wednesdays through Sundays at covers $15 and up. **Yoshi's Restaurant & Nightspot** (510 Embarcadero West, Oakland; 510-238-9200) has nightly shows featuring jazz greats like Max Roach, Joe Williams and Branford Marsalis, with covers ranging from about $8 to $30. Yoshi's also offers a Japanese restaurant, cocktail lounge and sushi bar.

SHOPPING

The East Bay offers plenty of malls, but the best shopping can be found by walking the neighborhoods. Start in North Berkeley, perhaps the East Bay's original gourmet ghetto. Beginning at Chez Panisse (see above) and walking toward Vine Street, visit **North Berkeley Wines** (1505 Shattuck Ave.; 510-848-8910), a serious wine shop with a nice selection of unfiltered California wines. Stop for a recharge at the original **Peet's Coffee** (2124 Vine St.; 510-841-0564). Back down Vine, peruse new and used books at **Black Oak Books** (1491 Shattuck Ave. (510-486-0698). Crossing Shattuck and heading back toward Cedar, pick up some bread and cheese at **The Cheese Board** (1504 Shattuck Ave.; 549-3183), one of the last collectively owned enterprises.

Next head to Rockridge, and start at the heart: **Rockridge Market Hall** (5655 College Ave.; 510-655-7748) houses specialty shops that rival any European food hall. Sample great breads and pastries at **Grace Baking** (510-428-2662), then pick up a cappuccino and gourmet chocolates at **Peaberry's Coffee & Tea** (510-653-0450). Head to **The Pasta Shop** (510-547-4005) for a fine selection of packaged foods, fresh pastas, imported cheeses, and a great deli counter. **Paul Marcus Wines** (510-420-1005) has a nice selection of French and Italian wines to serve with dinner prepared from your purchases at **Enzo's Meat & Poultry** (510-547-5839) and **Rockridge Fish** (510-654-3474). At the end of the hall, **Market Hall Produce** (510-601-8208) bountifully displays American, Asian and European produce. Stop on your way out to pick up a bunch of posies at **Bloomies Flowers** (510-547-0444).

Heading back into Berkeley, the Fourth Street area offers a growing enclave of upscale and gourmet shops. Visit **The Gardener** (1836 4th St.; 510-548-4545) for garden supplies and more, stock your home at **Crate and Barrel Outlet** (1785 4th St.; 510-528-5500) and find good deals on children's clothing at the **Sweet Potatoes Outlet** (1716 4th St.; 510-527-5852). **Hear Music** (1809 4th St.; 510-204-9595) allows you to audition CDs at listening booths or the listening bar.

There's plenty for the foodie to enjoy in East Bay: Line up for breakfast or lunch at **Bette's Oceanview Diner** (1807-A 4th St.; 510-644-3230), or lunch on the street with specialties from Bette's To Go (1807 4th St.; 510-548-9494). Try lunch or dinner at David Vardy's beautiful Japanese-inspired **O' Chamé** (1830 4th Street; 510-841-8783), or a Niman-Schell burger and fries or niçoise salad at **Café Rouge** (1782 4th St.; 510-525-1440). Café Rouge also offers a meat counter where you can purchase top-quality cuts to take with you. Next door, you'll find expanded outposts of Rockridge Market Hall: The Pasta Shop (1786 4th St.; 510-528-1786), Paul Marcus Wines (1784 4th St.; 510-526-9093) and Willy's produce shop (1788 4th St.; 510-527-5550). Don't miss Seattle-based **Sur La Table** (1806 4th St.; 510-849-2252) for all manner of culinary supplies, as well as cooking classes.

SIGHTSEEING

On a clear day, the East Bay offers glorious views across the Golden Gate and Bay Bridges to Marin and San Francisco. The East Bay Regional Park District offers many fine hikes through wonderfully tranquil, wooded areas. Berkeley's 2,078-acre **Tilden Park** (entrances at South Park Dr. and Canon Dr.; 510-843-2137) offers picnic areas and trails for hiking and bicycling.

In Oakland, **Jack London Square** (Broadway and Embarcadero) is named for the famous author, who lived in the area between his adventures in the Klondike. The waterfront features a variety of interesting shops and restaurants, and boasts a terrific Sunday farmer's market (10 a.m. to 2 p.m.). Ferry service from the waterfront terminal will take you to San Francisco's Fisherman's Wharf.

Other Oakland sights include man-made **Lake Merritt** (bordered by Grand Ave. and Lakeshore Ave.) and **Lakeside Park**, among the county's most beautiful municipal greenswards. **The Oakland Museum** (1000 Oak St.; 510-238-3401) has an international reputation as one of America's finest regional museums. Featured are exhibits on the art, history and ecology of California. Downtown, take in a show or tour at the **Paramount Theater** (2025 Broadway; 510-465-6400), an art deco masterpiece and protected national landmark that hearkens back to the glory days of the grand movie palace.

In Berkeley, stop in at the **University of California Visitors Center** in University Hall (University Ave. and Oxford St.; 510-642-6000) for campus maps. On weekdays, take self-guided or free student-guided walks around campus. **Sproul Plaza**, birthplace of the free speech movement, still offers a lively center for public opinion and street performance. The architecturally striking **University Art Museum** (2626 Bancroft Way; 510-642-0808) designed by Mario Ciampi houses an impressive collection of twentieth-century art. On the ground floor, the **Pacific Film Archive** features historic and avant-garde films. A short walk from the University, time-warped Telegraph Avenue features some of the area's best book shops, including **Cody's** (2454 Telegraph Ave.; 510-845-7852) and **Moe's** (2476 Telegraph Ave.; 510-849-2087), as well as street artists peddling their wares. Exercise caution in this area after dark.

WINE COUNTRY

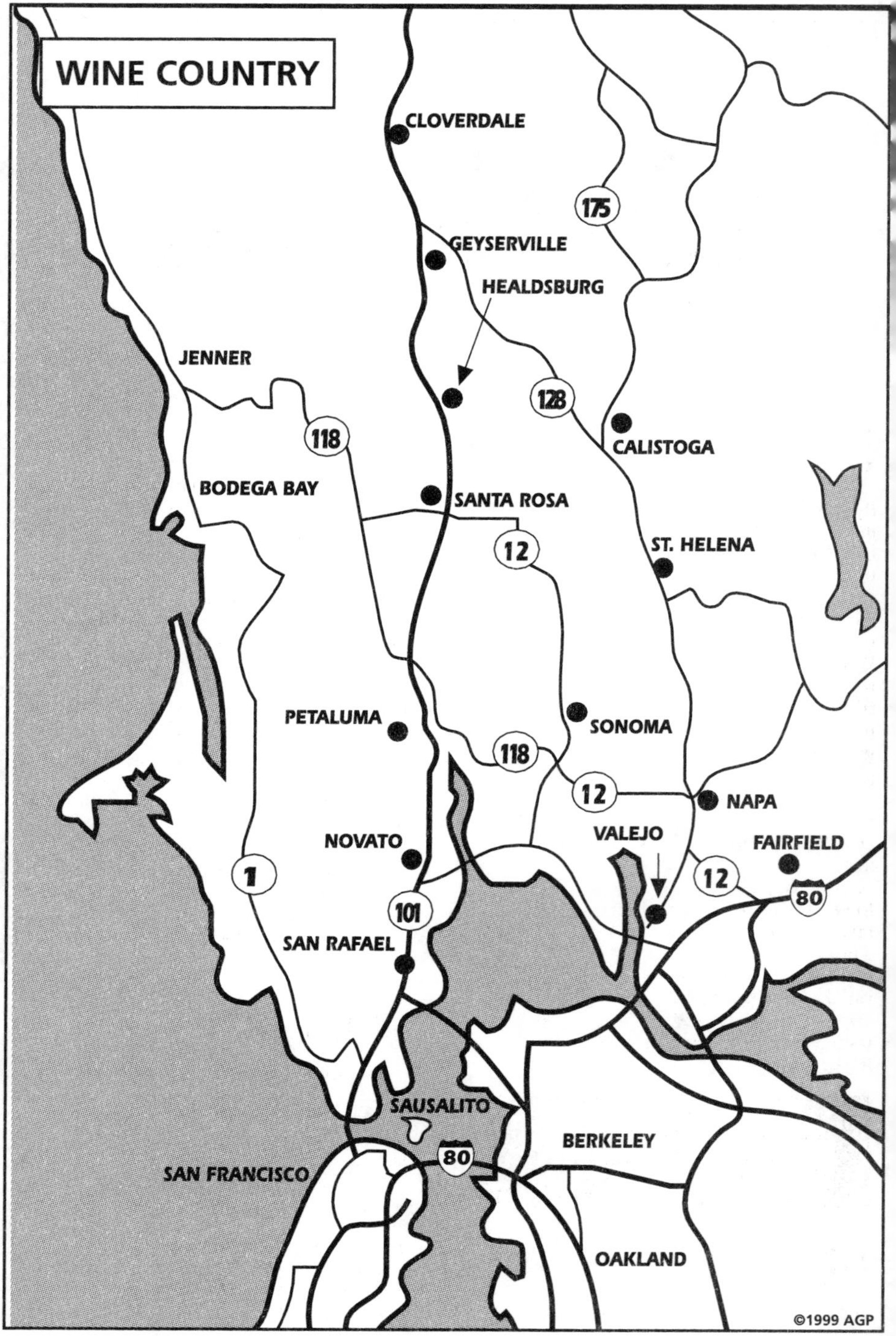

WINE COUNTRY
CLOVERDALE
175
GEYSERVILLE
HEALDSBURG
JENNER
128
118
CALISTOGA
BODEGA BAY
SANTA ROSA
12
ST. HELENA
PETALUMA
SONOMA
118
12
NAPA
NOVATO
VALEJO
FAIRFIELD
1
12
80
101
SAN RAFAEL
SAUSALITO
BERKELEY
80
SAN FRANCISCO
OAKLAND
©1999 AGP

AMONG THE VINES

Wineries can be found nearly everywhere in the state of California, but in all of the New World it is a bucolic area only 48 miles north of San Francisco that has captured the undisputed title of "Wine Country." Climate and soil conditions similar to those in the great grape-growing regions of France have rendered this part of California the premiere wine region in the United States. Winemaking is the focus of much of the region's culture and commerce. As a result, the area and its inhabitants have developed a unique collective character. A sense of quiet gentility prevails here, unlike the feeling you get in any other part of America. It is European in quality, owing in no small measure to the large number of French, Italian, and German expatriates who have settled here in recent years. For tourists, this combination of factors means good wine, good food, lovely lodgings and shopping that are of a quality rarely found outside of major urban centers. The several hundred wineries in the region offer as many architectural styles as there are varieties of wine; most are open to the public, and a great number of them offer tours and tastings of their wines (see "Wine Touring").

THE BIG THREE: NAPA, SONOMA & MENDOCINO COUNTIES

NAPA COUNTY

The most established, populated and affluent county in the region, Napa is home to over two hundred wineries, many top restaurants and innumerable luxury accommodations. Nearly all of the county can be accessed by traveling up Route 29. To the south, the city of **Napa** marks your entry into the Wine Country, but it does not compare in beauty to what lies ahead. Further north, the small towns of **Yountville**, **Oakville** and **Rutherford** have each developed individual personalities not only in the wines they produce, but also as tourist destinations. Even further north, beautiful **St. Helena** is home to many of the county's finest restaurants and shops. And at Napa's northernmost border, **Calistoga**, which has a more laid-back feeling, attracts many visitors to its spas built on natural geothermal springs. The rolling hills and verdant valleys, dotted nearly everywhere with vines, make Napa a delight to visit in the fall when the grape leaves turn a vibrant magenta, or in the late spring, when the budding vines are nearly overrun with bright yellow mustard flowers.

SONOMA COUNTY

Abutting Napa on the east and the Pacific Ocean on the west, Sonoma is more spread out than Napa and the pace of life here is decidedly more relaxed. Even the roads are less congested. Nevertheless, this county has come into its own as a wine producer and can no longer can be considered second best. From the south, Sonoma begins with the picturesque town of **Sonoma**; heading north, you'll pass through the towns of **Kenwood** and **Glen Ellen**. **Santa Rosa** is the cultural center of the county. Further north,

Healdsburg, **Geyserville** and **Cloverdale** each have numerous small wineries as well as many inviting bed and breakfasts. In addition to its wine, Sonoma is renowned for its agricultural bounty: vegetables, cheeses, ducks, rabbits and game of all kinds are grown here and featured in local restaurants and gourmet food shops.

MENDOCINO COUNTY

A favorite weekend getaway destination for Northern Californians, Mendocino County has lately seen its wine industry take off. The landscape still contains apple orchards, timber forests and sheep farms, but vineyards are growing over more and more of the land. Driving north on Highway 1 from the Point Arena Lighthouse, you'll pass through the funky town of **Elk**, through picturesque **Albion** and **Little River** and into the town of **Mendocino**, the entirety of which has been declared a National Historic Preservation District. Further north still is the town of **Fort Bragg**. Inland, the three-block-long city of **Hopland**, at the junction of highways 101 and 175, is the southern gateway to Mendocino's **Alexander Valley** wine country. Towns along Highway 128 each in turn possess an abundance of charm as well as some fine wineries.

DINING

Albion River Inn

CALIFORNIAN 13/20

3790 PACIFIC COAST HWY.
ALBION 95456
707-937-1919
Dinner nightly, $$$

Perhaps no other restaurant on the North Coast offers a better panoramic view of the ocean-and the food is almost as good. Chef Steve Smith takes advantage of his proximity to the sea, serving impeccably fresh seafood, including a signature dish of marinated grilled prawns with cilantro-lime butter. Medallions of monkfish come sautéed and served on a bed of sweet corn with sun-dried tomatoes and asparagus. The wine list, considered by many to be the area's best, wins awards.

All Seasons Café

CALIFORNIAN 12/20

1400 LINCOLN AVE.
CALISTOGA 94515
707-942-9111
Lunch Thurs.-Tues., Dinner nightly, $$

A black-and-white checkerboard floor, dark woods, marble tables and ceiling fans give this place a snappy bistro look. The menu presents many familiar and comforting items, and usually they are cooked with skill. For lunch, try a grilled leg of lamb sandwich on rosemary toast with grilled onions, portobello mushrooms and red peppers. At dinner, guests who know order pan-seared fish dusted with North African spices and served atop a spicy fennel-and-cabbage slaw, or choose the grilled pork loin with a potato-onion cake. This charming little spot also contains a wine shop with more than 800 selections, from which you can purchase a bottle (for $10 above retail) to accompany your meal.

Auberge du Soleil

FRENCH 13/20

180 RUTHERFORD HILL RD.
RUTHERFORD 94573
707-963-1211
Breakfast, Lunch & Dinner daily, $$$

Auberge du Soleil is undoubtedly one of the most romantic restaurants in the entire Wine Country, and it surely affords one of the most incredible views. To look over the fabled surrounding vineyards at sunset while sipping a wine from those very vines is a heady experience. The menu here supports the experience adequately and often with brilliance. The chef does a lovely roasted lobster sausage with minted lentil salad. Also worthy are rack of lamb and pan-roasted quail. Desserts are perfectly decadent, especially the white chocolate cheesecake.

Babette's

FRENCH 16/20
464 FIRST ST. E.
SONOMA 95476
707-939-8921
Café: Lunch & Dinner daily. Dining Room: Dinner Tues.-Sat., Café $$, Dining Room $$$$

Set back in a cobblestone alley off Sonoma Plaza, this petite restaurant and wine bar has had both diners and critics applauding since it opened in 1994. Skyrocketing chef Daniel Paterson and his wife, Elizabeth Ramsey, demonstrate daily their dedication to refined, French-inspired food purveyed in an artsy atmosphere all their own. In the dining room, dinner is a seasonal, five-course prix-fixe meal with three choices within each course. You might find rare ahi tuna suspended in lemon and black pepper gelée; a medallion of Sonoma foie gras with warm bing cherries; a ragoût of morels and ricotta gnocchi; and a duck breast served on a bed of French lentils, olives, and green garlic. Look for the dynamite coconut-and-banana napoleon with passion fruit sauce for dessert. A separate dining room is actually a tiny wine bar and café open every day from noon to 10 p.m. Choose a chair (or couch) in this funky living-room setting and order from a full, à la carte menu that you could easily find on Paris' Left Bank. Tempting dishes include pâté de foie gras with toasts and cornichons; thin, delicate sandwiches of watercress, cucumber and cream cheese; and, for dessert, a plate of tiny handmade truffles and cookies.

Basque Boulangerie Café

CAFÉ ¢
460 FIRST ST. E.
SONOMA 95476
707-935-7687
Breakfast & Lunch daily

Breads and pastries of countless shapes and varieties star at this bustling café off Sonoma Plaza. Breakfasts, ordered at the counter, can be as simple (and delicious) as a walnut-studded sticky bun or a fluffy omelet. At lunch, wine tasters stop in for filling sandwiches (prosciutto and Brie, for example), as well as salads and homemade soups. There's a small wine bar where you can sample Sonoma favorites by the glass.

Bistro Don Giovanni

MEDITERRANEAN 13/20
4110 ST. HELENA HWY.
NAPA 94558
707-224-3300
Lunch & Dinner daily, $$$

Situated roadside in Napa's southernmost wine-growing region and surrounded by vineyards, this huge, high-ceilinged dining room has seen a couple of unsuccessful restaurants come and go. The current owners introduced an appealing and straightforward Italian menu and have recently added a large outdoor patio with sculptures and a fountain. Start with individual pizzas from their wood-fired oven or a crispy fritto misto and go on to the handmade pappardelle with braised rabbit and chanterelle ragoût or the braised lamb shanks with Tuscan white beans—all are winners. We also urge you to order a plate of grilled Brie wrapped in grape leaves, marinated olives and roasted garlic for everyone at the table to share.

Bistro Ralph

CALIFORNIAN/FRENCH 12/20
109 PLAZA ST.
HEALDSBURG 95448
707-433-1380
Lunch Wed.-Mon., Dinner nightly, $$

The clean lines and spare décor perfectly match the chic food at this spot, which has become a favorite of wine industry locals. Chef Ralph Tingle starts his customers off with focaccia puffs-addictive nuggets of dough infused with fennel, olive oil and Pernod. He changes the menu weekly, but if he's offering Szechuan pepper calamari—rounds of squid, briefly deep-fried and seasoned with a dusting of black pepper, be sure to order a couple of platters. For dessert choose the crème brûlée with crushed vanilla beans on the bottom. Bistro Ralph has only 49 seats, so book in advance, especially on weekends.

Boonville Hotel

INTERNATIONAL 14/20

14050 HWY. 128 & LAMBERT LN.
BOONVILLE 95415
707-895-2210
Lunch Wed.-Sun., Dinner Wed.-Mon., $$

The wine-and-beer bar here is an entertaining place to hang out with locals, some of whom still know an old local dialect called "Bootling." The building also houses one of the most charming little hotels in California (see Hotels). Downstairs in the dining room, amid lots of blond wood and huge vases of colorful fresh flowers, talented chefs serve highly regarded international dishes. The duck quesadillas are exemplary, as are the hearty soups and stews. We were knocked out by the freshness of the ingredients, the simplicity of presentation and the extraordinarily lively flavors. The wine list here is similarly well-thought-out and, naturally, features local bottlings from the Anderson Valley region. Don't be fooled by the Boonville Hotel's out-of-the-way location (right across the street from the **Horn of Zeese** diner): this is a handsomely appointed, classy place.

Brava Terrace

CALIFORNIA/ITALIAN 12/20

3010 ST. HELENA HWY.
ST. HELENA 94574
707-963-9300
Lunch & Dinner daily May-Oct. (Closed Wed. Nov.-May), $$$

Chef-owner Fred Halpert abandoned San Francisco and opened this elegant little bistro to great fanfare a couple of years ago. De rigueur here are the cassoulet, risottos and garlic-mashed potatoes that are well-paired with either a grilled filet of beef or a piece of grilled fresh fish and a glass of local Merlot. Problems of sloppiness and inconsistencies exist when Halpert is taking a night off. Brava Terrace shares a parking lot with Freemark Abbey Winery and has a lovely back terrace replete with a brook that babbles charmingly in non-drought years.

Brix

CALIFORNIAN/ASIAN 14/20

7377 ST. HELENA HWY.
YOUNTVILLE 94558
707-944-2749
Lunch & Dinner daily, $$$

A

Remarkable Cal/Asian cuisine is the specialty of Michael Kawachi, who arrived in 1996 after cooking at the famous Roy's in Hawaii. Brix's airy dining room feels too big and is often too noisy for an intimate meal, but it remains a place to experiment culinarily with unlikely sounding combinations that usually work. How about crunchy coconut seafood cigars with pineapple-chili sauce; or smoked salmon spaghettini with fennel, capers, Maui onions and orange gremolata; or smoked rack of lamb with spicy peanut satay and Zinfandel glaze? For the less adventurous, the menu offers familiar green salads and unsurprising pasta dishes, such as rigatoni with rock shrimp in a tomato cream sauce. Ask for a table by the huge windows overlooking the herb gardens and vineyards. On the way out, pick up a bottle at Brix's wine shop—you'll find plenty of good choices.

Café Beaujolais

AMERICAN 15/20

961 UKIAH ST.
MENDOCINO 95460
707-937-5614
Dinner nightly, $$$

The husband-and-wife team of Margaret Fox and Chris Kump have accrued a sort of restaurant village on their large parcel of land (not far from the Anderson Valley wine country) where they run all their culinary concerns with care and skill. But it is the Mendocino dinner house that made the Café Beaujolais name famous. The simple but satisfying meals here feature ultra-fresh fish, poultry, or organic beef from the Niman-Schell ranch in Bolinas. Around back in the garden, the "brickery" turns out wonderful breads. Again, local products, such as vegetables and chèvre from a nearby farm, are the star ingredients. This place just keeps getting better and better.

Café Lolo

CALIFORNIAN 14/20
620 FIFTH ST.
SANTA ROSA 95404
707-576-7822
Lunch Mon.-Fri., Dinner Mon.-Sat, $$

You'll find no glorious vineyards in downtown Santa Rosa, yet this bistro on Fifth Street is worth trying. Chef Michael Quigley writes seasonal menus of quintessential Californian food: a goat-cheese-and-wild mushroom quesadilla, pan-roasted duck breast with an artichoke purée, and a sea scallop and potato napoleon with roasted beets, for example. Locals love this place for two more reasons: the friendly atmosphere created by Quigley's wife, Lori Darling (also known as "Lolo") and the reasonable prices on the wine list. Most bottle sells for less than $30, and decent wines are available by the glass for around $5 each.

Cantinetta

ITALIAN ¢
1050 CHARTER OAK AVE.
ST. HELENA 94574
707-963-8888
Lunch daily

In a small sandstone building draped with grapevines and wisteria, you'll find a wonderland of Italian food. Display cases are generously piled with soft foccacia, marinated olives, dipped biscotti, cured meats and fabulous salads. The chefs behind the counter will prepare thin-crusted pizzas and abundant sandwiches that rival the idyllic setting in which to enjoy them-a courtyard seemingly airlifted from Tuscany to Napa Valley. In addition, you'll find a good selection of top Californian and Italian wines, strong espresso drinks and many potential gifts, such as flavored oils, cookbooks and hard-to-find gourmet products.

Catahoula

CONTEMPORARY CREOLE 15/20
1457 LINCOLN AVE.
CALISTOGA 94515
707-942-2275
Lunch & Dinner Wed.-Mon. (Closed Jan.), $$$

Big flavors, big fun, big chef. Jan Birnbaum, previously of Campton Place in San Francisco and originally from New Orleans, holds center stage here in front of a wood-burning oven that faces an elegant, funky dining room. Rusted animal sculptures and large photos of dogs-the catahoula hound is the state dog of Louisiana-draw attention, but nothing stands out as much as the fabulous food. Birnbaum plays tribute to some traditional gumbos and other Southern classics with exciting twists. Get a load of sassafras-encrusted lamb with potato-salsify pie, or pork porterhouse steak with red-eye gravy, "sexy grits" and pickled cabbage or, better yet, Southern-fried rabbit with dirty rice and collard greens. Desserts change frequently (as do other items) but save room; they too nearly always satisfy.

Compadres

MEXICAN ¢
VINTAGE ESTATE MALL
6539 WASHINGTON ST.
YOUNTVILLE 94599
707-944-2406
Lunch & Dinner daily, Brunch Sun.

The well-made margaritas here come not only in several sizes ("uno", "dos" or "trés"), but also in widely assorted flavors. Check out such aperitivos as oyster shooters, Tijuana won tons and chingalinga. If you're still hungry, try the grilled pollo borracho (drunken chicken) marinated in booze. This stylish spot has a wonderful outdoor patio.

The Diner

CAFÉ ¢
6476 WASHINGTON ST.
YOUNTVILLE 94599
707-944-2626
Breakfast, Lunch & Dinner Tues.-Sun.
No cards

This is the Wine Country's answer to the sort of breakfast café so popular in Berkeley: raw ingredients are fresh and organic, and the food is free of salt and oils. A former winner of the "Best Breakfast in the Valley" award, The Diner may face more competition now than in the past, but customers can still enjoy satisfying waffles, pancakes, omelets and house-made spicy sausage here. With the addition of good, strong coffee, breakfast here is all you need to begin your day in Napa Valley.

Domaine Chandon

CALIFORNIAN/FRENCH 15/20 ♟♟
CALIFORNIA DR. AT HWY. 29
YOUNTVILLE 94599
707-944-2892
Lunch & Dinner Wed.-Sun., $$$

The revered restaurant at Domaine Chandon, the first winery in Napa to build a top-flight restaurant on its premises, remains excellent-even after chef Philippe Jeanty has left and his sous-chef Robert Curry has taken charge. The setting overlooking the vines is magnificent, particularly if you get a treasured seat outdoors. Curry's smoked salmon tartare with fennel-and-radish salad goes splendidly with the house sparkling wine; there's a loin of lamb with a ratatouille-goat cheese tart, caramelized scallops with truffle oil and foie gras sauce, as well as Sonoma duck breast with wild mushrooms and asparagus. A hot, moist chocolate cake is heavenly. The restaurant is open daily in the summer; menu changes daily.

Downtown Bakery & Creamery

BAKERY ¢
308 CENTER ST.
HEALDSBURG 95448
707-431-2719
Open daily
No cards

Chez Panisse alums Lindsey Shore and Kathleen Stewart have run this shop on the Healdsburg Plaza since 1987, and everybody in these parts knows that they turn out the best breads and pastries in all of Sonoma County. Sticky buns are wonderful, and scones are made with locally picked blueberries. For savory baked goods, try rosemary foccacia and an appealing tart made with polenta. The Bakery also serves fresh seasonal fruit and good house-made ice cream.

Freestyle

INTERNATIONAL 14/20 ♟
522 BROADWAY (HWY. 12)
SONOMA 95476
707-996-9916
Lunch Wed.-Sat., Dinner Wed.-Mon., Brunch Sun, $$

[VISA] [MasterCard] [●]

Wildly successful New York restaurateur Drew Nieporent (Tribeca Grill, Montrachet,

Nobu, and Rubicon in San Francisco) master-minded this new restaurant just a half-block off the Sonoma Plaza. Nieporent and his designer chose a country look, but went way too far with light woods, goatskin walls and precious touches—like butter served in miniature iron skillets. Fortunately, the food helps you forget the cutesy feeling as it runs-"freestyle"-all over the globe. Garlicky, crisp calamari are served with an Asian barbecue sauce. The Caesar-style salad comes with pancetta and croutons made from polenta. Someone at your table should order the salad of frisée, arugula and Asian pear, a dish served with duck confit as soft as butter. Winning entrées include oven-roasted chicken with polenta and spinach and an uncommonly good grilled salmon on a bed of potato purée, piled with watercress-crabmeat slaw and served in a pool of paprika oil. Desserts are of the gooey variety; best of all is the Valrhona chocolate cake with espresso ice cream and milk chocolate sauce. As we went to press, we learned that there was a new chef, so things may change.

The French Laundry

FRENCH/AMERICAN 18/20 ♟♟♟
6640 WASHINGTON ST.
YOUNTVILLE 94599
707-944-2380
Lunch Fri.-Sun. Dinner nightly, $$$$

There is a culinary wizard in the little town of Yountville and his name is Thomas Keller. In a vine-draped, two-story stone house he prepares dishes so dazzling and different that travelers accustomed to the best foods and wines of Europe and beyond call months ahead to reserve a table here. All of Keller's menus are prix-fixe-each offering four, five or nine small courses, and each an imaginative combination of classical technique and daring approaches to flavors. Plan on spending several hours sampling edible jewels such as crispy Scottish salmon with braised fennel, Picholine olives and preserved Meyer lemon; a medallion of New Zealand venison with yellow corn polenta cake and apple compote; or a sabayon of pearl tapioca with poached oysters and sevruga caviar. Between courses, Keller sends enchanting surprises to the tables: imagine, for instance, a white truffle custard, baked in an empty eggshell; a miniature ice cream cone filled with salmon tartare; or a single bite of foie gras with well-aged balsamic vinegar from

Modena. Outstanding. A meal here just might prove to be your ultimate Wine Country experience.

The Girl & The Fig

FRENCH 14/20

13690 ARNOLD DR.
GLEN ELLEN 95442
707-938-3634
Dinner nightly, Brunch Sat.-Sun.

Some serious food lovers have banded together in a bright café in tiny Glen Ellen to create the kind of restaurant they always dreamed of: French food cooked with passion, served with deftness and set in a contemporary atmosphere. Two chefs with strong backgrounds in San Francisco restaurants (Moose's, Café Kati, Postrio) show their class with items such as a crisp house salad of cool greens, shaved fennel, citrus wedges, blue cheese croutons and a tarragon vinaigrette. Briny, fresh mussels are steamed in garlicky broth and served with shoestring potatoes. No Chardonnays or Cabernets; you'll find only delicious Rhône-style Viogniers and Syrahs on the list. A cheese and port plate is a good dessert choice, since the owner is a fan of finding Sonoma's best artisan cheeses.

The Grille

CALIFORNIAN 13/20

SONOMA MISSION INN
8140 SONOMA HWY. (12)
BOYES HOT SPRINGS 95476
707-938-9000
Lunch & Dinner daily, $$$

The Sonoma Mission Inn is a European-style spa built on underground mineral waters. Overlooking its main pool and gardens is the Grille, a good place for a satisfying meal that carefully controls calorie content. Recent arrival Jeffrey Jake prepares a lovely corn risotto with wild mushrooms and Reggiano Parmigiano cheese and a roasted summer vegetable terrine with goat cheese and basil oil for appetizers. His leg of Sonoma lamb—roasted with whole wheat breadcrumbs and pistachios-and his version of orecchiette with smoked chicken and artichokes in a vegetable broth are admirable entrées. The interior of pink stucco walls and rattan chairs reminds you you're in a hotel dining room, but most hotels don't have such an impressive wine list: over 200 selections from California and beyond. For a tasty, low-cal dessert, try lemon chiffon with strawberry sauce.

Heritage House

AMERICAN 13/20

520 N. PACIFIC COAST HWY.
LITTLE RIVER 95456
707-937-5885
Breakfast Mon.-Fri. Dinner daily. Brunch Sat.-Sun., $$$

This 1877 farmhouse, perched dramatically on a cliff, has long been a destination for honeymooners and other lovers. A few highly regarded chefs have come and gone recently, but today Jason Hayter and Gerry Dimma share responsibility for their own version of American country cooking. Try local cod cakes with mustard sauce or a grilled New York steak with Cabernet mashed potatoes. This is a lovely spot, decorated with antiques and country-style accessories. At night couples huddle behind flickering candles, sipping wine from a thoughtfully selected, reasonably priced list. The view of the Pacific is spectacular.

John Ash & Co.

WINE COUNTRY 14/20

4330 BARNES RD. (B/W RIVER RD & HWY 101)
SANTA ROSA 9540
707-527-7687
Lunch Tues.-Fri., Dinner Mon.-Sun., $$$

John Ash, a pioneer of Californian cuisine, doesn't cook here anymore, but his preference for fresh and wonderful Sonoma County ingredients remains the kitchen's driving force. Some feel the décor is too corporate: pastel stucco walls frame big windows with panoramic views of vineyards. Monthly-changing menus, however, are always interesting. For appetizers we recently enjoyed a quintessential onion soup and a sassy salad of grilled portobello mushrooms, oven-roasted pears and Gorgonzola cheese. Entrées might be a lobster risotto, sautéed salmon or grilled filet of beef. Many vegetables and herbs are grown in an on-premise garden; nearly everything else on the menu is purchased locally from small farms.

Kenwood Restaurant and Bar

CALIFORNIAN 13/20

9900 SONOMA HWY. (12)
KENWOOD 95452
707-833-6326
Dinner Wed.-Sun., $$$

This little jewel of a restaurant has nothing to do with the local winery of the same name, but like the winery is housed in a vintage wooden building among the oaks of the upper Sonoma Valley. It's a popular, unpretentious place. Fresh Sonoma County ingredients are shown to advantage in such dishes as roast Petaluma duck served with cherry sauce and braised endive. Like the entrées, starters are filling and wholesome: try the grilled polenta with ratatouille, crab cake with herb mayonnaise. Desserts are homey and comforting, as in the case of the delightful chocolate walnut tart. Like so many establishments, the Kenwood's wine list features locally grown bottlings.

Lisa Hemenway's

CALIFORNIAN 14/20

714 VILLAGE COURT
MONTGOMERY VILLAGE, FARMER'S LN.
SANTA ROSA 95405
707-526-5111
Lunch Mon.-Sat., Dinner nightly, Brunch Sun., $$$

Recently returned from cooking trips to Indonesia and Singapore, Lisa Hemenway has brought Asian-inspired dishes to her little Santa Rosa strip mall café. Don't let this restaurant's location scare you off; there's enough warmth here to more than compensate. The simply decorated dining room is airy and light. Chef-owner Hemenway's eclectic menu, based on fresh Sonoma County products, is the main attraction. Recent entrées have included coconut- and peanut-crusted chicken breast with spicy ginger papaya sauce, bacon-wrapped filet mignon in a red wine reduction and oven-roasted duck breast in a blood orange demi-glace. Hemenway's desserts have always been crowd pleasers, especially her Hungarian nut torte, a fantasy of walnuts and caramel. The wine list contains a number of quality selections which pair well with the house cuisine.

Madrona Manor

CALIFORNIAN 13/20

1001 WESTSIDE RD.
HEALDSBURG 95448
707-433-4231
Dinner nightly, $$$

A

Chez Panisse alum Todd Muir established the dining room of this lovely former residence outside of Healdsburg as an outpost of reliable and satisfying Californian cuisine. Today Craig Linowski handles most of the cooking, drawing on top local ingredients including vegetables, herbs and edible flowers grown in the gardens surrounding this 1880s vintage mansion. The seared scallops dressed with a lemony beurre blanc show off Linowski's control of the classics. Even better is the roasted cashew-crusted salmon and the braised rabbit with mixed beans. You'll want to linger in any one of the three elegant Victorian dining rooms here—try doing so with a dessert like the white chocolate blueberry mousse cake. If you still can't tear yourself away, you may want to inquire about the inviting guest rooms upstairs (see Hotels).

The Meadowood Resort Restaurant

FRENCH/CALIFORNIAN 14/20

MEADOWOOD RESORT,
900 MEADOWOOD LN.
ST. HELENA 94574
707-963-3646
Dinner nightly, $$$$

A

This is the most formal (and best) of posh Meadowood Resort's restaurants, a place where the food resembles the décor: expensive ingredients presented with flair. The changing menu leans toward elaborate dishes like seared scallops steamed in corn husks with vanilla-bean butter and house-smoked sturgeon with warm potato fritters and osetra caviar. The wine list offers an exhaustive collection of Napa Valley bottlings (purportedly every Napa County winery is represented) and has good vintage depth. This is a dress-up kind of restaurant with the feel of a grand lodge, one that caters to a clientele of well-heeled Wine Country gentry.

Mustards

CALIFORNIAN 14/20

7399 St. Helena Hwy.
Yountville 94599
707-944-2424
Lunch & Dinner daily, $$$

This long-established Yountville bistro is often the first restaurant that many people think of when they envision Wine Country cuisine. The wide range of starters available here-tapas, canapés, grilled meats and veggies-are as good as ever, their generally strong (and sometimes wild) flavors pairing well with the good wines on Mustard's list. Our favorites still include deep-fried onion threads (try them with house-made ketchup) and crispy calamari with curry slaw. For entrées, baby back ribs and a grilled, marinated pork chop remain a meat lover's dream. For dessert, you can't go wrong with banana cheesecake served with a roasted banana-butterscotch sauce.

Oakville Grocery Café (Oakville)

CAFÉ ¢

7848 St. Helena Hwy.
St. Helena 94574
707-944-0111
Breakfast & Lunch daily

Since the 1970s the Oakville Grocery has been a popular tourist stop for upscale picnic supplies and expensive gourmet items. In 1997, the management took over a vacant restaurant space next door and began serving breakfast and lunch to travelers of this busy Napa Valley thoroughfare. Their house-baked muffins, scones and pastries are well done; so are breakfasts including decent omelets and frittatas. A decent lunch, featuring good foccacia sandwiches, pasta dishes and pizzas baked in their brick oven, is also available.

Oakville Grocery (Healdsburg)

DELI/CAFÉ ¢

124 Matheson St.
Healdsburg 95448
707-433-3200
Lunch & Dinner daily

Delicious sandwiches—smoked turkey with Brie, roasted pork loin with caramelized onions, eggplant with Fontina-provide the backbone of a menu that also includes wood-fired pizzas and vegetable salads. A full charcuterie of cured meats, dozens of artisan cheeses, wines sold by the glass and an espresso bar put lunch or dinner supplies within easy reach. You can take anything to go, or have your meal on an attractive outdoor terrace facing Healdsburg's town square.

Piatti Ristorante

ITALIAN 12/20

6480 Washington St.
Yountville 94599
707-944-2070
Lunch & Dinner daily, $$$

Piattis are breaking out all over! First in Yountville, then in Sonoma and now down the coast in Carmel. It's a winning formula: a little pizza, a little pasta, some grilled specialties-all served in the sort of warm, unpretentious trattoria setting that makes Italian food feel so familiar. What to order? The flatbread with local cheese and roasted garlic, a saffron pappardelle "fantasia," any of the rotisseried items (especially the succulent chicken) are best. Try the tiny roasted potatoes with crusty skins and sweet, fleshy centers. Nearly everything on the menu will satisfy your appetite for fine Italian country fare. The wine list combines Wine Country favorites with-you guessed it-selected Italian bottlings. Other locations.

Pinot Blanc

FRENCH 15/20

641 Main St.
St. Helena 94574
707-963-6191
Lunch & Dinner Tues.-Sun., $$$

A relatively new entry on Napa Valley's high-end restaurant roster, Pinot Blanc is the creation of famed Los Angeles chef Joachim Splichal (Patina, Pinot Bistro and Pinot Hollywood, among others). Sean Knight, who worked with Splichal at Pinot Bistro, is in charge of this kitchen, and ably produces a lengthy mix of hearty and light dishes reminiscent of European flavors. A tower of red and yellow beets served with a hazelnut vinaigrette and blood oranges, for example, makes a pretty and delicious mosaic. Large seared scallops are presented on a potato pancake made glorious with a salt cod purée. Ricotta cheese gnocchi are fabulously rich served with braised veal cheeks and baby artichokes. One dessert, chocolate croissant pudding, a dizzying dish of diced crisp croissant chunks baked in a vanilla bean custard studded with bittersweet chocolate, ranks among the best in Napa Valley. Serious wine drinkers will enjoy a list of over two hundred bottles—most of which the staff has never tasted, so if you don't know your wines, stick to the dozen or so available by the glass that the staff can describe. The atmosphere has a classic bistro feeling-lots of dark wood, graceful lighting, roomy booths and white linen tablecloths. If the brick patio is open, ask for a table there, where you'll enjoy the trellised grapevines and citrus fruit and olive trees.

Ravenous

INTERNATIONAL 13/20

117 NORTH STREET
HEALDSBURG 95448
707-431-1770
Lunch & Dinner Wed.-Sun., $$

No cards

This tiny, tucked-away bistro near Healdsburg's town square is a local favorite for creative cooking and a stylish setting. The menu changes frequently, but expect a lot of Mediterranean influences with other international cuisines. Recently, the kitchen's husband-and-wife team was serving grilled halibut with a chervil vinaigrette and braised fennel, posole (Mexican pork and hominy stew), and scallop brochettes with a green curry sauce. Many of the customers are winemakers, so the wine list also changes often enough to keep them interested. You'll find mostly Sonoma County bottles, with a dozen or so offered by the glass. Call for reservations, particularly on weekends, because the restaurant has only two dozen seats.

Rutherford Grill

AMERICAN 11/20

1180 RUTHERFORD RD,
RUTHERFORD 94573
707-963-1792
Lunch & Dinner daily, $$

In a region spoiled with innovative and artful food, this straightforward American restaurant calls out to people who want a thick steak, familiar side dishes and reasonable prices. Hungry for some barbecue ribs with cole slaw and potato chips or a prime rib sandwich? This is an ideal spot for a group of friends to take a roomy booth in the casual but classy dining room. Stand-out dishes include spit-roasted chicken, Maytag blue cheese potato chips and a homemade cookie and ice cream sandwich. You can expect friendly service inside and on the brick patio-the latter of which is very popular with the lunch crowd.

Terra

CALIFORNIAN/ASIAN 13/20

1345 RAILROAD AVE.
ST. HELENA 94574
707-963-8931
Dinner Wed.-Mon., $$$

Terra has a solid following among Napa Valley diners, for two very good reasons: chefs Hiro Sone and Lissa Doumani, both of whom worked for Wolfgang Puck at Spago. They've occupied this beautifully restored 1880s vintage stone structure for years now, turning out glorious food of imaginative design. Lobster tortellini in a chanterelle mushroom broth with tarragon is even better then it sounds; grilled New York steak with potato dauphinois and Cabernet Sauvignon sauce packs a big punch of flavor. A favorite is the broiled sake-marinated Chilean sea bass with shrimp dumplings in shiso broth. For dessert, try an apple and quince tart, house tiramisu or chocolate bread pudding.

Tomatina

¢

1016 MAIN ST.
ST. HELENA 94574
707-967-9999
Lunch & Dinner daily

The folks behind the wildly-successful Tra Vigne restaurant next door run this family-style pizzeria, whose menu includes home-made soups, fresh salads, warm pasta dishes and wide range of pizzas. Favorites pies are the margherita and the Mediterranean, but the kitchen encourages you to create your own with toppings like kalamata olives, Sonoma goat cheese and fennel sausage.

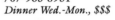

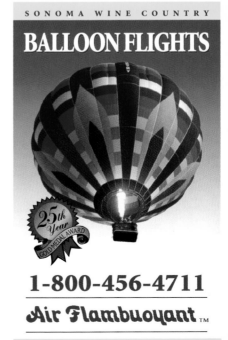

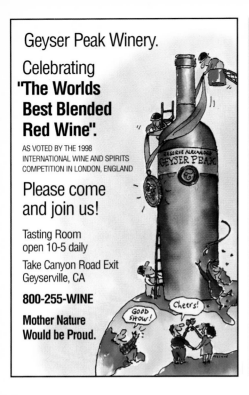

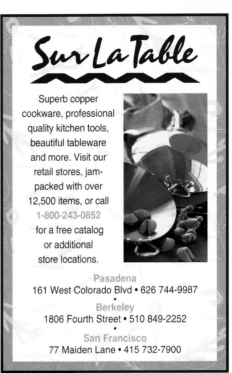

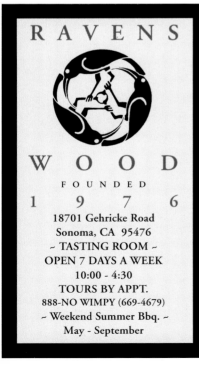

Tra Vigne

ITALIAN 15/20
1050 CHARTER OAK AVE.
ST. HELENA 94574
707-963-4444
Lunch & Dinner daily, $$$

Dining at Tra Vigne, one sees clearly how European influences have shaped Wine Country culture. Within this former wine cellar built of stone is an imposing carved-wood bar, frescos of pastoral scenes and enough marble and terra-cotta tile to fill a Tuscan villa. Italian art deco posters fill the walls and outside, a gurgling fountain in the courtyard speaks of the Old World. Fortunately, chef Michael Chiarello's food more than lives up to this setting. The trick at Tra Vigne is to order a bunch of dishes and pass them around: our favorite appetizer is mozzarella alla griglia, small romaine lettuce packets of tangy, creamy cheese and prosciutto grilled until the cheese is smoky and soft. Small pizzas ordered from the wood-burning oven—particularly one topped with roasted garlic and rosemary-are also quite wonderful. Breads baked on the premises are superb, and each table has a little tub of olive oil for dipping. Pastas are dreamy, featuring sauces of fresh seasonal vegetables and herbs, and grilled dishes, too, are treated with great finesse, as in the prawns wrapped in pancetta. The wine list offers excellent selections from Napa and Italy.

Wappo Bar

INTERNATIONAL 14/20
1226B WASHINGTON ST.
CALISTOGA 94515
707-942-4712
Lunch & Dinner Wed.-Mon., $$

This bar, which is actually a restaurant, is a brilliant change of pace from the dozens of Wine Country eateries offering trendy California food. Wappo's menu covers many culinary miles, but most items are rooted in South America. Critics rave about the chiles rellenos with walnut-pomegranate sauce; other signature dishes are brilliant gazpacho, seared Chilean sea bass with garam masala and chunks of braised pork in a dark chili-and-beer sauce. The interior of the small, narrow building is attractively designed with copper-topped tables and reddish-brown wainscoting, but the place to be in warm weather is the flower-lined brick terrace laced with grapevines. The service is usually excellent, with waitstaff always ready to refill your glass with wine or their phenomenal water flavored with fresh flowers and citrus. Entrée portions are big, but try to manage a bit of orange flan or strawberry-rhubarb pie for dessert.

Willowside Café

CALIFORNIAN 15/20
3535 GUERNEVILLE ROAD
SANTA ROSA 95401
707-523-4814
Dinner Wed.-Sun., $$$

Don't let the building fool you. Inside this funky roadhouse in the rural outskirts of Santa Rosa, top-notch restaurateurs are busy doing great work for a growing audience. A husband-and-wife team with many years in the San Francisco food scene (Greens, Postrio) combine efforts with Richard Allen, who cooked at the much-revered Chez Panisse in Berkeley before moving to the Wine Country. Every week, Allen creates a new menu, so it's impossible to say exactly what you'll get. He may serve chilled cream of cucumber soup with a smoked trout crouton as one of six starters, then perhaps quail with truffle oil onions, portobello gratin and roasted garlic as one of five main plates. Desserts are sometimes a little weak here, especially when the pastry chef tries too hard; stick to the simple recipes like lemon tart or nectarine crisp. Many local winemakers claim the best of all reasons to come here is the wine list, an ever-changing mix of hard-to-find bottles from Sonoma and wine regions all over the world.

The Wine Spectator Greystone

MEDITERRANEAN 15/20
2555 MAIN ST.
ST. HELENA 94574
707-967-1010
Lunch & Dinner daily, $$$

This massive stone building used to be home to Christian Brothers Winery and is now the West Coast campus of the Culinary Institute of America in New York. Diners gather in a large, colorful room with tasteful touches of tile, wrought iron and blond wood; cooks display their toques and techniques in three exhibition kitchens. The theme of the menu is Mediterranean, small tastings plates and such entrées as roasted duck glazed with honey and caramelized quince. The three vegetarian dips served with crackers and cod cakes napped with lemon aïoli are delicious. The all-California wine list offers many sought-after rarities. Wonder about the name? *The Wine Spectator* magazine donated the money to open this restaurant of the non-profit CIA. On a warm evening, get a table in the courtyard.

HOTELS

TOP OF THE LINE

Auberge du Soleil

180 RUTHERFORD HILL RD.
RUTHERFORD 94573
707-963-1211, FAX 707-963-8764
Suites $250-$900

There's no denying that Auberge is a very pricey place to stay; but then again you're paying for a room in a property that consistently turns up on respected lists of the world's finest inns. The "Inn of the Sun" has long enjoyed a reputation as the crème de la crème of Wine Country accommodations, and it caters to an accordingly—fancy clientele. Each of twelve adobe-style buildings contains four rooms-you can choose a one- or two-bedroom suite. Whichever you book, you'll find yourself in the lap of luxury, high on a hill amid an olive grove, with a valley of vineyards below. No suite here is without a view, nor a deck from which to appreciate it. Rooms have handsome terra-cotta tile floors and are tastefully furnished; they contain fireplaces and stocked wet bars. Guests receive baskets of fruit and other goodies and have access to the inn's tennis courts, a large swimming pool and the property's **Auberge du Soleil** restaurant (see Dining), which offers a lovely outdoor patio with the best view of any restaurant in Napa. Indulge yourself.

Meadowood Napa Valley

900 MEADOWOOD LN.
ST. HELENA 94574
707-963-3646, FAX 707-963-3532
Rooms/Suites $310-$675

Here's the kind of place this is: a resident wine tutor is available by appointment to instruct you in the nuances of the region's number one tourist draw. Get the idea? Meadowood's proprietors don't miss a trick at this truly luxurious resort. Comprised of a dozen New England-style lodges situated on forested acreage in a way that provides everyone a good measure of privacy, the resort offers 85 spacious guest rooms and suites. Meadowood has tennis courts, two swimming pools, a nine-hole golf course and croquet court and an endless list of recreational activities. The main lodge contains two dining rooms: **The Grill** is a casual spot and **The Meadowood Napa Valley Restaurant** (see Dining) is a dressy place for a special evening of dining.

Oak Knoll Inn

2200 E. OAK KNOLL AVE.
NAPA VALLEY 94558
707-255-2200, FAX 707-255-2296
Rooms $250-$350

One of Napa's hidden jewels, this charming four-room inn is situated amid vineyards on three-and-a-half acres, and offers serene luxury, terrific views and an excellent wine-and-cheese hour most nights of the week when winemakers from local boutique wineries come to pour and discuss their vintages with guests. Each spacious room has a king-sized brass bed and a wood-burning fireplace, and opens onto the patio, swimming pool and spa. Despite its size, the Oak Knoll has a knowledgeable concierge who is happy to plan guests' wine-touring and dining itineraries while in the Wine Country.

LUXURY

Albion River Inn

3790 PACIFIC COAST HWY.
ALBION 95410
707-937-1919, 800-479-7944, FAX 707-937-2604
Singles & Doubles $170-$260

Overlooking picturesque Albion Cove, where the Albion River meets the Pacific Ocean, the Albion River Inn comprises a number of quaint wooden cottages and several larger buildings. There are a total of twenty rooms here; most have ocean views and some have fireplaces, decks and tubs for two as well. The top accommodation ($260 a night), includes a Jacuzzi from which you can take in the Pacific in full panorama. In addition, there are lovely lawns and gardens on this property, located only six miles south of the village of Mendocino. A full breakfast is included with the price of your lodging.

Harvest Inn

1 Main St.
St. Helena 94574
707-963-9463, Fax 707-963-4402
Singles & Doubles $149-$499

A P

The Harvest Inn is located on St. Helena's main drag, but you'd never know it: this Tudor-style inn is surrounded by 21 acres of gardens and vineyards. Its 54 rooms are lavishly appointed and furnished with fine antiques; most have fireplaces, wet bars, refrigerators and vineyard views. Three rooms have their own adjacent spas, and a pool is available on the premises for the use of all guests. Some of the property's cottages-facilities with charming cobblestone fireplaces, oak-paneled walls, pegged oak floors and stained-glass windows-offer conference rooms for business meetings which, because they're usually occupied, somewhat diminishes the Harvest Inn's appeal as a romantic hideaway.

LaFleur Bed & Breakfast

1475 Inglewood Ave.
St. Helena 94574
707-963-0233, No fax
Rooms $165
No cards.

The rooms in this charming 1880s vintage Queen Ann Victorian are beautifully and individually decorated with lovely antiques. One, for example, is furnished with floor-to-ceiling hand-painted shutters: throw them open to reveal vineyard views from every window. Another faces a rose garden and contains a striking black marble fireplace. A third has a wall of bookshelves stocked with an intriguing array of titles. A full breakfast is served here. In the afternoon, you might want to pop in next door at the **Villa Helena Winery**, a micro-winery that specializes in Chardonnays.

Madrona Manor

1001 Westside Rd.
Healdsburg 95448
707-433-4231, Fax 707-433-0703
Singles & Doubles $155-$255

A P

Located on eight magnificently wooded acres, the Madrona Manor is a model of what every country guest house should be. The conversion of the old private Victorian mansion and carriage house on the property were carried out with taste and sensitivity. The mansion now has nine guest rooms; nine more can be had in the carriage house, and additional accommodations are available in two contemporary buildings on the property. (Needless to say, you want to be in the mansion or the carriage house.) All rooms have private baths, and some have balconies; there is a swimming pool on the premises. Breakfast at the inn's eponymous restaurant (see Dining) is included with your accommodations.

Silverado Country Club & Resort

1600 Atlas Peak Rd.
Napa 94558
707-257-0200, Fax 707-257-2867
Rooms & studio condos $150, 1-bedroom condos $280, 2-bedroom condos $385, 3-bedroom condos $485

A P

This 1,200-acre spread with its 800 condos (not all are available for guest lodging) is much larger-scaled than almost anything else in the Wine Country. Many of the condos are perfectly pleasant and, in two- and three-bedroom configurations, can accommodate entire families quite comfortably. But quaint or intimate the Silverado isn't. Golfers who flock here for the resort's two eighteen-hole golf courses, tennis players are in heaven with twenty tennis courts available and swimmers have nine pools to choose from. This place is neither self-conscious nor apologetic about its size: jogging trails wend around the property and you can rent a bike to get you from your room to the gift shop. A spa is coming in 1999.

Sonoma Mission Inn & Spa

18149 Sonoma Hwy. (12)
Boyes Hot Springs 95476
800-862-4945, 707-938-9000,
Fax 707-938-4250
Singles & Doubles $175-$395, Suites $395-$750

VISA MasterCard Diners Club International P

The Sonoma Mission Inn was established as a spa in the mid-1800s, and today still promotes good health in a region that's become famous for its concentration of Epicurean indulgences. Multiple-day lodging and spa packages offer various forms of exercise (aerobics, tennis, swimming and so on) and are accompanied by spa-cuisine meals. It also provides a number of beauty treatment packages. Though the ambience here is quite relaxed, guests rooms are befitting a luxury hotel. The Sonoma Mission Inn has a large repeat clientele, including many celebrities, socialites and titans of business and industry. Some insist on rooms in the main building, which is older and has more character; others want to lodge in the larger and newer rooms elsewhere on the property. Its proprietors have recently added several elegant suites and cottages.

Vintners Inn

4350 BARNES RD.
SANTA ROSA 95403
707-575-7350, FAX 707-575-1426
Singles & Doubles $178-$225

A P

John Ash put this small, 44-room European-style hotel on the map when he opened his restaurant here more than a decade ago. Ash has left but the restaurant and hotel remain in the middle of 50 acres of vineyard, perched on the flatlands not far from busy Highway 101. The hotel comprises four separate buildings, each covered in red tile; guest rooms are furnished with European antique pine pieces. Homemade breads and coffee cakes are part of a complimentary breakfast, but you're certain to want to visit John Ash & Co. (see Dining) for a full lunch or dinner.

Whale Watch Inn

35100 PACIFIC COAST HWY. (1)
GUALALA 95445
707-884-3667, FAX 707-884-4815
Doubles $170-$270

VISA MasterCard Diners Club International P

The appropriately named Whale Watch Inn comprises five buildings of varying styles, all of them poised among pine and cypress trees beside the cliff's edge. Each offers stirring views of the Pacific and the southern coastline. Our favorite accommodations are on the upper level of the main lodge (called Pacific Edge). The aroma of burning fireplace wood combines with the pines and the sound of the crashing surf to make a stay here a remarkable sensory experience. A fine breakfast is served in your room, then it's down a long, long stairway to a nearly-always-uninhabited beach. You're right on the ocean, and during the winter months you may sight migrating humpback whales from the windows of your room.

MODERATE

The El Dorado Hotel

405 FIRST ST. WEST
SONOMA 95476
707-996-3030, FAX 707-996-3148
Singles & Doubles $100-$160.

VISA MasterCard Diners Club International

Located on the plaza in Sonoma, the El Dorado dates to 1843 and was originally the residence of Don Salvador Vallejo, the last Mexican commandant of Sonoma. Hotelier/restaurateur Claude Rouas (proprietor of Napa's Auberge du Soleil and several Piatti restaurants) remodeled the 26-room inn some years ago, installing four-poster beds and private balconies in every room. A pleasant courtyard contains a swimming pool and provides outdoor seating for Rouas' Piatti Ristorante (see Dining) on the hotel's ground level. Room rates here include complimentary Continental breakfast, which is served in the lobby.

Embassy Suites Napa Valley

1075 CALIFORNIA BLVD.
NAPA 94558
800-362-2779, 707-253-9540, FAX 707-253-9202
Suites $144-$224

A

At first glance, the exterior of this 205-room hotel resembles the Sonoma Mission Inn. Its putative beauty is only skin deep, however: inside, this is a typical chain hotel lacking in individual character. Nevertheless, in a part of the state where it's often difficult to find an empty room, this property has its place. Suites are spacious and contain such amenities as a kitchen with microwave-this a good choice for traveling families. Indoor and outdoor pools are on the premises, as well as a sauna and spa. Full breakfast is included with a nightly stay.

Inn at the Tides

800 Pacific Coast Hwy.
Bodega Bay 94923
707-875-2751, Fax 707-875-3023
Singles & Doubles $124-$249

A P

This inn, tucked into hills along the rugged Sonoma Coast, is a bit off the beaten path of the usual Wine Country tour. But if you want to escape both city and heavily trafficked country, the complex of two-story, hill-hugging buildings provides a pleasant option. Most rooms have fireplaces and are appointed with cut fresh flowers and snack-stocked refrigerators. Guests receive a newspaper delivered to their room. Start your day in the Bay View dining room, which offers a sweeping view of the ocean. Inn af the Tides also has an indoor-outdoor heated swimming pool with adjoining sauna and massage facilities.

Mount View Hotel

1457 Lincoln Ave.
Calistoga 94515
707-942-6877, Fax 707-942-6904
Singles & Doubles $100-$170, Suites $190-$225.

A P

Jan Birnbaum's Catahoula restaurant is the jewel of this property, but the hotel's 32 guest rooms-each one art deco-themed and named for movie stars of the 1930s-are done with style and good humor and never seem precious. The hotel's suites are equipped with private redwood decks, Jacuzzis and wet bars. During the day you can sip fruit drinks by the pool or indulge in the spa, which offers baths, massages, facials and wraps.

Rancho Caymus Inn

1140 Rutherford Rd. (128 E.)
Rutherford 94573
707-963-1777, Fax 707-963-5387
Singles & Doubles $145-$175, Suites $245-$295

VISA MasterCard Diners Club International P

California history buffs will enjoy staying in the Rancho Caymus: its suites are named for Black Bart and other such colorful persons from the past, while public rooms reflect names like Bella Oaks Mine and the like. Artisan-made furniture of California oak, black walnut and fir lend the inn an air of solidity; Ecuadoran wrought-iron lamps and other appointments of the kind contribute character. Some rooms have fireplaces and Jacuzzis. Wherever you sleep, you'll probably want to take your complimentary breakfast in the pleasant courtyard, which seems always to have colorful flowers in bloom.

ECONOMY

Boonville Hotel

Hwy. 128 & Lambert Ln.
Boonville 95415
707-895-2210, No fax
Singles & Doubles $70-$150

A P

This little clapboard hotel in the heart of the beautiful and underrated Anderson Valley has been completely renovated in the last several years. Each of the eight rooms in the upstairs hotel is individually appointed in a creative and whimsical manner. With its excellent dining room downstairs (see Dining), it won't likely be the best-kept secret in all of Wine Country for long.

Sonoma Hotel

110 W. Spain St.
Sonoma 95476
707-996-2996, Fax 707-996-7014
Singles & Doubles $75-$85 (shared bath), $115-$125 (private bath)

VISA MasterCard Diners Club International

Once a combination dry goods store and meeting hall, this historic building is now a lovely seventeen-room hotel. It provides good value and is well located on the Sonoma Plaza. An era past is evoked by the hotel's antique furnishings. Complimentary Continental breakfast is served in the lobby with its beveled-glass doors and windows.

White Sulphur Springs Retreat & Spa

3100 White Sulphur Springs Rd.
St. Helena 94574
707-963-8588
Rooms $85-$185

VISA MasterCard P

Opened in 1852, White Sulphur Springs was California's first resort. Located three miles from the village of St. Helena, the retreat is still secluded and very rustic in an old-fashioned way. Think of this as the place to escape from your Wine Country escape:

four different types of accommodations are available on the property, including an ungentrified carriage house, one inn and nine cottages. But it's not luxurious accommodations that this place is about. You come for the 330 acres of redwoods, fir and madrone forests that surround you and through which you will want to hike on any of the numerous existing trails (several lead to splendid waterfalls). Obviously, you won't find TVs here: just those seeking to rest, hike, book a massage and enjoy a long soak in the Sulphur pool.

SHOPPING

The Wine Country, not surprisingly, contains several good shopping districts. **Vintage 1870** (6525 Washington St., Yountville; 707-944-2451) is a popular mall with more than forty independent shops and galleries. In Napa, the biggest tourist draw is **Napa Premium Outlets** (Hwy. 29 at First Street exit; 707-226-9876) showcasing heavy hitters such as Liz Claiborne, Esprit, Ann Taylor Loft, J. Crew, Timberland, Levi's, Harry and David, Tommy Hilfiger and Dansk. You'll find a smaller collection of factory stores at the **St. Helena Premium Outlets** (Hwy. 29, 2 miles north of St. Helena; 707-963-7282) including Brooks Brothers, Donna Karan, Joan and David and London Fog. There are wonderful clothing stores on **Main Street** in St. Helena, and around the historic **Sonoma Plaza** in the City of Sonoma there are numerous antique, clothing and gift shops, including the famous **Sonoma Cheese Factory** (707-996-1931) and the **Sonoma Sausage Co.** (707-938-8200). Of course any number of wineries in the area have their own gift shops, to say nothing of outlet stores at which you may purchase their wines. **The Book Cellar** (1354 Main St., St. Helena, 707-963-3901) specializes in books on wine and travel, and is a must for visitors to Wine Country.

SIGHTSEEING, ARTS & CULTURE

MUSEUMS

Nearly a dozen general interest museums are scattered throughout the wine country, such as the **Luther Burbank Home & Gardens** (the noted Santa Rosa horticulturist's former home, grounds and greenhouse; Santa Rosa and Sonoma; 707-524-5445), the **Healdsburg Museum** (exhibits focusing on life in this community, past and present; 221 Matheson, Healdsburg; 707-431-3325), the **Pacific Coast Air Museum** (aeronautics; Sonoma County Airport, Windsor; 707-525-7900), the **Carolyn Parr Nature Museum** (exhibits devoted to the fauna of the region; 3107 Browns Valley Rd., Napa; 707-255-6465) and the **Silverado Museum** (honoring the life and works of writer Robert Louis Stevenson; 1490 Library Ln., St. Helena; 707-963-3757).

GALLERIES

The Hess Collection (4411 Redwood Rd., Napa 94558, 707-255-1144; open daily 10 a.m.-4 p.m.), housed in the Hess winery, has on display paintings and sculptures of contemporary American and European artists personally collected by Donald Hess, founder of the winery. Hess' special interests in Abstract Expressionism and the work of Swiss artists are reflected in the collection. **Robert Mondavi** (7801 St. Helena Hwy., Oakville; 707-963-9611), **Clos Pegase** (1060 Dunaweal Ln., Calistoga; 707-942-4981) and several other wineries also have distinguished art collections on display.

PERFORMING ARTS

Music festivals and concerts are offered at many wineries throughout the year including the **Robert Mondavi Winery** (see above), **Charles Krug Winery** (2800 Main St., St. Helena; 707-963-2761) and **Domaine Chandon** (1 California Dr., Yountville; 707-944-8844).

Sonoma Valley Shakespeare Festival

GUNDLACH-BUNDSCHU WINERY
2000 DENMARK ST.
SONOMA 95476
707-575-3854
Performances Fri.-Sat.-Sun. in summer (call to confirm), 6:30 p.m. curtain
Adults $16, children under 12 free

Bring a picnic dinner and a blanket and find a spot on the picturesque hillside overlooking the Gundlach-Bundschu Winery. Works by The Bard are given high-spirited performances here by the Sonoma Shakespeare Company. Casual dress and comfortable shoes are recommended; you'll do well to arrive as close to the opening time of 5 p.m. as possible to get a place. Small picnic dinners are available at the winery.

LIBRARIES

Healdsburg Wine Library

139 PIPER ST.
HEALDSBURG 95448
707-433-3772
Mon. & Wed. 9:30 a.m.-9 p.m., Tues.-Sat. 9:30 a.m.-6 p.m.

Here, in the back of a regular branch of the Sonoma County Library, you'll find a great collection of wine books (some dating back over 100 years), wine memorabilia and wine-related periodicals. This library prides itself on its collection of oral histories featuring lengthy recorded interviews with many of the people who helped make the California wine industry what it is today. Wine librarian Bo Simons has a seemingly limitless store of knowledge on wine publishing; he can also show you how to use the on-line computer system.

Napa Valley Wine Library

ST. HELENA CITY LIBRARY
1492 LIBRARY LN.
ST. HELENA 94574
707-963-5244
Mon. & Wed. noon-9 p.m., Tues.-Thurs. 10 a.m.-6 p.m., Fri. 10 a.m.-6 p.m., Sat. 10 a.m.-4 p.m., Sun. 1 p.m.-5 p.m.

This unassuming branch library houses what is perhaps the most extensive collection of books and ephemera on California grape-growing, Winemaking, wine and wineries in the country. The countless treasures include rare lantern slides created as illustrations for a wine book published in 1889.

WINE CENTERS

California Welcome Center

5000 ROBERTS LAKE RD.
ROHNERT PARK 94928
707-586-3795
Open daily 9 a.m-5 p.m.

This facility's intention is to provide a central venue to promote the wines of Sonoma, thus raising public awareness of the region. The center contains a large relief map of the county, an interactive self-guided electronic tour through the region's various appellations, demonstration vineyards and a winery. A broad range of wine tasting classes, culinary seminars and Sonoma winery tours are conducted or organized here. And, of course, the center regularly hosts wine tastings.

Wine Discovery Center

ST. SUPÉRY VINEYARDS & WINERY
5440 ST. HELENA HWY.
RUTHERFORD 94573
707-963-4507
Open daily 9:30 a.m.-5 p.m.
Admission $2.50 (includes wine tasting)

Though the Discovery Center focuses on the wines of St. Supéry, it houses a good deal of information that's interesting and helpful to understanding wine in general. Inspect a display featuring cross-sections of grapevine roots, for instance, or a demonstration vineyard, bottling facility and barrel room and, best of all, something called "Smell-O-Vision," which allows you to experience at first hand the different aroma components present in wine.

ATTRACTIONS

Carneros Alambic Distillery

1250 CUTTINGS WHARF RD.
NAPA 94558
707-253-9055
Open daily 10 a.m.-5 p.m.
Admission $2

Only a handful of quality brandy makers operate in California and Alambic, owned by Rémy Martin, is the only one open to the public. The State of California says no winery or distillery may allow its customers to taste the product in the facility where it is made if the product has an alcohol content of 40 percent or more—so don't count on any tastings here. In the place of tasting, Alambic has instead developed a unique program of brandy sniffing. After a tour of the distillery (the pot stills here resemble the mad scientist's lab equipment in old horror flicks), you're invited to sniff various brandies from glasses in order to pick up their different aroma components. If the exercise leaves you a little light-headed, Alambic provides good, strong coffee.

Lake Sonoma Marina and Fish Hatchery

3333 Skaggs Springs Rd.
Geyserville 95448
707-433-2200
Open daily 7 a.m.-9 p.m. (summer), 9 a.m.-5:30 p.m. (winter)
Boat rentals from $15 an hour. Water-skiing/limo excursions $400-$800.

Located at the end of the Dry Creek appellation, Lake Sonoma is a 53-mile perimeter lake. You can rent all manner of boats here-houseboats, patio boats, paddle boats, canoes and fishing boats. You can even arrange a special ground and water tour involving a water skiing outing and a limo tour of the wineries in Dry Creek and Alexander valleys. On the lake is one of the most modern, state-of-the-art fish hatcheries in the country. Kids especially enjoy touring this facility to view its spawning and feeding tanks; everyone gets to feed the bass and the trout. The hatchery is open 9 a.m.-5 p.m. daily (707-433-9483).

Old Faithful

1299 Tubbs Ln.
Calistoga 94515
707-942-6463
Open daily 9 a.m.-6 p.m. (5 p.m. winter)
Adults $6, seniors $5, children over 6 $2, under 6 free.

This geyser, located about two miles north of Calistoga, is said to be one of only three such regularly erupting geysers in the world. The boiling water and vapor boil up and roar out of the ground at 350 degrees, shooting spumes more than 60 feet into the air. Eruptions generally occurs every 30 to 50 minutes; each one contains some 4,000 gallons of Sulphur-scented water.

Petrified Forest

4100 Petrified Forest Rd.
Calistoga 94515
707-942-6667
Open daily 10 a.m.-6 p.m. (5 p.m. in winter)
Adults $4 children 12-17 $2, children under 12 $1

Some three million years ago, an eruption of Mount St. Helena left the Napa Valley blanketed with volcanic ash. Then, a mere millennium ago, a solution of water and silica seeped through the ash and into the buried trees. You can find those trees today in this petrified forest located six miles from Calistoga. Excavations here have unearthed a number of giant redwoods, including a 126-foot long specimen. You can walk among the ruins of the forest and even picnic here if you like.

EXCURSIONS

TRAINS

Napa Valley Wine Train

1275 McKinstry
Napa 94558
800-427-4124
Brunch trains depart 8:30 a.m. Sat.-Sun., Lunch trains depart 11 a.m. Mon.-Fri. (noon on Sat & Sun), Dinner trains depart 6 p.m. Tues.-Fri. (5:30 p.m. Sat. & Sun).
$56.50 per person brunch, $63 lunch, $69.50 dinner.

This train makes a three-hour round trip commencing in Napa and extending eighteen miles to St. Helena and back. Lunch, brunch or dinner and, of course, wine, is served on board. It's a nice leisurely way to view the valley. In 1996 the Wine Train began offering an optional stop at Grgich Hills Cellars for a private tour and tasting.

Skunk Train

Fort Bragg Depot, Laurel Ave.
Ft. Bragg 95437
707-964-6371
Departs daily, 9:20 a.m. & 1:20 p.m. in summer months. Phone for winter schedule. Adults $26, $21 for half-day excursion; children up to 11 years old $12, $10 half-day.

Made up of vintage, no-frills passenger cars, the Skunk Train travels through deep Mendocino forest. No food or wine is allowed on board but its great fun for the kids. The Skunk goes all the way to the inland town of Willitts, where there isn't much to see. Passengers find it better to stop halfway at Northspur for a picnic in the woods and then meet the train on its return. This is the real thing as far as old trains are concerned.

SPORTS & LEISURE

BALLOONING

Adventures Aloft

Vintage 1870 Mall
6525 Washington St.
Yountville 94599
707-944-4408
Daily Departures 6 a.m.—weather permitting. Cost $185 per adult, $150 per child 6 to 12.

This Napa Valley balloon company offers thrilling flights over the vineyards of Napa. A celebratory brunch awaits you back on the ground.

Air Flambuoyant Hot Air Balloon Excursions

250 Pleasant Avenue
Santa Rosa 95403
707-838-8500; 800-456-4711
Daily departures at sun-up—weather permitting. Cost is $180 per person. Reservations are required.

Located in Santa Rosa, just 50 minutes North of the Golden Gate Bridge, Air Flambuoyant is the largest and most experienced, family owned balloon company in North America. They offer flights year around at sunrise, seven days a week—weather permitting—over the beautiful Sonoma wine country. The chief pilot's 3,000 hours ensures that you have a safe and carefree experience. Back on the ground, you'll enjoy brunch at a local restaurant.

BICYCLING

Napa Valley Bike Tours & Rentals

4080 Byway E.
Napa 94559
707-255-3377
Open Mon.-Sat., 9:30 a.m.-6 p.m. (4 p.m. in winter) Rentals $7 per hour, $22 a day; tours $85

For your fees, you're led on a 20-mile ride which takes you to three wineries for tastings. Bikes, lunch and water bottles are provided, and here's the best part: a van picks you (and your bike) up at the end of the ride and brings you back to Napa.

FLYING

Vintage Aircraft

23982 Arnold Dr.
Sonoma 95476
707-938-2444
Open by appointment
Cost $139 for 40 minutes

Charles Schulz, the creator of "Peanuts," lives not too far south of here, and now we know where he got the idea to put Snoopy in a biplane. Here at the old Schellville Airport near the Carneros district, they'll strap you into a WWII trainer and fly you around the Napa and Sonoma vineyards. If you're adventurous, you can request some aerobatics (upside-down flying, that is).

Calistoga Gliders

Calistoga Gliderport
546 Lincoln Ave.
Calistoga 94515
707-942-5000
Daily 9 a.m. $179 for two people per 1/2 hour, $119 for single; $129 for two per 20 minutes, $79 for single

Calistoga is a perfect site for gliding because, according to the experts, it has good "thermal activity," with great "ridge lift" and, in the winter, especially "nice waves." The Calistoga Gliderport has been here for more than 30 years; gliders launched from here get up to 3,500 feet in the air. From up there, you can see the vineyards of the Wine Country and as far as San Francisco and out to the coast.

HORSEBACK RIDING

Sonoma Cattle Co. & Napa Valley Trail Rides

P.O. Box 877
Glen Ellen 95442
707-996-8566
Call for reservations.
Horse rental & tour $35 and up.

The Sonoma Cattle Co. provides mounts for trail rides out of Sugar Ridge State Park and Jack London State Park in Sonoma, and Bothe State Park in Napa-all gorgeous locations. Choose from 90-minute rides, 2-hour rides, sunset rides and private rides for any length of time. The views are spectacular.

SPAS

The best-known and most luxurious of the Wine Country spas are located at the **Sonoma Mission Inn** (18140 Sonoma Highway, Boyes Hot Springs; 707-938-9000) and the **Meadowood Resort** (900 Meadowood Ln., St. Helena; 707-963-3646; see Hotels for both). There are about a dozen spas with mud baths, mineral baths and volcanic ash treatments in Calistoga; **Indian Springs Resort and Spa** (1712 Lincoln Ave., Calistoga; 707-942-4913) is perhaps the oldest. **Roman International Spa** (1300 Washington St., Calistoga; 707-942-4441) offers an unusually large range of spa treatments. **Dr. Wilkinson's Hot Springs** (1507 Lincoln Ave., Calistoga; 707-942-4102) is also very well equipped to pamper you. Take a mud bath!

WINE TOURING

Wine touring-visiting and tasting the wineries and wines of the region-is the quintessence of the Wine Country experience. Nearly all of the most famous and venerated California names are located in Napa, Sonoma or Mendocino; in a single day's time you can visit a veritable who's who of American wineries. Most of the wineries in this region are open to the public. Many offer tours and have tasting rooms, others at least have a sales outlet where you can purchase their bottlings. Many wineries are open by appointment, so phone ahead. For detailed maps and additional information contact the **Napa Valley Vintners Association** (900 Meadowood Ln., St. Helena 94574; 707-963-0148), **Sonoma Valley Vintners & Growers** (453 First St. East, Sonoma 95476; 707-935-0803), or the **Mendocino County Vintners Association** (P.O. Box 1409, Ukiah 95482; 707-468-1343). For comprehensive information on the wineries of California, see Gault Millau/AAA's The Best Wineries of North America (order form in back of book).

Napa Valley Holidays

707-255-1050

$30 per person, reservations required

Very friendly and knowledgeable Eli and Laura Glick will pick you up at the Embassy Suites or Marriott hotel (both in the town of Napa) and take you in a comfortable bus to three Napa wineries and a lunch stop. The cost does not include lunch.

Wine & Dine Tours

P.O. Box 513
St. Helena 94574
707-963-8930

Call for reservations & prices

If you'd like to see a few Napa or Sonoma wineries that are not open to the public and be treated to lunch and sparkling wine (perhaps in a wine cave?), this company will handle all the details, including your ground and air transportation, accommodations and spa treatments. A tour of three wineries plus lunch runs about $145.

WINERIES OPEN TO THE PUBLIC

Napa County

Beaulieu Vineyard
1960 St. Helena Hwy. (P.O. Box 219)
Rutherford 94573
707-963-2411

Beringer Vineyards
2000 Main St. (P.O. Box 111),
St. Helena 94574
707-963-7115

Caymus Vineyards
8700 Conn Creek Road
Rutherford 94573
707-963-4204 *(By Appt. Only)*

Chateau Potelle Winery
3875 Mt. Vedeer Road
Napa 94558
707-255-9440

Château Woltner
150 S. White Cottage Rd.
Angwin 95408
707-963-1744 *(By Appt. Only)*

Clos du Val Winery
5330 Silverado Trail
Napa 94558
707-259-2225

Cuvaison Winery
4550 Silverado Trail (P.O. Box 384)
Calistoga 94515
707-942-6266

Domaine Carneros
1240 Duhig Rd.
Napa 94581
707-257-0101, Fax 707-257-3020

Domaine Chandon
1 California Dr. (P.O. Box 2470)
Yountville 94599
707-944-8844

Domaine Napa
1155 Mee Ln.
St. Helena 94574
707-963-1666

Folie à Deux Winery
3070 St. Helena Hwy. (29)
St. Helena 94574
707-963-1160

Franciscan Estates
1178 Galleron Road
Rutherford 94574
707-963-7112

Freemark Abbey
3022 St. Helena Hwy. (P.O. Box 410)
St. Helena 94574
707-963-0554

Frog's Leap
8815 Conn Creek Rd.
Rutherford 94573
707-963-4704

Grgich Hills Cellar
1829 St. Helena Hwy.
Rutherford, CA 94573
707-963-2784

Groth Vineyards & Winery
750 Oakville Cross Rd. (P.O. Box 390)
Oakville 94562
707-944-0290

The Hess Collection Winery
4411 Redwood Road
Napa 94558
707-255-1144

Joseph Phelps Vineyards
200 Taplin Rd. (P.O. Box 1031)
St. Helena 94574
707-963-2745

Louis M. Martini
254 S. St. Helena Hwy. (P.O. Box 112)
St. Helena 94574
707-963-2736

Markham Vineyards
2812 St. Helena Hwy. North
St. Helena 94574
707-963-5292

Merryvale Vineyards
1000 Main St.
St. Helena 94574
707-963-2225

Mumm Napa Valley
8445 Silverado Trail (P.O. Drawer 50)
Rutherford 94573
707-942-3300

Niebaum-Coppola Estate
1991 St. Helena Hwy. (29)
Rutherford 94573
707-963-9435

Pine Ridge Winery
5901 Silverado Trail
Napa 94558
707-253-7500

Prager Winery and Port Works
1281 Lewelling Ln.
St. Helena 94574
707-963-3720

Robert Mondavi Winery
7801 St. Helena Hwy. (P.O. Box 106)
Oakville 94562
707-963-9611

Robert Pepi Winery
7585 St. Helena Hwy.
Oakville 94562
707-944-2807

Rombauer Vineyards
3522 Silverado Trail
St. Helena 94574
707-963-5170

Rutherford Hill Winery
200 Rutherford Hill Rd.
Rutherford 94573
707-963-7194

St. Supéry Vineyards & Winery
8440 St. Helena Hwy.
Rutherford 94573
800-942-0809 or 707-963-4507

Schramsberg Vineyards
1400 Schramsberg Rd.
Calistoga 95415
707-942-4558

Silver Oak Wine Cellars
915 Oakville Cross Rd. (P.O. Box 414)
Oakville 94562
707-944-8808

Stag's Leap Wine Cellars
5766 Silverado Trail
Napa 94558
707-944-2020

Sterling Vineyards
1111 Dunaweal Ln. (P.O. Box 365)
Calistoga 95415
707-942-3300

Sutter Home Winery
277 St. Helena Hwy. South
St. Helena 94574
707-963-3104

Trefethen Vineyards
1160 Oak Knoll Ave. (P.O. Box 2460)
Napa 94558
707-255-7700

Sonoma County

Benziger Winery
1883 London Ranch Road
Glen Ellen 95442
800-989-8890

Buena Vista Winery
1800 Old Winery Rd. (P.O. Box 1842)
Sonoma 95476
707-938-1266/252-7117

Château Souverain
400 Souverain Rd. (P.O. Box 528)
Geyserville 95441
707-433-8281

Château St. Jean
8555 Sonoma Hwy. (12)
Kenwood 95452
707-833-4134

Ferrari-Carano Vineyards
8761 Dry Creek Rd. (P.O. Box 1549)
Healdsburg 95448
707-433-6700

Geyser Peak Winery
22281 Chianti Rd. (P.O. Box 25)
Geyserville 95441
707-857-9463

Gloria Ferrer Champagne Caves
23555 Hwy. 121 (P.O. Box 1427)
Sonoma 95476
707-996-7256

Kenwood Vineyards
9592 Sonoma Hwy. (12) (P.O. Box 447)
Kenwood 95452
707-883-5891

Kunde Estate Winery
10155 Sonoma Hwy.
Kenwood 95452
707-833-5501

Landmark Vineyards
101 Adobe Canyon Rd.
Kenwood 95452
707-833-0053

Matanzas Creek Winery
6097 Bennett Valley Rd.
Santa Rosa 95401
707-528-6464

Paradise Ridge Winery
4545 Thomas Lake Harris Drive
Santa Rosa 95403
707-528-9463

Piper Sonoma
11447 Old Redwood Hwy. (P.O. Box 309)
Healdsburg 95448
707-433-8843

Ravenswood Winery
18071 Gehricke Rd.
Sonoma 94576
707-938-1960

Rodney Strong Vineyards
11455 Old Redwood Hwy. (Healdsburg)
(P.O. Box 368) Windsor 95492
707-431-1533

Sebastiani Vineyards
389 Fourth St. East
Sonoma 95476
707-938-5532

Stone Creek
9380 Sonoma Hwy.
Kenwood 95452
707-833-5070

Viansa Winery and Italian Marketplace
25200 Arnold Dr.
Sonoma 95476
707-935-4700

Windsor Vineyards
308 B Center St.
Healdsburg 95448
800-204-9463

Lake County

Kendall Jackson Vineyards & Winery
600 Matthews Rd.
Lakeport 95453
707-263-5299/263-9333

Mendocino County

Roederer Estate
4501 Hwy. 128 (P.O. Box 67)
Philo 95466
707-895-2288

Peninsula

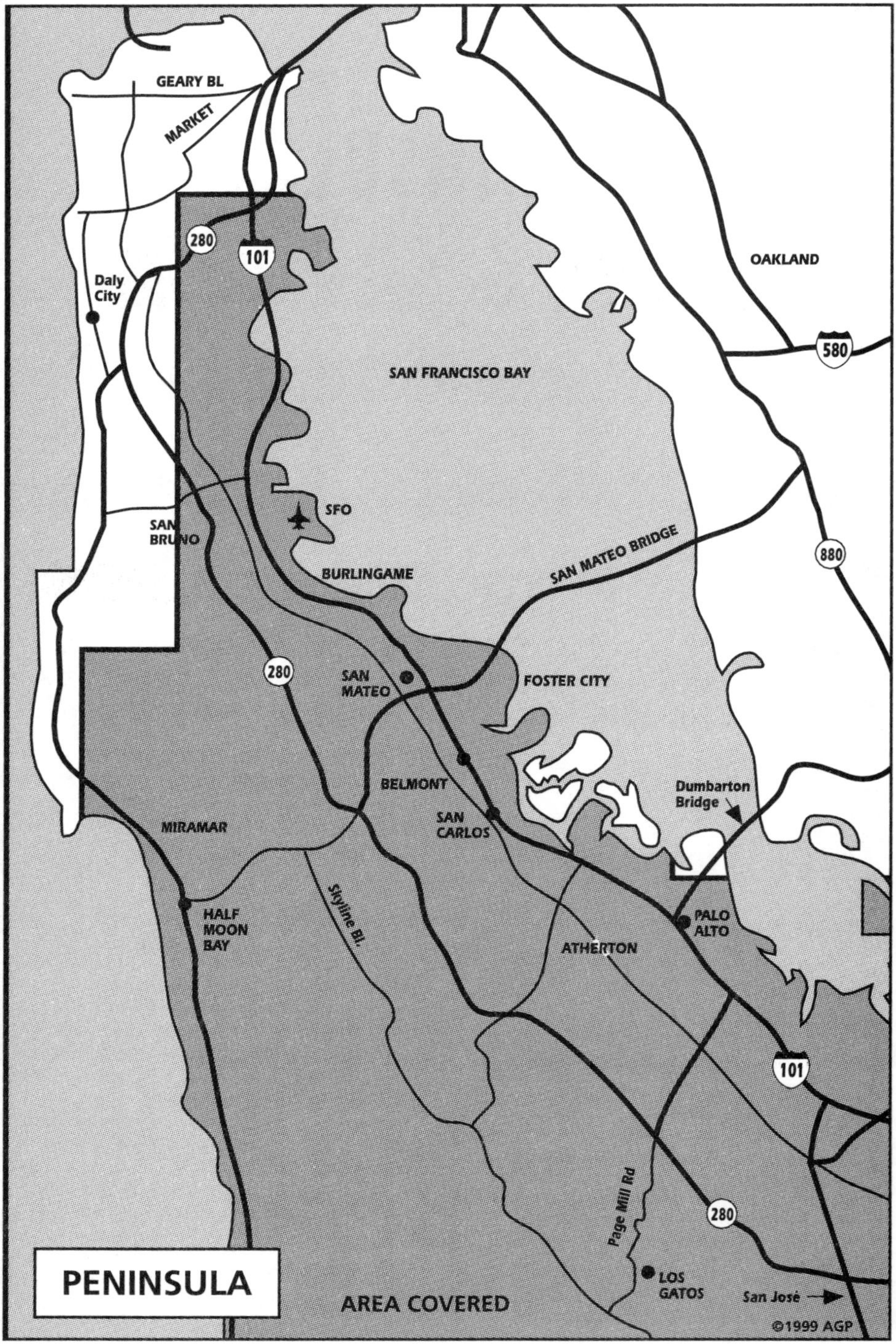
GEARY BL
MARKET
280
101
Daly City
OAKLAND
580
SAN FRANCISCO BAY
SFO
SAN BRUNO
SAN MATEO BRIDGE
880
BURLINGAME
280
SAN MATEO
FOSTER CITY
BELMONT
Dumbarton Bridge
MIRAMAR
SAN CARLOS
HALF MOON BAY
Skyline Bl.
PALO ALTO
ATHERTON
101
Page Mill Rd
280
LOS GATOS
San José
PENINSULA
AREA COVERED
©1999 AGP

SILICON & SUNSHINE

Settled at the turn of the century by wealthy San Franciscans in search of warmer summer climates, the Peninsula now is better known as the northern tip of **Silicon Valley**. Although the Peninsula retains some aristocratic airs, it tends to blend with neighboring **Santa Clara Valley** cities as the nation's high-tech hub. Technological innovation continues to draw creative minds to the area. Another important influence is **Stanford University**, a world-class center of learning. In addition, Stanford's sports teams mean big-time local intercollegiate competition.

The Peninsula's natural beauty has been preserved in the face of commercial development and population growth. Steeply wooded hills, plunging ravines, marshy Bayside wetlands and a foggy, rugged shoreline resist human interference. Coastal ranges offer undisturbed stands of redwoods, expansive natural parklands, family farms and scenic beaches. On the Peninsula you'll find such upscale communities as Burlingame and Woodside, along with burgeoning cities like San Jose and San Mateo.

Finding your way: **El Camino Real** runs the length of the Peninsula. In each town, however, the numbering of street addresses starts anew, as do divisions of north and south. Thus, although a restaurant at 3700 S. El Camino Real in Palo Alto appears by its address to be near 3500 S. El Camino Real in San Mateo, the two locations are, in fact, fifteen miles apart.

DINING

Barbara's Fish Trap

SEAFOOD 11/20
281 CAPISTRANO RD.
PRINCETON-BY-THE-SEA 94038
650-728-7049
Lunch & Dinner daily, $
No cards

Overlooking Pillar Point Harbor four miles north of Half Moon Bay, this cozy fish house is a longtime favorite of locals and visitors. Barbara Walsh still presides, though her daughter and son-in-law now run the place.

Birk's

AMERICAN 12/20
3955 FREEDOM CIRCLE
SANTA CLARA 95054
408-980-6400
Lunch Mon.-Fri., Dinner nightly, $$

A

The Silicon Valley archetypal bar and grill, Birk's is easily accessible off Highway 101. A decade-old interior by über-designer Pat Kuleto is attractive and noisy. Steaks and seafood are specialties.

Chez Sovan

CAMBODIAN ¢
2425 S. BASCOM AVE.
CAMPBELL 95008
408-371-7711
No cards

Sovan Boun Thuy's two Cambodian restaurants are longtime South Bay favorites. In Campbell, white tablecloths and murals define the place; the original location in San Jose (23 Oakland Rd., 408-287-7619) has a gritty ambience but the fish, chicken and pork seasoned with lime, garlic, ginger and banana leaves remain the same: superb.

Flea Street Café

CALIFORNIA 14/20
3607 ALAMEDA DE LAS PULGAS
MENLO PARK 94025
650-854-1226
Lunch Tues.-Fri., Dinner Tues.-Sun., Brunch Sun., $$

In small, parlor-like dining rooms, you'll discover owner Jesse Cool's love of Victorian-era lace and florals. The menu changes at least every other month, but it's always organic. A recent one included linguine with roasted beets and beet greens, maple-soy-glazed Muscovy duck and broiled lamb loin marinated in pomegranate juice and garlic.

JoAnn's Café & Pantry

COFFEE SHOP ¢
1131 EL CAMINO REAL
SOUTH SAN FRANCISCO 94080
650-872-2810
Breakfast & Lunch daily
No cards

Latin music rocks while diners peruse a menu of egg dishes ranging from countless omelets to JoAnn's Special (two eggs, choice of seven meats or sautéed spinach and mushrooms) with home fries, fruit salad and toast, muffin, bagel, scone or tortillas. For lunch, soothe yourself with house-made soup.

Peninsula Fountain and Grill

SODA FOUNTAIN ¢
566 EMERSON ST.
PALO ALTO 94301
650-323-3131
Breakfast, Lunch & Dinner daily

A

Serving thick malts and milkshakes in frosted metal canisters since 1923, the Peninsula Fountain and Grill recently underwent a well-deserved remodel and menu update. Now it offers a respectable wine list to complement its excellent burgers and chicken pot pie.

Spago Palo Alto

CALIFORNIA 14/20
265 LYTTON AVE.
PALO ALTO 94301
650-833-1000
Lunch & Dinner daily, $$$

A

The newest in celebrity-chef Wolfgang Puck's fine-dining empire, Spago Palo Alto is a beautiful (re)design (of the former Stars) by Adam Tihany. Executive chef Michael French and pastry chef Christine Law are firmly in command of the kitchen, and their dining room menu changes often to reflect seasonal offerings. Expect cutting-edge California cuisine with touches of the Orient and the Mediterranean. The Pavilion offers designer pizzas and an enticing bar menu.

The Village Pub

AMERICAN 13/20
2967 WOODSIDE RD.
WOODSIDE 94062
650-851-1294
Lunch Mon.-Fri., Dinner nightly, $$$

A

The Village Pub suits the community perfectly: its atmosphere is cushy yet welcoming and unpretentious, its fare fresh and sophisticated. Among many salads, the Caesar is excellent. Dinner entrées, too, are well done: grilled rack of pork is served with apples, bacon, frisée and whipped parsnip potatoes.

Zibibbo

MEDITERRANEAN 13/20
430 KIPLING ST.
PALO ALTO 94301
650-328-6722
Lunch & Dinner daily, $$

The current sensibilities of Silicon Valley are expressed by Cass Calder Smith's wonderful conversion of an old Victorian into a brash, bustling 280-seat restaurant, a space handsomely divided into patios, balcony, exhibition kitchen, indoor booths and spacious bar. Chefs Marc Valiani and Jody Denton bring signature dishes from Restaurant LuLu in San Francisco, including skillet-roasted mussels and rotisserie rosemary chicken.

AND ALSO...

Duarte's Tavern Artichokes

202 STAGE RD.
PESCADERO
650-879-0464
Breakfast, Lunch & Dinner daily, $$

Harvested from the local fields, 'chokes are fixed here pretty much any style-fried, souped or tossed into omelets.

The Fish Market

SEAFOOD
1855 S. NORFOLK
SAN MATEO 94403
650-349-3474
Lunch & Dinner daily, $$

These restaurants employ their own fishing fleet to haul in the fresh catch, so there's always ample choice. **Also in Palo Alto (3150 El Camino Real, 650-493-9188), Santa Clara (3775 El Camino Real, 408-246-3474) and San Jose (1007 Blossom Hill Rd., 408-269-3474.)**

Gordon Biersch Brewery

BREWPUB
640 EMERSON ST.
PALO ALTO 94301
650-323-7723
Lunch & Dinner daily, $$

Silicon Valley's original microbrewery. **Also at 33 E. San Fernando St., San Jose, 408-294-6785.**

HOTELS

TOP OF THE LINE

Hotel De Anza

233 W. SANTA CLARA ST.
SAN JOSE 95113
408-286-1000, 800-843-3700,
FAX 408-286-0500
Singles & Doubles $220-$245, Suites $250-$325

Built in 1930, this 101-room downtown San Jose hotel was renovated in wonderful Casablanca Moorish style and reopened in 1990. Today it is a national historic landmark. The ground-floor **Hedley Lounge** is a high-level gathering place and the restaurant, **La Pastaia** (408-286-8686) is one of the best in the region. Chef Forrest Gingold designs his menu with a classic Italian sensibility.

Stanford Park Hotel

100 EL CAMINO REAL
MENLO PARK 94025
650-322-1234, 800-368-2468,
FAX 650-322-0975
Singles & Doubles $240-$365, Suites $270-$365

With its cedar shingle and brick facade, copper gabled roof and dormer windows peeking out from the third story, this hotel, located near **Stanford University**, is attractively designed. Inside, rooms are well-furnished and come in several sizes and configurations; some have sitting rooms, vaulted ceilings, bay windows and/or fireplaces. The hotel offers a heated pool, fitness room, sauna and spa.

LUXURY

Mill Rose Inn ♫
615 MILL ST.
HALF MOON BAY 94019
650-726-9794, 800-900-ROSE,
FAX 650-726-3031
Rooms $165-$255 weekdays, $205-$285 weekends. Two-night minimum applies to Sat. night stays.

🅰 P ☎ ○ 💻

Each of the six plush floral-motif decorated rooms here offers a private entrance, feather bed and garden view; two are suites, and all rooms but one have fireplaces. Proprietors Eve and Terry Baldwin serve a full breakfast in the dining room or will deliver it to guests who don't want to leave their chambers. Guests enjoy an inviting sitting room (with tea and pastries in the afternoon), a library, rose garden and spectacular coastline just steps away. Their Website-www.millrose.com-provides a virtual tour of rooms.

Hotel Sofitel San Francisco Bay ♫
223 TWIN DOLPHIN DR.
REDWOOD CITY 94065
650-598-9000, 800-221-4525 OUTSIDE CA,
FAX 650-598-0459
Singles & Doubles $189-$259, Suites $259-$329

🅰 P ☎ ○ 💻

Decor in the skylit lobby and on the lagoon-side pool deck of this 319-room hostelry aims for Parisian chic. The premises are nicely designed, guest rooms are relatively spacious and the waterside setting is breezy and bright. Choose from **two French-themed restaurants** and a take-out market that sells fresh-baked pastries.

MODERATE

Fairmont Hotel San Jose ♫♫♫
170 S. MARKET ST.
SAN JOSE 95113
408-998-1900, 800-527-4727,
FAX 408-287-1648
Singles & Doubles $89-$109, Suites from $159

🅰 🍴 P ☎ ○ 💻

The heart of Silicon Valley hospitality beats to serve meetings and conventions, and the

Fairmont does it best, with 40,148 square feet of meeting and banquet space. High-tech amenities abound, as do homey touches like comforters and goosedown pillows. Among the Fairmont's 541 rooms, 41 are suites.

AIRPORT HOTELS

Of all the hotels near SFO, the **Marriott**, **Westin** and **Hyatt Regency** are perhaps the most popular, patronized not only by businesspeople and travelers needing to catch early planes, but also by locals for special events.

Hyatt Regency San Francisco Airport ♫
1333 BAYSHORE HWY.
BURLINGAME 94010
650-347-1234, 800-233-1234,
FAX 650-696-2669
Singles & Doubles $134-$249, Suites $299-$699

🅰 P ☎ ○ 💻

San Francisco Airport Marriott ♫♫♫
1800 BAYSHORE HWY.
BURLINGAME 94010
650-692-9100 OR 800-228-9290
Singles & Doubles $99-$225, Suites $295-$550

🅰 🍴 P ☎ ○ 💻

Westin Hotel San Francisco Airport ♫♫♫
1 OLD BAYSHORE HWY.
MILLBRAE 94030
650-692-3500, 800-228-3000,
FAX 650-872-8111
Singles & Doubles $117-$234, Suites $400

🅰 P ☎ ○ 💻

SHOPPING

Several Peninsula and South Bay towns have vital downtown areas worth a stroll for shoppers, such as **Burlingame,** with its dozens of clothing boutiques, and **Palo Alto**, where a **Borders** bookstore has revitalized the historic Varsity theater, on University Avenue. Other shopping destinations:

Draeger's

1010 UNIVERSITY DR.
MENLO PARK 94025
650-688-0688
Open Daily

A complete gourmet market under one roof, Draeger's offers everything from naturally raised poultry and fresh house-made sausages in its meat section, to French rolls and brown-butter-pear tarts in its bakery. You'll also find produce from local farmers, an excellent grocery section, an extensive wine selection and cooking classes taught by well-known chefs. **Also in San Mateo (222 E. 4th Ave., 650-685-3700) and Los Altos (342 First St., 650-948-4425).**

Stanford Shopping Center

180 EL CAMINO REAL
PALO ALTO 94304
650-617-8585, 800-772-9332
Most stores open daily

Bloomingdale's, **Nieman Marcus**, **Macy's** and **Nordstrom** anchor this tony regional shopping center, joining **Crate & Barrel**, **Tiffany** and the **Polo Store**. In all, 150 specialty shops are set among sculpted outdoor walkways lined with flowers, cafés, coffeehouses and gourmet groceries. **The University Shop** (650-614-0295) and the **Health Library** (650-725-8400), a resource of **Stanford Medical Center**, reflect the center's ties with the university.

SIGHTSEEING & ARTS

ARTS

Half Moon Bay Art and Pumpkin Festival

8 MILES ALONG ROUTE 1
650-726-9652

For weeks before Halloween, Bay Area residents flock to the farming community of Half Moon Bay to choose their pumpkins straight from the fields. Activity peaks on the final weekend of the Festival, with its food and crafts booths and lively entertainment.

Villa Montalvo and the Mountain Winery Concert Series

15400 MONTALVO RD.
SARATOGA 95070
408-961-5858

The wineries' concert lineup is best described as eclectic, ranging as it does from Tom Jones to the Juilliard String Quartet. The series runs most of the year, and takes place in four different venues. The arboretum gardens and art center are open daily throughout the year.

ATTRACTIONS

Raging Waters

EAST ON TULLY ROAD EXIT FROM HWY. 101
SAN JOSE 95113
408-270-8000
Open daily Memorial Day to Labor Day. Adults $20.99, children under 42 inches $16.99; under 3 free.

This waterslide park is essentially a kids' attraction, but adults can have a great time too. More than 20 rides now include a four-person water toboggan; certified lifeguards enforce safety standards. Ample picnic facilities lie just outside the entrance; no food can be brought in.

The Tech Museum of Innovation

145 W. SAN CARLOS ST.
SAN JOSE 95113
408-279-7150
Open Tues.-Sun. Adults $6, seniors $4, children 6-18 & students $4.

Due to inhabit expansive new digs in late 1998, this interactive celebration of technology offers mini-labs and exhibits. Visitors can design an aerodynamically-advanced bicycle or direct their own robot, among other things. Check the museum's Website at www.thetech.org.

SPORTS

San Jose Sharks

SAN JOSE ARENA
525 W. SANTA CLARA ST.
SAN JOSE 95113
408-287-4275

Tickets may be available at Arena box office Mon.-Sat., but it's best to check first with BASS, 408-998-BASS or any BASS ticket outlet. Event hotline is 408-287-9200.

Big-time sports have come to San Jose in the form of this professional hockey team. The Sharks have yet to win the Stanley Cup competition, but they're getting better every year. The franchise is justly famous for its dynamic color scheme (teal, silver and black) and its logo (a Great White crunching a hockey stick).

THE GREAT OUTDOORS

San Mateo County's extensive network of parks maintains thousands of acres of wildflower-studded grassland, chaparral, oaks and magnificent redwoods for public access. The **Midpeninsula Regional Open Space District** (650-691-1200) and **Santa Clara County** (408-358-3741) also maintain extensive hiking and walking trails. For general information about the region, call 650-363-4021.

If the ocean is your love, head west. The major roads to the Pacific are the turnoff to Pacifica from **Highway 280** (which becomes coastal **Highway 1**), **Highway 92**, and **Highway 84**. You'll find lighthouses at **Montara** and **Pigeon Point**, a harbor at **Princeton**, and fishing piers in **Pacifica** and **Princeton**.

WINE TOURING

From Half Moon Bay to Aptos, some 40 small, family-owned wineries reside in the **Santa Cruz Mountains**, where cool coastal climates and rugged terrain produce intensely concentrated fruit. Participating wineries open their doors for two weekends in June for a vintners' festival. Otherwise, many wineries are open only by appointment. Contact the **Santa Cruz Mountains Winegrowers Assn.** (7605 Old Dominion Ct., Ste. A, Aptos 95003 408-479-9463) for a complete list and map.

Bear Creek Vineyard
21428 Bear Creek Rd.
Los Gatos 95033
408-395-3718
(by appt. only)

Bonny Doon Vineyard
10 Pine Flat Rd.
Santa Cruz 95060
408-425-4518

Cooper-Garrod Vineyards
22600 Mount Eden Rd.
Saratoga 95070
408-741-8094

Cronin Vineyards
11 Old La Honda Rd.
Woodside 94062
650-851-1452
(by appt. only)

David Bruce Winery
21439 Bear Creek Rd.
Los Gatos 95033
408-354-4214; 800-397-9972

P. & M. Staiger
1300 Hopkins Gulch Rd.
Boulder Creek 95006
831-338-4348
(by appt. only)

Ridge Vineyards
17100 Monte Bello Rd.
Cupertino 95014
408-867-3233

River Run Vinters
65 Rogge Lane
Watsonville 95076
408-726-3112

Monterey/Carmel

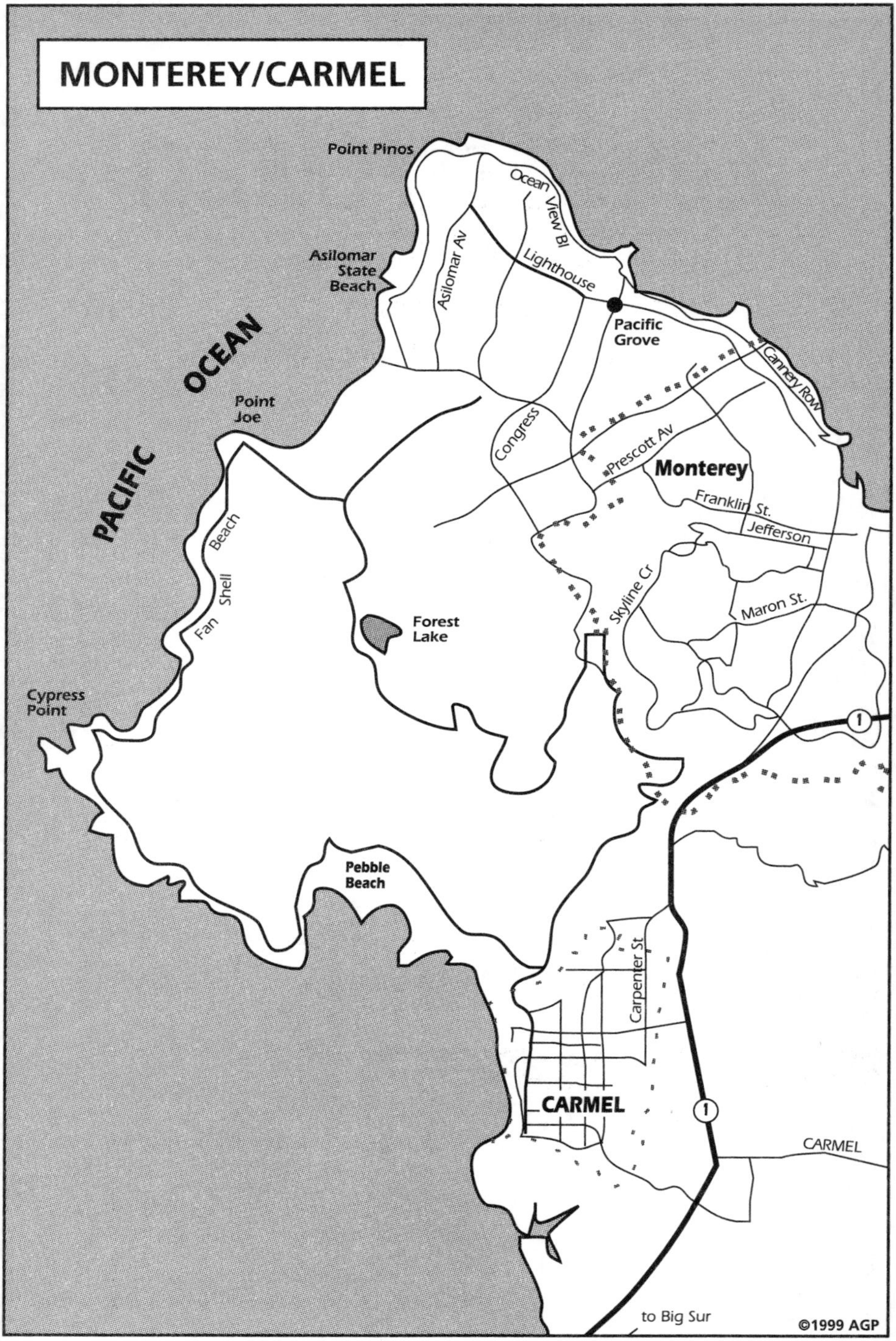
MONTEREY/CARMEL
Point Pinos
Ocean View Bl
Asilomar State Beach
Asilomar Av
Lighthouse
Pacific Grove
PACIFIC OCEAN
Cannery Row
Point Joe
Congress
Prescott Av
Monterey
Franklin St.
Jefferson
Beach
Fan Shell
Skyline Cr
Maron St.
Forest Lake
Cypress Point
1
Pebble Beach
Carpenter St
CARMEL
1
CARMEL
to Big Sur
©1999 AGP

CIRCLE OF ENCHANTMENT

The Monterey Peninsula is an Arcadian place, recognized the world over for the beauty of its rugged coastline dotted with windswept cypress trees. The region's main attraction is the pageantry of the **Monterey Bay**, now a National Marine Sanctuary. Almost every outing affords a glimpse of its sparkling waters, which lends a hand in preserving the Peninsula's status as a top destination by visitors from around the world. As California's first state capital, the Monterey Peninsula spins a historical tale as rich and resplendent as the bay that surrounds it. You'll see the elegant Victorians of **Pacific Grove** and **Carmel's** quaint cottages, the modern mansions of **Pebble Beach** and the weathered ranch houses of the **Carmel Valley**. Today, visitors will find scores of award-winning restaurants, exceptional accommodations, arts-and-crafts fairs and a host of cultural activities-a calendar of events is available from the **Chamber of Commerce, 380 Alvarado St., Monterey, 831-649-1770.**

DINING

Anton & Michel

CONTINENTAL 13/20

MISSION BETWEEN OCEAN & SEVENTH AVES.
CARMEL 93921
831-624-2406
Lunch & Dinner daily, $$$

A ☎

Original oil paintings line the dining room of this local favorite for more than a decade, an elegant setting further enhanced by gardens and two outdoor fountains. The menu features highly acclaimed rack of lamb carved tableside, fresh Monterey Bay seafood, filet mignon and grilled lamb medallions with mint pesto sauce. The catch of the day is always a good choice. Even the most discriminating wine lover can appreciate the restaurant's award-winning showing of California varietals from Napa and Monterey Counties. The regions of Burgundy and Bordeaux also have a prominent place on the list, as do many rare French wines. Exquisite desserts include bananas Foster and crêpes Suzette. The cozy cocktail lounge is a good meeting place for pre- or post-dinner libations.

The Covey

REGIONAL/CONTINENTAL 14/20

QUAIL LODGE
8205 VALLEY GREENS DR.
CARMEL VALLEY 93923
831-624-1581
Dinner nightly, $$$$

A ☎

Set in a tranquil country environment, this quixotic restaurant features a pleasant view of a shining lake, fountains, lush gardens and-of course-golfing greens. Chef Robert Williamson blends contemporary California-style cuisine with classic French techniques. His menu changes daily, but expect a variety of fish such as snapper, sole, salmon, seabass and other seafood. House specialties include roasted rack of lamb and seared ahi tuna in sesame-seed crust with shiitake mushrooms. Monterey Bay spotted prawns baked in lime butter are delectable with just the correct amount of chili heat. The Covey's extensive wine list renders a full page of half-bottles, highlighted with a good selection of California and Monterey County wines. Caramelized apple and almond cookies served with cinnamon ice cream and caramel add the crowning touch to a perfect meal.

The Fishwife

SEAFOOD ¢
1996 SUNSET DR.
PACIFIC GROVE 93950
831-375-7107
Lunch & Dinner daily (except Tues.), Brunch Sun.

This local treasure is within walking distance of Asilomar, making it the perfect place for dinner after a walk on the beach. Californian-Caribbean offerings include fresh chowder, grilled oysters, sautéed calamari and several seafood pastas. Well-chosen, moderately-priced, premium California wines are available by the glass or bottle. Key lime pie is a favorite dessert.

Fresh Cream

FRENCH 15/20
99 PACIFIC ST.
MONTEREY 93940
831-375-9798
Dinner nightly, $$$

Along with its posh interior, superb service, glittering Bay view and solid reputation, Fresh Cream has always had excellent food. Menu offerings include a selection of meat, poultry, seafood and vegetarian entrées. The filet of ahi tuna, one of the most popular menu items, is blackened and served with a scrumptious pineapple rum butter sauce. All entrées come with a salad of baby greens. A nice selection of California and French wines, carefully chosen to complement the menu, round out the wine list. Knowledgeable servers easily describe items on the menu. We recommend saving room for the Grand Marnier soufflé: it is divine.

Kincaid's Bistro

FRENCH 14/20
217 CROSSROADS BLVD.
CARMEL 93923
831-624-9626
Lunch Mon.-Fri., Dinner nightly, $$

A country-French setting with graceful archways, exposed wood-beamed ceilings, a cozy fireplace and walls that look like weathered stone. Chef/owner Robert Kincaid prepares classic bistro cuisine, adding his own touches. Signature dishes include roasted duckling with wild cherry sauce, grilled Holland Dover sole, presented whole on a platter, deboned at the table and served with a lemon-caper sauce. Polished service enhances the experience of dining here.

Pacific's Edge

CALIFORNIAN 13/20
HIGHLANDS INN
HIGHWAY 1
CARMEL HIGHLANDS 93923
831-622-5445
Lunch & Dinner Daily, Brunch Sun. $$$

A long-time favorite of travelers along famed Highway 1, this historic restaurant is one of the most enchanting spots on the California coast. Innovative regional California cuisine is well-suited to breathtaking ocean views accented by the craggy coastline and windblown cypress trees. Specialties include seafood dishes such as caramelized day boat sea scallops with chanterelles, pumpkin and black truffle sauce. To start, try an asparagus and artichoke terrine with tomato-anise vinaigrette. An award-winning wine list features many outstanding California wines, including several from Monterey County. The service is both gracious and prompt. Live music played nightly adds to the romance of this popular restaurant.

Roy's at Pebble Beach

CALIFORNIAN/ASIAN 14/20
THE INN AT SPANISH BAY, 2700 17 MILE DR.
PEBBLE BEACH 93953
831-647-7423
Breakfast, Lunch & Dinner daily, $$

As you enter Roy Yamaguchi's high-ceilinged restaurant, savor the tantalizing aromas wafting from the kitchen. His focus is on regional California dishes prepared with an Asian influence. Wood-fired pizza and traditional favorites are also served. We recommend ravioli of shiitake, spinach and ricotta accented with a sun-dried tomato-garlic cream sauce for starters. For a main course selection, try blackened ahi tuna, swordfish or lamb shank short ribs. Desserts are equally tempting: a hot-chocolate raspberry cake is beyond comparison. Roy's friendly, accommodating staff provides charming service.

Stillwater Bar & Grill

SEAFOOD 13/20
THE LODGE AT PEBBLE BEACH, 17 MILE DRIVE
PEBBLE BEACH 93953
831-625-8524
Breakfast, Lunch & Dinner daily, $$

Newly remodeled, Stillwater offers two-level dining overlooking the legendary 18th green of the Pebble Beach Golf Links. Start by sampling the celebrated crab cakes or visiting the Raw Bar, where you may choose among a medley of freshly shucked oysters, clams, mussels and more. Primarily a seafood grill, the restaurant's menu catalogs a variety of choices, including grilled sturgeon and salmon. If you enjoy the unusual, opt for applewood-smoked sea bass served with green lentil cakes or flavorful, house-made lobster sausage accompanied by saffron sauerkraut. Knowledgeable waitstaff can easily suggest pairings from the award-winning wine list. A warm flourless chocolate cake is perfect for dessert. Live jazz or classical music is played next door in the Terrace Lounge every evening.

The Village Corner

MEDITERRANEAN BISTRO ¢
DOLORES & 6TH AVE.
CARMEL 93921
831-624-3588
Breakfast, Lunch & Dinner daily

The quaint family atmosphere and solid reputation for good food have made the Village Corner a local favorite for 50 years. The menu includes mouth-watering lamb, pasta dishes and fresh fish. We recommend the saffron penne pasta with assorted local seafood. Beer and a variety of Monterey County wines are served; a chocolate espresso bread pudding for dessert is heavenly. Al fresco dining on the outdoor patio with a fireplace is especially pleasant.

AND ALSO..

Fandango

MEDITERRANEAN
223 17TH ST.
PACIFIC GROVE 93950
831-372-3456
Lunch & Dinner daily, $$

Flowers, baskets of fresh-baked bread and a crackling fire greet you at this cozy Mediterranean-style restaurant. The menu features everything from paella to pizzas from the wood-burning oven, along with such specials as osso buco, scallops in lemon-shallot butter or scampi with spinach in a tangy raspberry vinaigrette. The wine list includes offerings from all over the globe. There is a glass-domed terrace in the rear.

The French Poodle

FRENCH
JUNIPERO ST. AT 5TH AVE.
CARMEL 93921
831-624-8643
Dinner Mon.-Sat., $$$

A bastion of formal French cooking since 1961, this Carmel landmark has been under new ownership for several years. Excellent service and a fine wine list, along with such classic dishes as filet mignon with Madeira

Nepenthe

AMERICAN
HWY. 1 29 MI. SOUTH OF CARMEL
BIG SUR 93920
831-667-2345

Quite simply, Nepenthe has the most breathtaking view on the California coast. Named for an ancient drug that supposedly made one forget sorrow, Nepenthe, perched on a cliff high above the ocean, has been an inspiring stopping place travelers on Highway 1. Best dishes: the Ambrosia burger, the roast chicken and the four-layer chocolate cake. Do try to be there at sunset-on a clear day, it can be a truly spiritual experience.

Taste Café & Bistro

FRENCH
1199 FOREST AVE.
PACIFIC GROVE 93950
DINNER TUES.-SUN., $$
831-655-0324

No cards

A cozy European-style bistro where the décor is cheery and the menu features such homey favorites as herb-roasted chicken, escargots, pastas, soups and salads.

HOTELS

TOP OF THE LINE

Highlands Inn

HWY. 1 4 MI. SOUTH OF CARMEL
P.O. BOX 1700
CARMEL HIGHLANDS 93923
831-624-3801, 800-682-4811,
FAX 408-626-1574
Singles & Doubles $290-$475, Suites $475-$800

A P

The Highlands Inn has been a world-famous getaway since it opened in 1917, and after a $41-million renovation, its facilities are first-class. From its eleven-acre perch on the cliffs overlooking the ocean, the resort commands perhaps the single most awe-inspiring view of the central California coastline accessible to the public. The guest rooms have fireplaces, kitchens and double-spa baths. A swimming pool and several secluded outdoor spas are also available. With all that plus the Pacific's Edge dining room (see DINING) it's no wonder that this is a popular spot for honeymooners.

The Inn at Spanish Bay

2700 17 MILE DR.
PEBBLE BEACH 93953
831-647-7500; 800-654-9300,
FAX 408-644-7955
Singles & Doubles $305-$425, Suites $625-$725

A P

Imagine a day of tennis or golf on an oceanfront course, a walk in the woods or a stroll along a sandy beach. Is that bagpipes you hear at sunset and the continuous lull of the ocean as you drift off to sleep? All this and more awaits you at The Inn at Spanish Bay. The 269 guest rooms are spacious with fireplaces and views of either the beach or forest from a private deck or patio. Pebble Beach's newest hotel, The Inn also has a health club with a heated pool and an interesting array of shops, including the Ansel Adams Gallery. Choose from three restaurants including the stellar Roy's (see DINING).

The Lodge at Pebble Beach

17 MILE DR.
PEBBLE BEACH 93953
831-624-3811; 800-654-9300,
FAX 408-625-8542
Singles & Doubles $350-$475, Suites $1,000-$1,200

A P

From its beginnings in 1919, the Lodge served travelers to the forest and the rugged coastline in comfort and style. Only eleven of the 161 rooms are located in the Lodge itself; the remaining lie in twelve separate low-rise buildings; all are spacious and include every conceivable amenity. The four restaurants on site include Stillwater Bar & Grill (see DINING). Boutiques, 34 miles of forested bridle paths, a swimming pool, beach and tennis club and championship golf courses have made The Lodge internationally famous.

Quail Lodge

8205 VALLEY GREENS DR.
CARMEL 93293
831-624-1581, 800-323-7500,
FAX 831-624-3726
Singles & Doubles $295-$345, Suites $395

Surrounded by 250 acres of scenic rolling hills and oak-studded meadowland, Quail Lodge is a gorgeous retreat, complete with velvety expanses of grass, lakes (with swans), a magnificently landscaped, award-winning 18-hole golf course, tennis, swimming, biking, jogging, hiking and picnicking on the many nature trails behind the course. Most of the 100 rooms and suites have fairway views. Guests dine in the Covey (See DINING) or in the more formal club dining room.

Stonepine Estate Resort

150 E. CARMEL VALLEY RD.
CARMEL VALLEY 93924
831-659-2245, FAX 408-659-5160
Suites $295-$750

A

This luxurious estate in the bucolic Carmel Valley was once a country home of the Crocker clan; it contains the oldest working thoroughbred race horse farm west of the Mississippi. With only fourteen suites, it appeals to those who seek privacy in beautiful surroundings, with fine dining, tennis, swimming and horseback riding to boot.

LUXURY

Monterey Plaza Hotel

400 CANNERY ROW
MONTEREY 93940
831-646-1700, 800-334-3999;
FAX 831-646-0283
Singles & Doubles $175-$245, 1- & 2-Bedroom Suites $425-$735

A P

Spacious guest rooms (many with open-air balconies and sweeping views of the bay), all-day dining (in two excellent on-site restaurants) and the close proximity to Cannery Row has earned Monterey Plaza the status of being one of the best places to stay in the area. Patterned after the grand old hotels of another era, the hotel is furnished with eighteenth-century Chinese and Italian Empire period pieces.

MODERATE

The Cypress Inn

LINCOLN & SEVENTH STS.
CARMEL 93921
831-624-3871, 800-443-7443,
FAX 831-624-8216

P

Affectionately dubbed "Dog Digs" by locals, this charming hostelry has a sterling reputation for catering to pets in general and pooches in particular. For their owners, a bar and library lie downstairs, while on upper floors cheery rooms beckon with fireplaces, marble bathrooms and loads of amenities. Best of all, nearby Carmel City Beach is a rare stretch of sand that welcomes leashless canines. Cypress's charge is $17 for the first pet, $10 for each thereafter up to three total. Pet-sitters are available for $10-$13 an hour.

Doubletree Inn

2 PORTOLA PLAZA
MONTEREY 93940
831-649-4511, 800-528-0444
FAX 831-372-0620
Singles & Doubles $89-$279, Suites $215 -$300

A P

Located in the heart of Monterey, the Doubletree is just steps away from lively Alvarado Street, Fisherman's Wharf and the recreational trail. The hotel has 380 guest rooms, a swimming pool and spa, two restaurants and an attractive lobby lounge.

Green Gables Inn

104 FIFTH ST.
PACIFIC GROVE 93950
831-375-2095, 800-722-1774
FAX 831-375-5437
Singles & Doubles $110-$160, Suites $160-$225.

P

Recognized as the most popular bed-and-breakfast in America, Green Gables is set at the water's edge, and a stay here is unforgettable. Every detail of the exquisite Queen Anne Victorian, built in 1888, has been meticulously restored. Each room is unique: ask about the cozy namesake loft entered via ladder in the attic. The Inn serves a bountiful breakfast in the dining room overlooking the beautiful Monterey Bay.

Mission Ranch

26270 DOLORES ST.
CARMEL 93293
831-624-6436, 800-538-8221,
FAX 831-626-4163
Singles & Doubles $85-$225, Cottages $195-$225

A P

The former mayor of Carmel-and longtime movie star-Clint Eastwood owns this recently restored cattle ranch on land encircling the Carmel Mission. Nature trails crisscross the resort's 20 acres; it's just a short walk to a terrific white sand beach. There are eight tennis courts, and a restaurant and piano bar. At night, there's often live music in the former cow barn.

ECONOMY

Gosby House Inn

643 LIGHTHOUSE AVE.
PACIFIC GROVE 93950
831-375-1287, 800-527-8828
FAX 831-655-9621
Singles & Doubles $90-$135, Suites $160

P

This delightful bed-and-breakfast inn situated in the center of Pacific Grove, has been welcoming guests for over 100 years. The cheerful yellow-and-white Victorian mansion has 22 individually decorated rooms, many with sitting areas with fireplaces, a private patio entrance or window seat. The Carriage House features two deluxe rooms with a spa tub for two, fireplace and balcony. The staff is extremely friendly and helpful.

The Pine Inn

OCEAN AVE. & LINCOLN ST.
CARMEL 93921
831-624-3851, 800-228-3851,
FAX 831-624-3030
Singles & Doubles $95-$230

A P

Back in 1889, what is today the Pine Inn-the oldest hotel in Carmel-was the Hotel Carmelo, located up on high ground. Around the turn of the century, the old structure was rolled down the hill on pine logs to where it stands now, in the heart of this picturesque town. It has been remodeled on several occasions and is now an elegant, full-service hotel with a loyal following—many families have been coming here for years .

SHOPPING

The Monterey Peninsula offers literally hundreds of shops carrying most anything you're seeking in the way of household items, gifts, clothing, souvenirs, antiques and specialty foods. **Pacific Grove's American Tin Cannery** (125 Oceanview Blvd. 831-372-1442) houses 45 factory outlets in an old sardine cannery building. In **Monterey, Cannery Row Antique Mall** (471 Wave St., Monterey (831-655-0264) collects more than 130 antique dealers in the historic, 21,000-square-foot **Carmel Canning Company** warehouse, built in the 1920s. Besides being home to numerous unusual and ultra-chic boutiques. Carmel has a unique and rustic shopping area, **The Barnyard** (Hwy. 1 & Carmel Valley Rd., 831-624-8886)-gardens and brick walkways surrounding California barns that house over 40 one-of-a-kind shops and eight international restaurants. For the shopper seeking something out of the ordinary, **Total Dog** (2236 Carmel Rancho Lane, Carmel; 831-624-5553) satisfies dog (and cat) needs with unusual merchandise and comical greeting cards. In Pacific Grove's historic Holman Building, you'll find **Collage Design Studio and Workshop** (542 Lighthouse Ave., Pacific Grove; 831-642-0232) a unique collective of local artists featuring hand-painted furniture, watercolor paintings, linens, buttons, painted glass and whimsical collectibles.

SIGHTSEEING & ARTS

ARTS

Dispersed throughout the Peninsula are more than 60 galleries representing a diversity of painting, sculpture and photography. The area has a strong artistic tradition, and was home to such eminent photographers as Ansel Adam,s Edward Weston and Wynn Bullock.

For a gallery listing, pick up ***The Pine Cone***, Carmel's local paper, or one of the many tourist publications found at newsstands around the Peninsula. Several free publications are available in the rack just outside Carmel's Harrison Memorial Library the **Carmel Art Association Gallery** (Dolores and 6th Aves., Carmel; 831-624-6176), where you can view the work of many local artists. Although most Peninsula theaters are dark Monday through Wednesday, check the *Coast Weekly*, a free publication found at area newsstands, for performance schedules.

ATTRACTIONS

Carmel Mission Basilica & Museum

3080 Rio Rd. (off Hwy. 1)
Carmel 93921
831-624-3600
Open Mon.-Sat. 9:30-4:30 p.m., Sun. 10:30 a.m.-4:30 p.m.

This was Father Junipero Serra's headquarters until his death in 1784, and his body is buried beneath the church floor before the altar. The mission building has been skillfully restored, and contains a small museum and a reproduction of the simple cell where Father Junipero Serra slept on a hard wooden bed.

Monterey Bay Aquarium

886 Cannery Row
Monterey 93940
831-648-4888
Open 10 a.m.-6 p.m. daily. Adults $14.95, seniors & students $11.95, children 3-12 $6.95.

The new Outer Bay Galleries have nearly doubled the size of the Nationally acclaimed marine life center: imagine being 50 miles out to sea and several hundred feet below the surface, and you'll get an idea of what to expect from the Monterey Bay Aquarium's new wing. The centerpiece exhibit features 1 million gallons of sea water held back by the world's largest window. The exhibit is also the new home of blue and soupfin sharks, barracuda, pelagic stingrays, schools of tuna and other fast-swimming, open-ocean fish. Crowded as it is, the Aquarium is still among the best reasons to go to Monterey.

Point Lobos State Reserve

Hwy. 1, Box 62
Carmel 93923
831-624-4909
Open 9 a.m.-4:30 p.m. daily. Free admission for walk-ins, $7 per car.

Located three miles south of Carmel, Point Lobos reserve was once the site of a whaling station, a shipment point for coal and a cattle-grazing ground. You'll experience a feeling of seclusion here, of being wrapped in nature among cypress forests, meadows, sea cliffs and open rocky points jutting into the sea. Some 150 species of birds live in the reserve, making it a bird-watcher's delight. Sea life abounds—you might spot sea otters or seals in their natural habitat. Wear sturdy shoes and bring binoculars and a camera.

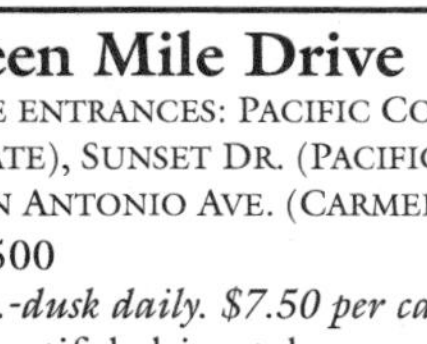

Seventeen Mile Drive

3 toll-gate entrances: Pacific Coast Hwy. (Carmel Gate), Sunset Dr. (Pacific Grove Gate) & San Antonio Ave. (Carmel Gate).
831-649-8500
Open 9 a.m.-dusk daily. $7.50 per car.

This beautiful drive takes you along the coastline, through the Del Monte Forest and Pebble Beach, past the famous Lone Cypress, into the Crocker Grove Wildlife Reserve and past world-class golf courses and fabulous houses. A must for visitors to the Monterey Peninsula.

WINE TOURING

Second only to Napa and Sonoma, Monterey County now ranks as the third largest premium wine-growing region in the United States. Thrice-yearly wine festivals make it possible for visitors to sample many of the local wines. Tastings are available any time of the year at several wineries tasting rooms and at **A Taste of Monterey on Cannery Row** (700 Cannery Row, 831-646-5446).

Listed below are a few of the wineries who welcome visitors. **Monterey County Wine Associates** (P.O. Box 1793, Monterey 93942; 831-375-9400) offers a free map with information on 25 local wineries. It's always best to call ahead for hours of operation. For comprehensive information on the wineries of California, see GaultMillau/**AAA's The Best Wineries of North America** (order form in back of book).

Bernardus
5 W. Carmel Valley Rd.
Carmel Valley 93924
831-659-1900

Bargetto Winery of Cannery Row
700 Cannery Row, Ste. L
Monterey 93940
831-373-4053

Calera Wine Company
11300 Cienega Road
Hollister 95023
831-637-9170
(by appt. only)

Chalone Vineyard
Hwy. 146
Soledad 93960
831-678-1717

Chateau Julien Winery
8940 Carmel Valley Rd.
Carmel 93923
831-624-2600

Galante Family Winery
1818 Cachagua Rd.
Carmel Valley 93924
800-425-2683

Georis Winery
4 Pilot Rd.
Carmel Valley 93924
831-624-4310

Jekel Vineyards
40155 Walnut Ave.
Greenfield 93927
831-674-5522

Las Vinas Winery Tasting Room
381 Cannery Row
Monterey 93940

Paraiso Springs Vineyards
38060 Paraiso Springs Rd.
Soledad 93960
831-678-0300

Sarah's Vineyard
4005 Hecker Pass Highway
Gilroy 95020
831-842-4278
(by appt. only)

Scheid Vineyards
1972 Hobson Ave.
Greenfield 93927
831-386-0316

Ventana Vineyards
2999 Monterey-Salinas Hwy.
Monterey 93940
831-372-7415

Practicals & Index

FREE & CHEAP THINGS TO DO

Tours

The Sunday Datebook section of the ***San Francisco Chronicle*** remains the best source for seasonal tours. **Friends of Recreation and Parks** (415-263-0991) offers free walking tours through Golden Gate Park, Stern Grove and McLaren Park. **City Guides Neighborhood Walks** (415-557-4266) offers free walks; schedules are available at Bay Area libraries. Most popular are their Victorian San Francisco, Japantown and Cityscapes and Rooftops tours. Walking tours of Davies Symphony Hall, the War Memorial Opera House and Herbst Theatre are available Monday on the hour, 10 a.m.-2 p.m.; tours of Davies on Wed. and Sat. by request (415-552-8338).

Concerts and Plays

The San Francisco Symphony (415-552-8000) puts on a free concert series every summer (mid-June to mid-August) in Sigmund Stern Grove, where you'll hear some of the world's great performers in a charming outdoor setting surrounded by redwood trees. Plan to arrive via public transportation; parking is tough. Also, don't miss the annual **Opera in the Park**, presented by the San Francisco Opera (415-864-3330) in Golden Gate Park every summer. Several theater companies perform outdoors in various parks as well, including the **San Francisco Mime Troupe** (415-285-1717) and **Shakespeare in the Park** (415-422-6041). For an afternoon of free comedy, watch for the annual **Comedy Celebration Day** (415-386-5035), held each summer in Golden Gate Park. The free event draws internationally known headliners as well a long roster of local comedians. In addition, various radio stations occasionally promote free concerts: the best come during the **Making Waves Festival**, a day of free outdoor music that takes place on stages throughout the city to celebrate the summer solstice (415-252-2590). Finally, check the ***San Francisco Bay Guardian*** and ***SF Weekly***, both of whom include free weekly performance listings.

Half-Priced Tickets

The epicenter for half-priced tickets remains **TIX Bay Area** (415-433-7287), the easy-to-miss kiosk on the east side of Union Square. When available, TIX has half- or reduced-price tickets for San Francisco Symphony, *Beach Blanket Babylon* and countless plays and musicals at large or small venues. TIX accepts cash only for half-priced tickets. For standing room or reduced-rate tickets to performances of the **San Francisco Opera** (415-864-3330) and **San Francisco Ballet** (415-865-2000), call their respective box offices.

Fairs is Fairs

Various free ethnic fairs each have their own flavor: **Chinese New Year** occurs in late January; Japantown's **Cherry Blossom Festival** take place in April; **Cinco de Mayo** happens the first weekend in May in the Mission district, and **Carnaval** the last. Most

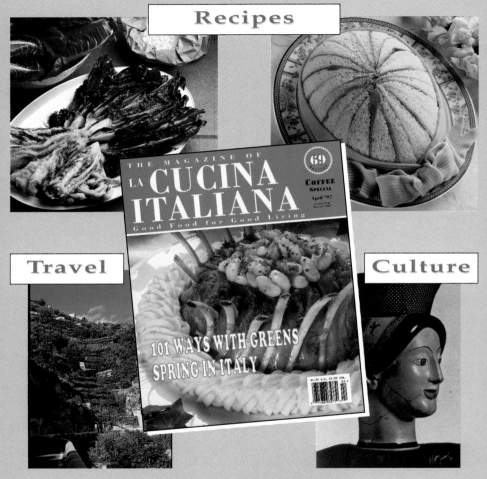

neighborhoods throughout the city have public street fairs one weekend in the summer. The **Union Street Festival of Arts and Crafts** is around June 1; the **North Beach Festival** in mid-June; Jazz and **All That Art** on Fillmore in early July; the **Folsom Street Fair** at the end of September; and the **Castro Street Fair** in early October. At press time, there is talk that the Haight Street Fair will be permanently canceled.

Window Shopping

Countless neighborhoods are great for window shopping: stroll the streets of **Union Square**, oohing and aahing at the couture shops: **I. Magnin**, **Tiffany**, **Hermès**—they're all here. Likewise is Union Street between Van Ness and Steiner worth a walk. For a change of sights, head to **Hayes Valley**—Hayes Street between Franklin and Laguna-where groovy clothing, shoe and houseware stores alternate with art and craft galleries. In the **Haight-Ashbury**, you'll find vintage clothing stores, along with a range of smoking paraphernalia, health food, and gift stores to peruse; the local color here is somewhat overwhelming. For a more ethnic slice of consumerism, head for Grant Street or Columbus Avenue in **North Beach**, where enticing Italian bakeries and delicatessens stand next to Italian potters and charming cafés. Likewise is **Mission Street** between 16th and 24th alive with Latin and Asian cultures; turn left on 24th Street for the most authentic Spanish-flavored avenida in town. **Chinatown**, too, is hopping with interesting shops and fascinating groceries—Stockton and Grant are the busiest routes. A final suggestion is **Fillmore Street** between Geary and Jackson, a long strip of eyeful treasures.

Cheap Eats

For the best in inexpensive dining, head for the **Mission**, where you'll find countless taquerías and pupuserías, bakeries, and take-out counters. Stroll down Mission Street from 16th Street to Cesar Chavez Boulevard, and take your pick. For the best in bargain dining, we recommend any listing marked as a "Quick Bite" in the Dining section of this guide. In addition, the city hosts a number of **Farmers Markets** (800-949-3276) at various locations throughout the week. On Sunday and Wednesday you'll find one at United Nations Plaza just east of Civic Center; on Alemany Boulevard beneath the US101 and Interstate 280 interchange on Sat.; and below the Ferry Building on the Embarcadero on Saturday and Sunday mornings.

Cheap Rides

The cheapest way to get around San Francisco for any long distances is via the Municipal Railway, a/k/a **MUNI** (415-673-MUNI), the unglamorous orange-and-white fleet of buses and streetcars. Fare is $1 (dollar bills are fine) which comes with a transfer for two additional rides within the next 90 minutes. The lines criss-cross the city, and Muni claims that no San Franciscan is farther than two blocks from a line. Maps are posted inside most bus shelters or are available from countless businesses. If you're seeing the city through the windows of an auto, keep an eye out for the seagull-emblazoned **Scenic Drive** signs that offer a prettier tour route. The best way to see the city inexpensively, however, is on foot: countless books on stairway walks, historical tours, points of interest and heart-pounding fitness tours are available. In addition, check weekly listings in the Sunday *San Francisco Chronicle Datebook* for new tours and walks.

Admission-Free Landmarks & Parks

The city's most scenic parks include **Golden Gate** (with countless diversions from pedestrian to exotic), **Alamo Square** (for a view of the famous "postcard row" Victorians), **Alta Plaza** and **Lafayette** (for breathtaking views of downtown) and **Sutro Heights Park** (for a vista of the Pacific coast). A trip up **Coit Tower** (and to view the incredible murals inside) is only $3 (415-362-0808). Countless activities on **The Presidio** (415-561-4323) are free or inexpensive, too. A **Cable Car** costs only $2 for a long, thrilling ride. And finally, there's no charge to view the **Golden Gate Bridge**, **San Francisco-Oakland Bay Bridge**, the Transamerica **Pyramid** or the gorgeous **Palace of Fine Arts**.

Free Museum Days

All major San Francisco museums offer free or half-price admission some time during the month. The San Francisco Museum of

Modern Art (415-357-4000) is free the first Tues. of the month, and half-price every Thurs. from 6 p.m.-9 p.m. Yerba Buena Center for the Arts (415-978-2787) is free the first Thurs. after 6 p.m. Both the Asian Art (415-379-8801) and the M. H. DeYoung Museums (415-863-3330) are free the first Wed. of the month, as is the Exploratorium (415-563-7337); the Palace of the Legion of Honor (415-863-3330) is free the second Wed. of the month. The California Academy of Sciences (and consequently Steinhart Aquarium and Natural History Museum, 415-750-7145) is free the first Wed. of the month.

In addition, various specialty museums are always free: the Cable Car Barn (415-474-1887), Chinese Historical Society (415-391-1188), Levi-Strauss (415-565-9159), National Maritime (415-556-2904) and San Francisco Performing Arts Library and Museum (415-255-4800).

Public Art Walks

San Francisco features more than 1,000 public murals, from political and historical themes to spontaneous, nonsanctioned art forms. Precita Eyes Mural Arts Center (415-285-2287) offers a variety of inexpensive tours highlighting mural arts in the city. Representatives from the Mexican Museum lead tours of the Diego Rivera Mural at the City Club on the first Wed. of the month. Another public art treasure is the recently renovated Beach Chalet (415-751-2766), where murals by Lucien Labaudt have been painstakingly restored and preserved. Enjoy this spot (and the trendy restaurant upstairs) after a long walk on Ocean Beach or through Golden Gate Park. One of the best artistic walks on the city is along the Embarcadero Promenade, which stretches from one end of the numbered piers to the other beneath the Bay Bridge. Historical signposts tell the stories of the city's earliest residents-sailing merchants, immigrant Chinese, prospectors for gold and silver-and a series of outdoor sculptures dots the path. It's especially pretty when strolled on a warm summer evening. If you'd rather stay indoors, you can't beat a trip to 49 Geary Street on the first Thurs. evening of the month, when several floors of fine art and photography galleries have new exhibitions on display.

What To Do With Kids

Critters!

A trip to the **San Francisco Zoo** (Sloat Blvd. at 45th Ave., 415-753-7080) is always well spent. Do not miss the delightful **Insect Zoo, Koala Crossing** or **Gorilla World**. The **Oakland Zoo** (Golf Links Rd., 510-632-9525) is an option for families traveling in East Bay. Both facilities have **Children's Zoos**. In Golden Gate Park, **Steinhart Aquarium** (Music Concourse, 415-750-7145) features more than 14,000 sea creatures, a hands-on tide pool and a delightful fish roundabout. Good with your admission to the **California Academy of Sciences**, Steinhart also features a pair of alligators and plenty of creepy reptiles. A colony of sea lions have permanently taken over a dock at **Pier 39** (Embarcadero and Beach St.)-you can easily spend an hour listening to them bark and watching them swim and flop about. And it's worth taking a trip north into the Marin Headlands to visit the **Marine Mammal Center** (Bunker Road near Rodeo Beach, 415-289-SEAL) where kids can learn about the care and feeding of injured or relocated seals, otters and sea lions.

Old Favorites and New

For six decades, the **Randall Museum** (199 Museum Way, 415-554-9600) has entertained youngsters with its petting zoo and art workshops, and with the tiny railway line that operates on weekends. It's a friendly place where kids will feel instantly at home. The **National Maritime Museum** (900 Beach St., 415-556-2904) is another kids' favorite for its many ship models and historical exhibits. **The International Children's Art Museum** (Ferry Building at Embarcadero and Market Sts., 415-772-9977) houses a permanent collection of some 4,000 international paintings and coordinates a "paintbrush diplomacy" program for young aesthetes to swap art and letters worldwide. Further afield, the **Bay Area Discovery Museum** (557 McReynolds Rd., Sausalito, 415-487-4398) offers an indoor/outdoor complex of historic buildings where kids can experiment with multimedia tools, learn about fishing and hydroelectric power, and discover microscopic creatures. From here, it's just a short drive to the **Bay Model Visitors Center** (2100 Bridgeway, Sausalito, 415-332-3870), where a one-and-a-half-acre Bay Model demonstrates the region's complex water system.

Something Completely Different

The **Exploratorium** (3601 Lyon St., 415-563-7337) remains the ultimate antidote to the stuffy museum experience. Its funky, informative hands-on displays will appeal to older kids, but a trip through the **Tactile Dome**—make a reservation in advance—is a treat for everyone. On the high-tech end, kids may like (but we're not crazy about) **Underwater**

World (Pier 39, 415-623-5300), which offers a diver's-eye view of Bay wildlife through long, transparent tunnels. Some content at the **Cartoon Art Museum** (814 Mission St., 415-227-8666) may be too adult for kids, but call in advance; many exhibits are fascinating. For a break from the noisy electronic arcades, give the kids a whirl through the **Musée Méchanique** (1090 Point Lobos Ave., 415-386-1170), which houses hundreds of vintage mechanical gadgets-photo booths, automated trinkets and clunky precursors to today's video games. From here, just west of the **Cliff House**, you're just steps away from the fascinating **Camera Obscura** (415-750-0415), a copy of Leonardo da Vinci's famous lens camera that slowly pans the shore (see also Museums).

Blinded by Science

The region offers many science hubs for children: across the Bay, the **Lawrence Hall of Science** (Centennial Drive, Berkeley, 510-642-5132) is a smart, well-designed space with exhibitions from animal behavior to astronomy. In the city, the **California Academy of Sciences** (Music Concourse, 415-750-7145) in Golden Gate Park features rotating exhibits on dinosaurs, spiders, and prehistoric cultures. You'll also find a full-fledged natural history museum, a planetarium, and an exhibit on earthquakes that mimics the 1906 temblor. For kids in the city's southern neighborhoods, the **Mission Science Workshop** (106 Bartlett, 415-550-4419) at **San Francisco City College** introduces kids to technology in a workshop setting.

Just For Fun

There probably isn't a child in the world who would not have fun at **Paramount's Great America** (Great America Parkway, Santa Clara, 408-988-1776), the nearest full-fledged amusement park to San Francisco, replete with over-the-top rides and thrills. For amusements closer to home, seek out **Jungle Fun and Adventure** (555 9th St., 415-552-4386), as 15,000-square-foot play facility with countless slides, tubes, and climbing nets. Jungle Fun has quieter activities, too—crafts, games, and birthday parties also happen here. Inside Golden Gate Park (Fulton and Masonic Sts., 415-831-2700), you'll find gaming tables, hiking and biking trails, paddleboats and rowboats to rent and horses to ride. While you're in the park, don't miss the **Children's Playground** (Bowling Green off John F. Kennedy Dr., 415-753-5210), which offers a diverse collection of climbing equipment, swings, and sandboxes; best of all, kids can ride a 62-seat restored carousel on summer afternoons. Across town, older kids and aspiring mountaineers will appreciate the **Mission Cliffs Rock Climbing Center** (2295 Harrison St., 415-550-0515), an indoor climbing facility with settings for all terrains and all levels of expertise.

History In the Making

The city offers a wide variety of historical exhibits for children. A stop at the **Museum of the City of San Francisco** in the Cannery (2801 Leavenworth St., 415-928-0289) fills kids in on local historical events, including the Gold Rush and the earthquake and fire of 1906. Likewise, a tour of the **Cable Car Barn and Museum** (1201 Mason St., 415-474-8887) is always fascinating. The city maintains a number of seagoing vessels to tour. The **Jeremiah O'Brien** (415-441-3101) is a **Liberty Ship** docked at Pier 32; the **USS Pampanito** (415-775-1943), the last of the WWII submarine fleet, is tied up at Pier 45. At press time, the **Scottish Balclutha** (415-556-2904), anchored at **Aquatic Park**, has had her decks recently furbished and is open again to tourists. Kids, too, love a trip to **Alcatraz** or **Angel Island** (Pier 41, 415-773-1188), to tour the old prison or the military garrisons built there. More historical information-plus a half a floor of multimedia equipment, computers, a fairy tale center and more-awaits inside the gorgeous new **San Francisco Main Library** (Larkin and Grove Sts., 415-557-4400).

You Make It, You Buy It

Kids love to watch industry in action, whether it be fortune cookies being folded and baked at the **Mee Mee Bakery** (1328 Stockton St., 415-362-3204) or the **Golden Gate Fortune Cookie Factory** (56 Ross Alley, 415-781-3956) or teddies being cut, sewn, stuffed at **Basic Brown Bear Factory and Store** (444 De Haro St., 415-626-0781). And the city is a mecca for excellent children's shops: **FAO Schwartz** (48 Stockton, 415-394-8700), located a block from Union Square, remains the king of all toy shops, and you'll find two **Toys 'R' Us** stores (2765 Geary, 415-931-8896, and 555 9th St., 415-

252-0607) strategically placed. Many parents prefer the **Imaginarium** (3535 California St., 415-387-9885), a kid-hospitable shop near Pacific Heights; the **Chinatown Kite Shop** (717 Grant Ave., 415-989-5182) is also a favorite for flying birds, dragons and various soaring monsters. And a stop to **Pier 39** (Embarcadero and Beach St.) is always a treat for kid shopping; you'll find another two-story **carousel** here (see also Children in Shopping).

Only (Kids) in San Francisco

The city nourishes several circus arts programs: the nationally touring **New Pickle Circus** (Info 415-665-6177) performs at Cowell Theatre every December, and in other parts of the Bay Area early in the year. **Make-A-Circus** (Info 415-242-1414) performs in the summertime, and the **San Francisco School of Circus Arts** (755 Frederick St., 415-759-8123), sponsors several workshops, seminars (in clowning, juggling, acrobatics and stilt walking) and performances throughout the year. A new circus arts group, **AcroSports** (639 Frederick St., 415-665-2276) offers summer camps in acrobatics and gymnastics. For their first trip to the city, kids love the views from **Coit Tower** (Telegraph Hill St., 415-362-0808) and the top of **Twin Peaks** (Twin Peaks Blvd.) as well as the steep descent of **Lombard Street** (at Hyde St.). Finally, a trip across the Golden Gate Bridge to **Muir Woods** (415-388-2595) is as popular as a ride on the city's **Cable Cars** (three lines, 415-673-MUNI).

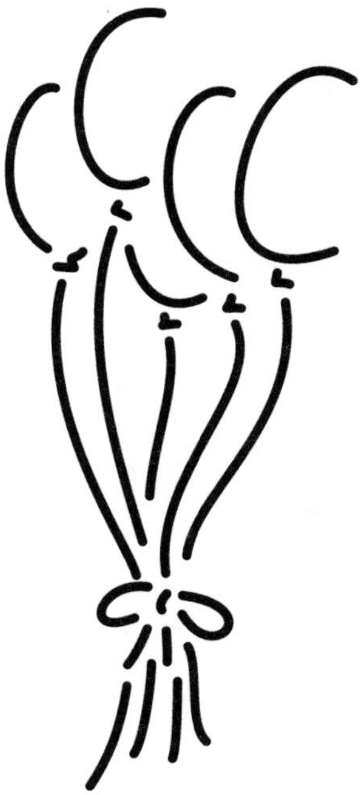

WINE SAVVY

The Emergence of California Wines

Though immigrant families started it in the late nineteenth century, California's wine industry did not flourish until the 1970s, when it fostered a new American interest in wine and a healthy increase in per capita consumption. California wine was thought to come of age at a blind tasting in Paris, where eminent French judges chose several California wines over those produced in France. The American media seized on this with a vengeance, much to the delight of the California wine industry. .

Meanwhile, other trends took hold in the popular segment of the wine market, including the seemingly unquenchable thirst for "a glass of Chardonnay, please." By the early 1980s, there was an influx of new talent into the California winemaking industry. Many of these new winemakers had been educated in viticulture and enology at UC Davis, while others were cellar rats who learned through on-the-job training. These young winemakers were committed to producing quality wine through better viticulture practices, proper utilization of soil and climate and better winemaking techniques.

A number of these winemakers struck out on their own, experimenting with different types of grapes while challenging the "varietal imperialism" of Cabernet and Chardonnay. Wines made from Rhône Valley varietals, like Syrah, Grenache and Mourvèdre, became increasingly popular and offered different flavors than the previous spectrum of California red wines. Plantings of Italian varietals, such as Nebbiolo, Sangiovese and Malvasia sprang up in order to take advantage of the Mediterranean-like growing climate of California.

The winemaking business fractured into many segments. While giant corporate wineries gained their market share, smaller artisan wineries also found their niche. Given the time and money, dreamers could build winery empires based on individual winemaking philosophies, whereas thirty years before, the rules of the game had seemed far more proscribed.

Today, California winemakers now understand that certain climates and soils that are good for, say, Cabernet, are not good for Pinot Noir. As more acreage is planted or grafted over, the most appropriate varietals are planted in the most appropriate environment. This not only increases the quality of the wines, but also furthers the movement of specialty wineries to the forefront. In essence, wineries no longer sell half a dozen different wines, but concentrate on only two or three-the best grapes from the best varieties that the region has to offer.

Today: More Wine, Better Vintages, and Lower Prices

In the late '90s, we are quite possibly entering the "Golden Age" of California winemaking. A new generation of vintners is fashioning wines with an intensity of flavor that is California's birthright, owing to its sunny climate and rich soils. They are refining their techniques to preserve the innate characteristics of the fruit, while at the same time building in more structure and complexity to enhance drinkability and longevity. Through their meticulous attention to detail, they are eliminating distracting elements from the wine in favor of creating a harmonious variety of complex aromas and flavors.

Today, in the best vintages, the wines are still powerful but now tempered with suppleness, finesse and depth. The most recent California grape harvest was a windfall for California winemakers. The 1997 crush was 2.87 millions tons, far outstripping the previous record set in 1993. For consumers, this translates as not only more wine but better wine (weather and growing conditions were near ideal) at lower prices, particularly for premium wines in the $10-$20 range. True, there will always be high-ticket "trophy" wines, like **Opus One**, **Dominus** and **Cardinale**. Good, solid, lower-priced wines that meet the needs of the everyday dining table, however, are also plentiful, due to both the bounty of the harvest and the recent influx of inexpensive imports.

In red wines, Cabernet Sauvignon is still king, though vintners are trying to catch up to the demand for Merlot by feverishly planting hundreds of new acres yearly. More interestingly, Pinot Noir—made in a smooth and silky style-has come of age, with excellent examples produced now in Santa Barbara, Carneros and the Russian River Valley (and Oregon's Willamette Valley). After a string of great vintages, Zinfandel is on the comeback trail, and is now being made in a more food-friendly style. Upstart red varietals, which have a long heritage in France and Italy, have taken their rightful place beside old standbys on wine lists: look to Sangiovese, Nebbiolo, Syrah, Mourvèdre and Cabernet Franc for intriguing flavors.

In white wines, the thirst for Chardonnay is seemingly unquenchable; it's far and away the white wine of choice. However, Sauvignon Blanc, at half the price, partners better with a wide variety of dishes, including many featuring seafood and chicken. A host of Rhône-style varietals, such as Viognier, Marsanne and Roussanne, are beginning to penetrate the marketplace, as consumers discover there is life beyond Chardonnay. The floral aromas of these wines are beguiling, and their flavors follow through with bright, refreshing fruitiness. Likewise, Italian varietals in California—like Pinot Grigio and Tocai Friulano, also offer unique flavor profiles, with a crispness and high acidity that cleanses the palate.

Guide to California Regions

It's been said that there are no climatic differences in California wine growing regions, as there are in Europe, and thus "every year is a vintage year" in California. Nothing could be further from the truth. For proof, merely contrast a 1989 Napa Valley Chardonnay (where it rained at harvest) and a 1989 Central Coast Chardonnay (where it didn't). The myth of statewide sunny weather also needs dispelling. There are certain pockets of land in California (usually associated with mountain ranges) that have vastly different weather and climatic conditions than the rest of the state. And from a viticultural standpoint, certain grape varieties that do well in one environment do not perform well in another. Check out a Pinot Noir from the **Sanford and Benedict Vineyards** in the (very cool) Santa Ynez Valley versus one from the (hot) Calistoga area of Napa Valley. Where the wine comes from does make a difference-the difference between a balanced, complex wine and a harsh, unpleasant one.

Alexander Valley

A largely unpopulated area of northern Sonoma County, the Alexander Valley is warmer than the rest of the county. There has been success here with Cabernets as well as Bordeaux style blends (white and red). The Chardonnays can be interesting.

Amador/Sierra Foothills

Just east of Sacramento, Amador County is home to some of the oldest continuously producing vineyards in the state. The principal wine is Zinfandel and its ubiquitous offspring, White Zinfandel. There is also Cabernet and Barbera, along with experimental acreage planted for Rhône varietals like Syrah, Mourvèdre and Grenache.

California

The use of this geographical term indicates only that all the grapes came from within the confines of the state.

Carneros

At the southernmost end of Napa and Sonoma Counties, this recently developed area borders on the cool San Pablo Bay. Perhaps the coolest area in either county, the climate is perfect for Pinot Noir and Chardonnay.

Central Coast

This is a very broadly defined area that covers coastal wine-growing regions from Santa Cruz on the north to Santa Barbara on the south. An entire spectrum of grape varieties is grown here, depending on which particular varietal is suitable for the individual microclimate.

Central Valley

Another broad area that covers the inland wine growing area from Sacramento to Bakersfield. This is the hottest, driest grape-growing region in the state. A wide variety of wines are made, most of them passable but few of them distinctive.

Dry Creek Valley

Parallel to and west of the Alexander Valley in Sonoma County, its relatively warm climate has produced good red wines, particularly Zinfandel and Cabernet. Chardonnay is a drawing card, too.

Mendocino/Lake Counties

The northernmost grape growing counties share a fairly cool growing season. Chardonnay, Pinot Noir, Gewürztraminer and Riesling can be particularly impressive.

Monterey

The cooling influence of the Monterey Bay has created a great environment for Chardonnay, while Pinot Noir has been less successful. Further inland, individual pockets of land have produced good Cabernets.

Napa Valley

The most famous wine-growing region in California and a top tourist attraction. The name "Napa" is synonymous with quality. Its long-lived Cabernets have achieved worldwide notoriety. Chardonnay, Pinot Noir, Sauvignon Blanc and sparkling wines have also proven themselves here.

Russian River Valley

A district of widely varying soils and climate in western Sonoma County; the cooler regions enjoy a reputation for Chardonnay, Pinot Noir and sparkling wine.

Santa Barbara County

Home to the Santa Ynez and the Santa Maria Valleys, it is the only region in California that has an east-west mountain range funneling cool ocean fog and breezes to the vineyards. That fact belies its southern California heritage that says it's too warm for grape growing. Pinot Noir, Chardonnay, Riesling and Syrah are prominent.

Sonoma County

Encompassing several different valleys with varying microclimates, it is probably the most versatile grape-growing region in California. Cabernet, Merlot, Pinot Noir, Chardonnay, Sauvignon Blanc and sparkling wine do well here.

Temecula

This southernmost grape-growing region, halfway between L.A. and San Diego, is also the most recently planted. Thus far its best efforts have been with Chardonnay and sparkling wine, while the red wines are on the rustic side.

Wine Touring

Visiting the wineries of Northern California can provide a pleasant day or two's break from the excitement of the city. The selected wineries below have tasting rooms and are open to the public on a regular basis. Nevertheless, you'll do well to phone ahead before setting out on your wine touring adventure. For comprehensive information on the wineries of California and Mexico, see **Gayot/GaultMillau/AAA's The Best Wineries of North America**. (Order form in the back of this book)

Coffee Savvy

THE ORIGINS OF THE COFFEE CRAZE

Nearly every culture in the world has a passion for coffee, and there are various stories about how it all started. One of our favorites has to do with a goat herder in ancient Abyssinia (Ethiopia) who one morning discovered his goats gleefully cavorting around a shiny, dark-leafed shrub with red berries. After nibbling a few of the red berries himself, the goat herder joined his goats in their spirited romp. Another story attributes the discovery to an Arabian dervish who, when exiled by enemies to the wilderness, survived by making a broth from water and the berries he plucked from coffee trees.

Regardless of which story is true, botanical evidence indicates that coffea arabica actually originated on the high plateaus of what is now Ethiopia in Africa. Traders undoubtedly brought it across the Red Sea to what is now Yemen, where it was cultivated from the sixth century on. Though at first coffee was used as a medicine-and by dervishes readying for a spin-it soon became a popular social beverage, resulting in coffeehouses where men exchanged ideas and gossip while sipping cups of hot brew in cities from Cairo to Mecca.

Though the Arabs jealously guarded their discovery, a few sneaky coffee fanatics managed to smuggle seeds from Arabia into India and Java, where it was cultivated with great success. By the seventeenth century, the coffee culture had spread to Europe. Coffeehouses attracted politicians, seafarers, merchants, authors and scholars, who often used the premises for discussions, reading, musical performances and even duels. At a time when Europeans wealthy enough to afford exotic luxuries were enjoying their two, three or four cups a day, the greatest French lover of luxury, King Louis XIV, supposedly built the first greenhouse to house a coffee tree given him by the mayor of Amsterdam. It's said that from the Sun King's royal coffee tree, sprang billions of arabica trees, including those growing today in Central and South America.

THE COFFEEHOUSE FOR THE NINETIES

Cut, as they say in Hollywood, to Seattle, in the rainy Pacific Northwest. Here, the current coffee craze was born just over a decade ago with a-then tiny-coffee company named Starbucks (after the first mate in the classic novel, *Moby Dick*). Starbucks re-invented the coffeehouse for modern times, creating attractive, relaxed and congenial meeting places where men and women exchange ideas and gossip-or read, work or simply think-while enjoying a cup of coffee. And we're not just talking about a cup of coffee. The choices of specialty coffee drinks made with "specialty" coffee beans-those of the highest quality-are endless, which is why we've put together this brief primer on the vocabulary of specialty coffees:

THE WORLD OF COFFEE

Like wine grapes, specialty coffee beans get much of their distinctive flavor from the growing conditions and preparation methods of the regions in which they're produced. We can classify coffee flavor and aroma according to geographic origin:

CENTRAL & SOUTH AMERICAN COFFEES

The most popular origins in the U.S. market, these are usually light-to-medium bodied, with clean lively flavors. Their balance and consistency make them the foundation of good coffee blending as well. Among these are beans from Colombia, Costa Rica, Guatemala and Mexico. Kona, though geographically a product of the Pacific islands, falls within this Latin American range of taste and aroma.

EAST AFRICAN COFFEES

These unique beans-from Kenya, Ethiopia, Tanzania and Zimbabwe-often combine the sparkling acidity of the best Central Americans with unique floral or winy notes, and typically are medium-to-full bodied.

INDONESIAN COFFEES

Usually full-bodied and smooth, low in acidity, and often possessing earthy and exotic taste elements, coffee beans from Java, Sumatra, Papua New Guinea and Sulawesi are an important "anchor" component of choice blends.

DARK ROASTS

Coffees from varying geographic origins are dark-roasted to provide a specific range of flavors, from the caramel spice of Espresso, to the smoky tang of Italian Roast, to the pungent French Roast.

BLENDS

Typically, a blend might play off Central American acidity with Indonesian smoothness, or spice up a delicate origin with the tang of a dark roast. At its best, blending coffee is high art, offering a balance or diversity which few straight coffees can match.

DECAFFEINATED

Some coffee-drinkers find the effects of too much caffeine unpleasant; others are looking for a hot cup to enjoy before bedtime. For that reason, coffee beans from many geographic origins are put through a decaffeinating process.

GLOSSARY OF COFFEE TASTING TERMS

THE BASICS:

Flavor: the total impression of aroma, acidity and body.

Acidity: the sharp, lively quality characteristic of many high-grown coffees. Acid is not the same as bitter or sour. Acidity is the brisk, snappy, spicy quality which makes coffee refreshing and palate-cleansing.

Body: the tactile impression of the weight of the brewed beverage in the mouth. It may range from watery and thin, through light, medium and full, to buttery or even syrupy in the case of some Indonesian varieties.

OTHER USEFUL TERMS:

Aroma: the fragrance of brewed coffee. Terms used to describe aroma include: caramelly (candy or syrup-like), carbony (for dark roasts), chocolaty, fruity, floral, herbal, malty (cereal-like), rich (over-used), rounded, spicy.

Bitter: a basic taste perceived primarily at the back of the tongue. Dark roasts are intentionally bitter, but bitterness is more commonly caused by over extraction (too little coffee at too fine a grind).

Bland: the pale, insipid flavor often found in low-grown coffees. Under-extracted coffee (made with too little coffee or too coarse a grind) is also bland.

Briny: a salty sensation caused by application of excessive heat after brewing. (The familiar smell of "truck stop" coffee.)

Earthy: the spicy, "of the earth" taste of Indonesian coffees.

Exotic: coffee with unusual aromatic and flavor notes, such as floral, berry, and sweet spice-like qualities. Coffees from East Africa and Indonesia often have such characteristics.

Mellow: the term for well-balanced coffee of low-to-medium acidity.

Mild: a coffee with harmonious, delicate flavor. Fine, high-grown Latin American coffee is often described as mild.

Soft: low-acid coffees such as Indonesians, that may also be called mellow or sweet.

Sour: a primary taste perceived mainly on the posterior sides of the tongue, characteristic of light-roasted coffees.

Spicy: an aroma or flavor reminiscent of a particular spice. Some Indonesian arabicas, especially aged coffees, evoke an association with sweet spices like cardomom. Others, such as Guatemala Antiqua, are almost peppery.

Strong: technically the relative proportion of coffee solubles to water in a given brew.

Sweet: a general term for smooth, palatable coffee, free from defects and harsh flavors

Tangy: a darting sourness, almost fruit-like in nature, related to wininess. A fine high-grown Costa Rican coffee is frequently tangy.

Wild: a coffee with extreme flavor characteristics; it can be a defect or a positive attribute, and denotes odd, racy nuances of flavor and aroma. Arabian Mocha Sanani nearly always exhibits such flavors.

Winy: a desirable flavor reminiscent of fine red wine; the contrast between fruit-like acidity and smooth body creates flavor interest. Kenyan coffees are examples of winy coffee flavor.

GLOSSARY OF SPECIALTY COFFEE DRINKS

***made by a Barista, an expert at preparing espresso drinks*

Espresso: A small but intense shot of coffee produced by forcing hot water under pressure through tightly packed coffee, one cup at a time.

Espresso Con Panna: A shot of espresso with a dollop of whipped cream.

Espresso Macchiato: Espresso lightly "marked" with foamed milk.

Caffè Americano: A shot of espresso diluted with hot, purified water, to produce a full-flavored but still mild cup of coffee.

Caffè Latte: A shot of espresso plus steamed milk, topped off with foamed milk.

Caffè Mocha: A squirt of chocolate syrup on the bottom of the cup, then espresso topped by steamed milk, a crown of whipped cream and a sprinkle of cocoa powder.

Cappuccino: Espresso topped with steamed milk and a generous cap of foamed milk.

Frappuccino: A cold and creamy low-fat blend of fresh-brewed Starbucks Italian roast coffee, milk and ice. Variations: with a shot of espresso (Espresso Frappuccino), with dark chocolate syrup (Mocha Frappuccino), or with a protein and vitamin supplement (Power Frappuccino).

The Glossary of Coffee Tasting Terms and Specialty Coffee Drinks was provided courtesy of **Starbucks Coffee Company**, *which has retail stores in the U.S. and abroad. Starbucks coffee and coffee products can also be found on major airlines, in fine hotels and restaurants, and in grocery stores (in addition to coffee beans, Starbucks produces wonderfully rich and delicious coffee ice creams).*

WATER SAVVY

Knowing Your Bottled Water

The bottled-water boom over the past decade and a half has transcended the elements of fashion, and has made bottled water a staple in American homes and restaurants. In 1995, according to Beverage Marketing Corp., bottled-water sales increased 8 percent, making it the fastest-growing segment of the beverage industry. Today, yearly sales of bottled water total about $3.4 billion. What spurred this need among consumers to buy what you can get out of the tap for free?

Baby boomers are maturing, and their tastes, as well as concerns over their waistlines, are guiding them toward more natural, less caloric beverages than the Cokes, Buds and margaritas they enthusiastically consumed in their younger party days. America's passion for fitness, combined with, in some cases, a near-prohibitionist attitude toward alcohol, has also driven consumers to seek PC beverage alternatives. Furthermore, the deteriorating taste and quality of tap water—and the fear of the contaminants it may contain—have made bottled water not just a choice for some people, but a necessity.

Trouble at the Tap

The basic belief that American tap water is safe to drink may no longer hold water. Virtually every day, the media reports incidents of contamination and pollution of our municipal water sources. Water quality varies from city to city, street to street and tap to tap. New York City is said to have better-tasting tap water than Los Angeles. Yet both are subject to such chemical treatments as chlorination, which kills bacteria but can produce trihalomethanes (THMs) when it interacts with organic matter in water. THMs have been found to be carcinogenic. From toxic dumps leaking into the aquifers to agricultural pesticides seeping into our reservoirs, our taps are under constant threat. Even the very delivery system that brings tap water from the reservoir to the glass has been found to contain contaminants: lead, copper, radon and a potpourri of other elements that can cause everything from severe headaches to cancer.

When we turn our taste buds to bottled water, we have a long list of "don't wants," but only a hazy idea of what things we do want in our water. Understanding all the bottled water options is the first step.

Not All Water is Created Equal

Within the bottled-water business there are two distinct divisions. The biggest, by volume, is the 5-gallon or jug-water business. Deer Park and Great Bear are among the leaders in this field. Bottlers also are capitalizing on consumers' fondness for their office water coolers, selling two-and-a-half as well as one-gallon containers in supermarkets. This type of bottled water is sold as an alternative to tap water. Premium—or "gourmet"—bottled waters, such as San Pellegrino, Poland Spring and Perrier, are sold as alternatives to soft drinks and alcohol. Packaging ranges from six-ounce to two-liter bottles, from custom glass and

PET plastic to aluminum cans. These waters are sometimes carbonated and may have added essences, juices or flavorings.

To make an informed choice about which of the various types of bottled waters is for you, scrutinize the labels. European bottled mineral waters come from springs, which are simply underground water sources that flow naturally to the surface. Waters labeled "spring water" must come from a spring source. Federal labeling standards in the United States, which came into force in May, 1996, now require that bottlers disclose on the label where the water originated.

Purified water is a different story—it's usually produced by distillation, de-ionization or reverse osmosis. This water can originate from either the tap or from ground water. Often labeled "purified" or "drinking water," this processed water often has minerals added to it to give it taste. If the water is produced by vaporization and condensation, it may be labeled "distilled water".

Eight Glasses a Day Keeps the Doctor Away

In Europe, bottlers tout the reputed healthful properties of good water. Almost every European bottled water is "bottled at the source," which means that it comes from a spring where people have gone for hundreds of years to "take the waters" in curative spa treatments. Spas like Vittel and Contrexeville have medical programs designed to address specific ailments. Most spa treatments involve consuming more than eighty ounces of water a day, which is said to remove toxins from the body and to be effective in the treatment of obesity. In Europe, these bottled waters—with their mineral contents listed on the label—are sold not only in supermarkets but also in pharmacies. Doctors even prescribe certain mineral waters for specific ailments.

In the U.S., however, bottled water is marketed with an emphasis on taste, its contribution to fitness regimens, and in some cases, its trendiness. The U.S. Food and Drug Administration does not recognize any therapeutic values of bottled water because the existing medical research does not conform to FDA guidelines. However, the therapeutic value of certain bottled waters is becoming a subject of discussion in American scientific and medical circles.

The Taste of H_2O

We have approximately 100,000 taste buds, each one connected to our brain by a nerve. Each taste bud senses four basic stimulations from various parts of the tongue; saltiness and sweetness are experienced from taste buds on the tip of the tongue; sourness is perceived on the outer edge of the tongue, and bitterness is perceived on the rear surface of the tongue. Aiding the total tasting experience are two nerves in the upper passage of the nose. The aromatics of a substance pass through the nose when we exhale. Experiment: pinch your nostrils closed and notice how much less vivid your sense of taste is. When evaluating water, it is important to draw the water into the mouth and cover all your taste-sensitive areas with it.

Tap-water taste varies depending on where you live and how your municipal water supply treats or processes the water. The slightly acidic taste of chlorine is one of the most commonly perceived tastes in municipal tap water. Chlorine and other chemicals can affect the taste of beverages, ice cubes, soups and even vegetables. Water impurities can also affect the taste of foods and beverages. Certainly, tea and coffee's natural aromatic constituents will diminish when made with poor-tasting tap water. In fact, Julia Child once said that her Santa Barbara tap water turns her "Chinese tea into mud."

When Carl Rosenberg became the chief baker at the Century Plaza Hotel in Los Angeles, he was asked to duplicate the famous dinner rolls baked at the Olympic Hotel in Seattle. Rosenberg tried out the recipe in Los Angeles, but the rolls' distinctive flavor and texture were both missing. He rechecked the ingredients, and all were correct and of the highest quality. "Could it be the water?" he wondered. After ordering several gallons of Seattle tap water, Rosenberg tried the recipe again. This time the rolls were perfect. Since it was not practical to ship Seattle water each time he baked the rolls, Rosenberg used distilled water, which produced better dough fermentation than L.A. tap water.

But though distilled water may be better to cook with than tap water, it does not score well in water tastings. At a recent "Homage to H20" held by The American Institute of Food and Wine, ten non-carbonated bottled waters were judged in a blind tasting. The distilled bottled water scored the lowest number of points, and judges used words like "dull" and "flat" to describe its taste. People tend to prefer drinking spring water because it tastes better than distilled water. Use distilled water to fill your car battery and steam-iron.

The taste of spring water reflects the different geologic strata underground, where the water absorbs minerals and trace elements—some over a year or two, and others over centuries. These minerals are described in the water's mineral analysis (printed on the label) and are perceived in its taste. Highly mineralized water can sometimes taste metallic; highly bicarbonated water can taste salty. Water with a high content of hydrogen sulfide tastes like rotten eggs, and water with a high concentration of iron can taste like a rusty nail. People tend to prefer their non-carbonated water with a range of 30 to 100 parts-per-million of total dissolved solids—that being the measure of these minerals and trace elements. For carbonated waters, higher levels of minerals are acceptable.

The taste of water can be affected not only by what's in the water, but what the water is in: Lower-grade plastic bottles can impart a plastic taste to the water. If the bottles are stored in the sunlight, the plastic taste can become even stronger.

Bubbly Water

The taste of carbonated water is effected by its level of carbonation—the more carbon-dioxide gas present, the more acidic the water's taste. This sensation, sometimes described by tasters as "bracing," "sharp" and "spritzy," can be positive or negative, depending upon which minerals are in the water. Certain minerals bind the carbonation into the water. Seltzers tend to lose their carbonation quickly because of the lack of minerals. In bottled-water tastings, the more highly mineralized carbonated waters have scored best.

Become bottled-water savvy with this brief primer about popular brands available in New York restaurants.

The Major Brands

CALISTOGA

Nestled at the north end of Napa Valley, Calistoga is a spa-resort town where a geyser second in size only to Yellowstone's Old Faithful shoots up from the ground, and people have been coming to "take the waters"—in pools and in mud-baths—since before the turn of the century. Of the town's three commercially bottled waters, Calistoga comes from water which emerges from the ground at 212 degrees Fahrenheit and is then cooled to 39 degrees F for bottling. The hydrogen-sulfide aroma is removed from the water at the bottling plant by filtering it through sand. The finished water is then ozonated and carbonated. Calistoga also bottles a non-carbonated water sourced from a Napa County spring.

CRYSTAL GEYSER

Also bottled in the town of Calistoga, Crystal Geyser water comes from an aquifer 240 feet below the bottling plant. The water surfaces at a temperature of 140 degrees F, and through a method of heat exchanges, is cooled, filtered to remove sediment, ozonated, carbonated and bottled. The company also produces the non-carbonated Natural Alpine Spring water near the town of Olancha, California. Its source is high in the Sierra Mountains, where glacial waters have seeped over eons through cracks in the granite rocks. Crystal Geyser also produces Natural Alpine spring water, which comes from a source near the base of Mt. Whitney.

DANNON NATURAL SPRING WATER

You know the name "Dannon" from the company's line of milk products. Now you'll find it on bottles of non-carbonated water. The source this newcomer to the bottled-water biz is a spring in the Laurentian region of Quebec, Canada. Test-marketed in Florida and Colorado, initial results showed that Dannon's brand name and moderate pricing produced positive sales, as consumers associate the name with taste, trust and natural products.

DEER PARK

Deer Park's source is a spring 3,000 feet above sea level surrounded by hundreds of acres of woodlands in the Allegheny Mountains, near Deer Park, Maryland. When it was first bottled in 1880, the non-sparkling water was called Boiling Spring because of the action of the water as it bubbled through white sand. The Deer Park Hotel and Spa, which opened in 1873, became a watering ground for distinguished guests, including U.S. Presidents Garfield, Cleveland, Harrison and Taft.

EVIAN

This famous non-sparkling European water comes from Source Cachat in France, where the water emerges from a tunnel in the mountain at 52.88 degrees F. The source is fed from the melted snow and rain that filters through glacial sand from the Vinzier Plateau over a period of 15 years. The glacial sand is surrounded by clay which protects the water from pollution. The water is bottled at a nearby bottling plant, which is highly automated and exceptionally hygienic.

GREAT BEAR

Great Bear Spring has been known since the Onondaga Indian tribe lived near the source in Central New York State, where it is protected by remote woodlands and sheltering rock formations. The spring water filters through layers of gray and white sand and fine sandstone gravel, emerges from the earth at a temperature of about 52 degrees F, and is bottled as a still spring water.

ICE MOUNTAIN

Early Indians were the first to discover Ice Mountain Spring, located in the remote woodlands of Mt. Zircon, near Rumford, in central Maine. They noticed it seemed to rise and fall with the cycles of the moon and called it Moon Tide Spring. The water was first bottled by the Abbott family In 1859, and is now bottled as both still and sparkling.

MOUNTAIN VALLEY

This water springs from a source in a 500-acre forest in the hills between Glazypeau and Cedar Mountains, in Arkansas. Adjacent is a timberland preserve, all of which protects the Mountain Valley aquifer. It was first bottled in 1871 and has been continuously bottled since then, both as carbonated and non-carbonated water. Mountain Valley's source emerges at 65 degrees F; the bottling plant draws approximately 50 gallons per minute from the spring. The source's aquifer is estimated to be at 1,600 feet below earth's surface, where the water filters through levels of shale, Blakely sandstone and limestone.

PERRIER

Dating back more than 100 million years to the Cretaceous Period, when limestone deposits began to form faults and fissures that captured water deep within the earth below what is now Vergèze, France. Hannibal's Carthaginian army is said to have paused by the spring, Les Bouillens, in 218 B.C. Remains in the area suggest that the Romans also refreshed themselves in the waters of Perrier, which have a bit of natural carbonation. When it is bottled, extra fizz is created by adding filtered CO2 gas captured at a nearby natural source.

POLAND SPRING

The history of Poland Spring, Maine, dates back to 1793, when the area around the spring was first settled and the Ricker family opened a small inn. Soon afterward Joseph Ricker lay dying, and to ease his fever someone fetched water from the spring. The story is that Ricker drank it and lived another fifty-two years to tell the tale! Iin 1845, Hiram Ricker began to bottle the water and, in 1893, Poland Spring was awarded the Medal of Excellence at the World's Columbian Exposition in Chicago. Today, Poland Spring comes both still and sparkling.

QUIBELL

The source for Quibell's sparkling product is a spring on heavily wooded Sweet Springs Mountain, West Virginia, at the pinnacle of the Great Eastern Divide. Geologists from Virginia Tech have indicated that the water flows naturally at about two million gallons per day. The water filters through limestone rock strata and emerges from the spring at 42 degrees F.

SAN PELLEGRINO

The spring of San Pellegrino is sequestered in the mountains north of Milan, Italy, and was first made famous by quenching the thirst of Leonardo da Vinci. Today the Fonte Termale, an opulent marbled drinking hall is a monument to the glamour of "taking the waters." San Pellegrino's sources are three deep springs which emerge from the ground at 69.8 degrees F. The waters come from an aquifer 1,300 feet below the surface, where limestone and volcanic rocks impart unique minerals and trace elements. Among its several bottled waters, San Pellegrino also bottles and imports to the U.S. Acqua Minerale Naturale Panna, a still water that comes from a spring in the hills of Tuscany near Florence.

SARATOGA

In the southern foothills of New York's Adirondack Mountains is the famous town of Saratoga Springs, where, in the Gay '90s, celebrities like Lillian Russell and Diamond Jim Brady drank Saratoga's carbonated water from monogrammed cups. Saratoga's original source was a hand-drilled well that went through 30 feet of sand and 150 feet of rock. Natural carbonation occurs in the water, although the water is re-injected with additional carbonation during the bottling process.

SOLÉ

The Fonte Solé Spring is located in the foothills of the Lombardy region of the Italian Alps, and has been revered for its health-giving waters since Roman times. In the Middle Ages, the source was controlled by a monastery when both plague and pestilence threatened the population. A belief grew up that those who drank from the spring would be . Today, the water is recognized as being low in sodium. The University of Pavia has declared it as being microbiologically pure. Solé is packaged in green glass bottles, both non-carbonated and lightly carbonated. The latter, be warned, is not the best mixer to use for spritzers because of the fragility of its bubbles.

SPA

First discovered by the ancient Romans, the source for Spa's non-sparkling mineral water is located in Belgium's Ardennes Valley. Spa was the first town to develop an international bottled water industry (in 1583, the water was exported to none less than King Henri II of France). In the process, the town inadvertently exported its name; since then, "spa" has been synonymous with most natural springs and health resorts. On the edge of the High Venn near Spa is the spring called Reine (the Queen's Spring). Rain and melted snow falls on a moss area of La Fagne, a plateau 575 meters above sea level. It percolates down through layers of clay, slate, flint, sand and quartz where it finally surfaces at 440 meters above sea level.

TYNANT

Springing from a source in Wales' Cambrian Mountains, this carbon-filtered sparkling water first made a name for itself in London's high-end hotels in 1989. Today, the lightly carbonated beverage is more widely distributed, and imported to the United States as well. Tynant is recognizable by its striking blue glass bottles, the hue that apothecary bottles were colored during the Victorian era.

VITTEL

This still mineral water comes from three springs in the small town of Vittel, protected within a 5,000 hectare forest in the Vosges Mountains in Northeastern France. Vittel Grande Source comes from an immense underground aquifer where rock strata and sandstone charge the water with calcium, magnesium and sulphates. The spring surfaces at 11.1 degrees C. and its waters are renowned for its stimulating effects on the kidneys, gall bladder and liver.

Arthur von Wiesenberger is the author of a number of books about water, the most recent, The Taste of Water (Best Cellar Books). He is also a consultant to the bottled-water industry.

INDEX

C

D

E

F

I

J

K

Q

R

T

RECEIVE
3 FREE
ISSUES OF

(A $15 VALUE)

BY FILLING OUT THIS QUESTIONNAIRE, YOU'LL RECEIVE 3 COMPLIMENTARY ISSUES OF "TASTES," OUR INTERNATIONAL NEWSLETTER.

NAME ____

ADDRESS ____

CITY ______________________ STATE ______________

ZIP ______________ COUNTRY ______________________

PHONE (   )   –

The Gayot/GaultMillau series of guidebooks reflects your demand for insightful, incisive reporting on the best that the world's most exciting destinations have to offer. To help us make our books even better, please take a moment to fill out this anonymous (if you wish) questionnaire, and return it to:

GaultMillau, Inc., P.O. Box 361144, Los Angeles, CA 90036;
Fax: (323) 936-2883.

1. How did you hear about the Gayot guides? Please specify: bookstore, newspaper, magazine, radio, friends or other.

2. Please list in order of preference the cities or countries which you would like to see Gayot cover.

3. Do you refer to the AGP guides for your own city, or only when traveling?

A. (Travels) .... B. (Own city) .... C. (Both) ....

(Please turn)

4. Please list by order of preference the three features you like best about the Gayot guides.

A. ....

B. .... C. ....

5. What are the features, if any, you dislike about the Gayot guides?

6. Please list any features that you would like to see added to the Gayot guides.

7. If you use other guides besides Gayot, please list below.

8. Please list the features you like best about your favorite guidebook series, if it is not Gayot/GaultMillau.

A. ....

B. .... C. ....

9. How many trips do you make per year, for either business or pleasure?

Business: International .... Domestic ....

Pleasure: International .... Domestic..........................

10. Please check the category that reflects your annual household income.

$20,000–$39,000 .... $40,000–$59,000 ....
$60,000–$79,000 .... $80,000–$99,000 ....
$100,000–$120,000 .... Other (please specify) ....

11. If you have any comments on the AGP guides in general, please list them in the space below.

12. If you would like to recommend specific establishments, please don't hesitate to list them:

Name	*City*	*Phone*

13. Do you often/sometimes use the Internet to buy goods & services? ❑ Yes ❑ No

We thank you for your interest in the Gayot guides, and we welcome your remarks and recommendations about restaurants, hotels, nightlife, shops, services and so on.

303/99

GAYOT PUBLICATIONS

GAYOT PUBLICATIONS GUIDES ARE AVAILABLE AT ALL FINE BOOKSTORES WORLDWIDE.

INTERNATIONAL DISTRIBUTION IS COORDINATED BY THE FOLLOWING OFFICES:

MAINLAND U.S.
Publishers Group West
1700 Fourth St.
Berkeley, CA 94710
(800) 788-3123
Fax (510) 528-3444

CANADA
Publishers Group West
543 Richmond St. West
Suite 223, Box 106
Toronto, Ontario
M5V 146 CANADA
(416) 504-3900
Fax (416) 504-3902

HAWAII
Island Heritage
99-880 Iwaena
Aiea, HI 96701
(800) 468-2800
Fax (808) 488-2279

AUSTRALIA
Little Hills Press Pty. Ltd.
Regent House, 37-43 Alexander St.
Crows Nest (Sydney) NSW 2065
Australia
(02) 437-6995
Fax (02) 438-5762

TAIWAN
Central Book Publishing
2nd Floor, 141, Section 1
Chungking South Rd.
Taipei, Taiwan R.O.C.
(02) 331-5726
Fax (02) 331-1316

HONG KONG & CHINA
Pacific Century Distribution Ltd.
G/F No. 2-4
Lower Kai Yuen Ln.
North Point, Hong Kong
(852) 2811-5505
Fax (852) 2565-8624

UK & EUROPE
World Leisure Marketing
Unit 11, Newmarket Court
Newmarket Drive
Derby DE24 8NW
(01332) 573737
Fax (01332) 573399

FRANCE
GaultMillau, Inc.
01.48.08.00.38
Fax 01.43.65.46.62

SOUTH AFRICA
Faradawn C.C.
P.O. Box 1903
Saxonwold 2132
Republic of South Africa
(11) 885-1787
Fax (11) 885-1829

TO ORDER THE GUIDES FOR GIFTS, CUSTOM EDITIONS OR CORPORATE SALES IN THE U.S., CALL OUR TOLL-FREE LINE.

THE BEST OF

SAN FRANCISCO & NORTHERN CALIFORNIA

We wish to thank our generous sponsors for their invaluable contributions which made this book possible

- **Air Flambuoyant**
  www.airflambuoyant.com
- **de Ladoucette**
- **Designers Center**
  www.designerscenter.com
- **Forbes FYI**
  www.forbes.com
- **Geyser Peak Winery**
  www.geyserpeakwinery.com
- **La Cucina Italiana**
  www.piacere.com
- **The Mansions Hotel**
  www.themansions.com
- **Oak Knoll Inn**
  www.virtualcities.com/ons/ca/w/caw9602.htr
- **Pan Pacific Hotel**
  www.panpac.com
- **Perrier**
  www.perrier.com
- **Ravenswood**
  www.ravenswood-wine.com
- **Ramos-Pinto**
- **Renaissance Parc 55 Hotel**
  www.renaissancehotels.com
- **Roederer**
- **Sur la Table**
  www.surlatable.com
- **Swaroski**
  www.swaroski.com
- **Vittel**